FATHERS AND THEIR FAMILIES

FATHERS AND THEIR FAMILIES

edited by

Stanley H. Cath

Alan Gurwitt

Linda Gunsberg

THE ANALYTIC PRESS

1989   Hillsdale, NJ   Hove and London

The Analytic Press

Distributed solely by

Lawrence Erlbaum Associates, Inc., Publishers
365 Broadway
Hillsdale, New Jersey 07642

Set in Schneidler type

Printed in the United States of America

Fathers and their families / edited by Stanley Cath, Alan Gurwitt,
    Linda Gunsberg.
        p.   cm.
    Includes bibliographies and index.
    ISBN 0-88163-052-7
    1. Fathers–Psychology. 2. Father and child. 3. Family.
    I. Cath, Stanley H. II. Gurwitt, Alan R. III. Gunsberg, Linda.
    [DNLM: 1. Family. 2. Father-Child Relations. 3. Fathers-
    psychology. WS 105.5.F2 F2515]
    HQ756.F3834 1988
    306.8'742–dc19
DNLM/DLC   88-14548

Contents

List of Contributors   ix

Acknowledgments   xiii

Introduction   xv

I DEVELOPMENT REVISED

Prelude – *Alan Gurwitt*   3

1/Fatherhood and Father-Child Relationships: Five Years of
   Research – *Michael E. Lamb* and *David Oppenheim*   11

2/The Paternal Imago – *Melvin R. Lansky*   27

3/Fatherhood from the Perspective of Object Relations Theory
   and Relational Systems Theory – *Roy Muir*   47

4/Fathers as Single Parents: Object Relations Beyond Mother –
   Peter B. Neubauer   63

5/Toiletry Revisited: An Integration of Developing Concepts
   and the Father's Role in Toilet Training—*Moisy Shopper*   77

6/Readiness for Grandfatherhood and the Shifting Tide—
   Stanley H. Cath   99

II TRANSITION TO FATHERHOOD

Prelude—*Alan Gurwitt*   121

7/Tomorrow's Fathers: The Anticipation of Fatherhood—
   Mary-Joan Gerson   127

8/Risk Factors in the Transition to Fatherhood—
   Howard J. Osofsky and *Rex E. Culp*   145

9/Flight from Fatherhood—*Alan Gurwitt*   167

III FATHER-DAUGHTER RELATIONSHIPS

Prelude—*Linda Gunsberg*   191

10/Fathers and Daughters: Early Tones, Later Echoes—
   Lora Heims Tessman   197

11/Paternal Influence in Early Child Development—
   Bernard L. Pacella   225

12/The Paternal Possibility: The Father's Contribution to the
   Adolescent Daughter When the Mother Is Disturbed and
   a Denigrated Figure—*Rosemary H. Balsam*   245

IV FATHER-SON RELATIONSHIPS

13/The Riddle of Little Hans—*John Munder Ross*   267

14/Lincoln and the Fathers: Reflections on Idealization –
   Charles B. Strozier and *Stanley H. Cath*   285

Interlude—*Stanley H. Cath*   301

15/Calcium Light Night and Other Early Memories of
   Charles Ives—*Stuart Feder*   307

16/Overstimulation by a Father: An Alternative View of
Charles Ives—*Lawrence Deutsch*   327

Recapitulation—*Stanley H. Cath*   337

V CULTURAL AND OTHER VARIATIONS

Prelude—*Alan Gurwitt*   343

17/Turkish Fathers and Their Families: A Study of Fathers
and Their Families in a Transitional Society—
Vamık D. Volkan and *Abdülkadir Çevik*   347

18/Black Fathers—*James P. Comer*   365

19/Papi, or the Child Is Father to the Man—*Saro Palmeri*   385

20/The Nurturing Male: A Longitudinal Study of Primary
Nurturing Fathers—*Kyle D. Pruett*   389

VI DISRUPTED FAMILIES

21/So Near and Yet So Far: The Nonresident Father—
Carol S. Michaels   409

22/The Noncustodial Father: An Application of Solomonic
Wisdom—*Albert J. Solnit*   425

23/Divorce and Fathers: Some Intrapsychic Factors Affecting
Outcome—*Richard N. Atkins*   431

Afterword—*Stanley H. Cath*   459

VII TREATMENT CHALLENGES

Prelude—*Linda Gunsberg*   467

24/Paternity and Transference: The Fatherhood of a
Child Therapist—*James M. Wallace*   473

25/Factors Affecting the Preoedipal and Oedipal Paternal
Relationship in Girls: The Collusion to Exclude Father—
Eleanor Galenson   491

26/Issues in Fathering and How They Are Reflected in the
Psychoanalytic Treatment of Men—*Linda Gunsberg*   507

27/Fathers of Psychotic Children: Clinical Observations and
   Approaches to Treatment — *Michael Schwartzman*   525

28/Conflict and Resistance in the Treatment of Psychiatrically
   Hospitalized Fathers — *Melvin R. Lansky* and *Ellen A. Simenstad*   541

   Epilogue   553

   Author Index   559

   Subject Index   567

Contributors

Richard N. Atkins, M.D. – Associate Professor of Psychiatry in Pediatrics, New York Medical College; Director, Division of Child and Adolescent Psychiatrity, New York Medical College.

Rosemary H. Balsam, M.R.C.P. (Edinburgh), M.R.C.Psy. (London) – Associate Clinical Professor, Department of Psychiatry, Yale University; Staff Psychiatrist, Department of University Health, Yale University.

Stanley H. Cath, M.D., (co-editor) – Medical Director, Family Advisory Service and Treatment Center, Belmont, MA.; Faculties, Boston University School of Medicine and Boston Psychoanalytic Society and Institute; former Associate Clinical Professor of Psychiatry, Tufts University School of Medicine.

Abdülkadir Çevik, M.D. – Associate Professor of Psychiatry, School of Medicine, Ankara University, Turkey.

James P. Comer, M.D. – Maurice Falk Professor of Child Psychiatry, Yale Child Study Center; Associate Dean, Yale University School of Medicine.

Rex E. Culp, Ph.D., J.D.–Director of Research, Child Advocacy Services, Inc., Kansas City, MO; Associate Professor and Director of Family Research Center, University of North Carolina at Greensboro.

Lawrence Deutsch, M.D.–Associate Clinical Professor, Yale Child Study Center; Clinical Associate Professor, Psychoanalytic Institute, New York University Medical Center.

Stuart Feder, M.D.–Faculty, The New York Psychoanalytic Institute.

Eleanor Galenson, M.D.–Clinical Professor of Psychiatry, Mt. Sinai School of Medicine, The City University of New York; Attending Psychiatrist, Mt. Sinai Hospital.

Mary-Joan Gerson, Ph.D.–Director, New York University Psychology Clinic (Doctoral Program in Clinical Psychology); Faculty, Department of Medicine, Mt. Sinai School of Medicine.

Linda Gunsberg, Ph.D. (co-editor)–Editorial Board, *Psychoanalytic Inquiry;* Graduate, New York University Postdoctoral Program in Psychotherapy and Psychoanalysis; private practice, New York City.

Alan Gurwitt, M.D. (co-editor)–Lecturer, Cambridge (MA) Hospital, Harvard University; Associate Clinical Professor, Yale Child Study Center, Faculty, Western New England Institute for Psychoanalysis, New Haven, CT, and Hartford (CT) Child Psychiatry Training Consortium.

Michael E. Lamb, Ph.D.–Chief, Section on Social and Emotional Development, National Institute of Child Health and Development, Bethesda, MD.

Melvin R. Lansky, M.D.–Staff Psychiatrist and Chief, Family Treatment Program, Brentwood Division, West Los Angeles V.A. Center; Faculty, Los Angeles Psychoanalytic Society and Institute.

Carol S. Michaels, Ph.D.–Chief Psychologist, Child, Adolescent, and Family Clinic, Postgraduate Center for Mental Health, New York City; Clinical Assistant Professor, Department of Educational Psychology, New York University.

Roy Muir, M.D. – Deputy Director, C. M. Hincks Treatment Center, Toronto, Canada; Associate Professor, Department of Psychiatry, University of Toronto.

Peter B. Neubauer, M.D. – Clinical Professor of Psychiatry, Psychoanalaytic Institute, New York University Medical Center; former Director, Child Development Center, New York City.

David Oppenheim, M.A. – Graduate student in Developmental Psychology, Department of Psychology, University of Utah; Research Associate, Department of Gynecology and Obstetrics, University of Kansas Medical Center.

Howard J. Osofsky, M.D., Ph.D. – Professor and Head, Department of Psychiatry, Lousiana State University School of Medicine, New Orleans; Teaching Analyst, New Orleans Psychoanalytic Institute.

Bernard L. Pacella, M.D. – Former Director, Child and Adolescent Psychiatry, New York State Psychiatric Institute, New York City: Faculty, Center for Psychoanalytic Training and Research, Columbia University.

Saro Palmeri, M.D. – Assistant Clinical Professor, Yale Child Study Center; Director, Clinical Child Development Program, Connecticut State Department of Health Services.

Kyle D. Pruett, M.D. – Clinical Professor, Yale Child Study Center; Coordinator of Training, Provence-Harris Child Development Unit, Yale Child Study Center.

John Munder Ross, Ph.D. – Clinical Associate Professor of Psychology and Psychiatry, Cornell Medical College; Faculty, Psychoanalytic Institute, New York University Medical Center.

Michael Schwartzman, Ph.D. – Faculty Member and Coordinator of High School Outreach at Child, Adolescent, and Family Clinic, Postgraduate Center for Mental Health, New York City; Clinical Instructor, Department of Psychiatry, Mt. Sinai College of Medicine.

Ellen A. Simenstad, M.S.W., L.C.S.W. – Mental Health Coordinator, V.A. Combined Clinic, Anchorage, Alaska; former Clinical Social

Worker, Family Treatment Program, Brentwood Division, West Los Angeles V.A. Center.

Moisy Shopper, M.D. – Clinical Professor of Child Psychiatry and Pediatrics, St. Louis University School of Medicine; Supervisor and Training Analyst. St. Louis Psychoanalytic Institute.

Albert J. Solnit, M.D. – Sterling Professor of Pediatrics and Psychiatry, Yale University School of Medicine and Yale Child Study Center; Training and Supervising Analyst, Western New England Institute for Psychoanalysis, New Haven, CT.

Charles B. Strozier, Ph.D. – Executive Director and Professor of History, Center on Violence and Human Survival, John Jay College of Criminal Justice. The City University of New York.

Lore Heims Tessman, Ph.D. – Clinical Psychologist, Psychiatric Services, M.I.T., Cambridge, MA; Co-investigator, Study of Adult and Career Development, M.I.T.

Vamık D. Volkan, M.D. – Medical Director and Professor of Psychiatry, Blue Ridge Hospital, and Director of Division of Psychoanalytic Studies, University of Virginia School of Medicine, Charlottesville, VA; Training and Supervising Analyst, Washington Psychoanalytic Institute.

James M. Wallace, M.D. – Child and Adolescent Psychiatrist, Hamot Medical Center, Erie, PA; Child and Adolescent In-Patient Coordinator, Pediatric and Neonatal Consulting and Liaison Service, Hamot Medical Center.

Acknowledgments

This volume has evolved over the last four years. In our review of its many chapters and of further thinking about issues in fathering, we have personally gained greater respect for the variety in the kinds of connections fathers have with their families and that we have with our fathers. We have many people to thank for helping us in significant ways during our very successful collaboration.

First, a very special thanks to our families for their enthusiasm and commitment to us while we worked on this volume.

From Stanley Cath, thanks to his wife, Claire, and his daughter, Sandra Cath Mahon, who helped him with some of the editing, and to his nephew, David Fishbein.

From Alan Gurwitt, thanks to his children, Rob, Jonea, and Andrea, and to his sister, Marcia Wofsey, and her family for all their wonderful suggestions.

From Linda Gunsberg, thanks to Steven and little Dana and Philip. And a special thank you to Sylvia Gunsberg, Ephraim Gunsberg, Hadassah Kenney, and David Goldberg for their sustained confidence and love over the years.

Our gratitude to the American Psychoanalytic Association for its support of the ongoing workshop on Issues in Paternity. It was through this workshop that the three of us met, learned about the work of many of this volume's contributors, and through the discussions and presentations in this group over the years heard so many interesting insights.

We especially express our appreciation to the contributors of this volume, not only for their thoughtful contributions and their willingness to consider editors' comments throughout the working stages of their chapters, but for their patience in what turned out to be a much longer period in completing this volume that we had initially anticipated.

We want to thank Joseph D. Lichtenberg. Early in our book, he endorsed the value of this volume with his personal support and confidence. It was he who referred us to The Analytic Press, our publisher.

We would especially like to express our gratitude to Paul Stepansky and Eleanor Starke Korbin of The Analytic Press. Dr. Stepansky initially guided us through the book contract stage and not only expressed his continued interest, but gave us much sage advice. Mrs. Kobrin edited our volume skillfully and with rare respect for the integrity of the work of all of our contributors.

Alan Gurwitt would like to mention certain colleagues who have been especially helpful to him. These include: James Black, Hugh Cardon, Paul Graffagnino, Roy Muir, Kyle Pruett, Ibrahim Orgun, and Lora Tessman. Always an inspiration have been Sally Provence, Albert Solnit, and Sam Ritvo of the Yale Child Study Center. And of great help, in terms of interest, searching questions and constructive discussion, were his students, especially Maureen Adair, Ilsa Bick, Mary Hennessy, Sherri Spielman, and James Wallace. His thanks also to Drs. Donald Cohen and John Schowalter of the Yale Child Study Center, Drs. Ken Robson and Paul Andrulonis of The Hartford Child Psychiatry Training Consortium, and Drs. Myron Belfer and David van Buskirk of Cambridge Hospital for both interest in this work and providing latitude in his teaching responsibilities to enable it to be done. His thanks to Charmian Proskauer for her considerable help in fathoming word processing and for her many helpful suggestions.

Finally, we would like to acknowledge our daily appreciation of two secretaries: Lois Ross Golliher in Boston, and Barbara Worrest in West Hartford. Both took on many additional burdens with patience, good humor, and good sense, tactfully expressed, and kept material for at least 40 papers flowing back and forth across the country and the Pacific.

Introduction

In the movie "Mac and Me" the United States satellite, in its explorations on another planet, accidentally sucks up a family of extraterrestrial creatures consisting of a young child, Mac, an older sibling, a mother, and a father. The family, once it is discovered on earth, is separated, with young Mac on his own and the rest of the family finding its way to a cave for shelter. Although there are many happy moments in this movie when Mac meets up with a lonely boy, Eric, who befriends him, there is the powerful and at times gnawing theme of Mac's wish to be reunited with his family. His nonverbal communications express his yearning to be with his family and his distress that he is not. The theme of family separation is reiterated and more subtly presented by Eric, who moves to a new house with his mother and older brother. There are several scenes where Eric clutches a family photo of a happy mother and father, himself and brother. But where is his father, whose presence, through his absence, is felt throughout the movie but is never directly expressed? While these two friends experience many interesting adventures, nevertheless they feel the same pain of being torn from their *full* nuclear families, families that include father.

While literature and the arts often portray the contributions of

Introduction

fathers to the well-being happiness, and sense of belonging within families, father's contribution to the family is sorely ignored in the writings of mental health professionals. Many professional papers and clinical presentations only pay lip service to the multiple roles of fathers in child and family development. We are puzzled and frustrated by the apparent reluctance of many researchers and clinicians to include fathers as significant and real objects. Most clinical and theoretical discussions are characterized by an intense focus on the mother-child dyad, which, while of course necessary for an understanding of the child's development, is not sufficient except when abuse, neglect, absence, or marked passivity are crucial and overt negative dynamic factors, fathers tend to be minimized. Often they are portrayed vaguely as primarily oedipal figures, symbolic but without substance. They are seldom represented as real people, real parental objects, with real relationships within the family—as people capable of making major contributions to the intrapsychic structure and external lives of their children at *all* phases of development. True, this minimialization often springs from fathers and mothers themselves, reflecting a pervasive societal pattern of overlooking paternal importance. But we accept too easily this obscuration of the real relationships, the subtle but very rich dynamics of paternal involvement.

The editors are convinced by the evidence of the currently flourishing fatherhood literature that there are many general and specific, actual and potential impacts of fathers on child and family development (and vice versa). We are wary, however, of drawing premature conclusions. Clearly, the study of fatherhood is in an early stage, with some well-documented findings, but also with major gaps, contradictions, and complexities. We are also wary lest our convictions can lead to preaching a new developmental gospel, selectively chosen to support our subjective notions. We have attempted to avoid social engineering, to strike a scientific balance, to report of a wide range of observations by many contributors.

Accordingly, it is to fathers and their families that this volume is primarily dedicated. The editors firmly believe that the father contributes a very vital sense of well-being for *all* generations in all of todays various forms of "living together." He is part of the seed bed, one of the biological originators, who adds his meaning to life and his structure to the personality scaffolding of his children. He will be remembered for his nature, his ability to protect, comfort, and communicate feelings. He may be of the past, but he is always psychically in the present whether or not he is in residence. He determines, along with mother and grandparents, the history and destiny of the family. The father has a profound and continuing impact on the personal lives of his children for generations. It is not surprising, then, that many adolescent children of Vietnamese mothers and American soldiers, in searching for new identities in the United States, engage in a quest for their biological fathers (Mydans, 1988). It is as if they yearn to complete their historical and psychological selves by reconstructing a whole family to enhance their sense of origin and belonging. Similarly, grown children of English war brides and American GIs from World War II have long searched for their fathers (Trucco, 1987).

In 1982, Stanley Cath, Alan Gurwitt and John Munder Ross edited *Father and Child: Clinical and Developmental Perspectives.* That volume was a response to the perceived relative lack of awareness of the significance and influence of the father throughout the developmental life span of the child, as well as of the significance of the child for the father's maturation. In that volume not only did the editors place great emphasis on the normative developmental considerations that arose from focusing on the father-child relationship as a dyad, but, as we do here, they drew attention to the paradoxical omission of the father as a force in dynamic theories of neurosogenesis and psychopathologies. The present volume, *Fathers and Their Families,* highlights the father more as a crucial member of the family system and explores the dyadic and triadic overlapping relationships with the family in more depth. Furthermore, it attempts to broaden the concept of the father by looking at the connections between children, fathers, grandfathers, and other idealized father figures, such as heroic or national leaders. Parenting, including fatherhood, is a multigenerational and extended social phenomenon whether or not members of the extended family are actively involved or actually present.

A man in his 20s (Cohen, 1986) beautifully writes about the meaning his father has for him. He speaks of father giving his son a name and the son naming the father in return:

> A boy has only one daddy
> and for such a short time
> who puts him to bed
> and watches him sleep
> and goes on watching
> when the boy is grown;
>
> who gives him a name
> and a vision

and a promise
he'll never forget

Because a name is a strange and powerful thing
it can conjure light from darkness
dredge from water dry land
split man from animal
or describe a tune
It can make a child believe
and belong. So today I complete that pact.

Years ago you named me
and now I name you back;
Father –
meaning you are
meaning you are mine.

A grandfather (Wessel, 1987) describes the similar closeness he feels with his son upon the birth of his granddaughter, the pride he experiences in seeing his son become a good father, the opportunity he now has to pass down memories cherished from his own childhood and to observe the same passage of history from his son to his grandchild.

Last summer I achieved through no effort on my part an important milestone.[1] I became a grandfather for the first time! I was pleased, excited and I'll admit a bit tearful with joy when my son phoned to share the news of the pregnancy. I anticipated eagerly the moment when I would be able to cuddle a grandchild in my arms. I counted the months until the baby would know me, or be ready to take a walk in a stroller, or to be read to, or to feed the ducks in the park, or visit the aquarium or zoo. I could hardly wait until he or she would be old enough to enjoy stories of the past introduced by phrases such as "when your father was a boy" or "when I was a child." I hoped that my grandchild would want to hear about Franklin Roosevelt, Vietnam, John Kennedy's assassination, Nixon's Watergate, the Nicaraguan struggle, or the story of the early space age when man first landed on the moon.

There is an aspect of being a grandfather which surprises me. I sense a new closeness, a glow deep inside of me as I observe my son caring for his baby and assuming parental responsibilities.

---

[1] contrast this reaction to Margaret Mead's

He looks, beams, touches and holds his baby daughter with confidence and pride. His whole being is preoccupied with his wife and baby.

I am just beginning to understand my feelings since my son has become a father, and I a grandfather. It is surprising how satisfying it is to see my son care for his baby and assume other parental responsibilities. He is enjoying this role as much as I did in his infancy thirty three years ago. I feel a new bond between us, since we are now both fathers sharing roles which establish a continuity in our two generations. I place a high priority on being a parent and to observe my son repeating this role with obvious pleasure is particularly satisfying.

This new volume reports on the continued work of many of the contributors to the first book, *Father and Child;* as well as the work of others. Some of these authors had the opportunity to meet and share the fruits of ten years of concentrated discussions at the Issues in Paternity Workshop of the American Psycholanalytic Association. Others represented here have independently given detailed attention to the study of the father.

This book is divided into seven sections, representing clinical, theoretical, and research contributions to developmental theory, transition to fatherhood, father-daughter relationships, father-son relationships, cultural and other variations, disrupted families, and treatment challenges. All sections deal with the real relationship between the father and his child within the family as well as the internalizations, representations, and paternal imagos of the father.

Several important ideas have emerged from the various contributions.

First, it has not been our intent to offer a coherent theory of fatherhood. Rather our goal has been to bring fatherhood more intensively and extensively under psychoanalytic inquiry and to underscore that any developmental theory of childhood must respect and incorporate the father as a profound and significant force in a child's life from birth and even after the death of the father.

Second, the nature of the child's attachment to both parents must be reexamined considering today's broad varieties of people living together – married or not; working fathers; mothers at home; both parents at work; or mother working and father at home taking care of the baby. Thus, Mahler's (Mahler, Pine, and Bergman, 1975) theory of symbiosis between mother and infant is now being reexamined to include consideration of other primary caretakers: father, grandparent, nannie, babysitter, older sibling. We need to study how psychobiological development differs for each child under all these conditions. We have only begun to appreciate the many "gatekeeper roles" (Atkins, 1982) that each parent plays for the other in facilitating emotional and physical access to the child. It may be that these roles are just as meaningful as the issue of "working mothers" or "latch-key children."

Third, as mothers establish competence in traditionally male areas (professional life, sports, intellectual pursuits) how does this effect the child's sense of both parents as introjected images or ego ideals? Earlier we thought of the mother as responsible for the child's inner world and the father as the bridge to the outside world. Is this still so? When both parents are active in the world outside the home it seems inevitable that the image of mothers and fathers will change for older children and older theorists, but not necessarily for children or theorists who have known no other arrangement. While the evidence is not all in, it is clear that some mothers thrive in dual-career families and others become "overburdened." It is equally clear that some fathers are more able to "pitch in," to become major supports for their wives and children in some of the desperate or overloaded circumstances that may arise. Their contributions are both direct and indirect, and often more than merely supportive.

Fourth, we need to know what prompts and enables a father to want to spend more and better time at home with his children and family. It has been observed in one study that fathers who report greater job satisfaction tend to be home less than are those who are not happy in their jobs. The latter play more and are involved more in the caretaking of their children (Grossman, Pollack, and Golding, 1988). This finding is reminiscent of Lamb's (this volume) that when fathers have more free time, they often spend it in the more personal pursuit of pleasure rather than sharing it with their family or children. Mothers with surplus time are more likely to do something connected with their role as mothers. This seems to reflect a difference between the character, motivation, and participation of each of the parents. But, like many other differences in their styles, it is not something to judge prematurely. The interplay of social, historical, and intrapsychic forces is complex. Lamb's finding and that of Grossman et al. may not be the final word. Changing social expectations of fathers may bring a change in behavior, but, encouraging all fathers to be more active and more sharing in the nurturing of their children is no wiser than urging all mothers to remain at home.

Fifth, several authors have commented on a disequilibrium that may take place in the adaptation of many expectant couples as they make the transition to a newly formed family triad. Just contemplating children may be so serious a challenge to age-specific imperatives and to the ongoing interests of either or both parents as to become a major deterrent to having children at all. The effects connected with having children may be influenced by experiences with past triads and by the meaning of such imagos when superimposed on an anticipated child. Some new fathers may indeed experience a sense of loss at the birth of an offspring in that they no longer remain the only center of the wife's attention. Some wives feel similarly or experience the child as a threat to an ongoing professional career. Still, some mothers readily give up careers or other income-producing jobs to gratify what they consider a natural predeliction to giving birth and caring for a child. It is equally challenging for the father to accommodate to these circumstances and not feel too left out, to be able to support his wife and still maintain the romance implicit in the earlier relationship. There is no question that the degree of mutual love and ongoing support between parents plays an important role in determining the character of the relationships with the child. The birth of a child may see a shifting balance when particular vulnerabilities and frailties in either parent are likely to emerge for the first time. But the timing of the felt discontent may vary as considerable interest, love, and idealized expectations are partially transferred from each other towards the baby.

Sixth, many contributors to *Father and Child* (Cath, Gurwitt, and Ross, 1982) emphasized the richness, complexity, and importance of the preoedipal relationship between fathers and their children. It is probably true that the positive character of the father-child preoedipal ties is crucial to the later transition through the oedipal phases. However, it appears that the father is not purely "an uncontaminated object." To what degree this coloration is an inevitable intrapsychic developmental feature in children and to what degree influenced by the father's ambivalence remains to be demonstrated.

Seventh, we have also begun to realize how the warm and nurturant qualities of the father are not simply and unilaterally based on maternal identifications. While a major source of these capacities may indeed have been maternal, the likelihood is they came from both parents. This is especially true, as some chapters illustrate, when one parent compensates for missing or decompensated qualities in the other parent, either in fantasy or reality. Warm and nurturing characteristics can even be created in fantasy, projected onto a missing parent, and later incorporated into an idealized self. Thus, the maternal and paternal contributions need to be reassessed and brought into line with the personal constructs of the child. We believe many qualities attributed to one or the other of the sexes may be more generally parental rather than gender specific. Bisexual identifications and imagos are so often confused by introjection and projection that it may be difficult to differentiate the maternal and paternal components. Pruett's (this volume) studies of primary caretaking fathers provide great opportunity to understand male nurturing in its various forms as well as many other aspects of basic primary caretaking.

Eighth, included in this volume are three contributions that take a close look at separation and divorce particularly as they pertain to fathers and fathering. The reader will note diversity in views represented here, along with some very important facts. Attempts to define guidelines for legal resolution have changed over time and probably will continue to change, informed, we hope, by ongoing study of the effects on *all* participants. It is likely that what is in the best interest of children, over the long haul, is intertwined to some degree with what supports the continuity of optimal parenting by both parents, albeit under changèd circumstances. We do not advocate any one position, for we believe that study of the psychological phenomena is a matter separate from legal customs. It appears at times that mental health professionals are overwhelmed by legal pressures and do not heed sufficiently the psychological implications.

Ninth, the assets and liabilities of men and women who devalue and denigrate the same-sex parent but who then engage in a search fo extrafamilial, more powerful idealized models are worthy of further exploration (Balsam, Gunsberg, Strozier and Cath, all this volume).

Finally, parenting is probably the most difficult, challenging, and gratifying undertaking life offers. Perhaps it is true that the character of fathering differs more from society to society than does mothering. If so, we feel inclined to move beyond the fathers and their families to look at the subculture or cultures within which many families exist. How do minority subcultures conflict with majority groups to alter the role and imago of the father? Does the interaction overtly or covertly either respect or denigrate the father's position? Perhaps a new volume should focus on connecting the father in the nuclear family with the father-at-large in the subculture in which the family exists.

Although we have not attempted to offer specific revisions of developmental theory with father as the focus, the contributors to this volume have pointed to the humbling need to reassess basic assumptions about the significance of father in all forms of child-parent and adult son-aging parent relationships. We hope that in reading this volume you will be challenged to widen your horizons in your own professional work, thereby becoming more aware of the fascinating and admirable attempts at parenting and fathering made by today's young people.

Stanley H. Cath
Alan R. Gurwitt
Linda Gunsberg

REFERENCES

Atkins, R. (1982), Discovering daddy: The mother's role. In: *Father and Child,* ed. S. H. Cath, A. R. Gurwitt & J. M. Ross. Boston, MA: Little, Brown, pp. 139–149.

Cath, S. J., Gurwitt, A. R. & Ross, J. M. (1982), *Father and Child.* Boston, MA: Little, Brown.

Cohen, J. (1986), *The Pact.* Unpublished poem.

Grossman, F., Pollack, W. & Golding, E. (1988), Fathers and children: Predicting the quality and quantity of fathering. *Develop. Psychol.* 24:82–91.

Mahler, M., Pine, F. & Bergman, A. (1975), *The Psychological Birth of the Human Infant.* New York: Basic Books

Mydans, S. (1988), They train to become as American as they look. *New York Times,* March 8.

Trucco, T. (1987), English war babies search for American fathers. *New York Times,* April 9.

Wessel, M. (1987). Liberation of being a grandparent. Connecticut Section, *New York Times,* April 27.

I

DEVELOPMENT REVISED

Prelude

This section contains a number of diverse chapters. They all touch to some degree on the character of the father's impact on child development, but in doing so they emphasize the family context and the mother-father relationship. Cath's chapter focuses on the grandfather and grandchild, yet the three generations are very much kept in mind. Except for Shopper's, these chapters contain relatively little detailed information about direct father-child interaction (see Cath, Gurwitt, and Ross, 1982, for greater specificity). Rather, they capture the basic essentials of the father's presence or absence, his impact on mother and child, and the character of the paternal image both within the family and within and between individuals in that family. While Lansky focuses on the "paternal imago," a carefully defined and far-reaching theoretical and clinical conceptualization, the percepts involved are discussed fully in the chapters by Muir, Neubauer, Shopper, and Cath. All the authors note the matricentric bias of developmental thinking especially within psychoanalytic literature, research, and clinical work, a bias that has obscured study of the preoedipal role of the father, paternal contributions in postoedipal phases, and the evolution of paternal development. Indeed, we believe that this bias may have caused an incomplete, if not skewed, view of child development. Neubauer states:

> We may wish to extend our psychoanalytic theory of develop-
> ment. [It] demands a clarification of concepts of preoedipal objects,
> the influence of *various* primary objects, and the emergence of
> object primacy. An assumption that the exclusive dyadic relation-
> ship between mother and child is the essential matrix of the
> evolvement of object- and self-representation and individuation
> implies that the early pathology of the child is always seen as
> reflecting a disturbance in mother-child interaction. Such a formu-
> lation seems too limited, for it does not include the child's capacity
> to form relationships with a number of meaningful objects, to
> adapt to different object relations and to benefit from it.

Lamb and Oppenheim, developmental psychologists, review some highlights of the research done in their field in the last several years. In examining questions about the extent and nature of paternal involvement, they characterize that involvement along three dimensions: *engagement, accessibility,* and *caretaking responsibility.* When father involvement in traditional families is compared with that in dual-career families, the latter have higher involvement as measured by the first two categories, but not in the third, an indication of which parent is truly the primary caretaker. It does not seem that fathers are doing more than in the past, or that a fundamental redefinition of roles has yet taken place, even if both parents have equal potential for primary parenting at the time of the birth of the first child. Parenting skills are learned "on the job." As mothers do more, assuming (no matter what the previously agreed upon arrangement) more of the traditional pri-mary caretaking responsibility, they become more and more compe-tent in that role and fathers less so.

That fathers indeed have the potential to become primary care-takers is seen in the research of Pruett (see Section V). When fathers do not become primary caretakers, stylistic differences between mothers and fathers tend to remain distinct (see Yogman, 1982); when they do become primary caretakers, some of the stylistic differences become less pronounced (see Interludes to Sections II and V for further discus-sion). The character of the mother-father relationship colors the char-acter of father involvement, a recurring theme in this section – indeed, in much of this volume (see also Atkins, 1982 and 1984). Specific factors in the background of the mother, especially the nature of her relationship with her own father, influence her facilitation or deterrence of her husband's involvement.

Lamb and Oppenheim found that 60-80% of mothers do not want their husbands to be more involved – supposedly greater involvement would change the power balance and other attributes of the marital relationship.[1] This is a very important factor in the degree and character of paternal involvement. *Both parents* play a significant part where major redefinitions of roles have not taken place.

Another deterrent is the nature of institutional policies. Yet even when these policies allow for greater participation of men in their families, for example, at the time of childbirth, many men are reluctant to use the opportunity. Why this is so needs further study (see Gurwitt, this volume) but one reason may be that there is a difference between a policy entitlement and an atmosphere that truly facilitates and encourages the exercise of that right.

In looking at the influence of fathers on child development, Lamb and Oppenheim reviewed only those studies where fathers were highly involved. Like Pruett, they note that in those families where both parents are very involved the children are advanced in their cognitive development and have a high degree of empathic capacity, less sex-stereotyped beliefs, and a more internal locus of control. Lamb and Oppenheim believe this is because both partners are highly motivated – and have each other's support – to be active parents. These parents can achieve a better balance of career and parenthood, and hence a greater sense of fulfillment. When fathers are forced to be highly involved without wishing to be so, the quality of fathering may not be as high. Lamb and Oppenheim comment: "What matters is not so much who is at home but how that person feels about being at home, for his or her feelings color the way he or she behaves with the children."

Societal changes (more distinct sex role expectations, for example, in the 1950s compared with a recent tendency toward sex role flexibility) and great variations in modes from culture to culture help define the character and quantity of father involvement. The amount of time fathers and their children spend together seems less important than what they *do* with that time and how mothers, fathers, children, and other important figures in their lives perceive, behave toward, and value the father-child relationship. Nonetheless, we believe the issue of the amount of time spent needs further study.

From a psychoanalytic-developmental perspective, there is a

---

[1]Grossman, Pollack, and Golding (1988) came to similar conclusions.

question as to whether both parents are indeed equally prepared to assume primary caretaking responsibilities. Pruett's work shows that fathers can do so, but is the fact that they generally do not purely a matter of social custom and on-the-job learning? Might it not be that the total spectrum of their childhood and adolescent experiences, identifications, parental imagos, and ego ideals – obviously different for girls and for boys – all add up to different positioning for parenthood? Furthermore, it is likely that biological differences matter a great deal (for example, see Notman and Nadelson, 1981). We are not proposing the existence of a "maternal instinct," nor are we ignoring the bisexual character of early psychological development. We simply are convinced about the importance of differential developmental pathways for boys and girls that have to do with their later parental modes as well as their gender role identities. (For example, see Ross, this volume, and 1982 a, b).

Lansky's chapter on the paternal imago is a theoretical paper strongly based on psychoanalytic concepts of the individual and family. It also has clinical underpinnings and implications. His conceptualization of the paternal imago expands and enrichens a useful construct. The paternal imago, he proposes, is more than an accumulation of actual experiences with the father. Maternal, familial, self- and other representations are involved. The paternal imago is a kind of screen representation, similar to screen memories, a set of recollections and views of the paternal object serving defensive and screening functions for self- and other object representations. It contains split-off maternal components, with each object representation or imago being colored by the other objects. (We might also assume that the maternal imago contains paternal components.) Splitting, that is, a schism, in the marital relationship is internalized by the child as a felt split within the family, compounding the child's normal dyadic ambivalence toward the father. Like other authors in this section, Lansky emphasizes the mother's coloration of the child's and family's views of the father. That coloration acts as a kind of gatekeeper, influencing the degree to which other attachments can be made by the child. Lansky thus concurs with the "transitive vitalization" concept of Atkins (1984). We think it reasonable to emphasize the importance of the child in shaping the paternal imago by the multiple interactions that trigger paternal responses.

Muir, a psychoanalyst and child psychiatrist trained in Canada and working in New Zealand, is well versed in the work of British object relations theorists. Here he particularly cites Winnicott and Fairbairn. Like Lansky, he emphasizes that the father is part of an internalized family relationship system consisting of a network of objects. He advocates not only the dyadic affective relationship between father and child, but seeing as internalized and part of the self the whole family's patterns of relatedness, with its defensive myths, distortions, and preferred modes. Acknowledging the great variations in paternal patterns from society to society, nevertheless, he notes, "the presence or absence of the father is always of considerable significance to the child." He spells out some of the general ways that fathers are significant, for example by helping to provide a suitable nurturing and holding environment for the mother and child, serving as an alternate attachment figure (libidinal object), helping to modulate negative and aggressive affect (see also Ross and Herzog, 1985), facilitating separation and individuation (especially when projective distortions might impair the mother-child relationship), playing important roles in the child's gender and gender role development, and during and after the oedipal phase encouraging group relatedness including within the family.

Muir believes there may be a "hierarchy of attachment figures that can, in preferential order, insulate the infant against the experience of aloneness, strangeness, and danger." He also sees the father as a modifier of maternal messages as well as a contributor to transpersonal modes and messages within the family. Like Lansky and Neubauer, he states: "It may also be that it is not the specific object relationship with the father or mother that is essential to the ego development of the child, but the continuity of nurturing relatedness and behavioral regulation within some kind of integrated family network that is of basic importance."

Neubauer addressed the question of the oedipal development of the one-parent child in his now classic 1960 paper. He returns to this theme more than 25 years later, reviewing his earlier findings and discussing them in the context of more recent developmental and clinical thinking in a setting of major social changes that include higher incidences of divorce and unmarried young mothers. Whereas his succinct review of his earlier paper shows his original conclusions to have stood up well over time, he now addresses the question of variable outcome in instances of loss or absence of one parent. For the children, the outcome depends on many factors: the conditions and relationships (dyadic and triadic) prior to loss, the age and stage of the child at the time of loss, the reasons for the loss, the postloss arrangements and conditions. Besides these and other external variables, the internal intrapsychic state of the child, before, during, and after the loss is crucial too. He notes the different developmental characteristics of boys and of girls, for example in the form and timing of rapprochement and the importance of the father in influencing the evolution of aggression in boys. (The father's role here is probably important for girls too; see Section III.) He calls for further study of these many variables in relation to outcome. We agree that more research is vital both for academic and pragmatic clinical purposes.

Neubauer points out that there can be ameliorating circumstances. The object-hungry child may be able to seek out and benefit from other caregivers, other adults or siblings. Studies of vulnerable and at-risk children demonstrate that survivor skills are present in some children, absent, unfortunately, in others. Furthermore, the remaining parent may be able to adapt some of the positive parenting characteristics of the absent parent that help to compensate to some degree for the loss.

Regardless of parent loss, other adult caregivers are important in early (and later) childhood. In this context, Neubauer spells out some of the newly recognized functions of fathers. Fathers are objects too, their direct and indirect contributions obscured in the past by the exclusive emphasis on the mother-infant toddler dyad, a vital dyad, but simply not the only object attachment of young children. Father and other adults provide similar and additional nurturant influences in the processes of separation and individuation, and the evolution of libidinal and aggressive growth and modulation (see also chapters by Osofsky, Galenson, and Pruett, this volume; Cath, Gurwitt, and Ross, 1982).

Neubauer, in pointing to research on divorce and the phenomenon of fathers occasionally serving as primary caregivers, asks a key question: Can fathers be "mothers"? This question is discussed in the introduction to Section V in relation to the chapter by Pruett. We propose that some of what is called "maternal" "might more properly be called "parental," that is, not gender linked, but, rather, characteristic of the primary-caretaking parent.

Shopper's chapter makes a major distinction between male and female modes of toilet training and emphasizes the importance of the father's direct role with sons. Lack of awareness of and attention to the father's preoedipal roles, plus a tendency toward a unisexual view of toddler development, which fails to distinguish different needs on the part of girls and boys, have combined to create a blindness to the need for differential approaches to toilet training. Shopper clearly spells out the different approaches ideally required and discusses the developmental and clinical reverberations of failure to use these distinctly different approaches. The implications go far beyond the specificity of toilet training.

Cath resumes his commentaries on grandparents in general and grandfatherhood in particular (see also Cath, 1982). The birth of a grandchild creates four grandparents, but what an array of reactions the grandparents may experience. Cath points out that theoretically there are three stages of grandparenthood (young, middle middle-aged, and elderly), and that the state of health and energy and degree of disengagement may influence those stages and the capacity to respond. His case examples illuminate intrapsychic phenomena that have the timelessness of the unconscious, reflecting lifelong developmental issues of the past, especially oedipal, as well as other basic attributes of the grandparent-parent relationship. Indeed, Cath sees grandparenthood as a developmental stage, the third individuation crisis, containing all the characteristics of previous crises and stages. There is a restructuring of the internal life, a review of past attachments, and an opportunity to revise how those past relationships, some still active and alive, are experienced. Preparation for this new stage in life probably begins long before the actual event. A new balance of narcissism and altruism can be achieved, as the meanings of life, work, leisure, and the like are reevaluated. There is a rescreening of the strengths and weaknesses of one's own parenting, enabling modifications and resyntheses of parenting concepts. While all of this is within the context of a race against time, the birth of a grandchild can be rejuvenating, a compensation for a time of decline for those grandparents able to make use of the opportunity.

The parents of the grandchild tend to serve as the gatekeepers in this instance, influencing the character of availability of the grandchild, the attitudes toward the grandparents, and the amount of time grandparents spend with their grandchild. But the opportunities for reworking the relationships between the grandparents and parent are considerable, catalyzed by the grandchild, enabling, for example, observations by the grandfather of his son's or daughter's parental caring and adaptation to parental responsibilities. These observations, linking grandparent and offspring parent, can establish new bonds.[2]

As Cath states, "Grandparenthood, then, initiates a whole series of changes within an enlarged and complex extended family structure. It will lead to various degrees of alliance, enjoyment, responsibility, centrality, loss, and conflict in various members' lives."

These authors—and we agree—state or imply: *The father is an object too.* This recognition alone requires a revision of developmental think-

---

[2]See Wessel (1987) for a beautiful description of his personal experience.

ing. As basic as it may seem, the concept has simply been missing in much if not most of psychoanalytic literature.

Alan Gurwitt

REFERENCES

Atkins, R. N. (1982), Discovering daddy: The mother's role. In: *Father and Child,* ed. S. H. Cath, A. Gurwitt & J. M. Ross. Boston: Little, Brown, pp. 139–149.

—— (1984), Transitive vitalization and its impact on father representation. *Contemp. Psychoanal.,* 20:663–675.

Cath, S. H. (1982), Vicissitudes of grandfatherhood: A miracle of revitalization? In: *Father and Child,* ed. S. H. Cath, A. Gurwitt & J. M. Ross. Boston: Little, Brown, pp. 329–338.

—— Gurwitt, A. & Ross, J. M., ed. (1982), *Father and Child.* Boston: Little, Brown.

Grossman, F. K., Pollack, W. S. & Golding, E. (1988), Fathers and children: Predicting the quality and quantity of fathering. *Develop. Psychol.,* 24:82–91.

Neubauer, P. B. (1960), The one-parent child and his oedipal development. *The Psychoanalytic Study of the Child,* 40:163–182. New Haven: Yale University Press.

Notman, M. T. & Nadelson, C. C. (1981), Changing views of femininity and childbearing. *Hillside J. Clin. Psychiat.,* 3:187–202.

Ross, J. M. (1982a), The roots of fatherhood: Excursions into a lost literature. In: *Father and Child,* ed. S. H. Cath, A. Gurwitt & J. M. Ross. Boston: Little, Brown, pp. 3–20.

—— (1982b), From mother to father: The boy's search for a generative identity and the oedipal era. In: *Father and Child,* ed. S. H. Cath, A. Gurwitt & J. M. Ross. Boston: Little, Brown, pp. 189–203.

—— Herzog, J. M. (1985), The sins of the father: Notes on fathers, aggression, and pathogenesis. In: *Parental Influences: In Health and Disease,* ed. E. S. Anthony & G. H. Pollock. Boston: Little, Brown, pp. 477–510.

Wessel, M. (1987), Liberation of being a grandparent. *New York Times,* Connecticut section, April 26.

Yogman, M. W. (1982), Observations on the father-infant relationship. In: *Father and Child,* ed. S. H. Cath, A. Gurwitt & J. M. Ross. Boston: Little, Brown, pp. 101–122.

1

Fatherhood and Father-Child Relationships

Five Years of Research

Michael E. Lamb

David Oppenheim

THE CHANGING ROLES OF FATHERS

A little more than a decade ago, Lamb (1975) described fathers as "forgotten contributors to child development." That label is certainly not accurate today. In the intervening years, we have witnessed a resurgence of interest in fatherhood and the roles that fathers play in the family (Lamb, 1986). Especially helpful have been attempts to achieve an interdisciplinary synthesis of the relevant research in a variety of disciplines, including sociology, psychology, psychiatry, sociobiology, and family history. These syntheses have greatly enriched understanding of the father's many roles in child development and promise to reshape research perspectives in this area.

In this chapter we focus on three areas in which substantial progress has been made in the last five years: literature concerning the extent, determinants, and consequences of paternal involvement in childcare. Research on these topics has been summarized more fully elsewhere (Lamb, Pleck, and Levine, 1985; Lamb, Pleck, Charnov, and Levine, 1985, 1987), and our goal here is simply to summarize the most important trends we have witnessed.

QUANTIFYING THE NEW FATHERHOOD

Much attention has recently been paid to the changing role of fathers, with particular focus on "the new father," who is, by definition, deeply involved in the day-to-day care and rearing of his children. Unfortunately, much of the evidence concerning the new fatherhood is journalistic in nature, and we do not know how representative the men featured in such accounts really are. Before pursuing our topic further, therefore, we need to ask: What does the average American father do, and how has that changed over the last several years?

The Extent of Paternal Involvement

Consider first figures concerning the degree of involvement by fathers in two-parent families in which mothers are not employed (Pleck, 1983; Lamb et al., 1987). The data suggest that in such families fathers spend about 20% to 25% as much time as mothers do in *engagement* (direct, one-on-one interaction) with their children. In the same types of families, fathers spend about a third as much time as mothers do just being *accessible* to their children (being available whether or not interaction is actually taking place). The largest discrepancy between paternal and maternal involvement is in the area of *responsibility*, defined by a perception of responsibility for ensuring that the child is appropriately cared for at all times, rather than simply being available to "help out" when it is convenient. As summarized by Lamb et al. (1987), many studies show that fathers assume essentially no responsibility for their children's care or rearing.

In two-parent families with employed mothers, the levels of paternal engagement and accessibility are both substantially higher than in families with unemployed mothers (Pleck, 1983; Lamb et al., 1987). The figures for direct interaction and accessibility average 33% and 65% respectively. As far as responsibility is concerned, however, there is no evidence that maternal employment status has any effect on levels of paternal involvement. Even when both mother and father are employed 30 or more hours a week, the amount of responsibility assumed by fathers appears negligible, just as it does when mothers are unemployed.

In light of the controversies that have arisen on this score, it is worth noting that fathers do *not* spend more time interacting with their children when mothers are employed (Pleck, 1983). The proportions cited here go up not because fathers are doing more, but because mothers are doing less. Thus fathers are proportionately more involved when mothers are employed, even though their levels of involvement, in absolute terms, do not change to any meaningful extent.

Overall, these findings reflect parents' perceptions of their respective roles, indicating that even when external circumstances (for example, maternal employment) call for a redistribution of parenting tasks, a fundamental redefinition of roles does not take place. This is especially true for the responsibility component, as it was defined here, which both parents seem to define as an exclusive attribute of the maternal role. The reasons for this probably lie in patterns of sex-linked power and privilege, which are discussed later in the subsection on *support* (Polatnick, 1973–74).

Behavioral Styles of Mothers and Fathers

In addition to evidence about the amount of time parents spend with their children, both observational and survey data suggest that mothers and fathers engage in different types of interaction with their children (Lamb, 1981a, b; Yogman, 1982). Mothers' interactions with their children are dominated by caretaking, whereas fathers are behaviorally defined as playmates. Mothers actually play with their children much more than fathers do, but as a proportion of the total amount of child–parent interaction, play is a much more prominent component of father-child interaction, whereas caretaking is much more salient with mothers. Even in play, furthermore, the behavioral styles of mothers and fathers differ. Mothers are more likely to initiate fantasy and joint positive play with their preschool children, whereas fathers are more likely to initiate rough-and-tumble play (Roopnarine and Mounts, 1985).

Although mothers are associated with child care and fathers with play, we cannot assume that fathers are less capable of caretaking. A number of researchers have attempted to investigate the relative competencies of mothers and fathers with respect to caretaking and parenting functions, and the results of these studies are fairly clear (Lamb, 1981a). First, they show that in the newborn period, there are no differences in competence between mothers and fathers – both parents can do equally well (or equally poorly) (Parke and Tinsley, 1981). Contrary to the notion of a maternal instinct, parenting skills are usually acquired "on the job" by both mothers and fathers. Because mothers are "on the job" more than fathers are, however, they become more sensitive to their children, more in tune with them, and more aware of each child's characteristics and needs. Belsky and his colleagues (1984), however, showed that both mothers and fathers adapted to their infants' development over the course of the first year, thus demonstrating their sensitivity and competence. Nevertheless, there were large differences between mothers and fathers with respect to the extent of interaction, a finding also reported by Lamb and Elster (1985) in research on adolescent mothers and their partners.

By virtue of their lack of experience, fathers become correspondingly less sensitive and come to feel less confidence in their parenting abilities. Fathers thus continue to defer to and cede responsibility to mothers, whereas mothers increasingly assume responsibility, not only because they see it as their role, but also because their partners do not seem to be especially competent careproviders. As a result, the differences between mothers and fathers become more marked over time, but they are not irreversible. When fathers are thrust into the primary caretaking role by unemployment or by the loss of a partner, or when they choose to redefine their parental roles and their parent--child relationships, they are perfectly capable of acquiring the necessary skills (Levine, 1976; Hipgrave, 1982; Russell, 1983; ch. 19, this volume). In reality, of course, most fathers never get as involved in child care as their partners, and so the differences between mothers and fathers tend to increase.

If we look at paternal involvement in terms of the three components mentioned earlier (accessibility, interaction, and responsibility), we find that increased involvement on the father's part brings about increased accessibility and interaction, but not increased responsibility. Responsibility seems to be the one component that clearly distinguishes fathers from mothers.

We speculate that from the child's point of view the unique quality and emotional investment of the "responsible" parent is a salient dimension that permits the child to distinguish between the kinds of experiences provided by father and mother. The father may provide exciting play experiences and may be salient and attractive because of his relative novelty, but from the child's perspective the mother is the person who "takes care of me." What happens when fathers are actively involved in caretaking: Do the differences in behavioral styles persist? Lamb and his colleagues (Lamb, Frodi, Frodi, and Hwang, 1982; Lamb, Frodi, Hwang, Frodi, and Steinberg, 1982) addressed this problem by comparing father–infant and mother–infant interaction in Swedish families, in some of which the fathers were highly involved. They found that the fathers were less likely to hold, tend to, display affection toward, smile at, and vocalize to their infants, *regardless* of whether they were highly involved or not. The infants also showed clear preferences for their mothers on measures of attachment and affiliative behavior–again, regardless of whether or not their fathers were highly involved (Lamb, Frodi, Hwang, and Frodi, 1983).

These findings suggest that gender has a more important influence on parental style than does extent of involvement. Thus, even when fathers are highly involved in caretaking, their styles remain distinctly different from maternal styles. Nevertheless, we must remember that even though the fathers in the Swedish studies were highly involved in child care, they were not exclusive primary caretakers, as mothers often are, and they had all experienced traditional sex-role socialization. Thus it is unclear whether the differences between maternal and paternal behavioral styles were of social or biological origin, and it would be interesting to determine whether fathers who assume the responsibility for their children's care, with the emotional investment this entails, adopt a more "maternal" behavioral style or assume parental responsibility while maintaining the typical paternal behavioral style. It may be that responsibility for child care is the key determinant of parental style, not parental gender. This is suggested by Pruett's (1984, 1983) findings indicating that primary-caretaking fathers adopt a nurturant style reminiscent of the behavioral style typical of primary-caretaking mothers.

THE DETERMINANTS OF FATHER INVOLVEMENT

Motivation

Four factors are crucial to understanding variations in the degree of paternal involvement (Lamb et al., 1987). First, there is motivation–the extent to which the father wants to be involved. Survey data suggest that 40% of fathers would like to have more time to spend with their children than they currently have available (Quinn and Staines, 1979). This implies that a substantial number of men are motivated to be more involved. On the other hand, the same data suggest that at least half of the fathers in the country do *not* want to spend more time with their children than they currently do. Clearly, there is no unanimity about the desirability of increased paternal involvement–an important point when one considers the need to evaluate parental motivations when attempting to understand parental influences on child development. Recent changes in levels of paternal motivation have taken place, however, and can be attributed primarily to the women's movement and the questions it raised about traditional male and female roles. In addition, media hype about the "new father" has also affected motivation levels.

Why do fathers want to be more involved in child care? Sagi (1982) distinguished between the "compensatory" hypothesis, which suggests that involved fathers want to compensate for their own fathers' unavailability by being more involved with their children, and the "modeling" hypothesis, which suggests that involved fathers emulate their fathers' high involvement. In his Israeli study, Sagi found that the more highly involved paternal grandparents had been (at least in the fathers' recollection) the more involved the fathers were, thus supporting the modeling hypothesis. Other findings are contradictory, however. Radin (1982) found no differences between the way highly involved and "traditional" fathers perceived their own fathers, and more recently Baruch and Barnett (1983) found that fathers who perceived themselves as having had relatively poor fathering experiences tended to be more involved, thus supporting the "compensatory" hypothesis, at least when mothers were not employed. These conflicting findings suggest that paternal involvement is multidetermined and that important variables, such as fathers' perception of their own fathers (and grandfathers perhaps), have to be viewed in conjunction with other variables (e.g., wives' perceptions of their fathers, employment opportunities, social support) when predicting degree of paternal involvement. In addition, as Russell (November, 1985, personal communication) pointed out, parents' recollections of their childhood experiences are fallible and may not tell us much about the actual circumstances in which parents were raised.

Skills and Self-Confidence

Men who claim to be motivated often complain that a lack of skills (exemplified by ignorance or clumsiness) prevents increased involvement. Sensitivity is also crucial (Lamb, 1980). This involves being able to read the child's signals, know what he or she wants, know how to respond appropriately, know what expectations are realistic. Sensitivity and self-confidence are abstract characteristics, both of which are probably much more important than specific skills. Specific skills however, may provide useful vehicles for developing sensitivity and self-confidence. Here again it is important to emphasize the family context in which the father tries to improve his skills and self-confidence. If the mother perceives her partner's increased involvement as a threat to her position, or if marital conflict is channeled into disagreements around child care practices, the father's attempts to increase involvement may be unsuccessful.

Support

The third factor influencing paternal involvement is support, especially maternal support. Radin (1982) confirmed this when she found that the major correlate of *paternal* involvement was a variable that had to do with *mothers'* past experience: Fathers were more involved when the mothers' recalled their fathers' involvement as gratifying, but of frustratingly limited extent. Interestingly, women whose fathers had been nurturant and accessible were apparently not noted for their encouragement of paternal involvement, but we do not know to what extent the mothers' selective recollections and the limited variability in recalled nurturance and accessibility may have influenced these results. Palkovitz (1984), too, found that fathers' concepts of their roles and their wives' concepts of their roles were of equal importance in determining the fathers' actual involvement. Baruch and Barnett (1983), like Radin, concluded that wives have the major influence on paternal involvement. One important variable was circumstantial (mother's employment status), and another was attitudinal (mother's nontraditional perceptions of the father's role).

Thus maternal attitudes, which are in part influenced by the mothers' perceptions of their own fathers, may have an important effect on the likelihood of paternal involvement. Yet, most mothers apparently do not want their husbands to be more involved. The same surveys that show many men wanting to be more involved also show that somewhere between 60% and 80% of women do *not* want their husbands to be more involved than they currently are (Quinn and Staines, 1979; Pleck, 1982). This suggests that although many mothers would like their husbands to do more, a substantial majority are satisfied with the status quo.

There may be many reasons for these attitudes. Some mothers may feel that their husbands are incompetent and that their involvement may create more work than it saves. More importantly, increased paternal involvement may threaten to upset some fundamental power dynamics within the family (Polatnick, 1973–74). The roles of mother and manager of the household are the two roles in which women's authority has never been questioned; together, they constitute the one arena in which women traditionally have had real power and control. Increased paternal involvement may threaten this power and preeminence. For many women, it may be preferable to maintain authority in the child-care arena, even if that means physical and mental exhaustion.

Women's attitudes toward paternal involvement have changed very little over the last 15 years or so (Polatnick, 1973-74; Pleck, 1982). Their resilience is likely to endure until fundamental changes within the society at large change the basic distribution of power. Even among those women who say they would welcome increased paternal involvement, there may be more ambivalence than survey results indicate.

The heterogeneity of maternal attitudes regarding paternal involvement raises very important issues about father involvement and its likely effects on young children. When deciding whether or not father involvement should be encouraged in particular families, one must take into account the preferences and attitudes of *both* parents. To do so involves the articulation of individual assumptions and values, followed by negotiation in an attempt to achieve some satisfactory consensus. Agreement between the parents regarding their roles in the family and in the child rearing process may predict family harmony and promote optimal psychosocial development in the children.

Because women's attitudes and assumptions about sex roles appear to be changing faster than men's, conflict between partners may become increasingly common. In this regard, it may be significant that in the two longitudinal studies of high father involvement, an unusually high rate of family dissolution was evident when families were later recontacted (Russell, 1983; Radin and Goldsmith, 1985). The researchers attributed this to the excessive strains experienced by nontraditional families. Thus even when both parents appear committed to nontraditional parental roles (as in Radin's subject families), there can be fundamental conflicts and ambiguities concerning roles and responsibilities that make it difficult for families to maintain nontraditional arrangements and that add stresses to the marriage. Such problems attend nontraditional or novel parental roles even though increased father involvement is desired by an increasing number of parents.

In addition to maternal opposition, lack of social support may inhibit paternal involvement. Russell (1982) reported that fathers who became primary caregivers complained about lack of support, especially from their peers, and this contributed to the return of most of the families to traditional constellations.

Institutional Practices

The last of the factors influencing paternal involvement comprises institutional practices. The needs of families for economic support and the barriers imposed by the workplace rank among the most important reasons given by fathers to explain low levels of paternal involvement (e.g., Yankelovitch, 1974).[1] Clearly this is an important issue for many men, and it will remain important as long as males take on and are expected to assume the primary breadwinning role. It is also true, however, that men do not trade off work time for family time in a one-to-one fashion. Survey data show that women translate each extra hour of nonwork time into an extra 40 to 45 minutes of family work (housework, childcare, food preparation, shopping, and the like), whereas for men each hour not spent in paid work translates into less than 20 minutes of family work (Pleck, 1983). Thus, while the pressures of work do have a significant effect on parental involvement, the effects on men and women are different, presumably because men and women are differentially socialized concerning the responsibilities to expect and to assume. As mentioned earlier, men are increasingly willing to "help" with child care, but women are still considered more "responsible" for child care. Being at work does reduce the amount of time that fathers can spend with their children, but even when they have time available, they spend only a small portion of it with their children, choosing instead to spend the majority on personal leisure. Fathers and mothers thus continue to be differentially motivated with respect to parenting roles.

Paternity leave is the most frequently discussed means of enhancing paternal involvement. This near-exclusive focus is really misdirected, because paternity leave is unlikely to provide *the* answer to increased paternal involvement (Pleck, 1986). Paternity leave facilitates involvement only during a very narrow period of time at the beginning of the child's life, although there is continuity over time in aspects of paternal involvement: Fathers who choose to take paternity leave remain more involved than peers who do not do so (Lamb, Hwang, Bookstein, Broberg, Hult, and Frodi, in press). The same is probably true of brief events like being present at the child's birth. As one study showed (Grossmann and Vollkner, 1984), those fathers who wanted to participate in their child's delivery were those who had attitudes favoring paternal involvement when the child was one year old, regardless of whether they did in fact attend in the delivery. This study and others emphasize the importance of paternal attitudes in determining increased involvement and the quality of parent–child relationships over and above mere availability.

---

[1]In addition to the constraints imposed by actual work time, it is also important to recall that the whole identification of fatherhood with breadwinning limits male involvement in child care.

Stability of Increased Paternal Involvement

In interpreting the research on families in which fathers are highly
involved, we must also take into consideration the stability of the
child-care arrangements, because when nontraditional arrangements
do not persist, the effects on children's development are likely to differ
from those that occur when the child-care pattern is maintained. When
Russell (1982) recontacted the families that had participated in his
study, he found that only 22% (four families) still had nontraditional
arrangements several years later, and Radin's (1985) follow up yielded
similar results. The small numbers of "persisters" in these studies
provoke speculation about the factors that fostered maintenance of
nontraditional arrangements. Radin found persistence more likely
when mothers had strong, and fathers weak, attachments to their
careers, or when both parents had strong career orientations but
flexible hours. In nontraditional families, mothers tended to have
grown up with employed mothers, nurturant fathers, and limited
experience in primary caregiving, whereas fathers perceived their fathers as nonnurturant and tried to compensate for that with their own
children. All Radin's subjects lived in a small university community
supportive of nontraditional patterns. In sum, according to Radin and
Russell, maintenance of nontraditional patterns depends on a combination of factors having to do with the parents' employment, early
experience, and environment.

PATERNAL INFLUENCES ON CHILD DEVELOPMENT

The focus of this chapter now switches from fathers' actions to fathers'
influences on their children's development. Over the decades of psychological research on this topic, three bodies of literature have
emerged; all are important to understanding paternal influences on
child development. These three approaches involve using correlational
strategies (in which paternal characteristics like masculinity were correlated with filial characteristics), examining the effects of father absence, and studying the impact of highly involved fathers. Only the
last class of studies is discussed here, albeit in abbreviated form, because
they have dominated research in the last few years; a more detailed and
comprehensive review is provided elsewhere (Lamb, Pleck, and Levine,
1985). Our goal here is to illustrate key features of the empirical
research that have prompted major changes in the conceptualization of
paternal influence patterns.

Studies concerned with the effects on children of increased father involvement, as exemplified by fathers who either share in or take primary responsibility for child care, have become a prominent feature of fatherhood research in the last few years (Russell, 1983; Radin and Russell, 1983; Lamb et al., 1985). The question has been addressed in three or four studies, which provide some remarkably consistent results with respect to infants and preschool-aged children whose fathers are responsible for at least 40% of the within-family childcare. Children with highly involved fathers are characterized by increased cognitive competence, increased empathy, less sex-stereotyped beliefs, and a more internal locus of control (Radin, 1982; Radin and Sagi, 1982; Sagi, 1982; Pruett, 1983; Carlson, 1984; Easterbrooks and Goldberg, 1984; see also ch. 19, this volume). Such findings beg the question: "*Why* do these sorts of differences occur?"

Three factors are probably important in this regard (Lamb et al., 1985). First, because the parents assume less sex-stereotyped roles, it is not surprising that their children have less sex-stereotyped attitudes themselves about male and female roles. Second, particularly in the area of cognitive competence, these children may benefit from having two highly involved parents rather than just one; this assures them the diversity of stimulation that comes from interacting with different people who have different behavioral styles. A third important issue has to do with the family context in which these children are raised. In every study reported thus far, high paternal involvement made it possible for both parents to do what was subjectively important to them. It allowed fathers to satisfy a desire to become close to their children, and it allowed mothers to have adequately close relationships with their children while also being involved in the pursuit of career goals that were important to them. In other words, increased paternal involvement in the families studied may have made both parents feel much more fulfilled. It is likely that as a result, the relationships were much warmer and much richer than they might otherwise have been. Our speculation is, therefore, that the positive outcomes obtained by children with highly involved fathers are largely attributable to the fact that the fathers' involvement created a family context in which parents felt good about their marriages and the arrangements they had been able to work out.

In all of these studies, fathers were involved because both their partners and they wanted this to be the case. The results might have been very different had the fathers been forced to become involved, perhaps because they were laid off while their partners could get and hold jobs. In such circumstances, the partners might resent their husbands being poor breadwinners who could not hold jobs and support their families, while the men resented being home doing "women's work" with the children when they really wanted to be "out there" earning a living and supporting their families (see Russell, 1983). This constellation of factors might well have adverse effects on children, just as the same degree of involvement has positive effects when the circumstances are more benign. The key point is that the extent of paternal involvement may be much less significant (so far as understanding the effects on children is concerned) than are the reasons for the father's involvement, his evaluation of that involvement, and his partner's evaluation of his involvement.

In sum, the "effects of increased paternal involvement" may in many cases have more to do with the context of father involvement than with father involvement per se. What matters is not so much who is at home, but how that person feels about being at home, for his or her feelings will color the way he or she behaves with the children. That parent's behavior is also influenced by the other partner's feelings about the arrangement: Both parents' emotional states affect the family dynamics.

The three genres of research on paternal influences together paint a remarkably consistent picture. First, fathers and mothers tend to influence their children in similar rather than dissimilar ways. The important dimensions of paternal influence are those which have to do with parental characteristics rather than gender-related characteristics. Second, the nature of the effect may vary substantially depending on individual and cultural values. A classic example of this can be found in the literature on sex-role development. As a result of cultural changes, the assumed sex-role goals for boys and girls have changed, and this has produced changes in the effects of father involvement on children. In the 1950s, sex-appropriate masculinity or femininity were the desired goals; today androgyny or sex-role flexibility is desired. And whereas father involvement in the 1950s seemed to be associated with greater masculinity in boys, it is associated today with less sex-stereotyped role standards in both sons and daughters. Third, influence patterns vary substantially depending on social factors that define the meaning of father involvement for children in particular families embedded in particular social milieus. Finally, the amount of time that fathers and children spend together is probably much less important than what they do with that time and how fathers, mothers, children, and other important people in their lives perceive and evaluate the father–child relationship. Easterbrooks and Goldberg (1984), for example, found that "qualitative" measures of paternal involvement (e.g., attitudes and behavioral sensitivity) had a more positive effect on many aspects of socioemotional development than did more quantitative measures (e.g., the amount of time spent in interaction). All of this means that high paternal involvement may have positive effects in some circumstances and negative effects in other circumstances; the same is true of low paternal involvement. However, we must not lose sight of recent historical changes in average levels of paternal involvement (Juster, 1986). If these trends continue, there will be increasing numbers of families in which greater father involvement would be beneficial.

SUMMARY

A number of issues pertaining to paternal involvement have been addressed, albeit briefly, in this chapter. The currently high degree of interest in paternal roles and functions on the part of scholars and researchers reflects the latest in a series of shifts in how American society conceptualizes and idealizes fatherhood (Pleck, 1984; Lamb, 1986). Consistent with the notion of a "new fatherhood," average levels of paternal involvement have increased in the last several years, although the increases have been modest. Mothers still spend much more time than fathers do in interaction with or being accessible to their children, and this remains true even when both parents are employed. Furthermore, ultimate responsibility for child care and child rearing remains the nearly exclusive province of mothers, while fathers "help out when they can" (or when it is convenient). A number of factors—including motivation, skills, and self-confidence, support, and institutional factors—appear to affect levels of paternal involvement, but many of these reflect manifestations of an underlying assumption: Men are first and foremost workers and breadwinners, whereas women are primarily nurturers.

Whatever the extent of their involvement, fathers do appear to influence their children's development, both directly by means of interaction and indirectly by virtue of their impact (both positive and negative) on the family's social and emotional climate. Because attitudes concerning appropriate levels of paternal involvement vary widely, this means that both high and low levels of paternal involvement can be either beneficial or harmful to child development depending on the attitudes and values of the parents concerned. It is thus critically important to recognize intercultural and intracultural diversity when exploring paternal influences on child development.

REFERENCES

Baruch, G. K. & Barnett, R. C. (1983), *Correlates of Fathers' Participation in Family Work: A Technical Report* (Working Paper #106). Wellesley, MA: Center for Research on Women, Wellesley College.

Belsky, J., Gilstrap, B. & Rovine, M. (1984), The Pennsylvania infant and family development project. I: Stability and change in mother-infant and father-infant interaction in a family setting at one, three, and nine months. *Child Devel.,* 55:692–705.

Carlson, B. F. (1984), The father's contribution to child care: Effects on children's perceptions of parental roles. *Amer. J. Orthopsychiat.,* 54:123–136.

Easterbrooks, M. A. & Goldberg, W. A. (1984), Toddler development in the family: Impact of father involvement and parenting characteristics. *Child Devel.,* 55:740–752.

Grossman, K. E. & Vollkner, H. J. (1984), Fathers' presence during birth of their infants and paternal involvement. *Internat. J. Behav. Dev.,* 7:157–165.

Hipgrave, T. (1982), Childrearing by lone fathers. In: *Changing Patterns of Child Bearing and Child Rearing,* ed. R. Chester, P. Diggory, & M. Sutherland. London: Academic Press, pp. 149–166.

Juster, F. T. (1986), A note on recent changes in time use. In: *Studies in the Measurement of Time Allocation,* ed. F. T. Juster & F. Stafford. Ann Arbor, MI: Institute for Social Research.

Lamb, M. E. (1975), Fathers: Forgotten contributors to child development. *Human Devel.,* 18:245–266.

_____ (1980), What can "research experts" tell parents about effective social-ization? In: *Parenting in a Multicultural Society,* ed. M. D. Fantini & R. Cardenas. New York: Longman, pp. 160–169.

_____ (1981a), The development of father-infant relationships. In: *The Role of the Father in Child Development,* ed. M. E. Lamb. New York: Wiley, pp. 459–488.

_____ (1981b), Fathers and child development: An integrative overview. In: *The Role of the Father in Child Development,* ed. M. E. Lamb. New York: Wiley, pp. 1–70.

_____ ed. (1986), *The Father's Role.* New York: Wiley.

_____ & Elster, A. B. (1985), Adolescent mother-infant-father relationships. *Devel. Psych.,* 21:768–773.

_____ Frodi, A. M., Frodi, M. & Hwang, C. P. (1982), Characteristics of maternal and paternal behavior in traditional and nontraditional Swedish families. *Internat. J. Behav. Devel.,* 5:131–141.

_____ Frodi, M., Hwang, C. & Frodi, A. (1983), Effects of paternal involvement on infant preferences for mothers and fathers. *Child Devel.,* 54:450–458.

_____ Frodi, A. M., Hwang, C., Frodi, M. & Steinberg, J. (1982), Mother- and father–infant interaction involving play and holding in traditional and non-traditional Swedish families. *Devel. Psych.,* 18:215–221.

_____ Hwang, C. P., Bookstein, F. L., Broberg, A., Hult, G. & Frodi, M. (in press), Determinants of paternal involvement. *Internat. J. Behav. Devel.*

_____ Pleck, J., Charnov, E. L. & Levine, J. A. (1985), Paternal behavior in humans. *Amer. Zool.,* 25:883–894.

_____ _____ _____ _____ (1987), A biosocial perspective on paternal behavior and involvement. In: *Parenting Across the Life Span,* ed. J. B. Lancaster, J. Altmann, A. Rossi & L. R. Sherrod. Chicago: Aldine, pp. 111–142.

_____ _____ & Levine, J. A. (1985), The role of the father in child development: The effects of increased paternal involvement. In: *Advances in Clinical Child Psychology,* Vol. 8, ed. B. S. Lahey & A. E. Kazdin. New York: Plenum Press, pp. 229–266.

Levine, J. A. (1976), *And Who Will Raise the Children?* Philadelphia: Lippincott.

Palkovitz, R. (1984), Parental attitudes and fathers' interactions with their 5-month-old infants. *Devel. Psych.,* 20:1054–1060.

Parke, R. D. & Tinsley, B. R. (1981), The father's role in infancy: Determinants of involvement in caregiving and play. In: *The Role of the Father in Child Development,* ed. M. E. Lamb. New York: Wiley, pp. 429–458.

Pleck, J. H. (1982), *Husbands' and Wives' Paid Work, Family Work, and Adjustment.* Wellesley, MA: Center for Research on Women, Wellesley College.

_____ (1983), Husbands' paid work and family roles: Current research issues. In: *Research in the Interweave of Social Roles,* Vol. 3, ed. H. Lopata & J. H. Pleck. Greenwich, CT: JAI Press.

_____ (1984), Changing fatherhood. Unpublished manuscript, Wellesley College.

_____ (1986), Employment and fatherhood: Issues and innovative policies. In: *The Father's Role,* ed. M. E. Lamb. New York: Wiley, pp. 384–412.

Polatnick, M. (1973–74), Why men don't rear children: A power analysis. *Berkeley J. Sociol.,* 18:44–86.

Pruett, K. D. (1983), Two-year followup of infants of primary nurturing fathers in intact families. Paper presented to the Second World Congress on Infant Psychiatry, Cannes, France.

_____ (1984), Children of the father-mother: Infants of primary nurturing fathers. In: *Frontiers of Infant Psychiatry,* Vol. 2, ed. J. Call, E. Galenson & R. Tyson. New York: Basic Books, pp. 375–380.

Quinn, R. P. & Staines, G. L. (1979), *The 1977 Quality of Employment Survey.* Ann Arbor, MI: Survey Research Center.

Radin, N. (1982), Primary caregiving and role-sharing fathers. In: *Nontraditional Families,* ed. M. E. Lamb. Hillsdale, NJ: Lawrence Erlbaum Associates, pp. 173–204.

_____ (1985), Antecedents of stability in high father involvement. Paper presented at the Conference on Equal Parenting: Families of the Future, Chico, CA.

_____ & Goldsmith, R. (1985), Caregiving fathers of preschoolers: Four years later. *Merrill-Palmer Quart.,* 31:375–383.

_____ & Russell, G. (1983), Increased father participation and child development outcomes. In: *Fatherhood and Family Policy,* ed. M. E. Lamb & A. Sagi. Hillsdale, NJ: Lawrence Erlbaum Associates, pp. 191–218.

_____ & Sagi, A. (1982), Childrearing fathers in intact families in Israel and the U.S.A. *Merrill-Palmer Quart.,* 28:111–136.

Roopnarine, J. L. & Mounts, N. S. (1985), Mother-child and father-child play. *Early Child Devel. Care,* 20:157–169.

Russell, G. (1982), Shared-caregiving families: An Australian study. In: *Nontraditional Families,* ed. M. E. Lamb. Hillsdale, NJ: Lawrence Erlbaum Associates, pp. 139–171.

_____ (1983), *The Changing Role of Fathers?* St. Lucia: University of Queensland Press.

Sagi, A. (1982), Antecedents and consequences of various degrees of paternal involvement in child rearing: The Israeli project. In: *Nontraditional Families,* ed. M. E. Lamb. Hillsdale, NJ: Lawrence Erlbaum Associates, pp. 205–232.

Yankelovich, D. (1974), The meaning of work: In: *The Worker and the Job,* ed. J. Rosow. Englewood Cliffs, NJ: Prentice-Hall.

Yogman, M. W. (1982), Development of the father-infant relationship. In: *Theory and Research in Behavioral Pediatrics,* Vol. 1, ed. H. E. Fitzgerald, B. M. Lester & M. W. Yogman. New York: Plenum Press, pp. 221–280.

2

The Paternal Imago

Melvin R. Lansky

THE CONCEPT

Laplanche and Pontalis (1973) defined the concept of "imago" as follows: "Unconscious prototypical figure which orientates the subject's way of apprehending others; it is built up on the basis of the first real and phantasied relationships within the family environment" (p. 211). The authors warn against simplifying this definition into something that would make "imago" closer in meaning to "image," that is a distillate of real memories of the person in question. Nonetheless, imago has commonly been felt to be a prototypic imaginary construct, a phantasied photograph as it were, codifying the relationship with the other. It would be, of course, naive to assume that such memory is undistorted. Memories or reactivations of attitudes toward persons resembling the prototype in some way are distorted by the defensive needs of the subject.

Common psychoanalytic usage places the paternal imago as one of many object representations colored by defensive needs but, like the maternal imago or other imagos, substantially derived from real experiences with that object. The common connotation of the paternal imago, therefore, is that of a defensively modified residue of the subject's relationship with father that serves as a template for reactions to those who, in some important way, signify father in later life. Data concerning the paternal imago is inferred from the patient's associations or responses to people in similar roles. Distortions woven into the (inferred) imago are unraveled *pari passu* with the unfolding and resolution of the transference neurosis. The transference neurosis provides insight into distortions based on provocation, hostility, devaluation, and other defensive operations that color, both positively and negatively, the subject's view of father.

I maintain that such a notion of the paternal imago, however straightforward it may appear, is oversimplified and, further, that this oversimplification may hold us captive, much to the detriment of theory, of clinical practice, and of the relationship between theory and practice. There is a superficial plausibility in conceptualizing the paternal imago as a buildup of associations, expectations, and reactions derived from actual transactions with father himself. But such a view, with its assumptions that data derive from the dyad, may arrange our receptivity to clinical data so as to close out an appreciation of the significance of the full scenario that is the basis for the patient's associations. In the clinical situation in which the paternal imago is the focus, the analyst's comprehension of what it is that the patient is associating to may be unnecessarily constricted by explicit or implicit theories about the paternal imago. Are the patient's thought associations to the paternal object representation? To aspects of the self-representation? To the maternal representation? Or to the entire family constellation composed of not only object representations but also their relations to each other?

A constricted and reified set of preconceptions foreclose an appreciation of the way in which the paternal imago illuminates a great deal about self-representation and other (especially maternal) object representations, and about internalizations derived from the parental marriage or the family as a whole. Oversimplified views of the paternal imago, then, widen the split between theory and practice, supporting either a rigidified theoretical view of internal representation that is of no clinical use; or, alternatively, a somewhat nihilistic view that views the imago as no more than another type of ideational material for analysis and without further theoretical significance. The purpose of this chapter is to work toward a clearer view of the paternal imago, one that puts theory and practice in a reciprocally enriching relation to each other, clarifies our theoretical notions, and contributes enhanced clinical understanding of the notion.

Scrutiny of the evidence that is the basis for inferences about the paternal imago reveals more complexity to the subject than might at first blush be imagined. *Observational data* that contribute to an understanding of fathering are more enigmatic than those that constitute mothering. Mothering is often thought of as feeding, cleaning, nurturing, cuddling, all experience-near and dyadic – that is, activities administering to regressed, somewhat childish needs if they take place in a clinical setting and behaviors that can largely be defined and studied by observation of the mother-child dyad. Fathering, however, is not an entirely analogous concept. Such functions as providing, protecting, guiding, leading, and those felt not only in common parlance, but also in conscious and unconscious fantasy, to be father's role often extend beyond the dyad and beyond the experience of immediate observation. Father's interactions with the child are both important and specific (Lamb, 1976; Tyson, 1982; Yogman, 1982), but they may be only a small part of the relevant data. Father may be represented as heroic and valiant, Olympian in power and discernment, by a mother who creates and sustains the illusion of such a father. Mother's contribution may so powerfully affect the child's appreciation of comparatively sparse data from interactions with father himself as to constitute the greater portion of what makes up the child's experience of fathering. Furthermore, a man with the attributes and behaviors of a very strong father may be represented in a light that emphasizes his undependability, his letting mother down, his self-centeredness, his absence, his arrogance, his lack of success or sexual prowess, or any other shortcomings. A mother inclined to integrate the family and promote a positive experience may cover over and compensate for shortcomings and convey an experience of marvellous fathering where in fact very little has transpired. The subject's experience of father may have to do with extended family, with sibling systems, and with others in a much more complicated fashion than the experience of mother usually does.

In *conscious fantasy,* the maternal and paternal object representations are, again, not symmetrical. The fantasy "I want my mother" is generally regressive and concrete, a wish for soothing, feeding, exemption from responsibility, harbor from hurt, and something dominated by the pleasure principle, that is, the wish for somebody to soothe one and free one from unpleasure. The fantasy, "I want my father," on the contrary, is more dominated by the reality principle, a wish for help, power, mastery, justice while one faces the world (as opposed to a regressive retreat from the world).

Our *theoretical understanding* of the paternal imago, then, is not based on the same dyadic relationship as is the experience of mother. Atkins (1982, 1984), writing about the mother's contribution to the paternal imago, has argued that that maternal contribution may form a large part of what the child feels to be experiences of father. Attitudes, moods, and occasional statements like "Wait till I tell Daddy" and "Won't Daddy be proud," "Won't Daddy be surprised!" may convey the sense of father's imminent presence, even throughout long absences or when father's actual contribution is, in fact, minimal. Likewise, even the best-intentioned father may be represented as a pompous, irresponsible, brutal, insensitive lout during his absence, and the child may pick up complaints that externalize blame from a mother who is depressed, upset, divisive, and discontent. The child's experience of the memory may be as something about father, rather than something about mother or family as a whole.

CLINICAL ILLUSTRATIONS

Example 1

A single attorney in his late 20s with difficulties in close relationships began analysis at a time when his girlfriend had gone on an extended trip. She complained that he was overly dependent on her. Early in the analysis, he described his immigrant family in idealized terms as close-knit, educationally aspiring, sacrificing and dedicated to professional excellence. As the analysis began to unfold, a more complex picture of the family developed. His recollections of his father were, at first, of a very rough, punitive man. Remembering a state of extreme anxiety at the age of four, he recalled that he used to cry at night, luring mother from the parental bedroom to soothe him. He recalled that on one occasion he had cried, expecting his mother, but was surprised that father was the one who burst in, angry, furious, and blustering. The patient was convinced that he had, at these times when he was three or four, interrupted sexual activities between his parents. This recollection came when the transference was replete with ambivalence toward the analyst and provocation on the patient's part. He devalued the analyst as overweight, not stylishly dressed, and probably not very successful – reproaches he also leveled at his father. Attention to the hostility and resultant anxiety in the context of the transference reduced his anxiety level and evoked more memories of father. A mild-mannered, nurturing companionable aspect of father emerged in his memories of that time. Father assumed a warm, even protective role with his business subordinates. He had sheltered the patient from competitive sports and had arranged vacation activities so that the patient would not be exposed to the athletic competition and peer harassment that he had always found difficult.

Later in the analysis, when the patient was at the point of breaking up with his girlfriend, who by then had become more committed to him and was pressing for marriage, he became increasingly clear about some of his anxieties about women. His associations went to his mother, a strong, educationally ambitious woman, talking of father and telling the patient in secret of father's potency difficulties after a prostate operation. This was at a point in mother's career where she wished to move from the small northwestern town in which they lived to a big city. She told the patient that his father's attachment to his own job and to his family showed how weak he was, how tied he was to his parents, and how unable he was to make progress in the world. She saw men as being basically weak, dependent, unadventurous, and contemptible. As the analysis progressed, the patient became aware of his own mixed reactions to these conversations with his mother. He was thrilled by these intimacies, by being given special status as his mother's confidant; at the same time he remained filled with anxiety. He was aware that there was something wrong with his relationship with his mother, and there seemed to be something deeply upsetting about the way women regarded men. This confusion was conveyed in his reports of his dialogues with his mother.

Only after many years of analysis did the patient realize that he had recalled *talks with his mother* rather than *actual transactions with his father.* As the analysis continued to unfold, the mother's castrativeness, seductiveness, and contemptuousness became increasingly evident, not only in his memories of her but also in his experiences with strikingly similar women whom he selected as sexual partners. These relationships tended to confirm an inner world in which men were held in contempt; they shed light on why he was both attracted to and frightened by serious attachments to such women. In retrospect, the dialogues with mother could be understood as divisive and seductive, binding him in a gossipy, hostile relationship that devalued father sexually and otherwise. Her complaining aggravated antagonism between the patient and his father and at the same time offered him a specialness so seductive that it did not seem to him an act of divisiveness at the time; nor did it until relatively late in his analysis.

Example 2

A man in his late 40s came for analysis after years of difficult relationships with women in which he had felt trapped and alienated. He came with criticisms of his third wife, whom he wanted to leave after many years of marriage. Early in the analysis he discussed his lifelong difficult relationships with women. As he recalled his family of origin, his associations went to his experiences with his father, a rough, punitive man who belittled him. The patient had been an overprotected youngster, whose home was an apartment in back of the father's business. He recalled daydreaming in his room, starting school late, being frequently absent from school because he was sick, hearing his father do business in the store, and being very frightened of his father. As the analysis continued, the scenes during which father blustered and yelled at him unfolded as ones in which father had felt that mother overprotected him and exempted him from responsibilities. He frequently stayed home from school and was pampered and cuddled by a very vulnerable mother. This woman had, for a short time after his birth, been unable to care for him. She had gone away for what had been called a "rest period," perhaps a postpartum psychosis, for several months before he was a year old.

Somewhat later in the analysis, he recalled that his family situation had changed dramatically when he was in early adolescence. Father had made enough money to sell his business and retire to managing his property. The patient recalled father as weak, servile, soft, even effeminate, lavishing praise on him and staying with the mother despite her disagreeableness and open contemptuousness. He wished that his father would either have stood up to his mother or left her. He recalled a conversation with mother, who had taken him aside and complained bitterly about his father, saying, "All I need is a real man," (meaning sexually) "That's all that's wrong with me." This intimacy in the conversation with the mother left the patient thrilled, but upset and confused. His attention was riveted to his father when he discussed these memories. Why had father endured such indignities? Why hadn't he put her in her place? Why hadn't he left? What had happened to his manliness? These preoccupations led straightaway to an analytic focus on the patient's seeing himself *as his father* in his many unsatisfactory relationships with women. He had picked extremely dependent, often dysfunctional partners in the hope that he would prove to be the strong one in the relationship and not, like his father, an object of contempt. Analytic attention to these fears led him back to more recollections of his conversations with his mother in which she talked contemptuously of his father. These recollections occurred when his difficulties with his wife had escalated in response to his threats to leave her. The current situation was in resonance with memories of his mother's debunking conversations with him about his father, and, for the first time, he was able to focus specifically on his fears of contempt and devaluation from women and to link these with his mother's discourse rather than with his actual experience with his father alone. It had taken him many years and several attempts at treatment to unravel the significance of her divisiveness and binding to him by an angry method of complaining that devalued, castrated, and belittled his father.

Example 3

A married woman in her early 40s entered psychotherapy complaining of difficulties with her second husband, a priggish, controlling man with whom she quarrelled constantly. She had a low-key clinical depression. The marriage had been a verbal battleground from the outset. The patient complained of her husband's withholding, controlling, and stinginess and (according to her) he, of her irresponsibility, wastefulness, and disorganization. Therapy intensified, and the patient began analysis. She talked in a warm, apparently unambivalent way to the analyst but spent many hours complaining. Analytic focus on the complaining illuminated her relationship to her mother, to whom she regularly complained about her husband.

She was the eldest child and only daughter of elderly parents, who lived near her. The parents' marriage had been difficult. This difficulty had been attributed by her mother to her father's gambling, drinking, and business failures, sources of shame and embarrassment to the entire family. The patient had been her mother's confidante for the mother's marital difficulties. In adolescence the patient did not bring friends home for fear that father's behavior would be seen and would embarrass her.

Her own difficult marriage was a focus of continued commentary from her mother. While she showed manifest sympathy and understanding for her daughter's plight, the patient's mother also bombarded her with admonitions to remain in the marriage and always to lavish on her husband caretaking that seemed excessive and unnecessary. She was advised not to take short trips or even to have evenings out with friends, lest her husband not have his meals prepared or his laundry done. Her efforts to deal with her husband straightforwardly were discouraged. Her only protests were ineffective, angry outbursts or episodes of financial irresponsibility that invited more discrediting of her, more control, and more withdrawal on his part. A similar provocativeness emerged in the transference; she had so arranged submission of insurance claims that she fell seriously behind in the payment of

analytic fees. Interpretive attention focused not only on the provocatively late payment, but also on the genetic (infantile) and current
(marital) parallels to what was transpiring in the analysis. These
included her fears of closeness to the analyst (father, husband), which
seemed to her to forebode either desertion or outright attack from her
mother. Just as she was gaining insight into the significance of these
struggles, she impulsively lost a large sum of money on a foolish
investment and decided to discontinue treatment for several months.

She resumed with a clearcut awareness of the self-sabotage that
had threatened the treatment and a fearful eagerness about exploring
her tendency to undermine herself. She bewailed her lack of accomplishment in life, her lifelong pattern of obsequiousness peppered with
angry outbursts, and the type of provocativeness typified by her
financial bunglings in the analysis and in the marriage that sabotaged
what seemed to be her own projects and her own credibility. She
increasingly saw herself as the author of her own unhappy marital
destiny and a person shockingly like her own mother, whom she saw
as contemptible because she complained about her marriage but did not
manage either to deal with the marriage or to leave it.

She was agonizing about her similarity to her mother, and she
began to focus on her mother's expectations that she complain about
her marriage continually but never change it. The undermining effect
of her emotional reliance on her mother became the central focus of
treatment for a long time.

In the meantime, self-sabotage both in the marriage and in the
analysis began to abate. She began to stand up to her husband, and she
insisted on changes. These desires were not undercut by irresponsibility on her part that allowed the husband to discredit her. She began
to distance herself from her mother, seeing her for only the time
necessary for her to manage some of her parents' affairs and to arrange
for needed medical treatment. She neither complained nor tolerated
complaining, and she became circumspect about her marriage.

In the course of a long and largely successful treatment, this
woman's views of her husband and of her father changed very little.
Her father seemed to her as he always had: weak, overly dependent,
ineffectual, and uninterested in anything but his own comfort. What
had changed was not her view of him, but her ability to modify factors
amplifying her shame about her mother and about herself. This shame
had been split off from her self- and maternal object representations and
were experienced as embarrassment about her father. Her husband
remained portrayed as constricted, rigid, and unsatisfying, but the
marriage improved and became a source of support for her young

children. She no longer evoked her husband's shortcomings to justify her regressive attachment to her mother. She had used the attachment to her analyst in the way she could never utilize the relationship with her father. She was able to separate from the regressive dyad with her mother, which was organized around self-sabotage and complaining. She became aware of her own provocation and irresponsibility, which confirmed her sense of identification with her mother. And she became able to assume leadership in her marriage and make it into a functional (if somewhat unsatisfying) union on which she and her children could rely.

Example 4

A man in his mid-30s entered analysis to deal with recurrent episodes of carelessness and self-sabotage that had ruined his career by plummeting him into personal and financial difficulties repeatedly when he was at the point of success. In the midst of one of these bouts, his wife had made an offhand remark about his lack of success in his corporate career. She was then convalescing from an abdominal operation. He had flown into a rage and left her for some months. Before he turned to analysis, they had sought first marital therapy and then pharmacologic help for his sprees of overactivity.

He represented his father as a cruel, competitive man who came home and singled him out for bullying and debunking. The patient himself had been a gifted youngster and described repeated encounters in which his attempts to impress father were met with ridicule. The patient's father worked excessively long hours, feared his business partners greatly, and never allowed himself vacations. The patient's mother, a near-psychotic eccentric, had taken to her sickbed, kept unusual hours, and never seemed to deal with her husband or nurture the children.

The patient maintained a warm, clearly subordinate but always collegial and friendly stance toward the analyst. In the early years of the analysis, there seemed to be no trace in the transference of the relationship he had described with his father. He did, however, treat his two sons in ways that were clearly derived from his view of that relationship. The elder he treated as an inept, presumptuous, bungling, irresponsible upstart; his rantings against this child were clearly reminiscent of the patient's recollections of his own father. (The patient, too, had been an eldest son.) The younger son, on the other hand, was treated as the child the patient himself would like to have been. He was loved, physically cuddled, praised, and cherished.

The patient's external circumstances took a marked turn when a close female associate became ill and unable to function. He became upset, sleepless, overtly terrified of the world, and furious at a host of female employees and at his wife again. He viewed himself as a bluffer, a fake, a failure who had failed to succeed in the world of aggressive men, one who hung around with women and depended on them for support because he could not exert his power in the world of men. Those issues reached the point of crisis when he decided that he was financially unable to continue in his current business situation and began to inquire about other firms. Only when a surprisingly good offer was made to him from a prestigious and cordial firm could his anxieties and sleeplessness be seen in relation to the analyst. He wondered what would happen if he took the job. He would earn more than the analyst. The analyst would resent it and feel the patient to be an upstart. Manifest anxiety became clearly associated, for the first time, to his fear of reprisal from the analyst. Interpretive attention to this transference anxiety led to his feeling much better and taking appropriate steps to establish himself in his new firm.

Further associations went to his provocations of his father that were designed to get nurturance and care when he was fearful of dealing with the world and could not get soothing from his mother. Behind the fear of retaliation, then, was the *wish* that he could be in a helpless, childlike state so that father could care for him, cater to his regressive needs, and provide soothing, nurturance, and support. Embedded, then, in the positive oedipal struggle were his fearful identifications with his dysfunctional mother and his wishes to escape the masculine role, with its risks and dangers, and obtain from his father what he had not gotten from his mother.

Both this patient's parents had left him with a sense of terror at what he saw as the male role. He viewed his father as ruthless, debunking, competitive, yet at the same time fearful of dealing with colleagues and clients in the business world and emotionally deserted by a wife who took to her bed for years. His mother was seen as regressed, self-centered, divisive, incapable of nurturance or support and able only to ease her own tensions. It was the failure of complementary and mutual support between his parents, combined with the terror of the competitive outside world, that so shockingly split this man's inner world into a rough, competitive, retaliatory, masculine world and a self-centered, incompetent, regressed, feminine one. His fears of women, precipitated by his wife's and colleague's illness, had to be analyzed before his view of the male world (i.e., his paternal imago) could be modified by analysis.

SCREENS OF FAMILIAL DYSFUNCTION

These patients report difficulties with their fathers in two ways: In Examples 1, 2, and 4, the early memories, negatively tinged, are of interactions with father himself and portray defensive reactions on father's part. He is gruff, rough, punitive – angry defenses that patients often will not be aware that they have provoked. Often such provocation involves a regressive coalition with mother. Other experiences of father, however, are reported (unawares to the patient) as dialogues with mother about father (Examples 1, 2, and 3) and show mother's omnipotent defenses. These dialogues leave the child with a sense that the memory is entirely about father, whereas the actual material reveals a discontented mother, bonding in a devious manner with her child and portraying father in a way that is divisive, devaluing, and contemptuous. In Example 4, the mother's failure to nurture figured powerfully in the patient's view of the terrors of the male role and his attempts to avoid it.

These examples, then, each convey a drama with a father seen prominently onstage and a divisive mother who is not only a co-actor, but also producer, director, narrator, and even writer of the script. This particular group of analysands had mothers in whom divisiveness, splitting, seductiveness, and absence of what Atkins (1984) has termed "transitive vitalization" – mother's capacity to allow the child to make attachments to the world and to develop outside of the mother-child dyad – are strikingly evident in the case material. Abelin (1971) has drawn attention to the father's role in the child's successfully traversing of the separation-individuation process. The father is the "other-other," the one who joins with the child to offset the tie to mother, which would otherwise become regressive, unmanageably ambivalent, and fraught with dangers of excessive closeness on the one hand and terrifying abandonment on the other. The clinical examples point to divisiveness and lack of bonding within the parental marriage that foreclose the possibility of such a stabilizing relationship for the child, not just in infancy but lifelong. In each case, the memories that provided data for inferences about the paternal imago contained a dialogue with a mother who employed a divisive kind of dyadic binding with the child instead of a transitive type of familial integration. Devalued aspects of the paternal imago are conveyed, then, in the narrative of a mother portrayed as complaining, disappointed, devious, and castrating, one whose pairings-off, rather than integration within the family, and whose omnipotent defenses are represented in the dialogue about the father.

This supradyadic focus has major implications for our understanding of specifics of the process of splitting and of internalization. If,
for the male, the view of father is compounded by the recollection of
mother's attitudes toward father as weak, impotent, and contemptible,
such a model for introjection (exaggerated by the youngster's oedipal
rivalry) is internalized as a damaged introject and powerfully affects the
patient's sense of self. With women, the same binding with mother
portrayed in memories of mother's complaining about father is taken
in as a message the manifest content of which concerns men, but
whose latent content activates the fear of attack or abandonment by an
envious and competitive mother if the young girl were to bind herself
in a secure way to her father. The split representation is based on an
internalization of a felt split within the family, not simply of the child's
dyadic ambivalence toward father. That is, the paternal representation
is split into a strong, primitive aspect (that often records father's phallic
narcissistic defenses when provoked) and a devalued, contemptible
aspect (that reveals mother's omnipotent defenses through a dialogue
between mother and child about father). The split paternal imago,
then, codifies not only the child's phase-appropriate ambivalence exerting a self-fulfilling force on the family, but also a divided family that
powerfully and destructively reinforces the child's ambivalence at the
expense of his or her development. Difficulties in that development are
encoded in the self- and maternal representations, both of which are
screened by the paternal representation.

IMPLICATIONS FOR THEORY AND PRACTICE

Clearly, then, that what we call, for theoretical and clinical convenience, the paternal imago might be called a screen representation, or at
least one that has a screening function – both revealing and masking
sources beyond the specific father-child dyad and powerfully mediated
by the patient's impression of the mother and her attitudes toward, and
relations with, the father. Hence, the paternal representation is not
simple ideation, in the sense that a photograph is a record of the scene
it captures, or even a composite version of that notion. Rather the
"representation" is a set of recollections or views of the paternal object
that serves important defensive and screening functions for self-
representation and other object representations considered in isolation
and for the family as a whole.

The notions of self- and object representations might well undergo the same scrutiny as did the notion of memory in Freud's 1899

paper, "Screen Memories." That work modified the very earliest theory, that of the early 1890s. There was a simple elegance to the earliest theory: all of its major precepts centered on clearcut notions of "ideas": *Pathogenesis* was accounted for by a traumatic event, represented by something like a picture of it–a memory, a photo, so to speak, of an occurrence that had a charge or a quota of affect attached to it. *Symptoms,* insofar as the patient had a *psycho*neurosis and not an *aktual*neurosis, were also representable by ideas–of a feared object in the phobias, of a dysfunctional part of the body in the conversions, of a forbidden impulse in the obsessions, and of a persecutor in paranoia. The *method,* as it remains today, was the association of ideas, and interpretation made the patient aware of complexes of ideas that elucidated unconscious significance. *Cure* was a discharge of affect by abreaction and a return of the walled-off memories to the mainstream of associative connections. Assumed here was that one event, especially a sexual one, can cause pathology. Hence the importance of memory, which was a record of the event. Symptoms were understood by explanation of the ideas involved in phobias, conversions, obsessions, and delusions. The association of ideas leads to certain interpretations by way of the understanding of complexes. The energy necessary to keep the memory out of awarenesses was thus liberated, and the mnemic ideas became free to enter the associative stream of ideas.

Freud's work deepened, and as he began to expand past an oversimplified seduction hypothesis and to appreciate the workings of fantasy and the role of infantile sexuality, he began to put less theoretical emphasis on what actually happened and how it was represented. The memory, therefore, became less central. This deemphasis continued as the structure of the psyche and the structural aspects of psychopathology became more and more understood. But before these changes took place, Freud (1899) wrote "Screen Memories." This work, in my opinion, is not taken seriously enough even now, although it should be at the very foundation of psychoanalytic work. Our conception of screen memories goes far beyond Freud's illustrative case, which was vivid, intense, and innocuous in content. Every memory can be viewed as an ideational product, woven afresh, and concealing as well as revealing. The memory, like the dream, has both manifest and latent content. Memory comes to be seen more like a dream than like a photo of an event. The memory, like the manifest content of a dream, is reworked and woven afresh for defensive purposes, or (if I may reify the way Freud did at that time) one memory defends against another. The level of the complexity of the 1899 paper is significant because it grants full importance to trauma, to fantasy, and to defense, that is, to both internal and external reality. It presumes that trauma and its reconstruction are important but also shows awareness of the fresh weavings of the mental product, the memory. Ideas that are memories, like those that are symptoms, or dreams, may be formed afresh. After 1905, emphasis came to center much more on the internal world and on infantile sexuality, so much so that interest in what actually happened tended to be neglected, especially theoretically. As a result, the theory of memory and of screen memories had less centrality than they had had in the days when an actual event was presumed to be a sufficient explanation of a psychoneurosis.

I dwell on these points because I think the same issues have appeared after the more or less Aristotelian turn in psychoanalysis that followed the advent of the structural theory in 1923, with subsequent emphasis on direct observation of the development of ego, id, and superego in the child and of the development of early object relationships. This introduction of concepts that are abstract distillates of anamnestic data moved away from an exclusive reliance on *the idea* and emphasized a notion of structure that was not as clearly related to discrete units of ideation (e.g., dream, joke, slip, symptom) than it had been in the heyday of the earlier topographic theory. There has, of course, been continued recognition of the fact that in the early lives of neurotic patients something did happen – not trauma as the result of one sexual event, but cumulative trauma, not necessarily capable of mental registration as a single event. The relation of such cumulative trauma to the patient's actual ideation about early familial relationships has nowhere near the theoretical tightness that it did in the times preceding awareness of psychic structure in the development. But *the "idea"* does persist in Hartmann's (Hartmann & Loewenstein, 1962) and Jacobson's (1964) writings, as self- and object representations. I cannot, within the scope of the present discussion, deal with the many advantages, nor the theoretical problems, that go with the usage of these terms. Self- and object representations, or imagos, are similar terms for the "idea" that one has about one's own or another's person. They are inferred by the analyst from affect-laden memories or from actions, cumulative or isolated, integrated or not. Frequently they are evoked in discussions of unintegrated or split-off parts of the personality. Questions arise regarding the concept of representations that are similar to those raised by the concept of memories in the heyday of the seduction hypothesis, namely, whether or not they correspond to some pathogenic event that actually happened. In the case of representation, this is a relationship rather than an isolated trauma. The same type of complexity applies to object representation, and the same analytic penetration is required for the representation that is for the memory. That is, one may imagine *screen representations* or imagos along the same line as one conceptualizes screen memories. The paternal object representation is colored by the emotional climates supplied by the mother (another object representation or imago) and by that which is disowned or repressed as an attribute of self-representation and often is detectable in the transference. So, the paternal imago may serve as a screen memory, as it were, for views of the mother or of the family or of the self, especially if, as we see so commonly in clinical practice, something about the self is either repressed or not representable in any simple way.

The maternal object representation, then, can be split and displaced onto the paternal object representation. We see in many clinical presentations what might be called screen paternal representations in the associations of patients of both sexes. Very real difficulties that the patient has with men (repetition of what is presumed to be a relationship embodied by the paternal object representation) are portrayed in ways that also screen difficulties of the mother in her relationship to the father and deemphasize loyalty conflicts within the family that threaten to overwhelm the patient with anxiety.

The history of psychoanalysis showed at the start awareness of conflictual oedipal predicaments, phalocentric, and organized around the father, and only later evolved an understanding of what was preoedipal, mammocentric, and organized around the mother. In our current, more sophisticated return to interest in the father, we are faced with the need to refine theoretical constructs from the psychoanalytic situation itself to allow for integration of purely psychoanalytic data with the results of direct observation of development. The predicament is similar to the one Freud was in when he developed the notion of screen memories. We will need much philosophical and theoretical clarity before our terms can be used in ways that do not prejudge the world on matters of fact. And we need to realize that what appear to be representations of one object, perhaps father especially, may derive from the relation of father with mother, with siblings for that matter, or from relationships and loyalties that can only be understood from observations of the whole family. Much clarifying work will have to be done to integrate material from direct observation into psychoanalytic theory and even to permit consistent usage of our terms.

Patients' recollections in the analytic situation of their fathers do reflect in part their direct experiences with father. These too often reflect his defenses when provoked by the patient. The provocations often become evident as the transference unfolds and is worked through. It is common for such memories to be supplemented with others that are more pleasant and mellow and portray satisfying or even terrifyingly intimate aspects of the relationship with father when consistent transference interpretation has resulted in working through (Examples 1, 4).

The paternal representation codifies a great deal about the self-representation, and, in men, about identification with a damaged or devalued paternal introject and a struggle against that identification (Greenson, 1954). The young male sees himself *as understudy to a male* – his father – *in relation to a female* – his mother. The value or lack of value of father as model is defined for the youngster much more by dialogue and experience within the home than in other areas. The paternal imago, then, contains a record of the patient's model for identification and an entire set of attitudes toward this model. Examination of devalued, or damaged, introjects and struggles against them or alternatively brutal and persecutory introjects, and provocations of them, form a large part of the work of analysis.

The paternal imago also encapsulates a great deal of information about how mother is seen and about the patient's fears and desires relating to her. The maternal imago in Examples 1, 2, and 3 is split, and projected bad parts are experienced by both patient and mother as belonging to father. Mother's defensive activities (that is, to protect her self-representation) so dovetail with the patient's defensive workings (which protect the self- and maternal object representation) that both mother and child take defensive opportunities to split off unacceptable parts of mother and experience them as either due to father or residing in father. Father, then, absorbs a great deal of ambivalence in the mother-child dyad. This is reflected in the paternal imago.

These considerations point convincingly to the fact that that which is internalized is not to be confused with self-representation, maternal, paternal, or other object representations, but rather a sense of self that comes from internalization of the family, that is to say, self as defined by father in relation to mother and to other children in the family. Split representations are reflective of splits in the family, which, in turn, induce or amplify serious splits in the ego that (as a manifestation of the compulsion to repeat) show up in later object choices that will preserve the same constellation of difficulties.

It is uncommon, in my experience, for patients in psychoanalysis or in psychoanalytic psychotherapy to have a relationship with their fathers that they see as strong and useful. Those paternal relationships that are hailed initially as good usually unfold in the patient's expanding perspective as seductive and divisive. In the rare instance where it appears that a very caring, supportive father has been in a close relationship with the patient, the mother is often found to have been highly dysfunctional or even psychotic. The paternal representation, negative as it so commonly is early in analytic work, provides us with a focus for analytic scrutiny not just for the relationship with father, but for mother's capacity to integrate and to allow meaningful attachments outside of the mother-child dyad and her toleration of otherness, or, on the contrary, her divisiveness or sabotage of attempts at separation from her. Persons with a strong positive relation with their fathers usually have a strong relationship with both parents. They are not often seen in the consulting room. Their satisfying recollections point not only to positive aspects of the relationship with the father, but also to the presence of a mother who can be assumed to be one who integrates, tolerates separation, and makes possible, and even promotes, such a relationship with the father. The patient with poor paternal relations, on the contrary, usually proves to have not only a poor relationship with father, but almost always an intensely ambivalent relationship in the dyadic situation with mother, that is, with a mother who cannot tolerate separation, tends to be fixated to dyads, and sabotages any attachment outside of the mother-child dyad.

We also learn from the "paternal imago" much about the self-representation. The paternal imago contains latent commentary about self in relation to father and mother. Behind a negatively portrayed paternal imago in the examples sketched earlier are the patients' divided selves, selves who seek out or are drawn into situations where the patient is a go-between and then experience the same seductive binding to one person and hostility coming from another, who is excluded (Slipp, 1984). The paternal imago, of course, like the dream and the screen memory, is not the bedrock of analytic thinking, but the subject for further analytic work. What the paternal imago tells us about the relationship with father is like the manifest content of a dream or a memory. Useful information is often conveyed, but the significance of the manifest content must be seen in the light of latent content, which must be reached by further analysis. It is this process that makes for modifications of the self-representation, maternal representation, splits in the family, process of internalization, and the capacity to be freed from dyadic fixations within the family. The paternal imago, then, when it reflects disturbance, is indicative of disruption radiating outward from the self. Vulnerabilities to personality disorganization show up as clinginess and fixation to the mother-child dyad. When the mother-child dyad becomes too hotly ambivalent and risks eroding the relationship with mother, displacement from the analysand's maternal imago may dovetail with the mother's defensive needs (to protect her self-representation) so that mother and child act in collusion against father. This collusive attitude is often combined with activities that provoke defensive reactions from father. These further confirm negative aspects of what is, in an oversimplified way, called the "paternal imago."

These considerations, then, set the stage for an analytic focus that gives us a good deal of feeling for the cohesiveness, sense of separateness, fixation to dyads, and methods of defense not only in the patient but in the family, and for the processes of internalization against which these patients so frequently struggle.

The paternal imago is a powerful indicator of the patient's internalizations. It reveals much about the capacity for binding or for divisiveness in the narrative of the patient or of that of others in the family. The narrative of the mother, especially, points to the patient's experience of her effect on cohesion or disruption in the family: either to her binding, transitive vitalization, integration, capacity to tolerate depressive anxiety (that is, Eros); or to her divisiveness, unbinding, detachment, castrativeness, sabotaging, or a retreat to the paranoid-schizoid position (that is, Thanatos). But the data that comprise the paternal imago provide sources for analytic understanding that are fed by expressive and defensive resonances not only from the mother-child dyad and the patient's relationship to the parental marriage, but also from the very earliest father-child dyad and from the family as a whole.

REFERENCES

Abelin, E. (1971), The role of the father in the separation-individuation process. In: *Separation-Individuation,* ed. S. B. McDevitt & C. F. Settlage. New York: International Universities Press, pp. 229–253.

Atkins, R. (1982), Discovering daddy: The mother's role. In: *Father and Child,* ed. S. H. Cath, A. Gurwitt & J. M. Ross. Boston: Little, Brown, pp. 139–149.

Atkins, R. (1984), Transitive vitalization and its impact on father-representation. *Contemp. Psychoanal.,* 20:663–676.

Freud, S. (1899), Screen memories. *Standard Edition,* 13:303–322. London: Hogarth, 1962.

Greenson, R. (1954), The struggle against identification. *J. Amer. Psychoanal. Assn.,* 2:200–217.

Hartmann, H. & Loewenstein, R. (1962), Notes on the superego. *The Psychoanalytic Study of the Child,* 17:42–81. New York: International Universities Press.

Jacobson, E. (1964), *The Self and the Object World.* New York: International Universities Press.

Lamb, M. E., ed. (1976), *The Role of the Father in Child Development.* New York: Wiley.

Laplanche, J. & Pontalis, J. B. (1973), *The Language of Psychoanalysis* (trans. D. Nicholson-Smith). New York: Norton.

Slipp, S. (1984), *Object Relations: A Dynamic Bridge Between Individual and Family Treatment.* New York: Aronson.

Tyson, P. (1982), The role of the father in gender identity: Urethral erotism and phallic narcissism. In: *Father and Child,* ed. S. H. Cath, A. Gurwitt & J. M. Ross. Boston: Little, Brown, pp. 175–188.

Yogman, M. W. (1982), Observations on the father-infant relationship. In: *Father and Child,* ed. S. H. Cath, A. Gurwitt & J. M. Ross. Boston: Little, Brown, pp. 101–122.

3

Fatherhood from the Perspective of Object Relations Theory and Relational Systems Theory

Roy Muir

In this chapter I will examine the contributions of object relations and family systems theories to the study of fatherhood. I shall attempt to show that the role of the father is significant in providing an optimal developmental ecosystem; that the father is an object, in the psychoanalytic sense; and that his relationship with his child is internalized as is the family relational system of which he is a part. Some modifications to the psychoanalytic theory of relationships are proposed that I believe facilitate our understanding of family processes and of fatherhood in relation to child development. I shall show that the father relationship offers several advantages to the child:

1. The mothering dyad is "held" by the father.

2. He provides an alternative and differently responding attachment figure (object).

3. Having two parents ensures there is someone to love when the other parent is hated.

4. He is a stimulus for individuation.

5. He offers an oedipal challenge and thus the initiation into group relations.

6. He contributes to the group relational patterns of the family, which are internalized by the child. Out of these internalizations role functions will be recreated in adulthood.

The biopsychosocial role of the father was neglected or avoided by developmental psychologists until the last decade or so. One of the reasons for this seems to be the great variety of fatherhood models manifest in different human societies. Motherhood, prescribed as it appears to be by more clearcut biological as well as cultural forces, is more often recognized as a factor in human development. This has tended to obscure the necessity to evaluate fatherhood.

Infant and parent-infant developmental studies have provided a large body of data challenging psychoanalytic developmental theory. New information challenges both drive theory and linear causal assumptions. Object relations theory and family process theory each offer new and interesting ways of interpreting and integrating this knowledge. This chapter attempts to show how these frameworks enable us to examine fatherhood without the constraints that classical drive theory, and to some extent structural theory, together with a dyadic methodology, have tended to impose on both developmental theory and observational opportunity. I shall describe in this chapter how certain modifications in structure and drive theory proposed by object relations enables us to incorporate the father in a more comprehensive psychoanalytic study of the family. First, however, I will discuss attachment theory as the drive theory that makes new syntheses possible.

ATTACHMENT THEORY

Studies of the nature of human attachment and comparative studies of other species have led to a coherent human psychobiological drive theory; *attachment theory.* The work of Bowlby (1958, 1970) has been a major impetus for this revised instinctual drive theory, which increasingly illuminates and extends Freud's later theories of anxiety.

In the last ten or fifteen years, significant new knowledge has been accumulated on the relational and perceptual capacities of the infant. Yogman (1982), among others, has shown how differentially responsive to the male and female adult a four-week-old baby can be.

Still, we tend to suppose that for several weeks or months there is a more or less undifferentiated mother-father image. During the first year of life, however, the infant becomes preferentially attached to one figure.

It has become clear that the father, or for that matter an older sibling, may become (or be from the beginning) the primary attachment figure for the child. Does this answer the question, Can the father be an object in the psychoanalytic sense? Of course, the answer has always been yes, an exciting oedipal object, for example – in line with the libido theory. However, attachment theory takes us further by positing a hierarchy of attachment figures that can, in preferential order, insulate the infant against the experience of aloneness, strangeness, and danger.

The work of Lamb (1976) and others suggests that there are very few quantitative or qualitative differences in the child's responses to fathers and mothers when a variety of test "strange" or "separation" situations are set up experimentally.

Clearly, the father who in ordinarily good-enough circumstances becomes an object of attachment may at times be the most important. What else should he be to a boy or girl at different ages and different stages? The variety of fatherhood models referred to earlier suggests that in the first months of life it is not only the direct relationship to the child that is important, but the part the father plays in regulating the environment around the child and ensuring the integrity of this nurturant, facilitating, and acknowledging environment. Winnicott (1960a) referred to this as the father's providing a protective covering around the mother-child unit.

THE OBJECT AND OBJECT RELATIONS THEORY

An "object" in psychoanalytic usage has two meanings: (a) It is the human figure (or part of that figure) that is invested with instinctual energy. This definition derives from Freud's (1905) source, aim and object. (b) It can also be the mental representation of the real object.

An internal object relationship is the establishment of an internalized pattern of relationship with an invested object that is evoked repetitively whenever the needs and affects associated with that relationship are mobilized.

Object relations theory derives from a movement within psychoanalysis, British psychoanalysis in particular. It owes much to Melanie Klein (1946), who elaborated Freud's theory of internalization and externalization in early ego development. Balint (1968), influenced by Ferenzi, outlined his ideas about early faults in the parent-child relationship and what he called "primary love" (1937), the earliest object love.

Balint, Fairbairn, Guntrip, and Winnicott (see Sutherland, 1980), each in his own way, emphasized the importance of the real object and its empathic, nurturant, and responsive capacities. It must be said, however, that the word "object" almost always implied the maternal object. With the exception of Winnicott, these workers ignored fatherhood in any practical sense, as much as other schools. To be fair, this neglect was largely due to the emphasis within object relations theory on so-called preoedipal development issues, which in turn has meant a focus largely on mother-infant relations.

Winnicott (1953, 1960c) also preoccupied with early parent child relationships is best known for his concepts of the transitional object and of the false self, as well as his reassuring notion of good-enough mothering and the simple but profound idea of the holding environment.

Fairbairn (1952), working in relative isolation, was the only one of these analysts to break with Freudian theory in any explicit way. He took issue with both structural theory (which he saw as inhuman and mechanistic) and the libido theory, which gives attachment bonds merely secondary drive or "cupboard love" significance. He stood the libido theory on its head in insisting that pleasure is the signpost to the object rather than the object's merely being the signpost to pleasurable discharge. Put another way, pleasurable sensual experiences cement relationships to the object, but object seeking is the primary drive. Thus, Fairbairn's ideas on drive as object seeking approach congruence with the work of the attachment theorists.

Fairbairn's argument with Freud's structural theory was based on the proposition that structure formation was a defensive adaptation rather than a necessary part of healthy ego development. Guntrip (1969), a pupil and interpreter of Fairbairn, described his basically different approach to the theory of psychic structure formation simply: Good object relations *become* a *part* of the *ego;* bad object relations become split off, repressed—a *foreign body* in the *ego.* Ego structures are therefore always pathological. This includes Freud's (1923) superego concept. More recently, Rubens (1984) reviewed Fairbairn's theory of structure formation and showed that the attempts of Kernberg (1976) and others to reconcile Fairbairn's ideas with Freudian and ego psychology viewpoints overlook this critical issue of the normality versus pathology of structure formation.

Regardless of which drive theory is used – libido or attachment theory – it is clear that the father must and does become an "object" in the psychoanalytic sense.

WINNICOTT'S CONTRIBUTIONS AND THE MOVEMENT TOWARD A RELATIONAL SYSTEMS APPROACH

Winnicott (1944) pointed out that the two-parent child has the advantage of always having a parent to love when the other is hated. This is a very significant advantage when we consider that hate for the object threatens the child's security more than any other emotion.

Winnicott provided many linkages with family process theory. Among them was the concept of "mirroring" (1960b). According to Winnicott, early affective mirroring is fundamental to the development of the ego. Mirroring is the face-to-face contact and preprogrammed stimulus-response linkages, empathically reciprocated, observed in the early parent-infant relationship. The early-linked emotional response cycles described by Brazelton and his associates (1975, 1979) appear to confirm Winnicott's earlier formulations.

Later, Winnicott (1967) extended his ideas on mirroring within the mother-infant relationship to the recognition that the family as a whole has a mirroring role.

FAMILY STRUCTURE AND FAMILY PROCESS

The wide variety of father roles makes it impossible to define anything approaching an ideal fathering formula. This variety and flexibility has increased with the breakdown of rigid cultural prescription of sex-role behaviors. Recently studies of primary fathering families have been initiated (see ch. 19, this volume).

Family process theories offer concepts that allow analysis of *parenting role* behavior. Currently, parenting as a joint responsibility is seen as desirable, rather than "mothering" and "fathering" in stereotypic assigned roles and duties. These days, we seldom encounter the biblical father, breadwinner, managing director of the family, ultimate judge, and executor of punishments. This type of father, who played little direct part in the emotional life of children aside from occasionally being charmed by daughters and appeased by sons, is now encountered only in certain fundamentalist sects and other ultraconservative groups (at least in westernized countries). Nevertheless, recent studies by Parke, Power, Tinsley, and Hymel (1979) suggest that the birth of the first child shifts most couples, however egalitarian in attitude, toward differentiation in parenting roles rather than similarity.

Quite early, the father seems to elicit a different set of responses (Yogman, 1982) than does the mother. He does this by approaching his infant with a different set of affectomotor stimulus patterns. He tends to be more aggressive, more exciting, louder; and, of course, the voice tones are different. The infant responds with quicker arousal – a shorter "plateau" and briefer disengagement. This different experience prepares the way for a wider potential for self-expression and object relatedness during and after separation-individuation (Abelin, 1975; Mahler, Pine, and Bergman, 1975). Siblings, grandparents, and other members of the family constellation contribute similarly to the emergence of different patterns of self-experience and expression.

Thus, a good-enough father contributes to the nurturant environment and provides an alternative attachment figure, a gender-orienting object, and a libidinal object. In addition, he will set limits and aid the development of behavioral controls in conjunction with the mother. Finally, he will intervene when projective distortions impair the mother-child relationship (as will the mother when the father is projectively enmeshed with a child).

Obviously, a child with a father who parents in this way is better off than a child with no father. Such a child gets good *parenting,* but this does not define the father's *specific* significance within the object relations frame of reference. Among the most important questions that remain unanswered is whether, as adults, fatherless children have significant difficulty with parent-role function. My clinical impression is that males especially do. It remains for long-term predictive research to answer this question.

DEVELOPMENT OF A RELATIONAL SYSTEMS
MODEL

Given the validity of the foregoing modifications in instinct and structural theory, the observations of 30 years of psychotherapy of whole families, and the recognition that relational deficiencies are sometimes more important than conflict in development, we can make progress toward a relational systems model of psychological development. It is proposed here that this model makes it possible to incorporate the father as a real object, as a parenting figure, and as a major contributor to the internal relational world of the child. The concept of transpersonal processes is an essential step toward this new frame of reference.

Laing (1967) emphasized the importance of family processes in development. While he did not specifically address the role of the father, his concept of *transpersonal defenses* paved the way for a psychoanalytic understanding of how family dynamics can be internalized in each family member. By transpersonal defenses, Laing meant those defenses which operated on the inner world of one's objects in the effort to stabilize one's own inner world. Earlier, Johnson and Szurek (1952) made observations on the role of family and more particularly parental processes in the aetiology of some kinds of delinquency. They postulated the transmission of defects in parental superego structures to a child. The transmission of these superego "lacunae" was of course mediated by *interactions* between parents and child. While the theory appears to be a deficiency model, as suggested by the term lacunae, these workers clearly noted the tendency of one or both parents to *actively,* if unconsciously, encourage dyssocial behavior in the child by smiling and other signs of pleasure, interest, or even fascination while verbally discouraging or prohibiting the behavior.

Stierlin (1972) later carried the psychoanalytic understanding of family processes further with his concept of family modes of relatedness, particularly in families with separating adolescents. He delineated three modes—binding, delegating and expelling; the delegating mode encompassing the phenomena Johnson and Szurek had described earlier. At times, parents may set up conflictual delegations. Again, it is important to remember that certain types of parent-child interactions *mediate* these modes. Clearly, the role of the father is critical in these transactions either as a principal in the delegation process or as a modifier of maternal delegations when he is able to maintain his parental objectivity and adaptive awareness of his child.

Family process practitioners and theorists have in recent years made increasing use of general systems theory (Von Bertalanffy, 1968) in their formulations of behavioral disorganization and psychopathology (Selvini-Palazzoli et al., 1978). Some, but not all (e.g., Watslawick, Beaven, and Jackson, 1967), have specifically excluded linear developmental concepts and even the notion of intrapsychic individual dynamics. All have emphasized the need to view motivation in circular systems rather than in linear perspectives.

SYNTHESIS

The author has elsewhere (1975, 1982) argued the necessity to integrate the object relations approach to individual dynamics with the
family group relations and systems theory approaches. This effort had
two main thrusts. The first was in a study of the psychoanalytic theory
of internalization (1975), where it was argued that Bowlby's (1970)
theory of attachment behavior, together with Fairbairn's (1952) critical
reevaluation of drive theory, better fitted our knowledge of affiliative
systems (families) than did classical Freudian libido theory. In that
paper I also argued that linear constructs of internalization, whether
primitive incorporation or higher, more mature order concepts of
identification, were, as Schafer (1972) said, not to be mistaken for
actual processes. They might represent *fantasies* of taking in the object
in some way, but the *actual processes* of encoding into the individual's
psychic structure seem more likely to be the encoding of *relational
systems* (affective/interactional patterns). Furthermore, these patterns
were not only self-object (child-mother or child-father) transactions but
also object-object (especially mother-father, mother-sibling, father-
sibling) patterns of relatedness. (See also Sandler and Sandler, 1978.)
Finally, it was argued that the whole family's patterns of relatedness,
with its defensive myths, distortions, and preferred modes of affective
regulation, would be internalized and become a part of the self.
    The second major line of thought in the author's attempts to
integrate these threads (Muir, 1982) brings us back to the nature of the
processes that go on between people, in infancy, in families and
groups. The role of projective identification, as clarified by Ogden
(1979), is central to this model in which Laing's (1967) work on
transpersonal defenses was developed into a theory of transpersonal
processes. I proposed that a mode of psychological functioning called
the transpersonal mode operates throughout life in conjunction with,
or oscillating with, an individual objective mode. The former is the
mode of empathy, of merger, and of many group processes. The latter
is the mode of individual and dyadic transaction in which individuated
objectivity is preserved. The capacity to function facultatively in this
latter, individuated mode is attained only on satisfactory completion of
the separation-individuation phase. The relational modes of the family
are critical in this transition.
    In classical dyadic psychoanalysis, these two modes alternate, the
analyst attempting to use the transpersonal mode in the service of
understanding the patient. Thus the transpersonal mode may be *adaptive,* as in the empathic identification of analytic work, or *defensive,* as in

the projective identification in child abuse, borderline states, and other situations where an internal state is recreated in the relational world.

The transpersonal mode incorporates the selfobject concept of Kohut (1978) and his followers and their revised theory of normal narcissism. In particular, the individual's need for mirroring from the group, for the maintenance of integrity and continuity of the self, is seen as congruent with, and contributing to, the synthesis of object relations theory and family process theory.

The implications of this bimodal theory for the study of father-hood appear to be that not only the dyadic relationship with the father will be internalized (and its negative aspects repeated), but also the relational system of the family as a whole, in which father may play a greater or lesser part. Both sets of internalizations may need to be addressed in analytic work (Muir, 1975). When the child matures and enters parenthood, not only the dyadic object related father set will be activated, but also the family structure sets involving father as a systemic member.

Parke et al. (1979) summarized the situation as follows:

> The importance of these findings (largely from parent-infant interaction research) is clear: In order to understand the father-infant relationship and its effects on the infants development, the total set of relationships among the members of the family needs to be assessed. Only in this way will the complex nature of such influences be understood [p. 31].

The following case illustrates some of the developmental implications of these formulations and gives some clinical perspective to the discussion that follows.

CASE ILLUSTRATION:
A MAN WHO NEVER HAD A FATHER

J., an articulate, crisply direct professional man in his 40s, asked for therapy following a separation from his wife and the initiation of another relationship. He had custody of his three teenaged children and was worried that he would not be able to relate to them emotionally, as he had always been intellectual, remote, and infuriatingly logical in his dealings with them. He was also concerned about two other aspects of his emotional life: first, that he would not be able to relate with sufficient depth of feeling to his new lady; second, that a pervasive lack of appropriate feeling might interfere with his social relationships. He did have a specific symptom: In any public situation where he or his work was in the limelight, he would feel extremely shy and embarrassed, blush, and be barely able to cope.

He and his ex-wife had had a very comfortable, understanding, merged kind of relationship since their marriage as kindred spirits nearly 20 years before. They had each had a couple of affairs, completely avoiding conflict; but in recent years his wife had signaled her interest in the female member of a couple they were friendly with. He had encouraged her, he said, not sure why, out of boredom maybe, and eventually his wife became deeply involved in a lesbian relationship and asked him for a separation agreement. He agreed without too much pain. Now, a year later, he was surprised at the depth of his ex-wife's bitterness and rage at him. He only slowly began to perceive that she might feel profoundly betrayed by him and his failure to "hold her" or to affirm her femininity. Meanwhile he became custodian of the children, who were painfully aware of their mother's status as a lesbian.

In his therapy sessions, he reviewed his history and in particular his merged, ambivalent, troubled relationship to his mother and his lack of a father, which at first he regarded as insignificant. His mother had married his father and conceived J. on the eve on her soldier husband's departure for the war. He was declared missing, and she ran off with a much older man when the patient was about a year old, alienating herself from family and community. She had four daughters by him over the next few years, but they never married. The patient remembers his mother taking enormous pains to hide her shameful unmarried status. There were several moves.

He was closely enmeshed with his mother and remembers long intimate discussions with her. He also remembers that she never gave him any encouragement and affirmation, but always made sarcastic or derogatory references to his achievements. He was a bright scholar, and his teachers realized he was university material.

He said of his stepfather, "He and I didn't have much to say to each other." He spoke indulgently but dismissively of the old man but revealed some envy as he described how his stepfather doted on his four beautiful halfsisters.

He was able to make good progress in his relationship with both his new lover and his daughter after exploring the intensity of his fear of his mother's grip on him and her power to denigrate any autonomous achievement. He realized that he and his mother had had from the start a special, if conflictual, relationship from which his stepfather was excluded. One day he learned that his stepfather was ill back in his home country. He angrily predicted that his mother would use this to manipulate his return home. He declared his horror of funerals – how he was affected, overwhelmed by other people's grief. He felt he could not go home.

At the beginning of the next session, he asked me directly what I thought of him. Recognizing that this was a very important transaction, I first acknowledged his need to know, then told him I would not answer, but that he needed something, perhaps affirmation, urgently. Could it be related to the news from home?

He looked stunned, then became tearful, and began to speak of his need to really have it out with the old man – really find out what he thought of J. He went on to talk of his anger with his stepfather for *not* interfering in his enmeshment with his mother, for not caring enough to rescue J. and his male identity and the abilities he had.

He recalled a male teacher who had taken an interest in him when he was a school boy. He had gone to visit this man on a trip home a few months before, only to be told that the man had died six weeks before. He cried as he remembered this.

He was able to visit his stepfather and talk about some important things. Coping with his aging mother proved easier than he had expected. His daughters were doing well, and his new relationship was progressing towards marriage. He terminated therapy with warmth and sadness, acknowledging how important I and his therapy, and his stepfather had been to him.

Discussion

This man's intense but denied need for interest and confirmation from a father was identified quite early in his therapy but reached full consciousness following the news of his stepfather's illness and his transference question. His own significance as a father to his daughters and his failure as husband-father to his first wife became poignant realities to this man, who could begin to acknowledge his own importance – his differentiated male importance – only after acknowledging his stepfather's importance to him.

Whatever his earlier contribution, the father in western cultures becomes more significant during the separation-individuation phase (Abelin, 1975). He provides an alternative attachment figure during the dissolution of omnipotence in the rapprochement subphase, with its sometimes exhausting battles – as Winnicott (1944) said, someone to love while the other is hated. He is not, as Burlingham (1973) suggested, merely a substitute for the mother.

When oedipal stirrings begin, the child discriminates not only his or her relations with a separate mother and father, but also their separate relationship from the child. The child also becomes aware of the father's separate role in the world outside the family "skin." The parents' sexual relationship and the way father and mother negotiate power and responsibility will all become aspects of the parents' relationship, which *are* internalized by the oedipal child. The author has reported elsewhere (1985) how oedipal stage strivings in the child may be heightened by family (transpersonal) reverberations derived from the parents' unresolved oedipal issues.

Masterson (1976), applying Mahler's (1975) ideas to the understanding of the genesis of borderline personality disorder, argued that the father, by failing to intervene in the overenmeshed mother-child relationship and offer a different and more individualized relationship to the child, shares by default in the pathology. The failure of the father to intervene effectively in a mother-toddler or mother-adolescent individuation struggle, sets up a deficiency in the adaptive dynamics of the family. This deficiency is as powerful as overt action in its impact on the child and is internalized by the child. An analogous situation is the mother who colludes silently in father-daughter incest. Thus, the psychologically absent father can be of enormous significance during these and other stages of development.

CONCLUSION

In this chapter I have attempted to show that the father-child relationship is significant in two ways. First, the father is an object in the psychoanalytic sense and as such is the object of an internalized relational system. Second, the father is a significant contributor to the relational system, the family, which in turn, is internalized by the child and which provides patterns for a variety of later role functions.

Numerous studies, those of Adam (1980) and Rutter (1977) among them, strongly suggest that the loss of a parent by death or separation affects children catastrophically only when the integrity of the surviving family fails. Children mourn, yes, but in ordinarily good-enough circumstances they recover and develop normally. While these studies refer to loss of a parent—and it is recognized that loss is different from not having a parent at all—it may not be the specific object relation with father or mother that is *essential* to the ego development of the child, but the continuity of nurturing relatedness and behavioral regulation within some kind of integrated family network. However, clinical experience suggests, as does the foregoing review, that the presence or absence of the father is always of considerable significance to the child.

I feel that cultural development toward a civilization in which empathic receptiveness and a child-centered parenting attitude are expected of fathers and fully supported by the culture is in its early stages. Even in western society, the father role ranges from mere impregnator at one end of the spectrum, to primary caregiver, nurturer, and provider at the other end. Given this variability and the wide cultural variations in father roles, it is obvious that no single father role pattern can be regarded as essential. The infant brings to the father a repertoire of relational needs that unfold as a series of relational modes, each with its phase-specific style of perceiving and responding to the object world. At each phase, there is an optimal response to the child, and in some of these the response of a father is critical.

I have proposed here that a developmental ecosystemic model of human relationships can be constructed using attachment theory, object relations theory, and family systems theory. Cultural processes can be readily assimilated into this model. In the belief that this extends the conceptual basis of the psychoanalytic theory of relationship into the group process field, I have introduced a concept of transpersonal processes. These formulations are offered in the belief that they enable an understanding of fatherhood in the context of a wider under-standing of human affiliative urges and needs, which later cement individual, family, and cultural identity.

REFERENCES

Abelin, E. (1975), Some further observations and comments on the earliest role of the father. *Internat. J. Psycho-Anal.,* 56:293–302.

Adam, K. (1980), Suicide and attachment. In: *The Place of Attachment in Human Behavior,* ed. C. M. Parkes & J. Stevenson-Hinde. New York: Basic Books, pp. 269–264.

Balint, M. (1937), Early developmental states of the ego: Primary object love. *Internat. J. Psycho-Anal.,* 30:265–273.

———— (1968), *The Basic Fault.* London: Tavistock.

Bowlby, J. (1958), The nature of the child's tie to his mother. *Internat. J. Psycho-Anal.,* 39:350–373.

———— (1970), *Attachment and Loss,* Vol. 1. London: Hogarth Press.

Brazelton, T. B. & Als, H. (1979), Four early stages in the development of mother-infant interactions. *The Psychoanalytic Study of the Child,* 34: 349–369. New Haven: Yale University Press.

_____Tronick, E., Adamson, L., Als, H. & Wise, S. (1975), Early mother-infant reciprocity. In: *Parent-Infant Interaction,* ed. R. Hinde. (Ciba-Geigy Foundation Symposium, No. 33). Amsterdam: Elsevier.

Burlingham, D. (1973), The pre-oedipal infant-father relationship. *The Psychoanalytic Study of the Child,* 28: pp. 23–47. New Haven: Yale University Press.

Fairbairn, W. R. D. (1952), *Psychoanalytic Studies of the Personality.* London: Tavistock.

Freud, S. (1905), Three essays on the theory of sexuality. *Standard Edition, 7*:, 135–243. London: Hogarth Press, 1953.

_____ (1923), The ego and the id. *Standard Edition,* 19:12–66. London: Hogarth Press, 1961.

Guntrip, H. (1969), *Schizoid Phenomena, Object Relations and the Self.* London: Hogarth Press.

Johnson, A. M. & Szurek, S. A. (1952), The genesis of antisocial acting out in children and adults. *Psychoanal. Quart.,* 21:323.

Kernberg, O. (1976), *Object Relations Theory and Clinical Psychoanalysis.* New York: Aronson.

Klein, M. (1946), Notes on some schizoid mechanisms. *Internat. J. Psycho-Anal.,* 27:99–110.

Kohut, H. & Wolf, E. (1978), The disorders of self and their treatment: An outline. *Internat. J. Psycho-Anal.,* 59:413–425.

Laing, R. D. (1967), Family and individual structure. In: *The Predicament of the Family,* ed. P. Lomas. New York: International Universities Press, pp. 107–125.

Lamb, M. E. (1976), The role of the father, an overview. In: *The Role of the Father in Child Development,* ed. M. E. Lamb. New York: Wiley, pp. 1–34.

Mahler, M., Pine, F. & Bergman, A. (1975), *The Psychological Birth of the Human Infant.* New York: International Universities Press.

Masterson, J. F. (1976), *The Psychotherapy of the Borderline Adult.* New York: Brunner/Mazel.

Muir, R. C. (1975), The family and the problem of internalization. *Brit. J. Med. Psychol.,* 48:267–272.

_____ (1982), The family, the group, transpersonal processes and the individual. *Internat. Rev. Psycho-Anal.,* 9:317–326.

_____ (1985), Transpersonal processes and the oedipal stage of development. *Brit. J. Med. Psychol.,* 58:111–118.

Ogden, T. (1979), On projective identification. *Internat. J. Psycho-Anal.,* 60:357–373.

Parke, R. D., Power, T. G., Tinsley, B. R. & Hymel, S. (1979), The father's role in the family system, *Seminars in Perinatology,* 3:25–34.

Rubens, R. L. (1984), The meaning of structure in Fairbairn. *Internat. Rev. Psycho-Anal.,* 11:429–440.

Rutter, M. (1977), Separation, loss and family relationships. In: *Child Psychiatry,* ed. M. Rutter & L. Hersov. Oxford: Blackwell Scientific.

Sandler, J. J. & Sandler, A. (1978), On the development of object relations and affects. *Internat. J. Psycho-Anal.,* 59:285–296.

Schafer, R. (1972), Internalization: Process or fantasy. *The Psychoanalytic Study of the Child,* 27:411–436. New Haven: Yale University Press.

Selvini-Palazzoli, M., Boscolo, L., Cecchin, G. & Prata, G. (1978), *Paradox and Counter Paradox.* New York: Aronson.

Stierlin, H. (1972), *Separating Parents and Adolescents.* New York: New York Times Books/Quadrangle.

Sutherland, J. D. (1980), The British object relations theorists: Balint, Winnicott, Fairbairn and Guntrip. *J. Amer. Psychoanal. Assn.,* 28:829–860.

Von Bertalanffy, L. (1968), *General Systems Theory.* New York: Brasilier.

Watzlawick, P., Beavin, A. D. & Jackson, D. D. (1967), *Pragmatics of Human Communication.* New York: Norton.

Winnicott, D. W. (1944), *The Child, the Family, and the Outside World.* Middlesex, Eng.: Penguin Books.

———— (1953), Transitional objects and transitional phenomena. In: *Collected Papers.* New York: Basic Books, pp. 229–243, 1958.

———— (1960a), The relationship of a mother to her baby at the beginning. In: *The Family and Individual Development.* London: Tavistock, 1965.

———— (1960b), The theory of the parent-infant relationship. *Internat. J. Psycho-Anal.,* 41:585–595.

———— (1960c), Ego distortion in terms of true and false self. In: *The Maturational Processes and the Facilitating Environment.* London: Hogarth Press, pp.140–152, 1965.

———— (1967), Mirror role of mother and family in child development. In: *The Predicament of the Family,* ed. P. Lomas. New York: International Universities Press, pp. 26–33.

Yogman, M. W. (1982), Observations on the father-infant relationship. In: Father and Child, ed. S. H. Cath, A. Gurwitt & J. M. Ross. Boston: Little, Brown, pp. 101–122.

4

Fathers as Single Parents
Object Relations Beyond Mother
Peter B. Neubauer

Since the publication of my paper "The One-Parent Child" in 1960, new conditions of family life have given this topic increasing significance. There is the accelerated divorce rate; there is now an ever-increasing number of unmarried mothers, many of whom are still in their adolescence; and there are fathers who have accepted the role of primary caregiver during the first years of their children's lives.

The resulting change in the traditional family constellation or cohesion, the absence of a nuclear family structure, raise many new questions about the influence of these conditions on the development of children. Furthermore, since more than 50% of the women in America today are employed, there is the additional issue of the effect of the absence of both parents during the day, the need for substitute caregivers, and their effect on the stability of the primary objects in the lives of children.

In order to profile appropriately the effect of these conditions, it is useful to restate some of the findings I presented in my earlier paper:

1. Children seem to idealize the absent parent. There is a longing for the unavailable parent; the child fantasizes that if that parent were present, he would fulfill its wishes and would help to overcome its difficulties. Furthermore, the absence of one parent does not permit

ever-changing experience in interaction to reduce the omnipotent image of the parent: "When a parent is absent, there is also an absence of oedipal reality. The absent parent becomes endowed with magical powers, either to gratify or to punish. Aggression against him and the remaining parent as well becomes repressed" (Neubauer, 1960, p. 308).

2. Children who suffer the loss of a parent search for an explanation and consistently arrive at a "theory" that may, over a period of time, assert an organizing influence on development. Cognitive demand asks for causation and, depending on the children's age, these fantasies distort reality and change the inner representational world. The child feels deserted by the absent parent and arrives at the explanation that he was not deserving of love or that the remaining parent has made it impossible for the other parent to stay with him. There is, then, the need to assign responsibility for the absence of the parent, and it is assigned either to the remaining parent or to the child himself.

3. Although the absent parent is idealized, and in the presence of conflictual feeling for the remaining parent, there is nevertheless a tendency for the child to cling to the available parent for fear that this parent too may abandon him; thus, aggressive feelings become repressed.

4. If the separation from a parent occurs in the first years of life, it will affect the conditions of the oedipal constellation and make the resolution of the oedipal conflict difficult. After all, the complex interaction within the triadic relationship is the basis for the oeidpal solution in which identifications with both parents should finally lead to an acceptance of both with the appropriate evolvement of a superego structure. Of course it may be difficult to consolidate the gender role identity when one parent is absent or when the idealization maintains omnipotent characteristics that not only are ascribed to the absent parent, but become incorporated in the child's own image.

Since we believe today that the triadic relationship is also part of the preoedipal constellation in the striving for the exclusive possession of the parent with ensuing rivalry, jealousy, and envy, the absence of a parent during this period may affect these processes of fermentation. We assume that identification with the same sex and the opposite sex parent is an essential ingredient for gender differentiation and the resolution of the oedipal conflict.

In the context of these complex processes, the "real" features of the relationship wil have their influence, but in the absence of a parent, the processes may succumb to idealization, fantasies, and wish fulfillments that may continue over years.

It is clear that such generalizations stemming from our assumptions about normal developmental sequences must be tested against the many individual conditions that occur in the interaction between child and parents and that may have a pivotal influence on the developmental outcome. If we take as a model our theories about traumatic conditions, we will have to take into account the prevailing condition before the traumatic event or, in the context of this study, those before the separation from a parent. This not only implies that we have to understand parental attitudes, but also includes our understanding of the child, his age, and the intensity of the tie that had been established to each parent when the separation occurred. It will depend on the information given to the child during the period when parental attitudes change and on the explanations offered to modify or increase the child's fantasies and theory formation. Of equal interest, moreover, are the circumstances during the postevent period. How did the remaining parent react to the absent parent in private or in direct interaction with the child; what were the circumstances for absence, that is, death, divorce, remarriage. Thus the event alone must be seen as imbedded in these sequences. This may either increase the traumatic effect or slowly lead to a recovery. In order to understand the full impact, one would need follow-up studies through the various adolescent stages.

The attitude of the present parent toward the child, as well as toward the absent parent, remains a pivotal influence. Thus, the parent's own preoedipal and oedipal organization will affect the outcome of the child's development and with it influence gender and sex identity.

When studying traumatic situations, we are inclined to pay particular attention to environmental circumstances and, as has been stated, to the sequence of events that may influence the child. But we have to consider with equal interest the child's inner psychic life, the stages of development, his disposition, his search for comfort or activation, his level of curiosity, and his individual developmental pull, in addition to the interplay between the maturational and developmental processes. All these factors are brought to bear on the environment, and they will influence what is selected from the environment as significant and as being traumatic.

The pursuit of the child's inner developmental need will, depending on developmental phase organization, determine the intensity of the child's wish for a complete family. It is a frequent finding that the child wishes for the reunion of the separated parents, a wish determined by the child's developmental and maturational demand to complete or at least to proceed with his own development. Such wishes can coexist with the child's acceptance of others in the environment as substitute objects.

When applying the propositions about separation-individuation sequences, one has to study the effect of the absence of a parent on the processes of separation as well as of individuation. One can expect that as the longing for the idealized absent parent continues, separateness and self–object differentiation are more difficult to attain.

The review of the literature at the time of my original paper revealed that the disorders associated with the death or absence of a parent ranged from minor characterological disorders to more severe disturbances. There is, then, the obvious inference that the effect of such an event can be understood only in the context of multiply determined factors, and therefore the outcome does not reveal a simple correlation. My own finding was that there is a specific disorder of an oedipal nature, for the prelatency child with one parent cannot sufficiently resolve the triadic conditions and therefore there is an incomplete resolution of the oedipal conflict.

Since that time many studies have examined the development of children with one parent, and there is an extensive literature addressing itself to conditions of children during and after the divorce of parents. The data from these studies appear significant for the understanding of children with one parent. However, these studies refer more to outcome than to the personality variables either of the parent or of the child. In this connection, it may be useful to consider the risk-vulnerability intervention model that Anthony (1974) proposed when he studied the children of psychotic parents. Such a model is useful because it consolidates the internal factors of vulnerability with the specific conditions of the environmental risks. In all these studies it is important to understand the degree of vulnerability or invulnerability of the individual child and therefore understand the effect that an event may have on the child's further development.

Gudrun (1978) offered no clues to the multifactional aspects to be taken into account for an understanding of the effect of such events. He summarized his findings from an evaluation of a few hundred parents and children:

> The immediate disturbing effects of the divorce process on the children were not easily separated from preexisting disorders or from disorders that continue following the termination of the divorce. . . . The risk for children for becoming disturbed is thus a complicated product of parental loss, parental welfare, the visita-

tion dramas. . . . The interaction between these risks and the vulnerability of the children influences the outcome of the divorce stress decisively. Of the 500 children, 140 were traumatized (28%) [p. 257].

Gudrun found that another 28% of the children appeared to improve, for they "may find a more stable environment, free from daily conflict, which may give them opportunity to master the trauma." Furthermore, those children with symptoms had suffered from emotional problems from early life on.

We are not surprised, then, to find confirmation of our clinical observations. We see here that the same external event may lead to different outcomes. There are those children who can overcome trauma; and there are those whose pretraumatic conditions continue and others for whom may be an intensification due to acute stressful conditions. These findings warn us not to arrive too hastily at conclusions when we examine the interrelationship between external and internal conditions, even when these are part of the basic relationship to the primary objects, the parents.

Reviewing these systematic studies of the one-parent child, one wishes that investigations would address specific issues, for instance, to compare the development of children who from the beginning of life had only one parent with those who lost a parent later. Similarly, it would be illuminating if the studies compared the effect of the absence of the parent of the same sex with the effect of the absence of a parent of the opposite sex. As I discuss later, we would need studies showing the influence of other available caregiving objects and compare these with those where there is only one primary caregiver. Furthermore, one would need for each of these categories long-term follow-up studies.

Wallerstein's (1980) extensive investigations and careful methodology give us useful findings. Her study of children and their parents involved in separation, divorce, and remarriage led to results I should like to paraphrase:

1. Often diminished parenting by both parents.

2. Conflicts between the parents (58% of the children witnessed violence at the time of the marital rupture).

3. Abandonment and loss. Not only is one parent lost, but also the intact family, the continuity, the sense of family cohesion. In the

United States, there is a distinct move toward the dissolution of joint custody.

4. Infidelity and demeaning of one parent by the other prior to, during, and after the break-up.

These factors contribute to the negative influence on children and seem to lead to consequences that markedly affect the establishment of a secure representational world, a healthy adaptive behavior, and developmental progression. But there are also other findings that alert us to the possibility that some children, under certain conditions, are able to overcome the trauma of separation and seem to find solutions which further their development.

My earlier study focused on the effect of loss of a parent during the preoedipal and oedipal period; I observed children only up to the age of six and have not undertaken a follow-up study. There is evidence that some children are able to form relationships and undergo experiences that permit them, later on in life, to compensate for earlier losses and deficits. The children can form new relationships that substitute for earlier experience and can draw on them to bring about a psychic reorganization and integration, which at an earlier stage one could not have observed or predicted.

Some children have an extraordinary striving to seek out new relationships. Their object hunger leads to new attachments, and they "adopt" other adults to serve as parental substitutes. Thus they are able to find objects that correct their wish for magical, omnipotent parents and assuage their sense of guilt, for they can now find evidence that they can maintain relationships, that one does not turn away from them, and thus they do not feel responsible for the absence of the parent. These corrective experiences can take place at many crucial stages of the child's life and throughout adult life.

Until recently, the one-parent child relationship was most frequently between mother and child, but now fathers are accepting the role of parenting for the first years of life. Without speculating about the reasons for this change, from a developmental point of view, the question arises whether the father as a primary caregiver in the first years of the child's life can carry out the task with the same success that mothers have had. Often this question is construed to mean whether fathers can be mothers, based on the assumption that the primary object has to be the mother, and that all other objects are surrogates or substitutes for her.

It is important that over the last several years studies have investigated the role of fathers, for they give us new information that changes our assumptions about the role of both parents in early child care. Not only do we find what Abelin (1975) described as the innate "father thirst", but also that he found that infants can form symbiotic relationships with fathers or with both father and mothers. Furthermore, symbiotic relationships then assert their influence on Mahler's phases of separation-individuation, that is that the refueling can occur with both parents. But Abelin's study did not address itself to the relationship of father and child in the absence of mother. And what is the assignment of roles of mother and father when both are present? The father may leave to his wife certain child-care functions that have traditionally been assigned to her, while he accepts the execution of these functions when he is sole caregiver.

There are indications that mothers are more comforting, whereas fathers lean more toward activation and stimulation of their children. When both parents are available, the children may turn to one or the other, depending on their needs at a given time or on their disposition and stage of development. Thus, the question arises whether in the presence of the father or mother as sole caregiver, a sufficiently varied quality of interaction occurs, and do these different interactions influence gender development? What is the contribution of these modes of interaction or sensorimotor, perceptual orchestration and stimulation and its effect on preoedipal and oedipal organization? Will boys living alone with father respond differently from girls on this level of earliest experiences or primary identification? We can speculate on the effect of mother's comforting and soothing action on a child in need of stimulation, or father's activating stimulation on a child in need of comfort and tension reduction. The "knowing," orchestrating parent will modify innate preferences of the child, at least to a certain degree, and we have to explore the possibility that availability of multiple caregivers will permit the child to select the caregiver who favors the dispositional and gender-oriented preferences.

To view earliest development, it may be useful to refer to Winnicott's (1960) idea that in the absence of an appropriate presence of mother's "holding," the child may turn to a defensive maneuver of self-holding and that "the development of a caretaker-self and the organization of an aspect of the personality that is false. . . . This is a defense whose success may prove a new threat to the core of the self, though it is designed to hide and protect this core of the self" (p. 210). Thus, if there were a deficit in the father–infant caregiving condition, we then must expect that such defensive maneuvers would give evidence of a possible failure of object- and self-differentiation. These formulations stress the maternal "holding," the primacy of early maternal relationship; and these propositions therefore alert us to the consequences of the absent holding quality of the parent, which may lead to a loss of the integration of the self, the loss of the sense of self, or the establishment of the cohesiveness of the self. When one views such issues, one is inclined to investigate the child's development of object representation to find how the child views the father when he is the sole early caregiver or when both parents share these functions.

Most of the available studies address observational data about the child's capacity for attachment and bonding. They are based on observations of parent–infant interaction,but they do not give us a view of the child's subjective experience and his evolvement of "his' representational world.

Many findings reflect the complexity of early object relations. For instance, we have the observation (Pederson and Robson, 1969) that by eight months the infant is able to form attachment to "both" parents and that the presence of both parents permits the child to differentiate objects, which then enhances the child's own capacity for differentiation between self and object. As we have said before, the presence of only one parent may be a disadvantage to the differentiating process and gender differentiation. Cohen and Campos, (1974) studied infants and their relationship to fathers and mothers. Among their findings was the observation that under stress the infants seem to prefer their mothers to their fathers, when they are in need of the comforting attitude of mother. We do not know yet whether this is due to mother's having been more frequently engaged in physical caregiving more than father.

In addition, we have to compare the development of boys with that of girls when there is an absent father. Kohlberg (1966) has stated that there is a difference in reaction of boys to absent fathers, for they are seeking objects like themselves, male figures, in order to achieve a more appropriate masculine role by identification. The girl, under the same circumstances, still has mother avaiable for early identification. We are speaking here of the first two years of life and not about the period in which triadic, oedipal interaction is required for higher gender identification and differentiation.

Tyson (1986) stated: "The girl without a father does not have the same difficulty as the boy, but she lacks the experience of *sharp contrasts* between mother and father when both are present. These contrasts help to further separation/individuation and to dissolve lingering symbiosis" (p. 18). Tyson goes on to discuss the effect of father's action on the vicissitudes of the aggressive strivings:

Loss of the father before the child can successfully internalize his own controls over aggressive themes seen in such children . . . that the child cannot be successfully learn to "turn it off" [the aggression] by internalized controls without the presence and aid of father, an achievement which is attained more gradually [p. 18].

In this respect we have to learn about the nature of the "sharp contrasts" between mother and father and for how long father's influence is required to tame aggressive strivings; for one must assume that the oedipal fermentation with superego participation will be required to restrain drive impulses.

Following the processes of separation/individuation of boys and girls, it is interesting to note Anni Bergman's (1985) summary of Mahler's work.

1. It seems that during practicing, boys experience more elation and expansiveness than girls. This could be related to the greater strength of the motor apparatus in boys.

2. The data suggest that the period of early rapprochement, from about 14 to 18 months, is one of special pleasure and elation for girls. It is a rather special pleasure that the girl experiences in social interactiveness that starts with mother but easily spreads to others as long as mother is approving. The daughter's mood and personality take on an individual character at this time, but she is also more sensitive to mother's praise or disapproval.

3. It seems that the rapprochement crises are somewhat more easily resolved by boys than girls. Boys seem to remove themselves more quickly and more definitely, and their interest in the outside world continues to develop. Boys seem to rapidly disidentify with mother, while girls, after removing themselves, become reinvolved in struggles with mother more intensely during the end of the second and beginning of the third year [p. 28].

These findings allow us to test our assumptions about the effect of an absent parent on the phallic development of boys and girls, and they sharpen our interest in describing the specific stage of development of the child and his reactivity to potentially traumatic events.

In addition to Tyson's findings, there are other studies that indicate the preference for antisocial behavior in boys. Rutter (1970) found that the disruption of relationships between boys and parents indicated greater vulnerabilities among boys compared with girls and that these very often lead to antisocial disorders. Block (1982), trying to explain the difference of reaction to stress between boys and girls, found that boys make adaptive changes to the environment by moving in different directions and by turning away from situations of stress. Girls, on the other hand, strive for assimilation and thus have a tendency to maintain internal continuity of relationships. Gamble and Zigler (1986) found that "if boys are somewhat more aggressive, coercive and exploratory than females to begin with, then any treatment which has an identical effect on both sexes will not affect the magnitude of the post-treatment differences, but merely shift the difference along the behavioral continuum" (p. 38–39).

So far I have discussed those factors which seem to be operative between parent and child, but over the years we have learned to be attentive to the relations between the infant and the young child to other objects in the environment, such as substitute caregivers, grandparents, and siblings. From a theoretical point of view, we have focused on the dyadic/triadic relationships between parent and infant and have outlined developmental sequences based on the consolidation of these relationships. In the past, other object relations were viewed as variations of this earlier mother–child relationship; they were viewed as substitute relations without enough weight being given to the capacity of the child to extract from various objects what he needs and to form different relationships with different objects very early in life. As I have outlined before, we have finally extended this notion to include the father–child interaction, with its own characteristics. In the past, we may have overstated the notion that the requirement for continuity of care implies the "exclusive" continuity of care by the primary object, rather than the continuity and the stability of caring human beings who provide the child with the basic sense of security. I do not think that we have enough evidence that multiple caregivers must bring about dilution of the role of the primary objects. When it does occur, it seems to be the result of relationships that did not allow attachment and bonding.

In the paper "Object Constancy and Early Triadic Relationships" (Solnit and Neubauer, 1986), we arrived at this formulation: "In the developmental line of incorporation and identification, we find stability and structural continuity. In the line of differentiation, we find the tolerance and awareness of incongruities which lead to individuation" (p. 29). This implies not only that deficits or overstimulation, points of fixation or regression contribute to pathological reactions, but that the uneveness and incongruities of a psychic system have their effect on separation-individuation and on the general course of development.

Solnit (1982) was referring to the multiplicity of causes and interaction when he stated that we must understand ". . . children's reactions to the temporary loss of parents, to parental deprivation and the children's recovery from such loss and deprivation" (p. 205).

Thus, we have to examine carefully the availability of other caregiving objects who, each in turn, may contribute to the child's development. Thus, no longer can we consider the absence of one parent as an inevitable situation of risk without taking into account the total human environment of the child.

We may wish to expand our psychoanalytic theory of development. As I have stated, such a theory demands a clarification of concepts of preoedipal objects, the influence of various primary objects, and the emergence of object primacy. An assumption that the exclusive dyadic relationship between mother and child is the essential matrix of the evolvement of object- and self-representation and individuation implies that the early pathology of the child is always seen as reflecting a disturbance in mother-child interaction. Such a formulation seems too limited, for it does not include the child's capacity to form relationships with a number of meaningful objects, to adapt to different object relations and to benefit from it.

As I have stated (1985):

> Under normal conditions of mother-child relationships, the simultaneous relationship to other adults and siblings during the first years of life does not inevitably dilute or divert the quality of the relationship to mother and father, but rather contributes to the shaping of primary objects and the primacy of the oedipal objects [p. 167].

From a clinical point of view, therefore, we have to explore the role of various early objects, and from a theoretical point of view, we have to extend the proposition of the basic and exclusive dyadic relationship to mother. We must undertake studies in which we can observe infants in various interactions with primary caregiving objects in their environment.

I have discussed the role of father as a single parent within the context of the broader parent–child interaction. This permits us to profile more clearly the characteristics of the father's attitude and its influence on development as we see it contrasted with other caregivers' attitudes and influences.

Originally, we described the incomplete preoedipal and oedipal conflict solutions reflecting the absence of a triadic constellation. The findings that are now available have added to our understanding of many factors that contribute to this and that allow us now to be more precise. The increasing knowledge about the differences between male and female development, the influence of fathers and mothers, have improved our awareness of the lines of development from the earliest sex characteristics as seen in the differences of the emerging ego equipment between girls and boys, their differences in responding to either mother or father, and thereby their gender evolvement and finally their sex identity.

In addition, expansion of our observation of the role of various caregiving objects in early life and of the infants and young child's capacity to form different and multiple relationships has sharpened our view of the effect of parental absence and the role these other objects may play to correct the deficiency. The factor of risk, therefore, may be due to the exclusiveness of a one-to-one relationship in addition to the nature of this relationship.

Thus our findings about the influence of the one-parent condition on the development of the child have enlarged our knowledge of normal development and of early psychopathology.

To close with a quote from Winnicott (1960): ". . . the object, if it is to be used, must necessarily be real in the sense of being part of shared reality, not a bundle of projections. It is this, I think that makes for the world of difference that exists between relating and usage" (p. 95).

REFERENCES

Abelin, E. (1975), Some further observations and comments on the earliest role of the father. *Internat. J. Psycho-Anal.,* 56:293–302.

Anthony, E. J. & Koupernik, C. (1974), *The Child in His Family.* New York: Wiley.

Bergman, A., Shuker, E. & Silverman, M. (1985), Preoedipal considerations in the individualization development of the family gender theme in adult feminity. *Bull. Assn. Psychoanal. Med.,* 25:28.

Block, J. (1982), Assimilation, accommodation and the dynamics of personality development. *Child Devel.,* 53:281–295.

Cohen, L. J. & Campos, J. J. (1974), Father, mother and stranger as elicitors of attachment behaviors in infancy. *Develop. Psychol.,* 10:146–154.

Gamble, T. J. & Zigler, E. (1986), Effects of infant day care: Another look at the evidence. *Amer. J. Orthopsychiat.,* 56:39.

Gudrun, B. (1978), Conflicted parents: high and low vulnerability of children to divorce. In: *The Child in His Family,* ed. E. J. Anthony & C. Koupernik. New York: Wiley.

Kohlberg, L. (1966), A cognitive developmental analysis of children's sex role concepts and attitudes. In: *The Development of Sex Differences,* ed. E. Maccoby. Stanford, CA: Stanford University Press, pp. 82–175.

Neubauer, P. B. (1960), The one-parent child and his oedipal development. *The Psychoanalytic Study of the Child,* 15:286–309. New York: International Universities Press.

—— (1985), Preoedipal objects and object primacy. *The Psychoanaltyic Study of the Child,* 40:163–182. New Haven: Yale University Press.

Pederson, F. A. & Robson, K. S. (1969), Father participation in infancy. *Amer. J. Orthopsychiat.,* 39:466–472.

Rutter, M. (1970), Sex differences in children's response to family stress. In: *The Child in the Family,* ed. E. J. Anthony & C. Koupernik. New York: Wiley.

Solnit, A. (1982), Developmental perspectives on self and object constancy. *The Psychoanalytic Study of the Child,* 37:201–221. New Haven: Yale University Press.

—— & Neubauer, P. B. (1986), Object constancy and early triadic relationships. *J. Child Psychiat.,* 25:23–29.

Tyson, R. L. (1986), The roots of psychopathology and our theories of development. *J. Child Psychiat.,* 25:12–22.

Wallerstein, J. S. (1985), Psychoanalytic perspectives on children in separation, divorce and remarriage. Report on meeting held in Hamburg, July 29.

Winnicott, D. W. (1960), In *The Maturational Processes and the Facilitating Environment.* New York: International Universities Press, pp. 140–152, 1965.

5

Toiletry Revisited

An Integration of Developing Concepts and the Father's Role in Toilet Training

Moisy Shopper

Psychoanalytic theory has been enhanced by the seminal work of 1) Mahler (Mahler, Pine, and Bergman, 1975) on separation/ individuation, 2) Stoller (1968) on core gender identity, and 3) Cath, Gurwitt, and Ross (1982) on fatherhood. These are contiguous areas of a child's development at age 18 to 36 months. Since they interdigitate, precise reconstruction of these three lines of development as separate entities is more the mark of a theoretician than a reproduction of the child's actual reality. It is only in the "reconstructed child," as opposed to the "actual child," that developmental issues are clearly demarcated and isolated (Shopper, 1976).

The "actual child," age 18 to 36 months, is at some point in his or her toilet training. Experientially the actual child is at the confluence of the aforementioned developmental lines and needs to balance, respond to, and, it is hoped, synthesize these three developmental lines. The "good enough" parent (Winnicott, 1965), who facilitates this synthesis, produces a less conflicted, stronger ego. When lines of development are widely disparate, contradictory, or disharmonious, the young child's embryonic coping and synthesizing abilities may be severely strained.

These recent theoretical contributions have yet to be correlated with issues of parent–child interaction vis-à-vis toilet training. This paper will attempt to do so and will differentiate the "female mode" of toilet training from the "male mode" and show how the latter, by actively involving the father, is more suited for the male toddler. In the "female mode," toilet training of the boy is done primarily by the mother, starts with bowel training, and does not differentiate between sitting or standing for the two different excretory functions. In the "male mode" of training the boy, the father initiates training, begin-ning with urination from the standing position, and offers himself as a model for bladder control.

REVIEW OF THE PSYCHOANALYTIC LITERATURE

Separation/Individuation

Mahler stated, "We do not have too clear a view of the relevance of toileting – to the separation/individuation process" (Mahler, Pine, and Bergman, 1975). She spoke of

> three paramount, anxiety-generating conditions of childhood, which . . . converge in the rapprochement period: 1) the fear of object loss; 2) there is a greater awareness of bodily feelings and pressures, augmented by awareness of bowel and urinary sensa-tions during the toilet-training period; 3) in most instances, there is a reaction to the discovery – rather earlier than we thought – of the anatomical differences between the sexes [p. 229].

Other than noting that toilet training often coincides with and complicates the rapprochement period, Mahler does little to correlate problems in toilet training with the problems of the separation and individuation phases. However, in speaking of "chance observations," that is, those "not expected by us" encountered during the analysis of the data of the second half of the second year of life, she found that prior to that time the children "fit into the various sub-groups – from the separation/individuation point of view" – without regard to the sex of the child. After this point, the complexity of the situation was suggestive of a "growing trend towards sexual differentiation and gender identity formation" (p. 269). Late in the second year of life "the consolidation of the personality is organized around maleness or fe-maleness (and to that degree) gender identity becomes a central focus" (p. 270).

Abelin (1971, 1980), from observational studies and theoretical constructs of the rapprochement phase, postulates a critical period at 18 months when the toddler involves the father in the toddler's "early triangulation" experiences. Abelin then notes that there are significant sex differences in meeting this phase. His emphasis is the integration of classical analysis's developmental stages with Piaget's work on cognition and the latter's implications for symbolic thinking and language development. Toilet training is not mentioned.

Fathers

Lamb (1976), in his review of the father's role in child development, has no index listing for "bladder," "bowel," "toilet training," or "enuresis." Nash (1965) pointed to the matricentric nature of most researchers of child rearing. His more recent article (Nash, 1976) focuses on the role of the father in many areas (gender identity, femininity, cognitive development, delivery room, etc.) but omits toilet training.

Similarly, Cath and his colleagues' recent book, *Father and Child* (1982), contains no index listing for "toilet training," "bowel," "bladder," or "enuresis," but does list "anal-sadistic phase" and "urination." Tyson's (1982) article specifically joins the father to issues of gender identity and urethral erotism. Tyson's focus on a libidinal phase (urethral erotism) approaches but does not integrate, as I am attempting to do, toilet training issues with the other three developmental lines. She noted Stoller's (1979) observation of the intimacy and symbiosis between mother and (transsexual) son, which precluded a paternal influence; and Mahler's (1966) emphasis on the "uncontaminated" father, who acts as a wedge in the mother–child symbiosis and is available to the child as a nonsymbiotic object. Tyson brings together the "practicing subphase," (at 9 to 13 months when the boy is attaining mastery over locomotion, bodily movement, sphincter control, and an increasing pride and pleasure in urination) with the boy's interest in the father and the father's genitals. Tyson notes that the boys' viewing of the father's genitals counterbalances his exposure to the mother's genitals. Thus it helps confirm his penis as part of his body image and becomes part of his masculine identification with the father.

Despite this recent recognition of the father's role in toilet training, his role has on the whole been neglected. Stereotypically, diapering and the cleaning of the child's bottom is regarded as "woman's work." Many a caring and participating father hands the child over to his wife once the child is wet or dirty. Such sexist attitudes are currently being challenged and are changing. Yet many fathers feel they should be free of diapering and cleaning chores. For many fathers the avoidance of diapering extends to an avoidance of toilet training as well. I believe it is important that these attitudes change, not just from considerations of equality in sex and parenting roles, but from considerations of the boy's optimal psychosexual development. Whether or not parents follow traditional sex roles in their marriage, the father needs to participate in the "male mode" of training his toddler son. It is the father's unique contribution to his son's personality development and masculinity.

Ross (1979) in his extensive review of analytic authors stresses the significant early involvement of the father and his child as a dyadic relationship in its own right. He feels that "a father's age-specific and his idiosyncratic contributions during the pre-oedipal and other developmental phases and their behavioral consequences have been underplayed. The dynamically evolving father-child dyad is not considered as such" (p. 324).

Gender Identity

Stoller (1968, 1975) regards the father as critical to the process of conveying to the child the gender role expectations of his gender assignment at birth. Stoller emphasized the young boy's difficulty (as contrasted with the girl's) in securing this gender identity since the boy needs to change his initial symbiotic identification with the mother (female) to an identification with the father (male), the latter being in harmony with gender assignment.

Greenson's (1966) and Stoller's (1966) study of a male transsexual youngster shows the nature of family pathology that precludes the formation of a male gender identity. They emphasize a) the maternal conflicts over penis envy, and b) the father's emotioinal distance, passivity, and acquiescence to his wife's pathological exploitation of their son. Toilet training is mentioned in passing. A close reading of the material reveals a classic instance of a male child who is toilet trained in what I call "the female mode." It is only when the transsexual boy has been treated "for several years and masculine traits start appearing does evidence of oedipal conflict develop. The boys start to value their penises (for instance, they now stand up to urinate where before they sat) . . ." (Stoller, 1975, p.28).

Greenson (1968), aware of Mahler's work, speaks of the boy's need to "dis-identify" himself from the mother, to

> replace the primary object of his identification, the mother . . .
> The male child's ability to dis-identify will determine the success

or failure of his latter identification with his father. These two phenomena, disidentifying from mother and counteridentifying with father are interdependent and form a complementary series" [p. 370].

Greenson notes that either mother or father could facilitate and/or hinder each process.

Pediatrics and Child Development

Spock and Rothenberg (1985), intent on furnishing practical "how-to" advice, include standard psychodynamic considerations regarding toilet training. They make no mention, either explicit or implicit, of separation-individuation issues, core gender identity, sexual differences in training, or the role of the father. Typically the parent is advised to train first for bowel control. They state, "Standing up to urinate comes later. . . . It isn't necessary to make an issue of this. He'll get the idea sooner or later when he has a chance to see older boys occasionally or his father once or twice" (p. 284).

In a frequently quoted article, Brazelton (1962) suggests "a method of training" which is "child oriented" and "starts at 18 months with a potty chair on the floor." With respect to urination and the boy, he states,

Teaching a boy to stand for urination is an added incentive. It becomes a part of identifying with his father, with other boys, and is often an outlet for a normal amount of exhibitionism. It is most easily learned by watching and imitating other male figures. It is better introduced *after bowel training is complete.* Otherwise, the excitement of standing for all functions supercedes [p. 124; italics added].

Interestingly, 8.2% were trained for urination first. It is not stated whether they were male or female. There is no mention of the father's role in the urinary training of the boy.

Ross Laboratories (1962), in its series of child rearing books for the pediatric waiting room, *Developing Toilet Habits,* suggests "sitting him on his toilet for a few minutes at the time that he usually has a bowel movement" (p. 6). Bladder control is discussed several headings later: "Bladder control usually takes longer to achieve than bowel control" (p. 11). It is felt that the mothers are more tolerant of wetness than of soiling, and consequently they don't push as hard for bladder control.

Fraiberg's (1959) guide to the developing intrapsychic child goes into great detail about the proper approach to toilet training, taking special account of the preverbal child. Nevertheless, she does not differentiate between the sexes and begins toilet training with bowel control. Although she states, "It will require considerable parental presure to get an active toddler to sit there for more than a few minutes, and such pressure or insistence will inevitably create rebellion and an inability to produce on the potty" (p. 96), she nonetheless favors the sitting position. There is no mention at all of the boy's need to learn urination in the standing position or to learn from older male figures in the family.

The tendency to think of toddlers as unisexual beings is a long-standing tradition of those who believe sex differences begin with entry to school or with entry in the phallic phase of psychosexual development.

The invisibility of the father in toilet training, not just in terms of opportunity to participate, but *also in those instances where the father did participate,* may have an explanation suggested by Abelin (1980). He suggests that before the rapprochement subphase processes are *presymbolic* and the father's presence in "early triangulation . . . cannot be reconstructed by the psychoanalytic method" (p. 164). The image of the early primordial father is "obliterated" by the more significant image of the symbiotic mother, and all interaction is subsumed and telescoped into the maternal imago. This inability to reconstruct psychoanalytically has unfortunately extended to our excluding the father's early dyadic role from our *observations* and theoretical constructions. As a result, our bias and our theory is matricentric and the actual father is all but invisible.

Sex Differences

Gesell (1940) did note block-building distinctions between boys and girls at age 18 months. Beller and Neubauer (1963) noted significantly more aggression, hyperactivity, lack of bowel control, and speech disturbance in the boy. "Defiance correlated only in boys with aggression, hyperactivity, and sleep disturbance. This suggests that these male children, not only have difficulty in impulse control, but actively resist or defy the mother's demand for compliance" (p. 424). The defiance of the mother is a crucial factor and will be discussed more fully later.

Similarly, Oppel, Harper, and Rider (1968) found that ". . . girls had significantly higher percentages of first attained daytime dryness and a higher prevalence of day dryness than did boys during the first two years" (p. 623).

Minton, Kagan, and Levine (1971) studied two-year-olds' obedience to maternal control. Boys had a higher rate of violations than girls for the "integrity of household goods" and were more often reprimanded for aggression toward the mother. Girls, on the other hand, were often reprimanded for failure to perform a task with competence. Girls were more likely to obey commands immediately, whereas boys were more likely to resist initially and obey later or be forced to obey. I would summarize Minton's work by saying that the boys were criticized for not being enough like the mother. In many ways Minton's work reflects the opinions of many mothers, namely, that girls are more obedient and more docile, whereas boys tend to be more active, disobedient, and negativistic.

Flappan and Neubauer (1972) spoke of the need to analyze preschool boy and girl groups differently. They "really constituted two different populations" and suggested different developmental lines and different standards of assessment. Like Mahler, they realized that their methodology may have led to possible errors or biases since their data was obtained only from women, mothers, and female teachers.

Douglas (1973), surveying 4,500 British children, found a marked preponderance of enuretic boys compared with girls, though the percentages vary with the age of the child. Rutter, Yule, and Graham (1973) in their Isle of Wight studies reported similar findings.

Sperling (1974) recognized the marked sex ratio in enuresis. She quoted Despert to explain the predominance of enuresis in boys. Despert spoke of the confusion

> . . . in the training period when the boy, unlike the girl, has to learn the sitting and standing position for defecation and urination. In the cases of mothers with unresolved conflicts concerning the sexual differences, this leads sometimes to grotesque training procedures with their male children and consequent enuresis of these boys [p. 328].

Davidson and Choquet (1984), in a longitudinal epidemiology study of 415 Parisian children (under 3 years of age), found that those with the highest incidence of symptomatology, that is, a "high risk group," were more than two-thirds boys.

Roiphe and Galenson (1984) note that "early development is the same for both boys and girls," both having an "upsurge in genital self-manipulation" in the first months of the second year. Concomitantly sexual curiosity emerges about the child's own genitals and those of parents, peers, pets, and toys. "It is at this point that we are able to discern significant divergence in male and female development, organized around the reaction to the observation of the anatomical differences between the sexes" (p. 436). They discuss this in the context of other developmental issues: anxiety about object loss and object dissolution, separation-individuation, father presence, body image, castration concerns, ambivalence, and splitting.

Lamb (1984) notes that by the end of the second year, boys, more so than girls, focus their attention on their fathers, seeking comfort and proximity, and consistently prefer their fathers. Lamb is, however, very cautious about seeing this as a significant determinant in the gender identity of the boy. He believes that there is "rather weak evidence that gender identity is established in the first two years of life" (p. 345).

"HOW-TO" BOOKS

The voluminous lay advice on toilet training addresses the following issues: readiness, age of the child when starting to train, resistance to training, regular toilet verses potty on the floor, and the use of training pants. Little mention is made of sexual differences in training or the role of the father. Interestingly, whenever an author gives an example of a child, it is usually boy and it is the mother who is having trouble and asking questions. Spock and Rothenberg (1985) initiate training with bowel before bladder, sitting before standing; their advice is essentially mother oriented. Fraiberg (1959) adds issues of feces/self-differentiation, narcissistic evaluation of the fecal product, the role of toilet fears and fantasies, cooperation and parental approval, and gift giving, but a "female model" of training is used. The female model is similarly recommended by Becker and Becker (1974), Leach (1978), Azrin and Foxx (1974), Levine and Seligman (1973), Salk and Kramer (1969), Beck (1976), and the U.S. Government guide, *Infant Care* (U.S. Children's Bureau, 1951).

Dodson (1973) differentiated bowel from bladder control and begins training with bowel control, stating that bladder control is "generally harder" to establish. However, he noted, "It is more natural to teach a little boy to urinate standing up by imitating Daddy or older brothers" (p. 139). Having mentioned "Daddy," Dodson next devoted an entire section to "How Mothers Feel About Toilet Training." In his subsequent book, *How to Father,* he referred the reader to the 12-page section on toilet training in his earlier book, *How to Parent.* Weisberger (1975) cautioned mothers to avoid delaying the training of boys because they are said to be "slower." "An expectant attitude is better for both sexes, and I would expect as much of a boy as I do of a girl" (p. 15). He noted that "your son may prefer to stand up to urinate" but advised mothers to use deflectors on the potty chair and only later to encourage him "to perform standing up" (p. 18).

Several authors have intuitively or idealogically anticipated my position. Klein (1968) saw the father as a fully participating parent who should be involved in all areas of the child's life, especially in such a "civilizing" and "important" area. She also stressed the importance of imitation. Using cross-cultural data, she suggested that our penchant for bathroom privacy makes toileting "a mystery" to the child. "A boy should be allowed to view his father urinating very early in life. The same is true for a girl and her mother" (p. 81). Eldred (1951) noted that "small boys can be trained much more easily if they are allowed to stand up and a small jar or bottle is used . . ." (p. 133) but otherwise followed tradition.

Brooks (1971) suggested that the mother sit the boy for urination (with a deflector) and that the boy stand later after following the example of an older sibling; once dryness is achieved, father praises him, as he does his daughter once she is dry. There are separate pictures and verses for "Johnny" and for "Susie," but other than the boy's standing for urination, training for boy and girl is essentially similar.

Mack (1978) was aware of the data indicating the quicker learning of girls than boys in toileting and that this may be related to the greater ease with which girls can imitate their mothers. Cross-culturally, the Ashanti father "takes the little boy outside to show him how and where to urinate. . . . It's especially good for fathers to teach sons – [he] can show a little boy to urinate standing up" (p. 20).

In my opinion, Mach was intuitively correct but approached it from a feminist ("toilet training is an equal opportunity employer") and learning (imitation) framework, although she later moved into what we would label "identification." Specifically she advised both parents to participate and show responsibility, the father more for boys, the mother for girls.

FEMALE PSYCHOLOGY AND THE "FEMALE MODE" OF TOILET TRAINING

What I am attempting here is simply to delineate more clearly the sexual dichotomy in toilet training and to stress its importance.

In the evolution of one's body image, one gains knowledge through visual and tactile explorations, and through stimuli arising from those areas as they function. With maturation there is progression from undifferentiation to increasingly more discrete differentiation of bodily parts and functions (Shopper, 1967). Unlike the boy, the girl is at risk in maintaining a "cloacal concept" of her excretory organs. This "unitary" concept of excretion is opposed to a binary neurophysiological concept of both urination and defecation. For the girl, the unitary cloacal concept is not only a result of greater anatomical and neurophysiological propinquity, but it is also a consequence of the girl's inability to see her own excretory organs or their functioning. The little boy can more readily see his penis and his urinary stream. In addition, the girl child is often subject to more maternal inhibition about touching and exploring her "bottom." This is because the girl is subject not only to greater maternal demands for cleanliness but also, I suspect, to greater prohibitions regarding discovery of the clitoris, labia, and vagina and their possible use in masturbation. Mothers of girls seem dedicated to repressing their daughters' sexuality early on. It is as though the little girl, if she discovers her genitals, will use them for pleasure and discharging excitement. Mothers reason that once their daughters are sexually awakened by masturbation, intercourse will quickly (and precociously) follow. Then, too, there are the dangers of pregnancy, disease, and a sharply curtailed adolescence (Shopper, 1984).

Bellman (1966) gives serious attention to gender differences in her survey of first graders in Stockholm. Bellman reports the following data: In the second year of life, 73.1% of boys and 60.9% of girls are wetting; in the third year, 22.2% of boys and 14.6% of girls; and by the seventh year, 7.2% of boys, 4.4% of girls. These gender differences are even more marked for bowel control. Bowel control is usually achieved first. Girls are at least six months earlier in control of defecation: 90% of girls are trained at 2 years 7 months, whereas 90% of boys are trained at 3 years 1 month. With respect to urination, 90% of girls are trained at 3 years 6 months; the same percentage of boys are trained at 4 years 10 months. Thus, boys are six months behind in defecation but *16 months behind in urination.* I regard these epidemiological findings as supporting data for the existence of a unitary cloacal concept in young girls. The cloacal concept helps us to understand the shorter time difference in the girls' attaining bladder *and* bowel control: 2 years 7 months for bowel, 3 years 6 months for bladder (11 months difference) versus the boys' 21-month difference (3 years 1 month for bowel, 4 years 10 months for bladder).

Additional validation of the unitary concept lies in the fact that after a few disillusioning tries at urinating standing up, girls (a) adopt a sitting/squatting position for urination as for defecation, (b) need to wipe themselves after either urination or defecation, and (c) are not able to see (only hear) either excretory process.

In sharp contrast, penis and rectum are anatomically distinctly separate; the boy can readily see his penis and urinary stream, and both are easily accessible to manipulation. (The boy wipes for defecation but not for urination.) The boy can urinate comfortably standing or sitting; if standing, rather than being prohibited from touching his penis, he is encouraged to touch it to better aim his urinary stream. If standing to urinate, the boy does not need to drop his pants as he would for defecation. Bellman's (1966) studies are compatible with the greater differentiation of bowel and bladder in the young boy. In all, the boy ends up with a more differentiated body image and a more distinct separation anatomically and functionally between urination and defecation, *provided that this potential is supported by parental child-rearing techniques.*

The female mode of training comes naturally to most mothers and, based on their own childhood and adult toilet habits, is appropriate for the training of their daughters. The female mode is characterized by:

1. Sitting down for elimination.

2. Wiping after elimination.

3. Minimal distinction between bladder and bowel training in technique, timing, or vocabulary.

4. Training started with bowel control.

5. Use of the mother herself on the toilet as a model for imitation and a greater tolerance for lack of bathroom privacy.

6. A tendency to train the girl somewhat earlier and more forcefully than the boy.

The female mode is compatible with and enhancing to the formation of a female gender identity. The child is encouraged to be like mother; by seeing mother's eliminative functioning, they have an intimacy with each other's body that fosters the girl's gender *and* sexual identity.

The sitting position is not as onerous to the girls, who, on the average, are not as motor-driven as boys the same age. Hence, sitting down and its enforced immobility is less likely to be a source of mother–child conflict. Toileting compliance for the girl, to the extent that it entails a regression to an increased mother–child unity, is not as anxiety pro-voking to the girl as it is to the boy. Regression to a less self/object differentiation is associated in boys with a loss of masculine gender identity. It is not just the boy's preference for an "uncontaminated" father in contrast to the ambivalently regarded mother (Mahler, 1966), but a father who also supports and mirrors the boy's budding mascu-linity. The female mode used with the boy in no way enhances the boy's potential for further body differentiation or supports the sexual differences between him and his mother. In fact, in many ways it is antithetical to the boy's maturation.

Is it any wonder that boys resent the impingement of toilet training (female mode) when it means (a) cessation of mobility, (b) regression from standing, (c) a loss of autonomy since it is done at the mother's initiation, (d) a blurring or loss of the boy's budding male gender identity, (e) a high degree of compliance, and (f) a threat to the boy toddler's growing self/object differentiation.

The female mode may be used by a mother because it "comes naturally"; that is, it is a reliving and reactivation of her own training experiences with her own mother. In some mothers it may be com-bined with various degrees of psychopathology. In these instances the female mode becomes the carrier for inflicting that pathology on the male child. As Sarlin (1963) noted, "In anality there is equality [be-tween sexes], but in the toilet training of the boy the mother has to confront urethral/phallic issue, i.e., inequality" (p. 800).

Esman (1977) saw enuresis as part of a difficulty in neurophysio-logical maturation. He advocated no therapy for the child, except for secondary or associated pathology, but advises parents to abstain from "pathogenic behaviors toward the child" (p. 156). Esman did not address the sexual differences in etiology. His single case example was male, and he did not give any clinical history of parental training procedures or offer any recommended procedures. Blum (1970), on the other hand, through the lengthy analysis of a mother of three enuretic girls, was able to show the mother's psychopathology in the urethral/bladder area to be a significant force in the etiology and maintenance of her children's enuresis.

Pierce, Mangelsdorf, and Whitman (1969) studied mothers of enuretic boys and found them either to have a casual nonchalance toward the symptom or else to actively encourage and abet the bedwetting for its unconscious gratification to them. When, through therapy, the women could renounce their unconscious gratification from their sons' bedwetting, the bedwetting ceased completely. One mother had her son participate in an experimental study of dreaming in enuretic children. This involved several nights of sleeping in a setting away from home under the care of a male therapist. The child suddenly ceased bedwetting. "His dreams indicated that identification with a doctor helped in a resolution of his masculinity-feminity conflicts. His mother's depreciation of father had made him feel masculinity was an achievement which would alienate mother" (p. 287). All mothers seemed to be "castrating females" who "verbalized their degrading, demeaning concepts of their husbands, specifically, and of all men generally" (p. 288). Despite being aware that specific maternal psycho-pathology played a significant role in the production of the boys' enuresis, the authors did not comment about the mothers' actions or attitudes at the time of toilet training.

"Castrating female" is not only a pejorative, but is in many ways an overly broad concept since it is used in connection with many developmental phases and issues. Toilet training entails issues of phallic narcissism for the boy, in the sense that the mother may admire or denigrate his phallus and its function, may aggrandize ownership of the boy's phallus, or allow him to own it and so incorporate it into his masculine body image. The mother's relationship to her husband will resonate with the mother's relationship with her boy, and, in that sense, toilet training of the boy is paradigmatic of the mother–father relationship and its difficulties.

THE "MALE MODE" OF TOILET TRAINING

The "male mode" is characterized by the following:

1. Active participation by the father and/or other male members of the family.

2. The male's modeling of urinary practices for the boy, and a greater tolerance for the absence of bathroom and toileting privacy.

3. Urinary training precedes bowel training.

4. Urinary control is taught as a stand-up procedure with emphasis on *skill, mastery,* and *fun.*

5. Control, function, and naming of urine is sharply differentiated from control, function, and naming of feces. (Girls tend to speak generically, i.e., "going to the toilet" rather than "making pee pee" or "making b.m.")

6. Encouragement to touch and control the penis so as to aim the urinary stream.

7. The emphasis is not on the regressive "pleasing mommy" or "staying dry" but rather on "making bubbles like daddy" or being a "big boy" (like daddy). In short, identification with *father* rather than compliance with mother.

8. Toilet paper need not be used to "wipe" the penis. Wiping after a bowel movement should be in the "male" direction, whereas girls are taught to wipe in the "female" direction, i.e., from front to back.

The male mode clearly is appropriate for the boy toddler, and the female mode is appropriate for the girl toddler. Other than providing a model for standing urination, the mother can carry out the male mode, although it is accomplished more easily and with more impact by the father.

The participation of the father, older brother, or other male household member provides a model for active identification not only with someone older but with someone male. The father thus helps in the separation-individuation process and in the disidentification process (Greenson, 1966) from mother and other household females. The disidentification process helps him to attain a masculine core gender identity. Participation by father and other males helps the boy toddler resolve more effectively the conflicts of core gender identity and separation-individuation. Standing for urination is a particularly male prerogative, and to the young mind it represents the one major difference between male and female.

Boys born with hypospadias usually have to urinate sitting down. Surgeons, eager to repair the hypospadias for functional and cosmetic reasons, also cite psychological ones, namely, to have surgical correction completed prior to school entry so that the boys will be "the same as" the other boys in their bathroom urination. This is not an inconsequential factor for the afflicted child, who will tolerate repeated procedures and even eagerly anticipate the next procedure so that not only will his genital be repaired, but he will be spared the humiliation of having to urinate sitting down – like a girl.

Nursery school teachers and day-care workers have reported to me that many young boys do not know how to urinate standing. They have to be taught, told, shown by teachers or peers. Although I have read of no formal study of this issue, many of these boys are raised in single-parent families headed by a female and with few or transient adult males.

Greenacre (1952), in her classic article on "Urinating and Weeping," noted that

> little boys may be taught to urinate from a standing position as early as 12 to 14 months – as early, in fact, as they have learned to stand firmly in an upright position. . . . By about 2½ most boys are standing urinators. . . . It is natural that the boy takes additional pride in this, just as children of both sexes have developed pride in the control of the time and place of urination, but the excess of pride in the boy may be enhanced by the fact that in his last weeks as a sitting urinator, his stream urination has actually made it difficult for him to urinate tidily in the toilet. . . . Urination soon develops game and contest possibilities, and it is his turn to laugh [pp. 114].

My remarks are not to be construed to mean that only fathers can or should train their sons or that mothers cannot or should not toilet train their sons. Many mothers, whether head of a single parent household or with an uninvolved or absent husband, can utilize the male mode. In fact, many mothers intuitively do so. They start training with urination, encouraging the boy to urinate standing up and to hold his own penis. Her rewarding remarks have to do not so much with pleasing mother but with ther son's growing up to be a "big boy like daddy." Further, the mother may encourage an awareness of the differences between and distinctiveness of the sexes early, as well as teaching the virtues of bathroom modesty and toileting privacy along gender lines.

Mothers whose psychological maturity allows them intuitively to use the male mode also encourage their sons to utilize men other than the fathers, such as older brothers, cousins, uncles, grandfathers, depending on their availability and their relationship to the boy. Akin to this issue is the age at which mother allowed her son to go unaccompanied to the men's room rather than into the ladies room with her.

It is not an infrequent occurrence to hear of difficulties and conflicts concerning toilet training plus symptomatic enuresis in the first-born male and to hear that the younger borthers had none. In those cases the younger sibling was trained without deliberate parental effort. Rather, he initiated imitative behavior by following his older brother into the bathroom and watching him urinate standing up.

CONCLUSIONS AND RECOMMENDATIONS

From the many detailed histories of toilet training taken from parents (only some of whom brought their children for specific excretory problems), I have come to certain conclusions and recommendations.

It must be recognized that the problems of separation-individuaion, core gender identity, and the child's increasing ambivalence toward the mother are all compelling reason for a different method of toilet training for the boy. When such a method is followed by design or by intuition, such boys train more easily and do not have enuresis. I consider the preferred method for the boy to be the male mode of toilet training, which is different from the female mode. Both rely on the child's understanding of and cooperation with the process. With regard for the boy's greater activity level and his increased awareness of the difference in gender between himself and his mother, it is advisable to start toilet training the boy for urination from a standing position. This obviates the need for a potty chair on the floor or toilet seat deflectors. The small stepstool used to reach the sink can be used to reach the toilet bowl.

Many mothers avoid starting with urination because they cannot teach this by imitation and because it is to some extent foreign to their own personal experience. However, other mothers intuitively are attuned to their sons' budding masculinity and begin toilet training with urination from a standing position. The fact that the boy urinates differently from his mother does not threaten his budding individuation. Nor does it threaten his emerging sense of maleness. Rather, it enhances both. The male mode also avoids the sitting position which, for active boy toddlers, may be resented simply because it interferes with motion. There are some mothers who cannot allow the male toddler to become more autonomous in his functioning and must hold his penis as he urinates (as mentioned in the case history of Freud's Little Hans). Not only is this unnecessary and seductive, but such a maternal attitude raises a question as to whether the boy's penis belongs to the boy or the mother. With the male mode, the boy's cpleasure in achieving bladder training is that he now receives permission to hold his penis and to aim it appropriately. This increases the value of his penis (and, for many a boy, makes of the penis almost a newly found toy). The boy's sense of power and importance is further heightened by the ability to aim, to make noise in the toilet bowl, and to create all sorts of bubbles and swirl patterns. All of this is immeasurably consolidated when the father or older sibling provides a model for this function. Thus, the male toddler is no longer conflicted about becoming toilet trained since training no longer carries the connotations of gaining his mother's love, submitting to her, and becoming like her. Much of the power battle and conflict so typical of the mother's toilet training of the male toddler can thus be avoided. Once bladder training is achieved, bowel training is made easier and is, by association, put into the same masculine category as bladder training. Once bladder training is initiated, the child should be placed in training pants. This strengthens the child's autonomy and maturity, since he can more easily care for his clothing while toileting.

From a consideration of the foregoing, I would like to offer some suggestions for those engaged in direct observation, longitudinal studies, and history-taking for research or therapy:

A. Toilet training should not be regarded as a single unitary procedure, either theoretically or behaviorally. Of dynamic significance is the degree to which training is handled as a unitary process (the female model) or as a differentiated, binary (male) process, as well as which sphincter is trained first.

B. There should be greater attention paid to the differences in training within the same family with siblings of the opposite sex, in terms of timing, techniques, and the differentiation between bowel and bladder control.

C. Special attention should be given to the role of the father (or surrogate) in the urinary training of the boy with respect to the extent of his interest and involvement and the degree to which he offers himself as a model for imitation and identification.

D. Techniques requiring special inquiry in the training of the boy are: a) standing versus sitting, b) the handling of the boy's penis by himself or others during urination, c) the use of toilet paper after urination, and d) the degree of exposure of the boy to both mother and father urinating.

E. There is need for further research in this area of child development. This should involve not only cross-cultural studies but also studies of the unique subcultures in our own country, as well as of alternative styles of family life, such as single fathers as heads of family, lesbian mothers rearing male children. Also open for study are the variety of families rearing opposite sex twins.

F. The behavioral practices involved in the mother's toilet training of her boy should be noted, especially the degree to which these practices are the behavioral embodiment of significant psychopathology. The mother's unconscious conflicts in the areas of self/object differentiation, male envy/hatred, body image differentiation, and anality need to be considered for an understanding of her toilet training practices and her child's pathology in those areas.

G. Those involved in training parental surrogates (day-care workers, nursery school teachers, nannies) and those professionals involved in the care of preschoolers from single-parent (predominantly female) families need to be apprised of the issues discussed in this paper. The developing phallic masculinity in the young boy needs to be recognized, accepted, and enhanced lest in later childhood/adolescence these boys rely on compensatory and hypertrophied phallic prowess, for example, rebellious gangs and narcissistic exploitation of women sex partners.

REFERENCES

Abelin, E. L. (1971), The role of the father in the separation-individuation process. In: *Separation-Individuation,* ed. J. B. McDevitt & C. F. Settlage. New York: International Universities Press, pp. 229–252.

———— (1980), Triangulation, the role of the father and the origins of core gender identity during the rapproachment subphase. In: *Rapprochement,* ed. R. F. Lax, S. Bach & J. A. Burland. New York: Aronson, pp. 151–170.

Azrin, N. H. & Foxx, R. M. (1974), *Toilet Training in Less Than A Day.* New York: Simon & Schuster.

Beck, J. (1976), *Effective Parenting.* New York: Simon & Schuster.

Becker, W. C. & Becker, J. W. (1974), *Successful Parenthood.* Chicago: Follett.

Beller, E. K. & Neubauer, P. B. (1963), Sex differences and symptom patterns in early childhood. *J. Child Psychiat.,* 2:417–433.

Bellman, M. (1966), Studies on encopresis. *Acta Ped. Scand.,* Suppl. 170:1–152.

Blum, H. (1970), Maternal psychopathology and nocturnal enuresis. *Psychoanal. Q.,* 39:609–619.

Brazelton, T. B. (1962), A child-oriented approach to toilet training. *Pediat.,* 29:121–127.

Brooks, J. G. (1971), *No More Diapers*. New York: Delacorte Press/Seymour Lawrence.

Cath, S. H., Gurwitt, A. & Ross, J. M. (1982), *Father and Child*. Boston, MA: Little, Brown.

Davidson, F. & Choquet, M. (1984), Epidemiological survey of functional symptomatology in pre-school age children. In: *Frontiers of Infant Psychiatry*, Vol. II, ed. J. D. Call, E. Galenson & R. L. Tyson. New York: Basic Books, pp. 531–539.

Dodson, F. (1973), *How to Parent*. New York: New American Library.

——— (1974), *How to Father*. Los Angeles: Nash.

Douglas, J. W. B. (1973), Early disturbing events and later enuresis. In: *Bladder Control and Enuresis*, ed. I. Kalvin, R. C. MacKeith & S. R. Meadow. Philadelphia: Lippincott, pp. 109–117.

Eldred, M. M. (1951), *Your Baby and Mine: How to be Better Parents and Rear Better Children*. New York: J. Day.

Esman, A. (1977), Nocturnal enuresis: Some current concepts. *J. Amer. Acad. Child Psychiat.,* 16:150–158.

Flapan, D. & Neubauer, P. B. (1972), Developmental groupings of pre-school children. *Israel Annals Psychiat. & Related Disciplines,* 10(1):52–70. Jerusalem: Jerusalem Academic Press.

Fraiberg, S. (1959), *The Magic Years*. New York: Scribner.

Gesell, A. (1940), *The First Five Years of Life*. New York: Harper & Row.

Greenacre, P. (1952), *Trauma, Growth, and Personality*. New York: Norton.

Greenson, R. R. (1966), A transvestite boy and a hypothesis. *Internat. J. Psycho-Anal.,* 47:396–403.

——— (1968), Dis-identifying from mother: Its special importance for the boy. *Internat. J. Psycho-Anal.,* 49:370–374.

Klein, T. (1968), *The Father's Book*. New York: Morrow.

Lamb, M. E., ed. (1976), *The Role of the Father in Child Development*. New York: Wiley.

——— (1984), Mothers, fathers, and child care in a changing world. In: *Frontiers of Infant Psychiatry*, ed. J. D. Call, E. Galenson & R. L. Tyson. New York: Basic Books, pp. 343–362.

Leach, P. (1978), *Your Baby and Child from Birth to Age Five*. New York: Knopf.

Levine, M. I. & Seligman, J. H. (1973), *The Parents' Encyclopedia of Infancy, Childhood, and Adolescence*. New York: Crowell.

Mack, A. (1978), *Toilet Training: The Picture Book Technique for Children and Parents*. Boston: Little, Brown.

Mahler, M. S. (1966), Notes on the development of basic moods: the depressive affect. In: *Psychoanalysis–A General Psychology,* ed. R. M. Lowenstein, L. M. Newmann, M. Schur & A. J. Solnit. New York: International Universities Press, pp. 152–168.

_____ Pine, F. & Bergman, A. (1975), *The Psychological Birth of the Human Infant.* New York: Basic Books.

Minton, C., Kagan, J. & Levine, J. A. (1971), Maternal control and obedience in the two year old. *Child Devel.,* 42:1873–1894.

Nash, J. (1965), The father in contemporary culture and current psychological literature. *Child Devel.,* 36:261–297.

_____ (1976), Historical and social changes–the perception of the role: the father. In: *The Role of the Father in Child Development,* ed. M. E. Lamb. New York: Wiley, pp. 62–88.

Oppel, W. C., Harper, P. A. & Rider, R. V. (1968), The age of attaining bladder control. *Pediat.,* 42:614–626.

Pierce, C. M., Mangelsdorf, T. K. & Whitman, R. M. (1969), Mothers of enuretic boys. *Amer. J. Psychother.,* 23:283–292.

Roiphe, H. & Galenson, E. (1984), Infantile origins of disturbances in sexual identity. In: *Frontiers of Infant Psychiatry,* Vol. II, ed. J. D. Call, E. Galenson & R. L. Tyson. New York: Basic Books, pp. 531–539.

Ross, J. (1979), Fathering: A review of some psychoanalytic contributions on paternity. *Internat. J. Psycho-Anal.,* 60:317–328.

Ross Laboratories (1962), *Developing Toilet Habits.* Columbus, OH: Ross Laboratories.

Rutter, M., Yule, W. & Graham, P. (1973), Enuresis and behavioral deviance: some epidemiological considerations. In: *Bladder Control and Enuresis,* ed. I. Kalvin, R. C. MacKeith & S. R. Meadow. Philadelphia: Lippincott.

Salk, L. & Kramer, R. (1969), *How to Raise a Human Being.* New York: Random House.

Sarlin, C. N. (1963), Feminine identity. *J. Amer. Psychoanal. Assn.,* 11:791–816.

Shopper, M. (1976), The real child vs. the reconstructed child. Presented to American Psychoanalytic Association, Baltimore.

_____ (1984), From (re)discovery to ownership of the vagina: A contribution to the exploration of the non-use of contraceptives in the female adolescent. In: *Adolescent Parenthood,* ed. M. Sugar. New York: S. P. Medical & Scientific Books, pp. 214–233.

_____ (1967), Three as a symbol of the female genital and the role of differentiation. *Psychoanal. Quart.,* 36:410–417.

Sperling, M. (1974), *The Major Neuroses and Behavior Disorders in Children.* New York: Aronson.

Spock, B. & Rothenberg, M. B. (1985), *Dr. Spock's Baby and Child Care.* New York: Dutton.

Stoller, R. J. (1966), The mother's contribution to infantile transvestic behavior. *Internat. J. Psycho-Anal.,* 47:384–395.

_____ (1968), *Sex and Gender.* New York: Science House.

_____ (1975), *Sex and Gender: The Transexual Experiment.* New York: Aronson.

_____ (1979), Fathers of transexual children. *J. Amer. Psychoanal. Assn.,* 27:837–866.

Tyson, P. (1982), The role of the father in gender identity, urethral erotism, and phallic narcissism. In: *Father and Child,* ed. S. H. Cath, A. R. Gurwitt & J. M. Ross. Boston: Little, Brown, pp. 175–188.

U.S. Children's Bureau (1951), *Infant Care.* Washington, DC: U.S. Govt. Printing Off.

Weisberger, E. (1975), *Your Young Child and You.* New York: Dutton.

Winnicott, D. W. (1965), *The Maturational Process and the Facilitating Environment.* New York: International Universities Press.

6

Readiness for Grandfatherhood and the Shifting Tide

Stanley H. Cath

Owing to the changing structure and dynamics of the American family, the tide is shifting for grandparents who are ready and longing to resume affectively salient, vitalizing, or supplementary roles within the extended family. For the 70% of persons over 65 who have become grandparents, readiness for this developmental task tends to be a marker of intrapsychic transition into aging. In this chapter, I shall first discuss some of the changes in self-image and family images facilitating this nomethetic transition into grandparenthood and, then, via clinical vignettes, illustrate some unique individual vicissitudes tending toward success or failure in the last parenting operation of the life span.

TRANSGENERATIONAL RESCREENINGS
IN LATE LIFE

With the birth of every child, at least four grandparents are created intrapsychically, whether near or far, involved or estranged. To be sure, not all elders respond in the same way. But to judge from subjective as well as research reports, of all human bonds, grandparenthood, especially in the young-old seems one of the least ambivalent,

easiest achieved, and most readily accepted (Robertson, 1977; Kornhaber and Woodward, 1981; Kivnick, 1981; Cath, 1986).

Webster defines the "grand" relationship as "one generation
removed." In "expectant" grands I have interviewed or treated, its
felicitous arrival seems to have stimulated in both prospective grandparents fond images of their grandparents and even their great grands.
From the ancient, ghostly halls of family introjects, as many as five
generations may be exhumed in an active, longitudinal inventory of
intrapsychic roots, characteristics, and determinants. Imagos of both
devalued and valued elders who were thought to have passed on
particular characteristics as well as national, cultural, or religious values
may be revived, even if only in a search for children's names or around
the institutions surrounding birth. Within the minds of new grandparents, a screening of their own parenting characteristics, memories of
their parents' and grandparents' behavior, family attitudes, habits, and
tendencies are likely to cover several generations of affectively laden
memories consisting of a mixture of reality and myth. Habits and
traditions from the past are now reconsidered in terms of their benefi-
cent fit with the new generation's needs. In all likelihood, this process
begins silently in the mid-years and gradually sets in motion a challenge to the balance between narcissism and altruism. This leads to
new interpretations of the past and an internal redefinition of "time
remaining." This Janus-faced reconsideration is usually accompanied
by various degrees of regretful reevaluation of self and new, hopeful
resolutions for the future. Thus this rescreening of the past may be
stimulated by hope for an improved, more loving future for all "selfob-
jects." This may be catalyzed by an age-appropriate realization of the
imperfections involved in the complexities, challenges, limits, and
ambivalences of having been parented, of having parented, and of
having lived in one's time and place in history. By the time of
grandparenthood, this shared inventory should have tested the limits
of omnipotent aspirations as well as the capacities to mold, influence,
and pass on to a new generation both personal values and the traditions
of one's past. The "revelations" of this intrapsychic silent rescreening
may lead to an internal reorganization of narcissistic-altruistic concerns. The relending of the self to a new generation triggers a search
beyond the self for ancestral or religious allies in civilizing a new brood
of offspring.

The birth of a grandchild, then, may be connected with archaic
longings for both a perfect child and a perfect version of the self as
parent. Accordingly, parenting concepts and values are recalled,
screened, modified, and resynthesized in a way not possible before this

opportunity presented itself. I believe this ongoing transgenerational shifting of mental representations of self, children, and grandchildren results in new aspirations, reinternalizations, and externalizations with mutative restructuring of the relationship between ego, ego ideal, and superego. This series of intrapsychic and social changes may puzzle and mystify the middle generation, as well as close others who ponder the discrepancies readily apparent in grandparental versus parental styles of coping with an offspring. This change in family dynamics may lead to the shift of certain transferences and conscious expectations from the shoulders of offspring to grandchildren or may even lead to a new set of transferences with different affective tones. In terms of social anchorages, the birth of a child more often than not increases in-law affiliations. Conscious and unconscious expectations may be even more idealized and related to archaic ego ideals. Still, they seem softer and mute the character structure and mode of relating of many grandparents to their own children. The pleasures and purposes of parenthood itself may be now redefined by a more mature, grandparental perspective.

GRANDFATHERS

It seems clear that for most men these shifts in psychic structure are subtly associated with previously disavowed longings for belovedness and ongoingness. Vicarious identification with the vitality of the grandchild may compensate for disillusionments of the past and for present and future depletions and concerns about death.

However, increasing awareness of the inevitability of death, especially in narcissistically vulnerable men, changes perceptions of relationships as well as of time past and time remaining. This altered time sense may have led to last-ditch efforts to achieve the unachievable or possibly to search for a chemical "fountain of youth." Lifelong repressed yearnings for an ideal father's or mother's love become intensified when one becomes a grandparent. Having been projected onto one's (adult) child or children with varying degrees of success, this poignant feeling may now seem inappropriate and be displaced, partially or wholly, on to one or more grandchildren. These highly charged affective expectations may convert a grandchild's receiving a prize at school or an athletic victory into a grandiose state of joy. For some grandfathers, the failure of a grandchild to achieve, especially as a male, that is, to compete successfully, may create new intensities of despair.

A relatively small number of grandfathers (I would guess 10%), avoid this major affective investment in a return from grandchildren. Some of these elders, overly preoccupied with preserving their own interests, bodies, and youth, may not make the transference of idealized, affective expectations to the youngest of the family. They may even ridicule those peers who seem to them to be overly involved with their grandchildren and have chosen to intensify less narcissistic–but, to be sure, similar–Faustian procrastinations through contacts with offspring. They listen with sardonic ear to such statements as, "If I can only live long enough to see my grandchild graduate . . . get married, etc." Still other grandfathers set up a late-life, intrapsychic, often one-sided bond with a favorite granddaughter. If this relationship is reciprocated, the elder will want nothing to change, often confessing that this relationship has been the most rewarding, the "purest love," of his life.

STAGES OF GRANDFATHERHOOD (YOUNG, MIDDLE-AGED AND OLD GRANDFATHERS)

But everything changes. How stable these revitalizing bonds and rescreened transferences can remain over time has yet to be adequately studied. What is clear is that the opportunity is timed exquisitely. For in many young to middle-aged grandfathers, grandchildren do provide a background for an enriched, emotionally refueling final phase of life. Indeed grandfatherhood may come at a time when life's meaning is in transformation, for example, in preretirement or disengagement, when ordinary, day-to-day life threatens serious alterations in purpose and function. In the background, nature relentlessly continues to take its toll from postreproductive, expendable creatures.

Many, to the end of their days, compensate beautifully by emotionally reinvesting in the young. However, almost invariably, if one lives long enough, a succession of inevitable tragedies will drain ego resiliency and resourcefulness. Knowing these tragedies are just over the horizon adds to the depth of emotional attachment and identification. Unfortunately, as was the case for 67-year-old, cancer-stricken Freud, should such a highly cathected grandchild die, the loss creates new levels of inconsolable grief. Heinerle's death was the only time when Freud was known to have shed tears (Jones, 1955). In my previous paper (Cath, 1986) on grandfathers I cited several cases documenting how late life illness may change the relationships between the grands.

PARENTS AS GRANDPARENTAL GATEKEEPERS

The mental representations of grands and the depth of the bonds can be "permitted," colored, and vitalized by the middle generation, who now become "vertical gatekeepers." In describing "access" to fathers, Atkins (1982) wrote:

> In the nuclear mother-father-infant constellation, the mother can either help to establish an affectively vital position for the father, or quite literally and negatively put him "in his place" as a hostile intruder. She can sign, through her affective valence, her attitude toward the father's holding and caring for their child, or her attitude toward the father's comings and goings. Her relative pleasures and unpleasures may manifest either as open expressions or be mediated through subtle changes in body contact while holding her infant. These shifts in her affective "body language" may register in her infant both as primitive affectomotor representations . . . and as signs communicating an anticipation either of father or the "father context." Such may well be the origins of the child's enduring positively or negatively charged father representations. This transaction may also provide a tableau for, or source of, idealizations or denigrations of the other.
>
> As the child develops, evocative representational capacities, fantasies, or mental images of father may remain linked to the mother's capacity to vitalize her husband even in his absence [p. 140].

Indeed, it is the nature of the ambivalent bond of the middle generation to their parents and to their in-laws that will serve as an armature upon which the third generation will sculpt images of their grandparents. Life decisions about living arrangements, geographic moves, and career choices often reflect these ambivalent affective imagos.

In contrast to enforced contact between grands, enforced separation by a gatekeeper is also possible. One daughter-in-law who refused to let her children either talk with or have meaningful contact with the paternal grandfather. She alleged to everyone it was his rigid authoritarianism that had caused their father's (her husband's) suicide.

By the time the grandchildren are adolescents, their image of their grandparent may be further modified as they witness the more intact, middle generation caring, or not caring, for a more feeble, infirmed, or disabled, aging one. Reconciliation with, or retribution against, parents will further alter identifications and relationships by adolescent offspring, usually with old-old grandparents (as well as others such as, aunts, uncles, teachers, and so on).

Mead (1972), reflecting from a cross-cultural perspective, wrote:

> The tag that grandparents and grandchildren have a common enemy is explicitly faced in many societies. In our own society the point most often made is that grandparents can enjoy their grandchildren because they have no responsibility for them—do not have to discipline them, and they lack the guilt of parenthood [p. 275].

Indeed the rebellious, separation-individuation thrusts of Western adolescents all too often conflict with their parents' more conservative tendencies, which likely reflect *a family coefficient of optimism-cynicism* characteristic of the middle of the journey through life. This coefficient may be determined by the actualizations of parental ego ideals, the successes or failures in marital as well as intergenerational relationships, and the like (Cath, 1965). Like Socrates', the middle generation's usually cautious, if not mistrusting, feelings about modern trends seem in conflict with the adolescent's push toward externals, his search for unlimited faith in idealized, charismatic others, and seemingly different values. Surprisingly, some teenagers find themselves more in tune with their grandparents than with their parents. Often the latter are in a similarly disillusioned, transitional, reaching-out phase (Cath, 1982a). And, as Mead (1972) implied, both may be struggling with autonomy from the middle, or "sandwich," generation, both searching for new identities, greater independence, and new anchorages. The tragedy is that one generation is more likely achieving these goals while the other more likely losing them. Vicarious mutual identifications are inevitable.

Should a "grand alliance" be established (as in the 1971 movie "Kotch"), old preoedipal and oedipal wounds will be opened and potentially rehealed in all generations. All in all, new opportunities for better relatedness will be possible. If such a struggle can be permitted, tolerated, and reworked, a creative restructuring of family bonds begins. This may contribute to the sense of a new or "best ever" self with more imaginative use of others, in Erikson, Erikson, and Kivnick's (1986) terms, new levels of integrity.

For some, even this third chance to participate in a more ideal parent-child interaction may not succeed, for the needs and priorities of the various participants may not remain "in synch." Even in midlife, serious emotional upheavals, often overlooked in family histories, may follow either the death of a grand or the abandonment of an old-old by a previously beloved but outwardly bound grandchild. Intermarriage may create a different affective tone in a previously harmonious "grand" affair. And there may be limited time for the return of the prodigal grandchild. In many elders the invisible organic decline plus this new failure in an idealized relationship may summate to trigger loss of immunocompetency and all the ensuing guilt. "I know my marriage killed my grandfather," reported one 40-year-old, childless woman.

Thus all generations may "use" or relate to grandparents for age-specific intrapsychic purposes and needs. As Ross (1982, this volume) has reminded us, Freud (1909) believed that little Hans promoted his father to grandfather in order to give himself a safer distance from oedipal concerns. As with parents, one can have too much or too little of them.

Grandparenthood, then, initiates a whole series of changes within an enlarged and complex extended family structure. It leads to various degrees of alliance, enjoyment, responsibility, centrality, loss, and conflict in various members' lives. In this regard Mead (1972) noted:

> I always have been acutely aware of how one life touches another
> . . . able to conceive of my relationship to all my forebears. . . . But
> the idea that as a grandparent one was dealing with action at a
> distance, that somewhere, miles away, a series of events occurred
> that changed one's status forever – I had not thought of that and I
> found it odd. . . . I had the extraordinary sense of having been
> transformed . . . through no act of my own but by the act of one's
> child. . . . I felt something like the shock . . . of being disenfran-
> chised . . . by the arbitrary act of some tyrannical government. . . .
> The point most often made (about grands) is they get along so
> well . . . because they have no responsibility . . . do not have to
> discipline . . . and lack the guilt and anxiety of parenthood
> [p. 275].

Mead's conflicted perspective may be illuminated by another of her sensitive cross-cultural observations: "Achieving grandparenthood . . . brings about intimations of mortality" (p. 276). Indeed, at a three-generation Thanksgiving dinner, with obvious relief, a five-year-old whispered to its mother, "You are not old. Grandma and grandpa are. You won't die, they will!" True enough, from this threatening vantage point grandparents are often the first fantasy or real contact a small child has with aging, depletion, and disease, informing the earliest memories around Eros, loss, and Thanatos.

But the nature of grandparenthood is much more complicated than implying a lack of guilty, anxious responsibility or having a common enemy. Depending on the family dynamics, grandchildren may have very different loving or hating imagos of mother's or father's parents (or family). In different developmental stages grandchildren may prefer one or another grand according to gender or, for that matter, may regard the very same person quite differently over time. Older children may have longer and sometimes more meaningful contact with one or more of their grands. Some, especially the youngest or those born to older parents, may have no direct contact with a senior generation.

CLINICAL VIGNETTES

The following is an excerpt from the analysis of an initially reluctant grandfather who had had no contact with his grands. Indeed, had he had them they might have provided much-needed affirmative sources of affection and vitality. This vignette also reflects and illuminates some of the complex factors involved in divorce and remarriage.

Case 1: Grandfatherhood as A Positive Maturational Force

Peter, a 60-year-old man in the process of terminating analysis, described his holiday on a Monday after a Christmas break:

> I feel incredibly flat. I should be happy. My daughter called. She thinks she's pregnant. Somehow I covered my feelings by joking about dancing in the street. I told her not to tell me until she was absolutely sure, so I wouldn't be a disappointed grandfather. It made no rational sense. Then I tried to be funny by thinking up all kinds of comical names for the baby. Sure, I don't want to feel disappointed, but I also don't want to act like a fool. Thinking about becoming a grandparent. It was the first thought I had when I woke. I never knew mine. They were kept in the dark, as if something was wrong, like a shameful family secret. It fits with last time, feeling I was the older generation, the next to disappear. But I've never been able to experience pleasure, or take enjoyment when it's right in front of me. I'm old enough to be a grandfather, God knows. I didn't even know a single grandparent.

I noted how upsetting it is for a child to mirror one of our weaknesses, like the inability to enjoy . . . or to reveal the experience of enjoyment. (Indeed, we had learned earlier that he acted like a clown to conceal deeper feelings. He responded:

> That would be like me, wouldn't it? I always hold back being open about pleasure with people, especially if I know they want it. I'm going to the movies with my wife this afternoon. She suggested it. I act flat, like I'm just going to please her.

He looked sad, blank, distant. I noted, "Like you feel now, here?" He answered, "I think about you in regard to my disappointing people as much as being disappointed in them, but I don't know why." He remembered that before Christmas I had commented on his complaint that he had no time to fill stockings; I had noted that he was usually disappointed in what he gave and what he received.

> It was the way I felt about my mother. She was always dissatisfied, busy, didn't have time. Either playing solitaire or doing something for other kids–not for me. She was always so flat. In our family we did things in categories; help with the meals, with the laundry; keep calm, help her save time. That's why I resent analysis so, being here on time, for only an hour . . . leaving when the hour ends . . . when I'm supposed to. Analysts are so busy and secretive. You must be a grandfather by now. I guess I feel you hold back from me. Especially on weekends. Just like she and my father did. Abandoned me on the weekends. I learned not to care. But, now I hold back from myself and my family too.

His annoyance at his busy, energetic, terminating analyst and his busy, abandoning mother led him back to the phone conversation with his daughter.

She had asked, "Aren't you pleased? Your voice doesn't sound overjoyed." He said to me:

> I guess she wanted me to share her enthusiasm, to welcome a baby. Instead I covered it by humor minimizing the reality. Why shouldn't she tell me? Damn, my mother always did that, covered her feelings with dry humor.

Maybe there were other reasons we still did not understand, probably in his feeling she should not tell him. His response was:

> I almost didn't tell you. My daughter said, "Don't tell mom [his divorced wife] about it yet. I want to tell her myself." I'm not sure

I was the first to know. But we have always had a special relationship. To me, telling her dad first was like it was our secret baby.

I doubt that there are any "grand" relationships not deeply triadic or oedipal in nature, often overlaid with intense competition over who will become the supergrandparent. With so many families involved in divorce and remarriage across generations, many grandfathers are reluctant, removed, secret, or absent. And the potential for unavailable grandfather idealization increases logarithmically. In many single-mother households other men may become "resident fathers," or children may for a period of time adopt a neighborhood grandfather. But, from the child's perspective, these men come and go in unpredictable sequences, and grandfathers tend to be more steadily available. In my clinical experience grandfathers are more likely to become stable, fatherly figures for their daughters' children. Like Peter's, the shared unconscious fantasy of the father and daughter may have been to create a secret, forbidden, perfect child.

I have encountered much envy of families with many males and believe it is endemic especially in certain mobile families in male-deficient sections of the country and in specific subcultures in which fathers tend to be minimally involved in the first five to ten years of their childrens' lives. Envy of those who have, or knew, grandparents may become a subtle, revived syndrome of the later years (a form of grandfather envy; see Cath, 1982c) as in Peter's case.

But let us return to his associations.

Maybe it's because it's my second marriage. I have no right to be happy there, any more than in my first. Anyway, if it's a three-party system, someone has to lose out. If wife #1 is happy, and we were to enjoy becoming grandparents it's like we will have an advantage over my second wife. Even if we are no longer married, we are all connected like *grand cogenitors* or something.[1] Maybe I can't be enthused because it's a time I want to exclude my first wife and can't do it without feeling bad. Hell, my daughter almost invited me to. I feel like she deserves to be excluded, although I imagine she feels that way about me. Damn!

---

[1] All "divorced" parents and grandparents have this secret, ambivalent "biological connection" whatever the ongoing relationships. It is part of each member's secret family image. The divorce of adult children affects the self-image of their parents as well as of their children – and remarriage complicates the already burdened in-law imagos.

I commented, "So flatness might relate to not being able to experience happiness without feeling bad and feeling guilty about excluding people. Could part of you want to exclude your second, as well as your first, wife in this fantasy 'our baby' with your daughter?" After a silence he said:

> My wife is waiting for me outside. She said maybe she would meet you today. I was disappointed when I came in and she stayed outside. It's as if she had to keep you excluded too. Lately I've been wanting to share you with her but I didn't tell her that.

The next hour: "This idea of withholding and concealing pleasure, of secrets and of excluding people, gives me goosepimples." I reminded him he had had goosepimples in the analysis once before when we talked of "forbidden pleasures." His thoughts took him back to becoming a grandfather. As if nothing had occurred in the last hour, he asked, "But what forbidden pleasures could that bring about?" He remembered he had always concealed enjoyment of his work from his first wife and enjoyment of weekend pleasures from me. He smiled.

> It fits exactly because while thinking yesterday of telling you I was about to become a new grandfather, I couldn't remember what I was thinking about when I first came in and felt so terribly flat. [He looks as if he is going to cry.] I guess I'm afraid of sharing anything. What comes to my mind is keep it to yourself. Like a command. Like my parents standing at the door of my bedroom saying, "Keep your hands above the covers." Maybe they were afraid I'd have hidden pleasures in my masculinity. I had to conceal that. Maybe I'm ready to enjoy being a grandfather at least!

By the time of the baby's birth, Peter had worked through more of his tendency to withhold. He did become more comfortable with pleasures in complex (grandfatherly) triangles. Of course, the conversion from reluctant to a ready, responsive grandfather was catalyzed by an alert and responsive grandson, an enthralled mother, and two grandmothers. He noted, "Even in flat people, grandfatherhood, with all its complications, is vitalizing." The family dubbed him a *great* grandfather.

For Peter, becoming a grandfather seems to have facilitated a working through of his capacity for pleasure as he recognized in the transference the underlying conflicts (masturbating, competitive oedipal, incestuous). This helped him come to terms with his withholding tendencies.

Case 2: Grandparenting: A Forced or Dreaded Experience

A man whose mother had died at his birth under the questionable circumstances of subintended suicide was raised by a busy, professional, now widowed grandfather and his housekeeper. In the patient's words,

> My mother's death and my arrival changed my father's life. He blamed my mother and me for the rest of his days. His revenge was to hand me over to my mother's parents as much as he could. My grandmother was so shocked, she quickly went senile and ended in a nursing home. My grandfather just hated having me or hated me, I never was sure which. But, I was determined to welcome my children and grandchildren and I did!

When a grandparent has been unwillingly pressed *in loco parentis,* the admixture of involuntary parenting and resentful grandparenting may limit the meaningful satisfaction of the role. Bitterness in the elder may be concealed publicly so that few but intimates and the grandchild know it is there. In teenage mothers, particularly in *serially divorced generations,* helplessness or a paradoxical sense of entitlement rationalizes dropping a child into a parent's lap. This also reflects a lack of understanding of the elder's conflicts, limitations, or readiness and may have serious repercussions for a child twice-rejected (by parents and grandparents). Although many elders do the best they can, some, worn by fatigue, illness, or time, have protested weakly to me, "God meant young people to have children."

In a similar vein, grandfatherhood may be associated with death. One expectant grandmother reported, "Although I was intensely attached to my grandfather, I dread my grandchild's birth. My granddad was both mother and father, but he was too tired and too old. I was too much for him. I helped put him in his grave. I am afraid that can happen to me!"

Not surprisingly, then, a variety of negative grand reactions can be observed. Some expectant grandfathers are threatened overtly by the new role. It may pose the threat not only of age but in some of painful repetition of the "bad seed" phenomenon. Furthermore, the role may revive unpleasant memories of reluctant, deteriorated, or demented aged grands. Then the dread of those images, plus the additional responsibilities, may outweigh the pleasures. Or, if it is not a shared pleasure, grandparenthood may trigger marital disequilibrium.

I have observed in my practice many single-tracked, healthy elders, who, like Margaret Mead, did not take the imposed "tyrannical changes" in priorities without great ambivalence: "I just don't have time." "I did my turn with the kids." "I'm not finished doing my thing." "When do I get time off?" "I'm too young (or too old) to be a babysitter." "Every time that kid comes I get a cold!" "This is just not the time."

But the atmosphere and scene may change by the time a second, third, or fourth grandchild appears. And each grandparent may have a favorite grandchild. Thus, with or without analysis, young-old men like Peter may become fine grandfathers over time. Occasionally heart failure, stroke, senility, or other complications of aging preclude even a limited degree of grandparenting in otherwise able and willing men (Cath, 1982a).

THE SOCIAL ROLE: GENDER AND TIMING IN GRANDPARENTAL DESTINY

The status of new grandparent may vary with age, sex, geographical distance, fashion, psychophysiological well-being, and the personality of the participants. Kivnick (1981), echoing Mead, observed:

> Due to pervasive geographic mobility, divorce rates, increasing longevity and earlier completion of the family, grandparenthood lacks clear social responsibilities and behavioral norms . . . providing an interactional freedom rare among interpersonal relationships [p. 40].

But, I believe, this lack of responsibility, this interactional freedom may be less the rule for women, especially for those who do not move, preferring to age *in situ* (95% of those over 65) (Lanton, 1980). Indeed, today some children in middle age are the ones most likely to move away, leaving grandchildren behind. When there are proximal, affectionate relationships, the family, including grands, remains the most stable caretaking unit in our society. When there are distal and hostile relationships, I have observed that the least loved children or grandchildren most likely will come forth to be involved to varying degrees in the role of primary caretaker. Then there are "the isolates," (Cath, 1982b) without children or grandchildren, but that is another story.

As noted in the clinical vignettes, in families with serious parental deficits it is more likely grandmother will become deeply involved as supplementary or substitute parent. Indeed, the lives of many "traditional" grandmothers have been sequentially organized around the care and nourishment of one or more parents, children, or grandchildren. In the past, then, this more optimistic notion of grand-parenthood as providing interactional freedom may have been associated with inordinate social and individual pressures brought into being, to be sure, by what may have been thought of as "a common enemy." The results might well be characterized by "incapacitating ambiquity" as well as very defined and constraining responsibility.

From my clinical perspective it is not possible to understand family dynamics and the multiple forms intergenerational bonds may take without reflecting upon the uneven bio-psycho-social and age-specific gender differences in various cultures at different times.

Thus, although most of what I have said can be applied to either sex, there are major differences. A striking factor is gender-determined immunocompetency. In all probability this is related to the differential longevity of the sexes–by age 65 there are almost three women for every man. In contemporary times, women live six to eight years longer than men. While many widows face lonely years in very changed emotional circumstances, in an extended family setting grand-mothers may become the "primary," most intact, most responsible, and most clearly remembered grandparent. In the transference, they often first emerge subtly from the mists of infantile repression. Such memories are not deemed by most analysts and therapists as formative or highly significant in transference interpretations; I believe they are underutilized, if not totally overlooked.

Whatever their psychophysiological state, longer life may place some grandmothers under considerable stress because of the power attributed to them by husband, society, children, and grandchildren. With the positive image of strength and endurance, the aging female may become a matriarch. But her revived maternal role may also contribute to the negative images of older women as witches, harpies, and implacable fates. In the words of one old man, "The old women in my family consume me." On the other hand, the less visible, less enduring grandfather, like an absent father a generation before, may be inordinately idealized, even though he is the first to deplete, decline, and die.

To highlight these late-life gender differences, let me contrast the female's unambiguous, sometimes exhausting, surrogate role I have just portrayed, with that of a grandfather recently reported by Kivnick (1986) as "Paul." Paul was an ideal and idealized retired grandfather, possessed of time, talent, and the rare capacity to play with both adults and children. These characteristics in general are similar to those that distinguish the earliest mother-infant and father-infant interactions (Lamb, 1977; Yogman, 1977); and they seem to persist all along the life span. For example, Paul's "masculine" joy in travel and an active lifestyle, plus the mature flexibility to change and redefine himself, helped him to become an unambiguous grandfather of considerable integrity and wisdom. This evolution may have been facilitated by the male's greater lifelong freedom to play with sons rather than to be responsible for raising them, a phenomenon that may forecast and facilitate some positive aspects of relationships with grandfathers. Echoing this observation, Lamb (this volume) cautions us that despite what we wish to believe about recent changes in the modern American father's role, his research affirms that the same gender distinction between mother's responsibility for rearing and father's time spent primarily in play remains as valid today as it was a generation ago.

From this broader life-span, gender-linked perspective, Paul's grandfatherly "integrity" may be connected to, if not dependent on, the qualities of the fit between himself and his wife and subsequently between succeeding generations. Or it may be only particular family settings that permit such distinctions to flourish. In clinical practice not too many elderly women find themselves either with the "freedom" to just be their best selves, as Paul did, or necessarily in a setting in which they can recreate in the grandchild interaction an image of an ideal, all-forgiving, understanding, playful parent. On the contrary, because of what is suspected to be a "vanishing" superior longevity, grand-mothers are often most remembered because of their more typical "matriarchal" qualities.

Whatever we may feel about the discrepancies just enumerated, research affirms the serious, vital importance of the need from cradle to the grave for play and for "time in between" (Sander, 1985). Indeed, these adaptive gender-role-linked capacities derived from the earliest interactions with both sexes may be the determining ingredients in later-life readjustments to disengagement and retirement. For later years will demand resiliency, patience, cohesiveness, wisdom, and the capacity for play and joy. I consider "mellowing," a term applied in the main to aging men, to be a semantic description of a complex, hormone-reinforced process. Indeed, elderly men may, for the first time, experience shared "time off" with grands as consolidating mutual complementarity rather than as the unwelcome interruption it was with a midlife spouse or their own young children. Mellowing changes, rooted in biology, along with a reordering of priorities by a more mature self may be fueled more by love than by duty. This may explain why some elders feel they have moved more deeply into their "true selves" and experience a new sense of revitalization. Family members, observing an aspect of father never seen before, may admire – and envy – the mellowed closeness they never knew before.

In contrast to late life for most grandmothers, that time of life for men still deeply involved in the mainstream may center on narcissistic priorities. Normative biological depletions and degenerations may be countered by a counterphobiclike intensification of the need to remain in the saddle or to drive even more forcefully toward achievement, money, and power. Such goals may delay, if not sabotage, age-appropriate reparative urges to compensate for losses or to seek others to engage in new life pursuits or in play (Cath, 1963a; Cath and Cath, 1984). Progressively enfeebled males, however, disengage first from extrafamilial relationships. Inasmuch as men at any age rarely have close friends, it is not surprising that elderly males seldom find the energy to move outside the family cocoon into new friendships. Consequently, large empty spaces are left in their daily life. Unless a man is suffering from the "la belle indifference" of early dementia, such voids add to his sense of life-space constriction. And isolation following widowerhood may add to depressive and increasing suicidal proclivities (Cath, 1983).

When they are available, inclined, and willing, talented, seductive grandchildren can reach across this void, even if they have to be forceful and intrude. In the process, they may learn to tolerate the ugly forms of human decline in increasingly ancient but still beloved ancestors. Not only do they donate refueling time off, but they have the eyes of another generation through which to see the past, the aging self, and the family's future. To this degree they add to the reservoir of people from whom elders can try again to relate lovingly and keep contact with the outside world. Sometimes grandparents experience new enthusiasm (en-theos, the God within) or solicit last-minute solace from the generation once removed. In one of my psychotherapeutic families, the death of an octogenarian, remembered by his children mostly for his irascibility and unpredictable temper, brought relief to all except a beloved, favorite grandson. The mother observed, "His were the only tears at the funeral."

Somehow from somewhere, then, grandfathers who in their

midyears were considered terrors by their own children may relate positively if not creatively with some, perhaps not all, of their grandchildren. Such well-situated elders may come to consider themselves successful at least in their last parenting operation. But such variegated circumstances speak against stereotypes. And elders and their internal dynamics have only recently come under psychoanalytic and research scrutiny as age barriers to therapy are lowered (Cath, 1982b).

TRANSFERENCE AND COUNTERTRANSFERENCE IMPLICATIONS

Thus clinicians need to keep an open mind about the potentials for positive growth and refueling inherent in late-life psychobiological relationships between generations. Overt dynamics seem less oedipal for elderly males and females who are most often comfortably involved in the same sex or "isogender" relationships (Blos, 1985). Early transference and countertransference manifestations of late-life relationships may not always be recognized as derived from "ancient," preoedipal, possibly isogender, loving grandparental introjects or the lack thereof.

The challenge/opportunity of becoming a grand is timed exquisitely. Beginning during the critical transition from mid to later life, it may be considered a fourth separation-individuation crisis (Cath, 1982b). While essentially intrapsychic, I believe it is different to the degree that it contains very real, in contrast to mostly fantasied, losses in self, substance, and loved ones (Cath, 1979). In this late life milieu of depletion and restitution, both sexes find that the gift of grandchildren provides a living backdrop in ongoing reality against which to restructure important past isogender and heterosexual relationships. Neurotic anxiety about intactness of the mind may lead to constant conscious and unconscious monitoring of the bio-psycho-social self (Cath, 1979). This screening of memory skills, energy levels, other internal messages, and external performance may consume increasing stores of emotional energy and interfere with the ability to concentrate and be productive. Dread of public exposure of aged ineptness, or the inability to keep up with current happenings, or to play a favorite card game logarithmically mounts. When tolerances for even normative, benign imperfections in mental agility are exceeded, self loathing and defensive withdrawals increase (Cath, 1963). As part of the efforts at reparation for such losses, as a countermeasure or restitution of self-body-other integrity, a young grandchild's availability, his appearance, development, performance, strength, or intelligence may be aggrandized and idealized. In response to such mirroring and other secondary gains, certain prelatency or latency grandchildren are predisposed toward a complementary aggrandizement of one or more of their grands. Each will forgive almost anything in the other. Understandably, with the dimming recent memory of their grandparents, grandchildren revive the early-stored images of lost loved ones past.

CONCLUSIONS

Thus, ambivalences notwithstanding, of all loving relationships, the grands may possess the greatest overall potential for late-life emotional refueling. And this comforting relationship simultaneously contains and screens one of the most virulent forms of separation anxieties in the whole life span, namely, that of a shrinking self and selfobject world.

Like parenthood, the process of transformation into a grand is neither universal nor universally pleasant. It seems to have no clear beginning and no clear ending. Like genetics, it may be seen as an invisible human organizing constant of our heritage wherever people gather together in families, clans, or larger groups. But never before on the stage of history has it occurred with such frequency, complexity, and intensity as in the longitudinous, rapidly shifting populations alive today. It may be that the world is in a deepening crisis in which one half seems to be abandoning the complexities of preserving the species while the other half, aided by new technologies, strives all the more for offspring. In some lands in the East, "single child" imperatives have been deemed necessary for survival; in the West "single parent" families are becoming the rule. Whether one has parented or not, well or poorly, little or much, may become a late-life accounting within and to the self. A recently marketed T-shirt depicts a middle-aged woman in tears and reads "I forgot to have children." In these circumstances, diminished intergenerational contact with limited potential for restitution may leave tumultuous individual and social currents in their wake. The destinies of many isolated grandelders will be seriously effected.

It is not surprising then that cross-culturally and over centuries, grandparenthood, in contrast to grandorphanhood (the state of being without grandoffspring), has traditionally held out a promise of more idealized psychic representations of the self as well as offering realistic assurance of continuity over time. In the past, grandparenthood was integral to the conclusion of many elders' lives. Not only was it a reflection of the changes possible in maturity (ripening), but, in the words of one of my friends, "It only takes one grandchild to feel loved a whole life long."

REFERENCES

Atkins, R. N. (1982), Discovering daddy: The mother's role. In: *Father and Child,* ed. S. H. Cath, A. Gurwitt & J. M. Ross. Boston, MA: Little, Brown, pp. 139–149.

Blos, P. (1985), *Son and Father.* New York: Free Press, pp. 24–27.

Cath, S. H. (1963a), Some dynamics of middle and later years. *Smith College Studies in Soc. Work:* 33:97–126.

―――― (1963b), Psychodynamics of the three generation home. *Tufts Folia Medica,* 9:88–98.

―――― (1979), Depression, depletion and dementia: A rational base for a comprehensive therapeutic approach to a specific condition of long lived people.In *Geriatric Psychopharmacology,* ed. K. Nandy. North Holland, NY: Elsevier.

―――― (1982a), Vicissitudes of grandfatherhood: A miracle of revitalization? In: *Father and Child,* ed. S. H. Cath, A. Gurwitt & J. M. Ross. Boston, MA: Little, Brown, pp. 329–337.

―――― (1982b), Psychoanalysis and psychoanalytic psychotherapy of the older patient. *J. Ger. Psychiat.,* 15:43–53.

―――― (1982c), Divorce and the child: The father question hour. In: *Father and Child,* ed. S. H. Cath, A. Gurwitt & J. M. Ross. Boston, MA: Little, Brown, pp. 467–479.

―――― (1986), Clinical vignettes: A range of grandparental experiences. *J. Geriat. Psychiat.,* 19:57–68.

―――― & Cath, C. (1984), When a wife dies: The race against time. In: *Psychotherapy and Psychoanalysis in the Second Half of Life,* ed. C. Colarusso & R. Nemiroff. New York: Plenum.

Erikson, E., Erikson, J. & Kivnick, H. (1986), *Vital Involvement in Old Age.* New York: Norton.

Freud, S. (1909), Analysis of a phobia in a five-year-old boy. *Standard Edition,* 10:3–149. London: Hogarth Press, 1955.

Jones, E. (1955), *The Life and Work of Sigmund Freud.* Vol. 3. New York: Basic Books.

Kivnick, H. (1981), Grandparenthood and the mental health of grandparents. *Aging and Soc.,* 1:365–391.

_____ (1986), Grandparenthood and a life cycle. *J. Geriat. Psychiat.*, 19:39–55.

Kornhaber, A. & Woodward, K. (1981), *Grandparents/Grandchildren.* New York: Doubleday.

"Kotch" (1971), Screen play by John Paxton from novel by Katherine Tompkins. Variety Film Review, New York and London (1971–1974).

Lamb, M. E. (1977), Father-infant and mother-infant interactions in the first year of life. *Child. Devel.*, 48:167–181.

Lawton, M. P. (1980), *Environment and Aging.* Pacific Grove, CA: Brooks Cole.

Mead, M. (1972), *Blackberry Winter.* New York: Simon & Schuster.

Robertson, J. (1976), Grandmotherhood: A study of role conceptions. *J. Marr. & Fam.*, 39:165–174.

Ross, J. M. (1982), The roots of fatherhood: Excursions into a lost literature. In: *Father and Child,* ed. S. H. Cath, A. Gurwitt & J. M. Ross. Boston, MA: Little, Brown, pp. 3–20.

Sander, L. (1985), *Biological Response Styles.* Washington, DC: Amer. Psychiat. Press.

Yogman, M. (1977), The goals and structure of face-to-face interaction between infants and fathers. Presented at meeting of Society for Research in Child Development, New Orleans, LA, March.

II

TRANSITION TO FATHERHOOD

Prelude

How do men make the transition to fatherhood? What factors influence these transitions? Are there really changes afoot as popularly believed? Why do some fathers interact comfortably with their children, but with others one can sense a strained distance, if not outright rejection? Are the colorations only dyadically determined, or are the mothers – even the marriages – involved?

Psychoanalytically informed researchers are actively looking at some of these questions. Considerable work on the roots of parental and paternal capacities has already been done (see Anthony and Benedek, 1970, and Cath, Gurwitt, and Ross, 1982). This section adds to that work, dealing with men's successful or unsuccessful transition to fatherhood and fatherliness. Two of the three chapters are based on studies of larger groups of couples from which the study groups were drawn. Although the focus here is on the husbands, there was opportunity for the researchers simultaneously to study the wives, to make comparisons, and to observe, at least in the Osofsky and Culp study, the nature of and changes in the marriage. The third chapter deals with unsuccessful transitions, looking at how and why men avoid fatherhood.

Gerson addresses an area practically devoid of previous direct

121

study, namely, the fantasies and thoughts of men, not yet fathers and whose wives are not pregnant, about their future children and fatherhood. While her subject sample is relatively small, of a wide range of ages, and primarily middle class, nevertheless her work provides interesting insights about preparental concepts of both these men and their wives. Important differences are noted. More than their wives, the men tended to downplay their roles with infants, more often fantasied relationships with male and oedipal age children, and tended to think about more structured and hierarchal situations in which they were teachers but within which the child was relatively independent. They also were more concerned about discipline and control, especially of aggression on the part of future children. Their images were more concrete and action oriented and seemed more based on narcissistic self-projections. They were more confident about their own future capacity to be good fathers, based on their family backgrounds and observations of peers. They were also more positive than their wives about their spouses' future pregnancies. The women saw everything as textually more complex, more reciprocal, presenting more dilemmas, more contained within a fabric of relationships, yet the women were more concerned with the child being an individual in its own right.

In response to one of the nine key questions posed, a question dealing more directly with the men's own parents, Gerson particularly focuses on the subgroup of five men who were least interested in having children. Noting important parental deficits in their backgrounds, she speculates that the absence of positive representations of *both* parents contributed to the reluctance to become a father. She concludes that, at least in these men, before they actually became fathers, their fantasies and identifications were of a traditional sort; these men tended to fall back on structured roles as educators and disciplinarians. Gerson wonders if these stylistic features and the absence of comfort in relating to infants reflected struggles with internal nurturant tendencies, struggles that stemmed from the need to reject maternal identification in favor of identification with the oedipal father.

These men simply had not been raised with the expectation that they would be the primary caretakers. While more removed than their wives from intimate tasks of parenting, they seemed less threatened by those tasks. Gerson notes that there could well be changes as these men and their wives later have children; she remarks on the crucial influence of the marital relationship and identification with the pregnant wife, seen in some of her study subjects as they indicated positive excitement about a future pregnancy. Gerson adds the important note that there are opportunities for early case finding and intervention. Indeed, all the chapters in this section have such major implications.

In the second chapter in this section, Osofsky and Culp report on the continuing research efforts in which they and colleagues have long been engaged in exploring normative and pathological factors in adjustment to pregnancy, birth, and early parenthood. Osofsky's background as both a psychoanalyst and obstetrician lends a special vantage point here. He and Culp emphasize the interdependence of roles and functions of all family members. After reviewing some highlights of the literature on the mother's pregnancy experience and noting the importance of Benedek's assertion that pregnancy and parenthood are developmental phases, they address the character of changes in and adaptive challenges to a marriage following the birth of a child, noting the shared and the differential reactions of new mothers and fathers. These changes in marital satisfaction, reported by others as well are of immense importance to the family (see Lamb, this volume). The relationship between the parental couple can never be quite the same. Whether the couple, as a couple and as individuals, grows in response to the new challenges depends on the character of the prepregnancy marital relationship as well as crucial formative historical patterns. Osofsky and Culp also review the literature on psychological adaptations of men in the transition to fatherhood, noting the past tendency to minimize or ignore the adjustments of normal males. Like Gerson, they underline the importance of the wives in sparking their husbands' parental capacities but observe that it is a mutual transaction, each partner influencing the other. The studies of pathological responses of men to their wives' pregnancies and the birth of offspring preceded and pointed the way to work on normal phenomena and recognition that pregnancy and birth are powerful events, indeed, developmental phases, for men as well as for their wives.

Osofsky and Culp, like Gerson, stress the importance of certain key symptoms as possible indicators for intervention. They point out the tendency – common in our experience – of patients and therapists alike to overlook the importance of pregnancy and childbirth as precipitants of moderately severe or severe psychopathology. We fully agree with their call for further studies of the key ingredients of stress, adjustments required, generalizability of findings, and development of strategies for intervention and support.

Earlier studies by Osofsky and colleagues, delineating both positive and negative phenomena experienced by men during their wives' pregnancies and labors and deliveries, are summarized. They note the regressive pulls, the unresolved conflicts, and the impact of various life circumstances. They describe common psychological events following the birth. No matter what the previously agreed upon allocation of child rearing tasks, the women in their studies assumed traditional primary caretaking roles, with men then commonly feeling left out. While not necessarily better prepared to take over the major caretaking responsibilities, women still tended to do so, learning by experience. As the wives became more practiced, their husbands, willingly or not, assumed secondary parental roles. A key divergence in the family then took place that had great significance for the mother-child, father-child, mother-father dyads and the whole family and resulted in particular intrafamily stresses (see also Lamb, this volume), stresses that may be only transient or may have long-term impact.

Osofsky and Culp then go on to describe and review the findings so far in a major longitudinal study of transition to parenthood, a study in its third year at the time of writing. The reader will see that their findings not only tend to confirm previous speculations and findings but also add some important new findings. Stresses and symptoms were not only a manifestation of psychopathology but *were common normative occurrences.* Also, their findings of a relatively high incidence of depression (29%) and of lowered self-esteem (47%) were unexpected, the exact origins and further outcome of which, it is hoped, will become clear as the study progresses.

The third chapter in this section addresses the questions of how and why some men avoid paternity (that is, biological fatherhood) or full psychological fatherhood. Using case illustrations to demonstrate some of the key psychological barriers to fatherhood, I outline a continuum of forms of "flight from fatherhood." While aware of social, economic, and historical forces coloring the character of parental roles, I focus on two aspects: 1) the formative, but flawed, intrapsychic developmental characteristics of some men that are reactivated with the new developmental challenge of possible or actual parenthood that limit or skew the further evolution of parental capacities; 2) and the important interactional phenomena between husbands and wives that influence the unfolding parental styles of each and may further limit the character of fathering. There are close correlations with the Osofsky and Culp chapter.

It is apparent that there are multiple factors at work for both men and women in the transition to parenthood. The past is crucial but is not all that matters. The marital relationship, other relationships, the cultural context, are among other important factors. Much more needs to be learned to guide future clinical strategies.

Alan Gurwitt

REFERENCES

Anthony, E. J. & Benedek, T., ed. (1970), *Parenthood.* Boston: Little, Brown.

Cath, S., Gurwitt, A. & Ross, J. M., ed. (1982), *Father and Child.* Boston: Little, Brown.

7

Tomorrow's Fathers
The Anticipation of Fatherhood
Mary-Joan Gerson

To judge from contemporary media coverage, fathers have been moved from their aggressive positions in the conference room and on the ballfield and are now supposed to be luxuriating in the warm ambiance of the nursery. It appears to me that these images of fatherhood reflect a form of magical thinking, a fantasy that profound changes can occur in human relationships if we merely wish them to. The growing tendency of the media to define and publicize social trends, often in distorted form, both reflects and facilitates this kind of thinking. We as psychoanalysts, however, are witness to the reality that our parental identifications and internal representations of experience are the templates from which cultural transformations are fashioned. For the individual, ideological and social change, like psychotherapeutic change, brings challenge and also conflict and resistance. So it is with fatherhood.

The study reported here is part of a larger investigation of the meaning of parenthood to young adults (Gerson, 1986). The study incuded, most relevantly for this chapter, an exploration of gender differences concerning the wish for a child. Though parenthood is a fundamental aspect of adult identity (Erikson, 1959; Gurwitt, 1982), there is still practically nothing in the literature concerning the fantasies, apprehensions, or anticipated psychological opportunities that the role of fatherhood evokes for young men who are not yet expectant fathers (Cath and Samaraweera, 1982). There has been somewhat more coverage of the psychological difficulties of making the transition to fatherhood (Benedek, 1970; Deutscher, 1981; Herzog, 1982), including its more pathological manifestations (Zilboorg, 1944; Freeman, 1951; Towne and Afterman, 1955; Lacoursiere, 1972a, b; Osofsky, 1982). There has also been a surge of interest, reflected in empirical investigations, of the special relationship of fathers and infants (Lamb, 1976; Parke, 1981; Gunsberg, 1982).

However, though there is a body of literature focused on the development of the wish for a child in women (Gerson, Alpert, and Richardson, 1984), for the most part the earliest starting point for the study of fatherhood in young men is in relation to their wives' pregnancies (Deutscher, 1981; Grossman, Eichler, and Winickoff, 1980; Gurwitt, 1982)–a subtle manifestation of the existing bias that fathers are second, not first, parents. In fact, clinical descriptions of the developmental impact of fathering often stress father in an ancillary role to mother: as the "breath of fresh air" that unclenches the symbiotic tie between infant and mother (Mahler, 1966) or as the barrier to symbiotic regression throughout childhood and adolescence (Loewald, 1951; Abelin, 1975; Greenspan, 1982). These are crucial developmental tasks; however, what the participating father experiences in fulfilling these responsibilities remains unclear.

Our attempt was to explore the meaning of fatherhood to young adult men who had never had children and to analyze the interplay of their available images, fantasies, and concerns about it as well as their recollections of being "parented." Though interview data lack the depth of material elicited in long-term analytic treatment, they have the virtue of being free of transference manifestations. Our goal was to begin to understand the normative aspects of conflicts about fatherhood, thereby deepening our understanding of gender identity and family structure as they relate to development. We hoped that any attempt to clarify normative dynamics would be useful to psychotherapists as a template on which to delineate complex, idiosyncratic issues.

METHOD

Twenty men between the ages of 22 and 42 were interviewed. Their average age was 30; twelve were in their 20s, seven were in their 30s, and one subject was 42. Subjects were recruited through their mates, who were approached at gynecology clinics in New York City when they appeared for routine examinations. Every man was involved in a long-term relationship; 14 were married for an average of three and a half years, and six were not married but had been living with their mates for an average of two and a half years. There was one black and one Hispanic male in the group of interviewees. Nine men were Protestant, six were Jewish, and five identified themselves as having another religion or no religion (ten were living with women of different religious backgrounds from their own). Their average income was approximately $30,000, which is likely an underestimation because of the ceiling on our questionnaire scale. Their occupations were extremely varied; we had an artist, an actor, a publisher, a lawyer, a journalist, several business executives. Demographic characteristics are reported in detail here because of the author's belief that cultural factors are part of any dynamic motivational matrix as well as a reservoir of images and metaphors for expressing wishes. In sum, these men were largely middle class, in terms of both original family background and present status. Using data from a questionnaire particularly developed to assess the degree of parenthood motivation (Gerson, 1983), we were able to categorize our 20 interviewees as follows: 12 of the men were eager to become fathers; three were ambivalent; five were rather uninterested in becoming fathers.

The interview data, as mentioned earlier, were part of a larger questionnaire-based study (Gerson, 1986) involving 113 women and 75 men recruited at metropolitan health centers when the women arrived for routine examinations. Subjects were randomly approached for participation in the interview segment. For the questionnaire study, a set of variables empirically and theoretically drawn from the literature on parenthood motivation (though the clear weighting here was to motherhood motivation) were hypothesized to predict the intensity of the wish for a child. Certain variables such as self-esteem and memories of father's love and care in childhood were significantly predictive for women. However, these variables were not relevant for the men. Thus the interview data appeared to be a particularly important base on which to begin to structure a phenomenology of anticipated fatherhood.

In one extended session each member of the couple was interviewed separately but simultaneously by two investigators. The male interviewer, who was married and had not had children, conducted all the male interviews; a comparable female interviewed the women. The interview schedule consisted of specific questions that the men were invited to answer at length. Nine questions that we believed would evoke the core issues of anticipated fatherhood were selected for analysis here; in fact, the first eight appeared as the first eight questions on the schedule. The answers to questions were subsequently coded by category for purposes of analysis. Patterns across categories are highlighted here to capture the major themes elicited by each question. In the presentation that follows, responses from the women in the sample are included whenever a particular theme can be enhanced or clarified by doing so. We will essentially "walk through" the interview by presenting the data as it flowed in response to the questions and delay summarizing across questions until all the data are in view. It must be stressed that our organizing themes and our final inferences constitute a somewhat impressionistic response to this material, requiring further study in empirical investigations and reports from in-depth analytic work.

THE INTERVIEW DATA

QUESTION 1: WHEN YOU PICTURE A CHILD, WHAT AGE IS IT? TELL ME ABOUT IT.

QUESTION 2: NOW PICK ANOTHER AGE FOR YOUR CHILD TO BE. WHAT IS THE CHILD LIKE AT THIS AGE?

Review of the data indicated that responses to question 2, allowing the subject a more delayed and perhaps less well-defended response, were not significantly different from responses to question 1. Thus we will consider them together, looking first at the projected age of future children and then at the kinds of images evoked.

Age of Child

Gender differences were marked in response to this first question. More than half of the men produced an image of an oedipal age child on the first go-round, whereas only 25% of their mates did so. Men thought of significantly fewer infants and toddlers than women. However, beyond the quantitative difference in category preference, there was an important qualitative difference characterizing the child's age. The male subjects did not imagine infants as needy and dependent, which is, in fact, the archetype of infancy in this culture. Instead their images reflected an attempt to bridge infancy and later stages of development, stressing autonomy and self-sufficiency. Mr. B. described his future baby:

> There's little things they do and ways they act that are indicative of whole aspects of their personality. . . . It's amazing to see. I mean they're cute and all that stuff you know, and that's nice, but they do things that you can see that . . . that's really going to be adult. I mean they're still going to have that same thing when they're adults.

Mr. P. imagined the potential neediness of an infant but tried to limit its scope:

> At that age . . . a child . . . ideally? . . . perhaps . . . I would say somewhat playful and . . . but you know, a fairly good child . . . an infant that's perhaps less demanding than my image of infants. I mean for me it's difficult to see infants. You know, that's what the problem is [laughs]. You know, they're just there. That's it. And you know I mean you're just satisfying their needs at that point, and their wants. It's really difficult to . . . I can't get into a boring situation or a social situation that's difficult . . . like infants I have trouble with . . . mentally.

For the second question, women consistently thought of teenagers, viewing the adolescent period as one of strain involving rebellion and separation that has to be tolerated and withstood. In contrast, male subjects produced a mixed assortment of age-related images. Notably associated with the questions about age was the finding that men more often than not fantasized about male children; women seldom identified the gender of the children they described.

Images and Fantasies

When these young men allowed themselves to imagine future children, they created images of fatherhood that were unelaborated and had a static and frozen quality. Some men had to be encouraged to produce any images at all. Ultimately the fatherhood scenarios that evolved almost always stressed well-tended boundaries between father and child. These boundaries were most easily constructed around a teaching or didactic function of fatherhood. A typical static set of images was projected by Mr. S., who first described what he envisioned as:

Mr. S. The first sight I saw was the four year-old son of a friend of mine, and then as you continued to ask I saw an infant. The first case is a pretty little boy, a blonde-haired boy, a kid who as a matter of fact my wife and I like very much. In the second instance I not only saw an infant but I saw an infant in somebody's arms.

Interviewer Is there somebody that you actually picture holding the infant?

Mr. S. No. Not that I did. I'd probably imagine it'd have been myself.

Interviewer What about the four year-old? Could you evoke a little bit more of what you saw of him? When it first flashed in your mind? What do you imagine happening when you think about a four year-old?

Mr. S. Really very little. I have a mental image of him, kind of standing on a sidewalk, outside in his house which is a couple of blocks from here, typically wearing some sort of a cap that's askew and untied sneakers, tee shirt hanging out. No particular activity though.

Incidentally, Mr. S.'s referring to a picture of a child he knew was a common characteristic of the male, but not the female, responses to these questions.

Father as educator was dominant in these projected interactions. Typical was Mr. R.'s saying, "I see a kid around three or four, and educating or enlightening—telling him something—I'm not quite sure what, but passing on information." The didactic relationship was generally pictured as hierarchical, with father the provider of information, whose resources could be tapped, but not enriched, by his children.

This sense of boundary as defining the space between father and child was also illustrated in descriptions of offspring whose inherent characteristics would be revealed to father without much psychological influence or interaction on his part. A fantasied child was often described as "its own person." A typical sequence of description was Mr. L.'s, whose second image, of an eight- or nine-year-old child was:

I don't know. One of the things that fascinates me about this whole process is that I can't wait to meet my kid. I want to see what the child is like. I don't imagine that much. I mean I think that I'm aware that the personality manifests itself quite early, but I think it probably establishes itself more and more. And by age either or nine, the child is going to be his or her own person, and I will find out what that will be.

Interestingly – and we will return to this later when we discuss confidence about parenthood – the spontaneous and first dramatizations of fatherhood were almost universally positive and problem free. Mr. L.'s first image was: "Ummm. Let's see . . . I imagine a child being very lively, active, inquisitive, questioning. I also imagine the child happy and playing. I realize there's certainly another side. That's not what I expect, but that is what I imagine."

In contrast, the images of the women interviewed were clearly more complex and textured and revealed fantasies about reciprocal relating and influence. Additionally, motherhood, right from the start, was imagined as laced with conflicts and dilemmas. The report of Mr. A.'s wife was typical:

> Say eight where it's definitely showing signs of not being identifiable. It's not defiant. I guess that's not too defiant an age (laughs). It's one where all the things that are not like you are . . . all the subtle things that you have influenced it with or haven't intended to, or are unaware of what you've done, start to – in the negative side – come back at you, and the positive side, perhaps is enlightening about you and the environment. Perhaps it's just showing the ability of the child to absorb other influences. I think that that's kind of exciting.

Also noteworthy in these global images of anticipated parenthood was that women spontaneously drew on their relationships with their own parents in imagining their future roles as parents. This was particularly salient when women portrayed teenage children who would reenact for them their own difficult adolescent period. Their narratives often reflected a wish to repair the hurt inflicted on their own parents. Not one male respondent drew on memories of his own parents in fantasizing about fatherhood. However, a few men speculated about a physical resemblance between themselves and their future children, which no woman did in these initial images. In general the link between parent and future child was more clearly embedded in a fabric of relationships for women than for men.

QUESTION 3: WHAT IS THE WORST TIME OF FATHERHOOD? WOULD YOU CREATE A PICTURE OF YOU AND A FUTURE CHILD AT THAT TIME AND DESCRIBE IT TO ME?

The answers to this question revealed a salient gender difference in concerns about anticipated parenthood. The men interviewed were strikingly concerned about issues of discipline, of being able to exert sufficient control over their children. Mr. L. stated, typically, "I think the major problem would be trying to have enough communication or enough relationship with the child to prevent your influence being overwhelmed by peer influence, you know, by the child's peer influence."

Several responses indicated that potential fathers were concerned about their ability to regulate aggression and were ambivalent about exercising control over their children. They wondered whether they could achieve a balance between what Mr. G. called "arbitrariness" and a "laissez faire" attitude. They were concerned that their children would hate them for being too severe. A dialogue that captured the issue of discipline was the following with Mr. C., who on the questionnaire identified himself as wanting a child "more than anything".

> *Interviewer* Can you imagine what would be the worst time of fatherhood?
> *Mr. C.* Oh God! I hope the kid skips puberty [laughs]. There are a lot of them. I hate little kids in the street when they're whatever age it is when they say 'no' to everything. I guess that happens a few times. And there's the wildness of just trying to break loose, and of course the kid never quite knows what he or she is doing, and always imagines it's something else, some burning issue, and I just hope I'm able to stay level-headed enough so I have an overview.
> *Interviewer* Could you create a picture of a child and you at the age you just described?
> *Mr. C.* The kid insisting on whatever it's chic and current to insist on for kids, whether it's staying out longer, or [catches himself] Eew! That sounds weird. What am I saying. I really haven't fleshed out a lot of thinking, I guess.
> *Interviewer* Do you see a picture of yourself talking about whether he or she is going to stay out late?
> *Mr. C.* Yeah. I guess what scares me about it is finding myself pressured by reacting to taking a very kind of authoritative kind of parental stand. I have a . . . I've never been that good at dealing with authority on either end, either being under it, or handling it and exerting it. And that scares me a lot, having to be the authoritative parent, saying a lot of "no."

QUESTION 4: WHAT IS THE BEST TIME OF FATHERHOOD? WOULD YOU CREATE A PICTURE OF YOU AND YOUR FUTURE CHILD AT THAT TIME AND DESCRIBE IT TO ME?

Perhaps because an invitation to reflect on positive images is less destabilizing to the structure of fatherhood identity in young men, answers to the question about the best time of fatherhood were less revealing. Furthermore, there were few clear differences between male and female responses to this question. Both men and women looked forward to sharing experiences with children (almost 50% of both groups); second, to watching children develop; and, third, to taking pleasure in their children's accomplishments. The images that men produced tended to be more focused and action oriented; those of the women often revealed a reluctance to pin down any specific age or offspring characteristic. A typical response is Mr. M.'s:

> I guess the accomplishments of the child. He brings home an "A" paper or rides a bicycle for the first time, or something of which the child himself feels proud, and he feels glad to show it to you. And he wants to convey his accomplishment to you—like, say "I did this good for you"—to realize that what he did was good and to congratulate him, or appreciate what he did . . . something like that.

Notably, four men chose the time of birth as the best time of fatherhood (Greenberg and Morris, 1982) and described it with great excitement; only one woman chose this moment. Mr. T. stated: "It would be ecstatic—having the nurse hold up the child and seeing this creation. I guess that's the ultimate vanity—to create something that looks like yourself." Or Mr. R., who elaborated: "It would be seeing a child that's mine for the first time—not really mattering if it's the first child or the second child or the third child. I don't think it would be the fascination of having a child, but it would be the fascination of having *the child.*

QUESTION 5: WHO WOULD YOU LIKE A CHILD OF YOURS TO BE LIKE MOST OF ALL?

The responses to this question very dramatically reflected self-projections. These projections sometimes embodied an idealized and perfected version of the potential father. Mr. R. stated: "I think like me. Conceited as it may be. Ummm. I think I have a fascination with a lot of things, and I'd like to be able to share it with someone. Of course strictly like me would be a little boring probably. It would probably be best to have a combination of us two . . . [wife's name] and I." Or, as Mr. C. put it:

> *Mr. C.* Well, God damn. I mean I would have to say me without making any of the mistakes. God does that sound corny. But

really that's what comes to mind. Kind of a very idealized picture of me.

Interviewer Why? Why you as opposed to someone else?

Mr. C. Well, because in many ways I don't think I fulfilled the promises and expectations that I had of myself at a younger age, and I'd like to see someone else live out those fantasies and do that.

Men who said they would like a child to combine qualities of themselves and their mates, or to resemble some other important person, nevertheless organized their fantasy around their own self-preoccupations. Women, on the other hand, often left themselves out of their idealized child images, focusing on significant others or the importance of the child being an individual in its own right.

QUESTION 6: HOW GOOD A FATHER DO YOU THINK YOU'LL BE? WHY?

QUESTION 7: WHAT, IF ANYTHING, IN YOUR LIFE HAS PREPARED YOU FOR FATHERHOOD?

These two questions were designed to explore the subjects' inherent confidence about fulfilling the role of father, however idiosyncratically defined. In general these potential fathers were impressively confident about their parenting abilities. Very few subjects were at all hesitant about their ability to father, and only one subject expressed serious reservation about his ability to relate to a child in a healthy fashion. Mr. S. was representative: "I fancy myself as pretty good. I think I have a fair amount of patience and I'm reasonably rational." Mr. A. replied to the interviewer: "I think I'll be a good father. No one's as good a father as they'd like to be, though, I would guess, but I'll be a good father. I'll be very sensitive to the child. I'd spend a lot of time with him."

A few men speculated that they would improve on their own fathers' ability; none of them felt that they would be inferior to their own fathers in either dedication, sensitivity, or general competency. These responses were somewhat different from those of their mates, who expressed more anxiety about competence in motherhood. A few women predicted that their mothering ability would be inferior to that of their own mothers.

Similarly, men always seemed to find something in their background that had managed to prepare them for parenthood, whereas women more often felt that they lacked preparation and were more vague about relevant experience from their pasts. Mr. T. claimed: "The fact that I was a child myself. I know what I liked and thought was done well." Mr. Z.: "I've travelled quite a lot. I don't think I've become bigoted; I'm open. The worst thing to do is hide your feelings . . . It makes him feel isolated."

> *Mr. F.* Hell if I know. I don't know. I think being around children, none in my family, but being around infants 'n stuff. You know, watching them and kind of learning how to be.
> *Interviewer* Is that hard to learn?
> *Mr. F.* No, not really.

QUESTION 8: HOW DO YOU FEEL ABOUT THE BODY CHANGES OF PREGNANCY?

Men were more positive than women in anticipating pregnancy. They generally viewed their wives' potential pregnancies with excitement and "fascination," or just as often were matter-of-fact about it as a natural part of motherhood. Only two men were negative – one with a visceral feeling that pregnancy was "grotesque," and the other concerned about his wife's putting on weight. In contrast, as many of the women were negative as were positive about pregnancy; they were worried about excess weight and physical discomfort. Very few were neutral. Mr. G. offered a characteristically positive response when he said:

> I think it's . . . I love it . . . It just . . . I know a couple of pregnant women and I've seen them . . . and touching their stomach and feeling the aliveness in their stomach and seeing in their face . . . You know it's an obvious process that brings about all this beautifulness in a person, in a woman. It really . . . It's really a . . . It's beyond words. It's something that you know you can't put into words. It's not something that man can explain away that simply.

A more neutral response was Mr. J.'s:

> Well I don't feel very strange about that at all. I guess since men start learning about women's bodies they learn there's things that don't go . . . that we don't have and so you more or less begin to . . . I mean you . . . either you can't take menstruation to begin with and therefore you couldn't take pregnancy, or anything else that goes with it from childbirth to miscarriage, to anything that could happen. If you understand or are understanding and loving with respect to any of those, I don't think any other ones would be a problem so I don't see any problem with . . . a tubby lady or anything like that.

QUESTION 9: PICTURE YOUR MOTHER: WHAT DO YOU SEE? HOW DO YOU WISH
YOUR RELATIONSHIP WITH YOUR MOTHER COULD HAVE BEEN DIFFERENT? PIC-
TURE YOUR FATHER: WHAT DO YOU SEE? HOW DO YOU WISH YOUR RELATION-
SHIP COULD HAVE BEEN DIFFERENT?

This data was particularly rich and quite complicated to analyze in
relation to fantasies and concerns about anticipated fatherhood. For
example, we found that, whether they reported their fathers as domineering or overly passive and permissive, the subjects focused on issues
of discipline when queried about the worst times of fatherhood. It
seemed most interesting, and parsimonious, to examine particularly
the responses of the five men who expressed very little interest in
having children. What was striking about their responses was their
basically negative portrait of both parents. The mothers of all five men
were described as emotionally aloof. Three of the fathers were portrayed as ineffectual, such as Mr. S.'s, who was "possessed with
enormous distaste and enormous ability to avoid anything he found
distasteful in life," or Mr. B.'s, of whom his son said:

> I see my father, a neurotic who has almost no hope of escaping it,
> and that's taken me a long time to realize, you know. When I first
> saw that image, the image is very graphic. One time I was visiting
> him and he was changing his clothes because he had just gotten off
> work and was just sitting down in the basement surrounded by all
> the things that he has in the basement, stuff, and he's just sitting
> there changing his clothes surrounded by trash, I mean not trash,
> but trash.

One of the fathers was described as too domineering and the
other as unavailable. No other subjects had negative images of both
mother and father, and of course all the others were more eager to have
children. Very tentatively it apears that the absence of positive representations of both parents is a necessary if not sufficient basis for
reluctance to become a father.

DISCUSSION

The results of this study indicate that the parenting fantasies of these
men were more buoyant and confident, but also less developed, less
textured, and less reciprocal or intimate, than those of the women with
whom they were involved. In general these potential fathers envi-

sioned themselves in traditional roles with regard to future children, that is, the role of educator or disciplinarian. Children were imagined in snapshot fashion – somewhat two-dimensional images lacking a third, empathic dimension.

What is problematic about these representations is that young men today expect themselves, and are expected by others, to become intimately involved with their children from birth. Unlike their fathers, they are not expected to delay the building of a fathering relationship until the child is clearly educable or primed for role socialization. The traditional mold of educator and disciplinarian has been recast by the media and by the feminist needs of young women; yet the contents of the mold, the identifications and fantasies of young men studied here, have remained traditional. This disjunctive transition in the function and parameters of fathering likely leaves young men feeling dislocated in the family. In fact, we have been almost overexposed to the difficulties of combining motherhood and career – as if this integration might be beyond reach of most women – but we are underexposed to the difficulties of negotiating a workable identity as father. Whether this is because men are generally less vocal about their psychological discomfort, or because young mothers are creating an illusion of intimacy between father and infant (which they might do for a variety of reasons), is not altogether clear.

What are some of the underlying dynamics that explain this anchoring in the traditional role? Men's emphasis on a structured role such as educator or disciplinarian may point to their strong need to suppress uncomfortable impulses or yearnings. It is likely that the yearnings arise from a reactivation of early maternal identifications, which are abandoned in the decisive developmental move toward father as active provider and organizer (Benedek, 1959; Greenspan, 1982; Kestenberg, Marcus, Sossin, and Stevenson, 1982; Ross, 1982).

Though the psychoanalytic literature, particularly in recent expositions, stresses that personality is fashioned from dual maternal and paternal identifications, there appears to be a disjunction in the development of a parental identity for men. Early experiences of maternal caretaking and its attendant identifications appear to be unintegrated with later paternal identifications. Dinnerstein (1977) wrote, ". . . the boy is likely to succeed more completely than the girl at incorporating subjectively the authority of the same-sex parent; but this authority was at the outset more finite. On a primitive, feeling level, female authority is far more awesome to all of us" (p. 87). Dinnerstein stressed that women feel linked to the magical caretaker of infancy through their own procreative potential and thus have a means of achieving mastery over the awe she evokes; for men, mastery is through a paternal identification, which unfortunately involves denial and repression of the primal emotion evoked in early dependency.

Thus, in terms of identifications that young men draw on, it appears that what has been traditionally defined as the oedipal, rather than the preoedipal, father is the silhouette on which fatherhood fantasies are sketched. Not that early experiences with father are unimportant; certainly the modification of aggression that Herzog (1982) described and the basic experience of father as protector (Ross, 1982) soften the tasks of educator or disciplinarian. The experience of father as protector is likely crucial to establishing the basic trust necessary for the boy to become "generative" (Erikson, 1959) and to incorporate fathering as a life goal. The passivity of the fathers of the young men who did not want children may have saddled the young men as toddlers with a sense of uncontrolled aggression (Herzog, 1982), precluding a stable parental identification. However, these early experiences serve as background, not foreground, in the representations of potential fathers. Relevant here is Slater's (1961) distinction between positional parental identification, based on perceived parental power, and personal parental identification, based on experienced nurturance. Slater emphasized that a wholesome identification with each parent is a composite. It remains problematic that the explicit fatherhood identifications of young men highlight positional identification. It is as though the nurturance of their fathers has become merged with their earlier experience of dependence on their mothers and thus is not easily integrated. Though young men today may be liberated to *act* more nurturant to newborns, internal psychological resources accompanying that mode of relating may not be readily available to them.

In fact, these young men, who feel somewhat distant from the experience of fatherhood, particularly its relational aspects, project an intense identification with the fantasied child. For the young man, the child seems truly to function as a selfobject in fantasy (Kohut, 1977) or as a projection of the "good-me," in Sullivanian terms (Sullivan, 1953). In a complex manner, because men may feel one step removed from procreation, they may be able psychologically to "use" their unborn child as an external expression of and organizer of their own self-cohesion. From another point of view, the degree to which a young man imagines his future child as either resolving or rescuing him from his ongoing psychological dilemmas seems to be a direct reflection of a man's sense that his offspring are his keys to existential survival (Benedek, 1970). This phenomenon of children embodying the ego ideal of the young man is the most intimate connection between the potential father and his future child (Gunsberg, this volume). It seems to take the place of the more interactive, reciprocal fantasies that perhaps are more natural to the female, who knows she will carry the child within her.

Of course, at birth, these ego ideal projections must be woven into an ongoing reciprocal relationship with an infant who has its own set of temperamental characteristics. Here the wife as facilitator of the husband's connection to the newborn is critical. If she welcomes him into the arena of symbiotic, nurturant care, he will be better able to bridge the psychological space between himself and his child.

Interestingly enough, our data indicate that young men can be most readily invited into the symbiotic, early phases of parenthood through an identification with their pregnant spouses. These men find the image of pregnancy quite wondrous and exciting, perhaps less threatening in fact than their fantasies of the early postnatal period. They seem to feel capable of identifying with the procreative female, even if the pregnancy is perhaps an exhibitionistic show of their own masculine prowess or a reaction formation to a deeper seated womb envy. Practically speaking, it appears that pregnancy is a facilitating time for therapeutic work with couples around issues of parenthood.

The balance sheet of this study indicates, as well, that though men feel more removed from the drama of parenthood, they also feel less threatened by failing at it. If in fact the representation of success in fatherhood is based on teaching and providing rather than attunement, then these are qualities that most men, particularly middle-class men, have been cultivating. Thus young men express little anxiety about being "good-enough fathers" and little concern about their preparation for fatherhood.

In sum, we can see that Erikson's (1959) concept of identity as a forge and amalgam of partial childhood identifications may in fact be more problematic for fatherhood than for motherhood. For women, the partial identifications of childhood, involving as they do a renunciation and yet identification with mother (Chodorow, 1978), provide a kind of structural integrity to motherhood identity. For men, the shift in identification from mother to father may lead to disjunctions in paternity that are mutable but real.

For men, working through the disjunctures and strains of achieving a multifaceted and yet coherent fatherhood identity may be the most dramatic and integrative psychological task of adulthood. Thus, psychotherapeutically we must be particularly alert to the distinction between cultural and personal conflicts and dynamics. Young men are caught in a rift between cultural change and intrapsychic patterning, which as it widens could cause increasing discomfort. Inasmuch as most young men appear to have traditional fantasied images of fathering, men with more pronounced nurturant or maternal identifications seem to be deviant and perhaps are the offspring of somewhat disordered psychological environments. But the new culture demands nurturance and softness, and thus these "deviant" young men may be best suited for the new fatherhood. We know that the authenticity of fatherhood – believing in and comfortably being oneself as a parent – is a crucial dimension of childrearing (Erikson, 1959; Kohut, 1977). It would be useful, then, for young men anticipating fatherhood to confront the discrepancies within their own psyches, between themselves and significant others, and within a society that promotes chimerical fantasies of change.

REFERENCES

Abelin, E. (1975), Some further observations and comments on the earliest role of the father. *Internat. J. Psycho-Anal.,* 56:293–302.

Benedek, T. (1959), Parenthood as a developmental phase. *J. Amer. Psychoanal. Assn.,* 1:389–417.

_____ (1970), Fatherhood and Providing. In: *Parenthood,* ed. E. J. Anthony & T. Benedek. Boston: Little, Brown, pp. 167–184.

Cath, C. & Samaraweera, S. (1982), Fostering the consolidation of paternal identity: the Tufts Family Support Program. In: *Father and Child,* ed. S. H. Cath, A. Gurwitt & J. M. Ross. Boston: Little, Brown, pp. 543–555.

Chodorow, N. (1978), *The Reproduction of Mothering.* Berkeley: University of California Press.

Deutscher, M. (1981), Identity transformations in the course of expectant fatherhood. *Contemp. Psychoanal.,* 17(2):158–173.

Dinnerstein, D. (1977), *The Mermaid and the Minatour.* New York: Harper & Row.

Erikson, E. H. (1959), Identity and the life cycle. *Psychological Issues,* Monogr. 1. New York: International Universities Press.

Freeman, T. (1951), Pregnancy as a precipitant of mental illness in men. *Brit. J. Med. Psychol.,* 24:49–54.

Gerson, M. J. (1986), The prospect of parenthood for women and men. *Psychol. Women Quart.,* 10:49–62.

_____ Alpert, J. & Richardson, M. S. (1984), Mothering: The view from psychological research. *Signs: J. Women in Culture and Society,* 9:19–49.

Gerson, M. J. (1983), A scale of motivation for parenthood: The index of parenthood motivation. *J. Psychol.,* 113:211–220.

Greenberg, M. & Morris, N. (1982), Engrossment: the newborn's impact upon the father. In: *Father and Child,* ed. S. Cath, A. Gurwitt & J. M. Ross. Boston: Little, Brown, pp. 87–100.

Greenspan, S. (1982), "The second other": The role of the father in early personality formation and the dyadic-phallic phase of development. In: *Father and Child,* ed. S. Cath, A. Gurwitt & J. M. Ross. Boston: Little, Brown, pp. 123–138.

Grossman, F. K., Eichler, C. S. & Winickoff (1980), *Pregnancy, Birth, and Parenthood.* San Francisco, CA: Jossey-Bass.

Gunsberg, L. (1982), Selected critical review of psychological investigations of the early father-infant relationship. In: *Father and Child,* ed. S. Cath, A. Gurwitt & J. M. Ross. Boston: Little, Brown, pp. 65–86.

Gurwitt, A. (1982), Aspects of prospective fatherhood. In: *Father and Child,* ed. S. Cath, A. Gurwitt & J. M. Ross. Boston: Little, Brown, pp. 275–300.

Herzog, J. (1982), Patterns of expectant fatherhood. In: *Father and Child,* ed. S. Cath, A. Gurwitt & J. M. Ross. Boston: Little, Brown, pp. 163–174.

Kestenberg, J., Marcus, H., Sossin, K. & Stevenson, R. (1982), The development of paternal attitudes. In: *Father and Child,* ed. S. Cath, A. Gurwitt & J. M. Ross. Boston: Little, Brown, pp. 205–218.

Kohut, H. (1977), *The Restoration of the Self.* New York: International Universities Press.

Lacoursiere, R. (1972a), Fatherhood and mental illness: A review and new material. *Psychiat. Quart.,* 46:109–124.

_____ (1972b), The mental health of the prospective father: A new indication for therapeutic abortion? *Bull. Menn. Clinic.,* 36:645–650.

Lamb, M. E. (1976), *The Role of the Father in Child Development.* New York: Wiley.

Loewald, H. (1951), Ego and reality. *Internat. J. Psycho-Anal.,* 32:10–18.

Mahler, M. (1966), Notes on the development of basic moods: The depressive affect. In: *Psychoanalysis–A General Psychology,* ed. R. Loewenstein, L. Newman, M. Schur & A. Solnit. New York: International Universities Press, pp. 152–168.

Osofsky, H. (1982), Expectant and new fatherhood as a developmental crisis. *Bull. Menn. Clinic.,* 46:209–230.

Parke, R. D. (1981), *Fathers.* Cambridge, MA: Harvard University Press.

Ross, J. M. (1982), From mother to father: The boy's search for a generative identity and the oedipal era. In: *Father and Child,* ed. S. Cath, A. Gurwitt & J. M. Ross. Boston: Little, Brown, pp. 189–204.

Slater, P. E. (1961), Toward a dualistic theory of identification. *Merrill-Palmer Quart.,* 7:113–126.

Sullivan, H. (1953), *The Interpersonal Theory of Psychiatry.* New York: Norton.

Towne, R. D. & Afterman, J. (1955), Psychosis in males related to parenthood. *Bull. Menn. Clinic.,* 19:19–26.

Zilboorg, G. (1944), Masculine and feminine. *Psychiat.,* 7:257–296.

8

Risk Factors in the Transition to Fatherhood

Howard J. Osofsky

Rex E. Culp

In recent years, much attention has been given to the transition to parenthood, with emphasis on developmental aspects for the woman and man as individuals, as a couple, and as prospective parents. During the pregnancy and following the birth of their infant, the couple experiences many rewards and gratifications as well as stresses and shifts in their relationship (Osofsky and Osofsky, 1984). Belsky and colleagues (1985, 1987) and Cowan and Cowan (1985, 1987) have described the importance both of the individual shifts and of the changes in the marital relationship that the parents must negotiate in order to achieve a successful transition.

In the last decade, in addition to studies focusing on the process, adjustments, and possible areas of risk for the mother in the transition to parenthood, interest has been paid to the psychological aspects of expectant and new fatherhood. Parke and Tinsley (1987) stress the importance of recognizing the interdependence among the roles and functions of all family members. They emphasize that to understand

The research described in this chapter is funded in part by Grant MH-39487 from the National Institute of Mental Health Center for Prevention Research, Division of Prevention and Special Mental Health Programs.

the behavior of one member of a family, the complementary behaviors of other members also need to be recognized and assessed. As these researchers trace the various patterns and styles that parents utilize in their interactions with their infants, they point to the shifts in roles that have occurred for both men and women, the quality of marital satisfaction, and the importance of support within the family, through the extended family, and within the community at large.

THE COUPLE'S ADJUSTMENT TO THE PROCESS OF BECOMING A PARENT: GENERAL CONCEPTS

The Mother's Pregnancy Experience

Pregnancy has been viewed variously as a period of psychobiological stress, a normative crisis, or a developmental phase. In Benedek's (1959) view, pregnancy represents a developmental phase, extending the continuum of earlier developmental phases. She suggested that personality development continues into adulthood under the influence of reproductive physiology and that parenthood utilizes the same primary processes of mental growth and development that begin in infancy. Just as each "critical period" of a child's development is influenced by present and past developmental conflicts, so pregnancy itself brings up earlier conflictual feelings that need to be worked through and resolved within the individual and between the couple so that a new level of maturation can be attained. According to Benedek, the maturational potential is influenced by both the level of evolved psychic structural development and psychobiological factors in interaction with a new reality experience of the period.

Bibring (1959; Bibring et al. 1961) described pregnancy, like puberty or menopause, as a period of crisis involving profound psychological as well as somatic changes. On the basis of their work with women whom they followed longitudinally with psychoanalytically oriented interviews, social work interviews, and psychological testing, Bibring et al. (1961) postulated that any disturbance in equilibrium at this time can create a temporary picture of severe disintegration; however, the outcome of the crisis leads more often to psychologically healthy than to neurotic solutions. These authors believe that the more severe the psychological disturbance before pregnancy, the more likely it is that dramatic problems will emerge during this period.

Caplan, who in 1957 described pregnancy as a crisis for the woman, later (1960) suggested that the woman's emotional state, which varies at different stages during the pregnancy, depends on her capacity to adjust to psychological and physiological changes and that her reactions to the sexual aspects of the reproductive process influence her emotional status during pregnancy. These reactions, according to Caplan, are associated with the nature of her personality structure and the vicissitudes of her sexual development; they also reflect her psychological development into the role of mother–a process influenced by her relationship with her own mother and other women who have served as important role models.

A number of studies (e.g., Shereshefsky and Yarrow, 1974; Leifer, 1977; Osofsky and Osofsky, 1980a; Entwisle and Doering, 1981) have clarified the normative psychological adjustment to pregnancy, the difficulties that may contribute to emotional disturbance during pregnancy, and the process of adjustment to anticipated motherhood. Others (Gordon and Gordon, 1960; Fein, 1976; Wente and Crockenberg, 1976) have applied their findings to clinical situations and to the development of intervention programs designed to lessen patient risk and difficulties in this transition period.

MARITAL SATISFACTION AND BEHAVIORS DURING THE TRANSITION TO PARENTHOOD

In attempting to understand the transition to parenthood for fathers, it is important to consider the couple and the alterations that occur in their relationship. Belsky (1981) has described the implications of marital change for parent–infant relations. In his studies, he found that high levels of father involvement and marital interaction covaried positively with each other (Belsky, 1979). More recently Feldman, Nash, and Aschenbrenner (1983) have presented findings indicating that marital quality is a powerful predictor of patterns of fathering during free and structured laboratory play situations.

Cowan and coworkers (1983, 1985) have studied couples during the prenatal period and up to six months following the birth of a first child and in a later study, up to 18 months postpartum. In the 1983 study, they reported a number of shifts in marital satisfaction with both husband and wife reporting less satisfaction following the birth of their infant. Shifts were noted away from romantic interactions and toward interactions around their infant. Couples who related comfortably prior to the birth of their infant tended to relate comfortably after the birth; however, some decline appeared to occur for the couples in general. After six months, a degree of improvement in the relationship was noted, not, however, to equal prepregnancy rates of satisfaction. These investigators also reported shifts in patterns of interaction, with the couple moving toward a more traditional division of roles. Husbands tended to be less involved in household tasks, family decision-making roles, and, to a lesser extent, style of baby care. These findings are consistent with those of Shereshefsky and Yarrow (1974) and Arbeit (1975). In the later study, Cowan et al. (1985) reported that the now expectable drop in marital satisfaction extends well into the second year of the infant's life. From six to 18 months postpartum, parents recorded an even sharper decline in marital satisfaction than was reported earlier from pregnancy to six months postpartum. They found that men's and women's satisfaction with marriage changed differently over time, with the fathers' satisfaction declining little in the first six months and markedly between six and 18 months and mothers' satisfaction declining sharply in the first six months and moderately thereafter. In general, the negative impact of becoming a parent is first felt by women and only later by men. Interestingly, the largest discrepancy between fathers' and mothers' evaluations of their marriage occurred when they had been parents for six months, at a time when their views of themselves might also be changing.

Consistent with the Cowans' studies, Belsky (1984; Belsky, Lang, and Rovine, 1985) found patterns of decline in the marital relationship when they compared ratings taken during the last trimester of pregnancy with those at nine months postpartum. In general, both husbands and wives become increasingly dissatisfied with the amount of positive behaviors offered by their partners. Husbands, who in general were less happy in this area than their wives, wanted their wives to behave more positively toward them. For husbands and wives, measures of satisfaction and love declined more steeply for the wives, although to a great extent this may have been due to their reporting initially higher levels of satisfaction. One area of discrepancy concerned the extent to which spouses characterized their relationships as romantic. A decline in romance over time and an increase in seeing the relationship as more of a partnership was more pronounced for husbands.

THE FATHER'S PSYCHOLOGICAL ADAPTATION
DURING THE TRANSITION TO PARENTHOOD

In any consideration of risk, it is important to consider individual psychological components involved in the transition to fatherhood in addition to tasks involved with parenthood. Until recently, developmentally and psychodynamically oriented studies of the coping processes of males during this important transition have received relatively little emphasis, and there has been a tendency to minimize the adjustments of normal males in response to pregnancy and new parenthood.

Parens (1975) suggested that significant maturation can occur in the male during the wife's pregnancy. Referring to Benedek, he stated that one can differentiate in the male an organization that, paralleling motherliness, directs the reproductive drive organization toward fatherliness. He added that fatherliness is a secondary developmental process compared with motherliness: a male's earliest security and his orientation to the world are learned through identification with his mother, and early identification is eventually surpassed by the need to identify with a male figure.

Benedek (1959, 1970), writing about the adaptational situation of fatherhood, referred to the normal maturational and developmental component of the process, the influences of early parent–child and sibling relationships, and the resolution of conflicts. Consistent with Parke and Tinsley's (1987) recent review in which they discuss the influence each spouse has on the other's views and behaviors during the parenting process, Benedek stressed the wife's role in influencing the husband's emotional response to pregnancy. She also pointed out that the emotional course of pregnancy may stabilize or disrupt the marriage, thus determining the psychological environment of the child.

Gurwitt (1976), utilizing a case study approach, reported on a male psychoanalytic patient's reactions before and during his wife's pregnancy. The couple underwent a remarkable sharing of psychological events during the pregnancy, and, through their new experiences and reexperiencing old issues, their relationship altered, faltered, and was strengthened as they grew. The husband's upheavals, which occurred around the conception and the unfolding stages of pregnancy were, in part, his reactions to the realistic events of the pregnancy. They also reflected significant events in the patient's early life, including his mother's becoming pregnant when he was quite young and his reactions to the explanations of her pregnancy and to the birth of his sibling. Gurwitt divided the husband's experience, beginning prior to conception and continuing through childbirth, into three periods: anticipation, entering the process, and coming to terms with it.

Herzog (1982) studied 103 men whose wives had given birth, at 25–39 weeks of gestation, to infants who were apparently premature. Retrospective, analytically oriented interviews for up to 24 months following the deliveries revealed marked differences in these men's experiences. Many of them appeared to experience preparatory, entry, and adaptive periods similar to those described by Gurwitt (1976). Thirty-five reported feelings and fantasies about the pregnancy. There were considerable shifts in their sexual fantasies, a reworking of feelings about their fathers, and, in some, a preoccupation with gastrointestinal symptoms. Aggressive fantasies, concerns about hurting the baby, and a sense of magic and mystery about the process of creation appeared especially after quickening. Although the numbers of men reporting feelings may have been reduced because of the retrospective nature of the study, and although the feelings described may have been influenced by the stress of the babies' being born prematurely, there are suggestions that for some of these men there were common themes and an orderly reworking of earlier issues.

A limited number of studies have focused on the male's development of emotional symptoms in response to his wife's pregnancy or the birth of their baby (Boehm, 1930; Zilboorg, 1931; Jacobson, 1950; van Leeuwen, 1965). Freeman (1951) studied six men with emotional difficulties whose symptoms began during their wives' pregnancies. He concluded that pregnancy precipitated these men's symptoms. Repressed thoughts and experiences from early childhood predisposed these men to react psychotically to their wives' pregnancies.

In Towne and Afterman's (1955) study of 28 hospitalized male patients, a temporal relationship was reported between the outbreak of a psychosis and a pregnancy or the birth of a child. All these men had unfulfilled, demanding dependency needs characteristic of their relationships with important people in their environment. Most of them were acutely disturbed on admission but responded to treatment fairly rapidly.

It has been suggested that psychopathological reactions to fatherhood probably appear with more frequency than is commonly recognized (Wainwright, 1966). Since the illness is usually attributed by the patient to other external stresses, the importance of the recent birth of a child may be overlooked by the therapist. Often both the treater and the patient are unaware of the intense reaction to fatherhood. Wainwright pointed out that the dynamic factors precipitating those reactions in men are not in themselves specific to people with mental illness; therefore, it would be well for supportive personnel to ascertain the meanings that fatherhood has for the spouse of the pregnant patient as well as for the woman herself.

Lacoursiere (1972a, b) reviewed the literature concerning the relationship between mental illness and fatherhood and presented four cases in which fatherhood had either precipitated or at least was associated with the development of severe problems. He concluded that no single type of mental illness is associated with fatherhood but that a wide range of symptoms and syndromes may be conducive to the development of postpartum psychiatric problems in the mother.

Men's envious reactions to their wives' ability to become pregnant and give birth and their rivalry toward the fetus or the baby have been reported by Ginath (1974). He described severe psychopathological reactions, such as psychoses, which were generated by unresolved childhood conflicts. Ginath cautioned that if men develop a psychosis during or after their wives' first pregnancy and delivery, further pregnancies and childbirths exacerbate the condition. This suggestion is consistent with the conclusions of Lacoursiere (1972a, b).

A few studies exploring the development of somatic symptoms in men during their wives' pregnancies have focused on psychological factors related to symptom formation. For example, Curtis (1955), who studied 55 expectant fathers, found that 17 had serious emotional problems, 14 had minor problems, and 24 had no apparent problems. Psychosomatic symptoms were common, especially among the more disturbed fathers, and marital tensions developed in a number of the families. These men were seldom aware of the association of their problems to expectant fatherhood.

Similarly, Trethowan (1965), in considering the development of psychosomatic symptoms in 327 expectant fathers in England, found that one in nine suffered from minor physical ailments, primarily of a gastrointestinal nature, during their wives' pregnancies. These men reportedly were in good emotional health prior to the pregnancies.

Cavenar and Weddington (1978), who reviewed the available literature on emotional difficulties in expectant fathers, also reported on three patients who experienced psychosomatic symptoms while anticipating fatherhood. Each man during his wife's pregnancy experienced abdominal pain suggestive of the couvade syndrome but for which no physical cause could be found.

These studies have provided evidence to support the proposition that mental illness may be associated with and precipitated by impending or new fatherhood. A wide range of symptoms and syndromes may develop in men, and their relationship to fatherhood may be overlooked by the treaters. Further determination of the significant changes that influence regression or growth, the adjustments that are required, the generalizability of the findings, and strategies for intervention and support are needed.

OUR EARLIER STUDIES WITH EXPECTANT AND NEW FATHERS

Concerns During Pregnancy

In earlier studies, utilizing psychoanalytically oriented interviews, we (Osofsky and Osofsky, 1980b; Osofsky, 1982) noted that men undergo considerable stress and upheaval during the course of a pregnancy and following the birth of a baby, especially a first child. The pressures that men have described appear to be related to regressive pulls, unresolved conflicts, and their life circumstances. For example, most men experienced a sense of excitement and pride when they discovered that their wives were pregnant. Even those men who were forced into marriage because of the pregnancy, after their initial anger, generally accepted the pregnancy and welcomed the forthcoming child. Frequently, these men felt more manly, no longer concerned about their virility and potency or about their wives leaving them for other men.

Following their initial sense of excitement and pride, some husbands described feeling strange – not totally themselves. Some worried and were frightened about the anticipated changes in their lives and in their relationship with their wives. A considerable number spoke about their own needs and their feelings of rivalry toward the baby. Most men described having a greater sense of responsibility, which at times was overwhelming. At such times these men became panicky, felt trapped, and wondered whether they were ready to settle down, have children, and accept the responsibilities of parenthood. A few actually questioned whether the child was theirs, and many wondered what kind of father they would be. Would they be like their own fathers or would they do things differently? Would they be adequate fathers and role models for their children?

Some men seemed to be envious of their wives' ability to reproduce. They felt like bystanders, unable to experience the beginning feelings of life or the changes in fetal growth. To compensate, some husbands engaged in their own creative efforts during pregnancy – writing books, planting gardens, breeding dogs. During the early months of pregnancy, some men gained weight; others were physically ill, mimicking the symptoms of their wives.

The men often had mixed feelings about their pregnant wives. Some men described being more comfortable with their wives, feeling great warmth and tenderness toward them and seeing them as more beautiful during the pregnancy; yet at the same time, at least intermittently, they also saw their wives as ugly and clumsy. Because of these mixed feelings, men often became confused and irritable and some of them engaged in fantasies about other women. A few had affairs during this time; many described their intermittent wishes to be out of the marriage, with subsequent feelings of guilt. Some men worried about whether their wives would be good enough for their children – whether they would measure up to their own mothers.

Fathers-to-be had special concerns if there had been difficulties with conception or if problems had arisen during previous pregnancies. When there had been a prior miscarriage, husbands tended to become extremely anxious during the current pregnancy at about the same time that the miscarriage had occurred in the previous one. Generally, these men were afraid of intercourse, worrying that the sperm or the sexual excitement of the uterine contractions would initiate bleeding or (later in the pregnancy) begin labor. When there had been a stillbirth, husbands tended to feel guilty about looking forward to the new baby. Because of their complex emotions, these men often became stoical and did not share their concerns with their wives. Thus, the couples grew apart and had difficulty communicating during the pregnancy.

Most men in the study had sexual concerns during the pregnancy. While some men were more sexually relaxed and more easily aroused during the pregnancy, others were tense and uninterested in sex. Some men even experienced loss of erection and a degree of impotence for the first time in their married lives. A few of them, feeling panicky about their sexual inadequacy, became attracted to other men, but this attraction seemed to be short-lived.

Concerns During Labor and Delivery

A number of concerns that had emerged at various times during the pregnancy reemerged during the labor and delivery experience. For example, some men worried about whether they would provide their wives with adequate support during labor, whether they would arrive at the hospital on time, or whether they would need to deliver the baby themselves. Others worried that somethign would happen to their wives and they would be left alone to raise the baby. They also worried that the baby would be stillborn or abnormal. Worries about whether they really wanted, or were ready, to be fathers also reemerged.

After they arrived at the hospital, most men tended to be upset about being in a secondary or ancillary role. They became more aware – sometimes painfully so – that their wives were the ones who were going to be giving birth to the babies. Some men were annoyed at being left out; they described a sense of being secondary, of being in the coaching rather than the doing role.

Following the birth of the baby, most men initially felt a strong sense of excitement, pride, and responsibility. For many men it was the most intensely pleasurable and meaningful time in their lives. However, it was also a time when other feelings surfaced. Following the initial excitement, some fathers felt let down and not as ecstatic or enthusiastic as they thought they should be. The baby might not meet the father's expectations; it might not be the right sex or look like him or a favorite relative. Men sometimes also experienced conflictual feelings: they should be strong and supportive, but they resented the fuss being made over their wives and babies, wishing to be cared for themselves. One husband said, "For the first time, women in the office began to look very appealing to me. I considered having an affair, but then I wondered; Did I really want another woman or did I want my mother to take care of me and make me dinner?"

Concerns After the Birth of the Baby

Many of the adjustments to new parenthood are common to both the mother and the father. We have found, for example, that both parents tend to feel overwhelmed and wonder, When will it end? When will things be back to normal? Both experience major upheavals and adjustments in their lives and in their relationships with one another. Fathers, however, tend to have additional feelings that are unique. For example, some fathers, feeling distant toward the baby, wondered if they were cold and unfeeling. Also, even though they spent more time outside the home, some men more than their wives expressed the need for more time alone as a couple.

Especially if the baby was a first born, fathers usually had a strong preference for a son. Yet after the birth of the baby, different and perplexing feelings at times emerged in the father. Many fathers described a particular closeness toward their daughters. Some fathers felt more awkward in relating to sons than to daughters, and some experienced discomfort when observing their sons nursing.

Conflictual feelings about sons tended to emerge at the time of circumcision. Fathers might go through considerably more inner turmoil about the procedure than did mothers, with temporary feelings of regret and concerns about what they "had done" to their sons. While feeling the procedure to be appropriate, fathers mentioned staying awake at night worrying about their sons and wanting to be available to console and comfort them.

Men also described a feeling of being left out during the early rearing of the children. They felt their wives to be occupied – even preoccupied – with their infants. Even though husbands valued their wives' motherliness, some felt that their wives had no time for them. As one husband said, "I felt that I came after the kids, the house, and the dog." With their own internal pressures to be better providers and with their wives' wishes that they be at home and more available, husbands at times felt torn in their role. One father poignantly stated,

> I constantly felt like a bigamist. I felt wedded to my work, with there being more and more demands being made upon me to be successful. When I came home I also felt that my wife was angry and resentful, making more demands upon me to be a good husband and father. I felt that each was jealous of the other and that I could satisfy neither.

Often men were intermittently critical of their wives as mothers, sometimes comparing them unfavorably to their own mothers. Some men described disquieting feelings of wishing that they could take over their wives' role in parenting.

Husbands also experienced new and conflictual feelings about their relationship with their wives. At times they felt closer and warmer to them; at other times they felt they and their wives were growing apart, that they had no time for each other. At times they might see them as beautiful, with the maternal role conveying a sense of warmth and deep affection. At other times they might be upset by their changing figures, their sloppy appearance, and, if nursing, their dripping breasts. They might feel jealous of or angry with their babies, at times wishing that they and their wives could go back to their old relationship.

New fathers frequently experience conflictual feelings and a period of adjustment about sex. Some men described being more sexually excited owing to the imposed period of abstinence, with a new sense of warmth and tenderness toward their wives. Other men said that they felt turned off sexually for a considerable period of time following the birth of the baby. In addition to some frustration about their wives' fatigue and preoccupation with the baby, they were concerned about whether intercourse would hurt their wives, whether sex would feel the same, and whether their wives' vaginas would be stretched. In addition, some men experienced psychological adjustment to having intercourse with the women who were formerly only wives but who were now also mothers and who reminded them of their own mothers.

CURRENT STUDY ON RISK FACTORS FOR PARENTS AND INFANTS DURING THE TRANSITION TO PARENTHOOD

We are now in the third year of a longitudinal study of the transition to parenthood in an attempt to learn more about the normative process and the factors that contribute to risk for parents and infants. We have recruited married couples who are expecting their first infant and who are receiving prenatal care at the University of Kansas Health Sciences Center. We hope to have 250 couples and infants in the study: 50 who are at low risk, 50 with psychosocial risk, 50 with maternal medical risk, 50 with infant medical risk, and 50 with multirisk situations.

Description of the Sample

The sample that has been analyzed to date consists of 107 marired couples expecting their first child. The mean age of the men is 27 years (range: 18 to 48 years) and of the women 25 years (range: 18 to 35 years). At the time of the initial prenatal visit, the couples had been married for an average of two and a half years (range: 1 month to 15 years). They are primarily middle class and well educated.

Overview of Procedure

The couples were recruited through the obstetrical group practice program of the University of Kansas Health Sciences Center. All patients, regardless of income, receive their care through this program in a private practice model with a team of consistent attending staff and residents. Initial contact with potential subjects occurred at a regularly scheduled obstetrical visit during the second trimester of the pregnancy. All women who were married, primiparous, and between 18 and 35 years of age and willing to participate were enrolled. Approximately 77% of the couples that met these criteria agreed to participate in the project. When the couples agreed to participate, the pregnant women were interviewed during subsequent regularly scheduled obstetrical visits. The men were interviewed when they came with their wives to the obstetrical clinic, or a packet of questionnaires was sent home for them to fill out and return.

Measures

In addition to extensive demographic information, individual measures of depression, self-esteem, and social support were collected from both members of the couple in order to learn more about the process and factors that contribute to risk. Assessments of the couple's relationship and style of interaction were also obtained.

Self-esteem was assessed using the Index of Self-Esteem (ISE) from the Clinical Measurement Package (Hudson, 1982). Depression was measured using the Center for Epidemiological Studies Depression Scale (CES-D) (Radloff, 1977) consisting of twenty items measuring current levels of depressive symptomatology. Family and nonfamily social support was measured by asking the respondents to list eight persons in their lives who were important to them, including people they feel close to, know well, and care about a great deal. After listing the eight persons, the respondents are asked to describe each person's relationship to the respondent, the frequency of their contact, and whether the person listed has children under the age of five years. Assessments of the couple's relationship and their style of interaction was also included in the interview and questionnaire packet. Two scales assessing different components of the marital relationship were used. One measures marital adjustment and marital satisfaction (Huston, 1983), and the other measures mutual role arrangements and role satisfaction with the Who Does What? Scale (Cowan and Cowan, 1983).

Results

Given the intent of this chapter, we will focus on the data obtained from the fathers. Data obtained from the mothers will be included primarily to help understand the father data, put it in focus, and point out discrepancies where they exist.

Individual Scores of Depression and Self-Esteem

The mean of the fathers' depression scores was 11.5. Twenty-nine percent of the fathers had scores of 16 or above, which indicated, according to this scale, that they were clinically depressed. The mean of the fathers' self-esteem scores was 28.8. Forty-seven percent of the fathers had scores of 30 or above, which indicated they had clinically low self-esteem. It was striking that a considerable number of these fathers anticipating a first child showed evidence of clinical depression or low self-esteem. We would point out that with both the depression and the self-esteem measures, the finding of clinical symptoms does not indicate whether the symptoms will be confined to the pregnancy or whether they will persist following childbirth. We are currently exploring possible continuities or discontinuities and how they relate to other individual measures, marital satisfaction, and patterns of parent–infant interaction. The fathers were divided into two groups depending on whether or not they had scores indicating clinical depression. The nondepressed group was composed of forty fathers, and the depressed group 17 fathers. The two groups were significantly different on the measure of self-esteem. Depressed fathers had significantly lower self-esteem than nondepressed fathers ($F = 7.89$, $df = 1$, $p < .007$). To determine that the measures assessed different parameters, the fathers were also divided into two groups on the basis of whether they had scores indicating clinically low self-esteem. Fathers with low self-esteem were not significantly different from those with higher self-esteem on the measures of depression, indicating the independence of the two sets of measures. Fathers with low incomes were significantly more likely to be clinically depressed than were fathers with higher incomes ($r = 0.29$, $p < .05$). However, fathers' income did not relate significantly to low self-esteem.

Fathers' scores on the Who Does What? measure of mutual role arrangements and role satisfaction related significantly to their depression and self-esteem scores. Depressed fathers reported having a lesser role in decision making as compared to their wives ($r = -.25$, $p < .05$) and were less satisfied with the decision making ($r = .31$, $p < .01$). Depressed fathers were members of couples who disagreed more about how decision making should be divided ($r = .38$, $p < .01$).

Who Does What? Scores

The six scores derived from fathers' reports of Who Does What? were intercorrelated. As might be anticipated, fathers who reported that they were satisfied with the decision-making process also described being satisfied with the division of household tasks ($r = .43$, $p < .001$). Further, fathers who reported being satisfied with the division of decision making agreed most with their wives about the division of decision making ($r = .54$, $p < .001$).

Marital Adjustment and Satisfaction Scores

The six Who Does What? scores were correlated with the three marital adjustment and marital satisfaction scores. Fathers' satisfaction about the division of household tasks correlated significantly with satisfaction with sexual activities ($r = .25, p < .05$). Fathers' satisfaction with the division of decision making correlated significantly with satisfaction with negative activities ($r = -.32, p < .01$) and satisfaction with sexual activities ($r = 0.4128, p < .001$). In other words, fathers who reported that they were more satisfied with the division of household tasks and with decision making reported fewer negative interactions with their wives and more sexual enjoyment. Decision-making awareness was correlated with satisfaction with positive activities ($r = .2853, p < .05$). Men who had greater agreement with their wives about how decisions were made, were likely to report more positive interactions with their wives. There were no significant correlations between the six Who Does What? scores and the three father social support scores.

DISCUSSION AND CONCLUSION

The research and clinical data collected on fathers in this study are consistent with past theoretical work on women's psychological adjustment to pregnancy (Bibring, 1959), indicating that many of the assumptions about the important psychological components during the transition to parenthood are relevant for expectant and new fathers as well as mothers. Consistent with Bibriing's broad definition of the woman's pregnancy experience, expectant and new fatherhood can be accompanied by and can offer a developmental opportunity for maturation and new growth. Prior to becoming a father for the first time, a man is a relatively self-contained individual, although he probably relates with closeness and affection to his mate. However, with his wife's pregnancy and his new parenthood, his relationship to his wife changes. She is now the cocreator and bearer of his offspring. Their child will be an individual but will also represent both of them, and together they will be responsible for his or her upbringing. The father will have a special relationship to his child, with identifications, concerns, struggles, and, over time, an ever-widening, conflict-free area of relating. The father will also have the opportunity to rework and resolve persistent conflictual relationships with his own parents. Not all men experience conscious severe upheavals. Yet it appears that all men, especially when they become fathers for the first time, undergo considerable shifts and internal disequilibrium, and few of them are the same as they were before their wives' pregnancy. On a conscious level, most men experience profound changes in their sense of responsibility, their relationship with their spouse, their attitudes toward their baby, and their feelings about themselves.

In our experience, even men without overt psychiatric symptoms before a pregnancy can experience considerable lability and unsettled feelings during the pregnancy and following the birth of the baby. These men demonstrate regressive pulls with conflictual themes similar to those described for more disturbed persons, although their overt symptoms may be less intense, more transient, and more responsive to supportive intervention. As with more disturbed persons, the nature and timing of symptoms and the adequacy of solutions appear to be related to unresolved conflicts and developmental difficulties. Life circumstances – including degree of economic stability, religious background and patterns, family and community supports, and the ability to make required maturational shifts in the marital relationship – all contribute both to symptoms and to solutions.

It is important, however, to understand the increase in symptoms at this time not only as a reflection of psychopathology but as part of a normative process. Erikson (1950, 1954), describing major steps in human growth, stressed that reactions and upheavals are part of the growth process. Considerable disequilibrium and crisis can herald the beginning of a new growth phase. The conflicts that have been observed in expectant and new fathers appear to be universal. The specific manifestations of the conflicts depend on the man's personality and life circumstances at the beginning of and during the process. Under optimal circumstances, expectant and new fatherhood should offer a man an opportunity for better resolution of past conflicts and an enhancement of the maturational process. In becoming a parent, in reworking the relationship with his wife, and in establishing a relationship with their child, a man has the opportunity – albeit with difficulties – for greater fulfillment of age-appropriate tasks and enjoyments. The burden may be greater for men with many unresolved conflicts; but even in difficult situations, better solutions are possible with appropriate support and intervention.

In recent years, it has been recognized more fully that the shifts that occur in each parent during pregnancy and following the birth of their infant can have a major impact on them as individuals, on their relationship as a couple, and on the parent–infant relationship and infant development. Psychological characteristics of each parent prenatally – for example, depression in expectant mothers (Elliott et al., 1983; McNeil, Kaij, and Malmquist-Larsson, 1983; Saks et al., 1985), and stressful life events (Paykel et al., 1980) – are associated with subsequent postpartum depression. Although, as noted previously, marital satisfaction in general declines for couples following the birth of their first child, the patterns of decline are related to prenatal marital adjustment and styles of interaction (Cowan and Cowan, 1985).

In our ongoing study, we are trying to delineate normative changes as well as risk factors for parents and infants. We have been struck by the relatively high incidence of clinical depression and lowered self-esteem in these married fathers expecting their first child. On the measures utilized, 29% show evidence of clinical depression and 47% low self-esteem. Further, the assessments seem to be measuring separate dimensions. Expectant fathers who have lower earnings are more likely to be depressed; however, low earnings are not predictive of low self-esteem in the fathers. Depressed fathers report that they have less of a role in making decisions within their marriages. They disagree more with their wives about how decisions are made and are less satisfied with the decision making.

There are also interesting relationships between the couples' mutual role arrangements and satisfaction with the role arrangements as assessed by the Who Does What? Scale and the measures of marital satisfaction. The division of tasks within the marriage does not relate to marital satisfaction. Rather, satisfaction with the process of decision making around the division of tasks relates to marital satisfaction. These data are consistent with those reported by the Cowans.

As the current study proceeds, we will be able to compare the prenatal data with information obtained at three, six and thirteen months following delivery. On the basis of our prior work, it is possible that some of the clinical depression and low self-esteem may be related to the psychological adjustments to pregnancy and that later assessments may result in different findings at varying time intervals following delivery. However, from the data previously cited concerning depression in women prior to and following birth, it seems likely that expectant fathers' depression and self-esteem will relate to findings on the same measures following delivery. It will be important to determine the changes in these findings over time as well as the impact of depression and low self-esteem on subsequent marital interaction and patterns of parent–infant interaction. One wonders whether some of the dissatisfaction and disagreements reported by depressed fathers are transient or are harbingers of future difficulties. Further, one wonders about the impact of further risk situations on outcomes, for example, the effect of maternal medical complications or infant vulnerability on fathers who are already depressed or who have low self-esteem and the impact on marital adjustment and parent–infant interaction. Future data emanating from the study will address these and other questions and, it is hoped, provide increased understanding about the important processes involved in the transition to fatherhood.

REFERENCES

Arbeit, S. A. (1975), A study of women during their first pregnancy. Unpublished doctoral dissertation, Yale University.

Belsky, J. (1979), Mother-father-infant interaction: A naturalistic observational study. *Devel. Psychol.,* 15:601–607.

_____ (1981), Early human experience: A family perspective. *Devel. Psychol.,* 17:3–23.

_____ (1984), Determinants of parenting: A process model. *Child Devel.,* 55:83–96.

Belsky, J., Lang, M. E. & Rovine, M. (1985), Stability and change in marriage across the transition to parenthood: A second study. *J. Marr. & Fam.,* 47:855–865.

Belsky, J. & Volling, B. L. (1987), Mothering, fathering & marital interaction in the family triad: Exploring family systems processes. In: *Men's Transition to Parenthood,* ed. P. Berman & F. Pedersen. Hillsdale, NJ: Lawrence Erlbaum Associates, pp. 37–63.

Benedek, T. (1959), Parenthood as a developmental phase: A contribution to the libido theory. *J. Amer. Psychoanal. Assn.,* 7:389–417.

_____ (1970), The psychobiology of pregnancy. In: *Parenthood,* ed. E. J. Anthony & T. Benedek. Boston: Little, Brown, pp. 137–151.

Bibring, G. L. (1959), Some considerations of the psychological processes in pregnancy. *The Psychoanalytic Study of the Child,* 14:113–121. New York: International Universities Press.

Bibring, G. L., Dwyer, T. F., Huntington, D. & Valentine, A. F. (1961), A study of the psychological processes in pregnancy and the earliest mother-child relationship: I. Some propositions and comments; II. Methodological considerations. *The Psychoanalytic Study of the Child,* 16:9–72. New York: International Universities Press.

Boehm, F. (1930), The femininity-complex in men. *Internat. J. Psycho-Analysis,* 11:444–469.

Caplan, G. (1957), Psychological aspects of maternity care. *Amer. J. Pub. Health,* 47:25–31.

_____ (1960), Emotional implications of pregnancy and influences on family relationships. In: *The Healthy Child,* ed. H. C. Stuart & D. C. Prugh. Cambridge, MA: Harvard University Press, pp. 72–82.

Cavenar, J. O., Jr. & Weddington, W. W., Jr. (1978), Abdominal pain in expectant fathers. *Psychosomat.,* 19:761–768.

Cowan, C. P., Cowan, P. A., Heming, G., Garrett, E., Coyish, W. S., Curtis-Boles, H. & Boles, A. J. (1985), Transition to parenthood: His, hers, and theirs. *J. Fam. Issues,* 6:451–481.

Cowan, P. A. & Cowan, C. P. (1983), Quality of couple relationships and parenting stress in beginning families. Presented at meeting of Society for Research in Child Development, Detroit, MI.

_____ _____ (1985), Pregnancy, parenthood, and children at three. Presented at meeting of Society for Research in Child Development, Toronto.

_____ _____ (1987), Couple relationships, parenting styles, and the child's development at three. Paper presented in a symposium on Normative Development and Risk Factors in Child Development, Baltimore, MD.

Curtis, J. A. (1955), A psychiatric study of 55 expectant fathers. *U.S. Armed Forces Med. J.,* 6:937–950.

Elliott, S. A. Rugg, A. J., Watson, J. P. & Brough, D. I. (1983), Mood changes during pregnancy and after the birth of a child. *Brit. J. Clin. Psychol.,* 22:295–308.

Entwisle, D. R. & Doering. S. G. (1981), *The First Birth.* Baltimore, MD: Johns Hopkins University Press.

Erikson, E. H. (1950), *Childhood and Society.* New York: Norton.

_____ (1954), Growth and crisis of the "healthy personality." In: *Personality in Nature, Society, and Culture,* 2nd ed., ed. C. Kluckhohn & H. A. Murray. New York: Knopf, pp. 185–225.

Fein, R. A. (1976), Men's entrance to parenthood. *Fam. Coord.,* 25:341–348.

Feldman, S. S., Nash, S. C. & Aschenbrenner, B. G. (1983), Antecedents of fathering. *Child Devel.,* 54:1628–1636.

Freeman, T. (1951), Pregnancy as a precipitant of mental illness in men. *Brit. J. Med. Psychol.,* 24:49–54.

Ginath, Y. (1974), Psychoses in males in relation to their wives' pregnancy and childbirth. *Israel Annals. of Psychiat.,* 12:227–237.

Gordon, R. E. & Gordon, K. K. (1960), Social factors in the prevention of emotional difficulties in pregnancy. *Obstet. & Gyn.,* 15:433–438.

Gurwitt, A. R. (1976), Aspects of prospective fatherhood: A case report. *The Psychoanalytic Study of the Child,* 31:237–271. New Haven: Yale University Press.

Herzog, J. M. (1982), Prematurity and the birth of the father. In: *Father and Child,* ed. S. H. Cath, A. R. Gurwitt & J. M. Ross. Boston: Little, Brown.

Hudson, W. W. (1982), *The Clinical Measurement Package.* Homewood, IL: Dorsey Press.

Huston, T. (1983), The topography of marriage: A longitudinal study of change in husband-wife relationships over the first year. Plenary address to the International Conference on Personal Relationships, Madison, WI.

Jacobson, E. (1950), Development of the wish for a child in boys. *The Psychoanalytic Study of the Child,* 5:139–152. New York: International Universities Press.

Lacoursiere, R. B. (1972a), Fatherhood and mental illness: A review and new material. *Psychiat. Quart.,* 46:109–124.

_____ (1972b). The mental health of the prospective father: A new indication for therapeutic abortion? *Bull. Menn. Clin.,* 36:645–650.

Leifer, M. (1977), Psychological changes accompanying pregnancy and motherhood. *Genet. Psychol. Monogr.,* 95:55–96.

McNeil, T. K., Kaij, L. & Malmquist-Larsson, A. (1983), Pregnant women with nonorganic psychosis: Life situation and experience of pregnancy. *Acta Psychiat. Scand.,* 68:445–457.

Osofsky, H. J. (1982), Expectant and new fatherhood as a developmental phase. *Bull. Menn. Clin.,* 46:209–230.

_____ Osofsky, J. D. (1980a), Normal adaptation to pregnancy and new parenthood. In: *Parent-Infant Relationships,* ed. P. M. Taylor. New York: Grune & Stratton, pp. 25–48.

_____ Osofsky, J. D. (1980b), *Answers for New Parents: Adjusting to Your New Role.* New York: Walker.

Osofsky, J. D. & Osofsky, H. J. (1984), Psychological and developmental perspectives on expectant and new parenthood. *Review of Child Development Research,* Vol. 8. Chicago: University of Chicago Press.

Parens, H. (1975), Parenthood as a developmental phase. *J. Amer. Psychoanal. Assn.,* 23:154–165.

Parke, R. D. & Tinsley, B. J. (1987), Family interaction in infancy. In: *Handbook of Infant Development,* 2nd ed., ed. J. D. Osofsky. New York: Wiley.

Paykel, E. S., Emms, E. M., Fletcher, J. & Rassaby, E. S. (1980), Life events and social support in puerperal depression. *Brit. J. Psychiat.,* 136:339–346.

Radloff, L. (1977), The CES-D Scale: A self-report depression scale for research in the general population. *J. App. Psychol. Measure.,* 1:385–401.

Saks, B. R., Frank, J. B., Lowe, T. L., Berman, W., Naftolin, F. & Cohen, D. J. (1985), Depressed mood during pregnancy and the puerperium: clinical recognition and implications for clinical practice. *Amer. J. Psychiat.,* 142:728–731.

Shereshefsky, P. M. & Yarrow, L. J. (1974), *Psychological Aspects of a First Pregnancy and Early Postnatal Adaptation.* New York: Raven Press.

Towne, R. D., & Afterman, J. (1955), Psychosis in males related to parenthood. *Bull. Menn. Clin.,* 19:19–26.

Trethowan, W. H. (1965), Sympathy pains. *Discovery,* 26:30–34.

van Leeuwen, K. (1965), Pregnancy envy in the male. *Internat. J. Psycho-Anal.,* 47:319–324.

Wainwright, W. H. (1966), Fatherhood as a precipitant of mental illness. *Amer. J. Psychiat.,* 123:40–44.

Wente, A. S., & Crockenberg, S. B. (1976), Transition to fatherhood: Lamaze preparation, adjustment difficulty and the husband–wife relationship. *Fam. Coord.,* 25:351–357.

Zilboorg, G. (1931), Depressive reactions related to parenthood. *Amer. J. Psychiat.,* 10:927–962.

9

Flight from Fatherhood

Alan Gurwitt

It is currently a popular notion that we are in an era when men, young and old, are more attuned than ever before to becoming and being fathers. Once having become fathers, they are presumed to be actively involved with their children, sharing equally in all child-rearing tasks in their dual-career families. Whether or not these changes are really occurring in the degree and form imagined (or, should I say, wished-for) is not clear (see Lamb, this volume); indeed, the evidence is controversial. While popular movies attest to the potential parental nurturing capacities of men, for example "Three Men and a Baby," and "Kramer vs. Kramer," these same movies also emphasize both the lack of interest on the part of some young men in siring and raising children and the clumsy comic manner–in these films, anyway–by which they begin the process of learning. In "Three Men and a Baby" (and the original, slightly different, French version) older women assist that learning (the landlady and the friendly neighbor in the French and American versions respectively, and the woman in the store in both). The men are devoted to their careers and the romantic adventures of single life, at least until some dramatic event or person triggers or forces a shift. Indeed, therein lies the heart of these stories, the "disavowed heart" (Tessman, 1988, personal communication), the comedy that is also bufoonery. We laugh at and take for granted the seeming ineptitude of the men. But we are also moved by the changes that unfold (changes showing capacities demonstrated by Pruett, this volume). Men can nurture,[1] under the right circumstances; they can be competent primary caretakers. They often do nurture, and occasionally are primary caretakers. They can form close attachments to their children, and the children to them. Some men, however, do not want or can not manage such attachments, such forms of nurturing, and the adaptations required.

It is a very old story that not all adults are eager to be parents. Some flee from the very notion and in doing so might be demonstrating a kind of wisdom that is right for them at a particular time, but a wisdom that often goes against the grain of societal expectations. Nonprofessional literature is filled with themes related to avoidance or abandonment of parenthood and specifically fatherhood, for example, the character of Charles Strickland in W. Somerset Maugham's (1919) *The Moon and Sixpense*. Strickland, an established businessman with a wife and two children, suddenly disappears, gone off to learn to be an artist, leaving a trail of outraged and saddened relatives and acquaintances behind. These themes also repeatedly are seen in the plays of Shakespeare (Kahn, 1981). It is also an old and very familiar story – often the core of our work – that adults pressured into parenthood, however reluctant they were, may be ill adapted to the role.

Flight from active parenthood should come as no surprise. It probably has been easier for men to escape into career choices that took them away physically and psychologically. Now, as women have wider choices about careers (and motherhood), our society, in examining who can and is willing to take care of the children, turns increasingly to the fathers.[2] As Herzog (1986) has pointed out, men who formerly could remain aloof from parenting now face a dilemma. Now men are apparently expected to be active and committed fathers. The social factors – customs, culture, history, economics – that have always been strong external factors influencing individual decisions

---

[1]The term "nurturing" has many meanings and forms. It is not specifically gender linked. Greenberg (1985) makes an interesting distinction between "interactional nurturing" and "caretaking nurturing," both being forms of nurturing but different types of activities. The former includes "holding your baby, cooing, singing, or talking to her, playing or dancing with her . . ." and the like. The latter includes "diapering, feeding and bathing" (p. 76).

[2]It is equally ironic that many women who choose to remain home with their children, leaving previous careers to do so, face second-class status with other women (Tessman, personal communication).

about parenthood are changing. What does not change readily are the psychological factors, external to some degree, but mostly internal, unconscious, and probably ageless, factors that can militate against active, pleasurable, competent fathering.

Some men avoid biological paternity, psychological fatherhood, or both, in effect taking flight in one form or another. This chapter addresses how and why they do so. I shall not attempt to touch on all forms of flight and all reasons – they are too many and too varied – but merely to highlight some common forms and causes that are clinically significant. Nor am I implying that there is a clearcut line between pathological avoidance and what lies within a normal range of reluctance. The variables are simply too complex. The case illustrations that follow demonstrate a continuum of forms of flight, from those who totally avoid paternity to those who are actually fathers but psychologically avoid some or all aspects of fatherhood.

CASE ILLUSTRATIONS

Reluctance to Become a Father

Mr. M., a young business executive, was referred for psychotherapy by his wife because of his reluctance to father a child. His wife, a professional who happened to hear a talk I had given, was eager to have a child. Mr. M. warned me at the outset that it was important to him that I take a neutral stand in regard to whether or not he became a father. He was interested in understanding what was going on, whatever the outcome. Why was the thought of fathering a child so abhorrent, he wondered? He knew he had a basically good marriage and his wife would be an excellent mother. Yet, he felt blocked by a variety of obstacles. On the surface he felt that the demands of his career and active social life were such that he could not afford the time, energy, and money required to be a parent. On the one hand sure of his wife's love; on the other, he was disinclined to share her with a child. He was concerned that she would not only have less time for him and their mutual interests, but would permanently be pulled away. He sensed that his apprehension stemmed from an earlier time. He also expressed serious doubts about his capacity to be a good father, anticipating an angry, jealous competitiveness with a child, any child.

We learned that a major source of his reluctance was his conflicted relationship with his father. His father, who had died a few years before, had been a stern, demanding man, seemingly inflexible

and solely devoted to his work as a craftsman. Early in life my patient
assumed a compliant attitude toward his father while secretly col-
luding with his seductive mother. Later, in adolescence, he openly
provoked his father. He saw him as an arch conservative, a defender of
the business establishment, unsympathetic to the poor and downtrodden. But his father's "most grievous sins" were his angry outbursts
toward the patient's mother and the patient. The patient's relationship
with his father contrasted sharply with his warm, tender, supportive
relationship with his younger sister.

We began to outline the sources of estrangement from his father;
his mother's seductive collusion, which excluded the father and led to
particularly severe oedipal conflicts; his father's troubled family background, including an unhappy relationship with his own father; Mr.
M.'s jealousy of his sister, which concealed a sense of betrayal by both
his mother and father for bringing her forth into the world; his desire to
be as warmly embraced, loved, and accepted by his father as his sister
was while, at the same time, being made anxious by the fantasied
closeness. In the transference, although he tended to idealize me, there
was a growing competitiveness and annoyance (particularly evident
one day when I had seen a child patient the hour before his appointment). There were frightening memories too, both directly in relation
to his father and indirectly in relation to early fears and repetitive
nightmares. We recognized the power of the previously unconscious
oedipal conflict, his mother's contribution to that internal battle, his
desire to be rid of his father, his own aggressiveness, his fear of his
father's rage – and his father's probable struggle with similar conflicts. It
was not all just fantasy: his father may well have been a jealous and
angry man. But he also began to see that his father had, in some ways,
been much less rigid than he had previously thought. He recalled
fragments of some very early experiences with his father that had been
exciting and happy. Love and admiration had flowed both ways, he
speculated, seemingly interrupted by his sister's birth. Indeed, his father
emerged as a man with some interests and hobbies, capable of some
playfulness, nurturing, and loving, although with serious limitations
stemming from the father's own background. Mr. M.'s father's angry
outbursts toward him, at times seemingly unprovoked and unpredictable, were not primarily of Mr. M.'s direct doing. He recognized his
sadness at his father's premature death and the loss of a wished-for
opportunity to "work things out," to become closer over time. This
wish included a fantasy that his father and he would eventually be
brought together by his causing the birth of a grandchild, a kind of
"anticipatory healing." But his ambivalence about this happening and

his fear that this child would be allied with his father against him were reflected in his previous avoidance of fatherhood and the anticipatory antipathy toward a child-to-be. At the same time, he was aware of a revengeful desire not to provide a grandchild for both his parents for he feared they would have taken over the child.

As he began to mourn his father's death, his relationships with both his mother and his sister improved. He began to take closer note of his sister's children and the fathering style of his brother-in-law and then extended those observations to friends and their children. It was at this point that he began to discern his own desire both to have a child and to be a father. Fantasies, both positive and negative, of what a future child would be like, made their appearance. He recalled that amid the childhood struggles with his father there had been times of pleasurable family gatherings that now caused him (and perhaps had as a child) to recognize an underlying wish to reproduce those scenes in his adult life.

Stirred by a dream about a bearlike colleague who, although he liked to appear tough, was basically kind, he recalled his own teddy bear and other stuffed animals whose comforting presence represented so many themes, including maternal *and* paternal generative, nurturing, and aggressive characteristics. All of these characteristics were part of himself and his teddy, yet he was not fully at home with them. Those seen as feminine and maternal were not welcome; they were attributes to come from his wife. *He* felt driven toward displaying a "masculine" fierceness, both to reflect the image of his father and as a challenge to him. Through the transference, this and other roots and functions of the "fierceness" became apparent. The recollection of the early positive experiences with his father, observations of his bearlike colleague and friend (who was such a good father with his own children) and his wife's reminders that he was very good with friends' children and was capable of being most nurturing towards her, all made him aware of his own potential. Yet he was still the child of the father, not ready to father a child.

While this work went on there were many significant changes, including in his aggressive work style, which he continued but now more flexibly and mellowed. The therapy ended a few months later with his wanting to defer any decision about future children.

Mr. M. called three years later for a follow-up to discuss a professional conflict with a colleague. In the course of two visits he mentioned that he and his wife now had a daughter and a newborn son. He was glad that a daughter had been born first "to pave the way," as it might have been more difficult if his son had been the first born.

He and his wife were very happy with their family, but the demands of parenthood were considerable and there had been some rocky times. Occasionally, after the therapy, he had been angry at me, thinking that I had not really been neutral but had been in collusion with his wife. At other times, he was grateful, wondering what I would do in certain situations he had experienced with his children. Maybe he would have grown up anyway, but having children was certainly a catalyst, he both boasted and complained. His mother seemed "to have grown up a lot" too; she was a very good and sensible grandmother, who indeed had not tried to take over her grandchildren. The more he thought about it, he said in the second visit, the problem with his colleague that had prompted his call was not his major motivation for coming back. We agreed that the birth of his son had triggered some of the old issues, displaced, avoided but still present to a lesser degree. At least he was aware of them, but what would the future bring? (Only as I was writing this did I realize the possible importance of his touching base with me, an older man, a father and a child analyst).

A Very Remote Father, as Seen Through the Eyes of His Adult Daughter

Dr. B. was 36 when she entered analysis following her realization that for the second time she was stuck in an affair with a married man who was not really going to leave his wife and children. She was also increasingly aware that her career as a scientist, modestly successful though it was, had been compromised by these relationships and a pattern of being only second in command. She wondered how she had "gotten into this mess" and how could she change the pattern. Generally, the analysis proceeded well, though repeatedly seen in the transference were her tendencies to play second fiddle to me, to see the analytic situation as a precise laboratory with all thoughts and emotions under control (otherwise it was dangerous), or as a confessional.

Dr. B. came from a large family. She was the eldest of five children, the only girl, reared in a strict Catholic family and educational system. She had always excelled academically, especially in scientific areas. While she had followed her father's footsteps in some ways – he was a physician with unrealized academic and scientific ambitions – she was initially conflicted both about the similarities to and the differences from his interests. He had passed on a considerable curiosity about scientific mysteries but without passion either for the search for knowledge or in his relationship with her. Her mother had been a nurse before marriage, yearning to return to her career, but forbidden to do so by her husband. Dr. B. thought she and her mother had been quite close, but as the analysis unfolded we realized that many factors had compromised the mother-daughter relationship. Her mother seemed increasingly overburdened and depressed by the number of children, miscarriages in between, and her husband's lack of active physical and psychological support. Dr. B.'s father was often away, on either professional or fishing trips, and when home he was emotionally remote from all in the family. Though the marriage and the family had started out on strong and cheerful notes, there seemed to be a decline, ending sadly with the demise of her mother from breast cancer after a long illness. This occurred when Dr. B. was in college. After her mother's death the father remarried quickly – too quickly, according to all the children. They had suspected his involvement with another woman. It was as if the family had died too, as the siblings scattered. Dr. B. tried, unsuccessfully in earlier years, to stay in contact with them, to maintain a family centeredness that her father seemed uninterested in doing. She was more successful in this endeavor in later years.

Within the family setting, my patient had become parentified. She was a "good daughter," responsible and responsive to both parents. She increasingly acted as a maternal presence with her younger sibs, helped her ailing mother with household tasks, and was her "father's favorite," a wifely helper, acknowledged as such but without expressed pleasure and pride. She recognized early in the analysis that she was repeating those roles in her adult life, secretly hoping and fearing that she would be glorified and rewarded by her father's (or lover's) intimate blessings. Indeed, such fantasies were a major source of her guilty self-denial and punishments, both for the felt disloyalty to and competition with her mother and for her rage at not succeeding. There would have been no chance at "success" anyway. Although she might have been her father's favorite child, there was little chance to be close to him. There probably was a period early in the marriage and during her first couple of years when the family got along relatively well, but the tone began to change during her mother's third pregnancy. It was not entirely clear what actually happened,[3] but as best as we could reconstruct it (including Dr. B.'s conversations with maternal and paternal aunts) the birth of the third and subsequent children, financial stress, and disagreements between her father and her mother's family all put a strain on the marriage and each parent.

---

[3]It took a while for us both to realize that we could never know exactly what had happened, nor was it vital. The psychic reality was what most mattered.

Her father weas a cool, remote, unemotional, "stiff" man. He had shown interest in her academic and particularly scientific achievements, and they could talk about school courses. Sometimes he seemed quietly critical of her, as he was with her brothers. He also had some interest in sports but refused to acknowledge and encourage her achievements, although he did so in a limited way with her brothers. He seemed to expect her devoted assistance to her mother – indeed he lectured on the importance of the family and responsibility – but showed no open appreciation of her efforts. Dr. B. sensed that there had been an earlier "blissful" period in the family and with her father. Attributing the change for the worse to herself, she fantasied that it was she who somehow had driven her father away, had caused sadness and frailty in her mother, and was partially to blame when her mother miscarried. In parochial school she had learned about evil thoughts and "knew" the badness inside her. There was little joy, warmth, pleasure, sensuality, or emotional expression in this dutiful family, and no positive affirmation, at least from her father, of her femininity. She grew up feeling unattractive, lonely, loved but without passion or pleasure.

When she began to rebel in adolescence, her father suddenly became attentive to her beginning to date, acting as if she were up to no good, embarrassing her and her friends with his terse and unexplained restrictions. Her mother tried to intervene, to soften, to ameliorate the tensions, but she was already ill and more depressed. A maternal aunt and her husband provided much-needed solace, some opportunity for enjoyable, relaxed relationships with her cousins, and respect for her total person.

In the later part of the analysis, after Dr. B. had terminated the unhappy affair that had precipitated her initiating the work and had begun to make major advances in her career, begun to accept the sexual and aggressive parts of herself, and experience pleasure without self-punishment, she could begin to forgive and better understand her parents.

She had long been enraged at them both for their failings, their remoteness, their rigidities. Her father had helped spark her interest in science but had not helped her to love and be loved. Now she began to realize the nature and implications of her father's background on his paternal behavior. His childhood had been one of repeated losses and moves. His father, a remote and harsh man, was often away; his mother was an alcoholic whose state was always unpredictable. Her father had had few friendships and little pleasure as a child. Dr. B. speculated that he yearned for close relationships and a family of a sort he had not had. For a brief time it looked as if this were possible, but it was an intellectual and moral construction without sufficient emotional underpinnings. Quite possibly, the birth of the third child was a critical point. In contrast to her childhood fantasies, she had not caused the decline. That decline had come about for a variety of reasons, one of which was her father's increasing unmet neediness as her mother focused her energies on the children. Some men – and some women – should not have children, or at least not too many, she concluded. Her father had drifted back to his isolated state, unable to nurture, to attune, to grow. Try as she might, Dr. B. could not change that.

Silent Father, Silent Son

Billy L. was 8 years old and in the third grade when he was referred in the spring by his pediatrician and school because of partial elective mutism. He was willing to speak occasionally in school, but only in a whisper. He had been able to keep up academically, calling for considerable patience and innovation on the part of his teachers, but they were concerned that he would have difficulty the following year and were puzzled by the lack of change. The school and pediatrician had ascertained that Billy was of above-average intelligence and had no learning difficulties or neurological problems in the areas of language in general or speech in particular. He had a few close friends, seemed well liked, but rarely participated actively with his peers. He was, however, a keen observer, showing considerable interest in what went on but usually hanging back. Occasionally he exhibited a "strong stubborn streak," at times was slyly involved in minor mischief, and had a quick temper when things did not go his way. One teacher and the pediatrician thought he was sometimes depressed.

Billy's parents came only at the urging of the school and only when I insisted that I would not begin the evaluation until both could come together. Mr. L. had said taking time off work would be difficult. Once in my office, Mrs. L. volubly agreed with all that the school had said but seemed little troubled by Billy's lack of overt speech. She was more bothered by his stubbornness at home, his fighting with his sister, and his tantrums. Mr. L., sullen and quiet through much of the first parent session, did not think they or Billy needed to come to see me. He thought that Billy would grow out of it as he had; he had been a quiet child, too. I noticed that he smiled mysteriously when his wife described events at home with Billy that left her angry and frustrated. Was there an unspoken complicity, I wondered?

In the second session, when we reviewed more of the developmental history, the character of the marriage, and the backgrounds of each parent, several themes emerged. While the parents felt they had a pretty good marriage and obviously were fond of each other, Mrs. L. complained about her husband's lack of involvement in recent years with her and the children but particularly with Billy. She acknowledged that he had a very stressful job (at which he spent too much time) and could understand his interest in his hobby of "tinkering with" old cars, but protested that Mr. L. should somehow find a way to spend more time with the children and to be less moody. He in effect had disappeared from the family scene except for silently watching TV programs with Billy and enjoying his daughter's guitar playing. Earlier he had been more active with their daughter but all along had left most of the child rearing to her, claiming, as he did with me, that he knew little about kids and had not been around them much. He did, however, have some very useful observations to make about Billy; but to enable him to speak up I not only had to encourage his contributing, but point out as tactfully as possible to Mrs. L. that, while berating her husband for his remoteness, she hardly let him get a word in. It was clear from then on that even though the father's relative lack of participation and silence within the family was probably a key factor in Billy's "mutism," both parents contributed to the situation. It was also likely that enabling Mrs. L. to make space available for Mr. L. in that session, with an underlying respect for the roles and importance of both parents, was a crucial step in beginning to establish a working alliance with both.[4]

Billy was a likable child, small for his age, shy, overly polite, anxious yet curious about who I was, interested in but initially holding back from play and conversation. He spoke in a barely audible whisper but made strong drawings of cars and animals, especially whales that swallowed up everyone and everything in sight. He avoided any direct response to my explaining my understanding of what the problems were, but his comments were followed by lots of car crashing. Only a year or so later, during the termination phase of twice weekly therapy, were we able to discuss his "not talking" problem. Not talking at first was acceptable to both of us as he gradually, *very* gradually, said much by other means. Within six months his mutism had gone, but his holding back, inhibitions, and some underlying depression took another year.

It was not easy to keep both of the parents engaged and sup-

---

[4]The establishment of a working alliance with both parents is always important but not always easy. Looking at basic interactional patterns in the family stirs much resistance. I was lucky here probably because of the good enough bonds between the parents.

portive of Billy's therapy initially. I saw them about every six weeks, sometimes more frequently. Early in the treatment Mr. L. came reluctantly, was often late, and spoke very little. As he became more engaged, as Billy began to speak up more at home and less compliantly so, and as Mr. L. began to be more active and outspoken in the family, Mrs. L. began to question the value of the therapy and expressed discomfort with the changes that were occurring. Yet they both continued to work, especially motivated and moved after the postevaluation session when Mr. L. described his early great reluctance to have any children, his ambivalent willingness to give it a try first with Billy's sister, and his feelings of abandonment, anger, and depression during his wife's second pregnancy. His wife had seemed caught up with her pregnancies and mothering. She threw herself into taking care of the children and had little time for him. Life together was not the same as it had been before their first child was born. Indeed, nothing was the same. He had never liked disruptions of his sense of order. He had had such forbodings during that first pregnancy, was it any wonder that he had retreated to his hobbies and male friends? The parents seldom went out now, and there was not much fun. He felt like a money-making machine without other purpose. Whenever he disagreed with his wife's ways of handling the children and intervened, she either put him down or undermined his suggestions. He had tried to spend time with their daughter – she was cute and responsive – but he felt inept with her. Mrs. L. said she wanted him to help out more, but when he did she was critical of him. Mr. L. had simply given up, not being sure he wanted to change things or even if things should be changed. At times he felt excluded, useless, angry, and jealous, all of which he was ashamed of yet which were very familiar. He knew he should not blame his wife for everything, because his own experiences growing up were painfully present. Mrs. L., initially talkatively defensive in that session, sensed the depth of feeling and importance of what was happening. We both listened quietly to what Mr. L. had to say, never said in that way before.

We learned over the next several months about Mr. L.'s background. He was the youngest of three children. He speculated that by the time he came along whatever had drawn his parents together was long past. His mother was a dominating influence, emphasizing neatness, order, obedience ("children should be seen and not heard"), without warmth, flexibility, acceptance. His father and mother had fought a lot, in part because the father was away so much, working (he "had to" travel a lot) and "having a good time," which he later learned meant (among other activities labeled as misdeeds by his mother) womanizing. He and his father had only a distant relationship, in part because Mr. L. somehow felt it would be disloyal to his mother (and dangerous for him) to fraternize with his father. His father hardly paid attention to him and, when he did, was critical. He was not at all close to his brother and sister; he was a lonely and sad child, devoted to school and hobbies that did not include others. His father died of a heart attack when he was 14; thus he felt he had never gotten to know him nor, as we saw, to mourn adequately for him. He occasionally had thought that he would be a more attentive father, like an uncle of his, but the dismal atmosphere of his childhood home had left him feeling very pessimistic and apprehensive about establishing a happier family of his own. He felt insufficiently parented himself.

Over the course of the therapy, it became clear to the three of us that the backgrounds of both parents had contributed to Mr. L.'s flight from fatherhood. True, Mr. L. had pulled away, but Mrs. L., by her exclusive possession of the children, had also pushed him out. It took two to accomplish the skewing, in a complex set of interactions. For Mrs. L. – raised in a large family, the oldest daughter, early in life given major caretaking responsibility for her younger siblings, in frequent disagreement with and highly critical of her mother, idealizing her quiet but usually physically and psychologically absent father – to *really* pull her husband into and actively include him in the family orbit was a foreign notion. For Mr. L. being pulled in and included, wanting to be an active father – whatever the forms of its expression – was equally foreign; indeed, it was a potentially dangerous trap. He had much to complain about from both the past and present but had instead kept mum, unknowingly drawing Billy into his silent protest. When at last he had license to speak and had spoken enough to begin vital changes within himself and the family, that license could also be granted to Billy. For Billy and his father to speak, and for Mr. L. to become an active parent, Mrs. L. had to make room and give her own form of blessing.

DISCUSSION

It has taken a long time since Freud's focus on the oedipal role of the father for us to begin to look at paternal contributions in other phases of childrens' development.[5] Although our understanding is still partial and fragmentary, a great deal has been learned. We know much more

---

[5]Freud's contributions included more than a view of the oeidpal father. Preoedipal and postoedipal aspects also were touched on (e.g., Freud, 1909, 1917, 1925, 1933).

about the multiple roles that fathers play throughout the life cycle (Cath, Gurwitt, and Ross, 1982); paternal contributions to the psycho-pathology of families and children (the "darker side" of fatherhood; for example, Steele, 1982; Ross and Herzog, 1985); the evolution of paternal roots in boys (Ross, 1982a, b, c); primary caretaking and nurturing capacities in men (Pruett, 1987 and this volume); specific contributions to the preoedipal development of children (for example, Galenson and Roiphe, 1982; Tyson, 1982; Shopper, this volume); new insights into the oedipal phase (Ross, 1982c); the similar and differen-tial paternal responses to girls and boys (Lamb, 1981); and the great importance of the relationship between mother and father in coloring much of what transpires (Atkins, 1982; Muir, this volume). Many of the chapters in this volume contribute to the growing knowledge.

The more we learn about all of these phenomena, the more evident it is that becoming and being a father is a complex challenge. While it has long been clear that some men avoid it altogether and others can only partially meet the challenge, there has been little direct study of how and why this avoidance occurs. For purposes of this discussion, I am going to look at three areas: biological factors and social forces; psychological impediments to paternity, fatherhood and fatherliness from earlier individual development; and influences from current life, including the marriage. The three cases described earlier illustrate some of the factors to be discussed.

Biological Factors and Social Forces

The power of the biological phenomena that are at work in pregnant women and nursing mothers, accompanied by significant psycholog-ical shifts, is simply awesome both to the women and those around. With regard to pregnancy, included are all the reverberations of the presence of the fetus inside and the many bodily changes. Certainly men respond to what is happening inside and outside of their wives and the many actual or implied changes in their lives together that begin to unfold even in the pregnancy. Becoming a parent is a signifi-cant developmental phase, if not a crisis, for both men and women. Men undergo significant psychological changes, too, in part echoing their wives, in part independently (Gurwitt, 1976; Herzog, 1982b; Greenberg, 1985). There are frequently biological echoes as well (Tre-thowan and Conlon, 1965). But the total biological impact on women is unique. Whether it leads successfully to setting the stage for moth-erhood and motherliness depends on many other factors as well. Notman and Nadelson (1981) state: "The biological basis of pregnancy does not have to be seen as implying a clear and sufficient source of maternalism and nurturance, although it proves a basis for women to start the experience of nurturance earlier and more intimately than men" (p. 193).

In addition, for nursing mothers unique biological phenomena act to shape the character of the parent-child relationship. Although men can certainly provide a bottle and cuddle their infants too and there may be some overlapping similarities, the biology is simply different. The reader may suspect hopeless romanticizing, hiding regressive chauvinism here. Am I sanctifying mothers? Will something equivalent to biology is destiny follow? No, of course not. But one cannot analyze women who are pregnant, men whose wives become pregnant and later nurse, and children whose mothers are pregnant and give birth without observing both the unique power of it all and the significant psychological reverberations throughout the whole family.

Furthermore there are social forces, varying from society to society (though probably varying less than they do for men) that more or less establish expectations of behavior for women and men, including maternal and paternal roles. These are forces at work from the very beginning of life coloring the character of childhood even when there are androgynous influences. It only takes observation of the play of children in a nursery school or day care facility to see that, while there may be some overlap, boys and girls play differently, teachers respond differently. Indeed we know there are distinctive differences in the response of men and women to sons and daughters (Biller, 1981). Interweaving of biological and socialization factors begins at birth to distinguish gender and gender roles (Tyson, 1982).

It is hard to believe, then, that even in this age of dual-career parents, distinctively different parental *anlagen* do not exist or that girls and boys grow up with totally similar parental destinies. Both boys and girls identify with their *mothers,* with their mothers' nurturing and other parental ways, and womb or pregnancy envy can be detected in boys. But much of this is repressed in boys as they disidentify with their mothers or strive to do so (Greenson, 1968). It is not that they suddenly then turn to their fathers; if their fathers had been there for them and with them, psychologically and physically, then it is probable that the scales of relatedness to the parents would tip. The maternal imago may remain, in latent form, to be tapped, to be integrated with other parental roots when called upon. As described by Lansky (this volume), the maternal, paternal, and family imagos are not simply identifications with the one parent implied. Perhaps it is when the maternal cannot be positively integrated, and when that which was paternal is unacceptable, that problems arise.

Biological and social factors both influence the different character of preparedness for parenthood in women and men. Though men can be primary caretakers (see Pruett, this volume), with sharp distinctions between what is maternal and paternal diminishing and though one could probably describe some genderless characteristics that are indicative of good parenting, there *are* differences. Why is this of importance here? Men may flee from what may be specifically *maternal*, from what is *paternal*, or from what could more generally be considered as *parental*. Mr. M., the father of Dr. B., and Mr. L. were probably avoiding all three aspects.

PSYCHOLOGICAL IMPEDIMENTS TO FATHERHOOD

Two areas regarding fathers that were among the first to be described were the impact of father absence and the outbreak of serious pathology triggered by imminent or actual fatherhood (for a review of clinical reports, see Gurwitt, 1976, 1988; see also Osofsky, this volume). The findings in the literature indicate the importance of becoming a father as a precipitant of decompensating stress and symptoms and provide a base of psychological understanding of the issues involved. Though the literature goes back a long way, it seems often to have been ignored in the profession. Many of the key conflicts pinpointed can now be seen as normative issues confronted by men achieving parenthood. It is when the conflicts are not successfully dealt with that strains occur.

Two more recent studies look at flight from fatherhood. Simons (1984) wrote a fascinating study of the Norwegian sculptor Gustav Vigeland. Simons focuses on several related phenomena: the impact of parent loss in childhood on development, the role of mourning, and the relationship of both to creativity. Vigeland, like the fictional Charles Strickland in "The Moon and Sixpence," abandoned his wife and two children to pursue his art, the only form of generativity he could tolerate. Simons traces Vigeland's "dread of paternity," stemming from highly conflicted paternal identifications among other roots. Herzog (1986) addresses the theme of the reluctant father, from those who avoid paternity altogether to those who leave their wives because the burden of fatherhood is too great.

From all of the foregoing sources and from my own clinical work (including the three cases described) and publications, the following psychological issues appear to me to be common impediments to fatherhood. They are listed in the order of developmental stages:

1. A fear of loss of oral dependent and narcissistic supplies to which one feels entitled, translated into a fear of loss of the wife, can be accentuated by previous experiences of loss brought about by births of siblings. (See Mr. M. and Billy case illustrations.)

2. Feared resurgence of a sense of a fall from grace and a sense of despair, triggered by sibling birth, plus anger at the parents, especially the mother, for bringing this all about. Seen in all three cases.

3. Recurrence, though not necessarily in conscious form, of child-hood womb and pregnancy envy; these may be accompanied by oral, and anal sadistic birth fantasies. (See Nelson, 1972; Gurwitt, 1976; Simons, 1984).

4. A conviction of having been inadequately parented, by one or both parents. Parental deprivation, maternal, paternal, or both, is a key theme. *Maternal* deprivation is a widely known set of clinical phenomena. *Paternal* deprivation is not merely a theoretical construct but is very real, evidenced in children by "father thirst" (Abelin, 1971) or "father hunger" (Herzog, 1982a). Crucial kinds of deprivation can be seen in the case illustrations. Mr. M.'s father's remoteness and paternal style left Mr. M. both angry and yearning for a more caring paternal presence. For Dr. B., forms of both maternal and paternal deprivation occurred; perhaps the most crucial was her father's inability to be a loving, nurturing man who could appropriately affirm her femininity and capacity to love and be loved in a form similar to what Tessman (1982 and this volume) calls "erotic excitement." (He did help her with "endeavor excitement.") Billy's father and mother combined, uninten-tionally, to exclude the father in many ways and did so because of parental deprivations of their own. Indeed, *characteristic of this and other impediments to fatherhood are the multigenerational origins,* as seen in all the cited cases.

5. Inadequate or conflicted separation and individuation from the mother, resulting from a combination of an overly close and possessive maternal attachment without appropriate paternal counter-balance. All the well-known sequelae – mother experienced as phallic

and overwhelming, untitrated anger and dependency in relation to her, a sense of abandonment by the father – can occur.

6. Lack of a good preoedipal direct relationship with the father that enables so many of the preoedipal father-son identifications and father-daughter attachments to occur without oedipal strains, establishing a base that helps the parents and child to survive later oedipal stage events. (Seen in all three cases.)

7. Revival of primal scene fantasies especially when colored by strife between the man's parents (Zilboorg, 1931; Jarvis, 1962; Gurwitt, 1976).

8. Great discomfort with highly conflicted feminine-maternal identifications, particularly in relation to pregnancy and pregnancy fantasies (Zilboorg, 1931; Gurwitt, 1976; Simons, 1984).

9. Oedipal rivalry, fear, and guilt stirred up by impregnation and paternity, with the wife unconsciously experienced as the mother. Seen in Mr. M. This is a *major* contributing factor. It occurs with the very fact of considering or becoming a father and reflects the two-sided rivalry of fathers and sons to which each contributes from generation to generation (Ross, 1982c). A son represents another rival in the oedipal drama, often linked with the father's father. When this potential rivalry is excessive, the result is often a preference for daughters, as seen with Mr. M. and Mr. L.

10. Resurgence of negative oedipal, homosexual conflicts in relation to a son and father (i.e., the grandfather). (Seen in Mr. M.; see also Zilboorg, 1931; Gurwitt, 1976.)

11. Postoedipal physical or psychological absence of the father that further impedes identification with the father. (Mr. M., Billy and his father.)

Usually there is a combination of many or all of these issues. Whether particular combinations lead to particular sequelae along the continuum of total flight from paternity to partial psychological absences during the childhood stages of the offspring is yet to be shown. What is clear is that the process of becoming a father can threaten the whole self-regulating mechanisms of a man. It is also evident from clinical experience that later adult developmental phases, interacting with earlier unresolved conflicts, color the reactions of parents to developmental stages of their offspring (Colarusso and Nemiroff, 1981). One outcome can be paternal distancing. Furthermore, the gender of the child may trigger latent conflicts, as seen with Mr. M., and the number of children before the father feels overwhelmed as seen with the father of Dr. B. and Mr. L., are both critical factors.

CURRENT LIFE INFLUENCES

Particularly important here is the character of the husband-wife relationship prior to the first pregnancy, during the first and other pregnancies, and during the parenting years (Gurwitt and Muir, 1985). Normally there are ups and downs (see Lamb and Oppenheim; Osofsky, this volume; Culp, this volume) when the marital bonds are tested by the stresses of pregnancies and child rearing. There needs to be not only an "alliance of pregnancy" (Deutscher, 1981), but a parenting alliance that is intimately tied in with the marital alliance (Cohen and Weissman, 1984). It is a two-way interaction requiring each spouse/parent to be empathic, supportive, and facilitative of the growth of the co-parent as an adult and parent. The father-to-be or father needs to actively take over at times to spell his wife. (Many of the father's supportive responsibilities are described in Colman and Colman, 1971, and Greenberg, 1985). The mother-to-be and mother may have special tasks too. Therein lies a crucial story.

During and after the pregnancy, given the ambivalence and even degrees of reluctance of many men to become and be fathers, the willingness and capacity of the mother to foster her husband's involvement during the pregnancy and later child care is absolutely key. Many men readily weather the transition to fatherhood and need little extra boost to become close to and actively involved with their children. Nonetheless, no matter what the previously agreed upon arrangements for sharing of child-care, it is usually the mother, even in a dual-career family, who becomes the primary caretaker (see Lamb,this volume). In that role, the mother in effect takes on a gatekeeping function (Grossman, Fichler, and Winickoff, 1980); that is, she is the monitor, permission giver, and controller of who else is involved with the child and the form of that involvement. As Atkins (1982, 1984) has so vividly described, the mother can color the child's attitude toward the father as well as vitalize the father's latent parental capacities. It is clear that the vitalization of parental capacities can be bilateral. Here the infant is a key actor for both parents. Here we can surmise that the father's readiness and skills for active parenting and fathering may need the mother's catalyzing activity. (Perhaps other women can serve this role in the absence of the mother. We can recall here the roles of the landlady-neighbor and the store assistants in "Three Men and a Baby"). The father's background and the mixed messages of our society may not have made the father ready to jump in. The mother here, like Mrs. M. in the first case, needs to help the father "hook up." (Dr. B.'s mother tried without success; Mrs. L. was not able to try.) Greenberg (1985) devotes a specific chapter to helping mothers do just this, by drawing the fathers in, making psychological space available, and enabling fathers to spend time alone with their children.

Factors outside the family can be influential. Obstetrical and pediatric practices in the past did not encourage father involvement. If anything they often discouraged it, making fathers feel unwanted, unneeded, and inept. Birth preparation classes and changed obstetrical practices now do tend to involve fathers. On the other hand, there has been relatively little governmental and corporate support in this country for fulfilling parental responsibilities,and for both men and women those responsibilities are difficult to carry out. Joining forces as parents seems particularly vital.

CONCLUDING REMARKS

Flight from fatherhood has multiple forms, roots, and reverberations. There is a spectrum from complete avoidance of paternity to full or partial psychological absence or reluctance. External socioeconomic and historical factors play a role, but my emphasis has been on intrapsychic factors from earlier development, in combination with the character of the marital relationship, that together can impede achieving full fatherhood.

I do not mean to imply that a decision (or nondecision resulting in the same effect) not to have children is necessarily pathological. While we have tended to see generativity in terms of parenthood as a necessary step for adult development, a developmental phase (Benedek, 1959, 1970), questions have been raised about this assumption. For example, Notman and Nadelson (1981), looking at the phenomenon of voluntary childlessness in women, wonder if the seemingly inextricable ties between childbearing and femininity are indeed inseparable. Other forms of creativity can be important to a woman's self-esteem and self-definition. Men have probably had more leeway in the past in regard to voluntary childlessness.

Once having achieved paternity, not to mature in fathering capacities is another matter having implications for wife and family. These men often exhibit early warning signs, and appropriate intervention (Samaweera and Cath, 1982) can enable the parents together and the father in particular to make significant changes. Knowing more about minor and major impediments within men and within the family can enhance the effectiveness of intervention.

REFERENCES

Abelin, E. (1971), The role of the father in the separation-individuation process. In: *Separation-Individuation,* ed. J. B. McDevitt & C. F. Settlage. New York: International Universities Press, pp. 229–252.

Atkins, R. N. (1982), Discovering daddy: The mother's role. In: *Father and Child,* ed. S. H. Cath, A. Gurwitt & J. M. Ross. Boston: Little, Brown, pp. 139–149.

_____ (1984), Transitive vitalization and its impact on father representation. *Contemp. Psychoanal.,* 20:663–675.

Benedek, T. (1959), Parenthood as a developmental phase: A contribution to the libido theory. *J. Amer. Psychoanal. Assn.,* 7:389–417.

_____ (1970), Fatherhood and providing. In: *Parenthood,* ed. J. Anthony & T. Benedek. Boston: Little, Brown, pp. 167–183.

Biller, H. (1981), The father and sex role development. In: *The Role of the Father in Child Development,* 2nd ed., ed. M. E. Lamb. New York: Wiley, pp. 319–358.

Cath, S., Gurwitt, A. & Ross, J. M. ed. (1982), *Father and Child.* Boston: Little, Brown.

Cohen, R. & Weissman, S. (1984), The parenting alliance. In: *Parenthood,* ed. R. Cohen, B. Cohler & S. Weissman. New York: Guilford, pp. 33–49.

Colarusso, C. & Nemiroff, R. (1981), *Adult Development.* New York: Plenum Press.

Colman, A. & Colman, L. (1971), *Pregnancy.* New York: Herder & Herder.

Deutscher, M. (1981), Identity transformations in the course of expectant fatherhood. *Contemp. Psychoanal.,* 17:158–171.

Freud, S. (1909), Analysis of a phobia in a five-year-old boy. *Standard Edition,* 10:3–149. London: Hogarth Press, 1955.

_____ (1917), On transformations of instinct as exemplified in anal eroticism. *Standard Edition,* 17:125–134. London: Hogarth Press, 1955.

_____ (1925), Some psychical consequences of the anatomical distinction between the sexes. *Standard Edition,* 19:243-260. London: Hogarth Press, 1961.

_____ (1933), New introductory lectures on psycho-analysis. *Standard Edition,* 22:3-182. London: Hogarth Press, 1964.

Galenson, E. & Roiphe, H. (1982), The preoedipal relationship of a father, mother and daughter. In: *Father and Child,* ed. S. H. Cath, A. Gurwitt & J. M. Ross. Boston: Little, Brown, pp. 151-162.

Greenberg, M. (1985), *The Birth of a Father.* New York: Continuum.

_____ Morris, N. (1982), Engrossment: The newborn's impact upon the father. In: *Father and Child,* ed. S. H. Cath, A. Gurwitt & J. M. Ross. Boston: Little, Brown, pp. 87-99.

Greenson, R. R. (1968), Disidentifying from mother: Its special importance for the boy. *Internat. J. Psycho-Anal.,* 49:370-374.

Grossman, F., Fichler, L. & Winickoff, S. (1980), Myths of parenthood reconsidered. In: *Pregnancy, Birth and Parenthood,* ed. F. Grossman, L. Fichler & S. Winickoff. San Francisco: Jossey Bass, pp. 244-255.

Gurwitt, A. R. (1976), Aspects of perspective fatherhood: A case report. *The Psychoanalytic Study of the Child,* 31:237-272. New Haven: Yale University Press.

_____ (1988), On becoming a family man. *Psychoanal. Inq.,* 8:261-279.

_____ Muir, R. C. (1985), Family development. In: *Psychiatry,* Vol. 2, ed. R. Michels & J. Cavenar. Philadelphia: Lippincott, pp. 1-12.

Herzog, J. (1982a), On father hunger: The father's role in the modulation of aggressive drives and fantasy. In: *Father and Child,* ed. S. H. Cath, A. Gurwitt & J. M. Ross. Boston: Little, Brown, pp. 163-174.

_____ (1982b), Patterns of expectant fatherhood: A study of the fathers of a group of premature infants. In: *Father and Child,* ed. S. H. Cath, A. Gurwitt & J. M. Ross. Boston: Little, Brown, pp. 301-314.

_____ (1986), The reluctant father. *Nurturing News,* 2:10-11.

Jarvis, W. (1962), Some effects of pregnancy and childbirth on men. *J. Amer. Psychoanal. Assn.,* 10:689-700.

Kahn, C. (1981), *Man's Estate.* Berkeley: University of California Press.

Lamb, M. (1981) ed., *The Role of the Father in Child Development.* 2nd ed. New York: Wiley.

Maugham, W. S. (1919), *The Moon and Sixpence.* New York: Modern Library.

Nelson, J. (1972), Anlage of productiveness in boys: Womb envy. In: *Child Psychopathology,* ed. S. Harrison & J. McDermott. New York: International Universities Press, pp. 360-372.

Notman, M. T. & Nadelson, C. C. (1981), Changing views of femininity and childbearing. *Hillside J. Clin. Psychiat.,* 3:187–202.

Pruett, K. (1987), *The Nurturing Father.* New York: Warner.

Ross, J. M. (1982a), The roots of fatherhood: Excursions into a lost literature. In: *Father and Child,* ed. S. H. Cath, A. Gurwitt & J. M. Ross. Boston: Little, Brown, pp. 3–20.

_____ (1982b), From mother to father: The boy's search for a generative identity and the oeidpal era. In: *Father and Child,* ed. S. H. Cath, A. Gurwitt & J. M. Ross. Boston: Little, Brown, pp. 189–203.

_____ (1982c), Oedipus revisited: Laius and the "Laius Complex." *The Psychoanalytic Study of the Child,* 37:169–200. New Haven: Yale University Press.

_____ Herzog, J. M. (1985), The sins of the father: Notes on fathers, aggression, and pathogenesis. In: *Parental Influences,* ed. E. J. Anthony & G. Pollock. Boston: Little, Brown, pp. 477–510.

Samaraweera, S. & Cath, C. (1982), Fostering the consolidation of paternal identity: The Tufts Family Support Program. In: *Father and Child,* ed. S. H. Cath, A. Gurwitt & J. M. Ross. Boston: Little, brown, pp. 543–555.

Simons, R. (1984), Creativity, mourning, and the dread of paternity: Reflections on the life and art of Gustav Vigeland. *Internat. Rev. Psycho-Anal.,* 11:181–198.

Steele, B. F. (1982), Abusive fathers. In: *Father and Child,* ed. S. Cath, A. Gurwitt & J. M. Ross. Boston: Little, Brown, pp. 481–490.

Tessman, L. H. (1982), A note on the father's contribution to the daughter's ways of loving and working. In: *Father and Child,* ed. S. H. Cath, A. Gurwitt & J. M. Ross. Boston: Little, Brown, pp. 219–238.

Trethowan, W. H. & Conlon, M. F. (1965), The couvade syndrome. *Brit. J. Psychiat.,* 111:57–66.

Tyson, P. (1982), The role of the father in gender identity, emotion, and phallic narcissism. In: *Father and Child,* ed. S. H. Cath, A. Gurwitt & J. M. Ross. Boston: Little, Brown, pp. 175–187.

Zilboorg, G. (1931), Depressive reactions related to parenthood. *Amer. J. Psychiat.,* 10:927–962.

III

FATHER-DAUGHTER
RELATIONSHIPS

Prelude

The papers in this section highlight the importance of the father's role in the girl's sense of self and in her feminine identity. It may be disturbing that the papers also highlight the sizable contribution of the father's unconscious and its influence on the directions the daughter's life takes, both positively and negatively. For example, Pacella's patient Madelyn was for her father a projection of his hated sister (Ross, this volume). Balsam's cases illustrate the intense pact between father and daughter that the daughter not be anything like the disturbed and denigrated mother. And then there is the power of the daughter's unconscious when she overtly becomes the father's selfobject but covertly loves the mother. This is the reverse of the scenario proposed by McDougall (1980) in her male perverse patients, who have a pact with mother to denigrate father but who secretly love the father. There are serious implications for both of these deviations in the oedipal scenario, since the child, whether boy or girl, believes he or she is an oedipal victor; and the father or mother, whoever is denigrated, is forced to witness the romantic love between the child and the more powerful parent.

It is clear from these papers that normal psychic development cannot occur until the child, adolescent, or adult female can establish adequate ties with each parent and acknowledge the marital bond between the two parents. Triangulation, both emotionally and cognitively, is essential to one's psychic identity.

One important issue for feminine development is whether the daughter is experienced by the father as the preferred child. Some fathers prefer daughters, but most have a preference for sons. Williamson (1976) states that cross-culturally men, more than their spouses, have strong preferences for sons. However, women also would like the first-born to be a boy, and, asked about their preference for more boys or more girls in their family, they also want more boys. There are only five societies that are considered daughter-preferring societies: the Mundugumor of New Guinea, the Tiwi of North Australia, the Garo of Assam, the Iscobakebu of Peru, and the Tolowa Indians of Northwest California. This preference – or lack of it – is bound to have an impact on daughters, especially those first born (Forrest, 1966).

Tessman's paper is an opportunity to follow in adult women the vicissitudes of her two concepts, endeavor excitement and erotic excitement, developed in her 1982 paper. Her emphasis on the father's role in endeavor and erotic excitement is an important psychoanalytic contribution. She has outlined endeavor excitement, which occurs in the second year of life, as the girl's interest in autonomy and exhuberance in her work and projects. She has outlined erotic excitement, which occurs in the third and fourth year, as an important basis for the expression of "passion in love." She sees the father as having a role as both the exciter and the model in the transformation of both kinds of excitement. The father enjoys projects with his daughter, gives her the sense that her accomplishments are valuable and that she is truly capable. The father receives his daughter's love, including its erotic component, by affirming her femininity and her expression of love toward him. Several important questions can be raised, however. First, is the father reactive to the daughter's excitement in these two areas? Tessman says he is the object of his daughter's excitement, implying that the agent is the daughter. Does the father contribute to his daughter's getting excited, and how does he do this? Or is his contribution an interaction between both, being the exciter and the object of his daughter's excitement? In Pacellas' and Balsam's cases, the fathers seem not to have been active in the promotion, encouragement, and response to their daughters' endeavors and erotic excitement in their evolution. Rather, they responded to both kinds of excitement only in puberty or adolescence. This paternal failure – that is, that the father did not contribute at a crucial developmental juncture – may be a crucial factor in the daughter's psychopathology. Second, because of Tessman's conscious efforts to focus on the father's role in endeavor and erotic excitement, she does not elaborate on the mother's contribution. Here the work of Biller and Weiss (1970) and Rees (1987) are important to consider.

Biller and Weiss point out that girls who develop masculine identifications and orientations very often do so as a result of not having mothers who are available to support the daughter's feminine identification. Balsam speaks to this issue, discussing the mother as dysfunctional and therefore as abandoning her daughter in many ways but particularly in terms of feminine development. Another arena for faulty feminine identifications is where the relationship between the father and the mother is suffering. Here, more specifically, a father may hold a very negative opinion of women (Balsam, this volume; Forrest, 1966; Levenson, 1986). In order to support the daughter's feminine identification, the father really needs, whenever possible, to respect the mother's feminine identity and to give the daughter the message that he would like his daughter to be like his wife. If that is not possible, for example, because of the mother's pathology, he needs to transmit a respect for a feminine identity that he can support. This is not the case with the fathers of Balsam's patients.

Fathers may unwittingly actually reinforce masculine identifications because of their own unconscious needs. However, in a more positive sense, as Biller and Weiss (1970) point out, the father, being different or contrasting in sexual identity with the daughter's feminine identity, can help in a very significant way to differentiate for the daughter between feminine and masculine modes. That is, a daughter can learn a great deal about femininity by contrasting herself with the masculine father. Biller and Weiss point out, however, that the father has to be able to support the daughter's relational nexus, her desire to care about others, her striving to be attractive, and her desire to communicate feelings. Furthermore, the daughter can identify with the father by taking in some of the father's values and attitudes, which do not necessarily interfere with her femininity even though they are embodied in a masculine father.

Rees (1987) alerts us to the fact that daughters turn more to their fathers as primary identification figures when the appropriate identification figure, mother, is not available because of illness. Masculine identifications can derive from an inability to identify with mother or other competent mothering figures, which was the case with Balsam's patients. Once the feminine identification with mother is secure, then the girl child can selectively identify with aspects of the father without adopting a masculine identification.

Mothers also foster endeavor and erotic excitement. Perhaps they are the motivators and even the first objects of these developmental achievements. The fathers may then react to these strivings in the daughter as autonomy and feminine identity issues come together. Ross suggests the latter in his discussion of Pacella's paper. This idea also supports a conviction of mine (Gunsberg, 1986) that the child gains a strong sense of self through his or her relationship with a mother who assimilates to the child and that the father, in general, places more of a demand on his child to be like him, to have similar interests to his, as evidenced in Tessman's and Balsam's chapters. Finally, as is always the case, we end up realizing that both the mother and the father contribute to all developmental achievements.

I find the issue of sex of therapist essential in the presentations by both Pacella and Balsam. Pacella tends to underplay this issue, while Balsam seems to recognize its importance in a fuller way. Let us look first at Pacella's case of Madelyn. The success of this case is due to many factors. First, Madelyn responded beautifully to the corrective emotional experience (as distinguished from transference) of having a paternal figure respond to her with respect and great interest. Second, the father was in his own treatment at the same time as Madelyn's therapy. There he began to understand how he had displaced onto his relationship with Madelyn his hostility toward his wife for being so enmeshed with Madelyn and therefore being unable to pay attention to her husband. Third, the father was often seen in parent meetings alone with Madelyn's male therapist. These meetings may have fostered a dyadic father-daughter relationship, with the therapist's approval, and, furthermore, the daughter's male therapist may have provided her father with a good fathering experience for himself. The daughter's therapist affirmed her need for her father, and the therapist was able to help the father see Madelyn as she really was, to be differentiated from his own hated sister.

Balsam makes an interesting and very valuable contribution in offering us the concept of "androgenous transference." She states that both fathers and daughters, in seeking treatment, shared as a primary treatment goal for the daughters that they not be anything like their mother. Balsam's patients had psychologically ill mothers who were housewives. Balsam was selected as therapist because she was different from the mothers—she worked and was not ill; she was as competent as a man. Yet, simultaneously and secretly, these girls yearned for a woman who could eventually help them acknowledge their love, albeit ambivalent, for their mothers. This was a secret treatment goal these daughters adequately disguised from their fathers.

The fathers were for these girls idealized saviors. My hunch is that one aspect of treatment success, although not discussed by Balsam, besides the girls' ability to move toward a feminine identification, was to come to terms with the psychopathology in their fathers as well. First, the fathers denigrated their wives and declared that they would, in no uncertain terms, have nothing to do with a daughter who was anything like her mother. Second, father saw himself as the "only parent," yet he was absent in significant ways in early years. Third, these fathers demanded that their daughters either be like them or become the kind of women they admired. In fact, each girl had been identified early on by the father as having a resemblance to him. This implies that another daughter may not have received this special treatment if she was not seen by father as "like him."

Androgeny may, therefore, be seen, as Balsam suggests, as a defense against fully accepting one's femininity. Another possible way of understanding the androgenous transference is that it serves as an interim way of holding on to both parents.

Certainly, development never stops. The women in Tessman's study and Balsam's female patients make us aware of the kinds of shifts that occur in relationships with parents when a girl becomes a spouse and mother herself. Very often, these developmental steps add new dimensions to her feminine identity, and, it is to be hoped, closer and more complex relationships with her mother and father can evolve. Here is another opportunity for denigration of one's parent to be turned into respect for one's parent. As we can see, this is also a central theme between sons and their fathers (Strozier and Cath, this volume).

Linda Gunsberg

REFERENCES

Biller, H. & Weiss, E. (1970), The father-daughter relationship and the personality development of the female. *J. Genet. Psychol.,* 116:79–93.

Forrest, T. (1966), Paternal roots of female character development. *Contemp. Psychoanal.,* 3:21–38.

Gunsberg, L. (1986), Father's accommodative style and mother's assimilative style: Implications for the daughter's identification processes and object relations. Presented at meeting of American Psychological Association, Washington, DC, August.

Levenson, R. (1986), Loyal ghosts: An exploration of women's difficulty in thinking. Presented at midwinter meeting of American Psychological Association.

McDougall, J. (1980), *Plea for a Measure of Abnormality.* New York: International Universities Press.

Rees, K. (1987), "I want to be a daddy!": Meanings of masculine identifications in girls. *Psychoanal. Quart.,* 56:497–522.

Tessman, L. (1982), A note on the father's contribution to the daughter's ways of loving and working. In: *Father and Child,* ed. S. Cath, A. Gurwitt & J. Ross. Boston: Little, Brown, pp. 219–238.

Williamson, N. (1976), *Sons or Daughters,* Monogr. 31. Newbury Park, CA: Sage Library of Social Research.

10
Fathers and Daughters
Early Tones, Later Echoes
Lora Heims Tessman

I love your majesty according to my bond
Nor more, nor less.....
Haply, when I shall wed,
That lord whose hand must take my plight
Shall carry half my love
With him.......

–Cordelia to King Lear, her father

Cordelia's love of her father survived his rejecting and banishing her at the height of his late life crisis in ambition. At the point of relinquishing his throne, he asked his three daughters to describe how much they loved him. Ruling his daughters' hearts had to supplant ruling the country; perhaps ruling the country had at one time symbolized ruling the mother. When his youngest, Cordelia, implied that true love of father also prepared a girl for love of a mate, Lear's rage blinded him to her devotion. Alienating himself from love, as well as his own loving-ness, Lear became vulnerable to his other daughters' false flattery,

An earlier version of this chapter was presented at the meetings of the American Psychoanalytic Association, New York, Dec. 1984.

which led him to his tragic fate. But Cordelia had been favored in her early years: she remained true to the tenderness between them, embracing her father with forgiveness in his madness (as he had embraced her in her childishness) and ready to share his exile. Were these the permanent echoes of early affective tones?

This chapter focuses on two questions about the father-daughter relationship. First, how does the father affect the formation of the daughter's ways of loving and working? Second, how are transformations during adult development colored by the early affective tones she experienced with him? The empirical material utilized to explore these questions consists of research interviews designed to elicit life narratives from adult women who were former students at the Massachusetts Institute of Technology.

Affective tones between fathers and daughters, and their developmental consequences for the daughter, have been one focus of my interest in trying to understand patterns of loving, playing and working in girls and women, as they appeared in my clinical practice. More recently, while I was doing research interviews with a nonclinical population of men and women about their life course up to age 30 and 40, hunches derived from clinical work generated further questions in my mind, especially about the later echoes of early patterns.

Before describing the research material, allow me to revisit the earlier premises (Tessman, 1982): The quality of emotional engagement between father and daughter frequently remains as a powerful undercurrent giving direction to that particular vision of *happiness* which may become one guiding force in a woman's life and affects her perception of the value or futility of her own efforts in striving toward it. Emotional engagement is, of course, complex: it continually changes and occurs at many levels of consciousness, involving perception, fantasy, and overt interaction. The daughter responds to her perception of the father's attitudes and feelings about a complex of changing strivings within her. Some of the strivings are 'gender linked' and some are not at all (p. 220). It seems that "the confluence of two kinds of excitement is directed toward the father, when he is available, during the time when individuation from the mother is proceeding (more or less successfully) with some momentum. These two kinds of excitement can be termed *endeavor excitement,* which begins during the second year of life and is eventually associated with autonomy, and *erotic excitement,* evident in the third and fourth year of life and gathering intensity throughout the oedipal period. These are the forerunners of later energies invested in work and love" (p. 221).

The transformation of endeavor excitement into later vitality in work optimally requires from the father something different from the transformation of erotic excitement into later passion in love. His view that her capabilities may not be gender linked strengthens her in the former, whereas an appreciation of her femininity, including an acceptance of her *emotionality in loving him,* affects the latter.

There are many connections between the two. For example, the wish to give herself erotically to a man can be expressed to some extent in an aim-inhibited and acceptable way if she is able to contribute positively to his or to their mutual endeavors. But, conversely, if he praises her skills but keeps himself greatly distant, her achievements may feel barren to her, as though the essence of herself has been rejected. In later life, she, in turn, may need to disentangle these two types of satisfactions sufficiently in order to value appropriately her autonomous endeavors" (p. 227). Father does appear to have a pivotal, but different, role in regard to both endeavor excitement and erotic excitement. His contribution revolves around his simultaneous role as object of her excitement and model for its transformation. If the daughter internalizes the ego capacity for transforming excitement in a way that is not only tolerable (e.g., becoming capable of delaying impulse discharge without turning against the impulse), but also pleasurable in affective tone with her father, then her knowledge of that potential happiness may remain as a bedrock of hope.

AN INTRODUCTORY EXCERPT: SHELLEY

Fragments of the father-daughter relationship recalled by Shelley will anchor my remarks. She is a vivacious, married urban planner, age 30.

> Once when I was little, I remember asking my father why *he* never won the Nobel Prize and his answer was "because I wanted to have dinner with you every night." I mean, he was a scientist who cavorts with scientists, some of whom have won the Nobel Prize. So it's not out of the question that he might have done – and his answer was that he had spent time with us.
>
> "What did that mean to you?" I ask.
>
> It must have struck me because I remember it and sort of think about my life that way – It was a very serious answer. Both my parents took their role as parents and as each other's friend very seriously. And that same issue has arisen for me.

She struggles over how far to carry her career ambitions.

To be at the top of my field, one has to make great leaps forward by committing enormous energy to one thing without stopping – and the way I see it now, I don't expect to be that person that people come to ask some earth-shattering decisions of.

Yet, as she describes her work, her enthusiasm for problem solving in her field and her attunement to its social ethical implications are clear.

Shelley explains how "my father spending time with us" echoes in her own life:

I feel that a relationship with another adult – you can put on hold for awhile – but still something important gets lost – when I'm very busy at work and we have house guests – which we do a lot – and I can't spend the time with people at home because I'm needed here, then I really hate that. I feel that what I'm giving up by not being with them is very important – and I'm only willing to forfeit that to a certain extent. You know, nobody at M.I.T. ever sat down with you and said: "These are the kinds of trade-offs you might have to make beforehand" – [she laughs] or maybe they say it and you don't hear it because you don't really know what it means until you come to that point in life where it arises as your own choice. You are in a different stage of life when you make that enormous commitment, to all the hours of work in school, and plan a career on the basis of *that*.

She views her career choice as combining her skills with what had been valued in the family: "Putting things together is what I'm really good at, combining different pieces into a whole concept, I think, is what planning is all about." Urban planning involves an integration of perception of physical structure (father's interest) and social structure with its consequences for people (beginning in adolescent idealism). There were childhood forerunners in physical and mental construction and in exploration of the world at large with father. These included constructing "a memorable tree house" (not urban, but suburban, planning!); a favorite geography quiz with father, accompanying her father alone to a meeting in Europe at age 11. "I come from a family that does lots of things, pays attention to the world, and really gets involved."

During her adolescence, Shelley's parents balanced being supportive with not being too intrusive. Rather than being restrictive, they conveyed trust in her judgment. She recalled:

They really never asked too many questions. I mean, they wouldn't have been too pleased if we had gotten involved with doing drugs too–but I guess they figured even then it would just sort of work itself out. I remember one big anti-war demonstration, November, 1969–there were about ten people staying at our house, and my parents just drove all of us downtown, dropping us off to go demonstrate. I mean, they were sympathetic and yet figured some of it was my own business.

Shelley's first love, when she was 17, was a 23-year-old graduate student, whom she described as "very intellectual, *wonderful* to talk with about everything!" Father liked him "because what my father *doesn't* want is to have somebody bring somebody home who sits at the dinner table and can't converse. It's okay to disagree with him, but you've got to talk!" The man she married is less like father, held less in awe, but no less appropriate for her. A dialogue with room for tenderness as well as argument is an essential dimension in Shelley's intimate relationships.

Three aspects of Shelley's story are a preview of the father-daughter relationships to be discussed. First, not only did Shelley's ego ideal involve father as a model for her enthusiasm in the pursuit of ideas, but she also admired the high priority he gave to connections to others. The echo in her own life was that she did not have to be a "superwoman" career-wise, though she had some nostalgic regret for giving up adolescent dreams of greatness. The importance of relationships, for example, being available to friends, was connected both to pleasure and to integrity about values that were reflected in her work. Second, father not only encouraged her curiosity and enthusiasm about developing skills by actively involving himself with them when she was little, but also was able to trust her autonomous judgment as she became more adolescent, allowing her to move out of the role of his "little girl." Third, the enjoyment of father occurred in the context of a sound and supportive relationship with her mother and an example of a lively engagement between her parents ("being each other's friend," as she put it).

In turn, aspects of a strong identification with each parent cohabit comfortably in Shelley. Like Cordelia, she prepared to have her lover "carry half my love with him" and chose someone who, like father, moved her with wonderful conversations. In young adulthood she attempted to recreate a balance between excitement in the pursuit of her career intentions and commitment in her personal relationships. She internalized this process from interaction with her father ("I remember it and I sort of think of my life that way"). In the research, she was scored as being high in "Intentionality."

THE RESEARCH PROJECT

The study of the life narratives of former women students at M.I.T. was a companion piece to the study of male students begun earlier.[1] In 1961, Dr. Benson Snyder launched a longitudinal study of the M.I.T. class of 1965 by interviewing a 5% sample (55) of students at yearly intervals during their undergraduate days. Between 1981 and 1984 a follow-up study was conducted of these men. In addition all the women of the 1965 class (26 women, who comprised just 2½% of the M.I.T. population then), as well as 5% of the men and women of the class of 1975 (women then were 10% of the population and are now over 33%). When interviewed, the men and women were just over 30 or 40 years old and had pursued a variety of paths from their original concentrations in math, science, or technologic fields. A larger proportion of women of 1965 chose majors in math and science (92%) than any of the other three samples. I interviewed the total sample of women of 1965, while four of us shared the interviewing of the class of 1975. The interviews were open ended and taped and ranged from between 1½ to 8 hours. They yielded surprisingly richly textured, meaningful material. Nonetheless, generalizations from this sample should be limited by at least two factors: (1) the distinctive characteristics of the sample and (2) the likelihood that access to unconscious meanings is far more limited in research interviews than it would be in its emergence over time in a psychoanalytic or psychotherapy process. The research posed questions about a range of phenomena having to do with the interaction between these men's and women's life course, the qualities in their sense of self, and the series of social contexts, from family, to school, to M.I.T., to their chosen field of work – each with its own agenda, value system, metaphors in models of problem solving, or demands – within which they have functioned.

The interaction between "intentionality" and the person's interpretation of what the social context wanted of him or her often became a central thread. Intentionality was defined as the tendency to direct one's energies toward a goal which has evolved from inner motivation, rather than primarily as a reaction to the wishes and demands of others. Its components include (1) making an inner choice or plan; (2) actively participating in trying to implement it; (3) being able to resist wishes

[1]The Study of "Career and Adult Development in Graduates of Technical Education" was made possible by Ford Foundation Grant #8100914A. I wish to thank Dr. Snyder, Principal Investigator, and to express my pleasure in his particular spirit of discovery, which enriched the study as well as our collaboration.

and expectations of others *when they are against one's better judgment.*
Intentionality is cousin to Kohut's (1971) "sense of the self as center of
initiative," but in the research was judged on the basis of more behavioral manifestations. Intentionality may be directed either toward
interpersonal goals or toward endeavors in the field of work, but
involves the capacity to experience and transform excitement into
vitality of involvement. Acknowledging rather than projecting responsibility for one's aims is a concomitant ego mode. Preliminary to data
analysis, the women's interviews were sorted into 21 different dimensions of content. "Description of father and relationship to father" was
one. For purposes of this chapter, this category *only* is singled out for
discussion. Preliminary findings in regard to mother–daughter patterns
in this group have been described elsewhere (Tessman, 1986).

Both mother and father become objects for love and identification
in childhood. As introjects, they people the inner dramas that underlie
the motivating life themes for the person. However, at different
periods of life the inner images of mother and father speak from
shifting positions and relative dominances. Such steps in the dance of
the introjects affect one's sense of contact with maternal or paternal
images during adult development, shaping one aspect of the inner
experience of one's identity. I will focus here on two different time
periods, referred to broadly as the "formative years" and as the period
of "transformations" during adult development.

RESULTS RELATIVE TO THE FORMATIVE YEARS

The first question has to do with the impact of the father on the
formation of the daughter's character: Can one discern patterns of
father-daughter interaction, within this sample, correlated with different functioning in the daughters? To approach this question, women's representations of the father-daughter interaction were scored
for the presence or absence of 20 categories referring to daughter's
descriptions of father as she grew up. Each category was operationally
defined, with examples of behavioral manifestations.[2] The result was
a cluster of categories that significantly differentiated the 25% of the
women who had been judged to be highest in "intentionality" from the
25% who were lowest in this quality. Intentionality, in turn, turned

---

[2]The scoring manual of operational definitions is available on request.

out to be closely and positively connected to the woman's sense of involvement and potential effectiveness in her role in life by age 40.

The data reveal a very significant association between high intentionality and a cluster of eight characteristics attributed by the daughter to the father and her early interaction with him. To summarize them briefly: the correlating categories revolve around the father's own self-image as expressive in initiative, an image transmitted through his active involvement with her. Daughter perceives father as attempting to steer his life in directions he finds interesting and rewarding; as innovative; as showing excitement or enthusiasm about either learning per se or specific areas of mastery such as prowess in mechanical competence; as not shying away from the untried or risk-taking thought or action when appropriate. In relation to the daughter, he is described as encouraging or stimulating her curiosity, exploration, or independent judgment; as involving her in joint endeavors with him; as showing trust in her growing capacities; and, finally, as enjoying a playful attitude or being playful with the daughter. The last category of playfulness was more variable than the other seven, seeming rarer in working class families. Exceptions to this overall pattern occurred when identification with father, not fueled by love, led to different developments than those modeled on the positive object relationship.

Low intentionality was correlated with a different cluster, of categories, of which several, but not all, were apt to be present. Father was pictured as either basically uninvolved and uninterested in daughter or as showing pride in her academic achievements, but not involved and participating in what she is enthusiastic about (so that getting A's was more valued than the learning process). Other variables included being restrictive or overprotective; discouraging or fearful about curiosity and exploration; actively disparaging daughter's interests or daughter herself, e.g., calling her "that ugly gawk"; highly punitive or competitive with her; restrictive about her aspirations on the basis of gender; passive and dependent, unable to intervene significantly in the mother-daughter interaction; fearful about jeopardizing security or asserting himself when appropriate. For these women, autonomy tended to remain in limbo, though the libidinal bond to father, especially if it was as his little girl, could persist.

Other characteristics, for example, whether father was described as introverted and ideational, versus sociable and expressive did not correlate with either high or low intentionality.

One implication of the apparent importance of the father's response to the daughter's assertive wish to explore, master, or construct (the content of endeavor excitement) may be this: assertive activity, from toddlerhood on, may be reacted to by the parent as though it were aggressive hostility, evoking a controlling, threatened, or angry reaction (Stechler, 1982). This can result in inhibition or negative self-evaluation about assertiveness, particularly in girls. The highly intentional women were often described, from early childhood on, as particularly curious, or headstrong about pursuing their interests. Thus, father's welcoming this quality and creating a companionship around it may have been particularly salient for the daughter's capacity to sustain and value it in herself.

TRANSFORMATIONS DURING ADULT DEVELOPMENT

> since feeling is first
> who pays any attention
> to the syntax of things
> will never wholly kiss you.
>
> — e.e. cummings

Transformations during the women's adult development are notable in the women's ego ideal, as well as in their actual relationships to their fathers. Changes in ego ideal for many of the women involved a new level of integration of affect, as well as a reintegration of identifications associated with mother. These changes tended to occur during the late 20s and early 30s.

Because the ego ideal remains more closely connected to desire than to prohibition (which characterizes the superego), and because desire becomes a central component of the little girl's wishes toward the father, she seems particularly prone to involve him in her ego ideal, even when her major identification is with the mother. Sex differences in ego ideal have been widely noted. Deutsch (1946) and Jacobson (1954) stated some decades ago that the female ego ideal is more enmeshed in her object relations than is the male's. More recently, Gilligan (1982), Miller (1973), Notman and colleagues (1986), and others have elaborated and deepened the thinking about gender differences in values and the associated models of morality. A woman's greater average concern with her relational nexus – that is, the great value she places on caring between people – is often central to her ego ideal and may conflict with what she perceives as dominant male values, especially in the workplace. Whether identification with an ego ideal involving the father is less a source of conflict for the woman who admires her father's qualities in relating to others as well as his work effectiveness than for the woman who does not is a question still unanswered.

Ego ideal development and its association with gender was a particularly piquant issue for the M.I.T. women of 1965. Pioneering as a 2½% minority, they entered a male culture that was highly skeptical about women's abilities, ambivalent about their accomplishments, and dedicated to problem solving by means of depersonalized principle and technologies. For most of these women, the choice of M.I.T. in itself represented their commitment to math and science and the concomitant high value they placed on the explanatory power of rationally derived abstraction, trusting rationalistic rather than intuitive ways of knowing. Their cognitive preferences, as well as their extremely high SAT math scores, placed them at a rarefied end of the continuum of qualities usually displayed by women, especially in the era of 1965. Many of the women felt that M.I.T. further put a premium on independence; by shunning signs of vulnerability and the softer affects one risks in intimacies.

It seems all the more striking, then, that for the majority of women definite shifts in ego ideal and associated life choices were prominant in their 20s and 30s. The women mused, with either puzzlement or glad conviction, about the changes in their cognitive approach. For example, the elegant economy of mathematical solution, while still exciting, was no longer sufficiently satisfying and seemed too far removed from connections to the real world, or what they now felt life is all about. It no longer reflected their inner sense of reality, a reality enriched during adult development. They described the change in a variety of ways: "The power of solving the puzzle paled beside the pull toward people I loved," said one woman. "The growth of humaneness in myself has softened my search for the absolute," said another. A third pondered, "Having less need to feel I can bring order to the chaos of the universe by understanding it through the laws of physics." A fourth talked of adult change as "giving up illusions of grandeur so that I can enjoy what really is." She regretted that her husband "tortures himself," unable to write up and publish his findings because he felt he had not solved the "big problems" in math and viewed what he had done as too little. Another spoke of the diminished need to have the "right" answer as revealing previously overlooked variables that complicated predictability. Some women spoke of having realized that their fathers' scientific thinking had limited them in human relationships. There is a social implication: the technologic magic of our times tempts social institutions toward simplistic solutions for complex human issues. These women were saying: "Wait, reality is multilayered, many sided, and partly in the eye of the beholder."

The shift in what had been viewed as cognitively rewarding affected aspirations. It often led to either a change in career path, or in the particular problem chosen within the field, or in a commitment to combining career interests with activity that had direct impact on human values, for example, the quality of life for students, or the establishment of a more supportive atmosphere toward colleagues in a department. In addition, the quality of intimate involvement with mate, children, or friends was given high priority by age 40.

Obviously, the sample I am describing is not representative; for many women the relational nexus is always a priority. For this group of science-oriented women with high intentionality, however, such priority was a gradual development.

Acknowledged closeness to mother was often pictured as being enmeshed with unwelcome affect until the woman felt confidently rooted in a separate life of her own. Father was more often drawn with laser-light clarity in terms of his inner attributes, whereas mother was apt to be defined as the sum of her behavior toward others, replete with contradictions between her wishes and role. Many women described the mother of their childhood as "kind of living through me" and felt implicitly obligated to make her happy, and guilty about wanting to separate their lives from hers. In this context, father lent himself especially well as a progressive force for emulation in the daughter's attempt to differentiate from, and master the early feelings about, the mother. In addition, many descriptions of mothers reflected the real contradictions in the mothers' lives. The mothers had been brought up in the 1920s and 1930s, years during which autonomy was seen as discordant with mutuality or femininity and needed to be adaptively muted by the mothers in many ways. To be different from mother was a conscious decision on the part of a number of the women (one by the time she was five) but tended, if *unrevised* in adulthood, to have a more precarious adult outcome. For many of these women, the shift in what was felt as rewarding marked a point in adulthood when they were able to reacknowledge the identificatory bond and closeness with mother, or other women, along with intuitive ways of knowing, affective yielding in relationships, and a recommitment to caretaking as a value. As the women spoke of these inner shifts, there were often allusions to the rediscovery of the values of mother or to a more conscious identification with her qualities. Jennifer is an example.

Excerpts from Narrative of Jennifer

Jennifer described M.I.T. as a garden of delights where she could freely experiment with original ideas with support for autonomy and fun-loving palships with "guys as friends." She made the most of her opportunities there. At age 40, Jennifer was dividing her time as a physician between original research involving high levels of abstraction and clinical work, in addition to raising her children, being a director in her husband's company, couple socializing with friends, and breeding horses. She told me humorously that she used to keep five different wardrobes, each fitted to one of the roles in her multifaceted life. Her adult relationship to her father included their being mutually colleagueal in what she called "a very strong interchange."

She started the interview by saying:

> She: I was strongly influenced by my father, who was an electronics engineer, and I was very oriented to science and problem solving, from the time I first started asking questions.
> I: Sounds like you started asking questions early. [She laughs.]
> She: Certainly the answers were there, and they built up a whole abstract world where problems could be solved, which made math and science a very comfortable place to be in.
> I: What kinds of questions occupied you together?
> She: I remember him using an orange to explain how a straight line could be a circle, depending on the geometry you were on. How, if you were an ant on an orange, and you were walking a completely straight line, you could still inscribe a circle. And so his explanation – while he would *do* practical things with you – his explanation would tend toward the abstract. So I really gained a lot of concepts, while we *did* a lot of things together. He gets excited by being the first to think of something, and I have a lot of that in me, too. There is a lot of influence from him in how I perceive myself and what I wanted to be. As a person, he's very withdrawn, but he does really fulfill himself, in his creations, making an abstract thing real, which he's been successful at. Let me contrast my mother and father, to give you some idea . . . my father is an ultrarational person. My mother is ultraunrational. And together they seem to do just fine. The problem is for someone who is rational to know how to deal with her, sometimes. My mother has lots of energy, she's very outgoing. Maybe she's not really unrational, as she suspects she is, but maybe just so much more social, trying to contrast with my father.
> I: Do you have the feeling that he in some way relies on her for that sort of emotional expression, and vice-versa?

She: Oh, he has to, because he doesn't have that himself, and she does supply it.

I: When you said "unrational," what is it that moves her in one direction or another? Clearly, as you put it, not the logic of the thing!

She: Well, she oscillates between her desire for happiness and her feelings of guilt. [We both laugh, familiar with the syndrome.]

Jennifer elaborated that mother had been taught "in the old European tradition that a mother is really subservient to all the needs of her family. She must, even to the point of losing her identity completely, subserve to them. Anything short of that is selfish and you should feel guilt." A picturesque example she gave of mother's "selflessness" was that "my mother had really, really long hair, like down to her knees – and to buy my first violin she sold her hair." So her hair, the border of self and not-self, was sacrificed to Jennifer. She felt that emotional separation from mother had been a long process, that she often had difficulty differentiating what she was feeling from what was mother's idea; with father this was never a complication. In her choice of mate, Jennifer resisted anyone who wanted her to be subservient; she married a man who encouraged her independent spirit.

By age 40, merged ego boundaries no longer loom as a danger in love or career. She talked of how her career interests had changed from originally valuing research most and the kind of rational and abstract thinking that shift had involved. She became involved in clinical medicine also, the aim of which she described as "people helping people." She currently works with a poor population with multiple social problems. I was intrigued by her description of how this change had come about:

Think of me coming out of M.I.T. with that strong science background without a lot of socialization, because I couldn't get into groups that were interested in me as I was, with me always wanting to take charge. And think of me, working in research, and then having children. That was a kind of turning point, a kind of exposure. First of all it was a reexamination of my own childhood. It was also exposure to that kind of nurturing and caring for someone. I mean, they are dependent individuals. And I've changed in my ability to support that. I think that most of the time before that, if somebody had been in trouble, I would have walked the other way rather than getting involved. *The fear, you know, of just my own emotions* – and I didn't have any defenses against other people's hurt – or pains. And no way of dealing with them.

But you learn when you're a mother, how to deal with these things. *You have to deal with it on two levels, an emotional level and a rational level.* And when I work clinically now, the patient comes first, before the interest in the disease. And this also supports my nurturing idea of medicine, my motherhood idea of medicine. My relationship with a patient, and what I give to them in a human sense is the most important thing for me. There are a lot of physicians who don't share that attitude, so I am again not in the mainstream.

But when I actually got into clinical medicine and started listening to people ... when you go in and do your first case histories as a medical student and people are telling you about the turn of the century, and the world wars, and giving you the kind of scenarios that previously I only got out of my reading – that were completely academic before *it suddenly opened up a real, real world of people instead of just a read-of world of people for me.* And I found that I could give them something, too, because somehow through learning how to cope with my children, I developed a way of listening and empathizing or sympathizing with them, so that they responded well to me. So there was a lot of positive feedback for me that was definitely rewarding to me.

Having become a mother, she demonstrated what her father had explained to her – how a straight line (of her development) can become a circle – and she could link her identity with her mother's once more. Meanwhile, colleagueal pleasure in her adult interaction with father continued to flourish, although he had a different function for her now than when she was younger and had struggled not to lose herself in the emotionality of the mother. With good reason, he now treats her as an equal even in those moments when her phone calls announcing a discovery in the lab have an unmistakable echo of her childhood exuberance: "Daddy, Daddy, guess what!" Confounding herself more than e.e. cummings, she pays attention to the syntax of things but does not forfeit the kiss.

TRANSFORMATIONS IN RELATIONSHIP TO FATHER

The young girl (and the woman she becomes) is willing to deny her father's limitations (and those of her lover and husband) as long as she feels loved. She is more able to do this because his distance means that she does not really know him. Because of the

> father's distance and importance to her, the relationship occurs
> largely as fantasy and idealization, and lacks the grounded reality
> which a boy's relation to his mother has.
> 　　—Nancy Chodorov (1978)

Growth of the father-daughter relationship can occur in a context opposite to that proposed by Chodorov; for a sizeable proportion of the women studied, the father was *not* distant, and increasingly in adulthood the daughter really did know him, rather than blinding herself to his "limitations." However, pleasure in being able to form a realistic evaluation of the father, with deepening acceptance, was most prominent, as Chodorov put it "as long as she feels loved." Some such women maintained multiple perspectives on father: While he was seen with all his foibles, he was also valued extraordinarily. For other women, particularly those of low intentionality, there were shoals on which the father-daughter relationship remained adrift; finally by age 30 or 40, these women might risk open confrontation over past differences and hurts. (Patterns evinced by the latter group are not further described here, while we focus on the women with high intentionality.)

Several daughters for whom father played a pivotal, positive role seemed highly motivated to evolve and maintain a *new* kind of connection to him, one in which the daughter could make an adult contribution. It might be based on a kind of collegial interchange (Jennifer); or empathic support of a new side on his nature, as she once felt supported by him (Cate, to be discussed later); or the loving acceptance and forgiveness of aspects of his character that may have pained her in childhood (Heather, to be discussed later). A prerequisite may be that she perceive his ability to accept her *now* as *both* autonomous and caring.

The striking echo of the early affective tone between father and daughter is this: the daughter whose father enhanced her early development by supporting her trust in her autonomy while still responding to her as feminine was often motivated in later adulthood to be actively supportive, in turn, of new features in her father's own later adult development. *She wanted to contribute to his continued growth as he had contributed to hers.*

The excerpts that follow describe two women (Cate and Heather) whose childhood bond with father was less than optimal in some areas. With Cate, autonomy was welcomed more clearly or comfortably than erotic longings. Heather experienced the loss of mother, and the disruptions with father in two divorces and frequent absences, but never doubted the reappearance—like sunshine—of his love. Recall that

Jennifer was secure in both areas. For each, the pleasurable affective tones, even when slightly off-key, were synthesized into powerful chords of caring in adulthood.

Excerpts from the Narrative of Cate

Cate, the oldest of three daughters of factory workers, felt a strong early alliance with her father. Having been caught in postwar unemployment, her family packed up a trailer with pioneering spirit (when she was three), borrowed $500, and moved themselves halfway across the United States to an area where they heard there were jobs – a risk-taking venture. They settled in a small rural town where the children walked several miles to school. The parents worked hard to progressively upgrade their economic situation.

> Dad and I would go to the hardware store together Saturday afternoon – I still love hardware stores – when he had to fix the car. My mother was one of those women who didn't know anything mechanical. It was as if my father expected nothing mechanical from her. So when he had to change the brake shoes, or the car had to be pulled out of a snowbank with tow chains, he would ask me – somehow I was the closest to him – though my father taught us all how to box, all three girls, just to be able to handle ourselves on the playground. We would wrestle, had dogs and bicycles. I remember what I liked best with a bicycle. I made a little wooden platform on my bike at the front and put a map on it and had a pin and as I would ride around I would move the pin. I remember having these elaborate forays, with the pin marking the destination riding off like it was some long trek. With my map and my pin for the destination and all my gear, it was sort of a *romance of the trek.*

"In that trek would you explore unknown territories too?" I asked. She answered, "In fact, *that* was the whole point. There were no repeats. It wasn't to find a path that you like in order to go back to. Once it was marked and done we went on to a new discovery." Intentionality, planfulness, and zest for discovery clearly had already fueled the bike rides of the scientist-to-be.

Cate's conflict with father began over her determination to go to M.I.T.

> At that time it was a flashing set of angry arguments between father and daughter – I can remember his saying, "When your

father tells you what to do, you do it, *right or wrong"* – and my saying "Oh, no, I'm going to do what I want to do, you can't make me." I had won a scholarship. In one argument he told me he was going to cut me out of his Will, and I came back with something like, "Well, that's not much!" So we were really estranged for three or four years while I was an undergraduate.

I asked why he had opposed her going to M.I.T.

He was scared of the East Coast and wanted me closer to home; scared of crime or my falling into a fast crowd – and of Republicans. I remember some disparaging remarks about going off to become better than oneself, that I wouldn't appreciate the value of a dollar or how the world really worked.

Her father had been raised in an orphanage and at age 13 had been adopted for hard farm labor. I said, "Sounds like losing you must have been difficult for him, must have complicated your adolescence and his letting you go." She answered:

I had no idea of that then though. It never occurred to me that he might miss me! I just put it in the realm of being told you had to tuck in your sweatshirt, ordering me not to go. And, of course, I was doing this thing in the *very spirit* of what he had done. He had just said, "The hell with it" and got up and left the farm when he was 18 to seek his fortune. In going to M.I.T., I was seeking mine!"

As Cate's career progressed to a full professorship in science at a university where women professors were few, she divided her energy between research and innovating programs that would improve the quality of learning experience for students. Her leadership qualities led to administrative posts; she influenced national educational policy. Like many other academicians from working class origins, she felt that estrangement from her parents which accompanied knowing that they could not possibly understand what mattered to her now. This phenomenon is often viewed in men who surpass their fathers in accomplishment or social economic status as having to do with guilt in oedipal competition. However, on the basis of these interviews with both men and women of M.I.T, I opine that this issue is also associated with a painful sense of loss of connection, evoking identity conflicts. The parents lose the sense of gratifying continuity in identity (or symbolic immortality) that echoes of the self reflected in children have.

Meanwhile, the child experiences the culture difference as a loss of the parent, who cannot follow him with appreciation and understanding (though pride may remain) in the new areas of interest. Cate described the gap:

> Certainly when I was doing postdoctoral work it took tremendous explanations of why this was a legitimate thing for me to do with my time. Why it would be that employers wouldn't ask me what the hell I'd been doing, not having a *job*? When I became a faculty member, it was a relief to them because "professor" was a word that was known. I mean, when you say to somebody who has never been to a meeting–except maybe a factory/union local–"I'm travelling across the country to go to a meeting." What can they say to their friends about what I'm doing?

Unlike many who accept the cultural gap with various mixtures of resentment, estrangement, loss, or inhibitions about being successful, Cate set out to bridge the gap. As she had been taught by participation, pleasure, and trust in her to solve practical problems, she introduced her parents, by way of direct participation to what mattered most to her now. Increasingly, dialogue and the expression of feeling have become salient for her.

She does this in a different way with each parent. She is on the board of trustees of a prestigious foundation that sponsors a "spouse program," financing spouses attendance at some of the meetings. Cate invited her mother to accompany her.

> She saw what it meant–if we talked about how minorities were doing in schools or youth unemployment she would hear the chit chat and would begin to pick it up; to notice things about the people involved and cut out articles in the newspaper after that about the issue to send me and then I would reply.

Thus, with her mother she broadened intellectual and social horizons. She felt her mother had been deprived of learning opportunities as a bright girl whose brothers had been educated, not she.

With her self-reliant father, in contrast, the dialogue was more personalized and around affects, a new experience for him:

> With my father, who would refuse to travel and was much less social than mother, I tried a different tack. I started with his birthday, making a date with him for the weekend. My mom went to my sisters. First I thought it was farfetched and my father

was just going along with it – it was odd driving up the first year – but there he was, sitting all dressed up in a rocking chair at the window, looking for me. When I came in, it was almost like a date. He asked me if I wanted a drink. And the next morning, he had made breakfast and told me he laid out the whole day. And we've done it ever year since then and gradually, more and more, he has begun talking about our family and then about his years at the orphanage and things he had never talked about to anyone when he was younger – like his loneliness.

At this point she knew that his battle with her over going to M.I.T. had to do with his shame about feeling vulnerable to loss.

A couple of features of Cate's adult development between the ages of 20 and 40 are salient. One has to do with the role of affects in her character and their impact on the values by which she lives; the second concerns the evolving changes in mentor relationships, which I believe prepared her for the changing relationship to her father.

Cate is aware of what she calls "my growth of humaneness." Like her age mates, she has grown somewhat away from "ambition" and more towards valuing feeling and sustaining relationships. She believes in offering sustenance to those who once offered it to her, living this out with both institutions and individuals. For example, she described the enhancing effect of different mentors in different aspects of her personal issues. In early relationship to mentors, she picked up at the point where she had gotten stuck with her father: support for autonomy in spite of disagreement. Describing a man who had a major impact on her, she said,

> Once you took an interest in his seminar, once he saw you as one of his individuals – he made it possible to come back to his office and spar with him. He was the first person I met with whom I could argue a difference of opinion about how I should proceed, or study, or whatever and the consequences were only that he would say, "Well, you'll see" and I'd say, "Yes, I will or won't I." You could go off and live your life. Then if you were right and he was wrong, you could come gloatingly back and say I was right. It had no consequence to your relationship. He didn't have the power to make you choose. But if he was right and I was wrong, then the code *I* would have about it is that one has to go back and say – you know, you were right. And that opened up different vistas for sparring.

She then, however, described a falling out with him, after which she did not see him for a couple of years while she was out of the country. But when she returned, "he made it very easy. When I came in the door, he didn't ask for an explanation so I didn't get the chance to say, 'Oh, yes, you were right.' He just looked at me and said, 'Hey, what took you so long?' We began a conversation about whether I would work for him." This relationship appeared to heal her adolescent impasse with her father (who had said, "When your father tells you what to do, you do it, right or wrong") and further strengthened her capacity for independent judgment.

Cate has continued her relationships with several of her mentors into their old age. She felt it then her turn to provide them with the emotional sustenance they had offered her earlier. Now that they are 70 to 80, she invites them to lunch or to university functions at a time when *they* feel unrecognized—that their faces and contributions have been erased in the memory of the very enterprises they helped launch. Thus, she reconnects them to their symbolic fathering. In this sense, her course with mentors differs from that of the men described by Levinson (1978). Levinson associates the stage of "becoming one's own man" in the early 30s with a necessary rupture in emulation of the mentor. Often mutual resentment takes the place of the former relationship, which if resumed is paled in intensity and meaning. The M.I.T. women more often maintained ongoing fondness for their mentors. For Cate there was the additional theme that what teachers received as students should eventually be returned to students—a further intergenerational bond. Thus, her adult generativity—in the Eriksonian (1959) sense—is extended in both directions at the same time.

I believe that, for Cate, conflicts in her love relationships are connected in complicated ways with early affective tones with father. Her pleasure in mastery, resourcefulness, and self-reliance, her capacity for long time spans in agendas are overt, strengthening aspects of identification with father. These were evident early at an affectomotor level of identification. The mutual pleasure in the object relationship was not acknowledged in other than "twinship" areas, reinforcing this mode of relating to him at that time. That is, father sought her out as his "buddy" in mechanical interests and problem solving, but became angry and fearful about the dangers of her feminine and other developments, which would make for differences between them. He fought these dangers in his opposition to her "falling in with a fast crowd," "becoming better than oneself," and the like.

An assumption of necessary self reliance was first developed by her as a fantasy in adolescence. "Somewhere between ages 12 and 16 I had a continuing saga to which I would add a new chapter each night before sleep—'almost like a TV series that dealt with the fact that you

had to cope.' " She pictured herself as " 'displaced from home . . .
having to survive . . . sometimes on a bicycle . . . raiding provisions at
the store, but eventually putting together a kind of traveling band . . .
going off to the country for a new settlement, and making the most of
every resource.' " In part, this fantasy was a vivid version of the
adolescent's psychic separation from parents and a resettlement of
libidinal energies around emotional resources shared with age-mates.
At another level, it was a preview of her rift with family before coming
to M.I.T., which she saw as an echo of the spirit in which her father
had left the farm in his adolescence to seek his fortune.

In addition, the affective component of this fantasy echoed the
father's own affective stance when, orphaned, he was left to fend for
himself. She returns to her father in caring form the sense of alliance he
offered her when she was a child. As he tells her of the festering
wounds of orphaned childhood loneliness, allowing himself finally to
recall the pain, he knows that in the context of shared weekend
activity, he can trust a celebration of his birth in which he does *not* have
to fend alone (Birthdays are always emotionally loaded for the adopted
and orphans who re-confront the absence of the person (mother) they
were with at the time of their birth).

The seeds of autonomy and pleasure in shared endeavors were
sown early in the affective alliance between Cate and her father.
Libidinal roots remained underground, emerging affectively later in
adolescent clashes instead of erotic longings. Yet, during adult development, Cate chose to use autonomy – both in intimate relationships
and in the various social systems on which she had influence – to foster
mutuality in caring: Autonomy in the service of mutuality.

Excerpts from the Narrative of Heather

Heather's experience of her father was more central for her development than for some women: he was the most reliably positive figure in
her life. When Heather was three, mother left husband and her
daughter and permanently disappeared. The child was told by the
paternal grandmother, with whom she lived, that her mother did not
want her. Father, an Air Force navigator, was often away but reap-
peared regularly "like sunshine" in her life. She was always "very
close" to him; his visits were always "a big time." When she was
seven, father took her to an island base where his squadron was
relocated. She then discovered that he had remarried, had a new baby
daughter, and this was the family she would join. For Heather sud-

denly to have to share the affections of her much adored father was first a painful trauma and then a challenge.

Yet, by age 30 she could accept father in spite of the fact that by extending his love to others he disappoints those who are already committed to him. He has divorced and remarried again, but only Heather has compassion for his loving more than one. The younger sister, who still needs him in a different way, can neither forgive him nor form the kind of good relationships with males that Heather has made. Heather can sustain emotional intimacy with her husband and her child. At the same time, she and her husband can allow each other space to pursue a career and other interests. (For example, she wants to learn to fly a plane next year . . . an echo of father.)

At age seven Heather first tried to come to terms with not being the only center of father's delight.

> It was either sink or swim with my stepmother and me – we didn't have much choice about working it out. It was rough getting used to each other because I didn't like sharing my father's affection so suddenly with the two of them, and my little sister had had him all to herself too, so it was just as hard for her. But after about three years, we were really a family.

She describes the flavor of their childhood interactions:

> He would share all kinds of things he was doing. Like he was good at carpentry and stuff like that, and if I wanted to do that with him, that was fine. I didn't really have any rules. There was nothing I *couldn't* do because I was a girl. When he was especially proud of me, he would tease playfully. He was very good with children. He also could be hard on you – if he didn't think you were thinking out a situation beforehand like you should – but never in the sense of restrictiveness, not in the sense of trying to make decisions for you, or run your life.

She believes his encouragement to make her own decisions helped to prepare her for M.I.T. and made her "a strong personality." He had told her as she began at M.I.T.: "Do something useful for the world – you have intelligence, you have talent, you should do something with it, but also enjoy yourself!" Heather, like Shelley, balances being inspired by her work with saving energy for "friends of the heart and friends of the road." She felt, when celebrating her 20th wedding anniversary recently, that she would have chosen the same husband again. A quality of her father's that she looks for in friends is if there's some curiosity, if they are really *interested* in things – I mean with some people a tidal wave could sweep them away and they probably wouldn't even worry where it came from – so if that spark isn't there, I have a hard time getting interested in the person – I'm sort of tolerant about just about everything, except dullness in interest, I'm a snob about that.

Father's terminal illness began shortly after he and Heather had celebrated an end to his feeling penalized for his ethics. He had previously rejected a particular promotion that involved politics, which he abhorred, and resigned himself to taking dull jobs to support his younger children and pay his alimony. Then an exciting job appeared which did not compromise his ideals, and he accepted. Soon thereafter cancer was diagnosed and Heather flew to his side:

> It was very, very hard on me because we were so close – but in a sense we had worked through most everything. He told me he had been *so worried* about telling me that he was married the third time because he didn't know how I was going to take it. But I felt like I was a grown-up person by then, and this was my father, and it didn't really matter what he did, it couldn't change what he was to me. In fact I get along fine with his third wife. Before he died, my feeling was that I didn't want to lose him, but we had sort of worked things through. It was harder on my sister because she had not forgiven him for divorcing her mother, and when he died. She still hasn't come to terms with it – she can't seem to make a good relationship with a man. But I felt different, like a grown, separate person, talking to another grown person.

At the funeral, friends and relatives came from far away. Even as she grieved she thought: "It *says* something that there is a somebody here from all three of these familes." She told me:

> She: You know, if my father had his way, he would have kept *all* his wives and *all* his children together. It was the *wives* who didn't like being – you know . . .
> I: Yes. I can understand that – but perhaps you are saying *some* men are truly able to love more than one person.
> She: Yeah, and the kids, I think any one of the four of us would tell you that we were his favorite. So that all would have been fine with the kids.

His death still deeply affects her:

She: One way I dealt with it, and still do, is by thinking about what he would say about something or how I might tell him about something I've been doing [her face glows as she says this]. You see, he was gone so much on a flight or the whole squadron would be gone for 30 days, so I was *used to that.*

I: You raise an interesting thought. You describe him as someone who was gone a lot of the time and then came in on, well, not quite on his white charger.

She: (laughingly) Yeah, he's still on it.

I: Okay, on his white charger, and it was an intense and lovely connection. And then he was away again. Now in death too, you've learned, I guess, to keep very lively the fantasy. I mean, just now you were starting a dialogue with him. (She: "yeah!") The fantasy was alive between visits. Sounds like he had something special, that he was able to make intimate connections that people valued.

She: Very, very much. You can tell by who showed up at the wake. There was a family joke about him getting into an elevator in London. There's somebody that he knows and every-time the elevator stops, somebody else he knows gets on who has no connection with anyone who got on before. It ends up with an elevator full of people and him, all knowing him. (The elevator scene evokes his three "unconnected" families arriving at his funeral.)

I: It sounds like you've been able to maintain both of those things. You're able to care about people even when you don't see them. You talk about friends of the road and friends of the heart — I bet your father was one of them.

She: Oh yeah!

I: . . . That you keep alive within you. And you have something of his spirit in the way you make connections that stay important to you. That's a piece of balance in the midst of your hectic schedule.

She: One of the things that I most admired when I was a kid was how *good* he was with children. Any strange child he came across would take right to him. It seemed to me that you have to be a good person for little kids to come to you like that and really accept you.

Heather has come full circle. Echoes of the child within her, like the other children she describes, accept him as he is, introjecting his curiosity and enthusiasm for useful work and for loving. To do that she had to face the poignant problem of forgiving him for his many "favorites," even while she needed him so. In part, her own rewarding adult life made this possible. In addition, the particular mental mechanism for coping with his absences by organizing her fantasies around the positive affective tones in their rich relationship shaped her way of transforming her bond to one in which she made the visits to him (in the hospital) on the level, as she put it, of "grown person to grown person." Just as her father had not deserted Heather as a child when she was abandoned by mother, in adulthood, she does not desert _him_ when he feels to blame for having multiple loves.

In Cate's case, needed defenses against vulnerability in the father were transmitted to the daughter, who in some way postponed – and adaptively so – giving into the fullness of erotic longing. For Heather, the father was not the steadily available parent all little children long for, but when he was present he made the kind of connection with her that led to a propensity toward a certain mental mechanism: the ability to give oneself to constructing and maintaining a motivating fantasy of the absent parent until he returned. This ability is often present in the children of divorced or deceased fathers with whom the tie had powerfully positive affective tones (Tessman, 1978). It can affect the future relations with men in diverse ways. Some such women are wary of binding commitments to heterosexual love. Others, when the libidinal engagement, often experienced by the child as shared affective pleasure, was more prominent than previous withdrawal or rejection, may want it to happen again, and they may attempt to master the trauma by doing what they can, in deed or symbolically, to bring this about: somehow to create or recreate the affective pleasure once more. This reaction is unlike the course of mourning other kinds of loss. Such woman may be particularly invested in maintaining an empathy with the loved man that heightens her sense of emotional engagement, and she may take special pleasure in attempting to fit herself to his libidinal wishes.

Such patterns make for individual variations in patterns of loving, complex and subtle, but not necessarily for psychiatric symptomatology or an impoverishment of emotional life. My point is this: even in less than ideal circumstances the power of early affective tones as organizers of the personality, as shapers of the central drama and its characters is considerable. The complex transformations of this drama – its eventual denouement in daughter's adulthood and father's older age – may depend on the vicissitudes of ongoing adult development in each.

SUMMARY

Former women students of M.I.T. were interviewed around age 30 and 40 in taped, open-ended sessions designed to evoke life narratives. The father-daughter relationship constituted one of 21 different areas for exploration. The sample is skewed for exceptional intelligence, rationalistic predilections, and career aspirations (in science and math), at odds with views of femininity common at the time they were students.

The impact of early affective tones between father and daughter in this sample is viewed during two time periods during the daughter's life, childhood and adulthood. Women with very positive adult development were differentiated by a cluster of eight characteristics in their descriptions of childhood interaction with father. Excerpts from the narratives of such daughters are discussed to illustrate the transformations in their adult relationships to their fathers.

Affective tones between father and daughter are viewed from two perspectives, process and content. The *process* of affective interchange is viewed as a paradigm for the transformation of instinctual excitement into eventual energies for love and work. The *content* of affect transmitted by father to a daughter may echo as a dormant chord in the daughter's adult agenda. The daughter for whom father played a pivotal positve role was highly motivated in later adulthood to be actively supportive, in turn, of new features in the father's own late life development. Her particular interest tended to echo what he had supported in her childhood (e.g. individuation). However, it occurred in a new context of changes in her (the) sense of inner reality, values, and cognitive approach that she now identified as feminine.

REFERENCES

Chodorov, N. (1978), *The Reproduction of Mothering.* Berkeley, CA: University of California Press.

Clark, W. & Wright, W. ed. (1864), *The Complete Works of William Shakespeare.* New York: Grosset & Dunlap.

Cummings, e. e. *Complete Poems, 1913–1962.* New York: Harcourt, Brace, Jovanovich, 1972.

Deutch, H. (1946), *The Psychology of Women.* New York: Grune & Stratton.

Erikson, E. H. (1959), Identity and the life cycle. *Psychological Issues,* Monogr. 1. New York: International Universities Press.

Gilligan, C. (1982), *In A Different Voice: Psychological Theory and Women's Development.* Cambridge, MA: Harvard University Press.

Jacobson, E. (1954), The self and the object world: Vicissitudes of infantile cathexis and their influence on ideational and affective development. *The Psychoanalytic Study of the Child,* 9:75–127. New York: International Universities Press.

Kohut, H. (1971), *The Analysis of the Self.* New York: International Universities Press.

Levinson, D. (1978), *The Seasons of A Man's Life.* New York: Knopf.

Miller, J. B. (1976), *Toward a New Psychology of Women.* Boston: Beacon Press.

Notman, M., Zilbach, J., Miller, J. B. & Nadelson, C. (1986), Themes in psychoanalytic understanding of women: Some reconsiderations of autonomy and affiliation. *J. Amer. Acad. Psychoanal.,* 14:241–253.

Stechler, G. (1982), Looking forward from infancy to the 25 year follow-up study. Paper presented at the spring meetings of the Massachusetts Psychological Association Symposium on Through Life with Pleasure: Longitudinal Perspectives.

Tessman, L. H. (1978), *Children of Parting Parents* New York: Aronson.

_____ (1982), A note on the father's contribution to the daughter's way of loving and working. In: *Father and Child: Developmental and Clinical Perspectives,* ed. S. H. Cath, A. Gurwitt & J. M. Ross. Boston: Little, Brown.

_____ (1986), Mothers and minds: Changing models for daughters. Paper presented at the annual meetings of American Psychiatric Association, Washington, DC.

11

Paternal Influence in Early Child Development

Bernard L. Pacella

The role of the mother and child-mother interactions in child development have been a major focus of research and clinical interest during the past 35 years. Particularly impressive during this period of time have been the studies and observations made by psychoanalysts, especially Spitz (1950, 1965), Winnicott (1956, 1965), Mahler (1952, 1958, 1963, 1967, 1971, 1972a, b; Mahler, Pine & Bergman, 1975), and Greenacre (1958, 1960). The formulations of Mahler, based on considerable observed clinical data, of a separation-individuation process consisting of four successive subphases during the first three years of life have had a significant impact on the psychoanalytic concepts of preoedipal development and on the theories of character formation, affect development, and object-relations development.

Only in the past 10 to 15 years has the role of the father in early child development been more carefully scrutinized and "respected" by psychoanalysts, such as Abelin (1971, 1972, 1975, 1977, 1980), Stoller (1975, 1979), and Ross (1977, 1979a, b). It is possible that the relative neglect of the father role is partially attributable to biological and

---

I am indebted to the late Dr. Margaret S. Mahler for her very important suggestions, comments, and advice in the preparation of this paper.

cultural factors, which traditionally have viewed the mother as the primary caretaker and protector of the infant and young child.

The purpose of this paper is twofold: 1) to attempt both a summary and a distillation (basic assumptions and inferences) of the prevailing psychoanalytic opinions concerning the role and significance of the paternal[1] influence on the developing child during the early years of life; and 2) to add some additional comments of the preoedipal paternal influence on the basis of material derived from two cases of children analyzed by the author.

A summary in outline form will be presented first so that the succeeding case material can be viewed to some extent within the framework of a structured background. The summary does not imply that all authors are in unanimity regarding each point, nor is there any attempt to rate the relative importance of each special influence attributed to the father. However, the outline probably represents a consensus of thought where little if any "violent" difference of opinion seems to exist.

Paternal Influence in early child development:

    A. The father enhances maturation by facilitating the separation-individuation process.

        1. He helps the child resolve the symbiotic pull to the mother by shifting some of the child's interest to the father and "diluting" the valence of the mother-child interactions.

        2. He facilitates the awareness of separateness and promotes the innate push towards independence.

        3. The father is uncontaminated by the ambivalences of the rapprochement child, and he is therefore important in the resolution of these ambivalences and perhaps in the formation of object constancy.

    B. The father aids the imitative and internalization processes in both boys and girls:

        1. in the formation of the ego-ideal and the forerunners of the super-ego;

        2. in the formation of self-esteem and confidence.

        3. in the development of core gender identity; gender role and sexual partner orientation, perhaps especially in boys. However, we might visualize a "push-pull" vector system in which the father "pulls" the boy toward him to imitate and identify with him while the

---

[1]It is implied that the father in these observations is regarded as an adequate or good-enough father, borrowing from Winnicott's (1971) use of the term "good-enough mother".

mother "pushes" him along the same direction. These vectors may be reversed in the case of the girl.

C. The father helps to modulate and regulate psychosexual development.

1. The system of early "triangulation" (Abelin, 1980) seems to represent a balancing system in which the father may facilitate the biologically prepatterned shifts of libidinal aims from orality to anality in the rapprochement phase to the phallic phase as object constancy and the forerunners of the oedipus complex are in formation. Thus, early fixations may be more readily diluted and have less opportunity to become too intense and pathological, at least in relation to mother. The mother-father relationship introduces a new awareness by the child that affects his perceptions of the mother's and father's roles in relationship to him, facilitates his own identity, including gender identity, and sets the stage for the development and ultimately the appropriate resolution of the oedipus complex.

D. The father promotes the development of the sense of reality (Loewald, 1951).

For the boy, the father provides an incentive to relinquish preoedipal attachments to the mother through the imitative and gender-identity processes, while oedipal attachments are loosened additionally by the pressures of castration anxiety. For the girl, the father becomes the preoedipal hero who facilitates the development of her secondary narcissistic interests in the direction of feminine gender identity and an increasing shift of libidinal cathexis to male objects. Under certain unusual conditions, of course – such as a father who is obliged to play a bigender role in which he must provide more of the caretaking functions because of an absent mother – some shifts in the paternal influences may occur. However, we are assuming that a relatively cultural norm of maternal and paternal influences prevails in a nonpathological family unit.

A short summary of two female children, aged five and a half and eight respectively, who were in analysis for over three years, will serve as a basis for further discussion of the preoedipal paternal influences in development.

CASE ILUSTRATION

Madelyn

Madelyn, age five and a half, was referred for analysis by a senior colleague who had seen her in several interviews over a three-week period. The presenting complaints by her parents and the school consisted of underachievement and poor socialization in the nursery school she attended. She had a very short attention span, feared making any mistakes, and as a consequence even refused to draw or undertake simple academic tasks. In the classroom she usually remained by herself and said very little. She occasionally burst into tears and impatiently waited for someone to take her home each day, feeling insecure about whether they would come on time or even come at all. The mother describes Madelyn as being very petulant, stubborn, defiant, demanding, negativistic, moody, given to extremes of moods with "screaming temper tantrums." During these angry outbursts Madelyn frequenty shouted that she wished she were a boy. The mother admitted to strong fluctuations in her relationship with Madelyn varying from intense affectionate "reunions" to violent episodes when she would verbally attack the child with streams of profanity and accusations. Within this emotional climate of intense fluctuating relationships, Madelyn was always anxious when mother left the house, would cling to her, and want to know exactly when mother would return. The mother also complained that Madelyn bothered her constantly at home, followed her about the house making demands, striving for constant communication and wanting to share in mother's activities. Although she constantly argued with mother, she wanted to be close to her yet never was demonstrably affectionate; she provoked fights and arguments with both brothers, especially an older adopted one, yet admired and respected him. When she was first brought to nursery school and subsequently to kindergarten, Madelyn exhibited considerable separation anxiety and demanded that her mother stay in the classroom with her during the first several days of each new class. The teacher described the patient as a "loner" and as having poor peer relationships.

Madelyn's mother was a friendly, attractive, outgoing, artistically talented, and emotionally charged person (in contrast to the father) enthusiastically involved in social and charitable community activities. She appeared to be quite devoted to the children, but was particularly attentive to her younger son.

The father reported that he had had very little interest in Madelyn until quite recently because she reminded him so much of his older sister whom he "hates." He had not spoken to his sister in over 15 years because of prior violent quarrels with her and added that he could not even stand the sight of her. "Madelyn acts like her, talks like her and behaves like her." As a consequence, the father avoided and ignored

Madelyn until fairly recently but, by contrast, heaped lavish praise on the patient's one-year-older adopted brother.

During the first five years of the parents' marriage, the mother was unable to conceive despite frequent treatments and consultations with the obstetrician. They finally adopted Andy, their oldest child, through an agency almost immediately after he was born. Shortly thereafter the mother became pregnant with Madelyn. Two years after Madelyn's birth, the mother became pregnant again and bore the younger son, Alex. The father described Andy as an extremely capable child who excelled in everything he undertook. He further characterized him exceedingly intelligent, brilliant academically and outstanding in athletic play. The father showered the boy with considerable affection and would always take him on various jaunts such as baseball games and other sports, while shunning his daughter. The father was also attached to Alex, who was almost three years younger than Madelyn, but stated that the youngest child did not appeal to him as much as the older adopted brother.

Madelyn had been seen for a psychological evaluation about two months prior to her visit with me. The psychologist's report described Madelyn as a highly intelligent child prominently displaying marked separation anxiety and fear of abandonment to which she reacted with clinging and aggressive behavior. The projective tests revealed pronounced ambivalent and hostile attitudes toward the mother, who took on aggressive yet protective features. At times a warm protective mother image was transformed into a dominating image who becomes dangerous and threatening. There was little spontaneous flow of fantasy, apparently related to obsessive-compulsive constriction in both cognition and emotional fantasy. However, there were manifestations of oral aggressive fantasies, narcissistic deprivation, and considerable negativism and denial. During the testing, Madelyn displayed considerable need to control the environment, lack of a trusting attitude, and uncertainty as to what she could share with the psychologist and what she would withhold. At times she showed little confidence in her abilities almost to the point of a pseudostupidity, yet her information level and vocabulary were superior. Her projectives suggested a strong anticonceptual trend, partially manifested in the Rorschach by a regressive reaction to the mother blot consisting of fragmented rather than integrated perceptions. The psychologist concluded that there was a core of depression and aggression associated with castration fears and insecurity about her feminine status within her household.

During the initial visit with Madelyn and her parents together in the consultation room, Madelyn stayed close to her mother. If she ventured forth to handle an object or toy in the room, she returned only to the mother; there was some verbal exchange between mother and child, but none with her father.

In the therapeutic sessions that followed, Madelyn exhibited a profound sense of distrust as to whether I would keep appointments with her on time. On two occasions when I was less than five minutes late in seeing her, she expressed irritation and some concern about whether I would show up for the session. I commented that she must often worry about people keeping their promises to meet her. She responded that mother was always late to appointments with her and sometimes let her wait for long periods of time before picking her up from school or from sessions with the therapist. When I asked her about trusting daddy, she replied that he was too busy to pick her up or meet her, but sometimes when he was supposed to meet her he forgot about it and would send the maid.

In the course of the first few weeks of analysis, on a four-times weekly basis, the patient gradually lost her anxiety about my being on time or whether I would show up for the session. Usually the maid brought her to the session, but on occasion the mother, and later on in therapy the father, brought her. Whenever the mother accompanied Madelyn to the session, the child would plead with mother to wait for her in the waiting room rather than leaving the office to do errands and returning later to get Madelyn since the mother usually would be late. During the latter part of therapy, the father was more active in bringing Madelyn to the session and grew to be punctual in picking her up at the office.

During the early part of therapy, Madelyn often wanted to play "hide and seek" after the parent (mother or father) left the room, hiding herself to be found by me. At other times she hid objects that I would have to find. These games, perhaps derivatives of the peek-a-boo game with mother, afforded me opportunities to comment on various aspects of her separation anxiety and on her need and her ability to master this anxiety. Later on, as manifestations of transference phenomena developed, I pointed out on different occasions how trusting she now had become of her father's interest and love for her.

On a number of occasions during the first year of analysis, Madelyn asserted that she had a penis like her brothers and that she would soon grow a big penis. In one of these sessions, she confided to me with much giggling and coy seductiveness that she had had a very good look at her father's penis and it was much bigger than her brother's and, she was sure, much bigger than mine. I commented on her interest and curiosity about penises, to which she responded only with more giggling. During a subsequent session, she was particularly exhibitionistic, demonstrating her gymnastic abilities with somersaults and standing on her hands against a wall in the playroom, causing her dress to fall down and exposing her panties. She had previously been careful to always keep her dress down or to see to it that it covered her thighs, to be sure that I would not see "underneath." During this phase of considerable exhibitionistic and voyeuristic interest, there was a session in which she confided, with considerable giggling, that she had seen daddy again come out of the bathroom after a shower and she saw his "whole front with lots of hair around it." She added that her brothers and a friend of the older brother did not have hair around the penis; she confided that she had seen them taking showers and going to the bathroom during the past summer when the family spent considerable time at their summer house. She admitted in a seductive and playful manner that she used to peek in at them without their knowledge and confided that she tried to arrange to catch her daddy in the nude. Toward the latter part of this session, she sat in a large chair with her legs widely apart exposing her panties and then suddenly interrupted as we were talking about her summer experiences and her voyeuristic explorations: "What are you looking at!" I replied, "What would you really like me to look at?" As though unperturbed she said, "I'll tell you what. I'll show you mine if you show me yours."

The recent summer period (which occurred after about nine months of analysis) must have been an occasion for considerable sexual excitement with mutual exhibiting and looking between her brothers and herself, and perhaps sexual play, which she was now manifesting as transference phenomena or displaced attitudes in the therapeutic situation. The relationship with her father, during this phase of treatment, grew increasingly affectionate in contrast to her previous aloofness and distancing from father. During one of his visits to me, in the second year of analysis, the father commented rather proudly that he had suddenly "found" his daughter. He now described her as bright, vivacious, independent, very stoic when hurt or hit by her brothers, more interested in being with her girlfriends, and even as good an athlete as her older brother. This represented a very substantial and significant change in the father's attitudes toward Madelyn, whom he had previously described as a "bothersome brat" with the "lousiest disposition."

In a session toward the end of the second year of analysis, the patient appeared particularly thoughtful and commented that she did not think she "can ever grow a penis". I asked her to tell me more about that idea. She appeared quite pensive for a few moments and then, as though she had arrived at a momentous realization, replied, "Well, I would have to be a boy first, and you know, I can't be a boy because I'm a girl." After another pause, she brightened up and remarked, "Gee you're stupid if you didn't know that." Then she asked me how I liked her new dress and the new bracelet her father bought her, holding her arm out for me to admire.

To recapitulate, in the course of the second year of therapy three significant developments occurred: (1) the father suddenly "found" his daughter; (2) the patient manifested oedipal strivings in relation to her father and to the therapist; (3) there was considerable diminution in the intensity of the ambivalence and the hostile acting out toward mother, coupled with less need to "shadow" mother when at home. Previously, on Father's Day in school, she had not wanted her father to appear in school; she would refuse to talk with or acknowledge him when he did show up, would not show him any of her classwork, and sulked or cried in a corner of the classroom. She now greeted him in the classroom very warmly, proudly displayed some of the work she was doing in first grade, and excitedly told me about daddy's visit to the school. At home, her behavior was reported as increasingly affectionate toward the father and as less intensely ambivalent toward the mother. Her heated arguments with mother every morning and during other times of the day became considerably less intense and more moderate. At the same time, her original distrust, anxiety, and hostility toward me were replaced by an increasing sense of trust and confidence. Occasionally she wanted to sit on my lap or play games where direct physical contact could be made. Several times I commented that she seemed to be a little excited in certain ways about me and also about daddy, which evoked variable reactions ranging from attempts to kick or punch me, to strong denials, or, later on, to seductive smiling or pretended indifference. But she would always distance herself from me when I made these comments as though she had to emphatically deny her wishes.

The course of therapy during two years was marked by considerable fluctuations in behavioral reactions and symptoms. Despite these variations, the therapy was progressively favorable with less hostile acting out, more effective academic achievement, and a remarkable improvement in social maturation. For example, she imitated mother's social activities by arranging her own parties for classmates, even calling their parents to obtain permission for the children to attend her parties and providing the mothers with all details concerning time arrangements, party dress, and so on.

In the third year of analysis the intensity of the ambivalence toward mother lessened considerably, so that Madelyn was ultimately described by her mother as having become "so reasonable about many things." There also appeared to be a continuing consolidation of the gains she experienced in the relationship with her father and continued to improve her social maturity.

Discussion of Madelyn's Case

In attempting to understand the shift in Madelyn's behavior and symptoms, it is important to be aware of a significant improvement in father's attitude toward her. Without this shift in the father's attitude, treatment might not have continued to progress as well as it did, or perhaps it would have run a more difficult course. There may be several reasons for the father's improved and more positive reactions to the patient. Madelyn seemed to be making increasingly positive gestures and overtures to the father in line with her oedipal strivings, which were clearly manifest in the transference situation. The regularly scheduled visits with the parents, which the patient was well aware of, were clearly understood by her as indicating a genuine desire on the part of the parents to understand her feelings and difficulties. She always liked the idea that her parents were visiting with me. During these sessions, which frequently were attended only by the father, father verbalized his affection and love for Madelyn as though she no longer was a representation of his sister but a little girl who was a separate person in her own right. He also came to recognize, through his own ongoing personal analysis with another analyst, that some of the hostility toward Madelyn was a displacement of anger toward his wife.

I believe that the father's earlier rejection and avoidance of the patient and his warm regard and apparent overidealization of Madelyn's older brother (actually the adopted brother) interfered with an adequate resolution of the ambivalence problem with mother during the rapprochement subphase of the separation-individuation process and perhaps even heightened the acting out of the love-hate interactions between both child and mother. Madelyn did not have the "dilution factor" derived from a "good-enough-father" to moderate and modulate the intense ambivalence existing between mother and child.

As a consequence, the natural movements toward a strong gender identity, with the development of "feminine" self-esteem, were inhibited. The preoedipal preparations for the drama of the Oedipus complex were significantly delayed as the child continued to remain bound in the struggles of the intense rapprochement phase, manifesting regressive behavior, separation anxiety, and excessive mother-shadowing, in addition to distancing from father as though he continued to be the "external person" intruding into the mother-child dyad.

The therapeutic situation provided Madelyn with a sense of trust and confidence, permitting a reduction in her separation anxiety as both parents cooperated in the treatment program.

At the age of eight, when treatment stopped, Madelyn was showing adequate development of sublimatory processes. She was now an excellent student at school, considered to be at the top of her class. Her writing, vocabulary, and use of the English language were considerably advanced for her age. She was also the best athlete in the class and a talented gymnastics performer. There was no acting out of sexual exhibitionistic or voyeuristic strivings in the therapeutic sessions during the latter part of the third year of analysis. In fact, she even seemed to have developed a certain shyness in this regard, which we would classify as "normal" behavior for her age level.

Karen

Karen, age eight and a half, an attractive, neatly dressed, blonde-haired girl of medium stature and weight, appeared for her first interview accompanied by her mother. The chief complaints about the child presented by the mother were the following: (1) marked stubbornness, provocative behavior and defiance at home, with frequent lying and temper tantrums; (2) underachievement in school despite high intelligence; (3) poor relationships with peers (she had been voted by her classmates as the most unpopular person in the class); (4) frequent baby talk since the birth of a half-sister 18 months earlier, (divorced father's child with his second wife); (5) overidealization and grandiose fantasies regarding her father, who had been separated from the mother since the patient was three years old; (6) incessant talking to mother and constantly following her around the house, yet being very demanding and argumentative; (7) intense hostility to mother's fiance; (8) attempts to attract the attention of strangers (she struck up intimate conversations with any adult stranger and discussed personal family matters).

The father deserted the family when Karen, an only child, was three years old. The mother described the father as an irresponsible person who shifted from job to job, and because he was a moderate but inconsistent income earner, she had to seek work in order to maintain a source of reliable and constant income. Since shortly after Karen's birth there had been increasing marital difficulties between the parents, considerable discord, and loud arguments.

The father was a good-looking, well-groomed man, fastidious about his dress and appearance, a convincing talker. He showed little interest in Karen and frequently made promises to the child which he rarely kept. After moving out of the house, he remained in New York for approximately a year and would occasionally have Karen spend weekends with him at his apartment. It was reported by the mother that he would take showers in the nude with Karen and would have Karen sleep in the same bed with him. However, he usually hired a babysitter to spend most of the time with the patient on these weekends. Very often after a weekend he would tell the patient he would see her the following weekend and take her to various places; then he would completely ignore the promises and plans and not see her for several weeks.

He finally moved to a distant part of the country when Karen was a little more than four years old, and remarried when she was five and a half years old. He maintained an inconsistent communication with the patient thereafter, infrequently phoning her and even more infrequently writing her a short note. On these occasions, he would promise to phone regularly each week and then would not call for four or five weeks or longer.

The mother, a very attractive woman in her mid-30s, was a graduate of an Ivy League college and held an M.B.A. from a top business school; she worked as a middle-level executive in a banking firm. She seemed to be a knowledgeable and sensible person with a well-integrated personality. She described herself as usually submissive to Karen's wishes and even excessive demands but admitted to not being demonstrably affectionate with the patient. At the time of her first interview with the therapist, she was engaged to Mr. F., an older man who was divorced and who was to become Karen's stepfather approximately six months after Karen had begun therapy. For about a year prior to their marriage, the man had been spending weekends at Karen's home, which Karen resented. For a while Karen demanded to be admitted to their room each night in order to kiss her mother goodnight. This became an increasingly prolonged ritual each time, so that the future stepfather insisted upon keeping the bedroom door locked and telling Karen that all her goodnights to her mother had to be done before the mother went to bed and before Karen went to her own room for the night. The patient was very angry about this and frequently reiterated that she hated him, especially because he was "forcing mother to marry him." Mr. F. was a somewhat obsessive-compulsive personality, well organized in his daily living routine and work habits. At the same time, the mother described him as a generous and kindly person, who tried to be good to Karen.

During the early weeks of therapy, the patient was very compliant, even seductive, frequently asking the therapist if he could marry her mother instead of Mr. F. In the meantime, the fiance, for all intents and purposes, played the role of a good father. Karen frequently complained that he was too strict, that he did not like her, that he often ignored her while paying considerable attention to the mother. In the third month of treatment, Karen became increasingly hostile to me and for the succeeding several months had outbreaks of almost uncontrolled, assaultive behavior in which she attempted to kick me or throw objects at me. This violent behavior occasionally erupted at home and was more often directed against the fiance rather than against the mother. In the playroom she would often shout and scream, saying that she did not need a "shrink," and accusing both me and her mother's fiance of taking mother away from her. She claimed that her "real" father would be glad to have her move to Texas anytime she wished and live permanently with him and her stepmother. All she had to do was to phone him and tell him tha she was on her way to live with him. On many occasions she referred to her father as her "prince," as a great, wealthy man who owned lots of territory, who was a sheriff and carried a gun. She said that if I acted kindly toward her, she would arrange for her father to give me one of his beautiful houses and any amount of land I wanted.

Her assaultive, aggressive behavior in the treatment session was much more likely to occur when she had been disappointed by her biological father either when he did not phone her after he had promised to call or when he did phone but reprimanded her severely because of her poor grades and poor conduct in school. Bad days in school or arguments at home with mother would also cause displacements of her hostility to the treatment situation. After the fifth month of therapy, her violent outbursts gradually subsided, although periodic flareups of verbalized anger would occur in relationship to disappointments and frustrations in the environment.

During the first summer vacation, which interrupted treatment for about six weeks, her mother married the man Karen hated. She attended the wedding and when treatment resumed in the fall, she told me that her mother cried, her grandmother cried, even she cried; it was a "beautiful ceremony" and everybody was happy "even though they cried." I commented that her "happy crying" at the ceremony was very different from the hate feelings she used to experience about Mr. F. marrying her mother. She replied, "Yeah, I guess so," and after a pause I reminded her that at that time she would turn some of those hate feelings onto me. She agreed and added, "Things are different now. Maybe I'm growing up."

Before the wedding, Karen had spent two weeks with her father and stepmother, who was in her eighth month of pregnancy. Karen noted that her "stomach was big as a barrel." She described her stay as "not bad" even though her father was frequently away from home during the evenings, presumably at business meetings.

In the course of the subsequent year of treatment, Karen developed an increasing fondness for her stepfather, who made every attempt to be a good father and who scrupulously attempted never to disappoint her. During the course of an interview with the stepfather, he expressed concern and some embarrassment about how to deal with Karen's attempts on several occasions to place her hand "accidentally" on his genitals, particularly when she sat next to him on the couch. On a few Sunday mornings, she would climb into his bed with him when he was reading the newspaper and her mother was in the kitchen preparing breakfast and would place her hand on his thigh near the groin. Each time he merely told her to "cut it out." Karen never discussed these incidents with me.

DISCUSSION

In attempting to determine the influence of the father on the development of the child, and his impact on the formation of psychic structure and function, on personality, character formation, and behavior, we are aware that we are dealing with multiple, complex factors. Among such factors are the personalities of the father and mother, their relationship with each other, their feelings and attitudes toward the child and siblings, and the impact of other persons in the total environment. Statistical studies of paternal influence that attempt to take into account some of the variable factors affecting this influence are certainly helpful, but the variability of these factors often tends to diminish the validity of such statistics despite research methods to establish controls. A psychoanalytic process that focuses on developmental psychic interest and cathexes and their distributions or altering valences over a period of at least two years or more of growth in the child may provide a more focused understanding of the paternal influence in addition to other influences impinging on the child.

The two cases presented here represent decidedly dissimilar family constellations and very different mother types. Madelyn's mother was an outgoing, intense, emotionally labile person, while Karen's mother was a reserved, quiet-spoken, "distant" person. Yet both children have in common certain characteristics of behavior in relationship to the mother, such as marked negativism, stubbornness, and violent temper tantrums during the rapprochement subphase of development. This information not only emanated from the patients, but was provided by the parents during the course of therapy.

One important similarity exists between the cases of Madelyn and Karen—both experienced paternal deprivation during their preoedipal years of development. However, unlike the paternal "turn around" in Madelyn's situation, Karen's father finally deserted the family when she was three and a half years old, saw her only intermittently for about a year after he left the home, and maintained an irregular communication with her by phone or short notes. The arrival of a "good enough stepfather" may have played an important role in facilitating a favorable therapeutic outcome, but certainly the dynamic changes incurred by the analytic treatment of the patient, in addition to communications with the parents during treatment, were significantly helpful. The role that a male therapist played in the treatment offers considerations we might speculate upon. My impression is that considerations of gender could be helpful in some instances, but I do not believe that the sex of the therapist is necessarily crucial.

REFERENCES

Abelin, E. L. (1971), The role of the father in the separation-individuation process. In: *Separation-Individuation,* ed. J. B. McDevitt & C. F. Settlage. New York: International Universities Press, pp. 229–253.

———— (1972), Some further observations and comments on the earliest role of the father. Presented at Margaret S. Mahler Symposium on Child Development, Philadelphia, May.

———— (1975), Some further observations and comments on the earliest role of the father. *Internat. J. Psycho-Anal.,* 56:293–302.

———— (1977), The role of the father in core gender identity and in psychosexual differentiation. *J. Amer. Psychoanal. Assn.,* 26:43–161.

_____ (1980), Triangulation, the role of the father and the origins of core gender identity during the rapprochement subphase. In: *Rapprochement*, ed. R. Lax, S. Bach & A. Burland. New York: Aronson, pp. 151–169.

Greenacre, P. (1958), Early physical determinants in the development of the sense of identity. *J. Amer. Psychoanal. Assn.*, 6:612–627.

_____ (1960), Considerations regarding the parent-infant relationship. *Internat. J. Psycho-Anal.*, 41:571–584.

Loewald, H. (1951), Ego and reality. *Internat. J. Psycho-Anal.*, 32:10–18.

Mahler, M. S. (1952), One child psychosis and schizophrenia: Autistic and symbiotic infantile psychoses. *The Psychoanalytic Study of the Child*, 7:286–305. New York: International Universities Press.

_____ (1958), Autism and symbiosis: Two extreme disturbances of identity. *Internat. J. Psycho-Anal.*, 39:77–83.

_____ (1963), Thoughts about development and individuation. *The Psychoanalytic Study of the Child*, 18:307–324. New York: International Universities Press.

_____ (1967), On human symbiosis and the vicissitudes of individuation. *J. Amer. Psychoanal. Assn.*, 15:740–763.

_____ (1971), A study of the separation-individuation process and its possible application to borderline phenomena in the psychoanalytic situation. *The Psychoanalytic Study of the Child*, 26:403–442. New York: Quadrangle.

_____ (1972a), On the first three subphases of the separation-individuation process. *Internat. J. Psycho-Anal.*, 53:333–338.

_____ (1972b), Rapprochement subphase of the separation-individuation process. *Psychoanal. Quart.*, 41:487–506.

_____ Pine, F. & Bergman, A. (1975), *The Psychological Birth of the Human Infant*. New York: Basic Books.

Ross, J. M. (1977), Toward fatherhood: The epigenesis of paternal identity during a boy's first decade. *Internat. J. Psycho-Anal.*, 4:327–347.

_____ (1979a), Fathering: A review of some psychoanalytic contributions on paternity. *Internat. J. Psycho-Anal.*, 60:317–327.

_____ (1979b), Paternal identity: The equation of fatherhood and manhood. In: *On Sexuality*, ed. T. B. Karasu & C. W. Socarides. New York: International Universities Press, pp. 73–97.

Spitz, R. A. (1950), Relevancy of direct infant observations. *The Psychoanalytic Study of the Child*, 10:215–240. New York: International Universities Press.

_____ (1965), *The First Year of Life*. New York: International Universities Press.

Stoller, R. (1975), *The Transsexual Experiment*, Vol. 2. London: Hogarth Press.

_____ (1979), Fathers of transsexual children. *J. Amer. Psychoanal. Assn.*, 27:837–866.

Winnicott, D. W. (1956), Primary maternal preoccupation. In: *Collected Papers*. New York: Basic Books, pp. 300–305, 1958.

_____ (1965), *The Maturational Processes and the Facilitating Environment*. New York: International Universities Press.

_____ (1971), *Playing and Reality*. New York: Basic Books.

DISCUSSION

John Munder Ross

For a researcher on fathers, it is indeed gratifying to see a clinical as well as developmental "respect" (to borrow from Pacella) accorded to the father's role in the emotional lives of his sons and, especially, his daughters. Pacella's chapter is a tribute to the tradition of the late Margaret Mahler (Mahler, Pine, and Bergman, 1975) in adumbrating the place in the prehistory of the Oedipus complex and later psychic structures of both parents.

After summarizing the current consensus regarding the father's developmental functions, Pacella presents two case histories of oedipal and postoedipal girls. In these he emphasizes a convergence of symptomatology—negative, oppositional "ambitendent" behavior—despite very different mothers (and indeed family circumstances). The author traces these to a preoedipal paternal insufficiency on the part of his patients' emotionally, and in the second instance, to physically, absent fathers. As a result, both girls remained stuck in the push-me-pull-you rapprochement subphase struggles with mother (see Mahler, Pine, and Bergman, 1975, pp. 76–108). The transference offerings of analysis eventually provided both girls with an object relational alternative, inviting them into a romance with a more nurturing, affirmatory father. Madelyn, in particular, took advantage of this second developmental chance to consolidate her core gender identity and then to elaborate a feminine sexual identity through the vicissitudes of the oedipal situation. Both analyses, incidentally, show the author's craftsmanly hand in facilitating these children's expression of their innermost yearnings.

Along the way, Pacella raises several questions that pertain to problems of isolating variables and tendering generalizations in research on father-child interactions and on development as a whole. Ours is still a fairly primitive discipline, after all, and caveats are in order lest we make facts out of heuristic devices. If people (and "people in progress") are noteworthy for the universals that seem to govern psychic life, they are also remarkable for their infinite variety, and complexity, and the existential twists and turnings along pathways otherwise predetermined.

First of all, Pacella borrows from Winnicott (1949, 1956, 1965) – as many of us have – the notion of the "good-enough parent," mother *or* father. Perhaps fathers lend themselves to this conceit even more than mothers do. After all, in research settings, as in many so-called traditional nuclear families, the father has largely remained a shadowy and, for all intents and purposes, a two-dimensional presence. Yet observers like Mahler, along with Escalona (1968), Brazelton and Als (1979), and others, have made note of complexities in the mother's character and quasi-transferential reactions to her growing and unique child. We have come to view the parent-child transaction as a layered interpersonal and object relational dynamism in which the caretaker is hardly reducible to any factitious constant. The concept of the "average expectable environment" (Hartmann, 1939) has become less and less useful as a working baseline in hands-on observational inquiry. Indeed, from the start, Spitz (1965) conceived of a *dialogue* between parent and child, one all too easily "derailed."

I see no reason that this should not apply also to the dyad of father and child, especially during the child's pivotal and responsive second year of life and perhaps even more so during the oedipal phase, when parental outlines are filled in by real experience and fantasy. In other words, fathers are people too, their perceptions and behavior shaped by external as well as intrapsychic influences. They change to some degree as their children grow – altering their representations of a son or daughter in accordance with subtle and often unconscious fluctuations in the interchanges between them. Children introject and internalize actual and implied aspects of their fathers and structure their wishes and ego-ideal accordingly. What fathers do intrapsychically – how their presence is assimilated and accommodated to affecting development – is thus a function of what they *do*, of how they are as represented in spite of themselves, and of what is released in them by the child in the way of instinctive parenting.

Wisely, Pacella demurs from speculating upon the sources of his change of heart, but certainly Madelyn's father offers a case in point of the conflictual and dynamic nature of a father's immersion or not in the life of a daughter. What was it, we may ask (and does Pacella have more information to offer us?), in his own history or in the family system that moved this man to reject his daughter in the first place – in a way experienced by her as a repudiation of her genitals and "feminine status"? We could learn more about the resonances of Madelyn with the hated sister, the place of this relationship early on and in later life, and its possible reenactment in the sticky mother-daughter relationship. In any event, the subsequent reciprocal love affair between father and daughter, rehearsed in the neutral climate of the analysis, becomes quite remarkable. *Perhaps*—and I emphasize the uncertainty in the absence of further clinical material—we are witness to the child's growing initiative and, with her entry into phallic and oedipal postures, her ability to evoke appropriate counteroedipal approbation— "minimal seduction," to borrow from Stoller (1975)—from her increasingly beloved father. As Madelyn became more libidinally available, so did he. A mutual feedback system seems to have been set in motion, which in the end enabled this little girl to meld what Tessman (1982) has called "sexual" and "endeavor" excitement under the evermore watchful and loving eye of an adoring Daddy. Karen was, of course, far less lucky and had to use analysis not to undo but rather to come to grips with the grim truth of paternal deprivation.

This clinical material also calls into question another of our habits of mind—our tendency, that is, to consider the actual family triangle (even excluding siblings) in terms only of dyads and of the influence of one or the other parent directly on the child or on the other's parenting. Seldom do we conceptualize the child's impact on the couple and their mature genital functioning. In turn, the state of the marriage certainly has its effect on parental readiness and capacity.

Once again, Madelyn's circumstances may tell of larger truths. Through analysis, she seems to have wrested herself from her entanglement with her mother, freeing herself for a fuller involvement with her father. At the same time, as the child overcame an apparent arrest in development, she may have liberated her mother as well, freed her from an overinvolvement, and, with this, an overidentification with a latterday toddler. Let go, Madelyn's mother could become more of a wife and woman (even at times a mother) to her husband. (We can only speculate on the web of mutual identification entailed.) With this, I conjecture, Madelyn's father may have become less resentful of the hitherto exclusive, if somewhat sadomasochistic bond between mother and child. Relieved of anger and guilt, he may then have been enabled to lavish libido on a daughter no longer so much *his* preoedipal rival.

In the analysis, Madelyn busied herself with the genitals of herself, her brother, and her father. Reviewing the chapter, I was reminded of James Herzog (personal communication), who has spoken of the penis-to-penis dialogues of father and son. In counterpoint,

Pacella's focus on fathers and daughters (not sons) – and their genital encounters – is rare and welcome. Girls are important too, despite the phallocentric bias of theorizing about fathers. I am glad that Pacella has righted an imbalance in which they have been given short shrift. In contrast to Abelin (1977), he suggests that fathers figure early on in the nascent erotic life of little girls – not merely during the oedipal years. I would only ask that he elaborate further on the relation of the father's role in resolving rapprochement ambitendencies to his part in a penis (or eye)-vulva transaction of father and daughter, and their impact on the consolidation of core gender identity. The interconnections are by no means clear, even though they intuitively seem unmistakable.

Thus, rather like Madelyn's sweeter flirtatiousness, Karen's cold, calculating coquettishness seems to bespeak some self-defining or narcissistic aim, the seductiveness of a toddler in search of a self, through an attachment to a new and more different "primary object" – one idealized in fantasy. Very often early deficits make for hidden agendas in caricatures of oedipal ambition. We have seen this sort of secret self-serving in the phallic narcissistic displays of boys and men inadequately disidentified from mother, secretly "father hungry." This idealization of the parent is typical where the reality is wanting in parental reliability and narcissistic supplies. What about counterparts in girls?

Both analyses, of oedipal and latency age girls (exhibiting a failure in latency), *manifestly* deal with phallic narcissistic and oedipal themes and conflicts, more so than with silent preoedipal and preverbal matters. In the process, however, as Pacella underlines, preoedipal, specifically rapprochement, issues are indeed revived and reworked. Apparently, in paying heed to the adaptability of the child, we must add to Mahler's emphasis on the child's capacity to *extract* from the supplies tendered (however meager or inconsistent) Erikson's (1963) stress on the child's dynamic plasticity and ability to recapitulate and rework earlier developmental journeys during later life crises.

To Pacella's conclusions then, I would add a consideration of 1) the idiosyncracies and dynamic reactions of a father; 2) the couple's relationship and the child's impact on this; 3) an elucidation of the formation of core gender identity in concert with rapprochement – the basic crisis of separation-individuation; and 4) the timelessness of the unconscious and our ability to revive and resolve archaic problems during later ones.

REFERENCES

Abelin, E. (1977), The role of the father in core gender identity and in psychosexual differentiation. *J. Amer. Psychoanal. Assn.,* 26:43–161.

Brazelton, T. B. & Als, H. (1979), Four early stages in the development of mother-infant interactions. *The Psychoanalytic Study of the Child,* 34:349–369. New York: International Universities Press.

Erikson, E. H. (1963), *Childhood and Society.* New York: Norton.

Escalona, S. (1968), *The Roots of Individuality.* Chicago: Aldine.

Hartmann, H. (1939), *Ego Psychology and the Problem of Adaptation.* New York: International Universities Press, 1958.

Mahler, M. S., Pine, F. & Bergman, A. (1975), *The Psychological Birth of the Human Infant.* New York: Basic Books.

Spitz, R. A. (1965), *The First Year of Life.* New York: International Universities Press.

Stoller, R. (1975), Healthiest parental influences on the earlier development in baby boys. *Psychoanal. Forum,* 5:232–262.

Tessman, L. (1982), A note on father's contribution to the daughter's ways of loving and working. In: *Father and Child,* ed. S. Cath, A. Gurwitt & J. Ross. Boston: Little, Brown.

Winnicott, D. W. (1949), The ordinary devoted mother and her baby. *The Child and the Family.* New York: Basic Books, 1957.

―――― (1956), Primary maternal preoccupation. In: *Collected Papers.* New York: Basic Books, 1958.

―――― (1965), *The Maturational Processes and the Facilitating Environment.* New York: International Universities Press.

12

The Paternal Possibility

The Father's Contribution to the Adolescent Daughter When the Mother Is Disturbed and a Denigrated Figure

Rosemary H. Balsam

When a girl's mother is significantly emotionally disturbed for long periods during the girl's growing up, a very involved father may play a more vital role than usual in his daughter's achievement of adulthood. This clinical paper explores some aspects of the heightened significance of the father in adolescence both in its positive aspects and in its potential to create inner conflict for the girl's burgeoning womanhood. The emotional constellations of my focus are mostly gleaned from the three-to-five-year analyses of college women in their late adolescence. Each of these patients chose a woman analyst, with the explicit or implicit goal that somehow they would be guided further along the lines they had chosen for themselves – the goal of how to be as unlike their mothers as possible. Their fathers all ostensibly supported their treatment aim, and the patients had none of the usual family problems of the ambivalence of launching a costly and lengthy therapy program. If the mothers had objections, they were quickly overruled in favor of father's and daugther's estimate that treatment with a woman analyst was a worthy venture.

Illustrative vignettes from five analyses will be given. They will be disguised to protect confidentiality. The findings are resonant with patterns in other cases with similar family dynamics seen in psychotherapy or supervision. These cases are dissimilar to young women with disturbed mothers and passive or uninvolved fathers; a father with a potential to share his gifted daughter's interests seemed an energizing aspect characteristic of this group under discussion. They are also dissimilar to patients whose parents divorced in the girl's early childhood, although certain common elements may exist in given cases. The trauma of actual separation or divorce at any early age often lends a particular caste to the patient's reenactment of ongoing concerns, such as an unconscious expectation of the disappearance of a parent. Therefore, I have excluded these special instances in the interests of simplicity.

THE FAMILY TRIAD

The five middle-aged fathers in this group were high-achieving professionals, caring and involved with the young women who at the time of presentation were between 18 and 20 years old. The five middle-aged mothers, all housewives, had longstanding diagnosed psychiatric illness: they included one woman with manic-depressive illness, two chronic alcoholics, a paranoid schizophrenic, and a severely obsessional and phobic woman. In short, they had all kinds of chronic disabilities that had inevitably affected the day-to-day interactions with their daughters from an early age. Two mothers had been divorced by their husbands when the girls were close to puberty. In each case, the daughters had, while in their early teens, acquired new, younger stepmothers – women who were extremely important to them and contrasted with their biological mothers. These stepmothers complicated the picture in generally positive ways, but they too proved internally conflictual figures.

I will not dwell on the details of the preadolescent home atmosphere. Such attention would include, at different phases of development, the specific problems between each girl and her mother, the thorny parental interaction, and the sibling relations. Of course, the individuality of each young woman was bound up with such issues, but it is too cumbersome for the purposes of this paper to elaborate these lines. Suffice to say that by late adolescence, albeit by individual historical routes, the consciously dyadic emphases in the triad had evolved and was weighted toward father and daughter. There was no common denominator of the daughters' birth order, but each had been identified early as having a resemblance to father. The fathers, in the girls' early childhood, had not been involved in direct child care. As one patient said, "That's when he was off making his name and his money." Universally the girls were aware early of a sense of his glamor and success in the outside world. They all expressed memories of early anger that he had failed to protect them from upsetting interactions with mother within the home. It was only in high school that these fathers became vigorously directly involved. Perhaps the girls' growing intellectual capacities, combined with their more unavoidable sexual presence, meshed with needs of these fathers arising from their own mid-life crises, in order to enhance the dyad.

The bright young women were all undergraduates. They were all excellent academically. School had always provided a refuge for them. Their fathers had admired and encouraged their advancing school achievements, and unanimously they verbalized their eager connections with their fathers in this area. Three of the mothers had undermined their ambitions, but that had never hindered school performance. In fact, in some instances it had spurred them to further honors in high school as a way of differentiating themselves from the difficult mothers and simultaneously vengefully to show their mothers up as worthless. Their career paths were almost set – they wanted to be doctors, lawyers, to go into business – to have major careers like their fathers. This was the area of their lives for which they felt best groomed.

The emotional tasks of adolescence can be condensed into three major areas. These women were in the process of mastering avocational choice. The other two trends, which should have been proceeding developmentally simultaneously, proved to be intertwined and sources of impasse: their internal psychological separation from both parents and the establishment of a relatively firm sexual identity (Irwin, 1977, p. 25).

PRESENTING COMPLAINTS

The overt complaints of these young women were, "I've had such a hard time with my mother and I do not want to turn out like her." The related major vulnerabilities were in attempts at forming stable heterosexual relationships. At this age, such problems are not necessarily malignant, but these patients felt a special urgency because of their dawning awareness of the potential destructiveness of their parents' marital problems. Two said, "I want to be married some day, but there's something wrong with my relationship with men." One who had a live-in boyfriend said, "I just weep all the time. I don't know why. He's getting fed up with me."

In brief, their mental states were characterized more by interpersonal anxiety and situational anxiety than by entrenched states of despair. None of the women were psychotic or severely dysfunctional. Two had concomitant eating disorders that had manifested themselves about age 15. These young women were obsessed with food and fatness, had been episodically bulimic but had never been physically compromised. Each patient had enough observing ego and awareness of inner conflict to warrant a psychoanalytic approach. These particular symptoms abated within a year of starting analysis.

The father plays a vital role in helping solidify the feminine identity of his daughter. Ritvo (1975) stated, "This has been so in the phallic oedipal period and again the pre-adolescent and adolescent stages" (p. 2). He is also pivotal in her relationship to her mother, weaving an additional thread in the formation of her attitude toward her own femininity. These patients, because of their uneven alignment between the parents, were blocked in the evolution of what Blos (1967) delineated as the second individuation process, "a component in the psychic re-structuring that winds, like a scarlet thread, through the entire fabric of adolescence" (p. 162). A loosening of the infantile object ties is desirable to "become a member . . . of the adult world" (p. 163). At presentation, they were overly involved with father and had dismissed mother, negating her as any influence in their lives. Their consistent denial of engagement with her was a defense against internal enmeshment with mother as a feared and hated infantile object. They presented this image unconsciously and were unable to test varying object- and self-representations in relation to her as a progressing adolescent will, in order to temper and remold earlier and later versions into a stable internalization.

In general terms, their development had begun to go awry as they shied away from any hint of becoming grown up, sexual women contending with the disturbing inner influences of their unconscious models of "true" femininity – their consciously denigrated mothers.

FATHER INVOLVEMENT

Their fathers, excellent models in dealing with the outside world, were uniformly greatly admired. They were all highly talented, educated, and achieving. Without exception, they had formed such close bonds, charged with active oedipal fantasies, that their fathers were consciously described as their best mates. The fathers, in turn, had relied heavily on the support of these daughters during crises with the mothers. In some instances, the girls had taken care of their younger siblings at the behest of father. One young woman, patient A, had been left at the age of 13 in charge of a household containing a separated mother so depressed that she neglected the home and the food and spent her time hiding in bed. Patient A, after school, used to organize her younger brother and sisters to do their homework and try to urge her sick mother out of bed. Father was a few blocks away in a new apartment with his lover, working in intensive therapy trying to get the courage to begin a new life. One night after mother had called father in a rage, threatening to murder the little ones, patient A ran away to join father and together they summoned help to rehospitalize mother. Patient A stayed with father from then on.

Patient B spent much of her time poring over academic projects with father, who joined in enthusiastically, ignoring mother. Father and daughter did athletics together, competing with each other. They cooked together. She was the only girl. Father would phone her often at college to try to dissect all her sulky moods after her brief visits home. Only when she reassured him that she loved him could they end each phone conversation.

Patient C would phone father for hours at a time to discuss her school papers. He advised her on how to handle her teachers. He would dwell on all his physical aches and pains, and she would advise him on which medical consultants in the town to approach. Mother would sit in stony silence in the background. This patient had an eating disorder.

Patient D would invite father to all her athletic events. He would cheer her, talk to her coaches, and plan her next strategy at a meet. Patient D and her father would go out for a beer together to talk about life. Occasionally he would bring a female companion with him, and the patient would spurn her. She would talk of the intractable troubles at home with mother. This daughter was much more in communication with her father than were his other daughters, who were in disgrace essentially for not being in sufficient supportive contact with him.

A downtrodden looking young women with an eating disorder, patient E had cut off any overtly dependent ties, except financial, to both parents. This represented a desperate, conscious attempt to become adult. On making the break for college, she chose to work with a female internist at the college health plan who oversaw her weight and nutrition, while she brought her psychological issues to analysis. In high school she had enjoyed close attention from father and had geared her achievements to reciprocate his love. As the intensity of their relation quickened, patient E developed her eating problem. Among other issues, it served to protect her from the sexual implications of the tie. Unlike her brothers, she chose to attend his college. Her relationship to father became revitalized during treatment. All of these fathers seemed to have delivered an overt message that if the daughters were to be loved by them, there was to be no behavior reminiscent of mother. For patient E, this behavior was obesity and overindulgence in alcohol.

Patient A had spells of depression after moving in with father. He would spend hours giving her pep talks on the virtues of becoming active and fighting adversity. Apparently he would become enraged if he thought she was spending too much time in bed, like her paranoid schizophrenic mother.

Patient B had her sulky moods and while visiting at home wanted to spend time in her room. Father would hound her to tidy her room, and he would visit her college room to inspect it, using her neatness as a barometer of her success in being unlike her alcoholic mother. Mother often lived in chaos in her kitchen.

Patient C kept telling father "not to worry" about his bodily complaints. The phobic mother used to become frantic, thinking he had cancer or a heart attack. All his bodily problems were treated by mother as dirty—she changed the plastic on the toilet seats at home each time he visited the bathroom. If patient C voiced any anxiety about her own body or her eating problem, he would end the conversation and turn away.

Patient D sometimes was injured in athletics. Because mother, a manic-depressive, had had many operations and finally had had a hysterectomy, the daughter felt it necessary to conceal all injuries from father. Indeed, if on occasion a confession emerged, he would berate her for being psychologically accident prone and thus held her responsible, compounding her guilt about body vulnerability and suggesting an attitude (which she shared) that she should be in control of her body at all times. Once she covered her blistered feet in tight, high-heeled shoes in order to have the pleasure of his company at a club. He danced with her all night, never suspecting her condition.

Patient E felt a failure and rejected by father because of her thin condition prior to college entrance. She was desperate to look better after a semester in order to go home on vacation. At college she ate sensibly and quickly acquired a preppy way of dressing, with many college emblems on her attire, a vivid contrast from her mother, who dressed from Goodwill stores. The most thrilling moment of her first visit home was when father resurrected his college blazer to solidify alliance with her.

The bilateral intensity of the relationship to father can be seen in these vignettes. Hopes to become a grown up were centered on amalgamated desires to be like him and therefore be pleasing to him by either "becoming" him, being enwrapped in the sphere of his self-love, or becoming his most beloved female. The new stepmothers of patients A and D caused turmoil in the young women, as they noticed their favorite conceptions of how to be maximally pleasing to father being called into question, for example by the stepmother's domesticity, lack of athleticism, or overt flirtatiousness with men other than father.

When a father is placed in such a key role in the girl's mind in adolescence, he becomes unconsciously not only the admiring adult male toward whom the second thrust of oedipal drives is attached. He *is* the patient's true husband in her mind. Thus fantasy becomes reality in all but overt sexual terms. The sexual fantasies are observed in attempts to seduce father, accompanied by intense frustration and inner puzzlement that he seems to give double messages in this way and also seems potentially rejecting.

Such a father, in addition, because of negation of the mother, becomes also the focus of fantasies usually directed toward the mother – traits of being like him/her, sexual competition with him/her combined with intense needs for the reassurance of continued nurturance from him/her. Yet, in order to preserve this ongoing relationship, these young women had attempted to split off and keep hidden the more tumultuous elements of their needs toward the wished-for mother in him. These particular fathers were especially ill at ease with neediness, which they perceived to be a feminine trait. Their wariness seemed due to unresolved issues with their own mothers, compounded by the demands of their wives.

A further aspect of such a father is his heightened capacity to become the young girl's major ego ideal. The lingering, strong, infantile tie, combined with the natural adolescent state of transmuting archaic superego into ego ideal, together with the protracted family enmeshment, places the father as the top of a hierarchy of ego ideals that the young woman would naturally seek in the extrafamilial world.

RELATIONSHIPS WITH YOUNG MEN

At the time of their felt need for help, these young women displaced all these combined wishes onto the young men with whom they attempted involvement in college. Their young male partners were unsatisfactory to them in every way. They were not as dashing as the fathers in these ideal and currently partially satiated oedipal roles. The young men's requirements for overt sexual activity were at odds with the girls' internal view of father and carried incest taboos. When the women did engage in close bodily contact, intense maternal desires were inflamed for tender nurturance with all the preoedipal tinge of repressed total needs to be "looked after," to be fed symbolically and actually, to be constantly approved of, and to have their wishes "known" without verbal expressions. These states also served as a defense against heterosexual desire. Since these women uniformly had had unsatisfactory experiences with mother in their early childhood (experiences that cannot be fully elaborated in this paper), their unconscious frustrations in these areas were particularly strong. And since these conflicts had to be focused on their fathers in adolescence, their young male partners became displaced and substituted objects for the full force of their difficulties in separation-individuation, their wishes to identify with and compete with them. The young men were also combined objects toward whom they experienced sexual arousal. It was no wonder that these first trials at heterosexuality fell foul. No young man, especially in late adolescence himself, could bear such a burden of this quality of wish. It was also no surprise that within these relationships the young women felt aghast at the shocking appearance of behavior that they had associated with their denigrated disturbed mothers. Their success in the isolation, splitting, denial and repression of these islands of primitive neediness had served a jealously guarded self-image in their earlier adolescence of being in control, strong, and self-sufficient. Thus, at one level, it was a tremendous blow to their self-esteem that they no longer were able to avoid reactivated behaviors and desires of earlier phases of their development, usually transmuted within the maternal matrix. Their self-repugnance was more marked than in the usual resistance to regression characteristic of adolescents in analysis. At stake was loss of honor, reminiscent of an impetuous and aggrieved aristocratic duellist of bygone days.

SEXUAL DEVELOPMENT

It was my impression that these young women were more open about or more actively engaged with masturbation than other women whom I have treated. Even in latency their autoerotic activities had off and on been knowing and intense. Tabin (1985) theorized that there is a reciprocity between focus and awareness of inner genital sensation and the degree of autonomy and integrity of body boundary achieved by the child. A premature sense of individuation from the early mother may have provided impetus in these cases for an ability to locate inner sexual stimuli, more akin to the normal development of a male child. Perhaps the lack of an effective maternal image yielded a less harshly organized superego in this area, resulting in a less restrained arena for erotic activity. The tie to the father seemed unevenly repressed from the classical oedipal phase, and suggestively from what Tabin (1985) called "the primary oedipal phase" (a term that grants the father a central role in what is usually termed the pregenital era in the first three years of life). In tune with the post-Freudian trend of finding critical periods of personality development earlier than the classical oedipal period, Tabin provided an integrative model for the development of the sense of self at about two years. She delineated the interaction of early genital sensation as it affects gender identity and ego formation, which in turn is in dynamic interaction with gender-based self-modelling toward the same sex parent accompanied by separation-individuation challenges. The universal view of themselves as victor over a vanquished mother provided these young women a powerful drive toward sexual self-discovery.

Masturbation had also long been a means of self-comfort, and fantasy had been a "cocoon of protection," as one patient expressed it, as they bulwarked themselves against maternal narcissistic blows.

It was also interesting that all five had repudiated doll play, preferring instead stuffed animals to cuddle in bed. Besides providing welcome psychological alignment with boys in daytime, the soft toys were sensually gratifying as breast substitutes and a reconnection with the reassuring transitional object stage of development by night. Dolls were too fearfully charged as defined artifacts of femininity.

Recalled childhood fantasies centered on a heady power of self-induced control over body stimulation and climax. They did not confine themselves to clitoral manipulation, but had explored the introitus and perineum, and in some cases the anus, but with no special preference for the latter. Formed fantasies included vague images of intercourse with males, fearful and exciting images of being penetrated by a large penis, romantic fairy tale encounters of being rescued by a prince, or images of becoming a powerful, graceful animal such as a magical black horse, a tigress, or a larger-than-life cat.

As soon as they achieved physical separation from home, all of these women became heterosexually active. In spite of all of their psychological turmoil, they seemed to have remarkable ease in achieving orgasm. The mechanics of the sex act were the least of their problem. This ease was, however, temporarily shaken in later phases of the analyses, when the women were preoccupied by previously unapproached images of being out of control in their female bodies. The legacy of their earlier autoerotic experience of orgastic expectation and bodily attention eventually emerged into playful and vital sexual connection with their partners, which also reflected mutual involvement with men rather than the use of their bodies as need-satisfying, masturbatory tools. (Tessman, 1982, reported similar findings in one of her cases.) Throughout their analyses, the women's sexual vigor was quite constant and readily included in their associations. (Later I refer to these qualities in connection with my comments on father excitement.) None of these patients had had intercourse earlier than college. They had avoided such consummation partly because of the distraught model of their parents' relationships, partly because of the intensified gratifying oedipal bond between themselves and fathers, and partly because of an inner awareness that each bodily attention would arouse both heterosexual passion and forbidden homosexual desires. When a real-life male entered the picture, his closeness stimulated a confused internal lack of clarity in relation to the male body per se. Who and what was actually male or female became unclear.

The young women's preferred modes of feeling separate, in control, defined, and independent emerged into images of wanting to be "on top" of the emotions engendered and distaste and disgust at feeling "unravelled" or vulnerable in sexual arousal with a mate. One patient was horrified that when involved with a young man she became "obsessed" by needing to see him all the time. She hated that her concentration on schoolwork suffered. In fact, all she seemed to want to do now, she explained, was to be in bed, to masturbate and daydream about the longing for his body. Fantasies often involved being on top sexually. "I want to give him orgasm after orgasm. I want to have that power—to let him see what it is like to feel that dependent." These fantasies expressed both the desire to show far more sexual power than the weak mother and simultaneously the desire to be a man as she conceived it. Aggressive, intrusive, and vengeful fantasies of intercourse also reflected unconscious anger at father. After all, if he were so powerful and so omniscient, then it followed that he must also be responsible for violating the mother, rendering her helpless and dysfunctional by, for example, "forcing" her to bear more babies. He thus was held to be the "cause" of mother's disturbance. In the vengeful aspect of the "ontop" sexual fantasy, the daughter was paying back her male partner on both her mother's and her own account.

The "on the bottom" fantasies of the female sexual role were ones of craven passivity. "You could go mad wanting a man that much," said the usually perfectly contained athlete, patient D. She and others were convinced that the experience of arousal by a man would stimulate such intense voraciousness that it would be uncontrollable. The appetites unleashed for unbounded experience were often associated with fantasies of early experience with the mother. Having an orgasm while in this state seemed to be a way of rediscovering self-definition in this phase of adolescence. Thus, the young man would be the recipient of both the desire for blissful fusion and also the delivery from that state. The young women then were absorbed in images of themselves as ill-defined, yielding, open orifices, blended with their vulnerable mothers in their fantasy of her intercourse.

Making the man solely responsible for their orgasms and redefined boundaries expressed wishes from all levels of their psyche to find safe refuge with the ideal of a better defined male who should "rightly" be in charge of them and their bodily needs. One young male partner, who was impotent, induced such rage in the woman that she bit him and beat him up after masturbating himself to climax. The body image of these patients in the act of intercourse cast internal doubt on their male or female habitus and genitals. Fluidly they shifted according to their inner needs with a male partner.

None of these patients was an overt lesbian in her choice of sexual partner. There was perhaps too strong a component of sexual desire toward the father and too powerful an overtly positive oedipal involvement and object relation with him, idealization and worship of the phallus. Men, after all, had been their saviors. This constellation seemed to outweigh their sexual identification with the father. Their yearnings toward women were unconscious. In fact, they all felt the need to work on their readiness to repudiate tender relationships with women friends, who were more threatening.

Images of their male partners were thus also self-representations of their own unconsciously bisexually perceived bodies, and their first choice of males was narcissistically tinged. This is, of course, typical of adolescents, but the androgeny had a special significance here as a defense against fully owning their femininity, which universally they saw as a trap.

TRANSFERENCE AND THE COURSE OF ANALYSES

In the transference initially, when it was even-toned, these patients often saw me, their female analyst, as a kindly man. Quickly this perception became sexualized in positive oedipal terms. They wanted to be the best, the greatest, the most admired both to defeat me as a woman and to gain my love as with a man; I should admire their young female bodies as though through the eyes of a man. Guilt about this oedipal transference was absent, as the mother was already destroyed and defeated. It was much later that they recognized the effects of repressed guilt and a sense of themselves as dangerous rivals. The excitement generated toward me also seemed a desexualized derivative of their connection to father as a highly valued person, free of gender definition.

Rage was a predominant affect in the early phases, as the patients struggled with entitlement and peevishness at the idea of other patients or my children as favorites. Some gloried in a fantasy that I preferred females. They tried to court and endear me along their favorite lines of seduction of their fathers. Analytic neutrality was hard for them to bear, for example, when it concerned my health (as with patient C) or their latest brilliant grades or athletic triumphs or defeats. They interpreted neutrality as rejection of them as oedipal victor. We thus lived through and worked through their current active oedipal transference and intense tie to father.

A deepening bond developed as the oedipal line was gradually interpreted and gave way to their seeing me as ideal parent. This was a female ideal with androgenous overtones. Unlike their own perceptions of their weak mothers, this male-type mother was strong, allowed separateness, but was an unfeeling model of female executive function. Perfection and clean lines of delineation veiled an androgenous confusion. Accent on surface appearance concealed a fear of what manner of beast was inside me. Fantasies centered on my activities. The patients would imitate my dress, pick up cooking magazines from the waiting room to learn to cook what they thought I cooked. One patient became aware that my husband worked nearby and that I met him at a local caf'e. She would make a point of crossing paths with her boyfriend during the work day, as she fantasized I did. That I keep my professional name signified militant feminism to several as they rehearsed how to become women who would not be engulfed by every aspect of their husbands.

Their penchant for seeing me as an ego ideal was, of course, a natural function of their adolescence. But the focused intensity stemmed in a major way from the idealization of the fathers, combined with dissatisfaction and denial of their own mothers, with a plea for me to teach by example how to become a woman. Associations on the couch to their real mothers were always devalued at this stage in treatment. Their urge was to remain, in their terms, reality bound – a tendency in adolescent analyses related to the ubiquitous resistance to regression noted by Blos (1967). The incorporative nature of the identification was most marked in the patients with eating disorders. They had a tendency to swallow whole every interpretation as undigested wisdom. The others also, in varying degrees, attempted to become like me, lest they discover their own internal complexity, containing as it did the influences of their own mother.

A further elaboration of an oedipal dynamic became manifest, this time with me as purely female. One young woman tried to arrange a meeting between me and her father over a billing issue. Part of this desire preconsciously was a wish that her father and I would fall in love and I would become her stepmother. All the women had had active fantasies of being the daughters of friends' mothers as they grew up. Associations to my being ideal opened areas of early adolescence where these patients had formed powerful bonds to female teachers. It was interesting that they chose older women rather than men as mentors.

Two of the analysands had attended boarding schools, where older women teachers had served the function of model, ideal, active, capable women who cared deeply about the girls. The ego ideal had the same ambiguously sexual nature as in the transference.

Gradually, and usually by nonverbal routes, earlier versions of their conflicts with mother or female infant caretakers began to emerge. Drawing attention to parapraxes or, say, leaving belongings behind in the office evoked repudiation, denial, or disgust. The contrast between themselves and the outer ideal of me was painful. My position as analyst and theirs as analysand stimulated comparisons with my "cool" (as they saw it), my control, my lack of "pouring out" in unbridled association. Their view of me was as an ideal of control, which they criticized themselves for not fulfilling. Their superego constraint was thus interpreted as part of their own self-criticism. They became angry because I was not serving the function that they and their fathers had consciously and preconsciously planned. I was a severe disappointment to them compared with their high school teachers or their adoring fathers. Where were the injunctions they wanted and had grown to rely on, to tighten up their performance, to excel, not to act spoiled or babyish? One young woman described herself at this stage as a blob of gelatin oozing all over the couch.

For months at a time, usually about two or three years into the analytic process, they would feel at sea in the sessions. What did I want of them? How could they please me if they could no longer unselfconsciously behave toward me as father or as their earlier adolescent ego ideals? Several almost interrupted treatment at this point with acting out behaviors to maintain their brittle sense of being grown-up. They declared themselves unable to bear the regression entailed in deepening analysis. Nevertheless, they weathered the storms within the process.

There were evidences of acute identity crises. "Who am I if I can't be strong, ordered, and neat? I hate you for making me so vulnerable." Thus I was beginning to be viewed as the early mother or caretaker. The young women saw themselves as reincarnations of the mothers they had denied. Once, during a rainstorm, patient A, having no umbrella or adequate shoes, came in soaked. She lay down on the couch, getting the covers wet. She wept for the first time. She felt angry and helpless and was full of expectation and hope of being scolded. If I was not angry, perhaps I did not love her as father or mother. The underlying wish was that I would have dressed her better for the storm. This was the girl, who at 13, prematurely pushed into motherhood, had had to oversee buying new underwear for her little brother when it had holes.

Weeping was anathema to these women. One told of how at age five she had wet her bed and had started to approach her parents' room for help, but had stopped herself, saying it was silly. Scarcely able to reach the shelf, she had taken clean sheets from the linen closet and fixed herself up, disturbing no one. Crying seemed to have been unbearable to all of these disturbed mothers. One patient had fantasies that I would beat her to "give me something to cry for." Many of their mothers had often dissolved in tears when overwhelmed, and the daughters' memories were of being afraid that they were the cause. They also accused themselves of being the "cause" of mother's entire disturbance. They would give mother a wide berth by delving into school work, or angrily they would take over mother's function.

The unfolding of the treatment can be summarized by saying that anything that reminded these women of childhood discomfort was seen as a sign of feminine weakness and revealed many unconscious hesistancies about their bodies. Childhood fantasies of a cloacal arrangement of the genitals, or castration fantasies and wishes for a penis, melded with dream images of blood or feces spewing out of them uncontrollably. Menstruation, either ignored by them or defensively glorified, became connected with anal material and infantile theories of birth. Current fears of pregnancy and the conviction that such an experience would destroy their bodies were intermingled. There appeared marked splits between their previous masturbation and the fuller acknowledgment of the sense of their sexual female bodies. Uniformly admitting such ideas and feelings to consciousness caused the patients violent distress because of associations to their troubled mothers and fears of rejection by the fathers. Concomitantly they mulled and readdressed their original stereotyping of male and female attributes, shifting self- and object representation in the context of their firmer female identities. One of the major tasks of these analyses proved to help these young women own the intensity of their wishes and fears vis-à-vis a mother-figure. Blos (1962) states that in order to reach maturity, the young woman has to "make peace . . . with her mother image" (p. 157). It took very hard work to separate off the image of themselves as mere caricatures of the troublesome mother whom they, father, and all men would find overburdening. As is always the case, each internalized sense of mother or early caretaker had to be considered in conjunction with the patient's own developmental demands of each psychosexual phase.

Characteristically, because of the active presence of their parents in their lives, the patients all evinced subtle changes in the relationship to their actual parents. Thus they separated themselves a little more from the idealized, possessive, and possessed fathers. In several cases, the fathers seemed relieved, and the patients spoke more of their interest in other women and their stepmothers. The father with physical complaints became acutely depressed, presumably suffering from the loss of his daughter's previously unrelenting support. He entered therapy.

The biological mother was now viewed independently from the father's perspective. Some of the women reconstituted richer connections with mother. For example, the daughter of one of the alcoholic mothers insisted that her mother never call her while drunk, but she would initiate shopping trips if her mother was sober. All of the patients rediscovered in their mothers talents they had previously overlooked, such as creative abilities, openness to feeling, tolerance of lack of perfection or abilities to act as they felt. They rehabilitated the image of mother in their own minds. They would often, at the same time, acknowledge flaws in the fathers and speculate about father's methods of exacerbating mother's vulnerabilities or his own needs to rely on the daughter in reaction to marital pain. By the close of treatment, all had experienced elements of closeness, intimacy, and genuine mutuality with young men. Newly awakened to their own oedipal dynamics, they viewed father's behavior with a certain indulgence as they struggled with the paternal side of the oedipal triangle to attempt a plane of adult equality. Interestingly, their original career commitments scarcely wavered throughout. Despite the tribulation of these analyses on the bilateral intimacy with the fathers, at termination the women maintained their loving and tender ties to one another. As patient A put it, "We still sing 'My heart belongs to Daddy,' but now we can joke about it too."

FURTHER COMMENTS

The outstanding feature of all these young women was an irrepressible life energy. There was a consuming desire to wrestle with their problems and become fully functional adults. Such qualities as determination, steadfastness, and lively commitment to academia, friends, adults, athletics, extracurricular activities, and their analyses were common denominators. At worst, they were driven under pressure. At best, they were joyful, intellectually curious, and sexually creative. They all had self-preserving elements of good judgment about their connections to the world.

There seemed a surprising paradox between their manifest ability to sustain vigorously both strongly positive and strongly negative ties to the therapist and to their early histories of often severe difficulty with the mother. Alternative caretakers had been available to these women, such as nursemaids, grandmothers, and aunts. While providing an anlage in a major way for islands of good-enough mothering (to use Winnicott's, 1971, term) to sustain the working alliance in analysis, none of these figures was granted the consistent force that would usually be attributed to an engaged mother. By the time the patients were five years old, these caretaking women had faded as figures who could withstand the developed, sexualized oedipal thrust, and thus internally they could not fully protect the young women from the later, highly charged, paternal relationship that flourished. The fathers had been involved with the girls as children, but it was especially at puberty and in adolescence that the exclusivity of the bond had caught fire. Greenacre, (1966) spoke of the "vigor and power" (p. 168) engendered in the small child through the participation with the father and believed this connection to be reflected in bonds of idealization toward the analyst later. Writers such as Herzog (1982) and others have observed and speculated about adult gender specific contributions to the quality of engagement with children.

The universal vivacity and willingness of these adolescent women to engage openly, experiment with, and experience change could be random features of self-selection for long-term treatment, or the result of the fluidity of the adolescent phase of development, or nonspecific, fortuitous, constitutional endowment. Because of the severe family problems, they may have acquired positive attributes of survival. Yet is is compelling to locate some of the quality of vigor as stemming from the relation to father per se. As the fathers were themselves highly energetic and achieving, identification with them would naturally carry these hallmarks. Defensively, the patients' fears of passivity, associated with their fantasies of basic ingredients of womanhood, may have provided a driving force toward this active involvement in treatment. These elements had become incorporated in their personalities as an adaptive and substantial way of being. Within the analytic process, the view of themselves as active agents in their environment allowed them to reenact, sustain, and analyze the long periods of passive fantasy and yearning for the analyst in the maternal transference and begin the discovery of themselves as possessing female bodies. The so-called feminine active pursuit of passive aims seemed cogent to what these young women claimed for themselves in the course of treatment.

The engaged father in a girl's life provides a focus for the direction and containment of high levels of general excitement. Tessman (1982) notes that not only is the father the object of sexual fantasy, but his engagement provides a psychic arena for the taming and modulation of general excitement, which yields fruit in the girl's ability to commit herself to work and to love. Tessman writes that "where sensuous interplay and mutuality have been lacking with mother, his response to her loving excitement may become more than usually crucial as the necessary force underlying her capacity for self-acceptance and ardor in adult life" (p. 229). Perhaps because of their diminished contact with nurturing mothers, these women were especially hungry for whatever stability the stronger, healthier father provided. The fathers certainly had behaved as if they alone were the source of positive parenting, consciously or unconsciously answering this need in their offspring. Perhaps the fathers also unconsciously compensated for an earlier potential deficit in the girls by an opportunistic overinvolvement in the second oedipal period. They seemed to be able to absorb both the erotic and the endeavor poles of the energies, so that the sexual aspect of the intimacy was not so terrifying as to provoke withdrawal. These fathers seemed to prefer daughters. The male siblings did not stimulate such attention, were more directly involved with the mothers, and often were in trouble with drugs, performed poorly in school, or were entangled with the law.

The sheer libidinal power of such active oedipal involvement in adolescence, in spite of its vicissitudes, may also have provided these young women with a greater than average ability to maintain self-esteem. They had internalized traits of self-worth and internal representations as people who could succeed if they worked hard. The patients felt especially chosen and supported by the fathers, and they represented themselves as entitled to glean the valued qualities perceived in the fathers, turning them to their own advantage. The fathers who remained within their marriages were taken as models for survival in tough conditions and the ability to weather discomfort without major disruption. Fathers who divorced were seen as being able to change their lives and not masochistically cling to problem lifestyles. Other interpretations could have formed central foci for sustained identification, such as their fathers' ungratifying choice of mates, but this did not become a viable option. The fear of repetition of the parental marriage was certainly present, but the women felt empowered to attempt better alliances. Two women have since married (satisfactorily by report), and it remains to be seen if the analytic intervention has been able to potentiate the kernels of strength that may coalesce to achieve the initial stated goals—to undo the threat of repetition compulsion of the fate of their own mothers. This will be especially tested when the young women themselves become mothers.

The very intensity of the father involvement that rendered the developmental impasse at the beginning of treatment proved to be the cornerstone of their bid to free themselves internally to become fuller women. I think that without such supportive fathers these young women would not, however arduously they tried, have been able to set their life course toward promising paths of satisfaction in life, work, and the social sphere.

REFERENCES

Blos, P. (1962), *On Adolescence.* New York: Free Press.

Blos, P. (1967), The second individuation process of adolescence. *The Psychoanalytic Study of the Child,* 22:162–187. New York: International Universities Press.

Greenacre, P. (1966), Problems of overidealization of the analyst and of analysis: their manifestations in the transference and countertransference relationship. *The Psychoanalytic Study of the Child,* 21:193–213. New York: International Universities Press.

Herzog, J. M. (1982), On father hunger: The father's role in the modulation of aggressive drive and fantasy. In: *Father and Child,* ed. S. H. Cath, A. Gurwitt, & J. M. Ross. Boston: Little, Brown.

Irwin, E. M. (1977), *Growing Pains,* Estover, Plymouth, Eng: Macdonald & Evans.

Ritvo, S. (1975), Female psychology and development in adolescence. A panel on the psychology of women: Late adolescence and early adulthood. Presented at meeting of American Psychoanalytic Association, Beverly Hills, CA, May.

Tabin, J. K. (1985), *On the Way to Self Ego and Early Oedipal Development.* New York: Columbia University Press.

Tessman, L. H. (1982), A note on the father's contribution to the daughter's ways of loving and working. In: *Father and Child,* ed. S. H. Cath, A. Gurwitt, & J. M. Ross. Boston: Little, Brown.

Winnicott, D. W. (1971), *Playing and Reality.* London, Tavistock.

IV

FATHER-SON
RELATIONSHIPS

13

The Riddle of Little Hans

John Munder Ross

In the last decade, researchers have repeatedly emphasized the fateful consequences of "paternal insufficiency" during the pivotal second year of life (Ross, 1979). During this critical period in the articulation of self and core gender identity, a lack of actual or felt fathering leaves a boy at risk on various fronts: his masculinity and selfhood uncertain; his elemental knowledge of sex difference befuddled; his fears of fusion and attendant emasculation pronounced.

The development of sexual identity does not end there, however, as well we know. There is, after all, the ensuing oedipal crisis and the organization of not only gender but sexual identity in its fuller elaboration. At this point – in the representational realm now more than in actuality – paternal deprivation makes for another and more conflictual dilemma. Faced with the seeming exclusivity of phallic and residual parental ambitions inherent in early maternal identifications, a boy gropes not only for a heterosexual but also for his procreative identity. Relative intrapsychic father absence further confounds the boy's efforts to answer the Riddle of the Sphinx. To be a man means to be barren; to make a baby portends castration; males do not "have" children – not yet.

It is in grasping and identifying with the father's fatherly role that a boy can more fully synthesize two opposing strains in his sexual identity (Ross, 1975). For only then are sexual union and the self-completion and fecundity it yields possible within the confines of his masculinity. Potentially perverse trends–and the part objects and partial identifications that they eroticize–also become subsumed by sex-specific genital fantasies and strivings.

LITTLE HANS: AN OLD CASE IN POINT OF A YOUNG BOY

In seeking out shared data on oedipal development–a common text, I will now turn to a psychoanalytic parable, the case of Little Hans (Freud, 1909a). In fact, much is known about Little Hans–later identified as Herbert Graf, stage director of The Metropolitan Opera and intendant of the Geneva Opera, as well as about his father Max, a musicologist and member of Freud's Wednesday night group (see Seides, 1987; Graf, 1941; Graf, 1942). In this exegesis, however, I have sought to deal only with the narrative data itself; with a clinical legacy, that is, available to all working analysts. A choice like this obviates the dangers of forced evidence and violated confidentiality in tendering clinical vignettes of one's own. It invites alternative readings and constructive disagreement.

Students of psychoanalysis and its history are familiar with "Analysis of a Phobia in a Five-Year-Old Boy" (1909a), which Freud used so brilliantly to embody the general propositions regarding infantile sexuality set forth in "The Three Essays" he had published four years previously (1905). For Freud, Hans figured as a case in point of the castration complex suffered by the little boy as he attempts to negotiate his oedipal passage–his *positive* oedipal complex in more modern parlance. He stressed Hans's wish to replace his father in his mother's bed, his ambivalence toward the man whom he loved and hated, and his fear of retaliation at the father's hand.

The neurosis, in which Hans's conflicts were displaced, projected, and externalized, engendering a fear of biting and falling horses, was set in motion by the birth of his sister, Hannah. His mother's screams, the bloody vessels and, notably for our purposes, Hans's confusion about the anatomical implications of the event set his castration fear in motion. As a consequence, he succumbed first to an agoraphobia of sorts and, subsequently, to the zoophobia detailed by Freud. Once Hans's father, "supervised," as it were, by the Professor, (as Glenn, 1980, has put it) had made Hans aware of his own intentions, of the imagined danger accompanying them, and of the anatomical differences, he was relieved of his neurosis. Freud (1909a, p. 128) himself, however, alluding to yet another thread in the story, noted that Hans's ignorance regarding the procreative function of the man remained to be addressed. It is this strain that I will pursue here, not ignoring the value of Freud's original formulations.

In the summary to follow, I augment these conclusions with a focus on Hans's ambisexuality. Speculating further, I attempt to reconstruct from its many derivatives a particular fantasy, which may very well have contributed to the genesis of the phobia and which was still in evidence at the close of his "treatment." Nor was Hans offered the opportunity during the oedipal phase to reorganize fragmented object images and various identifications into a heterosexual, paternal identity. Because of a failure to embrace a specifically fatherly identification, I submit, this first child patient ultimately resorted to what we now would label "a negative oedipal" position. Symptomatic improvement was effected by a sort of "transference cure," or so it all seems from the case material at our disposal.

THE CLINICAL NARRATIVE

Hans is introduced as a prototypic phallic little boy, enamored of his own "widdler," or "wee maker," and intrigued by those of others. His age-appropriate struggle with the genital distinction between male and female is chronicled repeatedly.

The narrators, Hans's father and Freud, tell us little of the boy's mother apart from her son's glimpses of her mysterious pubic region. The ambiguity of her responses to the little boy's questions about her genitals is highlighted as if somehow she were denying her apparent "castration." Early on she responds to her son's query, "Mommy, have you got a widdler, too?" with "Of course, why?" "I was only just thinking" (p. 7). The infantile idiom is confusing: does widdler or "wee wee maker" mean just that or does it refer only to a penis? Quite probably, Hans's mother is not asserting that she is in possession of a *male* organ. Rather this is Hans's, the father's, and even Freud's phallocentric inference.

Hans confuses a cow's udder with a penis. Pondering the boy's confusion about this quintessentially female beast, Freud emphasizes that this organ "plays an apt part as an intermediate image, being in its nature a *mamma* and in its shape and position, that of a penis" (p. 7). He then leaves the hermaphoditic motif behind, lacking as yet a theoretical framework in which to place it. At the time, what would only later (1910) be referred to as "the Oedipus *complex*" meant the positive Oedipus. Thus Freud concentrates instead on the external danger, namely, the mother's warning that should Hans dare to masturbate, "Dr. A." will be sent for to cut off the boy's penis. It is a threat with prophetic–yet, as we shall see, by no means self-evident–ramifications, and Hans's immediate reaction must be kept in mind in interpreting the plumber fantasies at the close of the case. Asked what he would widdle with then, he responds, "My bottom," thereby betraying what Freud (1909b) later described as Little Hans's underlying *cloacal* fantasies of reproduction.

Baffled because he cannot see or feel what his mother possesses, Hans exclaims that he thought she was so big that she should have a widdler like a horse. (Freud tells us to keep this analogy in mind.) But *where* is this widdler to be found?

It is in the context of this search that the "great" and pathogenic event in Hans's young life occurs–the birth of his sister, Hannah, when he was 3 1/2–though he would not succumb until over a year later. Freud describes Hans's impressions of the delivery: his mother's coughing; the doctor's bag in the front hall–perhaps the self-same doctor with whose gelding shears he was threatened–and the blood-filled vessels. Pointing to the bedpan, the boy observes, "But blood does not come out of my widdler" (p. 10). Dissatisfied by references to the stork, Hans attempts repeatedly to piece together the bits of information and sensorimotor experience that have come his way about the bodily reality of procreation.

He senses that sex differences are also at issue in making babies. Hans is confronted by little Hannah's unobscured vulva and becomes preoccupied by the absence, as well as the presence of male genitals. Yet he seems to know that there must be something more to the feminine anatomy, for simultaneously the little boy begins to play out telling birth fantasies, which intimate his dawning intuition into woman's recesses. He talks of the storeroom and, fetuslike, enters a W.C., exclaiming that he is widdling. These urethral enactments and imaginings most likely reveal an intuition into the male and female roles in procreation. Finally, at 4 1/2, Hans now laughs at the small size of Hannah's widdler as if deriding her femininity. Yet it is at this point that the father relays to Freud the outbreak of the boy's phobia.

With hindsight, the modern analyst–Silverman (1980), for instance–would stress the identification with his baby sister and preoedipal longings in the early stages of Hans's symptom neurosis. In January of 1908, when the case history proper begins, for example, he wishes, somewhat ambiguously, to stay home and "coax," to cuddle, to caress, with his mother.

The specificity of oedipal conflict and of symbolic representation, however, soon gives greater shape to the fear that a horse will bite him – a reference to earlier cautionaries and to outcroppings of his castration anxiety. Freud stresses the boy's masturbatory urges and activity and, according to the old anxiety theory, the conversion of repressed longings into *angst*.

Freud attempts to have the father, now his therapeutic proxy as well as journalistic observer, resolve matters cognitively. He is instructed to inform his son that his mother and all other female beings have *no* widdler at all. In the wake of partial enlightenment, his castration fear temporarily allayed, Hans improves.

A second significant event now occurs, however, which Slap (1961) called to our attention 50 years later. In early March, the father records perfunctorily that "after another week which he has had to spend indoors because he has had his tonsils out, the phobia has grown very much worse again" (p. 29). Remarking on the operation's pathogenic impact, Slap later underscores the representation of this realistic trauma in the subsequent phobia. Hans's ever more specific fear of white horses with black muzzles might be traced to the common costume of surgeons at the time, black masks and white gowns. In fact, it is not implausible that the infamous and ubiquitous Dr. A. may have indeed been involved in the procedure, lending even more substance to the mother's early warnings. Slap goes on to highlight the concretized paternal castration threat inherent in this ill-timed intervention, and its positive oedipal reverberations.

Additionally, I would *speculate* that Hans made an association between his own surgery and his impressions of his mother's delivery of little Hannah. I have in mind, for instance, his previous interpretations of his mother's groans and wretching as *coughing*, as well as his focus on the blood-filled vessels. Veiled references to menstruation may even have been suggested in the comment that blood did not emerge from his genital. Febrile states preceding the surgery, Hans's passive position before and after it, and the aftereffects of the anaesthesia would have confused the already tenuous distinctions between reality and fantasy in a phobia-prone five-year-old. How then would the boy have interpreted the surgical intrusion into one of his orifices, the cutting off of the two "balls" contained within its inner recesses, the blood, the swelling, and so forth?

To borrow from Bettelheim (1954), one might then infer that the surgery was suffered as a sort of "symbolic wound," a ritual cutting not only threatening retaliation but offering the promise of invagination, effeminization, and the assumption of child-bearing powers. Hans may very well have come to imagine that his mother had been impregnated in some similarly violent manner, as later fantasies indicate (the Grete play, for instance), or that somehow she had been given to exchange her penis for a baby in a genital/oral displacement and condensation. He may have construed his tonsillectomy as a variation on these primal scenes, one in which he himself was actually or symbolically impregnated or delivered of a baby. One day perhaps his penis, like his mother's, would be cut off as *he* prepared to give birth to an infant. The operation thus realized and partially gratified this little boy's conflictual desires to become a mother himself – his inarticulate and dreaded wishes to unman himself and submit to castration as the price to be paid for the woman's "painful prerogative." Now, this is, as I said, speculation. Yet there is ample evidence of Hans's ambisexuality and identifications with both mother and father.

Hans's earlier fantasy of the phallic woman, which foundered on the shoals of his abrupt "enlightenment," had already intimated hermaphroditic promptings – her anatomical bisexuality mirroring his own. When he was apprised of the mutual exclusiveness of phallic aspirations and maternal power, I argue, he succumbed to an intense *intra*systemic conflict, a crisis in sexual identity brought to a head by his mother's delivery of little Hannah and his own tonsillectomy.

The ensuing analysis of the phobia reveals an array of paradoxes in which male and female, intrusion and inceptivity are condensed. For instance, the father interprets Hans's notion rightly that, like a horse, his widdler *bites*. But the *language* is telling, possibly betraying unconscious interchanges in the dialogue between father and son. Counteroedipal feelings and intention permeate the case history. "Biting" inadvertently also implies that Hans's penis not only is stimulated but has an *incorporative* mode akin to that of the vagina, or the mouth for that matter.

Even more suggestive is Hans's famous "giraffe" dream or fantasy: "In the night there was a big giraffe in the room and a crumpled one and the big one crawled out because I took the crumpled one away from it. Then it stopped crawling out and I sat down on top of the crumpled one" (p. 37). Hans's father, aided by Freud, discerns in this wish fulfillment a typical incestuous possession fantasy. Yet might it not relate as well to the image of delivery – the crumpled giraffe representing not only the so-called defective, penisless female, but also the ill-formed (fecal) baby in childbirth? Hans says as much, and he may strive to steal the infant from the mother as much as he would wrest her from the father's dominion.

Similarly, Hans's wish for a gun to shoot people dead with seems an obvious phallic equivalent. But this, too, takes on added meaning by virtue of Hans's confusion of the German words for "shooting" and "shitting." He also wants raspberry syrup, suggesting that he too would like to appear to bleed (to menstruate) and be a child-bearing woman, a possibility that finds further confirmation later on, when we learn about its use as a laxative. Not only has intercourse taken place in the night in this boy's world, but childbirth as well. Yes, Hans is fascinated by projectiles, digits, and limbs, but also by spaces; entrances and enclosures are barred by policemen, prohibiting incestuous access and, with it, the vicarious assumption of womanly contours. The horse's whiteness is, incidentally, his mother's as well as his father's; both figure as self-protective and potentially vindictive authorities. And *both* are love objects.

In all events, interpretations of his phallic urges and rivalries fail to dispel his fear of these creatures. Freud's one encounter with Hans and ingenious interventions in this vein make, it seems, for a rather transient improvement. For one thing, they overlook Hans's growing fascination with and love for his father: he's fond of both Mommy and his father. More and more his rivalry and identifications seem to center on his mother as well – father's bedmate and Hannah's parent.

In fact, Hans's childbirth fantasies come to assume an *increasingly* negative oedipal cast. He becomes less afraid of horses' biting him than of their falling and spilling the contents of their carts, as repeatedly he enters the parental bedroom drawn by *both* father and mother.

Hans's incestuous and parental ambitions are further complicated by more passive desires evident in his fantasy of "standing by the cart and the cart driving off quickly and my standing on it and wanting to get onto the board and my driving off in the cart" (p. 47). At this point, the fear of horses with muzzles reemerges, which the father readily and rightly interprets as a reference to his own moustache, but one which, following Slap (1961) also hearkens back to the penetrating, invasive surgeons. Hans was passive then, anesthetized and somehow transported (in a cart of sorts), violated, perhaps in fantasy sexually transformed or at least mysteriously altered.

Hans's childbearing wishes intensify, overshadowing his castration anxiety. He becomes afraid of horses falling and making a row with their feet. Furniture vans obsess him. Big, fat horses are further sources of anxiety. He imitates the pawing and the "row," as if identifying with the woman in intercourse or childbirth. Nor is it simply that he fears the birth of another sibling rival, for Hans pointedly compares the horses on the streets with himself seated on the potty to make "lumpf," when he himself makes a row with his feet. And he does so within the context of commenting on his father's "lovely" whiteness.

It is now revealed that Hans has been subjected to repeated anal stimulation in the form of enemas. The father himself, the reader infers, is preoccupied with his own bowel movements, inviting identification in this regard. Hans, having seen his mother on the toilet making widdle and "lumpf," wonders all the while, too, about her complex excretory functions. Hans associates to pregnancy and childbirth, confirming Freud's findings about children's cloacal theories.

But the relation of these to phallic themes within the Oedipus constellation remains to be addressed. Hans tells his father the first of two plumber fantasies, which probably derive from his birth theories and from his mysterious wishes to submit to mutilation and, further, to penetration by a man as a means to parental power: "Daddy, I thought something. I was in the bath (like little Hannah) and then the plumber came and unscrewed it. Then he took a big borer and stuck it into my stomach" (p. 65). Hans's father interprets his fear of retaliation for his wishes to be in bed with his mother, the erotic personage who gives him his bath. Similarly, discerning the transference, Freud proceeds to emphasize the big penis with which the potentially castrating father drove him from the bed. Along with references to the actual surgery and the invasive analysis, however, the "thought" most probably betrays Hans's identification with the position of a woman in the primal scene (or the baby in utero). (See Freud's comments on Hans's notions about his father's procreative role: "With your big penis you bored [gave birth to] me and put me in my mother's womb" (p. 128).

As if intuitively, somewhat later the father does touch on Hans's identification with the *producing* mother. He underlines the fact that Little Hans has often seen horses doing "lumf" and concludes that "the bus horse that falls down and makes a row with its feet is no doubt a lumf falling and making a noise" (p. 66). Hans's fear of defecation, and of heavily loaded carts, is traced to his fear of a heavily loaded stomach or abdomen and to his sibling rivalry. But that Hans would *himself* like to be so encumbered and deliver himself of more vital concoctions—this unconscious fantasy still escapes the father's awareness. So do the boy's intuitive glimpses of the origins of babies in an instinctual encounter and of the mother's sexual role in this.

Had Hans's case followed that of his fellow protagonist, the Wolf Man (Freud, 1918), Freud would have had the developmental theory and language with which to render these or similar clinical inferences. He would also have had a frame of reference in which to consider the boy's musings on the mother's power over life and death and the threat posed by her even in an incestuous meeting of reengulfment.

Hans betrays his awe of a vitally omnipotent mother when he expresses his terror that she might let go of him, allowing his head to sink into the water, when she bathes him. It is not the big penis, but the big bath that concerns him at this point, an allusion to an engulfing womb. Once again, the father speaks to the periphery of Hans's perception of girls and women and his urge to be with and thus identify with them, when he stresses *only* the boy's death wishes, fears of retaliation, and sibling rivalry.

The riddle continues. With his glimmers of his mother's black pubic region, Hans draws equations between "lumfs," "lumfees," and "wumpfees," or children. Though he too has anal powers, making babies appears to be a woman's prerogative. And unlike him, she may even be able to retract when she has extruded, to reincorporate. Getting erotically involved has risks of its own, then, all the greater because of yet another yearning and dread—the *desire* to be a baby in the womb. There may even be a certain secret spitefulness in Hans's apparent sibling rivalry, a wish to destroy what mother alone has succeeded in making—a baby, who is not only Hans's competitor for her attentions but the envy of his would-be creativity.

More and more clearly aware of his mother's pregnancy, Hans would like to take something in and make something more of it. Hans remains, as earlier, more attuned to womblike equivalents—baths, boxes, and babies—than to penises. At times he endows his father with maternal capacities—for instance when he suggests that the stork came, unlocked the door, and put Hannah in the *father's* bed while his mother was asleep. Only when confronted does he correct himself, asserting that the stork put the infant in the mother's bed.

The father emphasizes his son's wish to possess her rather than his less discrete longings to be more fully, and variously, at one with his mother, to be mother and child, Mahler's dual unity (Mahler, Pine, and Bergman, 1975). Hans remonstrates that he is quite fond of Hannah and looks forward to nurturing her as well as babies of his own making. (Freud now remarks upon his failure to inform his proxy of the child's cloacal birth fantasies.) It is in the context of these transparent wishes to rear her that little Hans endows Hannah with a whip, implying that she, like the phallic mother, can have a penis. He wishes himself to be a baby and a mommy, yet to hold on to his phallus and masculinity.

Hans verges on a solution to the Riddle of the Sphinx: "Once I really did it. Once I had a weapon with the horse and it fell down and made a row with his feet" (p. 79). Attempting to reassert masculinity and, at the same time, to grant himself a role, a phallic-sadistic one, in the sexual making of babies, Hans gropes toward an understanding of paternity. He continues by saying that he would like to "beat" mommy and thereby make a baby. Again, his father fails to pick up on his son's reproductive aspirations, just as he has neglected to educate him about the male part in procreation.

His father's emphasis on heterosexual incestuous prohibitions has fallen short of the mark. As a consequence, Hans's fear of *horses with carriages,* symbolizing sexual union, increases, and he retreats indoors. Freud underscores an obscure sadistic desire for his mother and an impulse for revenge against his father.

Later in the month, his father reports a primal scene fantasy in which questions about the maternal phallus, the origin of babies, and the link between birth and the tonsillectomy are condensed:

> At lunch time I was told that Hans had been playing all morning with an India-rubber doll which he called Grete. He had pushed a small pen knife (like a scalpel) in through the opening into which a little tin squeaker had originally been attached, and had then torn apart the doll's legs so as to let the knife drop out. He had said to the nursemaid, pointing between the doll's legs, "Look, there's its widdler." . . . I tore its legs apart; you know why? Because there was a knife inside it belonging to mommy. I put it in at the place where the button squeaks and then I tore apart its legs and it came out there [p. 84].

Is the knife a phallus, a surgeon's knife, a baby—or all of the above? Do penises get cut off and turn into babies after penetration and sufficient gestation? While focusing on his mother's knife, presumably her penis, Hans also proclaims that both his father and he once laid eggs out of which a chicken emerged, thereby approximating her incorporative and generative power.

Freud concludes that by means of a "brilliant symptomatic act" Hans had said, "Look, this is how I imagine birth takes place"—not only birth, I might add, but conception. In fact, the boy again speaks of his wishes to make children and tend them—to have a baby himself.

To his father's suggestion that he would like to have a little girl, he responds, "Yes, he is going to have one and call her Hannah, too." His father asks, "But why isn't mommy to have a little girl?" "Because *I* want to have a little girl, for once!" "But you can't have a little girl." "Oh yes," Hans counters, "boys have girls and girls have boys," (righting the sexual imbalance and uniting maternal and feminine aspirations). "Boys don't have children – only women, only mommies have children," his father asserts again and again, as he becomes increasingly defensive. He omits the male role – his own, Hans's – in creating babies. "But why shouldn't I?" "Because God's arranged it like that." "But why don't you have one? Oh yes, you'll have one, alright, just you wait. . . ." Hans asks, "Does Hannah belong to me or to mommy?" His father answers, "To mommy," "Not to me? Why not to me and mommy?" Freud concludes, "So long as the child is in ignorance of the female genitals, there is a naturally vital gap in his comprehension of sexual matters" (p. 87–88). More in the way of sex education is indicated, it seems.

At last the parents tell him the facts about women and pregnancy: Children grow inside the mommy and are brought into the world by being pressed out of her like "lumf." All this, they add, gratuitously, involves a "great deal of pain." *Once again, theirs is but a half-truth; they neglect to tell him of the father's part and satisfaction in this whole process.*

Yet again the father errs in interpreting Hans's butting him one day only as an attack and expression of competition, rather than a sensorimotor, if sadistic, enactment of intercourse. Hans persists, telling his father that he would parent him. But the authoritative disavowal is too great. His inchoate theories of insemination ignored, Hans can only resort to the fantasy that babies are born from the behind, a compromise notion seemingly borne out by the bits of revelation offered him by his parents.

At last, Hans's father suggests to him that Hans would like to be a *daddy.* Immediately excited, Hans picks up on the cue, "Yes, how does it work?!" The father is taken aback. "How does what work?" he fumbles. Hans continues, "You say daddies don't have babies. But how does it work – my wanting to be a daddy?" His father's explanations have omitted the vital connecting link that might have helped resolve the boy's ambisexual conflict: penetration, ejaculation, insemination. Rather than educate, as he did earlier when the mother's genitals were at issue, he interprets instead: "You'd like to be a daddy and married to a mommy – you'd like to be as big as me and have a moustache and you'd like mommy to have a baby." And Hans seems to intuit a tacit injunction – the knowledge of the tree of life is God's alone, God the father's. Paternity lies beyond his cognitive grasp, and so he tempers his instinctual ambitions. "And Daddy, when I'm married, I'll only have one if I want to – when I'm married" (p. 92). All the while, he has reiterated his parental aspirations, seizing on having children in addition to oedipal possession in the suggestion that his progeny, not his wife, will always remain in bed with him.

When his father asks him later why he was always thinking of his children, Hans responds, "Why? Because I should like to have them." "The startling contradiction" (p. 93), in Freud's words, betrays Hans's intense conflict between wishing to produce babies and the dreaded outcome that is stressed throughout as a consequence of all *parental,* maternal and paternal, ambition – castration, from within or without.

The synthesis of a fatherly ideal denied him, Hans proclaims that he really was the *mommy* of the children at Gmunden. His motherly fantasies are amplified in the absence of possible paternal powers: "When I couldn't get all the children into bed, I put some of the children on the sofa, and some in the pram and if there were still some left over, I took them up to the attic and put them in a box. And if there were any more, I put them in the other box" (p. 94).

Oedipal access beyond him, his paternal future cloudy, his masculine anatomy irrefutable and seemingly barren, Hans again makes recourse to a negative oedipal fantasy. When his father asks him, "Who did you think you got the children from?" Hans responds, "Why *from* me" (p. 94). Simultaneously, he now becomes even more preoccupied with babies and behinds. He used to call the doors of the custom house "holes," but now refers to them specifically as "behind holes."

In counterpoint, he then proclaims his masculinity. When Hans's father comments on his playing with merely imaginary children, he responds, "I was their mommy before; now I'm their daddy" (p. 96). His penis has grown, he makes of his father a grandfather. Freud infers that

> things were moving toward a satisfactory conclusion, but little Oedipus had found a happier solution than that prescribed by destiny. Instead of putting his father out of the way, he had granted him the same happiness that he desired himself: He made him a grandfather and married him to his own mother too [p. 97].

The interpretation, however, omits the submission underlying Hans's new-found optimism. This is not the final but merely the penultimate transference fantasy. The next day Hans describes his vision of taking his children to the W.C., cleaning *their* behinds, and "doing everything one does with children," just as he himself had been treated by his parents. He is now freer to venture forth into forbidden territory and to confront horses and buses head on, yet he points to the bus and exclaims, "Look, a stork boxcart!" (p. 97).

The symptomatic improvement owes itself basically to Hans's *negative oedipal resolution to his many competing wishes and fears.* This is most evident in the fantasy that in fact climaxes his treatment, one that derives from the father's and surgeon's respectively psychic and physical examinations and intrusions:

> The plumber came, and first he took away my behind with a pair of scissor-pincers and then he gave me another. And then the same with my widdler. He said, "Let me see your widdler," which he also removed, giving him a bigger widdler and a bigger behind . . . [His father concludes:] Yes, like daddy's, because you like to be like daddy." "Yes, and I'd like to have a moustache like yours, and hairs like yours [pp. 97–98].

Hans's earlier fantasy is interpreted by Freud in the following manner: "The big bath meant the behind; the borer or screwdriver was as was explained at the time, a penis. The two fantasies are identical. Moreover new light is thrown on Hans's fear of the big bath. He dislikes his behind being too small for the big bath" (p. 98).

But what does this bigger *behind* stand for in the light of all the previous symbolism associated with it? Is it not also a would-be anal womb, rivaling the encompassing organ of his mother? And is Hans's not a fantasy of being in possession of ambisexual powers? More important, why emphasize the widdler and bypass the behind? That is, why ignore the submissive currents–the passive route to phallic power so typical of the homosexual quest? Indeed, Hans's construction has much in common with those pederastic *rites of passages* (described by Lidz and Lidz, 1977, and Stoller, 1985) in which boys surrender to adult males in order to be anointed as men while the collective fatherhood lays claim to birth-giving powers, that is, rites that take place long before puberty, in fact, and with boys who do not become actively homosexual.

The postscript gives more clues regarding the neurosis, pointing to all the etiologic factors emphasized by Greenacre (1953, 1955, 1960, 1969, 1971) and others (Gillespie, 1940; Bak, 1968) in the genesis of perversions. Hans was about four years old when he was moved out of the parental bedroom into a room of his own. Hence he possibly had been privy to primal scene experiences and to his mother's nude or nearly naked body, a circumstance that proverbially promotes a lasting bisexual identification.

The further suggestion is that there was a close, if ambivalent, relationship with his mother. Until the boy's illness, his father was only a sporadic presence in his life – notably during vacations at Gmunden – a presence inadequate to offset Hans's immersion in his mother's being and her femininity. With his intervention into the boy's psychic life, however, the father then became all too present – forceful, intrusive, and stimulating to a fault. Hans would suffer invasion, have his father wholly or not at all, while being discouraged from actively comprehending or identifying with his paternity.

Finally, Freud relates, while Hans enters a remission and refers to his phobia as the "nonsense that is past, nonetheless an unsolved residue remains behind. . . . Hans keeps cudgelling his brains," as his father puts it, "to discover what a father has to do with his child, since it is the mother who brings it into the world" (p. 100).

Freud concludes, "Yes, the doctor, the plumber, did take away his penis, but only to give a bigger one in exchange for it. Provocatively, he adds, "Each step forward leaves an unsolved residue behind" (p. 100).

CONCLUSIONS

I have emphasized Hans's identification with his mother and specu-lated about his fantastic interpretation of his fateful tonsillectomy not only as a paternal castration threat, but as a symbolic act of impregna-tion and birth. The but patchwork nature of the enlightenment offered him, and the parent therapist's apparent inhibitions regarding the reciprocal procreative functions of father and mother, seem to have left Little Hans adrift. Wanting babies and a penis at the same time, he resorted to a negative oedipal compromise in which he would suffer penetration and castration to produce life not as "Daddy" but in the manner of a woman. Had his wish to be a father been clarified, along with the mechanics of paternity, he might have progressed beyond the alleviation of his symptoms and arrived at a more adaptive and progressive resolution of a central conflict within the oedipal constel-lation; that is, between the wish to assert his emergent masculinity and the desire to participate in the generational cycle, to make babies. What Hans repeatedly strove for was a representation of father as a producer, male procreator, and nurturer by which to offset the intersystemic conflicts born of oedipal rivalry and the essentially *intra*systemic conflicts clustering about the wish of a phallic oedipal boy to give birth and to be a mother and therefore a woman.

A careful reading of the "Analysis of a Phobia in a Five-Year-Old Boy" (Freud, 1909a) reveals the clinical importance of *identification* with the *father qua father* to a resolution of *sexual identity* within the *Oedipus complex*. All are psychoanalytic concepts that were not yet available to Freud at the time. Freud himself would only name the Oedipus complex per se a year later (1910) and then elaborate clinically and theoretically on its negative and positive sides (1918, 1923). It would be some time before he would expound on the "phallic woman" (Freud, 1927) and the interweaving of early defensive disortions in object representations (A. Freud, 1936) as a consequence of uncertainty in one's own gender identity. And it would be yet another half century before students of Little Hans would be proffered Jacob Arlow's (1969) concept of organizing unconscious fantasy, in which elements of real experience and inner oedipal and preoedipal conflict become woven into a whole dramatic tapestry, a personal intrapsychic narrative determining the course of a life. Most recently, there is Peter Blos's (1982) delineation of the persistence and neurosogenic impact of the "negative," or negative Oedipus, motif on the eve of adulthood, long after the resolution or repression of the positive. With these developments, and with our current appreciation of fatherhood, a boy like Hans might have been even better understood and his heterosexuality truly secured.

Yet another postscript regarding the "real" Little Hans: All the indications are that Herbert Graf had a most successful life. Indeed, he married, fathered two children, worked creatively and nurtured many professional lives (see Holland, 1985, pp. 246–281). His parents, in contrast, fared less well, divorcing (as Freud noted) when he was still quite a young man. His father, Max, initially one of Freud's most zealous acolytes, later shunned and rejected the Professor (see Seides, 1987). Not only this, he was quite critical of his son's noisy "primal scene" staging while directing productions at the Met. To this the son is said to have responded, "My father is responsible for me, perhaps, but not I for him."

We can never know what went on psychically in Herbert/Hans's life as an adult: his dreams, fantasies, erotic experiences, everyday symptomatology. Negative oedipal resolutions, in any event, do not usually manifest themselves in any overt sexual symptomatology, which usually results from more profound preoedipal and narcissistic hungers. Rather, conflicts at the oedipal level tend to find more neurotic modes of expression in symptoms and character traits.

Nonetheless, it may very well be that the case history is as much about Max Graf's intrapsychic life as about his son's; *his* wish to mother the child better than his wife; *his* ambivalence in deferring to and later rebelling against a father figure in the person of Freud; *his* uncertainty about ceding his own paternal authority to his son. We will never know, yet the speculation is intriguing. Our cases and our legacy of clinical myths contain many hidden characters and mysterious dialogues. But these are the subject of another essay.

REFERENCES

Arlow, J. (1969), Unconscious fantasy and conscious experience. *Psychoanal. Quart.*, 38:1–27.

Bak, R. (1968), The phallic woman: The ubiquitous fantasy in perversions. *The Psychoanalytic Study of the Child,* 23:15–36, New York: International Universities Press.

Bettelheim, B. (1954), *Symbolic Wounds,* Glencoe, IL: Free Press.

Blos, P. (1985), *Son and Father,* New York: Free Press.

Freud, A. (1936). The ego and the mechanisms of defense. *Writings, 2.* New York: International Universities Press.

Freud, S. (1905), Three essays on the theory of sexuality. *Standard Edition,* 7:125–248. London: Hogarth Press, 1953.

―――― (1909a), Analysis of a phobia in a five-year-old boy. *Standard Edition,* 10:3–149. London: Hogarth Press, 1955.

―――― (1909b), Notes upon a case of obsessional neurosis. *Standard Edition,* 10:153–318. London: Hogarth Press, 1955.

―――― (1910), A special type of object choice made by men. *Standard Edition,* 11:163–175. London: Hogarth Press, 1957.

―――― (1918), From the history of an infantile neurosis. *Standard Edition,* 17:7–122. London: Hogarth Press, 1955.

―――― (1923), The ego and the id. *Standard Edition,* 19:3–63. London: Hogarth Press, 1961.

―――― (1927), Fetishism. *Standard Edition,* 21:149–157. London: Hogarth Press, 1961.

Gillespie, W.H. (1940), A Contribution to the Study of Fetishism. *Internat. J. Psycho-Anal.,* 21:401–415.

Glenn, J. (1980), Freud's advice to Hans's father: The first supervisory sessions. In: *Freud and His Patients,* ed. M. Kanzer & J. Glenn. New York: Aronson.

Graf, H. (1941), *The Opera and Its Future in America.* New York: Norton.

Graf, M. (1942), Reminiscences of Professor Sigmund Freud. *Psychoanal. Quart.,* 11:4:465–476.

Greenacre, P. (1953), Certain relationships between fetishism and the faulty development of the body image. *The Psychoanalytic Study of the Child,* 8:79–98. New York: International Universities Press.

_____ (1955), Further considerations regarding Fetishism. *The Psychoanalytic Study of the Child,* 10:187–194. New York: International Universities Press.

_____ (1960), Further notes on fetishism. *The Psychoanalytic Study of the Child,* 15:191–207. New York: International Universities Press.

_____ (1969), The fetish and the transitional object. In: *Emotional Growth,* Vol. 1. New York: International Universities Press, pp. 315–334, 1971.

_____ (1971), Perversions: General considerations regarding genetic and dynamic background. In: *Emotional Growth,* Vol. I. New York: International Universities Press.

Holland, N. (1985), *The Book of the I.* New Haven: Yale University Press.

Lidz, R.W. & Lidz, T. (1977), Male menstruation: A ritual alternative to the oedipal transition. *Internat. J. Psycho-Anal,* 58:17–31.

Mahler, M., Pine, F., & Bergman, A. (1975), *The Psychological Birth of the Human Infant.* New York: Basic Books.

Ross, J.M. (1975), The development of paternal identity: A critical review of the literature on nurturance and generativity in boys and men. *J. Amer. Psychoanal. Assn.,* 23:783–817.

_____ (1979), Fathering. *Internat. J. Psycho-Anal.,* 60:317–327.

Seides, S.W. (1987), Discussion of "The Riddle of Little Hans," Presented to scientific meeting of Psychoanalytic Association of New York, January 5.

Silverman, M. (1980), A fresh look at the case of Little Hans. In: *Freud and His Patients,* ed. M. Kanzer & J. Glenn. New York: Aronson.

Slap, J. (1961), Little Hans's tonsillectomy. *Psychoanal. Quart.,* 30:259–261.

Stoller, R. (1968), *Sex and Gender.* New York: Science House.

_____ (1985), *Observing the Erotic Imagination.* New Haven: Yale University Press.

14
Lincoln and the Fathers
Reflections on Idealization
Charles B. Strozier
Stanley H. Cath

Adults often search for idealized father figures in the public world of politics and culture. Sometimes this need for a superordinate surrogate father is particularly intense and takes shape psychologically as a drive for an omnipotent, grandiose figure of gigantic proportions. Clinicians are apt to encounter such dynamics in certain disorders of character often found in predisposing family patterns. One might see broad lines of similarity between these patterns and particular critical periods in history when certain kinds of charismatic, cultlike figures may emerge (Jim Jones and Hitler, for example). It is striking that, whether in the family or in history, women, truly the first source of goodness and power in the infant's life, have been rarely selected as objects of political idealization or converted to godheads. In our myth of cultural origins, a distinguished man talks to God the father on a mountain top. Our pantheon of cultural heroes, half men/half gods, includes figures as diverse as Abraham Lincoln, Rambo, even flashes in the pan like Oliver North. In this sense, Jim Jones was, for a moment in history, a perverted expression of his followers' ordinary and extraordinary human longings. Wherever one may look, men and their godlike substitutes seem to have a special hold on human imagination (Kohut, 1971, 1977, 1984, 1985; Strozier and Offer, 1985).

There are many converging individual and group sources for this pervasive pattern of idealization in all cultures. Political institutions foster it, the media glorify it, and religion sanctifies it. Individual helplessness, separation anxiety, disillusionment, and the intimidation of mortality feed into it. It may even be rooted in some unknown way in our biology. But idealization is also grounded firmly in the positive protective aspects of the family, that vital social institution where public and private intersect and from which public welfare will ultimately be served. Psychological images of greatness in the family are as diverse as the all-giving mother picking up the small, helpless child or, later, watching, with a gleam in her eye, as the toddler takes a few hesitant steps; or the magnificent father, first offering new ways of thinking, feeling, and acting, then coming home from work, seemingly all-knowing, teaching something crucial about the vast, mysterious world where he seems such a master.

Idealization, of course, can be distorted, indeed perverted, by family strains of diverse origin, especially the midlife decompensation of a previously idealized father (Cath, 1988). Our particular interest here is to examine whether there may be patterns of paternity that create a lingering need in offspring for unusually intense idealized paternal alternatives. We are particularly thinking of family constellations marked by patterns of early fatherlessness, father desertion, or deeply failed or unempathic fathers who abuse or "soul murder" their children (Shengold, 1979). We will explore this concept through the case of Abraham Lincoln, who as one of our most important and truly heroic men had his own driving need to recreate a world of political ideals. Psychohistory, at its best, attempts this kind of genuine sharing between the clinical world and the past.

In early January 1851, Thomas Lincoln, Abraham's father, lay dying in his home near Charleston, Illinois. Eagerly seeking some kind of reconciliation with his estranged son, Thomas apparently asked to see Abraham, sending messages through his stepson, John D. Johnston, and another relative, Harriet Hanks Chapman. Three letters piled up before Lincoln finally responded to Johnston on January 12, 1951 (Lincoln, 1953–1955, pp. 96–97): "[Although] you do not expect me to come now, you wonder that I do not write." From the context of Lincoln's letter, it is clear he understood that the reason for the flurry of letters to him was to urge him to visit Thomas. Lincoln rather lamely noted that writing seemed useless: "I could write nothing which could do any good." He urged Johnston to use his name, "if necessary, to procure a doctor, or anything else for Father in his present sickness."

Without a break, Lincoln then addressed the real issue – his failure to come visit – and gave three reasons why he was unable to travel to Goosenest Prairie.

The first excuse was that business was pressing. "My business is such that I could hardly leave home now. . . ." In fact Lincoln was busy then, as the Illinois Supreme Court was in session. Four cases with which he was associated were due before the court that week. But in three of these cases he was associated with other lawyers (in one case with Stephen T. Logan, and in two cases, with his partner, William Herndon) who could have made the necessary court appearances or arguments. In one case, due before the court on January 14, Lincoln alone represented the client. But in 19th-century central Illinois, as now everywhere, lawyers commonly substituted for each other in the event of a personal emergency. There was also the possibility of an extension or postponement of the case. And it was an emergency. Thomas died on January 17.

Second, Lincoln noted that his wife was "sick-abed." Mary had given birth to their third son, William Wallace, on December 21, 1850, more than three weeks before the date of the letter to Johnston. Mary was, of course, demanding, and there were perhaps some minor complications (though there is no indication of serious illness with either Mary or Willie). She may still have been grieving the death of her son, Edward, her father, and grandmother, all within the previous 12 months. Mary, however, was not still "sick-abed." Even Lincoln himself discounted the issue of Mary's illness as the reason for his refusal to visit his father. He said, "It is a case of baby-sickness, and I suppose is not serious." Lincoln had long since learned to ward off Mary's excruciating demands for attention when it suited his own needs.

The conclusion of the letter offers a deeper and more revealing insight into why Lincoln was not going to travel to see his dying father. "I sincerely hope Father may yet recover his health," Lincoln tells Johnston; "but at all events tell him to remember to call upon, and confide in, our great, and good, and merciful Maker; who will not turn away from him in any extremity. He notes the Fall of the Sparrow, and numbers the hairs of our heads; and He will not forget the dying man, who puts his trust in him." This passage, often quoted out of context, calls on God as Lincoln's substitute at Thomas' bedside. There is a note of hidden grandiosity here. God, who is ultimately caring and attentive, noting even the fall of a sparrow, will not neglect Thomas and will serve as an adequate substitute for Lincoln. This call on God is an effort on Lincoln's part to justify his own absence, which he finally explains succinctly immediately after invoking the Almighty: "Say to him [Thomas] that if we could meet now, it is doubtful whether it would not be more painful than pleasant. . . ." Since Thomas urgently wanted the visit, as Lincoln was well aware, the only reasonable conclusion is that Lincoln simply could not bear the thought of meeting with his father on his deathbed; he sent God in his place. The visit would have been too painful *for Lincoln* himself, something he was able to admit only parenthetically after inventing two specious excuses and offering a rather hollow praise of God's attentiveness.

Why was it so difficult for Lincoln to visit his dying father? (see Cath, this volume). There are any number of possible formulations. First, Lincoln's reluctance was a part of an initial series of responses to Thomas' death that all suggest profound ambivalence. After failing to attend his father's funeral, he never marked the gravesite, despite frequent resolves. After a decade, the grave lay "unmarked and utterly neglected" in the words of Lincoln's friend Ward Hill Lamon, who went there with Lincoln and his stepmother, Sarah, in January 1861. Lincoln vowed to order a stone marker for the site, but he seemed to forget the vow quickly. In any event, the marker was never placed on the grave. At the very end of the war, Lincoln apparently returned in his thoughts to that marker. On December 19, 1867, Mary Lincoln wrote to Sarah Lincoln, Abraham's stepmother (Turner, 1972): "My husband a few weeks before his death mentioned to me that he intended *that* summer [i.e., 1865], paying proper respect to *his* father's grave, by a head and footstone, with his name & age & I propose very soon carrying out his intentions" (pp. 464–65). Mary, however, in her state of emotional disarray after the assassination, was in no position to follow through on her commitment. The task of marking Thomas's grave fell to some local residents of Coles County, who finally erected a 12-foot monument at the grave in 1880–29 years after his death.

It is easy to neglect those we care for in the rush of daily life. Lincoln, however, seemed purposely to separate himself from his depleted and ailing father. While Thomas died, Lincoln remained in Springfield and then let the gravesite turn to dust unnoticed. Furthermore, in the 20 years before Thomas's death, Lincoln established an adult pattern of distance between Thomas and himself that the 90 miles (a one-day buggy trip) separating Springfield and Charleston hardly required. At first, during the New Salem years (1831–1837), Lincoln seems never to have visited his family, though the absence of evidence of any visits hardly proves they did not occur. One must be cautious. After about 1840, however, one can be more confident of the rhythm of father-son interaction. Lincoln's law practice on the circuit took him close to Goosenest Prairie twice a year. It seems he occasionally stopped by; at least his stepmother later reported (Lincoln, 1865) that Lincoln visited her "every year or two." Lincoln may well have visited *her* every year or two, for he adored his stepmother and only reluctantly paid his respects to the old man, who, at least until 1851, just came along with the bargain.

But however often or seldom Lincoln visited his father in Goosenest Prairie, it is certain that Thomas never visited Lincoln in Springfield, was not asked to attend his son's wedding in 1842, and never met any of his grandchildren (those born before his own death included Robert in 1843, Eddie in 1846, Willie in late 1850). Thomas never even laid eyes on Mary. Undoubtedly, Mary's social snobbery reinforced Lincoln's emotional distance from his father. She would probably have been markedly uncomfortable with Lincoln's backwoods relatives in her elegant home. Perhaps, as Herndon (1885) said, if they had come to visit "I doubt whether Mrs. Lincoln would have admitted them." But Mary hardly created the distance between Lincoln and his father. It came from within his own soul. Furthermore, Lincoln was accustomed to overruling Mary if it mattered to him. In this case, her inclinations coincided with his wishes.

Some additional evidence from the 1840s adds weight to this picture of alienation between Thomas and Lincoln. After Thomas and his family moved to Goosenest Prairie in 1831, Thomas made a number of unfortunate land purchases and generally appeared on the decline, while his responsibilities expanded. Sarah's children married, and two of them and their children moved into the two-room log cabin to share the meager pickings from the farm. In the mid-1840s there were 17 people in Thomas's household with whole families crowding into small lofts.

Perhaps inevitably, since he was so relatively well off by then, Lincoln came to play a role in supporting Thomas and his rural kin. In October 1841 Lincoln purchased 40 acres for Thomas. After that he periodically assigned legal fees to Thomas and gave him the power to collect on some notes (Lincoln regularly loaned money to friends and associates).

But Lincoln always seemed irritated when he had to deal with these money problems and at least showed open disdain for his father's plight. On December 7, 1848, John D. Johnston, Lincoln's stepbrother, requested for the illiterate Thomas a loan of 20 dollars to avoid the loss of his land. Johnston's (1848) letter is a curious document that reveals as much about Johnston as it does Thomas. It begins: "I [Thomas] and the old woman is in best of health" and "so is all of the relations at present." The letter noted with regret that Lincoln and his family had failed to visit Goosenest Prairie on their way to Washington where he was to serve his one and only term as Congressman. Thomas continued: "As you failed to come a past, I am compelled to make a request by Letter to you for the loan, of Twenty Dollars, which sum I am compelled to razes or my Land will be sold. . . ." Thomas was obviously embarrassed by having to borrow such a relatively small amount of money to avoid so great a calamity as the loss of his land. "I doe expect you will think strang at this request for that money & it was eaquely as strange, to me & John. . . ." Thomas explained that he had simply forgotten about an old judgment against him. He was under the impression that he had paid the judgment but had lost the receipt, "if we ever had one." The "we" here seems to be Thomas and Johnston, whose affairs were intermingled. There is a possibility that the debt was actually Johnston's and that Thomas was simply covering up for his wayward stepson. In any event, Thomas anticipated Lincoln's anger at the request, for he immediately added, "I now you can't appreciate the reluctance that I have made this request of you for money but I am compled to do so. . . ."

To his father's abject plea Lincoln (1953–1955) replied sarcastically and with heavy condescension:

> My dear father: Your letter of the 7th was received night before last. I very cheerfully send you the twenty dollars, which sum you say is necessary to save your land from sale. It is singular that you should have forgotten a judgment against you; and it is more singular that the plaintiff should have let you forget it so long, particularly as I suppose you have always had property enough to satisfy a judgment of that amount [vol. 2, p. 15].

Lincoln's scorn toward Thomas expresses itself vividly in this sarcastic reply. He says it is "singular" that Thomas should have "forgotten" such a small judgment and "more singular" that the plaintiff should have let it go so long. Lincoln clearly doubts his father's story and will not let him get away with a small lie to cover whatever need there was for 20 dollars. Such a sum was not an insubstantial amount at a time when a full-time domestic servant earned $3 a week, Lincoln's average law fee was $5, and the governor of the state earned $1200 a year. Thomas, supporting a clan of 17, had need of some cash. His distinguished and well-to-do son was the logical person to approach. Thomas got the money, but he also had to accept humiliation and sarcasm along with it.

Lincoln always seemed irritated with Thomas, who was never quite adequate in Lincoln's eyes. Around the time of the $20 loan, a distant relative wrote Lincoln asking for information about his family's background. In his account, Lincoln (1953–1955) stressed his father's ignorance, which Lincoln felt somehow cut his father off from his past:

> Owing to my father being left an orphan at the age of six years, in poverty, and in a new country, he became a wholly uneducated man; which I suppose is the reason why I know so little of our family history. I believe I can say nothing more that would at all interest you [vol. 1, p. 456].

Some 12 years later, in 1860, in a brief autobiographical statement, Lincoln described Thomas as a "wandering laboring boy" who had grown up "literally without education. He never did more in the way of writing than to bunglingly sign his own name." (vol. 4, p. 61) Lincoln's own smugness at being self-educated shows a brittle edge here in the emphasis on his father's dullness.

In sum, the evidence clearly suggests pattern of alienation between the middle-aged Lincoln and his elderly father. And this alienation seemed to have been sustained more by the son than by the father, for at this time there is no indication Thomas felt anything but fondness and respect for his smart and increasingly successful son. Many observers have noted a general decline in Thomas as he aged. Perhaps that explains Thomas's becoming partially dependent on Lincoln financially over the years. In his last decade of life, having raised one family, Thomas was still the patriarch of a vastly expanding clan that had to be supported on meager resources. Certainly Lincoln showed little sensitivity to his father's changing circumstances. Thomas apparently welcomed his son's occasional visits; at least none of the abundant oral histories taken of the Coles County relatives indicates otherwise. And, whatever went before, the dying Thomas or his family finally took the initiative to summon Lincoln to his bedside.

It seems reasonable to believe that something in Lincoln's feelings for his father was blocked and that the prospect of a bedside meeting with his dying father immobilized him. The ambitious and upwardly mobile Lincoln of the 1840s acted as if he were ashamed of his backwoods father. By then, Lincoln was wearing fine black suits, had married the scion of distinguished Kentucky clan, and had soaring political ambitions. His backwoods kin, especially his father, must have intruded on Lincoln's visions of upward mobility. But the alienation ran much deeper. In all his dealings with his father, Lincoln acted out of character. This most sensitive of men became almost cruel; this man noted for his empathy with people, showed harshness toward his father; warm humor turned to cruel sarcasm.

One way to gain perspective on these complicated issues is to look again at Lincoln's childhood and his early interactions with his father. Such an examination may be problematic, for the early determinants of such a significant figure as Lincoln lie shrouded in the darkness of his reticence. Furthermore, the historical evidence – especially the oral histories collected by Herndon and Weik – is clouded by time and the fantasies of various observers. One has to proceed cautiously and hope for a measure of consistancy in corroborating evidence.

A major theme in Lincoln's childhood emerges as Lincoln's rivalry with his father. Integral to this conflicted relationship is that Thomas may have abused his son. At least considerable evidence suggests such abuse. Dennis Hanks, the illegitimate cousin who grew up with Lincoln, noted that Thomas sometimes had to "slash" Lincoln for neglecting his work and reading instead, a punishment reported by several men for whom Lincoln subsequently worked. Lincoln's inquisitiveness also irritated his father. As Hanks noted (1865), "When strangers would ride along and up to his father's fence, Abe always, through pride and to tease his father, would be sure to ask the stranger the first question, for which his father would sometimes knock a rod." To be knocked a rod suggests a fearful hit that would have thrown Lincoln across the room. Sarah Lincoln also reported to Herndon that Thomas cuffed his son and interrupted his earliest speeches because they distracted others from their farm chores. Finally, it was reported by Dennis Hank's son-in-law that "Abe's father habitually treated him with great barbarity" (Lamon, 1872, p. 40).

The two had many run-ins over education, among other things. Thomas Lincoln was reported as saying (Whitney, 1908), "I suppose that Abe is still fooling hisself with eddication. I tried to stop it, but he has got that fool idea in his head, and it can't be got out" (p. 75). Another observer reported, "The cost of a blab school education was probably low on Tom's list of gripes and grievances as this litigious man suffered from drought, flood, intemperate neighbors, court trials over land deeds, lawyers and other serious complaints" (Suppiger, 1981a, p. 607).

There is some, less convincing, evidence to the contrary. Sarah, Lincoln's stepmother, expressed a gentler view of Thomas. "As a usual thing," she said (Lincoln, 1865), "Mr. Lincoln never made Abe quit reading to do anything if he could avoid it. He would do it himself first." Thomas, who was sensitive about his own lack of an education, wanted "his boy Abraham to learn, and he encouraged him to do it in all ways he could." Sarah, however, who was undoubtedly more understanding of Thomas, may have idealized the memory of Thomas over the years; he had died in 1851 and her account of his relations with Lincoln was given to William Herndon, Lincoln's law partner, in 1865. In retrospect, deceased husbands often seem mellower than they did while alive. Furthermore, Sarah only entered Lincoln's life when he was ten. By then, the pattern of tension between father and son, as well as possible abuse, could have been modulated by her gentle nature.

Abuse, of course, can have many meanings in different cultures and at different times. It was not at all uncommon in the 19th century for a father to whip a son. And that era was tinged with a certain personal violence foreign to the sensitivities of most contemporary middle-class Americans. In the South, many whites mercilessly beat their black slaves without being conscious of any special form of brutality. Men everywhere wrestled each other, and it was common to gouge out an opponent's eye. Thomas Lincoln, it was said, fought a vicious wrestling match with Abraham Enlow sometime around 1813 and bit off his nose. But not everyone in a given cultural setting is numbed to such violence. A boy who is whipped, even in a culture where whipping is common, may respond with lifelong pain and bitter, perhaps unconscious anger. Biography is not always congruent with social history.

Lincoln seemed to have been hurt by his father. It is fair to assume that early on, in the scene by the fence, for example, Lincoln manifested some oedipal need to displace Thomas by talking first to the visitor. In general, as Hanks (1865) noted, Lincoln was "rude and forward," testing, teasing, provoking his father as young boys are groomed to do by culture and biology. Among his peers Lincoln especially seemed to reach beyond his grasp and demand a unique kind of understanding. The response of an empathic father to such a son could be to tolerate, even encourage, such outward signs of assertive independence and eagerness to learn. Thomas, however, who may have granted some space to his testy son, had limits to which he seemed frequently pushed. When he responded with rage and "knocked his son a rod," as Dennis described it, Lincoln would drop "a kind of silent unwelcome tear."

The antagonism Lincoln felt toward his father expressed itself in many ways, some subtle and indirect. As a boy Lincoln and his stepbrother, John D. Johnston, cruelly dispatched Thomas' yellow hunting dog. The ugly cur had always announced the return of the boys from unauthorized absences. The two boys decided on a harsh punishment. They wrapped the skin from a dead coon around the miserable mutt. Attracted by the smell, three large dogs in the neighborhood gave chase and speedily killed the poor yellow dog. "Father was much incensed at his death," Lincoln commented laconically after relating this account (Herndon and Weik, 1889, p. 23).

Augustus Chapman reminisced that "Thomas Lincoln never showed by his actions that he thought much of his son Abraham as a boy . . . treated him rather unkindly than otherwise . . . always appeared to think much more of stepson John D. Johnston" (quoted in Suppiger, 1981b, p. 670). The animosity of father toward son appears to have been paid back with interest.

In debating whether Lincoln actually loved his father, Dennis Hanks decided "I Don't think he Did" (Beveridge, 1928). On the other hand, Dennis was convinced Thomas loved his son, though he never seemed to show it, frequently scolding and spanking the boy out of exasperation over his seeming indolence.

Throughout his working life, a kind of crudeness and downward mobility characterized Thomas. A neighbor of his, Nat Grigsby (1865) said that Thomas was not really "a lazy man, but . . . a piddler, always doing but doing nothing great, was happy, lived easy and contented." For most observers (e.g., Holland, 1866; Herndon and Weik, 1889) he was shiftless and irresponsible, roving, proverbially slow of movement, mentally and physically; was careless, inert and dull. He had trouble paying for his many land purchases because he never fell in with the routine of labor.

Research in the 20th century significantly changed some aspects of this harsh picture of Thomas that had emerged from the histories and the early commentators who used the oral testimonies. For example, in the 1920s it was discovered that in a local tax book in 1814 Thomas ranked 15th out of 98 people in ownership of property in the community where he lived. At least he may not have been the slouch then that some neighbors remembered later. It was also not uncommon for frontiersmen to have trouble with title to their land. Thomas lost property habitually and may have been litigious, but so were many in that age of unsettled land development. Thomas did attract two apparently outstanding women as wives to whom he seems to have been a loyal husband – or at the least they seem to have been loyal to him. He generally stayed sober (though, unlike Lincoln, he did not completely abstain), paid his taxes, went to church, and served on juries.

Still, there was something odd, indeed wrong, about Thomas Lincoln. One significant issue was sexual. Thomas became sterile because the mumps "went down on him," as they put it in the 19th century (Hanks, 1865). By various other accounts Thomas had castrated himself, had one testicle the size of a pea, had two testicles the size of peas, or had always been sterile. In all this contradictory evidence, Herndon, who detested Thomas, clung to one central idea: "Thomas' utter laziness and want of energy . . . is due to the fact of fixing" (note in unpublished ms.).

It can be said Herndon was intent on making Thomas irrelevant. This sexual issue was critical, for Herndon wanted to argue that Thomas was not in fact Lincoln's father. In a curious way, that determined effort of Herndon, the adoring biographer, reflected Lincoln's own, certainly upspoken, wish to be rid of his father. Herndon's bias, however, should not obscure the fact that the reports about the state of Thomas's genitals came to Herndon independently from numerous sources (at least as independently as one can hope for under the circumstances). The oral history material, for all its problems, remains a vital source. Granted, most commentators blithely dismiss it, but it can be understood in context, even while it is related to Herndon's complex psychology. That seems a more fruitful, not to mention more valid, historical approach.

One has to suspect that at some level Lincoln was keenly aware of what all the neighbors and relatives were whispering about his father. Certainly this knowledge fed into Lincoln's generalized sense of Thomas's inadequacy and helps explain some of Lincoln's disdain for and irritation with his father. In Lincoln's mind, Thomas was not good enough to be the father of such a smart, provocative, and ambitious youth as Lincoln saw himself to be. Even as a boy, Lincoln seemed to have aspirations that far surmounted his backwoods origin. In contrast, in the oral history reports, Thomas's inadequacy was consistently described as lazy, a piddler, a ne'er-do-well, illiterate, and on and on. But his inadequacy always seemed tied to sexual sterility or a lack of potency, or both. (The popular mind often fails to distinguish between sterility and impotency.) It is not unreasonable to conclude that young Lincoln harbored these same ideas, however confused and inchoate, about his father, based on their relationship set in this particular family setting—reinforced by whatever information or intimations reached conscious levels.

From a young boy's perspective, doubts of one's father's sexuality call into question the whole issue of origins: Who am I? Where did I come from? We may entertain the belief that these eternal questions had special meaning for Lincoln because in certain ways he was so markedly different from his surroundings. An early and gifted reader in an illiterate environment, he was sensitive in a rough and often crude world, full of soaring ambitions among peers who seldom thought beyond farming. The whispered rumors of Thomas's sexual inadequacy may have first undermined his legitimacy in his son's eyes. The real issues may have been vague for young Lincoln, for even precocious children cannot really understand such sexual complications until they are at least seven or eight years old. But one can be innocent and yet sense, from whispered rumors, some fatal flaw in one's father's manhood, especially a flaw that vaguely calls into question his legitimacy, masculinity, or potency.

If the rumors about Thomas raised doubts in Lincoln's mind whether Thomas was his real father, the question, then, is what psychological purpose might it have served, and what other ideas fed into the creation of what might be called a core fantasy? The sense one gets very quickly is that the possible illegitimacy or impotency of Thomas in Lincoln's mind, as garnered from garrulous and talkative neighbors, evolved into one piece of a larger and absolutely essential psychological construct. It is this larger context that helps clarify the issues regarding Thomas. The story leads directly to Lincoln's biological mother, Nancy Hanks Lincoln.

In 1850, Lincoln was riding in a buggy with his partner, William Herndon. They were traveling to court in Menard County to handle a suit that raised issues of heredity traits. Lincoln grew pensive and uncharacteristically shared with Herndon some important thoughts about his mother. "God bless my mother," he said (Herndon and Weik, 1889). "All that I am or ever hope to be I owe to her," Here Lincoln went on to say that she was the illegitimate daughter of Lucy Hanks and a well-bred Virginia farmer or planter. In fact, this Virginian had been the source of her (and therefore Lincoln's) traits – power of analysis, logic, mental activity, and ambition – that distinguished him from the Hanks family. Lincoln felt that "illegitimate children are oftentimes sturdier and brighter than those born in lawful wedlock . . ." (pp. 2–3).

The amount of exegesis on this confessional buggy ride is quite amazing. Some simply conclude it never happened, but to do so is to dismiss Herndon in the one area where all thoughtful observers feel he should be accepted: when he reports something Lincoln told him directly. Others have felt there is doubt about which mother Lincoln is referring to. But that is to read the passage incorrectly and focus only on the "God bless my mother" part. No one ever questioned Sarah's legitimacy, and besides, it would be irrelevant. The issue was heredity. In another context, Lincoln (1953–1955, vol. 4, pp. 59–61) also wrote of Nancy as his "mother" and Sarah, though she "proved to be a good and kind mother," as his "stepmother." He used words carefully.

The safest and now thoroughly tested conclusion over a hundred years of scholarship is that in the buggy ride Lincoln basically said what Herndon reported Lincoln's saying about his mother. That said, it proves nothing about Lincoln's geneology. Many formidable researchers have tried to uncover the facts of Lincoln's maternal line but without success. The crucial documents that would finally settle the debate have never been located. In the end, however, the geneological question is largely irrelevant. What matters is that Lincoln believed his mother was illegitimate. She may or may not actually have been so, but his firm belief that she was illegitimate is a psychological fact of great significance. Furthermore, Lincoln believed that his specialness was somehow related to his mother's illegitimacy and that it all started with "some Virginian" speculatively of the stature and character of Thomas Jefferson or George Washington.

This brings us to a speculative synthesis. A detestable father who may have abused his sensitive son was psychologically eliminated. Lincoln made him genetically irrelevant, a kind of generational stand-in for more exalted ancestors. His unusual personality derived from "some Virginian gentleman" who had sired his mother. This fanta-sized grandfather became, in the mind of the boy seeking alternatives to his real father, an idealized alternative of potent significance. His adored mother had imparted this special biological gift to him; she was a direct connection to fathers worth admiring, distinguished men in frock coats who had made revolution and wrote stirring documents of human freedom and dignity. Thomas had to be endured, but in the end he could be dismissed. There were other visions of greatness that inspired Lincoln and helped him during the threatened disintegration of his beloved country.

If it existed as we have described, it was an extraordinary core fantasy. It could explain, among other things, how he nourished his sense of specialness among the low-born. He probably memorized Weems's *Life of Washington* while other boys lounged about lazily. He practiced writing and spelling. He memorized Shakespearean solilo-quies and attended carefully to Bible stories his mother shared with him. He dreamed of greatness. He was from the backwoods but not of it. He worked hard to escape and never retained even sentimental attachments to log cabins (the "railsplitter" image was a David Davis campaign ploy in 1860). As soon as Lincoln began earning money, he married "up" and bought a respectable middle-class house that he eventually enlarged to be almost elegant. And he was, after all, elected – and reelected – President of the United States.

Such a core fantasy may provide a key to understanding Lincoln's relationship to his father. All the evidence suggests that Lincoln felt his father was inadequate. Thomas could only "bunglingly sign his own name," as he said in his autobiographical statement in 1860. He was tolerated grudgingly and was never to see his daughter-in-law or his grandchildren. Thomas was disdained. He became an irritating presence, which as he aged, became almost unbearable for Lincoln. And no wonder. He had always been an obnoxious presence for young Lincoln. In the core fantasy, Lincoln found his revenge. As a father, Thomas was out of his league, emotionally and genetically. Lincoln descended from one of the "real" fathers, the founders of the nation. Thomas was a kind of accident.

Finally, this core fantasy may provide the psychological basis for Lincoln's enormously significant attachment to the thought and deeds of the founders and the "temple of liberty" built by the founders. As early as 1838, Lincoln was talking of the "fortress of strength" that a careless, post-heroic generation was allowing to crumble. "We must hew new pillars for that temple from the solid quarry of solid reason" (Lincoln, 1953–1955, vol. 1, pp. 108–115). By 1854 Lincoln was calling passionately for a readoption of the Declaration of Independence.

> Let north – and south – let all Americans, let all lovers of liberty everywhere – join the great and good work. If we do this, we shall not only have saved the Union; we shall have so saved it as to make and keep it forever worthy of the saving. We shall have so saved it, that the succeeding millions of free happy people, the world over, shall rise up, and call us blessed to the latest generations [vol. 2, p. 276].

The war gave Lincoln a new urgency to define his unique relationship to the founders. Even as he left Springfield on February 11, 1861, Lincoln spoke of having a burden on his shoulders that exceeded "that which rested upon Washington" (vol. 4, p. 190). And in 1863 Lincoln spoke movingly of "our fathers" who "brought forth on this continent a new nation, conceived in Liberty and dedicated to the proposition that all men are created equal" (vol. 7, pp. 17–18).

Assuming this was Lincoln's childhood core fantasy, it linked him genetically, by way of his mother's illegitimacy, to Thomas

Jefferson or George Washington. It had the potential to solve the basic problems, pain, and incongruities of his childhood. Most of all, the fantasy could give him some rationalization for dealing with his troubling father, resolving the ambiguities of his father's obnoxious presence. Finally, the fantasy would attach Lincoln to specific idealized surrogates, whom Lincoln creatively reinterpreted for a generation caught up in division and war. Those founders were, after all, family.

REFERENCES

Beveridge, A.J. (1928), *Abraham Lincoln 1809–1858*. Boston: Houghton Mifflin.

Cath, S. (1982), Divorce and the child: "The father question hour." *Father and Child.* ed. S.H. Cath, A. R. Gurwitt & J.M. Ross. Boston: Little, Brown.

_____ (1988), Midlife decompensation of previously idealized fathers. Unpublished manuscript.

Grigsby, N. (1865), Statement to William H. Herndon, September 12. Herndon/Weik Collection, Library of Congress.

Hanks, D.F. (1865), Statement to William H. Herndon, June 13. Herndon/Weik Collection, Library of Congress.

Herndon, W.H. (1885), Letter to Jesse Weik, December 1. Herndon/Weik Collection, Library of Congress.

_____ & Weik, J.W. (1889), *Life of Lincoln,* ed. P. M. Angle. Cleveland, OH: World, 1930.

Holland, J.G. (1866), *The Life of Abraham Lincoln.* Springfield, MA: Gurdon Bill.

Johnston, J.D. (1848), for Lincoln, T. to Lincoln, A., Letter December 7. 1848, Manuscript, Illinois State Historical Library (see also C.H. Coleman, 1955, *Abraham Lincoln and Coles County, Illinois,* New Brunswick, NJ: Scarecrow Press, p. 73).

Kohut, H. (1971), *The Analysis of the Self.* New York: International Universities Press.

_____ (1977), *The Restoration of the Self.* New York: International Universities Press.

_____ (1984), *How Does Analysis Cure?* ed. A. Goldberg with P.E. Stepansky. Chicago: University of Chicago Press.

_____ (1985), *Self Psychology and The Humanities,* ed. C.B. Strozier. New York: Norton.

Lamon, W.H. (1872), *The Life of Abraham Lincoln.* Boston: Osgood.

Lincoln, A. (1953–1955), *The Collected Works of Abraham Lincoln,* ed. P. Basler, New Brunswick, NJ: Rutgers University Press, 8 vols.

Lincoln, S. (1865), Statement to William H. Herndon, September 8. Herndon/ Weik Collection, Library of Congress.

Shengold, L. (1979), Child abuse and deprivation, soul murder. *J. Amer. Psychoanal. Assn.,* 27:533–559.

Strozier, C.B. & Offer, D. (1985), *The Leader.* New York: Plenum Press.

Suppiger, J.E. (1981a), The intimate Lincoln, part I: The boy. *Lincoln Herald,* 83:604–694.

———— (1981b), The intimate Lincoln, part II: Growing up in Indiana. *Lincoln Herald,* 83:668–676.

Turner, J.G. & Turner, L.L., ed. (1972), *Mary Todd Lincoln.* New York: Knoff.

Whitney, H.C. (1908), *Life of Lincoln.* New York: Baker & Tayler.

Interlude

I have begun to plant thee
and will labor to make thee full of
growing

              –King Duncan to Banquo, *Macbeth,* Act 1

Why is it so difficult for most fathers to express enough love so that their sons will feel protected by their sires and "full of growing," or for most sons to sustain their fathers' kingship. Indeed, King Duncan spoke in gratitude to a heroic thane who had just helped save his kingdom from a "disloyal son." When it was foreordained that Banquo's issue would inherit the throne, this loyal subject soon became a traitor.

    In the compilation of this volume on fathers and their families I reluctantly revived many resonant memories of myself as an angry, unappreciated son, as an unempathic father, and as an inconsistent grandfather. With so many new insights into the essence of the narcissistic balance between men and their families, it seemed to me likely that many readers might feel the need to protect themselves from similar discomforts. For it became incontrovertibly clear that not only do our parents fill us with growing, but they simultaneously interfere with the process. Analyzed or not, we are all likely to subtlely repeat certain painful patterns with our own sons.

This particular section brought this disturbing, if not painfully throbbing, form of conscious stocktaking to a head. For these chapters illustrate these repetitive themes in ordinary and extraordinary unconscious interchanges between some famous fathers and sons set in the larger context of their families in the long ago. Thus these papers were not derived from formal psychoanalysis. Rather the insights they hold were revealed through analyses of personal and historical narratives, biographies, letters, and, in the case of Ives, lyrics and music.

In the familiar transgenerational oedipal context of who shall inherit the throne, a theme both Sophocles and Shakespeare exploited in their major tragedies, we often wonder just how much children accurately record or erase of their earliest nonverbal and subsequent verbal experiences. And, as a result of this immersion in father-son hostilities, do we then believe, as most ancient myths suggest, that whatever parents say or do will always be marred by deeply concealed, permanent, unconscious, negative motivations that echo silently the invisible necessities of unseen ancestors across generations?

In regard to this particular aspect of the historical perspective, there is a rich lode of information to be mined from Ross's (1984) many recent contributions on the Laius Complex. In this volume, his immediate focus is on the reinterpretation of the dynamics and therapeutic dilemmas involved in Freud's account of Little Hans, "a quintessential oedipal parable." Reading through several preliminary drafts of these Hans papers only enriched my appreciation of how complex clinical material can be and how it can be variously reinterpreted by clinicians in subsequent generations. In an earlier draft, Ross opined that psychoanalysts have tended to ignore the ambivalences at the heart of every little Oedipus and have been obtuse to the subtleties of the dialogue between fathers and children. He raises the question of the consequences of the failure of Hans's father and Freud to inform the boy of his biological destiny. Ross stresses Hans's fantastic interpretation of his fateful tonsillectomy not only as a threat, but as a symbolic act of impregnation and of birth. I would ask, does wanting a baby and a penis always lead to a negative oedipal compromise in which the male would suffer penetration and castration to produce life, not as a father, but in the manner of a woman?

There might be one other confusing contradiction in this paper. Ross speculates that Hans was not "offered the opportunity during the oedipal phase to reorganize fragmented object images and various identifications into a heterosexual paternal identity." But Hans became a father.

Can we really assume, as Ross suggests, that if the narrators had clarified Hans's "wish to be a father, along with the mechanics of paternity," Hans would have "proceeded beyond the alleviation of his symptoms and arrived at a more adaptive and progressive resolution of a central conflict within the oedipal constellation?"

In our lifetime, as in the lifetimes of our ancestors in this field, we can only continue to search for the tolerable degree of insight we are permitted with the conceptual tools at our disposal. Roazen (in press), a professor of social and political science and a keen critical observer of the psychoanalytic scene, cautions us on "the histiographic mistake of thinking what we now hold to be true must have somehow been missed by Freud." He adds, wisely, "the study of the history of ideas ought to expand the limits of our toleration and show us how different writers in the past came to terms with enduring human dilemmas."

The inherent human need for splitting, idealization, and projective identification of fathers and leaders has nowhere been so clearly significant and meaningful as in the self-images of great men (Strozier and Cath, this volume). The need to dissociate the idealized self from imperfect, limited, mortal, if not degraded, fathers plays a part in the relationship between all followers to all leaders (Cath, 1983; Strozier, 1985; Rizzuto, 1979). This interlude explores the role of these idealized self- and paternal imagos in our effort to understand and appreciate the work of artists and the lives of the great fathers of our historical and professional past.

Strozier and Cath researched three generations of the Lincoln family to understand better how the personal conflict between a brilliant and favored ambitious son (who may be said to have won the oedipal conflict) and a less intelligent, backwoods father became so meaningful to the 19th-century problem of preserving and equalizing the larger family of man. They find little to suggest that a reconciliation between father and son occurred during the midlife of our 16th president or at any other time before his father's death. Indeed, the historical records, including the recollections of those who knew Lincoln best, lead us to believe that he ignored and denigrated his biological father. The authors postulate that to fill the void he looked elsewhere for the positive substance around which to form his ego and maintain his ego ideals. His own narratives highlight the possibility of a father imago built on his mother's illegitimacy allegedly involving an aristocratic Virginian. He used this image to explain to his law partner his unique nature. This paternal imago was strikingly in contrast to that of his impecunious, abusive father, Thomas, whose stature gradually deteriorated with age. Strozier and Cath emphasize that Abe could not bear to be available in person before, during, or after his father's terminal illness. And despite promises to himself and to his wife, he failed to mark his father's grave before his own assassination. Furthermore, psychohistorical research, informs us that there is no real or written record that Thomas ever met Mary face to face or that he had ever been in his affluent son's home. It appears that his daughter-in-law and her Southern aristocratic family not only embarrassed the President by their Confederate leanings, but successfully screened the children from her husband's parents. As far as is known, the grands never met.

This pattern of avoiding a parent sensed to be shaming, cruel, and unempathic, both in life and in death, was repeated in the next generation. Robert, the only surviving son, was left with the burden of comforting and containing an embarrassingly impecunious, paranoid, if not intermittently psychotic, mother. At his death, he revealed his resentful alienation by refusing to be buried in the Lincoln family plot in Springfield, Illinois. Robert's grave is in the Arlington National Cemetery.

Strozier and Cath also attempt to tease out of existing historical documents other important strands of Lincoln's unique paternal-national imago. Not only did he extensively idealize his biological mother and her supposed aristocratic connection, but he did the same with a careful selection of the nation's founding fathers, including Washington. He seems also to have allied himself with the Bard of Avon, William Shakespeare. These collective strands of idealization so evident in his writings are hypothesized to be relevant to his creative quest for more heroic fathers and roots. It is not surprising that such a self-educated and eloquent man would find Shakespeare's concern with leadership and the transmission of political power a favorite source of comfort especially during the dark hours of the Civil War.

Lincoln, so familiar with Shakespeare, reframed Polonius's advice to a son into a homespun but brilliant soliloquy:

> "Beware of entrance to a quarrel, but being in [it], bear it so the opposed may beware of thee," is good but not the best. Quarrel not at all. No man, resolved to make the most of himself, can spare the time for personal contention. Still less can he afford to take all the consequences, including the vitiating of his temper, and the loss of self control. Yield larger things to which you can show no more than equal right; and yield lesser ones, through clearly your own. Better give your path to a dog than be bitten by him in contesting for the right. Even killing the dog would not cure the bite [Nicolay, 1912, p. 320].

Lincoln was always a contradiction in brilliance as well as brilliant in contradictions. When accused of being "common," this man, known for his humbleness, revealed a Job-like presumption (in effect, "I assume that I matter") when he responded, "The Lord prefers common people!" (Nicolay, 1912). After the election, when Governor Palmer of Illinois visited Lincoln in the White House while the President was being shaved, observed "Well, Mr. Lincoln, if anybody had told me that in a great crisis like this the people were going out to a little one horse town and pick out a one horse lawyer for President, I wouldn't have believed it." Lincoln whirled about in his barber chair, as if in a rage, but then answered earnestly, "neither would I. . . ." (Hertz, 1939, p. 629)

To appreciate better the conflicted contradictions Tom induced in his son, let us return to the revelatory power of Abe's letters. We will compare the taut abruptness contained in the message to his illiterate father with Lincoln's eloquent, comforting message to Fanny McCullough, the young daughter of a friend, who had just lost her father. He attempts to persuade Fanny to do with her father that which he seemed unable to do with his own a decade earlier (Strozier and Cath, this volume).

> Dear Fanny,
> It is with deep grief that I learn of the death of your kind and brave father; and especially that it is affecting your young heart beyond what is common in such cases. In this sad world of ours, sorrow comes to all; and, to the young it comes with bitterest agony, because it takes them unawares. The older have learned to ever expect it. I am anxious to afford some alleviation of your present distress. Perfect relief is not possible except with time. You can not now realize you will ever feel better. Is this not so? And yet it is a mistake. You are sure to be happy again. To know this, which is certainly true, will make you less miserable now. I have had experience enough to know what I say.[1] And you need only believe it to feel better at once. The memory of your dear father, instead of an agony, will yet be of a pure and holier sort than you have known before. Please present my kind regards to your afflicted mother
> Your sincere friend,
> Abraham Lincoln [Basler, 1953a, pp. 16–17]

Whether Lincoln ever knew his father as anything but "an agony" is a question that may never be answered definitively. But the

---

[1]In one of his deepest depressions, triggered by his request to be released from his engagement to Mary Todd, Lincoln wrote similar words: "Whether I shall ever be better, I can not tell. I awfully forbode I shall not" (Basler, 1953b, p. 229).

contrast between his unforgiving stance with his own father, as reflected in his behavior, and his faith in Fanny's ability to recover "memories of a pure and holier sort" of her father, suggests that Lincoln recognized the timeless, universal human need for a more loving father imago to sustain the self, especially in critical times. Abraham Lincoln was able to become that figure to a nation in need and over time to embody the best of fatherhood for an inordinately large segment of mankind.

Stanley H. Cath

REFERENCES

Basler, R. (1953a), *The Collected Works of Abraham Lincoln. Vol. VI.* New Brunswick, NJ: Rutgers University Press.

_____ (1953b), *The Collected Works of Abraham Lincoln, Vol. I.* New Brunswick, NJ: Rutgers University Press.

Cath, S.H. (1983), Adolescence and addiction to alternative belief systems: Psychoanalytic and psychophysiological considerations. *Psychoanal. Inq.,* 2:619–676.

Hertz, E. (1939), *Lincoln Talks.* New York: Viking Press.

Nicolay, H. (1912), *Personality Traits of Abraham Lincoln.* New York: Century Press.

Rizzuto, A-M (1979), *The Birth of the Living God.* Chicago: University of Chicago Press.

Roazen, P. (in press), Freud and his father.

Ross, J. (1984), Oedipus revisited: Laius and the Laius complex. *The Psychoanalytic Study of the Child.* New Haven: Yale University Press.

Strozier, C. (1982), *Lincoln's Quest for Union.* New York: Basic Books.

_____ (1985), *The Leader.* New York: Plenum Press.

15

Calcium Light Night and Other Early Memories of Charles Ives

Stuart Feder

What follows is an exploration of certain early memories of the composer Charles Edward Ives (1874–1954) to demonstrate how aspects of the paternal imago achieve symbolic representation in the music itself. At the heart of these memories are the composer's earliest experiences with his father, George Edward Ives (1845–1894), who was a village musician in a small town, Charles's most influential teacher and, indeed, the most important object in the composer's life. These experiences were related to attachment and to separation. It is important to note at the outset that the memories that are considered here were registered prominently in the auditory modality appropriate to a composer of music in addition to usual visual and kinesthetic ways in which memory enters the mainstream of mental life. Like all memories, they accrued histories of their own, but unique here is the manner in which they were incorporated within particularly innovative works of music at a significant later time. Thus, two pieces of music, *Calcium Light Night* and *The Pond,* will be analyzed musically and at the same time discussed from a psychoanalytic point of view. The early events that likely served as the raw material of memory are explored in biographical data and contemporary newspaper accounts of local events. Later accruals to this core of memory are supplemented with historical accounts stemming from late adolescence. Throughout, the nature of mental representation is sought in the auditory sphere. As a result, certain generalizations are suggested regarding the development of an exceptional musical talent, the enduring effect of specific objects who nurture it, and at least one of the earliest roots of later creativity.

GEORGE IVES, "PROFESSOR"

A unique birth announcement appeared in *The Danbury News* of October 28, 1874: "Ives' Brass Band has included among its soloists an infantile performer on the *vox humana.*" Thus from the very beginning was Charles Edward Ives associated with his father, George Edward Ives, a village musician in postbellum Danbury, Connecticut. The humorous notice attests to his visibility and popularity, although he was far from being the only musician in this burgeoning community. It was barely a decade since George Ives's discharge from the Union Army where, legend has it, he had been its youngest bandmaster. In the interim, he had established himself locally as a music teacher, organizer of musical groups, and sometime entrepreneur of concerts and even opera. He was truly a musical jack-of-all-trades, his life progressing countercurrent to the times and to family tradition. The Iveses of Danbury might be said to have been involved in virtually every trade and profession associated with a growing business community in laissez faire economic times with the exception, until Charles, of the then irrelevant business of arts and entertainment. George's father (Charles's grandfather) had started the local savings bank, and George's two older brothers owned the lumberyard and the largest hardware and home furnishings store in town. The family had been involved in every major civic endeavor, members of a small cohort of businesmen, as it was said, "a few families that *were* the town" (Perlis, 1974). Music and business comprised the double heritage that was to be Charles's.

George was 28 when Charles was born. Very much a family man despite his maverick vocation, he had married Mary Elizabeth Parmelee ten months earlier. The daughter of a recently deceased and not very successful businessman and sometime tailor in nearby Bethel, she did not have—nor did she ever achieve—the social status of the Iveses. What little has been said of Mollie, as she was called, points to a warm-hearted, generous woman of small stature; a good mother and grandmother in her time, uncommonly pretty but otherwise undistinguished in personality. Charles Ives's biographical writings are strangely silent about his mother, the more so in contrast to the idealized outpourings about his father. The major biographers of Ives, such as the Cowells (1955) and Kirkpatrick (1972), have been able to come up with little more. But from the first it appeared as if George were the more prominent parent. The humorous birth announcement in the newspaper seems to parallel Charles's perception and conscious experience: only his father is mentioned. Although this may say something about the public role of women at the time – at least in small-town America – there is more in this instance of both social and psychological consequence.

To say simply that George was charismatic would be to miss the essence of what it was to be a musician in that America. He might be the designated hero of the patriotic holiday strutting down Main Street at the head of the band. But most days his position was far from an exalted one. The term "Professor" accorded the musician carried with it an edge of contempt with connotations of alienation and denigration. This was far from the case for an admiring boy and his idealized father. And indeed during the first decade of Charles's life, George Ives was in his heyday in Danbury. Later, Charles could not avoid perceptions of his father as the devalued "Professor" (in his own word, "emasculated," within the context of the community) and the black sheep of the family. This would become at least one source of conflict among others in Charles's intrapsychic relationship with George.

Two important elements in this regard, which are developed elsewhere (Feder, n.d.), may be cited. The first relates to coming to terms with the alien affect of shame that was experienced with regard to an overvalued parental imago become assimilated into the self-representation. A second regards identification proper: The father who in early life conveys in all respects "be like me" also betrays an element of "don't be like me," which in this case would become conscious to both only later, in Charles's adolescence. There can be no question that conflict and resultant ambivalence about his father proved at length to be a strong motivating element in Charles's choices in life – not least of which was the decision to become the kind of private businessman-composer that he did, independent of art for income. However, our focus in this study is on a relatively unambivalent, precompetitive, preconflictual phase of life. It emphasizes more the preoedipal, idealizing, dyadic bond with father as described by Blos (1984), a bond whose fate lies in the formation of the ego ideal. As for the mother, relatively eclipsed in memory in the face of this activity, there will be more to say later.

MEMORY IN MUSIC

It is the purpose of this study to explore certain significant early childhood memories that the composer Charles Ives had of his father, George, and to consider their ramifications in life and in art. To begin with, I suggest that the events underlying these organizations of memory were experienced and, accordingly, recorded in two modes – that is, verbally and musically. In Charles's collected autobiographical notes, his *Memos* (Kirkpatrick, 1972), there are several reminiscences of George. That he called these notes "memos" at all makes concrete the very activity of the man, then in his 50s, in the act of remembering. The pace and rhythm of remembering is a part of that mental activity, which is of interest in itself although it has been little acknowledged save perhaps in the process of mourning.

In Charles's case, against the background of the flux of remembering that is regularly a part of "the libidinal milieu" (Glover, 1925), there were three spurts of relatively intense memorialization activity during the course of his life with respect to his father. The first was part of the immediate and expectable mourning process following George's death when Charles was 20; the second occurred around the time of Charles's courtship with Harmony Twichell, when in his early 30s, in the initial sharing of intimacy and with her encouragement, he told her much about his father in the course of which many memories were revived; the third was a part of the very beginnings of Charles's "summing up" in his fourth decade, which I have written about elsewhere (Feder, 1981), with the collecting of the prose *Memos* and in his three final culminating masterworks, the *Second Piano Sonata* (The "Concord"), the *114 Songs,* and the prose *Essays Before A Sonata.* For the rest, the vicissitudes of memory become obscure as Charles stopped writing and composing in his late 40s – at about the same age, 49, that George Ives was when he died. Charles, then, who lived until he was nearly 80, would outlive the composer in him.

My grouping together of the musical and prose works is purposeful and, I believe, responsive to the composer's intent and style. It also returns us to the point with which I started, that Charles's childhood memories of his father are recorded in his musical works in addition to his autobiographical prose statements. Further, it is my assertion that the nonverbal representation of these memories, even with their burden and challenge of ambiguity, are of a far richer and more suble nature than even the most feelingful verbal statements. Finally, those musical works themselves, of which these memories are a part, are of a special nature. They have a particular place in the *oeuvre* of Charles Ives. Composed during a relatively experimental period coinciding with his courtship, they are frequently innovative, if brief, and are from a technical point of view essentially exercises in one or another musical device. Moreover, they are often associated with certain specific affects characteristically related to memory, prominent among which is nostalgia.

THE POND AND CALCIUM LIGHT NIGHT

In what follows we will consider two examples of remembering in music. Both are short pieces for small chamber groups, and both were written in 1906, the composer's 32nd year. Ives had been in a "composer's slump" in 1905, when he was 31 (Kirkpatrick, 1980). With the beginning of his courtship with Harmony Twichell, there was a burst of creative activity yielding a number of short pieces, many of which proved to be markedly innovative studies that were instrumental in the formation of what would become a highly individual style. Among these were *The Pond* and *Calcium Light Night*.[1] I have chosen these two for consideration here because they afford an interesting contrast while at the same time representing typical components of Ives's characteristically heterogeneous style. *The Pond* may also be seen as a characteristic work in its similarity to what is probably Ives's single most famous piece, the ethereal, other wordly *Unanswered Question*, also written in the same year, 1906. As for *Calcium Light Night*, it incorporates one of the most idiomatic features of Ives's personal style in music in the use of the march. Thus, a polarity can be seen from the outset in this characteristic music of Ives: In musical time, *The Pond* scarcely moves; although a tune is quoted, it is slowed down past recognition toward a representation of timelessness and motionlessness. In contrast, in the march *Calcium Light Night*, there is created the clearest representation of the progress of time and, within it, of lively motor activity.

I (Feder, 1984) have discussed *The Pond* (Ives, mss. no date A.) elsewhere in another context and will here quote a brief descriptive summary:

---

[1]Both *Calcium Light Night* and *The Pond* may be found on a single recording: *Charles Ives Calcium Light Night*, Orchestra conducted by Gunther Schuller. Columbia Stereo MS7318. (Library of Congress Catalogue Number 70-750410).

In its original form of 1906, *The Pond* is a brief piece for chamber orchestra – a "song without words" – in which the actual words are written in below the lead line. The latter (which *may* be sung, however) is scored for trumpet or basset horn, two of George's instruments. There is manifest reference to his father in Charles' words, "A sound of a distant horn, O'er shadowed lake is borne – my father's song." *The Pond* is also to be found later as one of the *114 Songs,* retitled in the Index as *Remembrance* (#12). However, in

Figure 1. *Calcium Light Night.* Performing Version Arrangted by Henry Cowell in Collaboration with Charles Ives.

lieu of a title on the printed page a couplet by Wordsworth appears: "The music in my heart I bore/long after it was heard no more." . . . There are remarkable features in this brief work. (It occupies only 11 measures in printed full scores. . . .) For one, the "sound of the distant horn" is rendered literally with the spatial features emphasized in an echo. Distance is represented not only in space but in time, as the melody played by the trumpet (or basset horn; or vocalized) is repeated in canon a measure later by the echoing flute. All these instruments were those George played and the image of the composer's father playing from a distance across a pond, perhaps in the practise of one of his many musical experiments or "stunts" has been noted by several writers. Distance is emphasized in the instructions provided on the orchestral score: "PPPP (as in distance)." Similarly, on an earlier sketch (crossed out by Ives, characteristically using the same piece of manuscript paper, now upside down, for a sketch of something else) Ives scribbled: "cornet (in distance) taps, etc." (Kirkpatrick, 1960, p. 24). The tune itself is a rendition of a melody slowed beyond recognition. *Kathleen Mavourneen* is an Irish love song about parting and death: "Kathleen Mavourneen; the great dawn is breaking. The horn of the hunger is heard on the hill (beginning) . . . It May be for years, and it may be forever; Then why are thou silent, thou voice of my heart? (ending)" [pp. 336–337].

Calcium Light Night (Ives, mss. no date B.), probably written in 1907, is also scored for chamber orchestra but one of very different makeup. The nine instruments that constitute it suggests a marching band (piccolo, oboe, clarinet, bassoon, trumpet or cornet, trombone, snare and bass drums, and piano–the last used largely as a percussion instrument) (see Figure 1). The following is a verbal description:

After a drum-beat introduction of three measures, the trombone enters (triple-piano) with a tune which is soon imitated in free canon by other instruments. The tune, one of three Yale fraternity songs from Ives' college years, was written out with words in a shaky hand many years later when Henry Cowell helped Ives realize a performing version from his sketch: "And again we sing thy praises Psi U, Psi U, and again we sing thy praises, Psi Upsilon" (see Figure 2). Soon after, two other fraternity songs are introduced: 1) "When in after years we take our children on our knee, we'll teach them that the alphabet begins with T.K.E." [sic] (piccolo, measure 8); 2) D.K.E. Marching Song: "A Band of brothers in D.K.E., we march along tonight. 2 by 2 with arms locked close & tight" (trumpet, measure 15). The piece starts in "Slow March Time" and it is noted "accelerato/crescendo little by little until turning point." Thus at the center of the work the "band" is playing

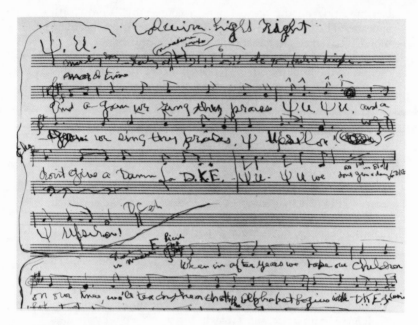

Figure 2. Musical "Memo" of Fraternity Songs Quoted in *Calcium Light Night* in Ives's Hand.

forte in an accelerated tempo, and, for emphasis, the section is repeated triple-forte even faster. From this climax, the "turning point," each section previously played is now repeated in more or less retrograde fashion, the music accordingly slowing in tempo and diminishing in volume, the piece ending as it began. Thus, the work aims toward as much symmetry as taste and judgment would allow. The effect upon the listener is that of a band approaching as if from a distance, passing in review, and fading away in the opposite direction. The volume is thus imitated quite literally while the tempo is distorted from its literal representation.

THE AUDITORY ENVIRONMENT AND EARLY LOSS

We will return to more details of the music later following a consideration of Charles Ives's early life. On the eve of Charles's birth, George Ives was approaching his prime as a village musician as evidenced by the number and range of musical activities in which he was engaged. These included teaching, leading, and performing in at least three bands that provided music for numerous patriotic, religious, civic, and social events of the town. Holidays such as the Fourth of July and Decoration Day were regularly commemorated with music. With cornet alone, George would lead the singing of gospel hymns during week-long summer camp meetings in nearby Bethel. During the summer season George also performed with a portion of his band on the steamboat from Norwalk to Rockaway Beach, New York, and, often, he would perform a second time with others of the band at social events weekend evenings. There were torchlight political parades and celebrations of local fraternal and quasi-fraternal groups such as the fire companies, advertising for local stores with impromptu band concerts, and even hiring out for serenades for favorite people (not, incidentally, limited to courting). There were, of course, the more traditional summer evening bandstand concerts on the green, in tiny Elwood Park right on Main Street. Later George was involved as an entrepreneur as well as a musician in the production of operas and operettas. These activities often took him to the neighboring towns of Ridgefield, Brookfield, and Brewster to which his reputation spread. Throughout, he taught privately the instruments he knew best, cornet, violin, piano, and flute.

Charles's early auditory environment was dominated by his father's music, the music germane to all of the aforementioned events. George practiced and taught naturally and regularly at home, a part of the expectable environment and as familiar as the people or domestic objects of everyday life. There is every reason to believe that the first-born Charles enjoyed an at least good-enough first human experience with his mother. Certainly, Mollie Ives would have had to be an extraordinarily sensitive and responsive mother to have gotten a child as exquisitely hypersensitive in the auditory sphere as Charles proved to be through the first 18 months of life. Her memorialization might in effect lie in the stabilization and equilibrium of psychosomatic equipment to which George was in effect the "disturber of the peace" among his other roles. Her reward was biographical silence, while Charles could never quite get over the impact of his father for the rest of his life. I believe, however, that Mollie Ives is not without her own memorial in Charles' music (for example *The Housatonic At Stockbridge*). The details will have to await another study, but relevant here are possible maternal contributions to the establishment of the paternal imago along the lines suggested by Lansky (this volume). In effect, might it be possible to detect elements of the missing mother in tracing her participation in the child's developing mental representation of the father? Mollie's marriage reflected upward social mobility, and there is no trace of dissatisfaction with her husband or his family, into which she was readily absorbed. Also, George may have represented for her the restoration of a beloved lost object, a recently deceased brother (Feder, n.d.). It is telling that, despite the generation of intense nostalgia within Charles, which, as we shall see was related to his father's absences at a critical time in life, depression, as distinct from nostalgia, was moderated. This may be the consequence Mollie's contribution. Finally, in her relationship with her husband she evidently did not insist on any complete division of domestic responsibility along lines of gender, although home was her chief source of esteem. Accordingly, in Charles's mental representation, George would come to encompass traditional features of father *and* mother.

George Ives was more of a presence at home than was usual, for already the characteristic American and urban pattern of father going out and away to work was fast developing even in a country town. In any event, George did not work what was considered normal hours in Danbury. His work (if townspeople allowed that it was "work") was performed mostly in the evening and on weekends and holidays (a pattern, incidentally, Charles was to follow in his musical work many years later). Furthermore, neither early on nor later in Charles's life did George seem uncomfortable in a nurturing role with his sons. Accordingly, he was available in several ways when Charles's brother, Joseph Moss, was born.

Moss, as they called him, conceived six months after Charles's birth, was born, then, at the first biological opportunity. George Ives was not only around the house but more than passively available to participate in parenting, apparently with Mollie's encouragement. He appears to have liked children, been an excellent companion to them, and not to have been embarrassed by what many considered "the woman's place." Among Charles's earliest memories of his father would be of George's playing music at home, and these were of both a visual and auditory nature. Mrs. Van Wyck, whose father was Charles's first cousin, related a portion of the family history:

> Charlie and Moss were born in the house. When Moss was coming, Mollie [Elizabeth Parmelee Ives] didn't want too much confusion, so George had to go up to the barn to practise the violin. Charlie who was under two was sent along where he sat happily in Uncle Joe's [Joseph M. Ives, George's oldest brother] buggy playing with the whip while his father practised. So Charlie's introduction to music began at an early age [Perlis, 1974, p. 7].

Actually, during more than half of that period when Moss was in the "coming," Charles was less than a year old! The music that he would have heard during this time, quite literally at his father's knee, would have represented a cross-section of late 19th-century American music as it was heard in a small town. It included all musical elements associated with George's round of musical activity through the spectrum of religious and secular and including every variety of vernacular music (patriotic, sentimental) and classical as well. These early experiences are reflected in Ives's stylistic habit of musical quotation. Kirkpatrick (1960) has catalogued all the quotations he could find in Ives's music, a list of some 142 individual tunes classified as hymns, patriotic, military, and popular and college songs (pp. 264–266). All but a few of these quoted tunes were written before the turn of the century, although the greatest portion of Ives's music was composed after. I suggest that this small anthology of 19th-century music became a part of Charles's musical vocabulary at least as early in life as the period in which he acquired verbal competence and perhaps even earlier.

If Charles perceived the birth of his own sibling as a turning away of his mother, what he himself had to turn toward was significant and decisive in his life, namely his father and music. Indeed, an early, preverbal, cognitive bond with his father may have rendered that with mother less intense and may have modified the impact of the birth of a sibling. From early on, his father was more like himself evolving than any other human being he would encounter, not merely in the usual biological sense that fosters identification but also in terms of specific cognitive and perceptual capabilities, a profound musical endowment. Both had, for example, not only perfect pitch but an acute auditory sensitivity to the sounds around them – their properties, associated meanings, and orientation in space. This is revealed by the father's practical (and impractical) experiments with sounds and the son's later musical compositions, which in many instances are derivative, albeit in a more sophisticated context. The difference would become that between the naturalist and the artist.

Greenacre (1957) has written of the "collective alternates" in the mental lives of artists, the investment of the raw materials of art – color, tone, form, physical objects, etc. – with the interest and involvement usually reserved for significant human objects. I suggest that where a parent shares that interest strongly and is similarly endowed, the process is more complicated. Both may share the investment in the art while at the same time intensifying a bond with each other that will affect all later stages of the child's artistic and personal development.

Later, as was the case with Ives, that parent may not only share and demonstrate but teach, becoming thus the bearer of rules that herald the beginnings of artistic morality. But, at the dawn of childhood, boundaries are indistinct. To the child Charles, father not merely introduced, shared, and taught music, he represented it: he *was* music. This degree of closeness was to have many ramifications in Charles's life. An early one was his prevailing in the sibling struggle. This could only have been a natural outcome of the current state of affairs, even if it went counter to George's conscious sense of fairness, a characteristic that Charles was to consciously share.

But the very public nature of George's work caused him to belong to others besides his small son and in any event created the conditions of inevitable separation if other factors of life, such as the birth of a sibling, had not. Within a day or two of Charles's second birthday on October 20, 1876, George left on a brief tour with a musical group called Lou Fenn's Alabama Minstrels, an ensemble of a kind increasingly popular at the time. Although the tour was brief, a week or two at the most, it was only the first of several during the course of the following two and a quarter years. George was not present at Charles' third birthday in October 1877, because he was touring Canada and the West with Fontescue's Burlesque for close to five months. He returned about the time of Washington's birthday, 1878. Later that year, in December, soon after Charles had turned four, George was on the road again for the Swedish Lady Vocal Quartet for more than a month, a tour that took him to Albany, Detroit, and Hamilton, Canada. Once again, he returned in February (all dates from *The Danbury News*). Thus, when Charles was between three years and four years four months, George was away for at least six months.

Except for day trips with the summer boat, which had started some time earlier, and brief trips locally, George seems not to have toured again. At first this appears to have been due to an increased amount and variety of work at home. But by the time Charles was five, George had achieved everything he would, musically speaking. Later, either his popularity diminished or his musical activities failed to meet his growing financial needs, particularly in anticipating schooling for his two sons. By the time Charles was eight, George already was working as a "bookkeeper" for one of the businesses other members of the family owned. But even earlier there had been signs that even if his star was not actually falling, not everyone held him in high esteem, in particular the extended Ives family. In Charles's fifth year the George Ives branch had to move out of the family home on Main Street where George had been born and, after him, Charles and Moss, and into another house a few blocks away. This move was in deference to the wishes of George's older sister, Amelia, to move into the Ives homestead after her marriage. Neither Mollie as executive mistress of the house (grandmother still lived) nor George as master could prevail.

THE MEANS OF REPRESENTATION

Some local musical events in Danbury, during Charles's early years, the details of which may be gleaned from contemporary accounts, are curiously resonant with certain details of his later music. They are of the kind already noted in a review of George's activities, and we will now look at a few in more detail. When George was home between tours during the second half of Charles's third year, he bought himself a new cornet. Its effect was reported in *The Danbury News* (February 13, 1878).

> We had the pleasure yesterday of hearing Mr. George Ives play the new Distin light-action cornet, with their patent echo, and were pleased with the beautiful effect it produced, sounding as if another instrument were playing a great distance off and yet clear, in fact, a perfect echo. This attachment is different from the mute, such as Mr. Arbuckle used here, in that the echo can be produced in any part of the piece, while the mute permits only the whole strain or piece being played with echo effect. Mr. Ives played us the "Sweet Bye and Bye," echoing each strain of the chorus instead of the chorus entirely, and this is what makes the delusion so complete. Mr. Ives will use this instrument in the Benefit Concert.

Later that year, in September, and only a few weeks before he was off on tour again, George repeated the performance at the First Congregational Church. If the three-year-old Charles did not hear the cornet at the performance, he certainly heard it at home. But very likely he was present, for the First Congregational Church was on the Iveses' property, George's father, George Wilcox Ives, having deeded a portion to the church during his lifetime. In fact, the barn of the Ives' homestead, where George would practice and which was later the family home, was in its path on Chapel Street.

I suggest that *The Pond,* considered earlier, is imbued with elements of memory of such early experiences. I have already noted, in the description of the music, the manifest references to George Ives certain spatial features (including echoes), and distance itself represented in both space and time. The words written by Charles, "A sound of a distant horn, O'er shadowed lake is borne – my father's song," suggest spontaneous reconstructions in the context of art forms of these early experiences. Distortion of memory and artistic imagination go hand in hand in creating these forms, each pressing the other into the service of accomplishing its goals. Distortion, for example, contributes to the richness and variety of imaginative detail and the artistic ambiguity it fosters. In turn, imagination may subserve distortions, which are variously motivated and have multiple functions in mental life. Additionally, secondary elaboration makes its contribution: an element of mourning stemming from a yet later date in the composer's life.

Among the functions distortion serves, screening is of particular importance. I have argued elsewhere (Feder, 1980) that certain clearly articulated musical memories of George Ives as hero of the Civil War (in Ives's *Decoration Day*) serve a screening function protecting the object from devaluation, with its attendant affects, and attempting to rescue the ego ideal. In that instance I questioned, along with Freud (1899) ". . . whether we have any memories at all *from* our childhood: memories *relating* to our childhood may be all we possess" (p. 322). Here, however, I suggest that authentic elements of childhood memory are recalled and revealed with that intensity imparted through artistic form. Elements that are probably literal are manifest and, in another sense, relate to manifest content. Created forms with multilayered meanings and ambiguities at the same time incorporate distortion. Here, of course, the forms of which we speak are musical forms – depending on one's perspective, musical, auditory, acoustical ideas. The composer is, after all, in the business of creating musical form.

For example, beyond any literalness of an early event and its possible representation in music, we search for something more, and something germane to the art of music – namely, the representation of affect. I assert that in this brief piece one finds a representation in crystalized form of an affect prevalent in the works of Charles Ives, nostalgia (Feder, 1982). The evidence for this surmise is fundamentally subjective, as it must be in any art – one's own experience and the consensus of that of others. Granted this, we may wonder about the relationship between this particular affect and the separations that Charles Ives experienced in the third year of life from an immensely significant object. In a childhood that we have every reason to believe otherwise lacked major trauma and was progressive and joyful, *a melancholy element* was introduced as a result of separation, which colored the composer's mental life and served as background to later mourning after George's death. It was not, however, frank depression. As I have shown elsewhere (Feder, 1981), this mourning proved to be prolonged, intricate, and full of creative issue. But, earlier in life, Charles had experienced a loss that was to modify even the pleasure of reunion. One suspects that Charles's first hearing of George's new cornet when he was three may already have been suffused with that particular variety of sadness which characterizes nostalgia. The affect thus established in mental life would undergo many vicissitudes as time went on. At length it would be pressed into service as a defense against the inevitable conflictual elements inherent in so close a human relationship as that between father and son.

We return to *Calcium Light Night*. Here, too, the manifest background to the work was an experience or series of experiences that the composer had during his early life. In the decade or two after the Civil War torchlight parades were popular around election time. Born of practicality and nurtured by tradition, they were also favored for the sheer excitement appropriate to political events. There are records of George's various bands participating in these at around the time of Charles' birth and after. A variety of sources of illumination would be pressed into service for this and similar out-of-doors evening events, in particular the calcium light – otherwise known as the "limelight" used in theaters. Since such lamps, large in size and on portable mountings, were often used by fire companies, these would also be deployed in nighttime parades of fire brigades. Typical of the time, the local fire companies in Danbury were also fraternal organizations characterized by a particular social class, religion, and ethnic group. The fire companies frequently held celebrations usually employing the local band. Again, in Danbury, this meant George Ives. There were many celebrations during Charles's boyhood, especially in the 80s. One such event, sponsored by the Kohanza Fire Company occurred on August 29, 1883 (two months short of Charles's ninth birthday). As reported in *The Danbury News,* it gives the flavor of these parades.

> The advertising of an organization's picnic by music and fireworks the night before is a new feature, and one worthy of this great picnic year. The display made by Kohanza boys was very fine. . . . The fireworks went off without accident or delay, and in the flaming red light the elegant carriage showed up admirably. The company preceded by the band marched down to the Park. Back of them a calcium light, mounted in a wagon, gave the procession the appearance of an enormous comet.

In *Calcium Light Night,* we have a reconstruction of a memory of such an event in the context of a brief and innovative piece of music. Here, too, the manifest reference is literal – a parade led by the composer's father, a representation of memory in music. But, like every recreation in memory, there is more to be sought – distortions of many kinds, revisions, accruals from later times, associated affects. Music is nonverbal but not necessarily nonrepresentational. Being nonverbal, it is fundamentally more ambiguous than the literary arts but may nevertheless subserve representation of a more subtle (if less readily decipherable) variety. In the approach and departure of the band in *Calcium,* we find a representation of presence and separation. This is not some spurious connection; it is enriched with associated affects. The excitement of anticipation is enhanced musically by a gradual quickening in tempo and increasing volume of sound (*accelerrando* and *crescendo*). The presence (actualized out of darkness) of the passing parade is rendered triple-forte, while a fading into the distance is highlighted by a gradual slowing and decrease in volume (*ritardando* and *diminuendo*). The music fades into that silence which here, in itself, is an important musical element starting and finishing the piece.

Marching bands, so important in Ives's auditory environment, are, of course, not actually perceived in this way. The volume of sound changes, but the tempo is constant. What may distort a tempo in actual performance has to do with an emotional element on the part of the performer. This may be seen in the child who, in the early stages of learning music, may in the process of becoming excited during the performance of a passage that is getting louder play it faster as well. (It can also be seen in the *rubato* of skilled performers.) This device appearing in *Calcium* may then constitute a regressive auditory reference to some earlier stage of Charles's life and musical experience. At the same time it draws our attention to the excitement Charles associated with his father and his father's music. Conversely, as the band fades, it becomes slower – distance being associated with slow time – and quieter, if not sadder, affects. The piece, marked "slow march time," never quite decelerates into a dirge.

The title of the piece is strongly evocative of those visual elements that might enhance the excitement of such an experience. The light is experienced as if at a distance, gradually reaching its fullest, most glaring intensity before fading into darkness. It is represented not only in the title but in the implied loss of boundaries between the two modalities of hearing and vision, a synesthesia in which the data of one perceptual modality is experienced in terms of another. We have a strong suggestion from other of his works that the composer had such experiences and could realize them in musical form. For example, at the climax of his song *The Things Our Fathers Loved,* vision and audition apparently merge (Feder, 1982). The genetic determinants are obscure, but the sexual implications are consistent with both positive and negative oedipal lines of development. Charles was unabashed in his love for his father, and it is no more surprising to discover a homoerotic side than it would be to find an ambivalent side.

In *Calcium,* seen as a reconstruction of memory, we have later accruals as well. In addition, there are further vicissitudes of the erotic in displaced and sublimated homoerotic elements. These again are characteristically represented in auditory terms. For example, the musical quotations in *Calcium Light Night* are specifically *not* those regularly used in those of Ives's work which are associated with his father and his father's music; there are no sentimental, religious, or patriotic tunes. Rather, they are apparently from another era of Charles's life, Yale fraternity songs of the 90s. Yet there is a matrix in mental life from which love of the father becomes a determinant in the love of other men and in their ideals. Charles was later to embrace fraternity life and indeed the very ideal of fraternity with the utmost seriousness. George died just after Charles entered Yale at the age of 20. His experiences enabled him to turn to other men, who further influenced the course of his most unusual life. In *Calcium,* written when Ives was 30, one may detect, then, a nostalgia for two earlier times, that of his own fraternity life in Yale and that in which the mental representation of his father was associated with groups of other men–the fraternal and quasi-fraternal groups of Danbury, and, above all, George Ives's own bandsmen. In fact, the very form in which the piece is cast, the march, is represented by the idea as well as the experience of men moving together. It was an experience dear to Charles, associated at one extreme with the feeling of being a part of a corpus of men and at the other with the ideals of patriotism, the love of his father's land. When Charles was five, dressed in the national colors, he reviewed the passing of the bands from the portico of the house on Main Street. By 13, he was playing in George's band, a part of its small, tight mass, playing in the rear on the snare drum with George at the head of the group. March music was an important element in Ives's style, and he incorporated it without exception in every phase of his career in composition and in increasingly more complex contexts. Yet, at times, a reference to a march might appear in a disarmingly simple form in a work, as if it were some fleeting reminiscence that had come to mind during the process of composition and simply been jotted down.

The layering of experience captured in artistic form that was suggested earlier can be observed in connection with a contribution from the era of Charles's college fraternity life to the composition of *Calcium Light Night*. It was the actual experience of an event that in certain respects was strikingly similar to the parade of the Kohanza Fire Company. This was the procession of the fraternities held each year at Yale during the election of members. It is described here by an alumnus contemporary with Ives (Welch, 1899):

> Each society robes itself in its appropriate color – D.K.E. in red gowns and hats, Psi U. in white, Alpha Delta Phi in green – and marches with full ranks, double file, behind a large calcium light. Each man is supplied with more or less fireworks, which makes it seem rather more interesting as the procession trails its way in and out of the campus and to different rooms in the dormitories where the candidates are quartered. Each member also reserves his voice to be specifically spoiled that night, by helping to sing the partic- ular songs of his fraternity in a voice louder than either of the other processions can sing the particular songs of its fraternity [p. 108].

MUSIC AS MATRIX

If music thus served as matrix for reminiscence, then in an important sense the reverse was true and can be seen in the examples considered in this study. In what was probably Ives's most experimental period, from 1902 to 1908, many of his most innovative works contain strong biographical reference much as the two works analyzed here do. Frequently reference is made to time, place, and person. Most com- monly (and more specifically), these were the old days now past, Danbury, and George Ives. As noted earlier, the composer's "slump" of 1905 appears to have dissipated in relation to Ives's courtship and a resurgence in spontaneous memory, induced reminiscence, and con- scious, artistic memorialization of his father. The year 1906 was the year of *The Pond* as well as the well-known and characteristic *The Unanswered Question*. *Calcium Light Night* was probably written the following year, 1907. The titles of some other short pieces of this period might suggest that they are superficial novelties rather than the product of Ives's fertile, creative mind and keen sense of humor. Nothing could be further from the truth. For the most part, each is an innovative study in one or another aspect of musical materials or in the development of some new musical idea. For example, *The Pond* can be seen as an exploration of certain temporal and spatial elements in music, here a tune slowed beyond recognition, transformed while appearing to be heard at some distance as if an echo. Similarly, *Calcium Light Night* is, among other things, an experiment in the temporal and volume qualities of music. Simultaneously, formal features are manipulated. If reminiscence, then, can serve as matrix for music, its sources are both richly overdetermined in mental life and timeless as well.

A final example with reference to *The Pond:* There are three actual ponds in the biography of Charles Ives. The "pond" that is contemporaneous with the composition of 1906 was the lake in Central Park, a short walk from Ives's bachelor apartment at 65 Central Park West. It served as background to another piece of that year: " 'A Contemplation of Nothing Serious' or 'Central Park in the Dark' in 'The Good Old Summer Time.' " An earlier pond was the one Charles in fact had constructed on his country property in Redding, Connecticut, in 1922, the year that saw the publication of his three great, final works when he was 48. Henry David Thoreau and Thoreavian ideals were major subjects of two of these; Charles's pond was his own, personal "Walden." The most remote pond of memory was that adjacent to the Ives plot in Worchester Cemetery, Danbury. George Ives had been the first of his generation to be buried there when he died at 49, and his resting place is on a knoll overlooking the pond.

One wonders, often in vain, about the sources of creative activity. Perhaps this was the attitude that led Freud to his well-known dictum that before the arts we lay down our arms. In the case of Ives, we may perceive in works such as those considered here both the spark and the creative blaze to which it was stimulus. Could it be that sparks such as these, created in the tie to the past, kindled by its objects and experiences, are at the source of the creative impulse? If so, they surely do not endow creativity; they enable it. But, given some extraordinary endowment, early objects may thus foster its cultivation, while the memories of experiences with and of these objects may in themselves promote the later exercise of creative acts. In Ives's music one can perceive traces of memory of these earlier objects, times, and experiences encoded in the music. It is of interest in itself to "decode" the memory as far as it may be possible. Of equal or perhaps greater interest is to observe how this element stimulates and enables the creative act itself. It is in this sense that memory and reminiscence may serve as matrix for musical composition.

REFERENCES

Blos, P. (1984), Son and father. *J. Amer. Psychoanal. Assn.,* 32:301–324.

Cowell, H. & Cowell, S. (1955), *Charles Ives and His Music.* London: Oxford University Press.

Feder, S. (1980), Decoration Day: A boyhood memory of Charles Ives. *Music Quart.,* 66:234–261.

_____ (1981), Charles and George Ives: The veneration of boyhood. *The Annual of Psychoanalysis,* 9:265–316. New York: International Universities Press.

_____ (1982), The nostalgia of Charles Ives: An essay in affects and music. *The Annual of Psychoanalysis,* 10:301–336. New York: International Universities Press.

_____ (1984), Charles Ives and the unanswered question. *The Psychoanalytic Study of Society,* 10:321–351. New York: International Universities Press.

_____ (n.d.), My father's song: The story of Charles and George Ives, Vol. I. Unpublished ms.

Freud, S. (1899), Screen memories. *Standard Edition,* 3: 303–322. London: Hogarth Press, 1962.

Glover, E. (1925), The neurotic character. In: *On The Early Development of Mind.* London: Imago, 1956.

Greenacre, P. (1957), *Emotional Growth,* Vol. 2. New York: International Universities Press.

Ives, C. (n.d.), *The Pond.* Photostat of full score; 5 pages with postface, Yale University Library.

_____ (n.d.), *Calcium Light Night.* Arr. by Henry Cowell, 10 pages, Yale University Library.

Kirkpatrick, J. (1960), *A Temporary Mimeographed Catalogue of the Music Manuscripts of Charles Edward Ives.* New Haven: Library of the Yale School of Music.

_____ ed. (1972), *Charles E. Ives–Memos.* New York: Norton.

_____ (1980), Charles E(dward) Ives. In: *The New Grove Dictionary of Music and Musicians,* ed. S. Sadie. Vol. 9. London: Macmillan, pp. 414–429.

Perlis, V. (1974), *Charles Ives Remembered–An Oral History.* New Haven: Yale University Press.

Welch, L. S., with W. Camp (1899), *Yale, Her Campus, Class-rooms, and Athletics.* Boston: Page .

16

Overstimulation by a Father
An Alternate View
of Charles Ives
Lawrence Deutsch

In analytic work with children or adults, we try to sort out and identify early pathogenic experiences from a myriad of contributing factors. One such item is trauma. Gillman (1986) noted:

> We think of trauma as a sudden or unexpected experience which, in a brief time, presents the mind with an increase of stimulus and excitation too powerful to be dealt with in the normal way. The customary barrier of defenses is overwhelmed. The child feels helpless in the face of its incapacity to deal with the increased internal or external excitation [p. 74].

For some years, I have been concerned with a different type of trauma, not a sudden overwhelming experience, but a sustained level of libidinal or aggressive overstimulation. The libidinal (falling short of genital contact) may be characterized by ribald humor, nudity, or repeated exposure to primal scene and can lead to impaired ego and superego formation.

Similarly, repeated aggressive overstimulation, such as verbal or physical battles between parents or between parent and child, that fall short of visible violence can have devastating psychological effects.

Elsewhere, I (Deutsch, 1986) have presented a number of case reports illustrating these points and the difficulties in identifying the sustained trauma and analyzing ego-syntonic material in patients who were, what I should like to call "covertly child abused" or "child misused" as a result of overstimulation.

We tend to think of overstimulation from an instinctual viewpoint, as libidinal or aggressive. However, there are two additional forms that are particularly pertinent to the subject of this essay. Sensory overstimulation, visual or aural, can interfere with growth and maturation. Similarly, there is a form of thought control exerted by some parents who impose their interests, ways of thinking, values, ideas, and ideals on their children in a repetitive, relentless manner.

I have reviewed the life of Charles Ives, one of America's most innovative composers. Considered by his biographers in a class with Bartok, Schoenberg, and Stravinsky, he had a strangely disquieting history. In Ives's life I believe that we can see the pathogenic role of overstimulation, particularly of the last two types that I have mentioned, sensory overstimulation and parental thought control.

In a larger sense, Charles Ives's affective adult life consisted of two major phases. Roughly from 20 to 50 years of age, he led the complex life of solid insurance broker and frenetic composer of musical works. After age 50 until his death at around 80, Ives retired from all forms of work and creativity. He withdrew from the public eye and did not write another composition.

When he was a student at Yale, Ives was at times humorous and a punster; at other times he was a recluse. Charles's friends had four distinct nicknames for him that attested to his wide mood swings and personality changes. After graduation from Yale, he undertook a career in business. In his insurance work he was staid, reliable, and creative and made a considerable fortune for himself. At the same time, every spare moment was given over to composing. Writing in an almost feverish manner, he jotted down musical ideas on scraps of paper. Ives worked evenings, weekends, and later, even into the business day.

Ives's compositions were different, often discordant, replete with quotation, and difficult to perform. However, he felt that not all music had to be playable. "Charles Ives was the most paradoxical man I ever met," so stated John Kirkpatrick (personal communication), Professor Emeritus of Music at Yale University, perhaps the only living person who knew Ives well. Once, when Kirkpatrick suggested a musical change to make a composition easier for the musicians, Ives defiantly said, "Damn simplicity." He seemed extremely upset with the suggestion. Ives could be negativistic, even enraged if one did not agree with him. Yet he also was kind and donated some of his music to posterity.

I shall review the childhood of Charles Ives from several vantage points in an attempt to understand the sudden dynamic change in his way of life.

The Ives family lived in Danbury, Connecticut. Its members were well educated and financially successful. The "black sheep" was George Ives, Charles's father, a well-known band leader in the area. He was a very gifted man, self-taught, played many instruments, and enjoyed the introduction of dissonant elements in his musical offerings. He passionately believed in sharing his talents by teaching and encouraging young people to love music. George Ives's wife, Molly, is described as originating from a lower socioeconomic background and as being loyal and supportive of George's profession.

When Charles was an infant and Molly was pregnant with his brother Moss, Charles was given over to his father for safekeeping. George practiced in the barn, and young Charles stayed with him, keeping time with a buggy whip. Thus, some of young Ives's earliest memories involved the sights and sounds of music making.

We know from biographers that Charles developed an enormous attachment to his father. In describing Charles Ives and his father George, all agree on the unusual bond between them. Kirkpatrick described it to me as akin to Chinese ancestor worship. Both father and son were alike in that they had perfect pitch, mastered a host of instruments, and were extremely sensitive to the nuances of tone, rhythm, meter. They enjoyed playing all manner of musical inventions and games together. Essentially the authors have painted a picture of little Charles attached with awe and glue to George, who filled the role not only of father, but of caretaker and teacher.

The driven quality that characterized Charles's early adulthood was followed by a period of prolonged apathy in midlife. To understand this change more fully, I feel we have to take into account (1) a 30-year extremely productive period, wherein much of the music Charles composed involved memorialization of his father (Feder, 1980, 1981, 1982, 1983, this volume). This era was ushered in when Charles was in his 20s, following his father's sudden death and (2) a second 30-year period following the productive one, which might be seen as a period of failure to resolve the mourning, a period of melancholia, of apathy.

Charles's early experiences included ongoing overstimulation of a child whose genetic makeup left him particularly vulnerable to the type of affective disorder that will be described.

MOURNING, IDENTIFICATION AND
MEMORIALIZATION OF FATHER

As Feder (this volume) has so carefully shown, memorialization can be found both in music and text. Elsewhere, Feder (1981) talks about the fact that Ives would work on various pieces at the same time and use the same musical material in different forms. He states, "As a result, Ives's music seems to be one vast opus, the result of a consistent lifetime of effort eventuating in a single creative product" (p. 269). I submit that this one vast opus is a result of a fusion between George and Charles Ives. Thus, even the very act of composing would constitute a lifelong memorialization of George.

In addition, Feder (this volume) discusses the use of quotation in music, which refers to a composer utilizing a passage, a theme, a melody, or words from another composer in a new opus. Ives's extensive use of this musical idiom illustrates in part not only the "possession" aspect of his father's influence, but also an aspect of his complexity and aggressivity. Ballantine (1979) compares the "quoted musical fragment" with dream fragments that have both a manifest and a latent content and are subjected to condensation and displacement. He discusses at length the use of themes of Americana as typical of Ives. At times some of the words and melodies seem to Ballantine not to be related to specific ideas and "suggest a 'secret' dimension to some of the music of Ives which can be revealed only by detective work" (p. 178).

I suggest, however, that where Ives uses American motifs independent of overt connections with memory traces, he still is eulogizing his father. Since George's music as a band leader in the Civil War was inexorably linked to American themes, any reference by Charles in his compositions to the splendors of America would be linked to his father.

Ives's use of quotation is instructive even when it appears not to relate to paternal remembrances. It is an admixture of styles and references from a whole spectrum of musical compositions that is both exciting and confusing. For example, Ballantine notes that Ives's *Second Symphony* has quotation from Brahms's *Second Symphony*, Wagner's *Tristan Und Isolde* and *Die Walkure*, Bach, Bruckner, Dvorak's *The New World Symphony*, Beethoven's *Fifth*. He notes, too, quotation from *America the Beautiful*, *Turkey in the Straw*, *Columbia the Gem of the Ocean*, *Camptown Races*, *Bringing in the Sheaves*, *When I Survey the Wondrous Cross*, college songs, *Reveille*, and various others (p. 179).

Kirkpatrick (personal communication) commented that Ives

abused the element of surprise. He added, "Charlie loved to shock people." This propensity revealed a glimpse of the aggressive side of Ives. We again can look to George Ives as the role model for some of this behavior. Charles's father took great pleasure in being inventive with sounds, often to the distress of those listening. Once he had two marching bands that were playing at different rhythms and in different keys approach each other from opposite ends of the town. As they came closer, they played louder and louder, and the result was a kind of discordant music. What was the motivation for this? Was it a prank? Did he enjoy seeing the discomfort of those about? Was he attempting to enrich those who heard it and those who played? Or was it a combination of all three? In a similar vein, Cowell and Cowell (1955) report that during the 15 years that Charles played organ at Center Church, he would deliberately insert dissonant notes into hymns. He would accompany a hymn melody with its overtones played high up on the treble of the organ. He would play sevenths, transiently change key, or decide on a brief syncopated rhythm. Lest people react too adversely to him (and complain they did), he continued after a brief interlude to play the music as it was written. What was the function of this behavior? It is not that I am challenging the creativity of Charles Ives; he certainly has been allotted a place as one of the prime innovators of his time. Rather I feel that in memorializing his father, Charles expounded not only on the libidinal aspects of his attachment, but on the aggressive identifications as well.

RETIREMENT FROM WORK; WITHDRAWAL FROM MUSIC

As Charles approached his 50th year, two pivotal events occurred that led him to discontinue his frenetic lifestyle. One was physical, a heart condition leading to an alleged heart attack; the other, psychological, the anniversary reaction of his reaching the age at which his father died. Ives's complex nature included a playful side. Cowell and Cowell (1955) note that in all of Ives's larger works there are humorous movements. For example, in the second movement of the *Concord Sonata,* he makes fun of going to church in an appositional, lighthearted way. Yet the very same Charles Ives now became eccentric and suspicious. Where he had been comfortable with friends in school and with the members of the band, successful in business, he turned into a cantankerous recluse.

Thus, this person who could alternately be friendly and friendless withdrew for periods of time, refusing visitors ostensibly because of a heart attack. His biographies contain frequent references to "break-downs" due to exhaustion. One might wonder if some of the so-called heart difficulty was a cardiac neurosis or hypochondriasis, hiding his reclusive nature and keeping him private.

Feder (this volume) has discussed the positive preoedipal ties that led to Ives's creativity. In the light of Ives's cessation of productivity, I question whether the relationship between Charles and George was, on balance, commendable or condemnable. In effect, the compulsion to write his music, the driven quality of his efforts, the sudden withdrawal in his middle years, and the decathexis of all outside interests, are suggestive of a progressive melancholic depression following a hypomanic period.

OVERSTIMULATION AS A CONTRIBUTION TO PSYCHOPATHOLOGY

Sensory overstimulation – exceeding the stimulus barrier – is often neglected as a pathogenic force. The latest techniques in delivery rooms tend to preserve quiet and only gradually expose the infant to noise. If the stimulus barrier is overwhelmed, ego development cannot but be impaired. It is likely that young Charles was exposed to massive visual and auditory stimulation when he was in his father's presence, playing musical games, experimenting with tonal structures, seeing and hearing the vibrant band leader during rehearsals.

His experience was, I imagine, similar to that of a patient who, describing his childhood, said, "It wasn't that my mother hit me, but it was the constant shouting at home. The noise was so loud that it was more than I could take and led me to feel totally disorganized. I still become confused in any situation where there is loud persistent noise."

In addition to the sensory overstimulation that I have postulated, there was in the intense father-son relationship both libidinal and aggressive overstimulation. Feder (1981, this volume) suggests possible homoerotic elements between the two, which would be a natural consequence of a relationship unconsciously perceived by Charles as a seduction. In addition, the passionate devotion of both to music may have resulted in Charles Ives's all-encompassing need to compose at a feverish pace after George's death not only as a memorialization, but as an introjection of the dead parent.

Current studies about father-child bonds may shed some light on Ives's dyadic relationships. We have come to realize that "the forgotten parent," as Ross (1982) calls the father, is very important indeed. Research has shown that in the first three critical years, the conditions for attachment to both parents are the same (Lamb, 1978) and are not solely or preferentially conducive to attachment to the mother, as was previously assumed. However, the nature of the attachment to the two parents differs. The typical infant experiences the father as being more separate and distant; the father's manner of physical play (rougher handling, being thrown into the air, etc.) teaches the child about gross affective states. In promoting differentiation and individuation, the father allows the child to explore in a more independent manner, both emotionally and cognitively. The father introduces the infant to a variety of new and unknown stimuli and acts as a balance to the relationship with the mother. Yogman (1982) states, "Fathers seem to provide infants with more intense, arousing, differentiating experiences, and such experiences, combined with others, may shape the infant's temperament" (p. 122). All the foregoing is predicated on an appropriately balanced triadic relationship, where the generic father has an important role to play in stimulating the child and serving as a role model. An excessive presence can be deleterious.

The influence of parents on the behavior and thoughts of children is well known and has been reported many times by many authors (see, for example, Fraiberg, 1959; Behrends and Blatt, 1985; Blos, 1985). Freud (1914) noted that parents can make children repositories and sources of their own vicarious fulfillment. Unconscious cueing between parent and child can lead the child to react at the behest of either parent, though more often the mother, in a manner similar to what we see in a posthypnotic state. An unanticipated finding in a study on the topic (Deutsch, 1986) was that in every instance there was highly significant libidinal or aggressive overstimulation that seemed a precondition for primitive nonverbal communication. In each of the cases the child felt an unconscious need to carry on with attitudes, beliefs and affects of a given parent, the parent responsible for the overstimulation. The most common result was an "as-if" child, whose behavior replicated that of the dominant parent.

I am reminded of a depressed patient, a striking woman with a brilliant, seductive smile, who was defensively functioning in a hypomanic manner. After many years of resistance to the analysis of character traits that made her the life of the party, enjoyed by all and respected by none, she suddenly associated in detail to what had been hinted at before, a covertly seductive relationship with her father in which he overstimulated her by hugging, kissing, and teaching her the pleasures of ear lobe and eyelid kissing. She also napped with him until she was well into her teens. She was aware of feeling a body warmth in her father's presence. As with Ives, her father died when she was 20. After his death she assumed his personality, and her shyness vanished. Her dress and behavior were geared to overwhelming all those around her in an unconscious memorialization of her father's effervescent style. Whereas she had been an excellent student through college, with the father's death her academic interests vanished. Like Charles, my patient rarely related to her mother, who outlived the father by 25 years. She carried her father's picture in her wallet and wept whenever his name was mentioned. As we worked this out, it was she who called her experience one of being possessed by a dybbuk, the soul of her father.

Another area of Ives's psyche that seems to have been influenced by the father-son relationship is the Oedipus complex and the difficulty in resolving it. Charles's relationship with his mother remains a mystery. He is depicted by his biographers as having been brought up in a one-parent family. It seems too facile to associate Charles's omission of his mother to a hypercathexis of his father alone or to his anger at his mother because she bore his brother Moss. I have not seen data indicating there was intense sibling rivalry. In fact, as Feder (1981, 1980) has noted, George Ives did travel a great deal and spent a considerable amount of time performing. He also taught music in the community. Thus, it is likely that Charles did spend time with his mother as well as his father. Furthermore, Charles chose as his bride Harmony Twitchell, the daughter of a minister. She is reported to have been a loyal, loving, tolerant, and helpful wife. In many ways she was like Charles's mother, who had similar qualities and supported George Ives's trade.

It has been reported, though, that Ives rarely, if ever, mentioned his mother. It was as if she did not exist. Kirkpatrick (personal communication) said that Charles would speak only to his wife about her. Ives only wrote one composition relating to his mother, *Songs My Mother Taught Me*. Eight years later, he renamed the piece *An Old Song Deranged*. Was Ives implying that the relationship with his mother was deranged, or was it distorted because of a pathological identification with his father? Did the fusion between Charles and George carry an unconscious injunction not to love his mother?

SUMMARY

The paradoxical man that was Charles Ives arouses a myriad of emotions in biographers, musicians, musicologists, and psychoanalysts. By and large those who knew or wrote about him were sympathetic. I agree with Feder (1980, 1981, 1982, 1983, this volume) that a major impetus for Ives's musical creativity was his need to memorialize his father.

I believe, however, that a necessary condition for Charles Ives to write music at the feverish pace he did was a specific type of pathological identification with his father, facilitated by both sensory and instinctual overstimulation. I further suggest that the abrupt end to his hectic pace of creativity has psychological meaning and is a consequence of the childhood that was described. Jacobson (1954), in her classic paper on psychotic identifications, defines the essential differences between ego identifications and the early infantile identification mechanisms: "The first are realistic insofar as they result in lasting changes of the ego. . . . the latter are magic in nature; they represent only a temporary-partial or total-blending of magic self- and object images, founded on fantasies . . . regardless of reality" (p. 243). Blum (personal communication) on the same topic states, "A gifted person is capable of transcending the identification with one or both parents. Even though infantile ties may remain, a truly creative ego matures with the passage of time."

Ives's attachment to George evidently did not allow such ego development. His frenetic period of almost undisciplined creativity after his father's death reflected some hypomanic elements as a defense against the depression he must have felt. The process of memorialization of his father through music helped contain these emotions. Perhaps overdetermined, yet convincing, Ives's identification with his father came full circle. That is, Charles Ives's productivity in business and music ceased when he reached approximately the same age that his father was when his father died. In this pathological identification with his father, he was not able appropriately to complete the mourning process, and now lived on the down side of what might have been a bipolar existence.

We are left with Ives's legacy of complex and commanding music. But understanding Charles Ives the man must take into account his unusual relationship with his father, who by parental overstimulation captured, raised, inspired, and eventually isolated this innovative composer from the rest of the world.

REFERENCES

Ballentine, C. (1979), Charles Ives and the meaning of quotation in music. *Musical Quart.*, 65:167–184.

Behrends, R.S. & Blatt, S.J. (1985), Internalization and psychological development throughout the life cycle, *The Psychological Study of the Child,* 40:11–40. New Haven, CT: Yale University Press.

Blos, P., Jr. (1985), Intergenerational separation-individuation: Treating the mother-infant pair. *The Psychological Study of the Child,* 40:41–56. New Haven, CT: Yale University Press.

Cowell, H. & Cowell, S. (1955), *Charles Ives and His Music.* London: Oxford University Press.

Deutsch, L. (1986), Unconscious communication between mother and child and its role in later psychopathology. Presented at Westchester Division of New York Hospital-Cornell University Medical Center, White Plains, NY.

Feder, S. (1980), Decoration Day: A boyhood memory of Charles Ives. *Musical Quart.,* 66:234–261.

_____ (1981), Charles and George Ives: The veneration of boyhood. *The Annual of Psychoanalysis,* 9:265–316.

_____ (1982), The nostalgia of Charles Ives: An essay in affects and music. *The Annual of Psychoanalysis,* 10:301–332.

_____ (1983), Charles Ives and the unanswered question. *The Psychoanalytic Study of Society, Vol. 10.* New York: Psychohistory Press, pp. 321–351.

Fraiberg, S.H. (1959), *The Magic Years.* New York: Scribner's.

Freud, S. (1914), On narcissism. *Standard Edition,* 14:69–102. London: Hogarth Press, 1957.

Gillman, R. D. (1986), Physical trauma and actual seduction. In: *The Reconstruction of Trauma,* ed. A. Rothstein. Madison, CT: International Universities Press, pp. 73–94.

Jacobson, E. (1954), Contribution to the metapsychology of psychotic identifications. *J. Amer. Psychoanal. Assn.,* 2:239–262.

Lamb, M.E. (1978), The father's role in the infant's social world. In: *Mother/ Child, Father/Child Relationships,* ed. J.H. Stevens & M. Mathews. Washington, DC: National Association for the Education of Young Children.

Ross, J.M. (1982), In search of fathering. In: *Father and Child,* ed. S.H. Cath, A.R. Gurwitt & J.M. Ross. Boston, MA: Little, Brown, pp. 21–32.

Yogman, M.W. (1982), Observations on the father-infant relationship. In: *Father and Child,* ed. S.H. Cath, A.R. Gurwitt & J.M. Ross. Boston: Little, Brown, pp. 101–122.

Recapitulation

The two foregoing chapters have stimulated some familiar, fascinating, but as yet unanswered psychoanalytic questions. Can we reconstruct from limited biographical data supplemented by a plethora of adult artistic sublimations, in this case a body of innovative music, some earliest core, preverbal memories? Will knowledge of the family dynamics deepen our understanding not only of the form but of the pattern and fate of creativity over this artist's life span? Can we estimate the influence the imago of a talented, musical father has in contrast to that of an "undistinguished" maternal figure when the son's extraordinary creative outpourings were terminated at the time of his father's death? Can we assume that the last statement more likely represents psychological dynamics when we learn that the only composition related to mother, "Songs My Mother Taught Me," was later retitled "An Old Song Deranged"? And do complex, shifting, despairing identifications with father connect with the abandonment of the creative drive in postmidlife self-confrontations?

While reading these two psychobiographies, echoes of selected themes in Mozart's life ran through my mind. Mozart too was nurtured, if not overwhelmed, in the auditory sphere by a musically talented father. Both his father and Ives's were initially idealized, subsequently disappointing, and ultimately devalued. Still they were the men who breathed their beloved art form into their sons' exquisitely sensitive ears from the earliest beginnings. And both composer-sons, "could not get over this impact from father" (Feder, this volume), became innovators of new musical forms or rhythyms. Of course, there are differences, for Mozart in imperial Vienna was probably not free to be as shocking as Ives in America. Mozart knew some public, even royal, acceptance in a way probably denied to Ives. Mozart had a talented older sister both as a model and as a rival. But despite the differences, certain common dynamic correlaries may be hypothesized. Both father and son Ives had perfect pitch. In another particularly illuminating description related to the possible difficulties in differentiation, we read "father was more like himself evolving than any other human being he would encounter." Can the same have been the case with the Mozarts? And can such formulations have any heuristic value? We leave that to our readers to decide, but inasmuch as we espouse both the value of individual and of psychohistorical studies, a few additional thoughts might be helpful.

At first reading, it may appear the Feder-Deutsch papers present almost contradictory views. Feder focuses more on the libidinal, intense memorialization of "relatively unambivalent, precompetitive, idealizing, verbal, musical memories, as reflected in the overt content of Charles "Memos" to his father, George. These seem to him "crystalized forms of affects of nostalgia" related to father's multiple absences. They were marked by "echoes of distance, time, and space." These approaching-distancing, crossroad concepts seem quite persuasive in understanding Ives's use of microtonal, polyphonic, dissonant, and Doppler-like chords. Feder beautifully traces out some of Ives's preverbal representations and correlates them with later-screened distortions of his memory-imagination. These combinations of sound are designed to adaptively and creatively preserve his ego ideal and his "unabashed love for his father." Feder notes: "If music thus served as a matrix for reminiscence, then in an important sense the reverse was true,. . . [Ives's] most innovative works contain strong biographical references . . . to the old days now past." The same may be true for the listener, who finds certain musical themes or genres revitalize or recontact nonspecific oceanic affects with biographical overtones.

Deutsch concurs that "the major impetus for Ives's musical creativity was his need to memorialize his father." But he adds a valid concern, namely, the *potentially traumatic effects* of Ives's sustained musical immersion so early on. He suggests this may be considered a form of "covert child misuse," reminiscent of an Australian patient (Cath, unpublished manuscript), who reminisced, "I could never rid myself of my bloody fatherweight." Such overstimulation could lead to an "as if" character with hypomanic "feverish" creativity even escalating after his father's death. Acknowledging the bond between father and son was "akin to Chinese ancestor worship," Deutsch considers that both father's and son's love of shocking people through discordant sound reveals a glimpse of their aggressive sides. And, (he speculates) Charles, unable to mourn, became a melancholic recluse upon reaching the age of his father's death.

For me these viewpoints, presented with such persuasive clarity, not only complement and highlight each other, but resonate with some of my own reflections on and responses to music. Most of us might agree with both authors that preverbal sensory memories can accrue affective histories of their own; or while initially stored in especially gifted (read prewired) individuals in one way, they may be elaborated upon by subsequent experiences, screened, and reinterpreted. Such a formulation, Deutsch believes, would more likely explicate Ives's transition from feverish creativity to a postmidlife musical death-like silence. I would add that the different emphases of the authors relate to other midlife shifts in narcissistic holding actions in which the value, significance, and identification with a talented, musical, idealized but blacksheep father no longer stem age-specific depletion anxieties associated with intimations of mortality.

Still, not everyone would agree on the creative aspects of Ives's form of contemporary music any more than they did with Mozart. Indeed, differences in the tolerance for music exist not only in various cultures but in males and females of various age cohorts in the same or different generations. In contrast to Freud, one of the few who could find little pleasure in and resisted experiencing the oceanic pleasures of music, a very large part of our population remains fascinated by the mysterious powers of various forms of music to soothe, shock, or excite moods and behaviors. I maintain a somewhat idealized notion that Freud would not be averse to exploring a greater understanding of the relationship of sound, speech and music with *inherently inaccessible aspects of human attachment, growth and symbolization,* as both Feder and Deutsch have done. Many researchers have related the capacities to integrate and utilize sound, speech, and music to the earliest interactions and multiple identifications with mothers and fathers. While attitudes toward and manipulation of music mayserve defensive purposes, they may also reflect the efforts of infants and adults not only to communicate with each other in non-verbal, nonrepresentational ways, but to transcend the limits of corporal reality in order to reach the consistent ethereal plane Beethoven defined as "a revelation higher than science or philosophy."

Stanley H. Cath

V

CULTURAL AND OTHER VARIATIONS

Prelude

Parents come in many shapes, sizes, ages, stages, and styles. While the first three are mostly biologically and genetically determined, the last two are less directly decided. Parenting styles and roles seem to be especially influenced by social, historical, political, and economic forces and patterns, as recently demonstrated by family historians and social psychologists. The far-reaching impact of the Crusades on feudal families (McLaughlin, 1974), of the industrial revolution on American families in the early 19th century (Demos, 1982), of the social and economic changes in this century on behavior considered adult (mature) (Modell, Furstenberg, and Hershberg, 1978), and of the challenges of childrearing in dual-career families (Rapoport, Rapoport, and Strelitz, 1980) are just a few examples of many-rooted historical trends or events that have colored the character of parenting.

Whether or not fatherhood is more variable in form from society to society than is motherhood is a question best left to the social scientists. Appropriate fathering certainly takes many forms. Even within one ethnically homogeneous country, Turkey, there are many different paternal patterns (Volkan and Cevik, this volume). Volkan and Cevik describe a nation in transition, heavily influenced by historical events and one major personality, Ataturk, who was seen as the father of the country. While they note four different family patterns that appear to be part of a continuum, standing out are the extremes. In the very traditional rural pattern, children are raised by a household of women; the father and men are portrayed as distant, stern, and dangerous. It is a patriarchal society where women, themselves positioned in a hierarchal manner within the extended family, dominate the home. When the boys reach a critical age, their rearing is taken over by the father and other men, as if to wrench their sons from maternal and feminine influence and expurgate all that is not considered masculine. A similar pattern has been described in certain families in India (Kakar, 1982). Thus, it seems as if gender roles become highly distinct and mutually exclusive, yet all may not be so sharply delineated. At the informal level of daily life, is the "traditional" Turkish father so remote, so stylized? Is there no expression of affection, tenderness, playfulness on the part of fathers, grandfathers, or uncles? Are the concentrated doses of maternal and feminine influence truly expurgated in boys, or are they merely repressed, later to be integrated into the adult and parental self? And what is the form of that integration? What defensive modes are necessary to encompass such contrasting, even conflicting, identifications?

At the other extreme, Volkan and Cevik describe "modern," city-dwelling families where gender and parental roles are not so distinct, where the forms of parental functioning are closer to those of the American nuclear family.

In tackling the task of describing and understanding patterns of Black fathers in the United States, Comer emphasizes the historical background. His is a sad and disturbing portrait of the forced destruction of African family styles, including traditional paternal and masculine roles. While the historical details are quite different, the story of the dysculturation of certain native American groups shares some of the same ingredients of loss of traditional social fabric, displacement, external rejection, and anomie without opportunities for reparative evolution and transition of the family within a friendly, supportive societal framework (Manson, 1982). There is a similiar outcome when constructive, reparative, supportive, and evolutionary forces cannot overcome destructive trends that dismantle what was, leaving only disconnected fragments: biological paternity becomes separated from active and effective fathering, and the many roles of the father within a family setting are lost. The resulting single-parent (mother only) families are fatherless, afflicted by all that that implies. There is impoverishment, not just financial, of all involved–children, their mothers, their fathers, their grandparents (see Neubauer, this volume).

Although Comer comments on important clinical considerations, his primary focus is on the kind of remedial social and educational efforts carried out by himself and his co-workers. These efforts
are a model of intervention, having a dual impact on educational
achievement and the strengthening of parental and family functioning.
And, we might speculate, they also provide for a kind of positive
communal family and paternal presence.

Paternal presence is very much evident in Palmeri's chapter. He
looks at the pattern of fathers (and mothers) in some cultural groups of
addressing their sons by the informal terms used for their parents.
These expressions not only become terms of endearment, but also
plant the seed of nurturing parental identity, to reflect the interchange-
ability of generations and to represent an interactive form of mutual
identification. Their use occurs only during the preoedipal years. This
chapter is a charming example of father-son relatedness that at an
informal level may provide different vibrations than does a formal
parent-child structure.

The chapter by Pruett is one of a series of papers and reports by
him of an ongoing longitudinal study of families in which the fathers
were primary caregivers for at least the first child. His is one of very few
studies of families with fathers providing the primary care. Pruett has
been following these children (now in latency) and their parents for
many years. While questions could be raised about the methodology
(the numbers are small, there is no control group, greater depth of data
would be desirable, other observers might have come up with other
data and conclusions, etc.) and other studies are needed to replicate the
findings, this is, nevertheless, an elegant and unique study. One reason
is its simplicity: it is research primarily done by one person with limited
time and assistance, without special funding, but with considerable
expertise in early child development. Second, Pruett's impressions and
findings are already of great importance, both to the children of these
families and to their parents. Third, what may well be of greatest value
is that this is both a longitudinal and pilot study that is hypothesis
generating. The study raises many crucial questions.

Pruett shows that fathers can be competent primary caregivers,
that they can catalyze parental and maternal capacities in their wives,
and that some of what we call "maternal" may not be gender linked
and might better be termed "parental." With regard to the last point,
one could argue that what occurs between a good primary caregiving
parent and the infant or toddler is maternal in origin and nature, and
that some men can do most of it merely shows their maternal side. On
the other hand, the finding that men can be competent nurturers and

experience many of the attachment phenomena that we call primary "maternal" preoccupation, that there is some degree of role reversal in terms of which parent provides certain kinds of stimuli, and that men in this study carried out these complex functions without loss of masculine traits and paternal style – all argue for reassessing what we call maternal, paternal, and parental. Some of the kinds of parenting that we have heretofore assumed to be maternal and feminine may not be gender specific but rather *role specific*, a function of primary care-taking parenting.

The study of fatherhood is still in its early stages. Cross cultural and intra-cultural variations will be increasingly important sources of further understanding.

Alan Gurwitt

REFERENCES

Demos, J. (1982), The changing faces of fatherhood: A new exploration in American family history. In: *Father and Child,* ed. S. H. Cath, A. Gurwitt & J. M. Ross. Boston: Little, Brown, pp. 425–445.

Kakar, S. (1982), Fathers and sons: An Indian experience. In: *Father and Child,* ed. S. H. Cath, A. Gurwitt & J. M. Ross. Boston: Little, Brown, pp. 417–424.

Mc Laughlin, M. M. (1974), Survivors and surrogates: Children and parents from the ninth to the thirteenth centuries. In: *The History of Childhood,* ed. L. deMause. New York: Psychohistory Press, pp. 101–181.

Manson, S. (1982), ed. *New Directions in Prevention Among American Indian and Alaska Native Communities.* Portland: National Center for American Indian and Alaska Native Mental Health Research and the Oregon Health Sciences University.

Modell, J., Furstenberg, F. E. & Hershberg, T. (1978), Social change and transitions to adulthood in historical perspective. In: *The American Family in Social-Historical Perspective,* ed. M. Gordon. New York: St. Martin's Press, pp. 192–219.

Rapoport, R., Rapoport, R. N. & Strelitz, Z. (1980), *Fathers, Mothers and Society.* New York: Vintage.

17

Turkish Fathers and Their Families

A Study of Fathers and Their Families in a Transitional Society

Vamık D. Volkan

Abdülkadir Cevik

Since the Turkish Republic arose in 1923 from the ashes of the Ottoman Empire, the Turkish people have gone through one cultural revolution after another. Modern communication technology, which now reaches the most isolated settlements, has brought wave upon wave of change. Thus it is difficult to make a valid study of the country's social and cultural conditions; statistics may need updating after even a year or two, and one must expect corresponding psychological effects to alter also. On the other hand, the rapidly growing influence on Turkey of western society and its technology has created unique opportunities for study, among them the chance to see fathers and their families on a spectrum from the traditional to the modern, to see the relationship between different external situations and the psychological adaptation of the people, both as individuals and groups, to these different external situations.

A PANORAMIC VIEW OF TURKISH HISTORY

Besides Turkey's 52 million inhabitants there are even more people outside the country who speak some Turkish dialect and are of

Turkish origin. Outside Anatolia, the Turkish heartland, there are Turkish-speaking people in Central Asia, Iran's Azerbaijan section, the Balkans, and elsewhere. And the Turks of Cyprus, concentrated since 1974 in the northern part of the island, declare themselves to be citizens of the Turkish Republic of Northern Cyprus. Since the 1950s, over one-and-a-half million Turks have settled in Germany and other indus- trialized European countries as *Gasterbeiter* (guest workers). (Readers interested in the cultural, social, economic, and psychological difficul- ties of the latter group are referred to Özbek and Volkan, 1976, and Suzuki, 1981.) In addition, there are about a half a million Turkish guest workers in various Arabic countries.

Turks, who originated in central-east Asia, belong to a group known as Ural-Altaic. It is thought they are related to

> the Finno-Ugrians (Finns and Hungarians), the Samoyeds, the Tungus and, in particular, the Mongols. It is practically certain that the earliest Turks known to history—although not called by that name—were the Huns. . . . Under the specific name of Turks (the meaning of which is uncertain), the Turks made their appear- ance, both in Chinese sources in the East and in the Byzantine sources in the West, in the sixth century A.D. in the territory that is now Mongolia, but very soon also over a wide area, expanding towards the south and west . . . . In the sixth century, a Turkish "Empire" existed in the northern part of what in modern times has been called Russian "Turkestan" [Cahen, 1968, p. 1].

Although it is hard to reconstruct their early history, we know that over about 2,000 years they swarmed over vast territories to reach the Indian Ocean, the Mediterranean Sea, and central Europe. They formed many empires, dominated many peoples, and assimilated different cultural and religious influences. Cahen (1968) noted that "the various elements of the Turkish people lost in unity what they gained in area" (p. 2; see also Stein, 1964, and Shaw, 1976).

A major group of Turks were the Oghuz, who began in the ninth century to migrate from Central Asia, going farther west than other Turkish tribes. They were known as Turkomans by those they attacked. As they came in contact with Islam they became converts. Descendants of the Oghuz, the Seljuks, entered the Middle East in the tenth century. The Battle of Manzigert, at what is now known as Malazgirt, in Eastern Turkey, fought in 1071 between the sophisti- cated armies of Byzantium and the nomadic Seljuk tribes, ended with the defeat of Byzantium and the establishment of Turkish settlements in Anatolia (Asia Minor).

The Ottoman Turks came into power with the decline of the Seljuk Empire. In 1453 Mehmet the Conqueror seized Constantinople (Istanbul), signaling a new era to follow the Byzantine. Ottoman Turks continued to expand their dominions across the Danube, over the Middle East and much of Northern Africa, appearing before the gates of Vienna at least twice. As Muller (1961) noted, legends about the "terrible Turks" led to very little appreciation of their amazing exploits, at least in Europe, and little was known of their art and culture. (For an excellent brief review of Ottoman history, see Itzkowitz, 1972, and for a detailed study see Shaw, 1976, and Shaw and Shaw, 1977.)

The Ottoman Empire reached its greatest glory in the 16th century; its decline and ultimate fall took 400 years. It was made up of many different national and cultural groups. After its fall, at the end of World War I, a new Turkish Republic was established, cohesive culturally but reduced in territory to Anatolia and Eastern Thrace in Europe. Mustafa Kemal, later known as Atatürk (Father Turk), became the first president of the Turkish Republic after leading his countrymen in a War of Independence following the loss of considerable territory in World War I. (See Volkan and Itzkowitz, 1984, for a psychobiography of this remarkable man.) An admirer of western culture, he abolished religious schools and did away with the caliphate, which had headed the Moslem world much as the papacy rules the Catholic Church and which had been taken over from the Arabs. In the course of educational reform, the Roman alphabet was substituted for the Arabic characters which, with a few Persian additions, had long been used, and the numbering system was westernized as well. These changes effectively cut off those Turks born after 1928 from the cultural heritage of their race. Penal and civil codes used in Europe were copied, along with business law, and all were secularized. Polygamy was outlawed, western dress was encouraged, and the wearing of a fez forbidden. But because the changes were made by fiat, from the top, once the God-like leader died, their assimilation – and modification – was slow and, indeed, is still taking place, almost fifty years later. Thus a considerable part of Turkish society is in a transitional state (Sümer, 1970; Öztürk and Volkan, 1971). What Berkes wrote about the situation in 1975 is still to a great extent true today: "Today's Turkey is neither a western nor a Moslem nation; it does not belong to a Christian, socialist, or capitalist community. It is neither Asian nor European . . . The dominant direction of Ottoman history has tilted more toward the west than turned toward the east" (p. 167). He goes on to say that since Turks have adhered to an eastern cultural reference, Europe has never seen Turkey as a member state.

THE HISTORICAL BACKGROUND OF TURKISH
FATHERS AND THEIR FAMILIES

We know little about Oghuz family life. Medieval and Arabic sources (see Friendly, 1981, for a summary) describe them as nomads who adopted what was basically a primitive kind of Islamic religion practiced at the borders and gave up shamanism as they moved westward. They were armed and were trained from childhood to hunt. Some of the prejudice with which they were described is apparent in such Arabian sources as that of Risala of Ibn Fadlan (quoted by Friendly), who expressed horror that pre-Islam Oghuz women wore neither veil in the presence of men nor appropriate covering for the body. He noted also that their people did not bathe after urinating, defecating, or ejaculating. A wife was acquired only after payment of enough camels, garments, or other valuables. Upon the death of a father, the eldest of his sons took the widow to wife if she was not his own mother. The Oghuz left their sick alone to recover or die by themselves although slaves attended them if they were wealthy. They buried their dead with shamanistic rites, especially those who had been rich. The only Turkish source of information about these people, either before or after they embraced Islam, is an oral epic of which the narrator is Dede (Grandfather) Korkut, who may have been a real person. (The Book of Dede Korkut was first translated into English by Sümer, Uysal, and Walker, 1972. See also Lewis, 1974.) Although it deals chiefly with the valorous acts of men,

> women are not absent from *The Book of Dede Korkut,* nor are they relegated to a greatly inferior position. Turkish women originally had almost equal status with men, the veil, the harem, and polygamy being Arabian institutions imported some time after the adoption of Islam. In the legends women are revered as mothers, loved and respected as wives. They are often good counselors to their husbands. . . . Reared in the hardships of nomadic life, Oghuz women came naturally by Amazonian attributes of the twenty-four women in the epic, three . . . engage

successfully in physical combat against male antagonists [Sümer, Uysal, and Walker, 1972, p. xvii].

By the time Seljuks and other Turkish tribes began to settle in Asia Minor, their devotion to Islam took the place of any national consciousness (Lewis, 1968) and altered the traditional family. The Seljuks – and later the Ottoman Turks – established many urban communities Turkish in character but influenced by Islam. Schools, colleges, fountains, hospitals, public libraries, and other facilities clustered around a place of worship; but Ottoman society as such developed in a bipolar way, life being very different in the country from that in these cities. The true Ottoman culture was that of the urban elite, who rigidly and ritualistically adhered to Moslem teaching, with common customs, celebrations, and superstitions. "Life was regulated by the houses of prayer, which were timed by the call of the muezzin, so there was no need for clocks. There were some sundials on public walls, and a few water clocks in mosques and medreses for fixing the time of prayers" (Lewis, 1971, p. 91).

The Ottoman Turkish family was patriarchal, patrilocal, and patrilineal. The male head of the family felt a great obligation to his Sultan and his extended family. As many as three generations often lived under the same roof, which sheltered all the unmarried women, children, and newly married sons with their brides, as well as any other dependent relatives. The wealthy household had servants and slaves in addition. Complete authority over such a community belonged to the male head of the family, although women, however unable to participate in a man's world they might be, often exerted a quiet power within the household. Wearing a veil and honoring many customs and rituals, the mother was in charge of all women and young males. Islam permitted four wives, and in the absence of the acknowledged "mother," the next eldest wife took over. The young bride joined her husband's extended family, submitting to her mother-in-law until she in turn gained seniority and dominance herself. The head woman often ruled the household with an iron hand and was responsible for its emotional tone and the psychological direction of its master, thus exerting considerable power. Turkish folklore depicts old women as omnipotent, with both benign and sinister aspects (Sümer, 1970). It is not possible to determine how much of this image comes from the Oghuz culture.

Women had a conscious preference for male children because of the prestige sons brought, but they may also have had conscious and unconscious wishes to control maleness in the society. Children of either sex were swaddled for at least six months and were spoiled within the confines of a world dominated by women. Most children went to district schools, which were under the auspices of religious communities; private tutors were employed by the very rich.

Boys were circumcised, usually just before puberty, and their release from the women's world came rather suddenly; along with the symbolic castration of circumcision, this led to strong denial of feminine authority and exaggerated emphasis on male superiority, which the culture approved. It was up to the father to decide, perhaps with subtle pressure from women in the family, when his son should marry; the mother often selected his future wife. All marriages were arranged and could be terminated by the husband's saying to his wife, "I divorce you," in any one of a number of ritualistic variations.

In the cities at the height of the Ottoman period, impressive provision was made for the care of the sick and dependent. The mentally ill were entertained by music and fed well, being given such delicacies as game birds. Sinan, an architectural genius of the 16th century, designed hospitals to soothe the sick (Stratton, 1972). However, during the 400 years of the Empire's decline, such institutions were not kept up. Death was attended by much ritual, and there was a firm belief that a good Moslem went to Paradise after death.

Rural life was quite different from that in the cities, an agrarian society having developed in Anatolia, where nomadic Turks had settled. The villages were remote, and life was hard there. It was not possible to adhere to urban ritual, and polygamy was not universal. The man continued to be the head of the household, but the women had to work in the fields and were assigned a lower status, although having their labor was an advantage economically. Rural poverty worsened as the Empire declined, and illiteracy, superstition, and a passive acceptance of fate were usual. Bloody feuds between regional overlords took place, ignorant religious zealots excited fear, and in spite of great emphasis on masculine power, most men followed authority passively.

TURKISH FATHERS AND THEIR FAMILIES TODAY

We will discuss the Turkish fathers of *today* in the categories indicated by Özbek (1971) and Cevik (1985), considering for our purposes here those living on the Turkish mainland in 1) rural locations; 2) small towns; 3) shantytowns *(gecekondus)* surrounding the metropolitan centers; and 4) metropolitan centers proper.

Those in the first category represent traditional Turkish fathers at the head of traditional Turkish families, although since the establishment of the Turkish Republic the old ways have gradually been giving way even in country villages. Nonetheless, even today some traditional values are adhered to in all categories, even in the fourth, among westernized Turks in the big cities.

Following Lerner (1958), Sümer (1970) called those who abandoned traditional ways *transitionals* and *moderns,* the former being Turks who were halfway on the road to change, clinging to traditional values while assimilating western ways; the latter were wholly westernized. Shantytown dwellers were considered to be transitionals.

Sümer estimated in 1970 that half the Turkish population were transitionals and 15% moderns, who were chiefly responsible for shaping Turkish life. Since that time further drastic political, economic, and social changes have occurred as the Turks "find themselves."

The Rural

At the beginning of 1985, about 48% of the Turkish population was rural; it had been 81% in the 50s, 75% in the 60s, and 60% in the early 80s. Considerable social change is apparent in this movement toward the cities.

Most of the 40,000 Turkish villages now have electricity, water systems, telephones, television, and access to passable roads to national highways. The government plans that by the end of 1988 there will be no village in Turkey without water, electricity, and access to national highways. In spite of all advances, however, village life continues to be dominated by tradition since their inheritance is that of the Ottoman village rather than of the elite. Although the family continues mostly patrilineal and patrilocal, the extended family seems to be undergoing change; Timur (1972) indicated that at that time 55.4% of families were nuclear. Psychologically, however, the apparently nuclear village family still functions as though it were extended, emotional ties to relatives remaining firm although the group no longer lives under the same roof. Family members still feel an economic responsibility toward one another. Timur held that rural people still idealized the extended family, but many could not afford it, so their idealization may have involved envy. We suggest, however, that prevailing child-rearing practices may have been a factor.

Özbek and Volkan (1976; Volkan, 1979; Volkan and Itzkowitz,

1984) saw the individual Turk living in a traditional (or modified extended) family as being in a *satellite state*. This term was originally coined by Volkan and Corney (1968) to describe a developmental compromise, a stable fixation in psychological orbit around the central figure from whose representation the individual fails to separate and achieve true individuation. This is a restrictive and potentially malignant state if adopted for any but cultural reasons. In a developmental sequence, the satellite state lies between a symbiotic relationship with the mother's representation and the ability to live intrapsychically apart from it without loss of identity. It becomes a way of life for some people, who, even after finishing school and undertaking a profession, always keep a representation of the mother around which to orbit.

Volkan and Corney originally used this concept to describe certain pathological dilemmas of patients, but Volkan and others later applied it to the understanding of a cultural phenomenon – the relationship of the traditional Turk to his traditional family. A Turk living in the country, where traditional ways are the norm, is not fully liberated from his mother's representation by becoming a freestanding person, intrapsychically, in his own right. Although he must remain near it, he fears being engulfed by it and so maintains some psychic distance from it. Since he can differentiate her representation from his own, he does not enter into symbiosis but is drawn toward the center when it represents the "good" mother and is repelled when it is the "bad" one. Like the circling moth so often described in Ottoman poetry and folk verse, he is suspended between two dangerous possibilities: he can be destroyed by flying into the flame or be lost in darkness by fleeing it. The traditional Turk is aware of his individuality, but his ego has to maintain the orbit. The bickering, nagging, and sulking that take place within the traditional extended (or modified extended) family reduces anxiety over the possibility of becoming genuinely symbiotic; but the family is quick to act as one in responding to outside influences, and its group self-concept seems, in stress, to prevail over the individual self-concept of any one member.

Complicating matters further is the ready availability of more than one mothering person. There is more than one flame for a moth to orbit around, and this accounts for certain psychological characteristics. The upbringing of a child in the extended family is not the sole prerogative of his mother; other women in the household feel entitled to mother him in their own way. When one "mother" frustrates him and becomes "bad," the child can turn to another to gratify him. She, then, is "good." Where the classic child–mother unit is stretched to include multiple "mothers," the frustrations of a child struggling for separation-individuation are unlike those of the child daily in a one-to-one encounter with the same woman. The child in the extended family has undue difficulty in mending the "good" and "bad" images of the mothering person and the corresponding "good" and "bad" images of himself. When he arrives at the oedipal age having adjusted to unmended self- and object images, he will have a great tendency to experience the father representation as unmended.

Although this situation might lead to psychopathology in a western culture, the adult who grew up in an extended (or modified extended) family not only is in a satellite state in relation to his family in a culturally expected way, but develops other culturally approved characteristics, being quick to classify those outside his own group as "good" or "bad" since he has not "learned" to integrate totally "good" and "bad" self- and object representations. This promotes greater externalization. As he goes through adolescence, the individual makes investment in people outside his family, but his childhood ways of adapting continue here too; the village – or part of it – becomes like the early mother representation around which he must orbit. He makes himself comfortable by investing heavily in his fellow villagers, making them "good" and making those in other villages the targets of the externalization of his devalued aspects. Kağıtçıbaşı (1976, 1980) has noted strong investment in a whole village.

There is great respect for authority, consistent with the dynamics of the satellite state, in which the individual is caught in either fusing with or escaping from his orbit's core, with consequent conflict in object relations. External authority is needed to handle this conflict and maintain the orbit. Respect for authority, whether sublimated or not, stems also from a need to deal with conflicts that arise in certain peculiarities in psychosexual development as a member of a Turkish traditional family.

Öztürk (1979; Öztürk and Volkan, 1971) examined in some detail longitudinal cross-section stresses faced by a member of a traditional family, and offer a summary. It is believed that the swaddling of infants for six to nine months does no real injury to motor development, but Öztürk holds that although it may at first offer womblike protection, the mother may utilize it to inhibit psychological and physical growth, depending on her own attitudes toward her child. The swaddled child actually receives much stimulation and is much handled by the many mothering figures in the household. The child may be kept at the breast until it is two or even three years old, but since this is seen as a means of birth control by many women, the introduction of modern contraceptives may make prolonged breast-feeding less usual. It is a practice that seems to encourage a search for and expectation of gratification from dependency needs, although it does not imply an altogether passive attitude; passivity clashes with the activity arising from prolongation of oral sadistic possibilities. Moreover, orality prolonged into the second year of life may promote interpenetration of oral with anal and phallic sadism. Defenses against and adaptation to such an accumulation of sadism must be initiated by the individual as well as by cultural norms.

The Turkish child is not toilet trained early or rigidly (Yusufoğlu, 1967); but, as Öztürk (1979) indicates, the culture discourages autonomous will and activity. One might suspect that this checks accumulated aggression but makes it clash internally with the prolongation of dependency. As the child approaches the oedipal stage, he is threatened with open references to a form of castration by the father (Öztürk, 1970). The need to displace castrating (and protecting) agents can be met when the child is preoccupied at this age with religious and supernatural tales of jinns and fairies. His other-directedness is condensed with the need for (supernatural) others to soothe the wounds of psychosexual development.

The circumcision of boys between the ages of four and eight has cultural sanction. The "castration" does take place, but the boy retains his penis! It has the psychological effect of being a social milestone in a boy's life (Cansever, 1965; Öztürk, 1966, 1973; Öztürk and Volkan, 1971). Girls, who are not circumcised in Turkey, may witness the procedure. This traditional event, as well as the open preference for male children, makes for a precocious and definite sex-role differentiation among children growing up in rural Turkey. During their adolescence they overhaul the psychosexual issues of their childhood and loosen their ties to early internal images; new identity formation then takes place (Blos, 1979). If the passage through adolescence is normal, the Turkish youngster firmly adopts stereotyped traditional adult roles, with their strong emphasis on sex-role differentiation. It is clearly understood what is the province of men and what is appropriate for women. Other character traits are assimilated to absorb residues of earlier psychosexual conflicts, such as the desire for but dread of feminine identification that stems from the mother–child relationship, and the fear of castration arising from paternal threats and ritual of circumcision. (The father himself, as indicated earlier, has a tendency to openly threaten his child with castration, but it is important to note that women in the family frighten the boy also by their creation of the image of a castrating father even when he is not present.)

The incest taboo is strong among men, and homosexuality is

scorned (Ekşi, 1982). Such displays of masculinity as those involved in patriotic rallies are approved. The Turkish villager is not lazy, but he keeps aspects of early dependency as an adult and looks to authority, transferring his obedience from his parents to the government without much questioning (Kağıtçıbaşi, 1980). There is no dating as one sees it in the west, and virginity has a high value, sexual restlessness being assuaged by early marriage.

The way the traditional Turk speaks of his sense of fatherhood reflects an unconscious modification of his own experiences as a child. For example, one patient reported that although he had been delighted when he became the father of a son, he had felt obliged to refrain from expressing his pleasure before his own father for fear of seeming unmanly to him; the free expression of emotion was a woman's prerogative. He reflected, indeed, that his infant would belong to his wife and the other women in the household until he became seven years old, when he would no longer go to the Turkish baths with women but be turned over to his father. Then he would truly "possess" his son, supervising his activities and acquainting him with the ways of the Turkish male.

What this man anticipated for his newborn son reflected his own life as a child. In the traditional Turkish household, boys are monopolized by the women for their first seven years of life, entering a man's domain only at the seventh birthday. The traditional father does see his sons before they reach the age of seven and may even eat with them; certainly, they speak with one another. Although the father clearly is proud of his small sons, they remain at the required distance, and he is more feared than idealized. The mother encourages this view of the father as stern and threatening, even dangerous and castrating, so it is a world of dangerous men that a boy enters when he turns seven.

Certain characteristics of the traditional Turkish man can be attributed to his efforts during latency to accommodate to this change, which help determine how he regards becoming a father himself when the time comes. He will feel that it is manly to suppress any open display of affection, to refrain from any play or physical contact with his child, and to play the role of a fearsome father. When his son enters latency or early puberty, the father will suddenly offer himself as a role model for him.

All children so abruptly introduced to the male world tend to identify in an exaggerated way with male attitudes and to suppress any "unmanly" displays of feeling. Since the change in their circumstances is so abrupt, the oedipal conflict does not lend itself to piecemeal resolution, so they externalize the untamed oedipal father image onto such authority figures as those provided by government, for example. That issue may be sublimated or, more likely, be subject to reaction formation, and an exaggerated respect for their elders (idealized oedipal fathers) may persist throughout life. The men will in turn assume the role of "the castrating father" for their children until the children reach latency.

The Turkish culture supports the boy's inner adaptation to the abrupt shift from a woman's world to a man's. Those unable to adapt become symptomatic in adult life, and it is usual for the father (or male extension of him) to care for the sick man much as he "took possession of him" when the child turned seven. His devotion will alternate with anger at the younger man's failure to become "one of them."

At the age of 27, the son of a rich villager entered psychiatric treatment. He was a compulsive eater, grossly obese, and unemployed. His father's first wife had died after bearing three sons, and his father then married her teenaged sister, who became the patient's mother. His father's advanced age reenforced his adherence to the traditional lack of involvement with a young son, so that the boy was dominated by a mother who felt herself to be in competition as a mother with her husband's first wife, her sister. Because of this attitude and the family wealth, attention was lavished on the child; one maid slept with him and helped him get to sleep by rubbing his penis, and another stood by when he played, holding bread and honey lest he have an urge to eat. When he rose to take part in the masculine world at seven, he could not adapt; and as an adult he created "instant mothers" – of restaurants, for example – and felt entitled to be given more than he could consume. He never had a job.

What interests us here is that his father and older brothers, rather than his mother, then felt responsible for him. They sought help for him from one physician after another and protected him from reality in many ways. Their sense of fatherhood demanded that they care for this "sick" adult male.

Small Towns

Most Turks who live in small towns are in modest business enterprises or engaged in farming. All are influenced by traditional values, some adhering to them in practice more closely than others. Basically conservative, they respect authority, but are better described as being somewhere between traditional and transitional than as traditional. The economy increasingly requires them to live in nuclear families, and improved communication is acquainting them with western values, which they heed along with Moslem teaching. Although appreciating the comfort and convenience of what comes from the west, they remain ritualistically involved in their own ways. Thus we see a modified version of the old extended family, with the senior male member still unofficially at its head. The women work, especially if they are poor, giving their earnings to the male family head; women who need not work enjoy higher status. But for all classes the difference between what is expected of women and what of men is very clear.

In small towns a modified kind of matchmaking arranges the marriages. Only 12% of women in small towns in 1971 made their own marriage choices, and 10% in the country. At the same time, 30% of women living in cities decided on a marriage according to their own choice, whereas 51% of urban men and 23.4% of rural men reported making marriage plans without family dictation (Öztürk and Volkan, 1971). Young men in the towns marry later than those living in villages. Öztürk and Volkan suggest that it is harder for the latter to handle sexual suppression.

Shantytowns

The metropolitan areas are attracting more and more of the population. Many are surrounded by shantytowns, in which between one third and one half of the current big metropolitan population lives. Although conditions there are more like those in villages, the people there are in contact with city life and evolve more rapidly than those living in villages and small towns. Their lives and psychological states have been studied rather extensively; a few examples from the literature will indicate their social and psychological turmoil in a situation of rapid change.

Although the people cling to their traditional values, life chips away at their belief systems. Seventy-two percent have nuclear families. The employment of women and young children reduces the traditional authority of the father. According to Yasa (1966, 1970), women are more and more involved in decision making, especially in respect to the education of their children; and men, who would have been horrified at the idea in the past, now help with housework.

Those living in shantytowns work in the city proper; one finds women working as maids in western-style households. They all are exposed to new ways of viewing the relationship between the sexes and become accustomed to seeing women physicians, lawyers, and even politicians. However, no new value system has entirely replaced

adherence to tradition. Gökçe (1973) polled parents in one shantytown
near Ankara concerning their willingness to have their children
friendly with members of the opposite sex: 51% were unwilling, and
only 33.5% found the idea acceptable. Those answering in the negative
felt that friendship between the sexes was against tradition (25.5%),
would make for bad morals (25%), or was prohibited by their religion
(7%).

Big Cities

Here live the "moderns," who seemingly accept most aspects of the
western way of life. The women no longer kiss the hands of their
husbands as a gesture of respect, but a remnant of male domination is
still felt in spite of more direct involvement of Turkish women in
political life. It is the "moderns" who lead Turkish intellectual life.

Interviews with a small sample of university-educated Turkish
fathers under 40 living in Ankara indicated a conscious attitude toward
fatherhood very like that held in the West. The following statement of
a man in his mid-30s with two preschool children, a son and a
duaghter, is typical:

> I believe that my main role as a father is not just to make a
> financial contribution to the family; I consider it to be a part, in a
> democratic atmosphere, of all considerations about the family.
> However, this is not new with me. I felt that my father also was
> involved with his family in a similar fashion. When my children
> were born I was extremely happy, and also, then and now, I am
> filled with feelings of responsibility and concern for their future.
> But now, thinking about this, I realized that my father also had
> similar feelings for his children. Perhaps I am more open in
> expressing this view. But my feelings about my fatherhood and
> the traditional feelings of fatherhood in Turkey – at least in rela-
> tion to my father's generation – are not in conflict, as long as those
> fathers of previous generations lived in big cities and were edu-
> cated. What is different between me and fathers of immediate past
> generations is in the actual behavior. Since my wife became
> pregnant I knew that I would share the actual work of looking
> after our children. We also decide together, in a mutuality, about
> things pertaining to child rearing. In any case, children demand,
> and they have a right to demand, that both parents respond to
> their needs in an appropriate mutuality.

The real father of modern Turkey is its founder, Atatürk, who
was too highly idealized for his death to remove him from the scene. It

is a circumstance perhaps without parallel to have a leader dead for half a century continue to have his shared mental representation still dominate his country. Pictures of Atatürk and symbolic representations of him are seen throughout Turkey today and are as sacred as the national flag. Politicians still make constant reference to him and cannot long enjoy popular favor without paying him homage. His photograph and his recorded or fantasied utterances appear almost daily in newspapers as though he still ran the country.

There are a number of reasons for this; he was in truth the savior of his country, which sees him as godlike even today. An empire was lost when modern Turkey was born, and the people needed to cleave to an idealized symbol to help assuage their grief (Vassaf, 1984; Volkan and Itzkowitz, 1984) over the loss of territories and power.

It is also possible that another cultural phenomenon is condensed in the need to keep alive his idealized mental representation. We have noted that the inability to solve oedipal issues in any piecemeal way tends to develop in the traditional Turkish man an exaggerated respect for his elders, who embody the idealized oedipal father, the representation of which we suggest is invested in a mental representation of Atatürk; the concept of the nurturing mother may underlie this also. In any case, the inability to mourn the death of Atatürk, which occurred in 1938, persists as a most important factor in Turkish life, particularly in respect to politics. In spite of political differences, Turkish "moderns" follow Atatürk's "wedge-shaped path of bon sens" (Hottinger, 1977) through the dense forest of Turkish tradition and politics. The Turkish family modifies itself by staying in this path, although this is not easy; a man must not only break with tradition in respect to "the sense of fatherhood," but must identify with an idealization of fatherhood in order to be "loved" by the representation of Atatürk.

Atatürk himself was born in a house of death – his mother was mourning the death of siblings he never had a chance to know. He tried to make his country happy and no longer addicted to grief, just as he tried to change his grieving mother into a happy one. During his efforts he consolidated his inner self again and again; this is reflected by his repeated change of name until he adopted that of Atatürk, which reflected his desired internalization of an idealized father image (Volkan and Itzkowitz, 1984).

The modern Turkish man has a fixed mental representation of a father figure that he shares with his fellow citizens and that directs them to become idealized and rather omnipotent. This process requires denial of painful aspects of manliness and the realities of fatherhood. As Turks continue to assimilate the drastic historical changes that have occurred, they will become able to combine westernization with valued tradition in an ego-syntonic way. Until then, the Turkish sense of fatherhood continues to evolve, being at the present time different among "moderns" from its manifestation among "traditionals."

REFERENCES

Berkes, N. (1975), *Türk düşününde batı sorunu (The western question in Turkish thought).* Ankara: Bilgi Yayınevi.

Blos, P. (1979), *The Adolescence Passage.* New York: International Universities Press.

Cahen, C. (1968), *Pre-Ottoman Turkey,* trans. from French by J. Jones-Williams. New York: Taplinger.

Cansever, G. (1965), Psychological effects of circumcision. *Brit. J. Med. Psychol.,* 38:321–331.

Cevik, A. (1985), Anksiyete Nevrozunun Psikososyal Yönü (The psychosocial aspect of the anxiety neurosis). *Toplum ve Hekim,* 38:18–21.

Ekşi, A. (1982), *Gençlerimiz ve sorunları (Our Youth and Their Problems).* Istanbul: Istanbul Universitesi Yayinlari.

Friendly, A. (1981), *The Dreadful Day: The Battle of Manzikert, 1071.* London: Hutchinson.

Gökçe, B. (1973), *Gecekondu gençliği (Youth in shantytowns).* Ankara: Harcettepe Yayınları.

Hottinger, A. (1977), Turkey's search for identity: Kemal Atatürk's heritage. *Encounter,* 48:75–81.

Itzkowitz, N. (1972), *Ottoman Empire and Islamic Tradition.* New York: Knopf.

Kağıtçıbaşı, C. (1976), *Insan ve Insanlar: Sosyal Psikiyatriye Giriş (Man and Men: Introduction to the Social Psychiatry).* Ankara: Sevinç Matbaası.

——— (1980), *Cocucun Değeri (The Value of Children)* Istanbul: Boğaziçi Üniversitesi Yayinlari.

Lerner, D. (1958), *The Passing of Traditional Society.* Glencoe, IL: The Free Press.

Lewis, B. (1968), *The Emergence of Modern Turkey.* London: Oxford University Press.

Lewis, G. (1974), *The Book of Dede Korkut.* London: Penguin Books.

Lewis, R. (1971), *Everyday Life in Ottoman Turkey.* London: B.T. Batsford.

Muller, H.J. (1961), *The Loom of History.* New York: American Library.

Özbek, A. (1971), *Sosyal Psikiyatriye Giriş (Introduction to Social Psychiatry).* Ankara: Ankara Üniversitesi Tıp Fakültesi Yayınları.

_____ & Volkan, V.D. (1976), Psychiatric problems within satellite-extended families of Turkey. *Amer. J. Psychother.*, 30:576–582.

Öztürk, O.M. (1966), Psychosocial effects of ritual circumcision in Turkey. *Proceedings of the 4th World Congress of Psychiatry,* ed. J.J. Lopez-Ibor. Amsterdam: Excerpta Medica Foundation.

_____ (1970), Anadolu Toplumunda Oedipus Kompleksi Teorisinin Geçerliği (The suitability of the theory of the Oedipus complex within the Anatolian population). *Hacettepe Cocuk Sağlği ve Hastaliklari Dergisi,* 13:1–7.

_____ (1973), Ritual circumcision and castration anxiety. *Psychiat.,* 36:49–60.

_____ (1979), Traditionally generated conflicts and their manifestations in certain belief systems. *Hacettepe Bulletin of Medicine/Surgery,* 2:89–100.

_____ & Volkan, V.D. (1971), The theory and practice of psychiatry in Turkey. *Amer. J. Psychiat.,* 25:240–271.

Shaw, S.J. (1976), *History of the Ottoman Empire and Turkey,* Vol. 1. Cambridge: Cambridge University Press.

_____ & Shaw, E.Z. (1977), *History of the Ottoman Empire and Turkey,* Vol. 2. Cambridge: Cambridge University Press.

Stein, A. (1964), *On Ancient Central-Asian Tracks.* New York: Pantheon Books.

Stratton, A. (1972), *Sinan.* New York: Chas Scribner's Sons.

Sümer, E.A. (1970), Changing dynamic aspects of the Turkish culture. In: *The Child and His Family,* ed. E.J. Anthony & C. Koupernick. New York: Wiley Interscience.

Sümer, F., Uysal, A.E. & Walker, W.E., eds. (1972), *The Book of Dede Korkut.* Austin: University of Texas Press.

Suzuki, P.T. (1981), Psychological problems of Turkish migrants in West Germany. *Amer. J. Psychother.,* 35:187–194.

Timur, S. (1972), *Türkiyede aile yapısı (The Family Structure in Turkey).* Ankara: Hacettepe Universitesi Yayınları.

Vassaf, G. (1984), Tarihsiz bırakılan toplum lidere sığınır, kolayca şartlanır (Without a link to its history a group comes into the influence of its leader and is easily conditioned). *Yeni Gündem,* 5:18–19.

Volkan, V.D. (1979), *Cyprus-War and Adaptation.* Charlottesville: University Press of Virginia.

_____ & Corney, R.T. (1968), Some considerations of satellite states and satellite dreams. *Brit. J. Med. Psychol.,* 41:283–290.

_____ & Itzkowitz, N. (1984), *The Immortal Atatürk.* Chicago: University of Chicago Press.

364 Turkish Fathers

Yasa, I. (1966), *Ankarada Gecekondu Aileleri (Shantytown families in Ankara)*. Ankara: Sağlik ve Sosyal Yardım Bakanlığı Yayınları.

_____ (1970), *Ankara gecekondu toplumlarında kentleşme* (Urbanization in Ankara shantytowns). Presented at 11th Conference on Urbanization, Ankara, May 21.

Yusufoğlu, N. (1967), Türkiyede Tuvalet Eğitimi Üzerinde bir Araştirma (A study of toilet training in Turkey). Unpublished research paper. Ankara: Hacettepe University Medical School.

18

Black Fathers

James P. Comer

Because of changes in the nature of work and modern life, people need a higher level of social and psychological development today than they did forty years ago. Families must rear – fathers must father – children in a way that allows them to function in a more complex world than that which existed before jet planes, television, and satellite communications. This puts families who were closed out of the economic, social, and educational mainstream, and related socialization, at a disadvantage. Groups whose historical experience in America did trauma to their culture, and who were excluded from the economic mainstream, have a disproportionate number of families in this situation. This is the case for Blacks, Hispanics, and Native Americans. In this chapter I will confine my discussion to Black fathers.

Black fathers are in many ways like all other American fathers. But because of historical and contemporary social conditions, there are important differences. Black fathers must accomplish traditional and changed manhood and fatherhood functions in a societal environment of neglect, abuse, or both. There are social, psychological, affective, even cognitive consequences of the "Black burden" that can interfere with the fathering process. Policy makers, clinicians, and all others who provide support services to families can be more effective if they understand the actual and potential effect of these different social conditions.

It should be noted that there is a broad spectrum of Black fathers – from those under great stress, the frightened and absent, to the secure and highly responsible, with many variations in between. In this respect too Blacks are like all other groups except that there is a disproportionate number of Black fathers at the end of the spectrum most under stress owing to adverse social conditions. Because of concern about the disadvantaged, the experience of the successful is often overlooked. This is unfortunate because it is the experience of the successful Black fathers that will provide us with clues to shaping social policies and clinical practice to assist the less successful.

It is important to understand the source of models and positive imitation and identification objects for Black fathers in a society that has created a disproportionate number of negative models. How has the Black family and community adjusted to protect itself and promote desirable growth and development in the face of social abuse? What are some of the specific positive coping mechanisms and strategies used by successful Black fathers, and how do they differ from those of unsuccessful fathers or those who experience excessive psychological pain?

But the intent of this paper is not to discuss clinical issues or treatment in great depth. Clinical issues and treatment are not much different in Blacks and in Whites. The problem, in my opinion, is that many therapists are not knowledgeable about the Black experience, the resultant interactional difficulties, and their own responses to them. Thus, in this chapter I attempt to discuss the Black experience in some detail and to alert therapists to interactional difficulties and their own possible troublesome responses.

Also, in this chapter I examine the obstacles to effective fathering by first reviewing traditional and emerging fatherhood expectations and then examining the unique experiences and adjustments Black fathers have made over time. I present several illustrative examples and then suggest social policy, support services, and clinical implications and interventions.

TRADITIONAL AND EMERGING FATHERHOOD EXPECTATIONS

The American father is expected to be the provider of basic needs for himself and his family – food, clothing, and shelter. He is also expected to provide a reasonable level of the experiences our society has deemed desirable – education, health care, and paid recreation. He is expected to create, through his interaction with his spouse, a climate that enables him to give his children a sense of belonging, worth, and adequacy and to help them grow along the critical developmental pathways – social, psychological, moral, speech and language, and cognitive.

Helping children grow includes interacting with them in such a way as to modulate and channel their aggression into the energy of work and play. It includes helping them control potentially harmful impulses, observe, think, and act in a way that meets their needs without compromising the needs of others. It includes being a model, guide, and mediator of the flood of information and experiences that come to the growing child. It includes helping the child interact effectively with other children, adults, and institutions in the family's own social network and in the larger society beyond it (Solnit and Provence, 1963).

Helping children grow is not easy. They need much nurturance and support to meet the tasks and to gain the skills necessary to become successful workers, heads of households, and citizens. Prior to the 1970s, nurturance and the day-to-day effort to rear children was more often the role of the mother. Our previous cultural notions of manhood created a pattern of emotional distance and authoritarian, aggression-promoting behavior between many fathers and their children, male children in particular (Demos, 1982).

Most fathers established the family ethos or culture – attitudes, values, and ways. Many served as the voice of authority or "court of last resort" when children challenged the expectations established by mothers. Thus, many fathers were providers first, childrearers and a source of nurturance and emotional support second – often a distant, sometimes difficult second.

A father's gratification came from being able to provide for his spouse and children, from making it possible for the mother to rear the children well (Lidz, 1963). This was possible when the father was able to secure food, clothing, and shelter from his labor – as an employee or an entrepreneur. As a result, a man's sense of identity, adequacy, value, and belonging in the society was largely determined by the nature of his work. Success at work and in the family and consequent respect from others motivated desirable citizenship behavior. Clearly, then, access to opportunities to earn a living wage was, and still is, important.

The effects of the economy and of science and technology on the nature of work, transportation, communication, and other aspects of life have changed male-female relationships and father-child relationships. More women must work outside the home. The nature of modern work attracts more women to the work-force even when it is not an economic necessity. These and other factors have led to more male involvement in child rearing and the nurturance of children.

HISTORICAL SOCIAL CONDITIONS

Most Blacks are descended from the pre-1850 societies of the west coast of Africa. While there were differences across the tribal-states involved, roles – including the male and fathering roles – were well defined. A person's work was determined by the kinship group into which he or she was born. Women had the traditional role of nurturing the young but also often played a role in economic functions, as farmers and merchants. Men were protectors – hunters, warriors, and farmers – and played a key role in governance and in the rearing of older male children (Gibbs, 1965).

Because these were communal societies, a man's sense of worth and belonging rested less heavily on his ability to provide individually for his family than it would in an entrepreneurial society. A man's sense of adequacy and worth came from being a competent participant in group – including economic – activities, from being a descendent of the lineage god (see Gibbs, 1965). Participation in social activities took place within age-grade sets (age cohorts who gave each other emotional and social support in life activities) and gave each individual a powerful sense of belonging. Because of the economic and psychosocial benefits of belonging, sanctions against the failure to live up to group expectations were effective. The appropriate care and preparation of children for adult life was an important expectation of parents.

Child rearing itself was to a degree communal. Although parents were the primary caretakers, any child within a tribal group could look to any adult in the group for protection and guidance and, in turn, was expected to accept and respond to any adult caretaking effort. Hence, parents were attentive not only because of the inherent satisfaction in caring for children, but because of the powerful positive social sanctions for doing so and negative sanctions for not doing so (Gibbs, 1965).

These conditions were significantly different from those of Western culture and were the opposite of the conditions of slavery. Again, in the pre-American culture of Blacks, one's sense of adequacy, value, and worth rested mostly on one's sense of belonging within a group, a sense derived more from adherence to group expectation than from independent achievement. And yet, desirable performance as a worker and a parent was promoted through strong group sanctions. In Western culture, adequacy and worth are based largely on individual productivity and achievement. This difference was highly problematic in slavery.

American slavery disrupted the pattern of societal and family life in Africa. Western culture, distorted by the nature of slavery, was imposed over about 250 years. The West African institutions and traditions that had provided a sense of adequacy, value, and belonging were destroyed or minimized. In slavery there was no opportunity to achieve as an individual and gain adequacy, value, and a sense of belonging independent of the slavemaster. Children were, in fact, the property of the master. Slaves existed in a totally dependent, degraded condition–with the old culture lost and a respected and socially and psychologically organizing position in the new culture denied.

The male slave was the greatest threat to the system and was therefore subject to more aggressive control. Aggression by the slave-master, and others promoted aggression among the slaves, often displaced from the White aggressors and directed against other slaves or manifest in passive-aggressive action against the slavemaster, for example, in slow, careless, or destructive work. Even without slavery, the greatly different western culture would have posed a formidable problem. Slavery in a different and abusive culture had a devastating effect on the "manhood" psychology and child-rearing or fathering practices of Black males.

Fathers could not be protectors in the West African tradition, and they could not be independent providers or achievers in the tradition of western culture. They were not raising their children to become competent, valued members of the larger society. They did not receive group-established institutional sanctions for either meeting or not meeting fatherhood responsibilities. In fact, many were not allowed to live with families, and even when they were allowed, the White master, not the Black father, was the real head of household. And unlike slaves in South America and the Carribbean, Blacks in the United States were a minority–five to ten slaves–on small plantations, where the master's power and control were directly felt in every aspect of life (Comer, 1972).

Relationship ties suffered. Some fathers had no responsibility for, and consequently little emotional tie to, their children. Because of the power situation and the "identification with the aggressor" defense mechanism, the children of the master, generalized to other Whites, were sometimes more valued by slaves than their own children.

Where slave families were frequently separated, establishing close emotional ties was to invite trauma.

Slave fathers served as models, guides, and mediators in a way forced on them by the conditions of slavery, ways needed to support the system. But what they modeled was harmful to themselves, their families, and their group. Many could not model attitudes and behaviors necessary to promote independent, goal-directed conduct or a sense of belonging, worth, and adequacy. Social, psychological, moral, cognitive, speech, and language development was distorted and limited by the conditions of slavery (Woodson, 1928).

Slave families lived under a spectrum of conditions ranging from that of lower animals to that of being almost members of the master's family. Those enjoying a quasi-family status were able, through positive identification with the master, to gain some sense of adequacy, belonging, and worth – but always as inferior persons belonging to an inferior group. And identification primarily with the master permitted a sense of well-being only on the master's terms – when one was a "good slave." Most successful Black families met their psychosocial needs primarily through religion or the Black church. Identification primarily with God permitted a sense of adequacy, worth, and belonging on less degrading "church" or religious terms (Frazier, 1963).

After slavery, Blacks attempted to establish families consistent with western cultural style. For most newly freed Black men, who had been denied independence, achievement opportunities, and a sense of adequacy or "manhood" during slavery, obtaining these conditions was of great importance. But oppressive conditions in the society made this achievement difficult or impossible for many. Socialization for slavery – self-destructive habits and attitudes – blocked the realization of these goals for others. And most were blocked–through legal racial segregation–from being a part of the social networks that held and transmitted job and other success skills, information, and opportunities. Blacks did not have the right to vote, a right necessary for effectiveness in the networks of political and economic power. Violence, terror, and subterfuge kept Blacks from voting in the localities where they might have had the greatest political power. Most Black males were forced to the bottom of the job market as sharecroppers, tenant farmers, industrial laborers, and domestic service workers (Franklin, 1961).

In the eight states that held 80% of the Black population through the 1930s, four to eight times as much money was spent per White student as per Black student in primary and secondary schools. In areas that were disproportionately Black, as much as 25 times as much was spent on Whites as on Blacks (Blose and Caliver, 1936). Similar disparities existed at the college and university levels. As late as the mid-1960s, the combined endowment of two prestigious White women's colleges was half that of Harvard University but equal to that of all the 100+ Black colleges combined (Council for Financial Aid to Education, 1967).

By 1900, Blacks were closed out of significant union membership, as well as the better jobs in industry and the associated economic and political power, a situation that prevailed until the 1960s (Spero and Harris, 1968). In short, all the major pathways to achievement in the societal mainstream—economic, political, educational—were blocked for most Blacks. As a result, just as during slavery, a large number of Black males could neither protect nor provide for themselves and their families. This state of affairs perpetuated for many, acting up and acting out, apathy and withdrawal behavior established in response to the conditions of slavery.

Of course, even during slavery, the combination of better conditions and religion permitted some families to live and work in a way similar to other families in the society, although they were denied basic rights and opportunities (Bennett, 1982). After slavery, much of the Black community organized around, and evolved out of, the Black church. Income, albeit marginal, and the psychoemotional and social support provided by the church permitted some Black men to serve as family providers and the voice of authority in their families, and to establish its culture. Black parents living under these conditions were able adequately to support the full development of their children. But after the 1940s, changes in the nature of work and life made it increasingly difficult for undereducated fathers to provide for their families.

Prior to the end of slavery, America was an agricultural society. And while it remained largely agricultural until the beginning of the twentieth century, the first stage of the Industrial Revolution took place roughly between the end of slavery, 1865, and 1900. The second stage of the industrial era occurred between 1900 to 1945. In the first stage, the heads of households could generally earn a living wage or at least provide for themselves and their families without an education or special training. The second stage required only a moderate level of education and training. And many previously poor White families rode the national rising tide of affluence, made possible through industrial development, to a middle income and better educated status.

Racial discrimination by unions and employers closed Blacks out of the better paying low or easily learned skill jobs of this era (Spero and Harris, 1968).

After World War II, or the third stage of the industrial era, better education and training became a requirement for better jobs and opportunities, even if they were not actually needed to do the job. In other words, education and training became the ticket of admission to living-wage jobs. Blacks, closed out of the rising tide of affluence in the first half of the twentieth century, closed out of educational opportunities, and without other sources of power were most adversely affected. A disproportionate number of Blacks were trapped at the lowest level of the job market. Nonetheless, the organizing effect of the Black church, adequate income (though barely), and the small-town or rural location of most Black families made adequate family functioning possible for most.

A massive Black south-to-north movement in the 1940s in response to the decline of agriculture and in search of better jobs, disturbed and weakened the impact of the church (Frazier, 1962). And in the late 1950s, as education became the key to better jobs, Blacks— undereducated in the south and closed out of trade unions and skilled training programs in both the South and the North—were less able to find primary job-market work. Because Black males were limited to low paying jobs, Black women often worked to provide an adequate family income—long before it became necessary among many White families.

That Black women and children did not receive the same support as Whites—in an age when it was expected—created the potential for greater male-female relationship problems and family stress. A severe blow to the Black male's sense of adequacy or manhood, it destroyed the confidence and will of some. In addition, because the attitudes of children toward their fathers are often a direct reflection of the mother's attitude toward the father (Atkins, 1982), increased male-female conflict—for whatever reasons—often resulted in stressful, negative father-child relationships. The subsequent emotional distress of not meeting generally recognized standards of success within either their economic or their social environments had a severely adverse effect on the psychological health of many low-income Black fathers. This, in turn, reduced their ability to provide their children with sustained emotional support and guidance (Meers, 1973). And before many Black males had ever had an opportunity to perform traditional manhood and fatherhood functions, changed societal conditions required changed relationships with women and children.

These factors combined to adversely affect Black family life. As late as 1960 two parents were present in almost eight of ten Black families. But, unable to provide for a family, a growing number of Black men avoided establishing one. Hopelessness and despair, substance abuse and crime began to increase. But siring children continued to be a way to find manhood and adequacy when most other ways were blocked. This combination of tendencies has led to increasingly high levels of stress and divorce, to the point that nearly half of all Black households today are fatherless (Edelman, 1987).

Nonetheless, despite the obstacles, many Black families and fathers have been able to function adequately, even to thrive (Berry and Blassingame, 1982). These are generally the families who were able to obtain education and stability through marginal income and the cohesion and support provided by the Black church and related subculture prior to World War II. It was this segment of the Black population that led the intensification of the Civil Rights Movement. And this segment benefited disproportionately from the voting rights and educational and economic opportunities that the movement made possible. For this reason the Black population appears to be going in opposite directions: the segment least stable before World War II, or deteriorating as a result of changed conditions, becoming an apparent underclass and the better functioning segment obtaining opportunities and status not available to Blacks until now.

But successful Black families still must avoid or overcome overt and subtle racial antagonisms in every aspect of American life – political, economic, educational, and social. And even when families are able to do so, these conditions engender responses ranging from wariness and distrust of Whites, and the larger social system, to anger and alienation. Success sometimes produces identification with the White power structure and low self- and group (Black)-esteem. It sometimes produces both, with ambivalence and antagonism toward the self, the Black group, and the White-controlled larger society (Greer and Cobbs, 1968).

BLACK FATHERS

Several synopses reflect the outcome of the Black experience and the problems and opportunities of Black fatherhood.

A 14-year-old Black father told me in 1968 that he had a child by his 13-year-old girlfriend because he wanted to give the attention and affection to his child that he did not receive from his own absent but known father. His mother–undereducated in the rural South in the 1930s–complained that she had to care for his baby because he was undependable and spent most of his time "ripping and running" up and down the street with his teenage buddies. The mother of his child continued to live with her own family because he could not provide her and the child financial and emotional support. He was still receiving an allowance from his older working sister.

A second Black father earned over $100,000 a year in a managerial position. But he did not have a college degree and had to overcome enormous obstacles. His son experienced some of the problems of affluence–the assumption of continued affluence without developing good planning and achievement habits and skills. The mediocre early performance of the son irritated the hardworking father. When, two years after graduation from high school, the youngster finally decided he wanted to go to college and work hard towards a goal, the father refused to send him.

A third Black father had experienced extreme racial prejudice in a previous all white college in the 1950s. Despite this he was an honor student and went on to become an outstanding professional man. In part, as a statement to the society that had held him in low esteem and attempted to block his development, he gave his children too much, too soon–high priced cars when they were 16 years old, expensive clothes, and vacations. They abused the privileges and experienced delayed social development.

A fourth Black father, with an elementary school education, worked as a steel mill laborer to provide adequate income for his wife and six children. The family was enmeshed in a social network of church and neighborhood friends and kin. In the family style common prior to the 1970s, he left most of the day-to-day childrearing to his wife but contributed, with his wife, to establishing family attitudes, values, and ways–the family culture. His emotional and financial support of his wife and children enabled all six to obtain a college education and become responsible professional people, family members, and citizens.

Such experiences–problems and opportunities–occur among all groups. In all of the foregoing cases, one hears the desire to function up to and above societal expectations. In all but the last case, racism, reflected in economic and educational policies and attitudes, adversely affected the behavior of these fathers. The undereducated parents of the 14-year-old were not able to provide him with the developmental experience that would allow him to be successful in school and competitive in the 1970s and 80s job market. He sought manhood in paternity. His own father had not been able to provide for his family and abandoned it after a period of domestic turmoil. The 14-year-old, with good intentions but limited resources, was repeating a modelled cycle.

The second father accepted society's rationalization for group and individual underachievement – a lack of individual effort. He had a pressing need to demonstrate his manhood in Western cultural terms – personal achievement. He made an extraordinary effort and expected the same from his son. He ignored the confusion, survivor guilt, and the effect of racist attitudes on the self-confidence and sense of belonging of Black youth from middle-income families. His effort to get ahead did not allow him to give his family the time and attention needed. His hard driving, aggressive, authoritarian childrearing style in an age when a more democratic style is more effective contributed to the problem. Without his being totally aware of it, his drive for individual success was tied to his ambivalence about being Black and his acceptance of negative attitudes or rationalizations about Blacks in the society.

The third case is fairly straightforward and common. Many Blacks do not want their children to experience the racial hardships they themselves experienced. Indeed, they want the opposite. Because this is not possible, they attempt to compensate by providing them with excessive material manifestations of success. In some ways this father expressed his anger and outrage against the society through his children – "White-controlled society, you tried to stop me and you couldn't, now I'll show you . . . I'll show you good!" A more constructive way to manage such feelings would be to support efforts to eliminate unjust societal practices. There is nothing inherently harmful about a reasonable amount of material possessions. But young people should be mature enough to appreciate them. This requires parental interaction, guidance and support based on the child's needs more than on the needs of the parent.

The fourth father and family utilized the most effective adaptive mechanism among Blacks. The father was from a church-based family and social network in the rural South. The attitudes, values, and ways of this subculture had survived the Black south-to-north movement and promoted a family situation of mutual support and respect. Overall family conditions allowed the father to provide security for his wife and children. As in many Black families, because it was less threatening to Whites, the wife took on the apparent leadership role as the family engaged with the larger society. But the father established the family ethos or culture.

The father's sense of adequacy came from his status in the church and the family social network and his ability to wring a living wage out of a low-status occupation. Education became a highly treasured value and focus of the family. There was an acute awareness of racial injustice. But family members were encouraged to respond through hard work and personal development except where it was absolutely necessary to directly attack racial injustice in order to accomplish one's goals. A secure wife and mother and this father were able to aid the growth and development of the children so that they were able to take advantage of better educational opportunities in the 1940s industrial North.

With education and social skills, the children were able to be successful in the postindustrial era job market after the 1970s. The males in the family, having grown up in a family with significant female leadership and having met manhood expectations through their own work performance, had little difficulty taking increased responsibility for child care and accepting more equal male-female relationships.

It is not possible to estimate the number of Black families and fathers that are functioning well as opposed to those with serious social and psychological problems and functioning very poorly. Between the 1870s and the 1950s, the style of the fourth family was on the increase. But the decline in two-parent families among Blacks, from 68.3% in 1970 to 55.1% in 1982, suggests that more males are not in a position to support themselves and their families (U.S. Department of Commerce, 1983). And while a number of better educated and employed Black fathers are participating more actively in childrearing or fathering roles, a large segment of Black families are under increasing stress and fathers are not present, not to mention being able to function in a different way. There are social policy, childrearing or fathering, and treatment implications for Black fathers in the situations and experiences just described.

SOCIAL POLICY IMPLICATIONS

The low-income Black father who successfully provided emotional and social support for his family reminds us of the critical elements of successful family functioning regardless of race. His situation was more often the rule than the exception before 1940. But with the sharp reduction of natural community supports, adequate fathering has become and will continue to be more difficult without appropriate social policy changes. The failure of the society to adopt social policies that would enable most Black fathers to function well has contributed greatly to the rise in the number of households headed by young females. Without needed changes in social policies, this segment of the population will continue to grow, with a devastating impact on Black communities and on the society.

To develop adequate policies, social policymakers in government, business, and education need a better understanding of the Black experience and its impact on Black males and families. Social policy needs to address the damage done to Black and White institutions, attitudes, values, and ways through slavery, segregation, racial abuse, and, most important, the exclusion of Blacks from full participation in economic, political, information, and educational institutions during the formative and fluid economic years of the country. It will not be enough to pass laws requiring equal employment opportunity when a disproportionate number of people are unprepared for today's job market and when racist attitudes, though more subtle, persist.

Some existing policies and social programs could have much greater positive impact if they were grounded in a realistic perception of our national past. Programs such as Affirmative Action, "set-asides" for minority business, incentives to draw business to minority communities, and the like could be more effective in conjunction with programs to help Black and White leadership and the public at large understand the need for such efforts and the adverse consequences for the nation without them.

Although social policy should encourage families to be as independent as possible, it is becoming increasingly difficult for many families to receive adequate income on a sustained basis in our modern economic system. We therefore can not continue to scorn income transfer payments such as public welfare, food stamps, subsidized housing and others. Without attitudinal changes about such programs, an increasing number of Americans, fathers in particular, regardless of race, are going to feel inadequate. This will interfere with the quality of family life, fathering, child growth and development, and, in turn, with the quality of life in the society.

Such political and social policy issues need to be addressed by business, government, foundations, and other leaders—working in collaboration with Black community leaders and organizations—if clinical intervention and adequate child rearing and parenting are to be promoted among greater numbers of Black parents, including fathers.

CHILDREARING OR FATHERING IMPLICATIONS
AND INTERVENTIONS

There seems to be a general assumption now that the plight of the growing underclass in this country is permanent. It need not be. The fact is that not very much has been done to provide the most troubled families and children with the knowledge, skills, and socioemotional support they need to be successful and break out of their predicament. School-based life and family preparation programs for future parents can be helpful for accomplishing this task. Other programs are also needed to tie future male heads of households to the mainstream job and economic systems. Properly designed, job and family life preparation programs could motivate young people to become effective family members and child rearers. This would enable them, in turn, to prepare their children better for education and future economic opportunities.

The notion of programs designed to tie low-income Black youngsters to the economic and social mainstream is based on an understanding that the major consequence of racist social policies and practices over the years has been to exclude and disconnect many Black families from the mainstream forces promoting adequate functioning, childrearing, and development, and, in turn, adequate learning, work, and citizenship. Life and family preparation programs can provide students with the skills needed for modern living. They can systematically provide – in a creative and interesting way – the requisite skills to participate successfully in families and to rear children, to participate in the economic system, in politics and government, and in spiritual/leisure time activities.

Working from this conceptual frame of reference, our Yale Child Study Center School Development Program, in collaboration with the New Haven School System, established a project designed to provide low-income Black students with mainstream social skills and the motivation to use them. With parent participation, this program entitled, "A Social Skills Curriculum for Inner City Children," was begun in 1968 in two elementary schools. Appreciation of the arts and academic and social skill learning were integrated through activity units in politics and government, business and economics, health and nutrition, spiritual and leisure time – areas in which students would need skills, competence, and confidence to be successful as adults. Parent participation made it possible for the students to imitate, identify with, and integrate the attitudes, values, and ways involved in these activities (Comer, 1980).

This approach led to dramatic academic achievement and social behavior gains. In 1968, students in the two schools involved were 19 and 18 months behind grade level on standardized achievement tests by the fourth grade. Attendance was the worst in the city, and there were serious behavior problems in both schools. In 1984–with no change in the socioeconomic makeup of the schools–students in one of the schools were a year above grade level in achievement by fourth grade and, in the second, seven months above grade level. Students in the first school were first in attendance for four of the five previous years. There were no serious behavior problems in either of the two schools. The project has now been expanded to include all the low income schools in New Haven and is being implemented in middle and high schools in the city, as well as in elementary schools in several other cities.

The middle and high school programs are addressing issues of sexuality, child care, and preparation for the world of work more directly. Our intent is to sustain the attitudes, values, and ways promoted in the elementary school and to help the students deal with the challenges of adolescence in a way that does not leave them vulnerable to the attractions of "the street." We are now working with local businesses and government to involve as many students as possible, so that the rewards of adequate social and educational development become apparent and motivating.

Such programs expose low-income youngsters to the same experiences many youngsters from better educated, middle-income or better functioning low-income families enjoy by simply growing up with their parents. Such programs help them learn to plan and organize their activities and develop the ability to stick to and complete long-range tasks. They help youngsters develop the skills to identify problems and opportunities–personal and external–and develop acceptable strategies and skills to overcome or take advantage of them.

Given the demands of today's workplace, students with social skills are more likely to be successful in the mainstream social and economic system. There is suggestive evidence that they will be better prepared to use political and economic mechanisms to reduce harmful racial practices and attitudes. We believe that as they succeed as students and adults, they will be better able to experience acceptance and belonging in their own primary social networks and in the society beyond them. This will permit more Black males to serve as family providers, will engender more nurturance and supportive fathering behavior, and will enhance the changing female role in the household.

Child-care programs in schools will enable teenage students, as parents and future parents, to learn the most helpful ways of rearing their children. Such programs provide models of cooperative male-female relationships; models of males as economic providers and adequate child rearers. On a large enough scale, such programs could begin to erode harmful fathering attitudes and behaviors born out of anger, frustration, and hopelessness and transmitted from one generation to the next. School programs designed to combine job preparation with learning about financial management of families and child care and development needs and costs will give greater meaning to all three areas and will allow many to be more successful workers and heads of households in the future.

Intervention programs require the involvement of constructive institutions within low-income communities as well as the institutions of the broader educational, business, and government communities. Thus, meaningful community-based institutions, such as the church, civil rights groups and others should sponsor such programs independent of schools or other public institutions as well as support such programs in them. The trust and emotional attachment of Blacks to churches and civil rights groups and the like could permit programs in schools, and other institutions outside of their social network, to promote desired change.

Black males with a mainstream orientation are involved in these Black community institutions. Programs can be structured so that these men can serve as models and guides for young males living in social networks with largely harmful models. In addition, the activities of various recreational programs—scouting, for example—could promote responsible manhood and paternity.

CLINICAL IMPLICATIONS AND INTERVENTION

Black males, like most other men, can be helped to adjust to more useful expressions of manhood or fatherhood. The aggressive, "macho" suppression of feeling and the nonnurturance characteristics of the past are not useful in creating desirable male-female relationships and supporting the development of children in a modern, science and technology-based society. Therapy, when indicated, should help men equate manhood with responsible personal behavior within their families and society. And family success should be viewed as an achievement as important as work and career success. The task of the Black male is distorted and more difficult because of the historical and contemporary racial conditions the group has experienced. Thus, treatment issues are both the same as and different from those for White fathers.

Several years ago I noticed a White colleague in a family treatment room looking perplexed and confused after a session with a Black family. She had been trying to help the father confront the meaning of his abusive treatment of the children. His wife pulled her aside and said, "You don't understand. . . . That's the Black man's way." My colleague was concerned that she might be breaching a cultural norm. But this was not the case. Child abuse is child abuse in every culture. Again, the controlling, authoritarian, aggressive, even violent and exploiting behavior of too many low-income fathers – a disproportionate number of them Black – is a reaction to their own sense of powerlessness, abuse, and rejection in the society.

A major task is to help the patient identify the underlying causes of anger and anxiety, manage them, and develop more appropriate problem-solving behavior. This is a difficult task for at least two reasons. Racial conditions are not the only cause – and usually not the overt cause – of excessive anger and anxiety in Black males and fathers; yet, given the continued racial problems in the society, race remains a focus in Black families far in excess of that of Whites. Second, in interracial therapy, transference problems can make it difficult for client and therapist to sort out and manage their feelings (Ellis, Comer, and Rubenstein, 1979).

Some Black patients will not be able to establish trust and will withhold feelings, attitudes and behaviors that need to be confronted. Other Black patients will use the therapist as a symbol of an oppressive White society and discharge anger without working through other conflicts in order to establish problem solving behavior. Some patients first express great anger with the controlling White society. Later, the target of expressed anger is often reversed. They then express – and act out – harmful attitudes and behavior toward themselves and other Blacks.

Some Black therapists overidentify with such patients and promote excessive discharge without moving toward problem resolution. Some non-Black therapists experience personal guilt and unconsciously utilize defensive rationalizations or antagonisms in work with Black patients. Some do not know the Black experience well enough to know when to empathize with the Black reality or to confront excessive discharge and distortion. Some have difficulty tolerating the level of Black anger, particularly more threatening Black male anger. This sometimes leads to bending over backwards to the point where the patient is not held accountable. Without awareness of patient and therapist vulnerabilities, interracial and some same-race therapy where the symptoms are related to racial conditions can be ineffective. The training and treatment implications are obvious.

Despite the problems in interracial therapy, most well-trained, sensitive (or willing to be sensitized) non-Black therapists can be effective with Black patients. In the foregoing illustrative cases, for example, directly race-related treatment issues are intertwined with personality and other social issues. It would be important for the therapist to be able to appreciate and acknowledge the indignation and rage related to direct racial injustice and to indirect racial injustice such as limited education, employment, and other life opportunities. The therapist could then help the patient move toward realistic problem-solving understanding and behavior, whether problems are race related or not.

As the treatment moves toward problem solving, the therapist would need to help the father understand the harmful nature of his adaptive responses to the self and family – in one case, identification with societal rationalizations for Black community problems coupled with high level individual achievement and unrealistic expectations of his son; in the other case, excessive materialism as a social status statement, which, in turn, interferes with his son's social and psychological maturation.

The problems of low-income Black males – uneducated and socially underdeveloped, as in the first case presented – are more difficult. Where psychotherapy is indicated and possible, the same basic approach is useful. But often it is important to try and help such persons to involve themselves in meaningful and supportive social networks that promote the social and psychological well-being of the father and his family. Supportive social networks are particularly useful for youths. Thus, social and community mental health workers in schools and other institutions can play an important role here.

Schools as well as recreational, religious, and other programs can be structured to provide low-income youth with mainstream educational, employment, and family functioning skills. It is in this context that individual therapy has the greatest possibility of success. This point suggests the need for simultaneous intervention at the social-policy and decision-making level of society, institutional and family service, and the clinical level.

REFERENCES

Atkins, R. (1982), Discovering daddy: The mother's role. In: *Father and Child*, ed. S.H. Cath, A. Gurwitt & J.M. Ross. Boston: Little, Brown.

Bennett, L. (1982), *Before the Mayflower*. Chicago: Johnson.

Berry, M. & Blassingame, J. (1982), *Long Memory*. New York: Oxford University Press.

Blose, D. & Caliver, A. (1936), *Statistics of the Education of Negroes, 1929–30; 1931–32,* Bull. 13. Washington, DC: U.S. Dept. of Interior, Office of Education.

Comer, J. (1972), *Beyond Black and White*. New York: Quadrangle.

_____ (1980), *School Power*. New York: Free Press.

Council for Financial Aid to Education. (1967), *1964–1965 Voluntary Support of America's Colleges and Universities*. New York: Council for Financial Aid to Education.

Demos, J. (1982), The changing face of fatherhood: A new exploration in American family history. In: *Father and Child,* ed. S.H. Cath, A. Gurwitt, & J.M. Ross. Boston: Little, Brown.

Edelman, M. (1987), *Families in Peril*. Cambridge, MA: Harvard University Press.

Ellis, W., Comer, J. & Rubenstein, S. (1979), Socioeconomic and racial considerations in the psychotherapeutic treatment of children and adolescents. In: *Basic Handbook of Child Psychiatry,* ed. J. Noshpitz. New York: Basic Books.

Franklin, J. (1961), *Reconstruction After the Civil War*. Chicago: University of Chicago Press.

Frazier, E. (1962), *Black Bourgeoisie*. New York: Collier.

_____ (1963), *The Negro Church in America*. New York: Schocken.

Gibbs, J., Jr., ed. (1965), *Peoples of Africa*. New York: Holt, Rinehart & Winston.

Greer, W. & Cobbs, P. (1968), *Black Rage*. New York: Basic Books.

Lidtz, T. (1963), *The Family and Human Adaptation*. New York: International Universities Press.

Meers, D. (1973), Psychoanalytic research and intellectual functioning of ghetto-reared, Black children. *The Psychoanalytic Study of the Child,* 28:395–417. New Haven: Yale University Press.

Solnit, A. & Provence, S., ed. (1963), *Modern Perspectives in Child Development*. New York: International Universities Press.

Spero, S. & Harris, A. (1968), *The Black Worker*. New York: Atheneum.

U.S. Department of Commerce, Bureau of the Census. (1983), *America's Black Population: 1970 to 1982*. Washington, DC: U.S. Government Printing Office.

Woodson, C. (1928), *The Negro in Our History*. Washington, DC: Associated.

19

Papi, or the Child Is Father to the Man

Saro Palmeri

A young father was chasing his son, a little toddler, who was playfully running away from him, in a park: "Careful, Papi," he said in Spanish, "You may get hurt. Careful, Papi."

Why would a father call his own son Papi (or Papito), the Spanish equivalent of Daddy? It is common practice in some families of Hispanic background for parents, especially fathers, to address their young sons as Papi. In a time when the evolution of fatherhood and its formative influence on children are receiving deserved attention, it seems fitting to report of this custom and to advance a psychological significance.

This practice always occurs in a milieu of emotional warmth, during moments of affection and mutual gratification, when the father seems to receive from the child as much as he offers to him. The father might say to the child, "Sit by me, Papi," or "Eat all your food, Papi," or "Go, Papi, get your toys." The word is usually used within the context of a sentence; occasionally alone, in place of the child's proper name, which Papi, however, never entirely displaces. Although clearly a term of endearment, there may be, in the sentence within which Papi is used, a tone of exhortation, but never one of anger.

Mothers may use Mama (or Mamita) for girls, but they may also, independently, address boys as Papi. The custom begins with the onset of communication in toddlerhood, flourishes during the preschool years, and fades during the oedipal years, when the need for closeness and infantilizing practices is mutually repudiated by the child and by the father. Mothers may carry the custom well into adulthood and into the middle ages of their sons (J. Suarez, 1986, personal communication).

When asked about this custom, adults invariably smile, slightly embarrassed, like lovers caught in an innocent act, unaware of what they're doing and why. The answers are always inadequate: "It is an expression of affection," or simply "I do not know." These parents clearly use Papi not by design, but with an unconscious motivation that perpetuates a practice that they may have experienced as children.

The child knows his proper name and he himself calls his father Papi. Still, he accepts the practice, enjoys it, and never questions it. But, question we must, for why should a father use for his child the same appellative that society intended for the parent?

The practice may begin with the following possible and manifest linguistic explanation: "Come [to] Papi," with the *to* conveniently left out but understood. As the practice linguistically expands, however, it becomes so discrepant and inappropriate as to betray an unconscious motivation. There is all the appearance of an identification of the father with the child, and of a role reversal. At least in the parents' unconscious mind, the boundaries between the self and the child appear indistinct. The message is out to the child that his very existence gives the father pleasure, gratification, comfort, and nurture, just as these feelings once came to the father from his nurturing parents. The father can now relive, and continue to thrive with, the memory of those wishes and experiences. In fact, not to take anything away from the child's positive experience, the object of this love affair is, in the parent's mind, never far from the subject. Attachment and identification combine with a measure of narcissistic gratification, at the roots of father's motherliness, so to speak.

In conclusion, with Papi parents seem to enact the equivalent of a parapraxis, within the context of their own developmental stage as parents, the late recapitulation of earlier stages. Other cultures may not be as intense as the Hispanic in vicariously revealing paternal parenting, but they can, of course, be equally nurturing. On the other hand, with the practice of Papi, the child himself becomes subtly aware of his own nurturing capacity (albeit toward his parents). The seeds for parenting may be cultivated this way. The child will have greater opportunities for identification with his loving father, a process that

will favorably influence the quality of his attachments, social relationships and the richness and quality of his personality growth.

"The Child is father to the Man" is the poet's metaphor (Wordsworth, 1948), recently borrowed by Pruett (1985) and by Glueck
(1986), the latter author writing in support of the notion that the
genesis of atherosclerosis is found in childhood. In fact, Papi is more
than a Freudian slip of developing parents. In the evolving developmental cycles of the human species, Papi is but another demonstration
of a fundamental biopsychological propensity for species-specific identification and for the need to nurture and to be nurtured. Human
psychological development always requires both the genetic psychological propensity for nurturing and the nurturing experience. Papi here
suggests that the former, when cultivated early, persists through life to
reemerge when appropriately evoked.

THE OTHER SIDE OF THE COIN–A POSTSCRIPT

As with Papi, observers of the Hispanic culture will just as quickly note
that aunts and uncles may use the Spanish equivalent nouns (Tia and
Tio) to extend bits of their own selves to nephews and nieces. The
dynamics here, of course, proportionately diminish in intensity and
quality. Of interest are similar practices of Papi in other countries such
as I have observed among Southern Italians, and Sicilians in particular
(where Papá is used instead), in the areas of Italy that had, centuries
before, been under Spanish rule and culture. One should not be surprised to discover similar practices in yet other countries of the Medi-
teranean basin.

As in all natural phenomena, however, beyond the range of what
may be considered innocuous, developmentally positive, or even nurturing, there exists in the Papi phenomenon the potential for the
interfering influence of too much of a good thing. What kind of
psychosexual message does a Puerto Rican boy experience when an
unmarried mother who addresses him as Papi also indulges in excessive
emotional and physical closeness such as sleeping in the same bed? Let
alone the homosexual, incestuous connotation when the message is
carried out by the father? For many sensitive little boys, this message
may be intolerable. How will this custom affect the resolution of the
oedipal complex? The child may be caught in a terrible bind, having to
love his father more than he would have otherwise. He may be torn
with guilt over the difficult choices he must make. Castration fears
invariably emerge, perhaps heightened by the closeness of the relation-

ship. Pride and guilt will compete for the primacy of the child's emotions when, among his siblings, he represents the chosen heir apparent for the perpetuation of the father's self (M. Suarez, 1986, personal communication). For if the oedipal phase should stem from a natural biopsychological propensity, then attachment, identification, and sexual identity should relate to one even more arcane natural propensity, this one laden with more serious psychopathological vulnerability.

REFERENCES

Glueck, C.J. (1986), The child is father of the man. *Pediat.,* 78:364–368.

Pruett, K.D. (1985), Oedipal Configurations In Young Father-Raised Children. *The Psychoanalytic Study of the Child,* 40:435–456. New Haven: Yale University Press.

Wordsworth, W.M. (1948), My heart leaps up when I behold. In: *Anthology of Romanticism,* 3rd ed., ed. E. Bermbaum. New York: Ronald Press, p. 217.

20

The Nurturing Male
A Longitudinal Study of Primary Nurturing Fathers
Kyle D. Pruett

This chapter summarizes a prospective, empirical, clinical investigation of intact families in which the father is the primary caretaker of the family's infants and young children. Previously reported observations (Pruett, 1983, 1984, 1985) have focused on careful delineation of the developmental profiles and characteristics of the infants and toddlers reared in such circumstances. Herein are clinical data and beginning speculations about the fathers in such families with a special focus on the psychodynamic profiles of these men. First, a brief description of the study and some preliminary findings.

At the outset, the study was conceived as a small-scale, hypothesis-generating, pilot investigation of a clinical phenomenon so unstudied that some clinical observations were required before relevant research questions could be framed. I began the inquiry as the sole researcher, thinking I could enlist aid if and when it was required. The study addressed itself broadly to four different areas: the development of the infants, the psychodynamic characteristics and nurturing patterns of the fathers, and their relationships to the infants' mothers.

Portions of this chapter first appeared in *The Nurturing Father* by Kyle D. Pruett, © 1987, and are included here with the permission of the publisher, Warner Books.

A small group of 17 families was recruited from general pediatric practices in a large New England industrial and academic community. The criterion for recruitment was that although the parenting might be shared, the father must, in the clinician's judgment, bear the major responsibility for parenting. The arrangement need not necessarily be considered long term and might consist of a working mother, unemployed father, student-father, or so-called dual-career family. Whatever the nurturing circumstance, it allowed for the formation of a primary affectional tie between father and infant. Though not by research design, the infants available for study all were firstborn into families that ranged across the socioeconomic spectrum from welfare through blue-collar and white-collar workers to professional. The children ranged in age from 2 to 22 months at the time of entry into the study, with a mean of 8 months for females and 12 months for males. Sex distribution was eight male and nine female infants. The parents ranged in age from 19 to 36, with a mean age of 24 for fathers and 25 for mothers.

Here I can offer only a cursory review of the initial findings: (1) Children raised primarily by men can be active, robust, and thriving infants. These infants also may be especially comfortable with, and attracted to, stimulation from the external environment. The majority of study infants functioned above the expected norms on standardized tests of development. The youngest group of infants (2–12 months) often performed problem-solving tasks on a level of babies four to eight months their senior; personal and social skills were two to six months ahead of schedule. The older babies in the group (12–22 months) performed as well. (2) These fathers could form the reciprocal nurturing attachment so important in the early development of the thriving human organism. (3) The style and choice of caretaking seemed to have been drawn from the father's own adaptive, though often narcissistic, wish to nurture and be nurtured. The time-honored mechanism of parental projective identification with the helpless, omnipotent infant in promoting empathic attachment to, and attunement with, one's infant, so well appreciated and researched in mother-infant caregiving, clearly is at work here as well. But the actual caregiving style is not merely that of a mother's substitute ("in loco matris"). (4) The paternal caregiving style is a distillate of selected identifications with the important objects in his own life. Therefore, such nurturing capacities do not seem wholly determined by either genetic endowment or gender identity.

Interestingly, the manner and chronology in which these families decided on this caretaking system had little bearing on how well the children developed. The decisions could be grouped roughly into thirds: the first third decided *before* the pregnancy, the second, *during* the pregnancy, and the third, during the *neonatal period*. The last group usually was pressed into the choice for economic reasons, that is, father lost his job, mother did not. The timing of the decision could not be correlated with how the child did on developmental examination.

The main support for the preliminary findings lies in the clinical material from the study. With the use of retrospective, analytically oriented interviewing techniques, the fathers were interviewed first at home while caring for their infants. Extensive histories were taken, and naturalistic observations were recorded of the father–infant dyad in the process of typical child care. Within one to two weeks of this initial interview, the babies were examined in a laboratory setting at the Child Development Unit of the Yale Child Study Center. The Yale Developmental Schedules were used to assess in detail their developmental competence in gross and fine motor performance, adaptive problem solving, language skills, and personal-social function. A final interview, again preferably at home and usually the most extensive, was conducted with both mother and father to obtain a marital history and to record further naturalistic observations about the family triad. Two years after entering the study, all the original families (except for one who had left the area) were studied again using the original, somewhat expanded, investigation method with increased emphasis on paternal development. Seven of the families had borne second children. The father continued as the primary caregiving parent in half of these families, as well as in four of the remaining only-child families. For six of the 16 families, fathers had returned to work or school and had ceased to serve as the primary parent. There had been one divorce, with the father retaining custody.

As before, the children's performance on the Yale Developmental Schedules was especially strong in the areas of adaptive problem-solving and personal-social function (Pruett, 1985). Also, the benefits of a biparental nidus of nurturing, where active though differentiated parenting flowed from both mother and father, were corroborated further (Pruett, 1984, 1985).

Buoyed by the reassurance that father care is not inherently noxious to the human infant or its family, we turned our attention to the father as a developing organism in his own right. What of *his* developmental profile? What are these men actually like? What of their histories? Are there unique, idiosyncratic profiles that set them apart from their more remotely nurturing peers? What of their adolescent growth and differentiation? Are there any harbingers or predictors to be gleaned? In addressing these questions, especially the last one, I must mention a shortcoming of this study. I first met these men when they had already fathered a child, and all, except for one, were, at least by chronological measure, adults. Therefore, almost all the clinical material regarding these men's childhood and adolescent years is retrospective, consciously remembered and reported data about a period of life that, in the case of the adolescent years, in particular, is notoriously inaccessible to conscious recall, even though only recently concluded. Moreover, before we begin to consider the clinical material itself, another caution regarding the study size is warranted. The study originally was designed as an hypothesis-generating clinical inquiry. Therefore, its small size invites speculation and hypothesis generation but probably precludes statistically rigorous conclusions.

First, a broad sketch of this group of 17 self-selected men ranging in age from 19 to 36 and stretching across the socioeconomic spectrum, though predominantly middle class. All 17 reported themselves as having been parented traditionally. Thirteen of the men came from intact families. The other four had lived predominantly with their mothers until beginning their own families. The average number of siblings was 2.6, ranging from none to seven.

Six men had attended private school for all or part of their secondary education. Fifteen of the 17 men spent most of their first post-high school year living away from home, the other two remaining with their families. All 17 reported that, as teenagers they had seemed headed toward the expected role of worker and father as protector and provider. *None* would have predicted as teenagers that they would be rearing their children.

Few recalled giving any thought when they were adolescents to what might be gained or lost for them personally through nurturing a child. The immediacy of attending to, and controlling, their own instinctual needs during that era seemed to eclipse interest in or reflection about any other children in their lives. When these men did think about fathering, it was in terms of phallic pride in siring an offspring through exhibited fertility and genital potency, and not through fulfillment of nurturing competence.

Three of the 17 men reported having undergone some form of either psychotherapy or counseling for a brief period during adolescence, and there were no reported hospitalizations. Only four of the 17 men reported active memories of having had anything more than casual involvement with young children or infants. Three of these men had been involved with infants born into their immediate families during their adolescence. One man lived transiently during his adolescence with a family friend who sheltered at-risk foster children.

Simply stated, based on retrospective reporting, these men appeared to themselves, as they quite possibly might have appeared to us, as having developed within norms concomitant with their social and familial variables. Taken as a whole, it was an unremarkable group with little to distinguish it from any other self-selected group of young men. However, some subtle subgroupings proved interesting.

Five of the six men who had chosen earliest (prior to conception) to serve as the primary nurturing parent tended to describe their fathers as uninvolved in their lives, most particularly during adolescence. Only here, at the extremes of the spectrum of parental choice, do we see any clustering of common experience. These men who chose early (with their wives) to serve as primary parent tended to report their own fathers as "absent . . . gone a lot . . . distant." These early choosers, with their perception of paternal absence coupled with a particularly vivid maternal presence, seemed as a group to demonstrate a "preadaptation" to being actively nurturing. Their nurturant role identifications seemed more strongly to be with their mothers. They seemed to pair in marriage primarily with women of more independent strivings who did not seek their primary fulfillment in life through nurturing. This raises the strong possibility of a kind of triggering mechanism in which particular women who were less predisposed to a lifelong nurturing role "triggered" the expression of that role in men possibly predisposed for it. This may have been especially determinative among the small group of "early chooser" first births.

It is important to note that this was a minority subgroup of the study population. This group was differentiated not only by the early choice to nurture, but also by higher income and more advanced education. These families tended to have long-range goals and timetables, but formal and casual, to achieve them.

Interestingly, those women who assumed the primary caregiving role after the second pregnancy tended to report their own mothers as being "unhappy . . . cold . . . unavailable." They felt more strongly affiliated with their fathers, who were generally experienced as nurturing and supportive. These women also reported feeling less competitive with their husbands and tended to identify positively with their nurturing of the first baby.

Eight of the remaining 11 men spoke of their families in predominantly positive terms, irrespective of how physically available the father was. The virtual absence of a middle group is intriguing; this will be discussed at greater length later.

Well, what of these identifications, dis-identifications, and predilections to fatherliness or, perhaps more accurately, nurturing? To elucidate some of the real changes these men experienced within themselves prior to and during the process of primary parenting, let us review the stories of two men.

CASE ILLUSTRATION

At 19, Mr. Ames, tall, bearded, wiry, intense man was the youngest father in the study. I first met him behind his rented house in a structure that served as a photographic studio and darkroom. The decor was notable in that its chief motif was some half dozen 2' × 4' enlargements of the ultrasound Polaroids taken of his daughter, Susan, in utero during the last trimester of his wife's pregnancy. Susan now was bouncing up and down animatedly on a Jolly Jump Up stretched between two tripods while she drooled and contentedly gummed an unemployed lens cap. Mr. Ames described himself as "being high for two weeks when she was born; she nailed me right there in the delivery room." (Susan was now 8 1/2 months old, and Mr. Ames still looked rather intoxicated to me.)

In describing his family of origin, he called it one of "your typical American composites." Each of his parents was still in the community and still quite involved in his life, although each had remarried after divorcing when he was 16. He had one older brother and two younger stepsisters.

He reported that his experience with his parents' marriage had been quite an unhappy one, and during his first intense relationship with a girl as an adolescent, he felt himself panicked when she asked for a third date. "I always thought I'd rather die than marry." Although he still has strong and positive relationships with both parents, Mr. Ames reported initially that he "felt funny and kind of odd whenever I fed Susan in front of my mother or father. I don't think she liked it much, either. We've just learned not to do it when they're around."

Mr. Ames had moved out of his home when he was 15 and gone to live with an aunt and uncle who lived two miles away from his parents' home. He reported that his relationship with his mother and father got better instantly, and he was able to be of some support to each of them when they divorced a year later. He continued in high school after leaving home, and his grades and social status improved. Living next door to his aunt and uncle was a family who offered temporary shelter for many battered and abused children. Mr. Ames found himself spending long periods of time in that home, being drawn to young children and their riveting life stories and what we clinicians probably would call their indiscriminate friendliness.

By 18, he had finished high school, married, and was hired as a commercial photographer by a small advertising firm. His father, who had worked as a successful advertising promoter, had taken an early interest in his son's talents in drawing and sketching and had, over his wife's objections, supported his son's interest in the graphic arts.

Mr. Ames reported that his favorite subjects for his photography were children. "I took a lot of pictures of kids for their families, albums, and Christmas presents. I could not stand to see the parents push the kids around during shootings. Soon I realized I could handle many of the kids better than the parents could in my studio and got much better pictures besides."

Mr. Ames spoke animatedly about how profound his experience as a father had been, though not without complicated feeling and affect. "When I became a father I stopped feeling like a punk. It was like I was more my own father's equal."

Although this young father feels his child is the most important thing in his life, he sometimes is distressed at the envy he feels over the attention and affection his daughter receives. It is as though this 19-year-old feels a narcissistic competition with his own child, indicating that his own adolescent closure may not be fully achieved yet. He reported some similar feelings during the end of his wife's pregnancy: "I had this monster baby dream about three times. It was funny that I actually remembered it was like the monster that used to scare me a lot when I had dreams at summer camp when I was 12 or 13." In spite of all he was feeling about the importance of his daughter in his life, he seemed to be suffering—and I suspect this is not rare—what Benedek (1970) described as "the flow of repressed memories and emotions of the father's developmental experiences which may become mobilized in response to the child's development" (p. 173).

As this interview was concluding, Mrs. Ames turned to the topic of his marriage. Mrs. Ames, two years older than her husband, was a head waitress at a successful, established local restaurant. Her job and salary were upgraded just at the time, shortly after Susan was born, when her husband lost his job in his family's auto parts business. His wife asked him how he'd "feel taking over with the baby for a while." He casually agreed (typical of several of the "late deciding" families), and "Susan didn't seem to mind."

How was this decision affecting his marriage? Mr. Ames commented that his marriage seemed to be off to a good start.

> That's really important to me. My parents were very unhappily married; they fought like George and Martha in 'Who's Afraid of

Virginia Woolf?' I guess I was kind of lucky. I got a chance to move out while I could still keep a good relationship going with both of them, even my mother, who was really giving me the silent treatment. I'm not sure any good feelings would have lasted if I had stayed.[1]

As I turned to leave, I commented on his daughter's enjoyment of her father's photographic equipment. "You know, it's weird," he said, "my mother was a weaver, and she wove this scarf for me when I was about ten. I still wear it around my neck, even when it's not winter. I guess it's important to have a piece of the old love around."

Meanwhile, what *were* those "old loves" thinking about all of this? The acceptance of this child-care arrangement by the grandparents varied widely—a not unexpected reaction from a very heterogenous group of adults who spanned three decades. At the time of entry into the study, the youngest was a 42-year-old grandfather, the oldest a 71-year-old grandmother.

Typically the fathers found very little support from their own mothers *or* fathers at the beginning, though there were prominent exceptions. The fathers' fathers, as a group, initially seemed to be bewildered, confused, and even saddened that their sons had chosen to "stay home" instead of doing things that more closely resembled the wishes and values the grandfathers "thought" they shared with their sons. The majority of the grandfathers seemed to act this out by withdrawing from the new parents and their offspring. The fathers' mothers, though often just as confused and saddened as the grandfathers, tended to withdraw less and remained more actively curious, talking more frequently with their sons about child-care methods and, as one father reported, "generally trying to promote good 'mothering' habits." Judged empirically, it seemed a bit easier on both grandparents if their son was caring for a grand*daughter,* presumably because the cross-gender male-female attachment carried fewer tabos than the same gender, male-male attachment.

Nevertheless, this initial universal distancing of the grandparents was painful and confusing for these fathers. Some were angry, some depressed, some denied feeling "anything" about the initial withdrawal. These early complex reactions usually were compounded by the fact that their spouses were undergoing similar rebuffs with their

---

[1]It is tempting to conclude, although "speculate" is more disciplined, that Mr. Ames may have found his adequate mothering by "being" an adequate "mother" to his child, thereby actively mastering a passive deficit.

own extended families. Their responses differed slightly in that the mothers' mothers seemed especially troubled, or as Mrs. Ames described it, the "idea of it just blew my mother away. There was *no way* I could make her understand our choice. It was like I was talking a foreign language to her." Mothers' fathers, though often as bewildered, stayed in closer touch, usually with piqued curiosity.

In the end, however, all the grandparents had closed the gap by the two-year followup. The study parents almost universally credited the babies. Mr. Ames reported, "She just wore 'em down with that smile. They never had a chance."

CASE ILLUSTRATION

I first met Mr. David, a medium-built, athletic, clean-shaven, easygoing man of 24 in the small kitchen of their new condominium, where he and his 12-year-old daughter were preparing dinner. "I do the work; she provides the music," referring to her animated babbling as she followed him about. The oldest of five children, with two younger sisters and two younger brothers, he was from an upper middle-class, suburban family, led by a father who was in the foreign services.

Like all the other men to varying degrees, Mr. Davis found himself in "hot water" with his family of origin when he originally announced his plans to leave his job and raise their children when it was born. Both he and his wife of two years, also 24, became employees of a utility company upon graduating from college. He had been quite unhappy with the way the institution was dealing with him, while his wife enjoyed a series of promotions and salary increases. He was contemplating a job change and had decided, to his wife's surprise and delight, that in the interim he would like to raise their planned child. (The Davises thus fit into the early deciding group.) Mr. Davis had been deeply involved in the pregnancy, as evidenced by his ten-pound weight gain, primarily the sequel of consuming large quantities of milk and crackers. He was "profoundly moved" by the delivery and set about his task with enthusiasm and vigor.

Gradually he became keenly aware of the social isolation of being the only father he knew who was raising an infant. He was invited by several women in the neighborhood to join them on their morning strolls with their babies around their pleasant suburban community. He resisted initially, reporting a very vivid memory of the times his sisters tried to urge him to play dolls with them. "I hated it at first. But then I noticed that it was a relief from the loneliness and tedium of the soap operas and industry. I began to feel some admiration from them of what I was doing and the job I was doing raising our daughter. Now we're all fast friends."

Mr. Davis described his own childhood as quite comfortable, full of friendships, enough sexual activity as a teenager to "keep me from feelig freaked out," some mild drug experimentation, and an increasingly close relationship with his mother. He felt important to her in helping her manage the large family and described her as "the boss, but she stopped short of domineering."

His father was away for extended periods of time on diplomatic missions. Occasionally, between absences, he was home for long stretches and very involved, but then he would disappeare again for months at a time. During his son's adolescence, his father was gone seven months out of the year. Mr. Davis spontaneously reported, "This was probably not a bad plan, even though I'm sure he didn't work it out that way on purpose. It was when I was beginning to think he was really kind of a turkey that he left, and I often managed to feel a little better about him while he was gone."

He described his mother as

> my model. . . . I helped her a lot, and she taught me how to become quite a good cook. Her mood was always light and stable. We certainly had our times, but not for long. You might think this is surprising, but it was really my wife who wanted kids first, not me. I really wanted to get my job rolling. She had been previously married for a short time and had had to have an abortion. I really felt we needed a little more time, and I wanted to get my career established, which I did. When we began to think about kids and how to divide the child care appropriately, it seemed quite natural for me to consider taking this break in my career to raise our daughter.

While we were talking, his daughter, Sarah, crawled up onto his lap and buried her head on his chest. He paused and looked longingly into the eyes of his daughter, who was just beginning to stir in his arms, and said, "But I'm not sure she's ever going to get rid of me."

This theme of resisting separation from the important objects in his life already had affected his feelings about Sarah. He had had to leave for two weeks on what he called a "job safari" when Sarah was ten months old, which marked the first prolonged separation between him and his wife and their daughter. He was stunned to find out from his wife during his absence that Sarah's appetite had decreased, her mood and temperament had "fallen apart," she became clingy, and she was tearful almost constantly. He reported that he had felt so awful upon hearing this that he lost his *own* appetite. He said, "I'm sure I blew an interview, maybe even on purpose."

Mr. Davis feels that his father has been much more supportive of his choice than his mother has been, although he feels "she's coming around, mostly thanks to this dynamite little number." He tousled his daughter's curls. He reports occasional waves of envy as he watches his father play with his daughter. He longs for active memories of his father having been that involved with him, but none seem to come. "My father had really been a pal when he *was* there, but, for the most part, what I remember most is his being gone."

DISCUSSION

There are many paths down which this clinical material might lead us. Where we want to go is toward an understanding of the fathering manifest in these men and its possible relationship to their own development. We also want to generate the appropriate questions to be addressed in more definitive, prospective studies on fathers who proceed with their lives in this way. This is important now, particularly because of the remarkable historical shift that has brought fathers into increasingly direct contact with their own infants and often the mothers into correspondingly less contact.

It has been interesting throughout this work to speculate why so much has *not* been done in this area. I am fond of Benedek's (1970) explanation:

> The psychobiology of fatherhood seems to have evaded investigation as if it were hidden by the physiology of male sexuality and by the vital socioeconomic function of fathers as providers. While biology defines the role which the male invariably plays in the propagation of the species, the role of fathers as providers changes with cultural and socioeconomic conditions [p. 167].

In this effort to repair such deficits, let us return to thinking about this material with specific reference to certain developmental constructs. I would like to summarize the clinical material typified by Mr. Ames and Mr. Davis with regard to several different constructs of male adult development – arbitrarily, but I hope wisely, chosen – that seem to highlight these men's developmental experience and preoccupations. For most of the men in the study, adolescence was a trek only recently completed. Thus, its normative characteristics weave an important backdrop for their choice to become primary nurturing fathers.

"Masculine identity" seemed to preoccupy the typical study father through the wish to grow as much as possible in *size* during adolescence. Physical strength was important in compensating for awkwardness. Unlike competitiveness, tenderness and intimacy typically were reported as unwelcome feelings or demands (in relationships). "Stand up to Dad [and other males]" was the rule, rather than the exception. Sixteen of 17 had held jobs during high school, typically to make money. Though they often chafed against, and longed for, their father's authority, admiration by friends, especially girlfriends, seemed a much greater prize.

Alienation was only a transient, minor condition for these men. Almost all the study fathers described themselves as richly befriended during adolescence, when membership in social, athletic, and religious organizations, both formal and informal, provided stability as they age-typically experimented with a variety of roles. There was little delinquency or involvement with authoritarian social or community agencies. "Belonging" was seen by most of the men as important in managing the limbo of the adolescent years. Only one of the 17 men had embraced alienation as a personality style during adolescence as a carefully crafted "hippie." He was amused by it now, as though it had been a ruse.

For the majority of the men in the study, becoming a father in such a devoted and focused manner seemed to provide a secure anchorage for the whole of their adult development. It was, or became, a choice and commitment of such great depth that it served as an ongoing, growth-promoting experience, encouraging personal flexibility and empathy. It also promoted confidence in a generous and capable self that was crucial to the very survival of another human being.

Conversely, might the mother's work, especially if she was able to *choose* to work, serve as a secure anchorage for her young adult development, freeing her from a possibly premature maternity? This seemed especially operative in those women who chose to come home after the birth of the second sibling and take over the role of the primary nurturing parent.

As far as social adjustment was concerned, 14 of the 17 fathers reported that they had begun dating by their last year in high school. This is a percentage similar to that reported in Offer and Offer's (1975) study of normal adolescence. Typically, most of the men did not see their first dating experiences as either friendships or especially important relationships. Affirmation of their own sexual identity seemed more crucial. Intimacy was not a hallmark of their early experiences. Looking at social class variables as a predictor of later interest in fathering, I would share, from this small study, the conclusion with Vaillant (1977) in the thirty-year Grant Study of male psychological health that

> social variables played no role in distinguishing poor fathers from good fathers. Subjects who had grown up in upper class families buffered from their parents by many servants did not make worse fathers than those who had grown up in more closely knit middle class homes; the latter did not make better fathers than the upwardly mobile, socially disadvantaged men who had more of an economic struggle in the early years after college. Many upwardly mobile men are bad fathers, but so are many downwardly mobile men [p. 318].

Having reviewed these normative constructs, let us turn to some areas of interest that seem especially poignant in a population of men who find themselves professional, if unpaid, nurturers: paternal identification, maternal identification, and experience with infants.

Paternal Identification

Signs of rivalrous or competitive relationships with fathers during adolescence were quite obvious from descriptions of these men's relationships with their own fathers. Yet, in these traditionally raised men, who now were being so *untraditional* in their own fathering, would we find idiosyncratic forms of identification with the father? During the second individuation process of adolescence described by Blos (1967), it is the final establishment of a strong identification with the father as a competent male figure that reinforces the son's strivings for independence from the mother. The men in this particular group were either quite close to or quite distant from their fathers during adolescence. These men, through nurturing their own babies, either were chafing against conflicts felt about unavailable fathers or were reveling in the strong identification of a nurturing, protecting, feeling father.

Interestingly enough, however, few of the men in the study could be called neutral. Soule, Standley, and Copans (1979), studying 70 prospective fathers in a longitudinal study of parent–infant interaction in an attempt to delineate father identity, found that men who had very high father-identity scores on interviews tended to report either very negative or very positive early relationships with their own fathers. Does this suggest that a strong sense of oneself as a father may be rooted in the family of origin, in which the father saw his own father as being psychologically distant and now is looking forward to constructing emotional ties with a new family of his own making in which he will be the longed for parent? Pleasant memories of being fathered or, conversely, lingering dissatisfaction with the relationship may impel a man either to repeat or to remake his past. A vital sense of fatherliness seems to have strong roots in either one's own father's caring or perceived emotional distance.

Maternal Identification

As all of these men were raised traditionally, their primary nurturing relationship had been with their own mothers. Curiously, although mothers often were described as important, "the boss . . . sometimes wearing the pants," there was not a domineering or hostile mother described in the group. Valliant (1977) reported as one of his most impressive findings that

> the image of the dominating mother seemed more a reflection of a young man's immaturity or of his mother's poor mental health than a reflection of actual strength or dominance in the mother . . . dominating mothers were rarely strong women, and in fact were often emotionally ill. Their power to dominate came more from their, or their son's, view of reality than from their own too loving or powerful nature [p. 136].

Yet how have these men managed to find themselves so thoroughly "mothering"? Articulating a feeling shared in some fashion with all the study fathers, Mr. Davis thoughtfully concluded toward the end of our first interview, "Talking about this makes me think how odd it is that I have become both a mother *and* a father. I really love it . . . so far." Clearly, the identification with mother is quite strong, particularly in the subgroup of men who chose to be primary parent earlier rather than later.

How have these men arrived at their own idiosyncratic ego ideals of what a father should be? If they have so thoroughly identified with their mothers' *acts* of nurturing, what are we to assume they have internalized of their mothers' *ideals* of what a father should be? It seems most unlikely these men were enacting or fulfilling their mothers' paternal ideas, given how initially unhappy most of the mothers were with their sons' choices. Nor, for that matter, can we make a strong case for such behavior or wishes being passed from father to son. Witness all the initially unhappy grandfathers.

I believe such questions are of vital interest, yet no clinical material, save a random anecdote here and there, has appeared yet to explain adequately this model of the paternal nurturing ideal: a very fruitful area for further inquiry.

For all men who have struggled and mourned over never bearing a child conflicts exist between the desire for intimacy with a child and the sublimation of work. The men in this study have found, at least for the present, particularly fulfilling sublimations that have allowed them to both father and mother in ways that have been quite ego-syntonic for them and often for their wives. I suspect the success of the sublimation also is evident in the relative, though far from complete, absence of rivalry and competition between these couples, especially the younger ones, where more might be expected.

Experience with Infants and Children

It was surprising to find so little previous experience with young children in the study population. In the Soule et al. (1979) study of father identity, merely *liking children* appeared not to be a significant source of fatherly feelings, but men who did have extensive experience with infants seemed to be "fathering enthusiasts." This also was true of the men who had chosen earliest to nurture their infants. Possibly the more interesting segment of the study population are the six who did not have extensive prefathering experience. Often they had to overcome their reluctance to assume the nurturing role – and in some cases resentment over having had it thrust on them. Nonetheless, they went on to achieve intensely mutual, need-satisfying reciprocity with their own infants.

Finally, might we be looking at a three-generational flow of the psychodynamics of fatherhood, strongly influenced by the far-reaching economic and social sequelae of what Lasch (1982) has called our "age of narcissism"? What of the qualities of genuine fatherliness that these men exhibit toward their infants? Given that the diversity of their fathering equals the diversity of most families' mothering, it is clear that there is no generic primary nurturing father discernible or describable here. Benedek (1970) defines fatherliness as

> an instinctually rooted character trend which enables the father to act toward his child or all children with immediate emphatic

responsiveness. It is not rooted as directly as fatherhood, itself, in the instinct for survival in the child, yet it is derivative of the reproductive drive organization. Its sources can be traced to the biological bisexuality and the biologic dependency of the mother. . . . It is the result not only of memory traces originating in the infant boy's oral, alimentary experiences with the mother, but these become integrated with memory traces of the boy's developmental experiences with his father [p. 175].

Would such fatherliness have been evident in all the men who self-selected themselves for this study had we been privileged to meet them earlier? I somehow doubt it. The *capacity* to father certainly is rooted more broadly in the biological matrix than is the *expression* of fathering. Although it is not the subject of our discourse, it is vital that we not neglect the enormous capacity of the infant to elicit, evoke, promote, provoke, and nudge fathering from men.

Further evidence of the strong attachment between father and child appeared when almost two-thirds of the men who returned to work or school, even those who did so after the birth of the second child, experienced some reluctance to leave the child in their wife's care. One middle-class father, who returned to his real estate firm, called from the commuter train station daily for weeks "just checking to make sure everything was fine. I was embarrassed feeling that way, but I got paranoid once wondering if I should leave her with my wife. Can you believe that?"

My secret hope at the outset of the study to at least begin to delineate a description of a nurturing character or predisposition in men who become primary nurturing parents has fallen short of fruition. With the small exception of the early-choosing fathers, no generalizations about "typical characteristics" of either the men doing the primary nurturing or the women letting them are yet possible. It is conceivable to me, now that I've come to know this diverse group of families over time, that there never may be such a list. In any case, much more data need to be harvested before such profiles or their lack are defined.

In summary, neither these men nor their wives are an unusually homogeneous lot with strongly delineated idiosyncracies that predict and determine their parenting choices and behavior. Instead, we find a predominantly healthy, heterogeneous group of men (with some subtle predispositions, such as paternal absence in the early choosing group) who are deeply committed to raising their children in ways that are of paramount importance to them and their spouses. A compelling quartet of powerful people makes them tick–mother, father, mate, and baby.

So . . . is the child father to man? . . . any man?

In closing, I'd like to open a fascinating linguistic window on who is nurturing whom that recently was shared with me by Saro Palmeri, M.D. He long has noted a prevalent tendency among Spanish fathers, during moments of affection and mutual gratification with their children, to address their children as *Papi,* the Spanish equivalent of "Daddy." The lesson starts early (see ch. 18, this volume).

REFERENCES

Benedek, T. (1970), Fatherhood and providing. In: *Parenthood,* ed. E.J. Anthony & T. Benedek. Boston: Little, Brown, pp. 167–183.

Blos, P. (1967), The second individuation process of adolescence. *The Psychoanalytic Study of the Child,* 22:162–186. New York: International Universities Press.

Lasch, C. (1978), *The Culture of Narcissism.* New York: Norton.

Offer, D. & Offer, J. (1975), *From Teenage to Young Manhood.* New York: Basic Books.

Pruett, K.D. (1983), Infants of primary nurturing fathers. *The Psychoanalytic Study of the Child,* 38:257–281. New Haven: Yale University Press.

_____ (1984), Children of the father-mothers: Infants of primary nurturing fathers. In: *Frontiers of Infant Psychiatry,* Vol. 2, ed. J. Call, E. Galenson & R. Tyson. New York: Basic Books, pp. 375–380.

_____ (1985), Oedipal configurations in young father-raised children. *The Psychoanalytic Study of the Child,* 40:435–456. New Haven: Yale University Press.

Soule, B., Standley, K. & Copans, S. (1979), Father identity. *Psychiat.,* 42:255–263.

Valliant, G. (1977), *Adaptation to Life.* Boston: Little, Brown.

VI

DISRUPTED FAMILIES

21

So Near and Yet So Far
The Nonresident Father
Carol S. Michaels

In clinical case studies, the absent father has been recognized as a powerful force (Neubauer, 1960; Burlingham, 1973; Wolfenstein, 1973). Absent fathers often appear in the play, fantasies, and thoughts of father-absent children (Bach, 1945; Thomes, 1968; Wallerstein and Kelly, 1975). Freud and Burlingham (1939–45) reported that children construct father fantasies even when the father-child relationship is almost nonexistent in reality. Early father absence is associated with greater vulnerability, causing more deleterious and longlasting effects in cognitive development, scholastic achievement, and the attainment of a masculine self-concept than does later father absence (Santrock, 1970; Biller and Bahm, 1971; Blanchard and Biller, 1971; Radin, 1976; Thompson, 1978). Few manifest differences exist in the masculine behavior of kindergarten black and white father-absent boys, but black boys make less typically masculine choices in sex-role orientation than do their white counterparts (Biller, 1968). Such subtle differences

This chapter is a condensed version of the original report of this research project. More detailed information pertaining to the statistical data, instruction and scoring manual, demographic facts, pilot studies, and samples of the measuring instruments are available in Michaels (1981).

raise questions about the varying impact of father absence on children of different ethnic groups (TenHouten, 1970; Radin, 1974; Adams and Horovitz, 1980).

The bulk of the literature on father absence pertains to boys. Even if hypotheses seem easier to formulate and investigate for boys than for girls, research studies suggest that father-absent girls also have difficulties, usually related to their sense of femininity and well-being (Hetherington, 1972; Kristal, 1978). Although the frequency of contact between the young child and the absent father has received little attention, Wallerstein and Kelly (1975) observed that the father-child relationship often became more consistent and affectionate if the absent father remained in contact with his preschool child.

Many theorists believe that when father is absent, the mother assumes an even more influential position from which to interpret the father to the child (Cath, 1982). As the remaining parent, her attitude to the father and child seems as crucial to development and adjustment as is the father's absence (Biller, 1971a; b; Siegler, 1983). Clausen (1966) believes that the mother's attitude toward men in general is also influential.

To date, the major research study that explored children's fantasies about the father considered fantasies of school age children whose fathers were away at war (Bach, 1946). Their fantasy father was more affectionate, more fun, more predictable, and less hostile toward his family than the fantasy father created by children whose father was present. However, little is known about the young child's view of today's absent father.

The research reported here was precipitated by the paucity of studies that explore the effects of father absence during the child's first three years, although early father absence seems the most detrimental, and the first three years of childhood are widely accepted as critical to the developmental process. The project was designed to ascertain father fantasies of father-absent preschoolers and examine the relationship between these fantasies and the date the father left home, the amount of father contact, sex and ethnic background of the child, and the mother's attitude toward the child's father. The focus is on paternal absence caused by divorce, permanent separation, or abandonment, rather than death; there is a growing number of preschoolers without fathers living in the home due to circumstances of divorce, permanent separation, or abandonment. Clinical and research findings suggest that paternal loss through death constitutes a different experience for both mother and child than does loss by other means (Santrock and

Wohlford, 1970; Hetherington, 1972; Santrock, 1972; Furman, 1974; Clower, 1978).

Although comparative statistics from a control group would have been desirable, inclusion of a control group turned out to be unrealistic. This study should therefore be viewed as exploratory rather than conclusive in nature.

Several terms require defining. *Nonresident father* refers to fathers who left home for reasons of divorce, separation, or abandonment. This term is preferred over the more usual term, father absence, because it emphasizes the actual living situation without implying that father is not an active physical and psychological presence in the child's life. *Onset age* refers to the age of the child when father ceased living at home. *Frequency of contact* refers to the amount of direct personal contact between nonresident father and child, characterized by spontaneously or regularly planned visits and is categorized as follows: never (0), seldom (1-12 days per year), regularly (13-52 days per year), and often (53-352) days per year). While the majority of children saw their nonresident fathers 1 to 52 times per year, the frequency scores for all of the children were normally distributed among the four categories. *Maternal attitude to nonresident father* refers to the mother's feelings and opinions about the nonresident father and is measured by the Maternal Attitude Toward Nonresident Father Scale (MANRF) constructed for use in this study. The scale consists of statements such as "I hope that my son/daughter will grow up to be like his/her father" and "My child's father is someone I trust." *Maternal attitude to men* refers to opinions about men and male-female relationships as measured by the Male-Female Antagonism Scale (MFAS) constructed by Taleporos (1974). *Father fantasies* elicited by the doll play technique are defined by symbolic play actions that involve and pertain to the father doll. Fantasies are grouped into "good," "bad" and "silhouette" categories. The "good" and "bad" definitions are borrowed from Bach (1946). These designations are not meant as judgments or to imply that such dichotomies are easily distinguishable. Rather they represent an attempt to operationally grasp and define the child's view of the nonresident father based on our understanding that preschool children tend to comprehend in concrete and polarized terms. "Good" father fantasies are assumed when affectionate, heroic, sexual, and elated mood actions or interactions with the father doll are manifest. "Bad" father fantasies are assumed when doll dramatizations are characterized by aggressive, authoritarian, withdrawn, sad, or depressed mood. The "silhouette" mode created for this study is derived from Bach's (1946) stereotyped category. "Silhouette" father fantasies are indicated by passive, stereo-typed actions that are expected and predictably occur. These include typical greetings such as hello, good morning, or good night. For example, the father doll mechanically enters and says good morning or leaves for work with no other accompanying play interaction. The expansion of Bach's stereotyped fantasies into the "silhouette" cate-gory was intended to further our understanding of the child's use of this type of fantasy and to detect a sense of father that seems more like a caricature than a real, lifelike, and individualized person.

METHOD

Ninety-six pairs of consenting mothers and children in attendance at publicly funded urban full-day preschool programs participated in the study. The participants were from diverse religious and ethnic back-grounds. Of the 53 girls and 43 boys, 33.3% were white, 27.1% were Hispanic, and 39.6% were black. All of the nonresident fathers had left home before their children's third birthday. The children, now be-tween five and six years of age, had experienced at least a two-year adjustment period since their fathers' departures. This precluded any acute or transitory effects of father absence at the time of this study. Nonresident fathers were not included in the project. A sufficient number of them could not be contacted and the request to do so precipitated so much anxiety and antagonism in the mothers that it threatened their participation.

Several measuring instruments were used. The first, the *Maternal Questionnaire* (MQ), addresses specific variables such as onset age, fre-quency of contact, and other pertinent demographic information.

The second measure, the *Maternal Attitude Toward Nonresident Father Scale* (MANRF), is a summated rating scale with high reliability (alpha = .92). It consists of statements that reflect either positive or negative feelings toward the nonresident father. Respondents indicate the ex-tent to which they agree or disagree with each statement. A high score indicates a more positive attitude (range 20-100). Since 60 represents a neutral score, the mean score for the mothers in the study ($M = 46.04$; $SD = 16.96$) reflects a slightly negative attitude. The results showed that mothers feel better toward fathers who see the child more fre-quently and who left home later. It was found that women who had more contact with their own nonresident fathers had a more positive attitude toward the nonresident fathers of their own children. The study showed that as the maternal attitude to the nonresident father becomes more positive, the woman's perceptions of male-female antagonism become less antagonistic.

A third measure, Taleporos's (1974) *Male-Female Antagonism Scale* (MFAS) depicts men and male-female relationships as negative and characterized by exploitation and dominance. For example, women agreed or disagreed with statements like "No matter how sincere a man seems, he usually has a ulterior motive for being nice to a woman." The MFAS retained high reliability (alpha = .84) for use with single-parent women. Findings showed that the women in this study did not perceive men as especially negative nor relationships between men and women as particularly hostile. The MANRF is affected by variables that relate directly to the child (length of father absence, frequency of contact), whereas the MFAS is unrelated to these variables. This suggests that the two scales measure different facets of womens' attitudes to men.

Symbolic games are most prominent in four- to seven-year-olds whose coherence of thought is more readily displayed in play than in verbal expression (Piaget and Inhelder, 1969). Doll play was selected as the measure of the dependent variable (father fantasies) since it accommodates the limitation and variance in expressive verbal abilities in preschool children. And, most important, it considers the potentially anxiety-provoking and emotionally laden issue of the nonresident father in a relatively benign manner.

The doll play technique used is also adapted from Bach (1946). Children provided with a doll family and apartment were asked to make up stories. The dramatizations and verbalizations of the dolls were quantified by raters using an observational scoring system. The child's doll play actions were considered his fantasies; those responses which pertained to the father doll were considered the child's father fantasies.

Each doll action constituted a separate fantasy. The fantasy score was based on the number and type of fantasies produced. Twenty-three categories found significant in the theoretical and research literature were operationally defined: nurturing; playful; supportive, instructive; caretaking; protective; daredevil acts; admiration; romantic; curiosity, exploratory; elated, happy; depressed, sad; killing; hurts, injuries; oral aggression; inanimate; commands, orders; physically forces; hiding, escaping; submission; staring, gazing; standing, sitting, lying; stereotyped; unclassifiable.

DATA COLLECTION

Mothers received a letter explaining the project. The MANRF, MQ, and MFAS were given to mothers who volunteered to participate. Children were eligible to participate on the basis of their mother's responses to the MQ and verification of father's nonresidency. The children were observed during three consecutive and standardized 20-minute play sessions. These were held at least one day apart and within a ten day period.

FINDINGS

Father fantasies were tested within a multiple regression framework. Analyses were evaluated using $p < .05$. The results provided interesting information and some surprises. The children produced 18,846 father fantasies. Almost half of these fantasies (45.85%) include father, and most (21.04%) fall into the good fantasy category (see Table 1).

As expected, the independent variables of onset age, frequency of contact, maternal attitude, ethnic background, and sex, when considered together, were found statistically significant in the formation of both good and bad fantasies. Contrary to the hypothesis, these same variables were found statistically insignificant in relation to silhouette fantasies.

Of the variables considered, only maternal attitude, as measured by the MANRF scale, proved to be an independently statistically significant variable in relationship to good father fantasies. The more positive the maternal attitude to the nonresident father, the greater

Table 1
Children's Fantasy Responses
N = 96

Variable	Sum	M	Percentage of Total Responses
Total responses	18,846	196.31	
Father fantasies	8,8640	90.00	45.85
Good	3,966	41.31	21.04
Bad	1,629	16.97	8.64
Silhouette	2,844	29.63	15.09
Unclassifiable	201	2.09	.01
Mother fantasies	8,028	83.63	42.60
Fantasies without father	10,206	106.31	54.14

number of good father fantasies produced by the child. A less positive maternal attitude to the nonresident father decreased the number of good father fantasies produced by the child. This only partially supported the anticipated result that children whose mothers had more positive attitudes toward the nonresident father would have more good father fantasies whereas children whose mothers had more negative attitudes would have more bad father fantasies. Although, as predicted, bad father fantasies were related to the variables of ethnic background, sex, onset age, frequency of contact, and the MANRF, mothers attitudes to the nonresident father alone does not account for any statistically significant fluctuation in bad father fantasies. Children whose mothers had more negative attitudes toward the nonresident father did not have more bad father fantasies although they had fewer good father fantasies.

Only gender is statistically significant in relation to bad father fantasies. Boys with nonresident fathers had more bad father fantasies than girls with nonresident fathers. The importance of gender was anticipated because Biller (1969, 1974) stressed the early vulnerability of father absent boys. However, gender differences were few, limited to the bad father fantasies, and seem related to the expression of aggression.

Neither sex, ethnic background, frequency of contact, nor maternal attitude toward the nonresident father were statistically significant in regard to silhouette father fantasies. Yet these father fantasies comprised a substantial proportion of the father fantasies (15.09%). Silhouette fantasies project an obscure, static, stereotyped image and appear important, but they remain unexplained by the variables considered in this study.

Surprisingly, neither ethnic background, onset age, nor frequency of contact, when considered independently, showed a statistically significant impact on father fantasies, as was expected. The current sociological shifts in the white family, the legacy of the father's power in the Hispanic family, and the central role of the matriarch in the lower socioeconomic black family underlay expectations of ethnic differences. No qualitative differences in black, white, or Hispanic subjects were found for father fantasies, mothers' attitudes toward the nonresident father, or antagonism to men.

The quality of the fantasy findings were in the same direction as Bach's (1946). Most good father fantasies were both affectionate and sexual in nature. Boys and girls equally imagined father as a romantic figure who aroused sexual curiosity as well as nurturing and caretaking thoughts. In fantasy, he initiated more loving and caretaking activities toward mother and child than any other kind of action. Fantasies about father as a daring figure to be admired were minimal, but boys had more fantasies of this type than girls. This statistically significant difference supported the idea that boys, in their normal developmental quest for sex role definition and identification, strive toward the image of a father who is actively competent and assertive, in addition to his other qualities.

Most bad father fantasies portrayed themes of harm, departure and disappearance and were shared equally by boys and girls. The overall similarity in boys' and girls' perceptions with the specifically limited differences related to physical force reflected variations in style of aggressive expression rather than quantitative differences in aggression associated with father.

Fantasies depicting action between father and child were prevalent. Both boys and girls imagined that father approached children more often than children approached father. Boys and girls viewed father and mother as initiating limited but equal amounts of activity with each other. Furthermore, data showed girls had more fantasies about mother than father while boys had more fantasies about father than mother. This implies that these children were confronting age-appropriate identification issues.

DISCUSSION

The most striking findings of this study relate to the undeniable presence and overwhelming goodness of the fantasy father and the strong impact of the maternal attitude to the nonresident father upon good father fantasies. The maternal attitude toward the nonresident father correlates with increases or decreases in the number of good father fantasies but does not, when considered alone, influence the production of bad father fantasies. This finding is provocative. It seems to contradict the commonly held belief that mothers' negative views of fathers influence their children's negative views of the father. While this notion may be correct, it does not specifically pertain to the bad father fantasies of preschool children with nonresident fathers.

All youngsters in this study, regardless of gender or racial differences, were interested in father. The magnitude and proportion of father fantasies substantiate clinical impressions that even if physically absent, father is very much on the minds of his children. His symbolic image occupies considerable psychological space and time. Although limited contact may hinder attachment to the actual father in reality, it does not inhibit attachment to a mental representation of father in fantasy.

Father's presence in children's fantasies is developmentally appropriate. Fantasy is a vital coping device employed by young children for reality-adaptive and/or defensive purposes (Gould, 1972). It is used to compare real and imagined elements as children comprehend and organize their thoughts about the role and place of father, mother, and self in work and family life. The fantasy father of children with nonresident fathers serves adaptive purposes by enabling them to keep father available to support development and growth through creative play.

Fantasies also serve wish fulfillment purposes. The sheer number of father fantasies, especially of good aspects of father, indicate an exaggerated interest in and hunger for the father object. It appears that even if, as experienced in clinical practice, libidinal desires relating to father are seemingly renounced in real life, father can still be a wished-for and longed-for figure.

Fantasy content can reflect a denial in fantasy of the objective reality (Freud, 1936). Young children often ameliorate pain associated with specific thoughts and events by denying their existence in play (Gould, 1972). For the children in this study, concentration on the good aspects of the fantasy father implies that these fantasies may be understood as the child's denial of the objective reality, as attempts to provide the safety and security that may be associated with father, and as attempts to cope with pain. Furthermore, it may act as a defense against anxiety associated with the nonresidency as well as a defense against the original, repeated or feared separations. Father fantasies can help fuel a creative search for replacement and/or defend against the loss of one's father (Tessman, 1978). Thus, children can find gratification and comfort in father fantasies.

Like the youngsters in Bach's (1946) study, children observed in this project viewed father as an affectionate and nurturing figure who is rarely authoritative or hostile to his children. He infrequently initiates angry, cruel, or demanding action. He is seldom bossy, harsh, punitive, or hurtful to his children. The overwhelming proportion of good father fantasies to bad father fantasies reflects that minimal attention is given to the bad aspects of father's behavior and personality. This suggests that these children are inclined to hold an idealized vision of father that lacks the ambivalence usually characterizing ideas of father for five- and six-year-olds. Theoretically, the ambivalence helps to form the basis for the more mature, realistic conceptualization of father as a person with both good and bad features. It continues to develop through adolescence and is important in the achievement of mature sexual identification, desire, satisfaction, and self definition (Abelin, 1971, 1975; Machtlinger, 1976; Tessman, 1978). Interference with this achievement may have profound effects on future development since it can diminish resources, derived from a more realistic view, that are important in the child's integration of father into his self concept.

Clinical observations (Weisman, 1963) suggest that an idealized perception of father extended into later years can hamper, retard, or distort the resolution of the intrapsychic struggles of the oedipal phase and affect the outcome of development. Research findings that establish difficulties in sex role orientation and identification for father absent boys (Donini, 1967; Biller, 1968; Biller and Bahm, 1971) and interpersonal difficulties for father-absent children of both sexes (Biller and Weiss, 1970; Hetherington, 1972) may reflect the problematic outcome of these intrapsychic struggles and may be related to the findings of this study, that is, the persistent invention and preservation of an idealized good fantasy father by preschool children with nonresident fathers.

The significant relationship between MANRF and good father fantasies supports clinical intuition and impressions that mother is influential in the creation of the father fantasy. The mother's positive attitude toward the nonresident father may wittingly or unwittingly give permission and even encourage the child to explore his own desire and yearning for a good father and promote an opportunity to satsify these wishes in fantasy. Conversely, children may limit or keep secret their vision of the good father in an effort to remain loyal to mother and not threaten their still necessary relationship with her. Thus, a mother's attitude is crucial to the development of the child's fantasied relationship with a good father, since it can inhibit the development of a good father fantasy and deprive the child of the adaptive aspects of wish fulfillment as well as the development of trust in a desirable, loving and good fantasy father to use in support of further development. The wish-fulfilling aspects may also reflect the mother's struggle with her own ambivalence and her own longing for an affectionate and loving partner. However, although important, the influence of mother's attitude to the nonresident father may be limited. While it can enhance or inhibit the development of the good father fantasy, it does not seem to enhance or inhibit the creation of a bad fantasy father.

A negative attitude toward the nonresident father does not necessarily imply a negative attitude toward men or a wish to be without a man. Mothers' attitudes toward nonresident fathers reflect feelings and experiences related to specific factors concerning the nonresidency that are unrelated to attitudes of male-female antagonism. The popular assumption that a woman who is furious with her ex-mate generalizes this feeling to all men is simplistic and does not consider the complex relationship between the two attitudes. The high remarriage rate in our society, generally neutral attitude toward men, and only slightly negative attitude toward nonresident fathers found in this study attest to the caution and doubt, as well as the hope and desire, of single-parent mothers for fulfillment in male-female relationships in spite of past failures and disappointments. Perhaps both mother and child continue in a search for a good father for the child.

The preponderance of sexual and affectionate father fantasies appears to reflect age-appropriate concerns regarding sexual exploration and identification. However, the idealized quality, comparatively fewer heroic, supportive, and playful fantasies, and limited gender differences suggest that the fantasy father created by the children in this study is still firmly rooted in earlier attachment and need-fulfilling images. These find satisfaction in nurturing and caretaking activities rather than in later, more admiring, powerful, and protective ones. The children's fantasy father can be seen to possess qualities similar to those associated with early mothering and may confirm the view of mother or the activities associated with mothering as the center of life for these young children, who are away from mother for long periods of time. These qualities, associated with the preoedipal period, coincide with the time that father left home (before the child's third birthday). One might speculate that mother is the most available model to the child and that the fantasy father is derived from her model, early recollections of father, and need satisfaction in attentive care. Adaptively, the fantasies simultaneously serve the purpose of keeping father and obtaining care. However, they also suggest that while ego capacities continue to develop and expand, preschoolers with nonresident fathers may be prone to fixations in libidinal development.

Themes of father's withdrawal highlight the prevalence of thoughts concerned with father's nonresidency, attempts to master father's departure, and the wish to reclaim father as a good rather than a bad figure. The peekaboo quality found in long fantasy games of hide and seek again hint that the children are focused on preoedipal concerns. It suggests that the father fantasy supports object constancy by permitting the children emotionally to hold the father in their psychological lives.

Most fantasies involve father or mother giving aid and comfort at bedtime, feeding, or toileting. There is much dyadic interaction between parent and child, but relatively little interaction between father and mother. There is little evidence of mother and father as a couple, with the accompanying sense of exclusion, or the rivalrous and competitive themes usually prevalent in play of children this age.

The lack of triangulated themes suggests that father is too narrowly and immaturely defined to reflect the more extensive gender differences associated with oedipal development. Thus, in spite of the apparent confrontation with age-appropriate issues, the quality and quantity of the fantasy material suggests that the father fantasies are not available to support greater expansion and differentiation in the father's role, encourage and refine sexual understanding, exploration, longing, desire, and identification. The fantasies do not reflect the higher level of organization necessary to successfully, even if only temporarily, resolve the intrapsychic struggles of the oedipal period. This cautions us that preschool children with nonresident fathers may be particularly vulnerable to disturbances and distortion in their oedipal development, as discussed by Neubauer (1960) and Siegler (1982).

The substantial proportion of silhouette fantasies complements the idea that the father concept is inhibited. These fantasies emphasize the extent to which these children have a mechanical notion of father. The quality of affect associated with these fantasies is artificial, flat, and distant. When not wonderful, father seems a static, nonthreatening, robotlike personage lacking in vitality and on the periphery of the child's world. This is probably a reflection of the actual experience of the children in this study. It is as if father were a stock figure based on a storybook version of a loving father. Perhaps he reflects a vision presented to the child by mother in an attempt to shield the child from pain and assuage her own guilt over father's nonresidency. While such a vision adaptively permits the child to sustain a good father to use in development, silhouette fantasies reflect a cost in the movement and willingness to confront or permit other than good aspects necessary to development.

The protection of father from any badness is glaring. The low proportion (8.64%) of bad father fantasies supports Neubauer's (1960) belief that aggression against the absent father is repressed. The general quality of the fantasies hints that aggressive feelings may not only be unexpressed but also inhibited. The children are reluctant to imagine father as bad, and they are unwilling to challenge father's goodness in fantasy. The low proportion of bad father fantasies can be understood as a defensive maneuver that serves an adaptive function. This defensive maneuver minimizes anxiety by keeping the good father "psychologically" alive and present as someone to stand in opposition to mother.

Children with nonresident fathers seem to have a minimal number of bad-father fantasies regardless of mother's attitude toward the nonresident father, onset age, quantity of contact, or ethnic background. It may be that the presence of more bad father fantasies would make it difficult to use thefather in the healthy developmental push toward self definition. Challenging father's goodness is supremely dangerous. It is tantamount to challenging mother's goodness, if father is considered another version of the early, preoedipal mother. The existence of bad aspects of father in actuality or fantasy is perhaps more dependent on father's presence than on his absence, and a luxury that preschool children with nonresident fathers cannot afford.

REFERENCES

Abelin, E.L. (1971), The role of the father in the separation-individuation process. In: *Separation and Individuation,* ed. J.B. McDevitt & C.F. Settlage. New York: International Universities Press, pp. 229–259.

_____ (1975), Some further observations and comments on the earliest role of the father. *Internat. J. Psycho-Anal.,* 56:293–302.

Adams, P. & Horovitz, J. (1980), *Psychopathology and fatherlessness in poor boys. Child Psychiat. & Human Develop.,* 10:135–143.

Bach, G.R. (1945), *Young children's play fantasies. Psychol. Monogr.,* 59:2.

_____ (1946), Father fantasies and father typing in father separated children. *Child Devel.,* 17:63–80.

Biller, H.B. (1968), A note on father absence and masculine development in lower class Negro and white boys. *Child Devel.,* 39:1003–1006.

_____ (1969), Father dominance and sex-role development of the male child. *Devel. Psychol.,* 1:87–94.

_____ (1971a), The mother-child relationship and the father-absent boy's personality development. *Merrill-Palmer Quart.,* 17:227–271.

_____ (1971b), *Father, Child and Sex Role.* Lexington, MA: Heath Lexington Books.

_____ (1974), Paternal deprivation, cognitive functioning, and the feminized classroom. In: *Child, Personality and Psychopathology,* ed. A. Davids. New York: Wiley, pp. 11–52.

_____ & Bahm, R. (1971), Father absence, perceived maternal behavior, and masculinity of self-concept among junior high school boys. *Devel. Psychol.,* 4:178–181.

———— & Weiss, S.D. (1970), The father-daughter relationship and the psychological development of the female. *J. Genet. Psychol.,* 116:79–93.

Blanchard, R.W. & Biller, H.B. (1971), Father availability and academic performance among third-grade boys. *Develop. Psychol.,* 4, 301–305.

Burlingham, D. (1973), The preoedipal infant-father relationship. *The Psychoanalytic Study of the Child,* 28:23–47. New Haven: Yale University Press.

Cath, S. (1982), Divorce and the Child: "The Father Question Hour." In: *Father and Child,* eds. S. Cath, A. Gurwitt & J.M. Ross. Boston: Little, Brown, pp. 467–479.

Clausen, J.A. (1966), Family structure, socialization and personality. In: *Review of Child Development Research* (Vol 2), ed. L.W. Hoffman & M.L. Hoffman. New York: Russell Sage Foundation, pp. 1–54.

Clower, V.L. (1978), The effects of divorce on children. Presented at the meeting of the American Psychoanalytic Association, New York, November.

Donini, G.P. (1967), An evaluation of sex-role identification among father-absent and father-present boys. *Psychol.,* 4:13–16.

Freud, A. (1936), *The Ego and the Mechanisms of Defense.* New York: International Universities Press, 1966.

———— & Burlingham, D. (1939–45), *The Writings of Anna Freud. Vol. III.* New York: International Universities Press, 1973.

Furman, E. (1974), *A Child's Parent Dies.* New Haven: Yale University Press.

Gould, R. (1972), *Child Studies through Fantasy.* New York: Quadrangle.

Hetherington, M. (1972), Effects of paternal absence on personality development in adolescent daughters. *Devel. Psychol.,* 7:313–326.

Kristal, J. (1978), The influence of the early father-daughter relationship on feminine sexual behavior. (Doctoral dissertation, University of Texas at Austin, 1978). *Dissertation Abstracts International, 39,* A4580B. (University Microfilms No. 79-00, 590).

Machtlinger, V. (1976), *Psychoanalytic theory: Preoedipal and oedipal phases with special reference to the father. In: The Role of the Father in Child Development.* ed. M. Lamb. New York: Wiley, pp. 277–307.

Michaels, C.S. (1981), Father fantasies of preschool children with nonresident fathers. (Doctoral dissertation, New York University, 1981). *Dissertation Abstracts International, 42,* 4935B. (University Microfilms No. DAB210930).

Neubauer, P.B. (1960), The one-parent child and his oedipal development. *The*

Psychoanalytic Study of the Child, 15:286–309. New York: International University Press.

Piaget, J. & Inhelder, B. (1969), *The Psychology of the Child.* New York: Basic Books.

Radin, N. (1974), Observed maternal behavior with four-year old boys and girls in lower-class families. *Child Devel.,* 45:1126–1131.

———— (1976), The role of father in cognitive, academic and intellectual development. In: *The Role of the Father in Child Development,* ed. M. Lamb. New York: Wiley, pp. 237–276.

Santrock, J.W. (1970), Influence of onset and type of paternal absence on the first four Eriksonian developmental crises. *Devel. Psychol.,* 3:273–274.

———— (1972), Relation of type and onset of father absence to cognitive development. *Child Devel.,* 43:455–569.

———— & Wohlford, P. (1970), Effects of father absence: Influence of the reason for the onset of the absence. *Proceedings of the 78th Annual Convention of the American Psychological Association,* 5:265–366.

Siegler, A.L. (1982), Changing Aspects of the Family: A Psychoanalytic Perspective for Early Intervention. In: *Day Care: Scientific and Social Issues,* ed. E. Ziegler & E. Gordon. Boston, MA: Auburn House, pp. 57–71.

Siegler, A.L. (1983), Groupwork with single mothers. In: *Ego and Self Psychology,* ed. E. Buchholz & J. Mishne. New York: Aronson, pp. 95–111.

Taleporos, E. (1974), Women's liberationists and pseudo-liberationists – Their beliefs about sex role socialization, opinions about social issues and perceptions of male-female relations. Unpublished doctoral dissertation, New York University.

TenHouten, W.D. (1970), The black family: Myth and reality. *Psychiat.,* 33:145–173.

Tessman, L.H. (1978), *Children of Parting Parents.* New York: Aronson.

Thomes, M. (1968), Children with absent fathers. *J. Marr. & Fam.,* 30:89–96.

Thompson, B. (1978), The effects of father absence on the arithmetic achievement self concept and school adjustment of elementary school children. Unpublished doctoral dissertation, University of Georgia.

Wallerstein, S.S. & Kelly, J.B. (1975), The effects of parental divorce: the experiences of the preschool child. *J. Amer. Acad. Child Psychiat.,* 14:600–616.

Weisman, P, (1963), The effects of preoedipal paternal attitudes on development and character. *Internat. J. Psycho-Anal.,* 44:121–131.

Wolfenstein, M. (1973), The image of the lost parent. *The Psychoanalytic Study of the Child,* 28:433–457. New Haven: Yale University Press.

22

The Noncustodial Father
An Application of Solomonic Wisdom
Albert J. Solnit

Most divorces in families with children are not associated with custodial conflicts. However, with the advent of new societal patterns – or are they tendencies?[1] – we are more aware of fathers claiming their interests in their children (Wallerstein and Kelly, 1982; Cath, 1982) by requesting assignment by law as the custodial parent or in asserting their rights and privileges as noncustodial parents who wish to maintain significant relationships with their children. This chapter focuses on that vast majority of divorcing fathers who do not wish to be, or could not be the custodial parents, who want their former wives to have the primary custodial responsibility for their children but who want to maintain a significant relationship with their biological children.

Usually such a father does not require a court order to describe, to limit, or to characterize his rights to be with his noncustodial child. In most such divorces, the courts refer to reasonable visitation in characterizing the way in which personal contacts can be determined. The courts usually do not enter into other areas of communication and

---

[1]Statistical trends and comparisons are too readily used to create and promulgate stereotypes of how children, mothers, and fathers behave.

contact that are significant ways in which absent adults and their children, especially the older ones (above five or six years of age), can stay in touch with each other. These include telephone talks, letters, birthday and holiday cards, gifts, audio and video tapes, and messages sent by other persons or through other indirect means. After all, the aim of a relationship is not only personal physical contact, although for children under the ages of five or six such concrete contact is essential. And for older children (and for adults) the awareness of the psychological-emotional presence of the absent parent usually must be based on sufficient previous physical contact. Of course, physical contact and a physical presence is also advantageous for older children when it is realistic and the circumstances promote a psychologically desirable experience.

This concept is based on the way in which psychological relationships develop between children and significant caregiving adults. The relationships develop primarily out of the needs of the child and the needs of the adult.

For the child, the need begins with the helplessness of the newborn infant, who dies if there is not an older person (usually an adult with the motives of a parent) to feed and protect him, to keep him warm, clean and emotionally secure, to provide the stimulation and expectations that enable the infant to unfold his potential as a rapidly maturing and developing individual who can make a unique contact and relationship with the adult or adults who care for him.

For the adult, the need begins with having been an infant, toddler, child, and then adolescent who, as an adult, wants to have a child whose care and parenting will provide the opportunities for fulfillment as a competent parent. It also expresses a unique preference for an extension of self by begetting and raising children.

As with intact marriages and families, the relationships between children and parents move from the physical to the psychological, from dependence toward independence, from passive to active roles in the relationship, and from child–parent to adolescent–parent to adult –parent relationships. Parents never stop being parents in intact and continuous relationships as their children grow to adulthood.

NONCUSTODIAL FATHERS

In the large majority of current divorces (well over 70%), spouses agree, because of practical or preferential reasons, that the mother will be the custodial parent and the father will live separately from the mother and children. Of course, there are exceptions, as indicated by the 15–20% of divorces associated with the custodial conflicts that are brought to court. It is possible that this trend will be reversed; it did change radically at the turn of this century. Prior to that time fathers most often were granted custody (Derdeyn, 1976) if they requested it.

Currently, the vast majority of divorced fathers are noncustodial parents. It is essential, in the best interests of children of divorced parents, for the parents to understand the difference between the adults' preferences and the children's needs. Children need at least one adult, one parent on whom they can count on an hour-to-hour, day-to-day basis for the continuity of affectionate care; for establishing a safe and stimulating environment; for setting limits; for the transmission of parental value preferences, customs, and beliefs; and for the interpretation of societal realities that enable the child both to be buffered from those realities and to adapt to them in a constructive manner.

Part of the child's reality when parents divorce is the recognition that parents have separated, usually physically and always in a vital, psychologically symbolic way. Helping these children, especially the younger ones, to recognize and cope with this reality of divorce is often resisted and warded off by parents and those courts that coercively order joint custody or that the children shall be available for visitation by the noncustodial parents according to a prescribed schedule. Such orders are usually not in the best interests of the child but are instead a manifest attempt to provide fairness for the parents (like the Solomonic challenge) and in a profound sense to pretend that only the parents are divorced but that their children can continue to have two primary psychological parents. (See Goldstein, Freud, and Solnit, 1979a, b; Goldstein, Freud, Solnit, and Goldstein, 1986.)

The noncustodial father who understands what divorce means to his children will accept the reality and gradually be able to restore and maintain their relationship. In this way, they can cope with and gradually overcome the reality in a constructive, development-promoting process.

Going beyond this recognition, the noncustodial parent realizes that he will be an important visitor, one who can become accepted as a trusted close friend, a vital adult person for the child. During the separation and divorce process, the child often loses, or feels a substantial weakening of, the primary psychological relationship that existed or was developing with the biological father, who now lives in a separate domicile. To become a trusted visitor or friend, he can try to become a vital supporting resource for the "single" mother or, later, in many instances, for the mother who remarries another adult.

By seeking to become a dependable support-resource, the noncustodial father strengthens the mother–child relationship. In so doing, the separated father insures that he will be trusted and that he will have as good as possible an opportunity to remain or become a beloved fathering person who understands the hierarchy of relationships essential for children as they grow and develop, and as they extract identifications from their close relationships with adults that are as conflict free as possible. In a crucial sense, the noncustodial father demonstrates that the custodial mother, who has the primary responsibility for the day-to-day care of the child, also has the primary authority to carry out such responsibilities. A caring father will want no less.[2] A rivalrous, quarrelsome, competitive former husband may lose sight of his child's needs and best interests.

In one instance, a father was given liberal visitation rights by the court, but the mother hated the visits and ordered her ten-year-old daughter, Jane, to refuse to visit. Though the father could have asked the court to insist on these visits, he accepted advice to try persuading his former wife to hate him less and to help set up visits between him and their daughter that would be friendly, comfortable, and as free of conflict as possible. This effect took several years.[3] Gradually, especially as Jane became older, positive visits took place. In the interim, Jane's father was able to maintain communication that the mother could tolerate – phone calls, letters, gifts, and other remembrances.

Jane's father was not an angel. He was furious with his former wife but realized that his wishes to litigate, to gain revenge, to bring about visits as ordered by the court – to win a Pyrrhic victory – would have created a huge psychological burden, possibly a trauma, for Jane. Later he also progressed from intellectual realization to emotionally felt conviction that his wish to win the battle with his former wife would have seriously jeopardized and weakened Jane's increasingly sound, warm relationship with him.

Although the case vignette about Jane and her parents may seem to be idealized, unrealistic and to require parental responses that we do

---

[2]The mother, of course, would be well advised, in the best interests of her child, to facilitate conflict-free visits between her child and the child's father. In fact, such an attitude is vital to strengthening the mother–child relationship.

[3]It might have been a shorter or longer period of time. From the point of view of the child, the shorter the time, the better.

not find easily or frequently, the lessons learned are logical and hard-headed. Until professionals understand the full implications of court-ordered visitation and joint custody, it is unlikely that the courts will change. The principle of "in the best interests of the child" and that, once the marriage has been broken, "the child's needs and rights shall be paramount" has been honored more in the breach than in the observance. Fathers, who constitute the great majority of noncustodial parents, and the professionals who advise them, need to know that by failing to support their children's custodial mother financially, socially, and psychologically, they are undermining the father–child relationship in a significant and corrosive manner.

Fathers can and do make excellent custodial parents (Pruett, 1986). In principle, the lessons to be learned by noncustodial fathers also can fit the conflicts and available choices of noncustodial mothers. This is not to deny that children will respond to the differing patterns of adaptation of mothers and fathers to separation and divorce; nor is it to avoid recognition that children's identifications with mothers and fathers represent differences in, as well as a composite of, their common or overlapping roots.

It becomes increasingly clear that the biblical story of how King Solomon decided to whom the disputed baby belonged or should be given carries with it a dynamic view of best interests of the child, namely, that the baby cannot be divided surgically, psychologically, or emotionally without being put into repeated jeopardy. The noncustodial parent, usually the father, has the opportunity to help his child and to work toward assuring a sound future relationship with his child, by minimizing the injuries that divorce causes and by maximizing the child's ability to cope with the divorce. By supporting the custodial mother's authority and becoming a trusted supporting person, the father enables the child to take advantage of being reared within a less conflicted marital relationship and to have as good an opportunity as is feasible to resume or continue a progressive development with appropriate and proportionately useful identifications with each of the parents.

CONCLUSION

As clinicians, our attention in divorce and family break-up cases has been focused on custody or placement conflicts. The principles that have emerged from our clinical experiences and studies (see Goldstein et al., 1979a, b; Goldstein and Solnit, 1984; Goldstein et al., 1986) are the same for those situations in which there is agreement as for those in which there is disagreement about who shall be the custodial parent.

The principles suggest an adaptation of the Golden Rule–to protect what is in the best interests of the child (least detrimental alternative), it is essential that the father do for the mother as custodial parent what he would like her to do if he were the custodial parent. This insight, or common sense, not only is in the service of the child's best interests, but also is crucial for protecting the husband's interests as a father who wants to have a significant, satisfying relationship with the children from whom he is separated as a result of the family break-up.

REFERENCES

Cath, S. (1982), Divorce and the child: The father question hour. In: *Father and Child*, ed. S.H. Cath, A. Gurwitt, & J.M. Ross. Boston, MA: Little, Brown, pp. 467–479.

Derdeyn, A.P. (1976), Child custody contests in historical perspective. *Amer. J. Psychiat.*, 133:1369–1376.

Goldstein, J., Freud, A. & Solnit, A.J. (1979a), *Beyond the Best Interests of the Child*. New York: Free Press.

———— ———— ———— (1979b), *Before the Best Interests of the Child*. New York: Free Press.

———— ———— ———— & Goldstein, S. (1986), *In the Best Interests of the Child*. New York: Free Press.

Goldstein, S., & Solnit, A.J. (1984), *Divorce and Your Child*. New Haven, CT: Yale University Press.

Pruett, K.D. (1986), *The Nurturing Father*. New York: Warner.

Wallerstein, J., & Kelly, J. (1982), The father–child relationship: Change after divorce. In: *Father and Child*, ed. S.H. Cath, A.R. Gurwitt & J.M. Ross. Boston, MA: Little, Brown, pp. 451–466.

23

Divorce and Fathers
Some Intrapsychic Factors Affecting Outcome
Richard N. Atkins

Married life used to begin in religious institutions, and, with "till death do us part" as its watchword, it was supposed to end in such institutions as well. But, in the last decade, what now starts in churches or synagogues to bind couples together as the beginning of a new family, frequently ends in the law office or the courtroom to divide them and to conquer their children. No fewer than four couples in every ten see their marriages end in divorce.

Divorce is not only a fulminant social phenomenon; it is also a family-centered crisis. Consequently, investigators have tried to outline the emotional impact of the family's dissolution on its *more vulnerable* participants—the children (Hetherington, 1966, 1972, 1979, 1981; Hetherington, Cox, and Cox, 1976, 1978, 1979; Wallerstein, 1977, 1983, 1984, 1985; Wallerstein and Kelly, 1974, 1976, 1980a, b). Yet, relatively little attention has been paid to its *equally affected* participant—the father.

In divorce, fathers are viewed as more often responsible for its causes and more often hurt by its effects. Father more regularly blame themselves and are blamed by mothers for the divorce (Kitson and Sussman, 1982). Divorced fathers are nine times more likely to be hospitalized for acute mental illness than their married counterparts

(Bloom, Asher, and White, 1978), a rate three times higher than its corollary for divorced mothers.

Yet, the sources of a father's psychic struggle and emotional pain are varied and complex. It is possible that they can only be uncovered by studying the natural history of fathers in the divorcing process. In that context, I present here a preliminary report of 14 fathers who were divorced *during* an ongoing psychotherapy, which was begun for reasons other than marital discord. I was able to identify two constellations of dynamic variables in these fathers. Each constellation focused itself on the fathers' difficulties with aggression. Some fathers believed that the ex-wife was hurting them in deeply scarring intrapsychic ways; other fathers believed that they were hurting their ex-wives. The two patterns of fantasy and behavior seemed to relate both to the quality of the father's subsequent coparental relationship and to the difficulties he experienced in parenting his children. But, to clarify that discussion, I must first review some of the causes of divorce, the general effect of divorce on the family matrix, and the processes of coping and adaptation required of parting parents.

DIVORCE: RATES AND CAUSES

The United States has the highest divorce rate in the world. If one was married, for example, in 1979, then the probability that the marriage will terminate in divorce is 49%. Although there is some current evidence of their plateau, the rates have generally increased each year and remain hovering at close to 50% (Hacker, 1983).

During the last ten years, the total population of children has declined by over 12%. But the number of children in single-parent households, many of these the result of marital dissolution, has increased by more than 44%. At least 40%, and probably closer to 50%, of all children born during the last decade will spend some of their childhood years living with only one custodial parent (Hetherington, 1979). Thus, the idea of a stable nuclear family has literally become only a half-truth in contemporary America, as over one million children have their lives changed through divorce and custody every year (Steinman, 1981). In such divorces, nine mothers out of every ten receive sole custody of their children.

It is not entirely clear what factors have contributed to the mounting divorce rate in contemporary American society. The studies that attempt to identify the causes of divorce rely, by and large, on the *post hoc* recollections of one or both parents. Such after the fact reviews of precipitants are, of course, subject to considerable secondary elaboration, and the reliability of such reviews, as more than the reporting of idiosyncratic perceptions, may be doubtful. For example, in an interesting study, when reviewers were asked to blindly pair divorcing wives' and husbands' written accounts of their marriages, they were able to do so correctly in only about one-third of the cases (Hetherington and Hagan, 1986).

The existing research data suggest that complaints from each partner center on the other partner's lack of tenderness, affection, sexual availability, and the like (Hetherington, Cox, and Cox, 1976). My own clinical investigation reveals that a parent's ambivalent feelings about family-based duties, responsibilities, and requirements; a professed breadth of extrafamilial obligations and involvements; and complicating motivations around success and accomplishment also play an important role. They tend to make both parents' ostensible wish for intimacy difficult to meld with their inevitable exhaustion or emotional preoccupation (Atkins, 1986b; Lansky, 1986). Thus, I believe that the mother's accusations and the father's self-blame for the divorce (Kitson and Sussman, 1982) frequently derive from unconscious neurotic issues, particularly narcissistic fixations or regressions, surrounding intimacy and self-definition on the one hand or oedipal conflicts around sexuality and guilt on the other.

I will have more to say about this shortly; for now the following example will highlight some of these points. A 32-year-old account executive in a brokerage firm, father of two small children, sought psychotherapy because he was unable to "service a stable of clients" sufficiently well to help them meet their financial objectives. As soon as two new clients would be referred, he would lose three old ones, and financial worries plagued his wife and his young family. Within three months of his three-time weekly psychotherapy, marital difficulties became more clearly focused in the treatment. His wife blamed him, seemingly incessantly, for his lack of sexual tenderness. Yet her busy professional schedule – she was a social worker – seemed to make adequate time for sex difficult to find. The patient also tended to avoid his wife sexually, except for the purpose of "making babies to keep her happy." The thought that his wife could want, or need, his body as part of her sexual fulfillment terrified him. Although his worries became difficult to engage in the treatment. It was not until much later that I learned that this man had fears of annihilation with every orgasm and that this fantasy had dated from the time of the first ejaculation. A year after he entered treatment, he impulsively decided to leave his wife as a solution to his intrapsychic problems.

Although his intention to act out was interpreted, he proceeded nonetheless. Two trial separations were begun. Each time he would return to his wife because, though he could not live intimately with her, he also needed her for the implicit requirements of narcissistic stabilization. After the second separation, his wife threw him out of the house and, with exasperation, demanded a divorce. Because he no longer had the anaclitic marital relationship, his anxieties became even more profound. As the patient marched a thin emotional line between his wife's claims that he had caused the family dissolution and his own anxious insecurity, he began to displace his conflictual relationship with his marital partner onto his two young sons. Suddenly finding a chaotic internal determination, he demanded regular contact with his children, and he took quick, decisive steps to insure that he got it. He hired a well-known female matrimonial lawyer, whom he viewed as having "the fastest gun in the East," to insure his patrimonial purview. When he had his children with him, he was manifestly calmer, but he also guiltily reported taking them to bed with him as "my little teddy bears." In this example, it is clear that such psychosexual and self-definitional issues are important derivatives of the father's response to divorce, his subsequent coping with and adaptation to the divorce, and the quality of his relationship with the children.

In other cases, changing sociocultural attitudes seem to play a role in the epidemiology of marital ennui. A parent's fears of intrusive, damaging penetration or castration are mirrored in a labile and inconsistent attitude toward the protective value of *family*. This accentuates the inordinate quantity of "me-firstisms" in our contemporary society–a society that promotes and tolerates an extraordinary disjunction between an individual's determination and the common good.

For example, a 29-year-old female psychologist sought treatment for a host of obsessive-compulsive symptoms. She had divorced her husband about two years before, and the two shared custody of their three-year-old son. In the course of the first few interviews, she decided to try to assure herself, by grilling me, that my orientation to psychoanalysis was not overly directed by "Freudian dogma about women and female sexuality." When I asked her about these concerns, she explained that she had been significantly influenced by the women's movement. In fact, she had insisted on a divorce when her husband had, allegedly, refused to participate equally in home-related activities after the child was born. Unfortunately, her version of equal often meant that he should do what she did not want to do. At the time, she viewed herself as successful enough and capable enough to rear a young child without a present father, that she "came first." She drew support for her position from her particular feminist ideology, which she regularly quoted me, chapter and verse. As her protestations became thinner during the next few months, it became clear to both of us that her demands of her husband had been quite inconsistent and that, no matter what he did (which admittedly was not much), she would complain about something that he failed to do. She suggested, with some satisfaction, that she had made her husband "chase his tatil" during the last few months of their marriage. Sexually gratifying experiences with men were difficult for her to identify and she admitted that she was unable to have an orgasm except through masturbation. Ultimately she acknowledged that her shrill espousal of ideology was intended primarily to defend her sexual conflicts and her anxious fantasies about sexual intrusion, physical hurt, and intimacy.

Another issue that certainly contributes to marital dissolution involves the apparently increasing incidence of extramarital affairs. While the research literature identifies that heterosexual affairs affect the decision to divorce (Furstenberg and Spanier, 1984), there is relatively little discussion about the role of homosexuality, particularly as it appears, in clinical practice, among fathers. While the anguish of the truly homosexual man (or woman), fettered to an unfulfilling life with a spouse and children is not to be dismissed lightly, the preponderance of "experimental," purely pleasure-seeking, or narcissistically twinning homosexual contact seems also to be increasing despite health caveats to the contrary. For example, a 35-year-old woman in psychoanalysis began consciously to surmise that her husband of ten years had been involved in numerous heterosexual and homosexual affairs. Every time that his business (at which he was quite good) required important decisions, he would disappear for several days to "think, calm his nerves, and seek the advice of a male mentor" whom his wife had never met. His homosexual adventures during these times became clear when he returned after one of them and sheepishly owned up to a venereal infection.

THE PHASES OF DIVORCE AND FACTORS AFFECTING ADAPTATION

The divorcing process is distinguished by three broad phases, which Wallerstein (1938) has suggested are, for each parent, successive and nonoverlapping. As I will demonstrate, I believe that the separate nature of each of Wallerstein's phases is less absolute in the population of fathers that I studied.

The *acute phase,* precipitated by the decision to separate and to terminate the marriage, can be marked by intrapsychic and interpersonal upheaval, occasionally intense. Sadness, anger, envy, guilt, jealousy, loneliness, regressions, and problems in self-esteem regulation in either or both parents can exist, reciprocally, with behaviors like spousal acrimony, sexual promiscuity, social withdrawal, self-destructive activities, or verbal (or physical) aggression. In such situations, the interpersonal and intrapsychic tumult feed on each other, as in the previous vignettes and as I will continue to demonstrate. Although the degree to which such psychic and behavioral phenomena are expressed or externalized will vary, children can certainly be witness to and participate in a bizarre or terrifying world created by their parents. Often these new parental behaviors are totally dyssynchronous with the child's previous experience of mother or father.

The acute phase, it is suggested, can last up to two years. As coparental relationships are modified, intrapsychic disruption is worked through and social experiences broaden outside of the dissolved marriage. The *transitional phase* marks a period of internal and external growth and development that can consist of several intermediate years of fluctuating progress and regression. Ultimately the *postdivorce phase* defines the period when coparental households acquire individual stability and autonomy.

I believe that fathers who adapt less well to divorce, as in my clinical population, and whose neurotic or characterological problems become actively remobilized by it, show the least clear discrimination between the acute phase and subsequent phases. All phases seem to blend into an ebb and flow of acute symptoms and behaviors.

The research evidence also suggests several factors that are important to the postdivorce adaptation of both fathers and mothers. Critical in this regard is the development of satisfactory postdivorce "peer" relationships, including sexual relationships (Trombetta, 1981). As the stages identified by Wallerstein (1983) suggest, the resolution of the acute phase depends on the establishment of pleasurable and supportive new relationships. But this factor may need to be modified by a clinical caveat. The divorcing experience all too often drives one or both partners into defensive relationships that either only camouflage the intrapsychic sequelae of divorce or duplicate (and neurotically, compulsively repeat) the experience with the divorced spouse. Also, new relationships are sometimes sought in an effort to undo the previous marriage. In such a situation, one or the other spouse may abandon the children because the children are wholly associated with the traumatic marriage or traumatic divorce.

For example, a 34-year-old physician who divorced his wife of seven years began, during the course of the marital dissolution, to live with a 19-year-old model. This younger woman affirmed the vitality of a man who was terrified of growing older. On the day that his divorce decree became final, he married his girlfriend in a civil ceremony. Abruptly, he and she moved to another city. Heralding the genetic conflict with his mother, the patient claimed that he wanted as much distance from "the old woman" as could be managed. After his second marriage dissolved three years later, he sought psychotherapy. His first wife was quite disturbed emotionally, he was not without his own difficulties, although they were hard for him to acknowledge. He had not seen his children in close to four years. He kept referring, early in his treatment, to the youngsters as "her children" in an effort actively to split and project all elements of imagined "badness" onto the external world.

So far I have discussed the development of satisfactory interpersonal relationships as important to each ex-spouse. Trombetta (1981) suggests, in addition, that the amount of cooperation and emotional support that both partners receive from their ex-spouses directly correlates with their positive adaptation. The research evidence argues that coparents whose relationships are, or come to be, supportive enjoy the easiest postdivorce adjustment.

Moreover, the length of the marriage before divorce, the continuity in personal experience of role and lifestyle, the amount of contact and interaction with the children, the age of the parents at the time of divorce, and the response of the children to the divorce are important parameters that influence each parent's coping and adaptation in the phases of divorce. The longer that partners were married prior to divorcing, the more difficult is their adjustment to single life. Older parents tend to adjust less well than younger parents. The more that each partner's postdivorce lifestyle continues its predivorce pattern, the easier the process of adaptation becomes. Children who have preexisting behavior problems, whose problems become exacerbated by the divorce, or who have poor ability to adapt to stress tend to make things harder for their parents' accommodation. Finally, and perhaps most important to the father's accommodation to divorce, the amount of either parent's postdivorce contact with the children directly predicts the extent of his or her adaptation.

For children, postdivorce reactions and adjustments often mirror those identified for parents. Reactions are to some extent related to the age of the child. Generally, however, for preschool and school-age children, parental adaptation strongly influences the child's adaptation.

That is to say, if parents ultimately adapt well to divorce and can resume parenting, then their children come along emotionally, sooner or later. Also, as Wallerstein (1983, 1984, 1985) has indicated, children react to divorce by and large according to age-appropriate developmental norms. The more attuned parents are to the developmental imperatives in their children, the more favorable are the outcomes for these youngsters. For instance, young school-age children, invested in the sequelae of oedipal fantasies, mourn the losses and separations of divorce with thoughts of being usurped and replaced or with intensely idealized family romances. Furthermore, positive outcomes in children seem to be related to the amount of sustained contact with the noncustodial parent. Greater contact between children and the "other" parent forecasts more favorable child-centered (Hetherington, 1979; Trombetta, 1981; Wallerstein, 1983) and parent-centered, and particularly father-centered (Greif, 1979; Jacobs, 1982), adaptation to divorce. Yet, such contact between noncustodial parents (these are fathers in 90% of divorces) and children must certainly exist within a certain "pleasurable window." The father who sustains an emotionally detached relationship with this children or who uses the relationship for ulterior motives – for example, competitively overgratifies the children with gifts, vacations, and the like – promotes poorer postdivorce accommodation. A child's reactions to divorce are also related to the quality of the relationship between the divorced parents. Again the greater the cooperation between the divorced spouses, the more favorable is the adaptation in their children.

But coparental cooperation implies that fathers and mothers will agree about important postdivorce issues, most of those concerning the children. Moreover, coparental conflict, in larger studies of divorced populations, seems only to imply the presence of manifest anger directed at the spouse. Little attention is paid to the reciprocal vicissitudes between interpersonal and intrapsychic aspects of such conflict, including those intrapsychic variables that lead to self-destructive as well as object-directed aggression. This is important because ongoing parental acrimony, overt and covert, is likely to be the variable that exacts the most pernicious effect on a child's emotional well-being (Bernstein and Robey, 1962; Derdeyn, 1983; Atkins, 1986a). Such acrimony is certainly not unique to the divorced population, but it is probably more destructive, distinctive, and intense among parting parents (Hetherington, Cox, and Cox, 1976). While it is important to note the origins of parental acrimony and its direct abusive impact, some of its indirect effects on children also need to be identified. For example, school-age boys in sole custodial placement with their mothers (who also have little contact with their fathers) may have more behavior problems and difficulties in sex-role identification that do same age boys who have more involvement with their fathers (Hetherington, Cox, and Cox, 1976). It is not clear how much an embittered mother's proclivity to *transitively* denigrate the father and maleness (Atkins, 1981, 1982, 1984) holds sway, in her child's mind, over the absence of the father-as-parent.

WHAT HAPPENS TO FATHERS IN DIVORCE

Perhaps the most important outcome in the population of divorced fathers is that they do lose at least some contact with their children in the five years after a decisive marital separation. According to Furstenberg (1982), while the range of diminished contact with children is probably quite broad, and contact with children may transiently increase in the acute postdivorce phase, as many as half of divorced fathers may stop seeing their children pretty much altogether in the immediately postdivorce years.

The reasons that fathers and children become alienated from one another is, however, far from clear. Ninety percent of the children of divorce ultimately find themselves in sole maternal custody, with the father allocated varying amounts of visitation with them. Some of the decrease in contact clearly derives from the manifest changes in family structure. Some researchers see divorce as the father's "child centered crisis" (Jacobs, 1983). A father who is deprived of his average expectable contact with his children is likely to suffer considerable emotional pain. The father's deprivation may be further exacerbated by a vengeful wife, thus increasing his propensity to depression, emotional withdrawal, and physical isolation. The father, then, becomes the divorce's victim. Externally imposed termination of contact with the children that has generated much support both for fathers' self-help groups, like Rights For Fathers and for legally mandated joint custody.

On the other hand, other investigators suggest that diminished fatherchild contact derives from the sequelae of the mother's victimization (Weitzman, 1985; Chesler, 1986). In particular, it is the father's narcissistically motivated retaliations against the mother that lead to his financial and emotional neglect or abuse of his divorced family. Diminished contact with the children is just another manifestation of his "getting even" with the mother and her universe.

There is also no clear evidence that given the option a previously "involved" father will continue his active parenting function in the postdivorce period. A father's prior fathering patterns do not predict his postdivorce involvement with the children (Hetherington, Cox, and Cox 1976; Wallerstein and Kelly 1980b). In a few cases when the father was relatively divorced from active parenting during the marriage, he became far more involved with his children after the decisive separation from his wife (Friedman, 1980), although such fathers were engaged in psychotherapy to accomplish that aim.

A mother's (or his own) remarriage and possible relocation can contribute to any father's involvement with his children. Eighty percent of divorced men and 75% of divorced women remarry within the first several years of marital dissolution (Hacker, 1983). The number of previously divorced coparents who subsequently marry other divorce(e)s is increasing. Children from prior marriages then become coupled to each other and to new children from the current marriage, thus potentiating both interfamilial and intrafamilial loyalty conflicts and other problems with both biological and stepparents.

While a host of reality-based circumstances or demands and a plethora of superficial motivations can limit a father's contact with his children and his ability to parent them, he is obviously subjected to complicated emotions during the acute postdivorce period. These emotions are poorly studied. Often the emotionality in the father is described in phenomenologically global terms, for example, anxiety, depression, loneliness, grief, anger, despair, without reference to their deeper, unconscious, psychodynamic correlates. Moreover, the correlations between such complicated affects in divorcing fathers is, are my knowledge, completely unknown. It would accordingly be useful if certain constellations of feelings, fantasies, and behaviors could be identified as belonging together to describe distinct populations of divorcing fathers. Such an elaboration of dynamic issues could also facilitate the prediction of the kinds of and intensities of coparental acrimony that may be part and parcel of the divorcing process.

To that end, I began to review the clinical records of 14 fathers seen in private psychotherapy or psychoanalysis at some time during the last ten years. I (Atkins, submitted) attempted to identify some of the intrapsychic variables that contributed to or were mobilized by the decision to divorce. All the fathers studied were white, middle-class, and between the ages of 29 and 45 at the time of marital dissolution. All had sought psychotherapy at least ten months prior to the decisive separation, and all remained in treatment for at least 15 months following this event. All the clinical case material was reviewed until the 15 month after divorce. None of the fathers had come into treatment for a designated problem of marital discord, and none thought initially about impending separation or divorce. Eleven had sought intervention for generalized feelings of anxiety, depression, dissatisfaction, or chronic boredom. Most complaints focused initially on the work environment or work requirements. Some problems were fiscal; some difficulties concerned work in unrewarding occupations or professions; some issues concerned chronic inability to get along with employers. Four of the fathers had one child; five had two children, three had three children; and two had four children. At the time of the divorce, the children ranged in age from seven months to 15 years.

Each of these men was seen at least twice weekly in psychoanalytic psychotherapy; three were seen in four-time weekly psychoanalysis; and two were seen three times weekly (one on the couch, one not). The manifest content of the complaints invariably gave way to reports of considerable conflict, unhappiness, or anger with their wives, inevitably in the sexual sphere. Disagreements and arguments with their wives became more regularly reported within the first three months of treatment. In nine situations, the acrimony centered at first monetary disputes, but, in all these, battles around finances masked more complicated difficulties with sexuality. Among these 14 men, ten wives had initiated the divorce. Eleven men had had at least one extramarital affair within the two months prior to separation. Nine of these affairs were with women; one was with a man; and one father was ambitendently involved with both women and men. Although final agreement in custodial disposition had not been determined in six situations at the 15 month postseparation, three mothers had been awarded, by "mutual" agreement, sole custody. These fathers had regular visitation ranging from one-third to close to one-half of the year. All the other coparents had initially agreed to or were working toward some form of joint custody, with the children in residence with their fathers from approximately one-third to one-half of the year.

Twelve of the fathers at first coped fairly well to poorly in response to the divorce. As noted earlier, those fathers with more significant psychopathologies, for example, severe personality disorder, fared less well in the acute postdivorce period and were less interested in cooperative relationships with their ex-spouses and with their children. But even those fathers with apparently more stable object relations and more evidence of classically oedipal neurotic conflict, such as the need to regressively mess up work-related successes, were not spared intense, often chaotic reactions to the stresses they intrapsychically viewed as part of the divorcing process. The trauma of the divorce, like that of other catastrophic stresses, reawakened primitive conflicts or fixations that had, until that time, remained relatively repressed. Unfortunately this reawakening was a premature precipitant in the treatment, and, while the degree of symptomatology varied, it was greater than it would have been had the conflictual material emerged anamnestically.

The 12 fathers exhibited essentially two constellations of fantasy material that governed their behavioral reaction. Although there was some overlap, each of these constellations derived from problems with aggression.

THE FIRST SUBGROUP

In the first subgroup, which consisted of seven fathers, reactions tended to revolve more around the idea that the lost wife was hurting them in one way or another. Whether the divorce was initiated by the wife or by the husband, the loss was viewed as castration, sadistic penetration, absence of the mood-stabilizing mother, or total annihilation. Sometimes intense, narcissistically based anxieties promoted considerable affective lability. To a variable extent, all the fathers noted feeling lonely, although whether what was missed was the true partnership of the wife or was, instead, an aspect of the damaged self-representation depended on the severity of the perceived insult.

To compensate for narcissistic injury, most of these men would engage in frequent, occasionally sustained forays into relationships with other women. "Getting laid" became an important watchword, although wishes for intimacy did not necessarily go along with the pressure for sex. Rather, sex was a confirmation of the man's phallic capacity and self-esteem. Revenge for the imposed hurt was inevitably the source of whatever retaliation the father wanted to muster against the wife. Although the enactment of such reprisals was a variable phenomenon, the wish to engage in retribution was discussed with regularity.

At its best, contact with the children was sustained, but a new intensity was invested in parenting activities that had previously been thought of as mundane, like trips to the park or museum, appearances at school conferences, or visits to child-oriented sports or cultural events. At its worst, there was an increased demand for time with the children, often for the apparent reason of "just having them." This vitality of apparent interest in child-centered activities or "possession" of the children was difficult to talk about honestly; it was frequently defended by "It's my right," "She can't do that to me," "I want them as much as she does," and the like. Yet it was quite clear that contact with the children involved some aspect of self-stabilization and that contact with them was different from what had existed or had been required before the separation. Now the children served, in part, as an inner confirmation of one's role as father/parent, served as a parenting substitute displaced from the lost wife, or functioned as a kind of transitional object.

In all cases, the intensity of the acute reaction became more subdued as time went on, but anxieties could return to high levels in the face of any unresolved legal issue, especially custody. Often, after custody had been determined, the emotional heat associated with the father's vituperations would dissipate. While the acrimony was intense, the pressure for contact with the children was at its height. As the fathers in this group became less involved with their ex-wives or were otherwise preoccupied, their interest in their children diminished and more nearly approached my understanding of their predivorce involvement with their youngsters.

Interestingly, three of the fathers became depressed when they could not fight with their ex-wives, as if their affective vitality on their sadistic involvement with the woman. Although there was nothing to stop them from having contact with their children, during their low periods, these fathers did not pursue greater involvement with them. Instead they complained that whatever contact was taking place was insufficient and was contributing to their poor self-esteem. They inevitably regarded the contact as less than they had had before the divorce. Although this did not seem to be qualitatively true, it was less contact than they pursued in the several weeks immediately after the divorce.

Again, the complaints about lack of contact with their children were displacements from the ambivalent feelings about the ex-wife and the ambitendencies toward narcissistic reunion. For example, one father turned away from his ex-wife and entered into an active affair. When the new woman moved in with him two months later, he was considerably less interested in having his children come to visit than he had been.

Case Illustration

Aaron was 38 years old when he sought psychoanalysis for work-related ennui. He had been essentially unemployed for the two years prior to his first consultation, although he had been a jeweler for the five years before that. He had sold his diamond concern, his most recent business, at a considerable profit. Several years before that, Aaron had been a partner in a fur trade, another business that had been sold for "millions" after his two years working in it. A master at buying and selling of businesses, Aaron had been supporting himself and his family on the proceeds of his sales, but he had not found another job or business. Yet he loved his money with a ferocity that mimicked the lioness's protection of her cubs. When he decided to spend it, he was generous to a fault. But if someone were to ask him for some, he became "weak in the knees, suspicious, and miserably anxious."

Periodically he wondered about his "staying at home," for he believed that his failure to work might have had something to do with his excessive tendency to drink. When he would reel into his house after a night on the town – and there were three or four of these weekly – he would accuse his wife of being unfaithful. She would literally hide under the covers as she waited for his drunken harangues to end with Aaron's passing out on the bed. The next morning he would apologize profusely and guiltily skulk out of the house in an effort to "find something lucrative to do." But each of these searchers was to no avail; he would return home without a single business venture in mind. At first, Aaron rationalized that he was "extremely enterpreneurial" and that it was very difficult to "put together business deals in lucrative areas, like real estate. At any rate," he concluded, "the last good land deal occurred when the Dutch got Manhattan for a song!"

Aaron described Evie, his 37-year-old wife, as a "handsome woman." They had been married for 13 years. Evie had been working for ten years as a stock consultant to a major financial institution. As she assumed increasing responsibilities for the design of the institution's portfolio, she claimed greater and greater professional achievement, although she could not achieve the kind of astronomical financial success that Aaron could manage "on a lark." The couple had two "charming daughters," ages ten and eight. The youngsters were in the fifth and third grades at the same exclusive private school, well-adjusted, and doing well academically. The girls were reared primarily by Evie. Aaron would shower them with gifts on their birthdays and other holidays, but he rarely became involved in the children's day-to-day lives.

Aaron claimed to have been the "singular case study of 'miserable childhood'." He was the elder of two children, his sister having been born when he was four years old. This sister, Eileen, came into the world as a Down syndrome baby. When his mother, Ellen, was told that her daughter was mongoloid, she fell apart. Although Aaron had scant recollection of his life before Eileen's arrival, he clearly remembered the day that mother and child came home from the hospital. Eileen was deposited with a housekeeper as Ellen went to her room, locked the door, and took to her bed – she did not emerge for almost two years. When Ellen did reenter the world, Aaron claims that she was "transformed," as was her relationship to Eileen. Her retarded daughter became her pet, and Aaron and his father became the source of his mother's grief. Ellen blamed her husband for the "mess that he had created" in Eileen. Ellen's berating became so effusive that Aaron's father constructed in the basement a "private sanitarium" for himself, with a lock on the door. Father, when not lost in his work as a dentist, would disappear into televised baseball or football in the cellar. With a beer in his hand he could dull himself to the screaming overhead.

Aaron thus bore the brunt of his mother's rages. No matter what he did, he was bad. If he was late for dinner, he was bad. If he got "a 90" on a test, he had, according to his mother, "missed ten points." Occasionally he was deemed a "good boy" if he brought his mother something that she needed at the moment, but there was usually a follow-up complaint about the "foul manner" that Aaron had used to serve her.

Aaron met Evie in high school. She was his only girlfriend, and it was not until the second year of his treatment that Aaron intuited that there "might just be something to the fact that my mother is Ellen, my sister is Eileen, and then I picked out an Evelyn for myself!" Aaron described Evie as totally captured by his bravado – when they met – she had an inner conviction that he was going to be a millionaire at 25. The couple went to university together, and, when she completed graduate school, they married.

Initially Aaron made his money by dealing drugs, mostly marijuana. Although he used the drug occasionally, he claimed to have always been much more interested in the "investment potential of weed" than in its soporific qualities. While Evie would leave their home each day to work "her balls off," Aaron would stay in their kitchen carving up kilograms of marijuana and "play at traveling salesman." Aaron correctly recognized that his income, which was considerable, was tax free, since he had no intention of reporting the nature of his cash business to the Internal Revenue Service. As money came into the house, he would pour it out, mostly into a Bahamian bank account. When he felt he had enough, he purchased, for cash, an enormous residential loft in an emerging fashionable neighborhood.

When he was 28, his elder daughter was born. With one of the finest homes in "nouveau Manhattan," Aaron believed himself to be on top of the world. A year later, he was on the bottom of it. His father died. As he put it, a "piece of my spirit died with him." He became depressed and began to drink heavily. One night, between sips of scotch, he found himself cradling Evie's new mink coat. He loved the texture and the smell of the fur, as if it had a kind of ambiguous "perfume." Later in the analysis, he would associated this fragrance to the memory of climbing into bed with his mother and father before his sister was born. But, at the time, without this piece of still unconscious information, he became determined to get into the fur business "like a rocket." He almost maniacally built his company but became bored after its success and retreated home to his collection of fur samples qua security blanket, and his bottle to mourn the loss of his father.

Initially in the treatment, he claimed that his relationship with his wife was "excellent," that Evie was "regular and reliable, and she never complained." As the first months of his four-time weekly psychoanalysis drew to a close, he began to introduce material suggesting that the relationship with Evie was not always so copascetic. In addition to the behavior surrounding his drinking that would cause Evie to hide under the covers, he would frequently tease and prod her. When she would explode at him to quit being such a pest, Aaron would sulk around the house, poor himself a drink, and complain that she did not love him. At times, his insistence that she was unfaithful or did not love him sounded bizarre. It seemed to us that Aaron was "being as crazy as his mother," driving Evie into her personal cellar under the covers, as Ellen had done to his father.

But the real cause of the problem began to emerge in the treatment. As part of Aaron's considerable insecurity, which was at times boundless, he attempted to consolidate his self-image by visiting brothels and gay bars. In neither institution did he receive sexual favors, but he would actively solicit. If he found a woman who "came on to him," he would pay her the required fee simply to be titillated by her telling him of his large penile size and sexual capacity. At gay bars, he would eagerly wait to be approached, his glee that much greater if he viewed the other man as handsome and "well endowed." "After all," Aaron mused, "he must think I'm bigger and better." When he returned home, usually drunk, he would vituperatively attack Evie as having been unfaithful, expiating his guilt and externalizing his conflict. He would race into the bathroom to masturbate, relieving himself of "mounting sexual pressure."

Although intercourse was neither easy nor regular with Evie, she did not complain about it. Indeed, she seemed to prefer her plodding, methodical involvement with her work to sexual intercourse. When

Evie and Aaron did make love, she thought, according to Aaron, that he was a good lover. As much as she wanted, she seemed to get.

That situation prevailed until, five months into Aaron's treatment, Evie decided that she wanted another baby. Evie had been offered another promotion, which, if she accepted it, would force her to postpone becoming pregnant for at least a year. Since she was close to 40, she assumed that having a new baby was now or never. That decision was neither callous nor impulsive, yet that is exactly the way Aaron interpreted it.

Whatever preliminary progress he had made during the first few months of his treatment was completely derailed by the "demand that I [Aaron] make a baby." He was hysterically anxious and angry, both in his sessions and outside of them, particularly at Evie. At his calmer moments in the treatment, he would repeatedly obsess, with great agitation, "How could she want something more? I don't have anything more to give. Think what a child will cost. She wants to drive me to the poorhouse." Sometimes he would add a final seasoning: "Of course, you know she is having an affair. She has never been able to make as much money as I, and that's all *she* craves. She will take me to court and try to get half – and then more for those kids!"

Of course Evie was not having an affair, and in his more rational moments, Aaron knew it. He was briefly able to entertain the idea that his rage at Evie had something to do with what he called his "money mishegas" and that he was not genuinely perturbed about the idea of a child at all. The fantasies of being "bled dry" by the unpredictable woman were much more important.

Unfortunately, such brief insights were not mutative to any degree. If Aaron managed not to torture Evie on Tuesday, he would become twice as horrible to her on Wednesday. The angrier that Evie would become in response to Aaron's verbal abuses, the more fright he would experience because she never gave in. At first he was miserably guilty about his temper, and he would try to make up with her, usually sexually. Since she was not much interested in that commodity, if not for the purpose of procreation, she would reject him. His anger would flare up all over again. Then he would get guilty. As he sat with his whiskey, he would imagine himself to be contracting cirrhosis of the liver. He dreamed that he was dying in a pool of blood that streamed out of his nose and rectum.

One day Aaron reported that Evie had left. He discovered that most of her clothing and the children's possessions had been evacuated from their domestic war zone. His level of remorse was considerable, and he blamed himself for her departure, professing tearfully and fitfully that he could not live without her. This hacking guilt lasted two days, until Aaron learned that she had set up household in another apartment, purchased with her own money. That she had squirreled away funds that Aaron did not know about rekindled his wrathful fire. When he was served with papers suing him for divorce, he responded by retaining the "most expensive" matrimonial lawyer he could find. He simply could not fathom why she had left him after all he had "given her over the years." He thought that any introspective investigation of his behavior during the last months was relatively senseless. At the same time, he began to cry regularly in his sessions with me, feeling emotionally deteriorated through Evie's departure, claiming that he missed her, loved her, and needed her. At the same time, he responded angrily to any interventions that I made, especially interpretive ones that frustrated or annoyed him. He also cried in fear that I would abandon him if his behavior did not improve.

As the weeks wore on, Aaron manifestly calmed down. I subsequently learned that his overt calm was, in large part, produced by his single-minded attempt to curtail any additional support for Evie. He refused to pay the private-school tuition for the girls. Though Evie could maintain a household, she could not also bear educational expenses and the children's day-care costs. Aaron initially suggested that she quit her job and stay home with the kids, "because her income was only a tax drain on all concerned."

Then Aaron further opened the doors to his prolific arsenal of vindication. He offered to settle all financial scores with Evie if she would agree to joint custody and coequal visitation for the children. She accepted. When I reopened a discussion of his interest in parenting, he claimed that he had "discovered the importance of his children." He had been to school each week to have conferences with the teachers. He had enrolled the children in music school and dance school. As Daddy, Aaron had begun to overinfuse the children with his attentiveness, concern, and personal and financial investment.

After a short period of time, the couple's lawyers constructed an agreement regarding finances and custody. Both Aaron and Evie signed it. An initial quarterly payment of $15,000 was due to Evie, but Aaron sent only $12,500, claiming that he was "short." He indicated through his attorney that the balance would be forthcoming the following month. Though Aaron might in fact have been temporarily in financial straits, Evie would have none of it. She immediately declared the agreement null and void and filed in court for sole custody of the children. Aaron, predictably, hit the ceiling, and, from his lofty perch, screamed that Evie was violating his constitutional rights. For the three weeks thereafter, Aaron visited brothels and gay bars with a vengeance. He allowed himself to be soliciated by a man who offered to fellate him and charged $15 an inch." Such a bizarre solicitation appealed to Aaron's considerable narcissism.

Because of the respective legal maneuvers in the situation, everything remained quiet between the two for nearly a year. The children visited back and forth, and although Aaron occasionally attempted to define his custodial purview, he virtually sat back and let Evie resume the role of principal parent. Since Aaron was so self-assured of his position and "right" to joint custody, he could work in the analysis in a much more productive way.

With productivity came a certain pain, as Aaron came to realize how pernicious and pervasive the workings of his psyche had become. He began to understand the intricacies of his sour relationship with his mother. Memories of his having been "spoiled rotten" by his mother before his sister was born emerged in the analysis, and these recollections were vitiated by the misery that occurred after Eileen's arrival. He understood aspects of his mother's fragile self-esteem – and of his own. He intensified his perception that mother blamed men for her "bad seed" daughter and that, in an effort to stabilize her own defective self-image, she attempted to reduce Aaron's "little boy effectiveness" through denigrations and symbolic castration. He recalled that, at the age of five, he had been impressed with his capacity, through urination, to "make bubbles in the toilet." Ellen simply accused him of making a mess and admonished Aaron to "keep that thing" in his pants.

He toyed with the idea, that while he professed love for Evie, he needed her to help himself stabilize. Evie comforted him, but money was his greatest source of inner integrity. In the long run, he inferred that it was Ellen's relative financial security that had kept her affect storms at bay; she could calm herself with regular and great "personal presents." Not only could money soothe him, but it, Aaron believed, was also the "way to a woman's heart." Unfortunately, in that sense, as a phallic extension, would compete with Aaron's sense of his phallic capacity and integrity, which helped to explain his counterrage when Evie exploded that he had "shortchanged her."

Though immediately prior to the final divorce proceedings Aaron again attempted to prove his "undying interest in the children," his efforts on their behalf were short lived. Evie was granted sole custody of the children, but Aaron was permitted unlimited visitation. Aaron rarely asked to see the children, but he actively responded when they asked to see him.

Three years later, Aaron purchased a construction company and, using favorable tax advantages, built the company into increasingly more profitable situations. He remarried six months later and recently had a new child, a little girl. A genuine interest in his new fatherhood has caused him to take greater and equally pleasurable interest in his other children.

THE SECOND SUBGROUP

Whether or not they initiated the divorce, the other group of (five) fathers viewed themselves primarily as hurtful to their wives and children (rather than being hurt) in the divorcing process. They responded to the requirements of the process with varying amounts of guilty reactions to their perceived aggression. For example, one father who had left his wife remained incapable of keeping an appointment with an attorney until the wife, quite uncertain about her interest in the separation, forced him into action through the service of papers. On occasion, some fathers would engage in fits of self-destructive activity, like drinking binges or getting fired. All of these men responded in one way or another as guilty partners to their own or their spouse's long-standing apparent ambivalence toward sexual penetration, gratification, or fulfillment. Holding to their own decision to divorce, or responding in a self-caring, self-protective way to a wife's decision to terminate the marriage or to her method of separation, was inevitably viewed as a phallic act with serious aggressive consequences.

Four of the five men in this group suffered periods of depressive withdrawal, internally convinced that they were dangerous men and had committed dangerous acts. They kept in contact with the children only in an effort to work through their guilty feelings and not for the pleasure in it. They were often overly and inappropriately sensitive to the children's positive or negative experiences in being with them, frequently overgratifying them with gifts but withholding themselves. Contact with sons was preferred to contact with daughters; three of the fathers were extremely guilty about the conscious discrimination.

Social activities with women tended to be avoided in the first several months after separation, but these fathers would pal around with male friends. The need for male companionship was sometimes so intense that such socialization became for some a nightly event, with intense feelings of loneliness, betrayal, and guilty self-accusation if it did not occur. Many of these sought-after male friends were married, and these men served the intrapsychic function of parenting the guilty, abandoned little boy that these fathers felt themselves to be.

One father, so intensely affected by his kindled conflicts with aggression directed toward women and femininity, spent the four months after his separation frequenting gay bars and searching for homosexual contact, thus avoiding women and guiltily identifying himself as the abused wife.

Case Illustration

The situation was somewhat different for Stanley, who was 32 when he entered psychoanalytic treatment. A lawyer of profession, he never practiced, nor did he take the state bar examination until after his first year of therapy. According to his own description, he had "inherited the Midwest" from his father, who had been an enormously successful land developer and financier. His mother predeceased his father, and he was an only child. He was born late in his parents' lives because of alleged fertility difficulties. He was conceived, "circumstantially," when his father was past 50 and his mother was well into her 40s. Money was the bane of Stanley's existence, for although he had plenty of it, he could not stand it. It made him atrociously guilty. Every time he tried to spend it, his thoughts would reverberate around conscious, obsessional conundrum. His father was frugal to a fault, and he continually imagined the "old man's punishments" if he spent a dime in what was considered an "unhealthy investment." Almost by definition, anything Stanley wanted was a fantasied bad investment, although he did have, in fact, reasonable business sense. He derived his greatest satisfaction from giving his money away as philanthropic contributions, through famiy trusts and foundations on which he served as a principal trustee.

Stanley married Rebecca while he was still in law school. She was described as a somewhat homely woman from a poor and disorganized family, but she knew what she wanted. She wanted Stanley's checkbook. Within the first year of the marriage, she had convinced him, through her arguments about "share and share alike," to place half of his liquid assets in her name. Overnight, Rebecca became worth 20 million dollars. She, in turn, made her parents millionaires and proceeded never to speak with them again.

Stanley was always terrified of what he called Rebecca's "self-certainty." In fact, he cowered in the face of her anger, which was prodigious whenever Stanley frustrated her. That occurred, unfortunately, with regularity. He was afraid of her as a sexual object and he kept his distance. She complained that he was a coward with no social savoir-faire, and she tried to teach him how to get along with people.

Stanley decided to collect wine and spent many hours with his "new friends" in the wine cellar of his brownstone. Rebecca decided to begin an analysis to learn how to tolerate Stanley's reticence. A month after she began her treatment, she persuaded Stanley to seek a professional consultation. I had been recommended by one of his friends.

Stanley and Rebecca had three children, a son 8, a daughter 4, and another daughter 2. All of the children were reported to be doing well, and Stanley liked them all, although he admitted that he did not do much with his daughters because he feared that "they would break."

Within the first four months of the analysis, Stanley reported that Rebecca wanted another child. He had entertained the idea of many children. He believed himself to be genuinely fortunate that his financial circumstances permitted a large family while others were not similarly blessed. Because his father and mother had waited so long for his birth and had wanted him so much, he had no trouble with the thought of spending his money to raise children. He just hated sexual intercourse. Making love to Rebecca engendered fantasies of a Brunnhilde waiting to pierce his genitals with her spear. As Stanley continued to avoid Rebecca, he did try to understand his lack of motivation in the analysis. Although his psychoanalytic work had begun in earnest, Rebecca announced to him, shortly thereafter, that her analyst had "recommended that she get a divorce, because Stanley was incurably schizoid."

Shocked, Stanley agreeably and guiltily left the house and moved into his own apartment. He obsessed, in the treatment, about the ways that he had hurt Rebecca. He believed that he was indeed hopelessly schizoid. His guilt about hurting her was assuaged by the adoption of this psychic plague. He stopped seeing his daughters, because he believed himself to be a threat to their emotional well-being. He did continue to see his son periodically, as he felt more of an allegiance to this child. It was a phenomenon he could not immediately explain.

Stanley's psychological difficulties responded fairly readily to psychoanalytic interpretation. While it was clear that he was the pride and joy of his parents' existence – "the Isaac that Sarah had waited until 90 to bear" – his history was somewhat complicated. His mother had died in an automobile accident when Stanley was 6. He had been in the car with her. Until the analysis, he had not remembered that on the day of the accident she had picked him up from school. Excited by his kindergarten prowess, Stanley proceeded to show his mother the art work that he had constructed for her that day. Both of them became so wrapped up in a model of the Statue of Liberty that Stanley had made out of colored paper that Mother did not see a slick on the road. The car spun, hit a tree, and she was killed. Stanley was seriously injured, lost consciousness, and next remembered the hospital room where he remained for week.

His father never remarried, and he doted in a special way on his prized son. He offered him every educational opportunity and advantage, but Stanley had difficulty making use of any of them. Stanley's reticence was mirroed back to him by his father as a serious shortcoming. His father chronically worried that his son would be a "ne'er do well." As Stanley began to reconstruct aspects of his father's conversations with him from childhood on, it became clearer that, although father deemed the automobile accident "God's will," he also looked on mother's death as the boy's fault. Certainly Stanley himself had no difficulty explaining the accident in those terms.

Accordingly, Stanley's passivity was understood as part of continuing retribution for his childhood crime. As the issues became clearer in the analysis, he was able to begin to work productively in real estate law. But his conviction that he had married Rebecca for all the wrong reasons continued to plague him. He understood that his passive acceptance of her as "wife" perpetuated a punishing fantasy that he should never have anyone as good as his mother. He continued to have trouble visiting his children for the next year because he admonished himself regularly for bringing children into the world from a "foul union."

As the analysis progressed, Stanley understood that his fantasies of a "foul union" long predated his relationship with Rebecca. He remembered how, before his mother died, his father would leave for work in the early morning and he would immediately run to his mother's bed to "snuggle with her." During the analysis, he began to dream of a torrential storm beating its way into his apartment, sweeping his bed into a raging sea of oblivion. He associated to a children's book about mythology that he had read with his mother. He remembered the picture of Thor, with lightning bolts springing from the god's great hammer. He thought that the picture of Thor, with his blond hair, resembled pictures of his father in his youth.

As these overtly oedipal themes became clarified in the treatment, Stanley's work inhibition diminished further and he came to regard his daughters as less dangerous. He began to include all of his children in quality family time. He is now struggling to find the courage to establish a more coequal relationship with Rebecca. But she resents the fact that he is dating other women.

CONCLUDING REMARKS

So we see that the traumas of the past can also be critical. Understanding the intrapsychic derivatives of the trauma often helped to
predict or to confirm many of the other subsequent interpersonal or
psychosocial variables which affected these fathers in the acute phase,
like the ease, proclivity, inhibition, suffering, or anger associated with
setting up, reorganizing, or maintaining a household; legal and financial obligations; or employment and professional responsibilities. The
degree to which the fathers possessed or acquired a greater capacity to
delay and to reflect before acting also forecasted a more flexible repertoire in coping and adapting, especially as changes in the family or
social milieu posed additional stresses on already taxed individuals.

Fathers in each group catalogued a veritable inventory of pain.
But such pain emerged, as I have demonstrated, from dramatically
different sources. While the two groups of divorced fathers are not
meant to exhaust the list of potential clinical constellations, and while
the clinical case vignettes often represented people at the extremes of
the respective spectra, they do provide us with an initial way of
organizing our thinking about fathers in divorce, their participation in
its causes, and their reactions to marital separation as a life stress.

But, hopefully, this study has shown that certain of the "well-
established" effects of divorce on fathers are caused by more than the
stress of divorce, *per se.* For example, as I noted above, the literature is
replete with descriptions of divorced fathers as "depressed." It has
become facile, although not always incorrect, to assume that such
depressions are inevitably the result of object losses in marital dissolution: those of spouse and children.

I believe that I have demonstrated that such "depressions" can be
considerably more complicated. In the first subgroup of divorcing
fathers, depression was more regularly correlated with the inability to
fight with ex-wives, as if emotional vitality were dependent upon a
sadistic outlet. In the second subgroup of fathers, depression emerged as
the product of guilty recriminations for their fantasied *a priori* sadism.
Thus, while depression may be a final common pathway, a vulnerable
divorcing father seems to arrive at that emotional destination from
very different psychic routing. Looking very narrowly at sadistic
fantasies, one group can't live with them; the other group can't live
without them.

Even this very narrow focus on sadism can help us to understand
a root of ongoing coparental acrimony among divorcing parents.
Subjects among the first group of fathers may well need to stimulate

continuing acrimony in order to preserve their illusory (and quite debilitated) emotional homeostatis. Among the second group of fathers, some individuals may promote, or not terminate, parental acrimony in order, unconsciously, to continue to feel punished for their imagined transgressions.

If ongoing parental acrimony, as a phenomenon, is closely correlated with poor emotional adjustment among the children of divorcing couples, then a word or two about prevention seems in order here. For close to a generation, there has been increasing momentum behind legally mandated *a priori* joint custodial dispositions for the children of divorce. It has been argued by the proponents of joint custody that prescribed coparental involvement and contact with the children lessens acrimony in the population of disenfranchised, and thus embittered, fathers who, in 90% of cases, would otherwise find their children in sole custody with their mothers.

To be sure, there are divorced fathers who are inappropriately constrained from developing ongoing, meaningful relationships with their children. But certainly there are also divorced fathers who abuse the privilege of joint custody in the service of their own, often unconscious, aims. For example, as I (Atkins, 1986a) have pointed out, some fathers in the first group utilized their aggressive pursuit of joint custody in order to torment their ex-wives. The torment is the important component of the act, while the joint custody and the children who are a part of it are simply vehicles in the act. Children who are caught in the emotional maelstrom between such parents are further victimized by this process in divorce.

Even fathers among the second group were not always easily able to fulfill their requirements as joint custody fathers. For example, a 39-year-old father of two children was asked for a divorce by his wife of ten years because of "sexual incompatibility." During the course of his treatment, his own and his wife's sexual conflicts and identity problems became more apparent. She could not tolerate sexual contact, and he "could never get his penis focused" in order to try to please her. Shortly after the divorce, his wife became relatively controlling about his contact with his son and daughter, limiting it to her "convenience." Despite the control, she manifestly agreed to joint custody. As the patient's early memories of maternally administered enemas for failures to have a daily bowel movement ("misbehaving") became more available to him, he devised less guilty strategies for dealing with his wife in the immediate postdivorce period. His greater determination began to please her, and the children came and went with him by mutual agreement. His new "toughness" impressed his ex-spouse, and she began to talk more openly about possible remarriage. Nevertheless, he declined each overture. When he began to develop a relationship with a woman of whom he was genuinely fond, his ex-wife invoked new court papers demanding sole custody unless the girlfriend was given up. In this case, even resolution of the father's early problems, potentially an asset to the children, was not enough.

DISCUSSION

As we look at the effects of divorce on parents, it is critical that we set our sights beyond the *secondary psychological consequences* of marital dissolution. Without question, the ex-wife who is tortured with financial and job insecurity by a withholding and vindictive ex-husband or a sexist society will have extraordinary difficulty accommodating to the effects of divorce. Similarly, an ex-husband who is deprived of contact with his children, for no reason beyond revenge, is going to suffer significantly. We need social policy decisions and legislation that protect the interests of ex-partners who are unfairly exploited by circumstances.

But we must also recognize that such social policy and legislative remediation deal only with the aftershocks of an earlier cataclysm. Accordingly, it is important that we, as mental health professionals, look beneath the surface of divorce and marital discord to understand the *original* psychic difficulties of men and women who marry poorly and separate with varying amounts of warfare and terror. Only then can we assure ourselves that we are on the road to understanding – and then, it is to be hoped, affecting – what has become a social nightmare.

REFERENCES

Atkins, R.N. (1981), Finding one's father: The mother's contribution to early father representations. *J. Amer. Acad. Psychoanal.,* 9:539–559.

———— (1982), Discovering daddy: The mother's role. In: *Father and Child,* ed. S.H. Cath, A. Gurwitt & J.M. Ross. Boston: Little, Brown, pp. 139–146.

———— (1984), Transitive vitalization and its impact on father representation. *Contemp. Psychoanal.,* 20:663–675.

———— (1986a), Single mothers and joint custody: Common ground. In: *In Support of Families,* ed. M. Yogman & T.B. Brazelton. Cambridge, MA: Harvard University Press.

_____ (1986b), Pathological preoccupation: Psychosexual issues. *Internat. J. Psychoanal. Psychother.,* 11:427–433.

_____ (submitted), Fathers in the decision to divorce.

Bernstein, N.R. & Robey, J.S. (1962), The detection and management of pediatric difficulties created by divorce. *Pediat.,* 45:950–956.

Bloom, B.L., Asher, S.J. & White, S.W. (1978), Marital disruption as a stressor: A review and analysis. *Psychol. Bull.,* 85:867–894.

Chesler, P. (1986), *Mothers on Trial.* New York: McGraw-Hill.

Derdeyn, A. (1983), The family in divorce: Issues of parental anger. *J. Amer. Acad. Child Psychiat.,* 22:385–391.

Friedman, H.J. (1980), The father's parenting experience in divorce. *Amer. J. Psychiat.,* 137:1177–1182.

Furstenberg, F.F. (1982), Conjugal succession: Reentering marriage after divorce. In: *Life-Span Development and Behavior Vol. 4.* ed. P.B. Baltes & O.G. Brim. New York: Academic Press, pp. 107–146.

_____ & Spanier, G.B. (1984), *Recycling the Family. Remarriage After the Divorce.* Beverly Hills: Sage.

Greif, J. (1979), Fathers, children, and joint custody. *Amer. J. Orthopsychiat.,* 49:411–419.

Hacker, A. (1983), *U/S A Statistical Portrait of the American People.* New York: Viking Press.

Hetherington, E.M. (1966), Effect of parental absence on sex-typed differences in Negro and white preadolescent boys. *J. Pers. Soc. Psychol.,* 4:87–91.

_____ (1972), Effect of parental absence on personality development in adolescent daughters. *Develop. Psychol.,* 7:313–326.

_____ (1979), Divorce: A child's perspective. *Amer. Psychol.,* 34:851–858.

_____ (1981), Children and divorce. In: *Parent-Child Interaction,* ed. R. Henderson. New York: Academic Press, pp. 33–58.

_____ , Cox M. & Cox, R. (1976), Divorced fathers. *Fam. Coord.,* 25:417–428.

_____ (1978), The aftermath of divorce. In: *Mother-Child, Father-Child Relations,* ed. J.H. Stevens & M. Mathews. Washington, DC: NAEYC, pp. 149–176.

_____ (1979), Family interaction and the social, emotional and cognitive development of children following divorce. In: *The Family,* ed. V. Vaughn & T.B. Brazelton. New York: Science Medicine, pp. 71–87.

_____ (1981), The effects of divorce on parents and children. In: *Nontraditional Families,* ed. M. Lamb. Hillsdale, NJ: Lawrence Erlbaum Associates, pp. 233–288.

_____ & Hagan, M.S. (1986), Divorced fathers: Stress, coping, and adjustment. In: *The Father's Role,* ed. M. Lamb. New York: Wiley, pp. 103–134.

Jacobs, J.W. (1982), The effect of divorce on fathers: An overview of the literature. *Amer. J. Psychiat.,* 139:1235–1241.

_____ (1983), Treatment of divorcing fathers: Social and psychotherapeutic considerations. *Amer. J. Psychiat.,* 140:1294–1299.

Kitson, G.C. & Sussman, M.B. (1982), Marital complaints, demographic characteristics and symptoms of mental distress in divorce. *J. Marr. Fam.,* 44:87–102.

Lansky, M.R. (1986), Pathological preoccupation. *Internat. J. Psychoanal. Psychother.,* 11:409–425.

Steinman, S. (1981), The experience of children in a joint custody arrangement: A report of a study. *Amer. J. Orthopsychiat.,* 51:403–414.

Trombetta, D. (1981), Joint custody: Recent research and overload courtrooms inspire new solutions to custody disputes. *J. Fam. Law.,* 19:213–234.

Wallerstein, J.S. (1977), The effects of parental divorce: Experiences of the preschool child. *J. Amer. Acad. Child Psychiat.,* 4:600–616.

_____ (1983), Children of divorce: The dilemma of a decade. *Psychiat. Update, Vol. 3.* Washington: American Psychiatric Assn., pp. 144–169.

_____ (1984), Children of divorce: Preliminary report of a 10-year follow-up of young children. *Amer. J. Orthopsychiat.,* 54:444–458.

_____ (1985), Children of divorce: Emerging trends. *Psychiat. Clin. of N. Amer.,* 8:837–855.

_____ & Kelly, J.B. (1974), The effects of parental divorce: The adolescent experience. In: *The Child in His Family, Vol. 3.,* ed. E.J. Anthony & C. Koupernik. New York: Wiley, pp. 479–503.

_____ (1975), The effects of parental divorce: The experiences of the preschool child. *J. Amer. Acad. Child Psychiat.,* 14:600–616.

_____ (1976), The effects of parental divorce: Experiences of the child in later latency. *Amer. J. Orthopsychiat.,* 46:256–269.

_____ (1980a), *Surviving the Breakup.* New York: Basic.

_____ (1980b), Effects of divorce on the father-child relationship. *Amer. J. Psychiat.,* 137:1534–1539.

Weitzman, L.J. (1985), *The Unexpected Social and Economic Consequences for Women and Children in America.* New York: Free Press.

Afterword

Since World War II, the wrenching apart of families in the West has reached epidemic proportions. Currently at least 50% of marriages end in divorce, and about the same percentage of those who stay together "till death do us part" contemplate divorce seriously at some time. Six thousand divorces a day leave six million sons and an equal number of daughters with their mothers as the single head of their families (U.S. Bureau of Census, 1982). At least 86% of children of divorce live primarily with their mothers as fathers tend to become more and more "nonresidential" and less emotionally involved, a finding confirmed by the three contributors to this section, Atkins, Michaels, and Solnit. Divorce may seem a long time in coming as two out of every three couples, previously intimate best friends, for a time become worst enemies, publicly humiliating each other and demanding partisan loyalty from their young and vulnerable children. Vicious retaliation seems at the base of the sticky cement that paradoxically holds dysfunctional and dissolving couples together.

When litigation proceedings ensue, extremely destructive forces are unleashed. Kelly and Wallerstein (1980) found that only one third of the children who came from families where both parents were able "to restore their parental functioning" were in good psychological health. Emotional disorders were directly related to continued parental conflict. All family members, including children and grandparents, in witnessing the shattering of the golden rules of family life, experience some regression and diffusing of self- or ego boundaries. Even when separation and divorce are followed by "the second chance" of remarriage, few children in this state do not experience the fear "they too can be divorced" or that the remaining parent might abandon them, a form of double jeopardy. Uncharacteristically good behavior frequently emerges, at least until restabilization through some form of maternal reattachment permits what is repressed in the child a degree of expression. In the dissolution of psychobiological attachments, all participants are challenged: Who they are? To whom do they belong? What determines their value to the proximal and distal, comforting others? These participants may include relatives of the nonresidental father with whom new modes of relating and behaving must now be evolved. Hanson (1985) reminds us that children do not necessarily benefit from a parent's new love affair, exciting career change, remarriage, or from step-sibs, or a parent's therapy (the so-called trickle down effect).

For some time now, Solnit and co-workers, Anna Freud and Joseph Goldstein (Goldstein, Freud, and Solnit, 1979) have offered us basic guidelines for handling some of the divorce-custody issues "in the best interest of the child." Utilizing the analogy of "Solomonic wisdom" in the 15-20% of divorce cases that reach court, Solnit in this volume has addressed himself to those instances: "That vast majority of divorcing fathers who do not want to be, or could not be, the custodial parent, but who want . . . to maintain a significant relationship with their biological children." He implies that except for children under the age of five or six, it may not be desirable for both parents to be equally involved. Indeed noncustodial parents, mostly fathers, should, in Solnit's view, accept that reality and retreat to become "dependable support resources." He advocates that fathers accept the position of visitor and friend with the hope of a better relationship at a later date. He reports a clinical case involving a girl for whom, after many years of father's therapy, such an outcome was possible. Gradually father even "persuaded his daughter's mother to hate him less," thereby setting up a more comfortable and satisfying relationship between father and adolescent daughter. But, as Atkins's chapter suggests, it may be important to know who initiated the divorce. Or how often such an approach without intensive therapy might be feasible for boys or for girls. Solnit's advocacy of a therapeutically induced altruistic transition by the noncaretaking father to the point where he becomes a peace-keeping visitor might disrupt the peace of mind of many readers. It is always clear what is the optimal contact between the noncustodial parent and his children? Is it possible that in the long run the best interest of all involved is that a father's need for a relationship to his children and theirs for him be satisfied in ways that disrupt the mother-child relationship least?

In Atkins's study of 14 men in psychotherapy, the majority of separations (10) were initiated by the women, who accused their spouses of one or more forms of neglect. Often the responsibility for the conflict was heaped upon men who tended toward self-blame and acute mental regression. Atkins found he could differentiate two groups: those who feel hurt and those who feel they have been hurtful to others. To correct damage to self-esteem and a failed image of themselves as fathers may require two sets of defenses. The first revolves around issues of aggression and retaliation ("getting even") and the second a newly vitalized thrust to establish themselves as truly interested in and involved with their children "even in activities previously regarded as mundane." However, as new relationships are sought to undo the sense of failure generated by divorce, one or both parents may reduce investments either in each other or in their child. Let me condense and paraphrase some of his observations.

> "The greater the cooperation between parting parents . . . the more attuned parents are and the more the sustained contact with the noncustodial father the more favorable the outcome." In contrast "ongoing parental acrimony, overt or covert, is likely to be the variable that exacts the most pernicious effect on the child's emotional well being. . . . It is not clear how much an embittered mother's proclivity to transitively denigrate a father and maleness holds sway in her child's mind over the absence of a father. . . . While the acrimony was intense the pressure for contact with the children was at its height." The majority of divorced men and women remarry or somehow restructure their lives. And in the five years following divorce, 50% of fathers will lose significant contact with their children.

All our authors share the concern that legislated custody complicated by both economic and psychological considerations may facilitate the conversion of a shared child into a shared weapon and that, under these circumstances, diminished contact with, and real return, from a divorced father is most likely.

But Michaels reminds us that no matter what the parents, courts, or therapist do, nonresident fathers, near or far, are "compellingly present, alive, and good" in the voluminous, wish-fulfilling fantasies of very young children. In the preschool child, the idealized imagery is of a father overwhelmingly affectionate, romantic, and nurturing rather than heroic, powerful, and protective. There is only minor interest in or perception of father and mother as a couple. "Bad father fantasies" make it difficult to use the father imago to separate from mother, thereby impeding separation-individuation from her and boding poorly for the resolution of some of the triangulations of the oedipal phase. Mother indeed becomes the "pivotal figure," for to preserve her as a constant object may demand remaining loyal to her to the exclusion of father. Some children may modify the enhanced vision of the good father held in their fantasy. But Michaels questions as too simplistic the assumption that a woman who is furious with her ex-mate will generalize this affective image to all men. Even when these invisible attachments lack healthy, aggressive, more oedipal qualities, they still may play a significant, impelling, creative role in subsequent affective, cognitive, and social relationships. In the service of ego autonomy in all the participants, these imagos remain operative in "comprehending and organizing thoughts and ideas about the role and place of mother, father, and self in work and family life." In that some fathers and mothers do become better parents after divorce, we can only echo Atkins words, "Considering the consequences, it is particularly incumbent upon mental health professionals to understand the divorcing process in the context and setting of individual members."

Many researchers have documented that diminished contact with fathers is hardest on boys, who are likely to manifest declinations in self-control, sleep, cognitive skills, and academic motivation. A striking concordance is that both boys and girls living with the same-sex parent after a divorce do better in terms of social competency, superego development, and general maturation. An interested father seems to be what a boy needs as an identity model and role model. Without father, boys are likely, as much as six years downstream, to experience father deprivation, manifested by various forms of reactive depressions, social incompetencies, or aggressive acting-out behaviors. Indeed, Hanson (1985) reports that boys in joint custody do not differ significantly from sons of happily married couples or sons in sole custody of fathers.

It is not surprising that many authors call for greater scrutiny of the reflexive tradition of awarding sole custody and control to mother while assigning a substantially limited role to father after a divorce (Kelly and Wallerstein, 1976; Slipp, 1987).

A clear example of how differently a mother and son may respond to the disappearance of the father can be gleaned from the dialogue between Lady MacDuff and her son. MacDuff has fled the wrath of his irrascible king, Macbeth, leaving his vulnerable wife and son unprotected in their castle. In her helpless rage, Lady MacDuff, understandably enough, cries to the kinsman who has come to warn them of their danger: "To leave his wife, to leave his babes, his mansions and his titles, in a place from whence himself does fly? He loves us not!"

Lady MacDuff turns to her son playing nearby, and the following dialogue ensues:

Mother: Fathered he is and yet he's fatherless, Sirrih, Your father's dead. And what will you do now, how will you live?"
Son: As birds do mother.
Mother: What with worms and flys.
Son: With what I get, I mean; and so do they. My father is not dead for all you're saying.
Mother: Yes he is dead: How wilt thou do for a father?
Son: Nay, How wilt thou do for a husband?
Mother: I can buy me twenty at any market. . . .
Son: If he were dead, you'd weep for him: if you would not, it were a good sign that I should quickly have a new father.
Mother: Poor prattler! How thou talkest.

Both mother and son speak the truth—but their words arise from vastly different reservoirs of experience and need.

Disrupted families are a developmental challenge many children handle, survive and adapt to as best as they can. Disruption is not likely to become a catastrophe unless the integrity of the protective surround fails to protect from the bitter acrimony of parent—thereby adding inordinate hostility to the intrinsic fears of abandonment and annihilation of the child.

Stanley H. Cath

REFERENCES

Goldstein, J., Freud, A. & Solnit, A. (1979), *Beyond the Best Interests of the Child.* New York: Free Press.

Hanson, S.H. (1985), *Dimensions of Fatherhood.* Beverly Hills, CA: Sage.

Kelly, J. & Wallerstein, J. (1976), The effects of parental divorce: Experiences of the child in early infancy. *Amer. J. Orthopsychiat.,* 46:20–32.

_____ (1980), *Surviving the Breakup.* New York: Basic Books.

Slipp, S. (1988), Issues in joint custody. *Amer. Acad. Forum,* Spring:32:1.

U.S. Bureau of the Census (1982), *Statistical Abstract of the U.S. 1981.* Washington, DC: U.S. Govt. Printing Office.

VII

TREATMENT CHALLENGES

Prelude

The last 15 years have brought about an enthusiasm regarding the father's role in the family. Fathers have been invited to attend childbirth preparation classes, even participate in the birth of their children, and many now are active participants in child psychotherapy. This enthusiasm has naively assumed that all fathers should be in all these activities, right from the beginning. Fathers who are not comfortable participating may feel guilty and awkward; yet there are many and varied ways to involve the father. Timing and motivation are crucial factors.

In treatment, who is it that wants the father in the psychotherapy of the child? Is it the child, the mother, the father, the therapist, or a combination of them? Is he there because his influence is a primary focus in the treatment of the child? Is he there because he is the target of blame for the child's problems? Is he there to help with a dysfunctional spouse and mother? Why is he being called in? Along with the enthusiasm about the father has come an enthusiasm for treating the entire family. But the question can be asked, is it not possible that the family or triadic focus may even undermine the more specific and, in some cases, most essential work with a particular dyad, for example, mother and child? Nowadays, treating a dyad is often seen as excluding one partner. However, this is not necessarily the case. We must remember that psychic reality and fantasy bring into the treatment room the entire case of family characters. As long as the therapist is open to the child patient's representations and fantasies about the father, the father is alive and hardly forgotten.

The question can then be raised, how open is the particular therapist to the father's influence? A therapist often must underemphasize the parenting function of the child's parents, with a consequent increase in professional self-esteem – the therapist can feel he or she is of great help to an at-risk child. Beginning therapists often have this problem. They do not yet truly understand the distinctions between being a child therapist and being a child's parent. Moreover, always keeping in focus the existence and importance of the real parents can facilitate the treatment, since helping the parents improve their parenting skills will also make the child better.

Furthermore, one of the issues in treatment may be the difficulties encountered by the child, mother, or father with triangulation, that is, the ability to perceive, experience, and internalize various dyadic and triadic relationships within a family. This symbolic and emotional process very often becomes a treatment focus, with apparent problems in achieving triangulation requiring therapeutic attention.

Thus, the need to include or exclude the father in treatment can have adaptive and maladaptive elements that need to be carefully understood (Ferholt and Gurwitt, 1982).

The father himself may wish to be included, for either good or pathological reasons, or excluded, for good or pathological reasons. Each of the papers in this section addresses in a central way how the father is included in or excluded from the psychic life of the patient, the mother, and the therapist.

Wallace is personally proud to be a father for the second time. He wishes to convey to his child patients this event in his life in order to help them understand his disappearance for a few weeks around the time of his baby's birth. He wonders whether telling his patients will facilitate work on their conflicts and issues in family relationships. He seems very open to the realization that for some of his patients this news was disruptive and caused regressive episodes. He had been working under the classical assumption of a paternal transference to him rather than seeing that in a very real way he was experienced by some of these children as a real father. Thus, the news was devastating for them. A possible issue he himself was addressing was how to break the news to an older sibling of the birth of a younger sibling. This news jolted his patients in terms not only of fathering issues but of parent-hood and motherhood issues as well. We can, of course, understand how becoming a parent is a truly exciting step in one's life and one we all want to share. Female therapists, of course, have the natural advantage of exhibiting their news physically. Along with our pride, however, is our guilt in having children, when our little patients look to us, very often in a real way, as their good parents.

Galenson offers another model of treatment and way of focusing on the father. The mother and the child are seen in two separate treatments simultaneously, with two different therapists, who share information. In one case, she shows how a mother repeats her relationship with her own father in her choice of husband. In particular, this patient's father did not enter her life until she was older. This pattern then was repeated with her daughter and her daughter's father. The mother's ability to analyze this is in her treatment paved the way for allowing her husband to be involved with her daughter earlier than her own father had become involved with her. As the mother became more open to her own paternal yearnings, she made room for her husband to play a significant role in her daughter's life. Perceiving her mother's openness, the daughter, having made her own treatment strides, was now ready to move toward her father. Here the father was not directly involved in the treatment, but he was vital in the psychic life of the mother, daughter, and the therapists.

In a chapter on treatment of men, I emphasize the defensive aspects of the position of many patients who come into treatment stating that their fathers were and still are inadequate. I show how the father, via the female analyst, may be revitalized in the treatment process. The chapter illustrates that many patients have mothers who for many reasons have needed to denigrate or devalue the father as a person and his role as a father in the family. On a concrete level, to have a therapist who now represents paternal inclusion and respect without maternal denigration and disrespect and approves of a father-son relationship provides an optimal environment for growth in masculine identity, triangulation, and in stimulating more adequate paternal development in the patient himself. The therapist faces the task of bringing in for the patient, by reminding the patient, the positive memories and images of the father. Consequently, the maternal imago, which has included everything good from both the mother and the father, becomes less encompassing. Recognizing father with his positive and negative contributions can now facilitate the formation of a differentiated paternal imago (Lansky, this volume, Paternal Imago).

Schwartzman, in his study of two fathers of young psychotic boys, focuses on the profound disappointment these fathers feel in their sons' inability to recognize, appreciate, and experience them as fathers. He shows how these fathers need a psychoeducational approach, one that is sensitive to their psychological feelings and yet helps them very specifically in their interactions with their sons. This psychoeducational approach can take the form of working with the father alone, with the father and child, with the father and mother, or in father groups. From Schwartzman's descriptions of the father-son interactions, what emerges is a particular parenting style adopted by these two fathers, who seem different in terms of their individual personalities. However, they also employed a similar controlling and at times intrusive style with their sons in order to keep the boys engaged with them.

Lansky and Simenstad emphasize a major reason why the psychiatric hospitalization of men fails so often. What seems to be missed by staff is the chronic despair and sense of failure these men have as fathers to their children and as heads of their families. Group work with these men, focusing on fathering issues, essentially failed, and the authors try to understand why. I would like to suggest a few possible reasons for this treatment failure. First, there may be a lack of agreement in treatment focus. Staff wants these men to regain their fatherhood status, and patients are saying that they have come to the hospital to avoid the suffering and humiliation they have endured and still feel as failed fathers. They came to forget, whereas staff wants them to remember. As therapists, we do encounter mothers who do not wish to be mothers and fathers who do not wish to be fathers. We tell ourselves that there must be conflict and that there is a part of these people that needs strengthening, that yearns to be a parent. Is this always so, or ought we not recognize our own limitations in achieving this? Can we help some of our patients move away from these roles without disgrace and disrespect for themselves and from their therapists? Perhaps the hospital staff could tolerate these men as emotionally ill but could not tolerate that these men wanted to be fathered (and mothered) and not be fathers themselves. These men may have felt they were protecting their families by leaving, and we as therapists must be open to this possibility.

Paternal idealization is something we all hold on to. Working with fathers and bringing them into treatment may shatter the paternal idealization for the patient and for the therapist. We are thus presented with a delicate and important treatment challenge: how do we look at the difficulties in fathering a man is having and still maintain respect for his journey as father to his children and perhaps as father to his wife, himself, and to the therapist?

Linda Gunsberg

REFERENCES

Ferholt, J. & Gurwitt, A. (1982), Involving fathers in treatment. In: *Father and Child,* ed. S. Cath, A. Gurwitt & J. Ross. Boston: Little, Brown pp. 557–568.

24

Paternity and Transference
The Fatherhood of a Child Therapist
James M. Wallace

It has been my experience that patients react in a variety of very powerful yet understandable ways to the knowledge that their therapist is becoming a father. My interest in this subject was kindled earlier in my training in a large, primarily inpatient hospital setting by the reactions of adult and adolescent patients to the birth of my first child. Their reactions fell into certain groupings that seemed to reflect the patient's level of development, the ongoing transference relationship, and current environmental influences.

Sexuality and gender issues, sibling and parental relationships, and current struggles with intimacy became open subjects for discussion. Protective feelings toward me and my family, fears of losing me, and anger toward the implicit competition with my family for my attention and affection were brought into therapy. Along with these discussions came a variable amount of stress, anxiety, regression, and behavioral problems both within and outside the therapy hours. These were major concerns that turned out to be short-term problems that were manageable within the inpatient setting. Overall, it seemed that many important recent and historical issues of my patients came to the foreground and were available for exploration as a result of their knowledge of my paternity.

473

The purpose of this paper is to demonstrate the same phenomena in a different population and setting through the presentation and discussion of five outpatient child psychotherapy cases. I hoped that the frank honesty of child patients would clarify and substantiate my impressions from my experience with adult and adolescent patients. My hypothesis was that patients of all ages and developmental levels would react in understandable ways to the fatherhood of their psychotherapist and that the exploration of these reactions could be beneficial.

The decision to disclose my paternity was a difficult one for three conscious reasons and perhaps many more of which I was less aware. First, the setting in which I work is not very private, and the chance that my patients might find out incidentally was quite high. Second, my projected two-week absence was necessarily unscheduled. This was atypical and would require some sort of disclosure in order to maintain the achieved level of trust and honesty within the therapeutic relationship. Third, my experience led me to believe that disclosure would be an overall benefit to my patients by bringing into treatment some important issues that were, as yet, unexplored.

Possible covert or unconscious reasons for my disclosure were not then, nor are they now, entirely clear to me. Perhaps they can best be represented by a dream I had as I was in the process of making this decision. I dreamed I was standing on a mountaintop, joyously shouting my announcement to the world. After a few moments, I heard my voice return as an echo, and I felt somewhat foolish and embarrassed. I walked back down the mountain, hoping I had not done anyone any serious harm. The dream demonstrates some of the mixed feelings I had about the disclosure. I tried to understand and account for these feelings in my decision making so as not to either burden or protect my patients because of unconscious urges and fears.

In reviewing the literature on the subject, I found no reports on the reactions of patients to the fatherhood of their therapist. In contrast, a small but growing number of female therapists have reported a broad spectrum of reactions of child patients (Browning, 1974; Ashway, 1984; Harnett, 1949; Lax, 1969; Nadelson et al., 1974; Underwood and Underwood, 1976; Cole, 1980; Fenster, Phillips, and Rapoport, 1987) to their therapists' pregnancy and motherhood. In essence, they suggest that their pregnancy and motherhood enhanced ongoing transference issues (Lax, 1969; Browning, 1974; Nadelson et al., 1974; Underwood and Underwood, 1976; Cole, 1980; Ashway, 1984; Fenster et al., 1987) and contributed to important conflict resolution and growth (Ashway, 1984). They also reported that the nature of the transferential relationships and reactions to their pregnancies and motherhood were determined by the patients' developmental level and degree of psychopathology.

Of course, motherhood and fatherhood are vastly different experiences for therapists and their patients. There is no possibility of anonymity for the female therapist during pregnancy. In contrast, the male therapist can wait until close to the expected delivery date before disclosing his paternity. In some treatment settings he may even have the option of totally withholding the information. The pregnant therapist often feels physically ill or tired, experiences fetal movements, and undergoes massive changes in self-and body images. There are no exact parallels for the male therapist, but there is no reason to expect his internal psychological reactions to his wife's pregnancy to be different from those of other men (Gurwitt, 1982). Beyond these reactions, toward the end of the pregnancy he may fear for the health and welfare of his wife and child, as he waits expectantly for a phone call to send him to the hospital. For these and other manifold reasons, the momentous inner experience of the therapist who is to become a parent is dependent on the sex of the therapist.

For the patient, the therapist's parenthood often reenforces the maleness or femaleness of the therapist in a very direct way (see Fenster et al., 1987). Sexuality is introduced quite blatantly into the therapy as patients are reminded of the therapist's active sexuality and involvement with an opposite-sexed partner. A commitment to a member of the opposite sex and an emotional life outside the treatment setting are clearly and unambiguously demonstrated. Anonymity and clinical neutrality are shattered as patients find out, either directly or indirectly, of the imminent parenthood. These are very basic issues that are related to, and have a powerful impact on, the ongoing transference relationship. They are also important ingredients of patients' reactions to the parenthood of their therapist and differ according to the sex of the therapist and the patient.

The role of the father in child development was largely neglected until recently (see Cath, Gurwitt, and Ross, 1982). As fathers and fatherhood become better understood, so will the importance of paternal transference phenomena for both male and female patients. It is not the purpose of this paper to explore the entire complex field of paternal transference reactions. Instead, it is to suggest that the reactions of patients to the paternity of the therapist may be one avenue for discovering more about the nature of paternal transference issues and the role of fathers in development.

The methodology for this study was structured around practical issues. The information was disclosed in a controlled setting prior to the patients finding out incidentally. Enough time was allowed for the important groundwork of clarifying the information and opening the topic for discussion. Between two and three weeks prior to the expected delivery date, the upcoming paternity and two-week absence of the therapist was announced. The statement was concise and was repeated as needed for each patient. The patients' parents were also informed either directly or by the parent therapist, depending on the treatment model being used. At that time, eight individual child psychotherapy cases were being seen in weekly 50-minute sessions. The patients ranged in age from four to fifteen years. While all of the reactions were interesting and noteworthy, the five cases described here had been in treatment for the longest periods of time. The patient–therapist relationships were fairly stable; consequently their reactions were more easily understood. Data was collected through detailed process notes, as it was felt that the sudden introduction of a recording device would affect the patients' reactions more than the inaccuracies of memory.

CASE ILLUSTRATION

Vinnie, a ten-year-old boy in a special school, had been in treatment for behavioral problems and depression for the previous two years without any major improvement. He was bright and verbal and had progressed academically despite a chaotic family situation. His parents had undergone a stormy separation and divorce during the current schoolyear and his mother was planning remarriage the following summer. He made strong attachments to peers and adults and had some ability to struggle with his internal and external conflicts in psychotherapy. His 16-year-old brother was streetwise and aloof, and his two-year-old brother received whatever soothing and nurturance was available in his family. Vinnie was described by his mother as being "just like his father"; he was becoming increasingly sociopathic, with frequent acts of theft, vandalism, and fighting, and was scheduled to go into residential placement at the end of the school year. Recent therapy hours had revolved around his limit testing, bragging about his sociopathic exploits and essentially keeping a very "macho" profile. This was often punctuated by long silences that bubbled with sadness.

Three weeks before the scheduled absence of the therapist, (about midway through a mostly silent session), Vinnie was told of the upcoming paternity.

> T: Vinnie, at the end of this month I'm going to miss two weeks because my wife is going to have a baby. After two weeks I'll be back to work.
> V: (mumbles inaudibly)
> T: I couldn't hear you.
> V: It's good to spend time with your baby.
> T: You think so?
> V: (silent)
> T: You have a baby brother, don't you?
> V: Yes! (mood brightening) I like him. You know, I take care of him sometimes.
> T: He must like that.
> V: (glowing) Yes, he does.
> T: What do you do for him?
> V: I feed him. I play with him. I used to give him a bath with my mother. Not now, though. I don't change his diapers.
> T: You don't?
> V: No, my mother and grandmother do that.

In further sessions, Vinnie was solicitous and sad but was unresponsive when the therapist commented on this behavior. He was truant from school and missed one session before and two sessions after the therapist's absence. He told his teachers and peers directly that he had skipped school because he did not want to see the therapist. Eventually, the therapist approached him informally in his classroom, and Vinnie reluctantly began coming to his scheduled appointments. He talked of his jealousy toward the therapist's baby and of being angry at both the therapist and his mother for being involved with other people when he was feeling so bad.

In subsequent sessions, Vinnie revealed that he had found out the sex and name of the newborn child. He made a graffiti sign of the name for the therapist to take home and give to the baby. He would not disclose his source and seemed quite pleased with himself. When he was reassured that the therapist kept the things he made in therapy in the office file, he seemed relieved. He then asked what kind of bicycle the therapist's baby rode so he and his friends would not "accidentally steal it."

In summary, Vinnie's initial reaction seemed to be a sullen, envious identification with the baby, which reflected his ongoing environmental influences and early life experiences. Later, as a caretaker of his brother, he found some joy in identifying with the therapist and other nurturant figures. He was protective of the baby and seemed genuinely concerned about his belongings. After the announcement of the pending birth, there was some increase in behavioral problems, with truancy and avoidance of therapy hours. With encouragement he was able to continue in school and return to therapy as regularly as before. He still required residential placement, but his overall emotional involvement in treatment was improved. His behavior, other than his initial avoidance, did not significantly worsen even given his family situation, his termination with his therapist and special school.

CASE ILLUSTRATION

Fred was an 11-year-old boy who was in Vinnie's class and had been his friend for more than two years. His behavior was impulsive and aggressive. He was self-centered and very controlling in his relationships with his peers and adults. He was the only son and third child of an unwed mother. All three had the same father, who left the mother during her pregnancy with Fred. The mother described feeling "overwhelmed" during the last months of pregnancy and after Fred's birth. She named Fred after his father, who saw him once when Fred was four months old and not again until Fred was seven years old.

Recent sessions had alternated between provocation and remarkably sensitive discussions that revealed Fred's increasing empathy toward his peers. He had not spoken of his father since his initial evaluation.

During the session in which Fred was told the facts surrounding the therapist's upcoming two-week absence, in much the same way as Vinnie was told, the following interchange took place:

F: Two weeks, that's too long. How about two days?
T: No, two weeks, and then I'll be back.
F: I like babies. I have a neighbor's baby and a stepsister's baby, they're okay.
T: So you know some babies.
F: (smiling) Yes, I do.
T: Do you ever help take care of them?
F: No, no. I'm no babysitter. Why are you taking so long? Why not two days?
T: You don't like me being away so long.
F: No. (silent)
T: I'll be . . .
F: (interrupting) I'm going to have babies some day.
T: You're going to be a father?
F: Sure, and I'll be a good father.

T: How will you do that?

F: Just be good, stupid.

T: Okay.

F: (silently dealing cards)

T: I guess your father wasn't around much for you.

F: (sadly) No, I only saw him once when I was a baby and now he hardly ever visits.

T: That's not much.

F: (interrupting) I don't want to play any more, I want to go back to class.

T: I guess you get pretty upset talking about your father. We don't have to right now if you don't want to.

F: (calming) Let's play hide the cards.

T: Okay.

In the remainder of the session Fred became uncharacteristically intimate—putting his arm around the therapist, leaning against him and wanting to take a scrap of paper out of the waste basket back to class with him. For the first time, he was polite and appropriate on returning to class.

In one further session prior to the therapist's absence, Fred suddenly announced that he had to go back to class early because, "You have to go see your wife." He said, "Next week I want to talk about the baby and I want you to tell me if it's a boy or a girl." Asked what his prediction was, he said glowingly, "A boy like me, of course."

During the first session on the return of the therapist, Fred quietly cursed the therapist out, asking where he had been the previous week. He was very controlling and finally said that he was mad because there had been a school meeting and the therapist was not there.

F: (scolding) You weren't at that meeting. That was important.

T: I know it was, and you're disappointed in me that I didn't go.

F: Yes.

T: I wish I could have but I couldn't.

F: (silent) How's the baby?

T: Fine, thanks for asking.

F: (silent) I've got to go back now.

T: We have 20 more minutes. I guess you're mad because the baby interfered with our sessions and kept me away from the meeting.

F: (silent)

T: I don't blame you for being mad and it's okay if you tell me if you want to.

F: Next time maybe.

T: Okay, next time.

In further sessions, Fred was able to talk of missing his father and hoping to be a good father some day. He was less able to speak of his anger and resentment toward the therapist or the baby or toward his father. His anger was being expressed through his behavior in the classroom.

In summary, Fred initially experienced the announcement of the therapist's absence and paternity as a narcissistic wound. He returned often to this theme after brief periods of identification with the therapist as a father. Eventually, he was able to discuss early paternal deprivation and in his play acted out an idealized father transference toward the therapist. He was empathic to the distraction of the therapist and concerned with the needs of his wife the day before the delivery. He showed another identification with the baby that he cloaked in humor. Upon return of the therapist, Fred again felt wounded and resentful but contained these feelings and spoke of missing his father.

Early in May, his family lost their rent-controlled apartment and suddenly moved to another city to live with Fred's maternal grandparents. The mother did ask for a referral for Fred prior to leaving. During the last session, Fred handed his therapist a card that said, "Dear Doctor, I will miss you."

CASE ILLUSTRATION

Sharon was a nine-year-old girl who had been in special programs since age three. Born prematurely, she suffered anoxia. She had an abnormal electroencephalogram and was developmentally delayed in all academic areas and in her interpersonal relationships. She was the youngest of three siblings, the only girl, 15 years younger than her next oldest brother. The family was overly close and protective. The adult siblings lived at home and were intimately involved with Sharon, her parents, and maternal grandparents. Sharon's mother had numerous somatic illnesses and complaints and was phobic of leaving home or driving. She projected many of her fears onto Sharon. She put all of her energy into Sharon's care, which she claimed "keeps her out of a wheelchair."

Recent sessions had involved ritualistic washing of puppets and some complicated puppet play where Sharon expressed feeling constantly observed and directed by adults in her play at home.

When told of the upcoming paternity leave, she said nothing and went over to a doll she had never touched before, picked it up, and said:

S: Can we wash the baby?
T: Sure.
S: (putting the clothed doll in a sink full of water)
T: First we have to take the baby's clothes off, don't we?
S: I can't get them off. (Suddenly they came off and she dunks the baby under water.)
T: Is it okay to hold the baby under water like that?
S: The baby can pee. The baby can pee.
T: I wonder if the baby can breathe.
S: (letting the doll up) Let's wash the baby.
T: Do you know any babies?
S: No.
T: Do you have any dolls at home?
S: Yes.
T: Do you take care of them?
S: Yes.
T: How do you do that?
S: I wash them. (walking away from the doll in the sink)
T: The baby is still in the sink.
S: Will you get the bowling pins? Let's play with puppets.
T: Who should I be?
S: Grandpa.
T: Grandpa wants to talk to Sharon.
S: Hi, Grandpa.
T: Hi. Sharon. You seem kind of mad at the baby doll today.
S: Yes.
T: Do you get mad when Dr. W is away?
S: Yes, I get mad. And I get sad.

Sharon's speech was at times somewhat distorted by perseveration and echolalia, and a meaningful exchange was often difficult to interpret. Nonverbal communication was often more reliable with her, and in the next hour she drew a picture of a very round woman and then superimposed what looked like a baby over the woman's abdomen. When the therapist observed that it looked like a baby inside the woman she said, "No, that's an angel on her shirt."

After the return of the therapist, Sharon made no mention of the baby or the absence. When she entered the office in the next few sessions, however, she looked over at the baby doll. If it was lying on top of the blanket, she would interrupt her play sometime during the session, go over to the doll, and wrap it in the blanket and gently lay it in its crib. When asked about this, she acted as if nothing had been said and resumed her play where she had left off.

In summary, Sharon showed that she understood the therapist's announcement and immediately included the doll in her ritualistic washing. She showed one aspect of her ambivalence initially by drowning the doll and later expressed it via puppet play in her discussion with Grandpa. Later, she showed primarily nurturant and protective feelings by gently wrapping the doll in the blanket.

CASE ILLUSTRATION

Jerry was a softspoken, eight-year-old boy who had been in treatment for severe separation anxiety manifested in tantrums and aggression. Four years older than his younger sister, he was the middle of three children. His mother admitted feeling most comfortable relating to infants and toddlers. As Jerry and his siblings got older, she had begun to take in foster infants and worked briefly in a daycare facility. His father was a quiet, distant man who worked many hours a day away from the home. There was a very close community and family network, and Jerry had been involved with a number of "parental" adults.

These incidents came approximately three months before Jerry's planned termination from treatment. His therapy hours had been focused on family relationships. The primary concern was the mutual overattachment with his mother, which was now being confused by her involvement with foster care. He enjoyed being allowed to develop more age-appropriate activities and skills with his siblings and cousins, but he wondered if his mother was mad at him for doing so.

After the announcement, he said nonchalantly:

> J: We have babies at our house.
> T: Really?
> J: Yes.
> T: What babies?
> J: My mom takes care of babies sometimes.
> T: Is she now?
> J: Yes.
> T: Can you tell me about the baby?
> J: (laughing anxiously) This one is a little boy. He looks kind of funny.
> T: What's he look like?
> J: (drawing a picture) He's kind of bald and fat and has big ears.
> T: You seem not to like him too much.
> J: No, I don't like babies much.

T:How come?

J: They can't really play. And they cry a lot and really make too much noise.

T:How's that for you?

J: I don't like noise, so I go out and play.

T:How about your mom?

J: She doesn't mind the noise, I don't know why.

T:How about your dad.

J: He doesn't like babies either.

T:No?

J: No. He watches TV or goes to work.

T:Does he every play with you?

J: He watches us sometimes.

T:Do you like that?

J: Yes, I guess so. He just sits on the steps and watches us play.

In a later session, Jerry was playing with a kangaroo that had a baby in its pouch. He started laughing, saying that the baby kangaroo looked like a puppy.

T: Baby people, how about them?

J: What?

T: You said they look kind of funny, too.

J: (giggling) They look kind of like puppies, too.

T: Do you remember when your sister was a baby?

J: Yes. (quiet) I wasn't very nice to her.

T: You seem sad about that.

J: I was pretty mean to her.

T: Do you remember that?

J: I used to punch her and hit her.

T: You must have been mad at her.

J: I guess. I got in trouble a lot. Not anymore.

T: Do you like your little sister more now?

J: Yes. Now she's big enough to play.

T: And you like that better?

J: Yes.

Jerry often brought up his dislike for babies and his relationships with his siblings. He reacted to the therapist's announcement by focusing on his unresolved ambivalent feelings toward babies, which related to past sibling experiences. He identified with his father's avoidant reactions but hinted at how important his father's limited involvemnent was to him. He was able openly to discuss both his guilt for mistreating his younger sister and his growing fondness for her.

CASE ILLUSTRATION

Sandy was eleven years old when she was transferred to a new therapist from a female therapist (Dr. A), who was leaving the clinic. Coincidentally, this happened furing Dr. A's third trimester of pregnancy. Soon thereafter, Sandy's parents' divorced. Her mother had begun dating a man who planned to move in with the family. Typically, Sandy was very domineering and unempathic toward her peers and felt compelled to be the best at all scholastic and athletic activities. She denied ever having had an angry or sad moment in her life. She had been referred for treatment at age five following a suicide gesture of scratching her wrist with her play scissors. She was very bright and precociously verbal, as was her ten-year-old sister. Recent sessions had focused on her mixed alliances with her father, mother, mother's new boyfriend, and therapist. She felt pulled in many different directions at once. At times, she felt close to her therapist, but this was also a powerful source of guilt. She alternated between drawing closer to and pushing away from her therapist.

> S: (whispering) Whoopie!
> T: Whoopie?
> S: That's nice. I hope it's a girl.
> T: How come?
> S: Girls are nicer.
> T: Really?
> S: Yes, like me.
> T: Oh, do you know any babies?
> S: Yes, my neighbor has a girl. She cries too much. (thoughtfully silent) Don't change the diapers.
> T: Why?
> S: They smell bad.
> T: I heard that.
> S: My mom said that when I was a baby my diapers didn't smell bad.
> T: Really?
> S: Yes. My sister's did but not mine. (painting a picture of a girl, she then wrote her sister's name boldly across the face) I guess I wrecked her face.
> T: I guess you did.
> S: Did Dr. A have a boy or a girl?
> T: I don't know, why?
> S: I think you'll have a girl and she'll be nice.
> T: You think so?
> S: Yes, I don't know why but I just think so.

> T: After Dr. A had her baby she stopped working here.
> S: Yes, she went to work at another hospital. You'll come back, right? You're not a girl.
> T: I'll be back after two weeks. What do you mean, "you're not a girl"?
> S: Sometimes girls stop working when they have a baby.

The next session happened to be the day before Sandy's eighth birthday. She started by painting a series of red beachballs she said were full of air or gas. She then came over to her therapist's painting and started to paint on it. She started smearing and splashing paint until she had to be stopped and the paints put away. She was still angry and wanted to play hide and seek, eventually hiding under the sink and refusing to come out. While sawing at the drainpipe with her barrette she said:

> S: I'm not coming out.
> T: What do you mean?
> S: Don't ask me questions. You said we don't boss each other around, and you're forcing me to move my mouth.
> T: I wonder which questions you don't like.
> S: All of them are stupid. Don't make me talk. You're stupid, ugly, nerdy, and I hate boys. Dr. A wasn't mean. You're the meanest and if you're coming next week, I'm not! Why don't you just quit and get a girl.
> T: Get a girl?
> S: Yes, have a girl teach me. I hate boys. How about your wife, when she's done with the baby?

In the next session, the last before the absence, Sandy was silent throughout the hour. She sat in a chair turned toward the wall, left her coat tightly zipped, and hugged her Cabbage Patch doll. It was later learned from her mother that her father had visited her for her birthday, stirring up both longing for and resentment toward him. She told her mother about these feelings, adding "I'm not telling anyone else about this."

In the first session following the therapist's return, Sandy was tentative but soon asked about the baby and engaged in active, competitive play. During a quiet moment she was asked if she remembered the last session, the silent one, which she initially denied. She later explained, "I must hve been tired." When asked about the time before that, when she had hid under the sink, she said:

S: Yes, I remember that. I must have been tired that day, too. Didn't I say I wanted your wife to teach me?

T: Yes, you did.

S: I remember that. (She walked around the office and then to the windowsill where we had started some plant cuttings. She poured the water out of the cup and laid them out on the table, breaking up the styrofoam cup. After a pause she picked up the cuttings and smashed them between her hands until they were a green pulp.)

T: Boy, you really smashed them.

S: Yes, I killed them.

T: I guess you did.

S: No more baby plants. Don't worry Dr. W, my mom said plants can't feel anything.

T: I guess you got rid of the plants.

She then went on regressively to pour water all over the table until it was flowing onto the floor, when the therapist asked her to sit down and help figure out what to do. She quickly calmed down and helped clean up.

In further sessions, her therapist reflected on the incident with the baby plants and asked if it might have been related to the new baby, which she denied. She said that she had started some baby plants at home with her mother.

In summary, Sandy's initial reaction was excitement and an identification with the baby. She briefly mentioned some unresolved issues with her former therapist's pregnancy. In the next session she regressed to paint smearing and refused to come out from under the sink. She repeatedly showed her interest in the therapist's wife as a rival and potential caretaker. These feelings, coupled with her birthday and her father's visit, resulted in the silent session just prior to the therapist's absence. On the latter's return, she immediately inquired of the baby and engaged in competitive play. When recalling the two previous sessions and her bid for the therapist's wife as "teacher," she aggressively destroyed the baby plants with the affect of a women spurned. Strong oedipal issues appeared to be intermingled with more regressive early developmental features.

Further sessions showed that she was working on oedipal issues and boundaries as she clarified the confusion over the destruction of the cuttings. She said, "Dr. W, it's okay for you to have baby plants in your office, just not with me." Her play became less seductive and more competitive, with her practicing and trying to master new games that she learned in school and at home. The paternity had precipitated a sort of oedipal crisis, and its resolution seemed to help Sandy to move into more latency-type play.

DISCUSSION

These cases illustrate quite clearly that personal information about the therapist, when it is in keeping with major transference issues, can enhance these issues and bring them more clearly into view. For some patients, there was an immediate enhancement of the related transferential components of the therapeutic relationship. For others, there was a temporary impairment due to the magnitude of the issues that were introduced. This proved to be temporary but was associated with behavioral changes that could potentially be dangerous. For each patient, the disclosure provided an opportunity to explore and perhaps improve core paternal experiences. Each of these children showed strong reactions to the disclosure and expressed new areas of conflict and concern.

Sharon's developmental delay and current life situation were in evidence as she expressed ambivalent preoedipal feelings. She seemed to struggle with her family's overbearing nurturance and resistance to her individuation. She showed a close identification with a nurturant, protective maternal figure as well as aggression, which she directed toward the doll. Jerry felt primarily an upsurge of the ambivalent relationships with his siblings and foster infants in his home. He described his anger and his guilt over that anger. He discussed his father and his importance as a distant but valued onlooker. Fred historically had suffered paternal privation, and his reaction was primarily a narcissistic disappointment that the therapist would become unavailable to him. He was able to discuss his "father hunger" (Herzog, 1982) and tried to imagine his own potential as a father. He showed protective feelings toward the therapist and his family and a recurrent identification with the baby. He always returned to his feelings of entitlement and resentment at being denied.

Sandy showed a whole range of developmental levels in her reactions, which reflected the rocky course of her development and unresolved issues at many stages. She was rivalrous with the therapist's wife and seductive toward the therapist. She became angry at the idea of the baby and then regressed to more primitive play. After surviving the initial upheaval, she seemed to have worked on some major oedipal issues. Another important factor for Sandy was the ongoing experience of the loss of her father through divorce. This loss, combined with the disclosure, made her therapy hours very difficult for her to tolerate. In fact, she seemed to be able to tolerate the situation, in part, only because her usual mode of expressing frustration and anger was verbal and direct, and this mode was available to her within the therapeutic setting.

On the other hand, Vinnie was also experiencing the loss of his father through divorce, and there was general chaos in his family. In addition, he was prone to avoidance and antisocial behavior and tended not to express affect verbally. There was concern that the disclosure would precipitate a behavioral crisis. In actuality, he did become more avoidant and depressed but was able to verbalize some of his feelings within therapy. As far as is known, he has not increased his antisocial behavior, although this continues to be a concern.

In retrospect, it appears that if treatment is conducted in a setting where it is feasible to withhold the news of an upcoming paternity, it may be desirable to do so with patients who are prone to dangerously impulsive behavior (antisocial, homicidal or suicidal) or to psychotic regression. This would be especially true for patients in an outpatient setting, where there is little or no support or structure outside the therapy hours. Although patients may all show a useful enhancement of important ongoing transference issues, the level of risk must certainly be considered.

Why there is a dearth of reports on the paternity of the therapist is not clear. In part, it may be due to the therapist's countertransference reactions. Fatherhood has not been extensively studied, and reports on the experience of prospective and actual fatherhood are rare (Jarvis, 1962; Liebeuberg, 1967; Cole, 1980; Herzog, 1982; Benedek, 1984).

When the author first became a father early in his training, he was reluctant to disclose his paternity to his patients or focus on their reactions. Exploration of this reluctance in some depth revealed it to be very complex. Discussions with colleagues showed it to be not uncommon). Discussions with a number of male adult and child therapists who became fathers revealed strong resistance to exploring patients' reactions to this issue. In most cases, the therapists went to great lengths to keep this information from their patients. In many settings, the information finds it way to patients inadvertently, as was the case with the majority of the therapists interviewed. When secrecy was not possible, therapists often viewed the questions and curiosity of their patients as a form of resistance. In those cases, the issue was not whether or not to disclose but whether or not to work with the patients' reactions to the disclosure. In most cases, this work was minimal.

There were no theoretical or technical discussions in the literature on this subject at the time of this writing, and many therapists seem to overlook the impact on their patients. An exploration of the psychodynamics of male therapists may help explain this silence about an experience that is so common, in a field that is built largely upon introspection and the reporting of important experiences and observations. This is itself a topic for further consideration and may yield important information about "manhood" and the experience of paternity.

The purpose of this paper was to demonstrate that many aspects of the therapeutic relationship were enhanced by the fatherhood of the therapist. Issues such as sexuality, gender, sibling and parental relationships, and ongoing conflicted relationships were opened up for therapeutic exploration. An opportunity was presented to explore many of these complex feelings when they were available within the affect-laden therapeutic relationship. This exploration increased understanding of many important issues for the individual patients. It also suggested patterns of paternal transference phenomena that may further our understanding of the role of the father in both normal and abnormal child development. This sort of clinical observation may also help therapists to understand their role in the growth and development of their patients and may help them to maximize the therapeutic impact of their interactions.

Many unanswered and unasked questions remain regarding the nature of paternal transference phenomena in psychotherapy. At the same time, there is a very limited but growing body of knowledge of the role of the father in child development. The interface between these two growing bodies of knowledge may help therapists to understand some of the potentials of their work as well as possible hurdles resulting from countertransference phenomena. The data presented here may certainly be understood differently as our knowledge grows. The intent of this preliminary report was to begin to focus attention on an important, but heretofor neglected, event – the fatherhood of the therapist.

REFERENCES

Ashway, J. A. (1984), A therapist's pregnancy: An opportunity for conflict resolution and growth in the treatment of children. _Clin. Soc. Work,_ 12:3–17.

Benedek, T. (1984), Fatherhood and providing. In: _Parenthood,_ ed. R. Cohen, R. Cohler & S. Weissman. New York: Guilford Press, pp. 167–183.

Browning, D. H. (1974), Patients' reactions to their therapist's pregnancy. _J. Amer. Acad. Child Psychiat.,_ 13:468–482.

Cath, S. H., Gurwitt, A. & Ross, J. M., ed. (1982), _Father and Child._ Boston: Little, Brown.

Cole, D. S. (1980), Therapeutic issues arising from the pregnancy of the therapist. _Psychother. Theory, Res. Prac.,_ 17:210–213.

Fenster, S., Phillips, S. & Rapoport, E. G. (1987), _The Therapist's Pregnancy._ Hillsdale, NJ: The Analytic Press.

Gurwitt, A. R. (1982), Aspects of prospective fatherhood. In: _Father and Child,_ ed. S. H. Cath, A, Gurwitt & J. M. Ross, Boston: Little, Brown, pp. 275–299.

Harnett, F. (1949), Transference reactions to an event in the life of the analyst. _Psychoanal. Rev.,_ 36:69–81.

Herzog, J. M. (1982), On father hunger: The father's role in the modulation of aggressive drive and fantasy. In: _Father and Child,_ ed. S. H. Cath, A. Gurwitt & J. M. Ross. Boston: Little, Brown, pp. 163–174.

Jarvis, W. (1962), Some effects of pregnancy and child birth on men. _J. Amer. Psychoanal. Assn.,_ 10:689–699.

Lax, R. (1969), Some considerations about transference and countertransference manifestations evoked by the analyst's pregnancy. _Internat. J. Psychoanal.,_ 50:363–372.

Liebeuberg, B. (1967), Expectant fathers. _Amer. J. Orthopsychiat.,_ 37:358–359.

Nadelson, C., Notman, M., Arons, E. & Feldman, J. (1974), The pregnant therapist. _Amer. J. Psychiat.,_ 131:1107–1111.

Underwood, M. M. & Underwood, E. D. (1976), Clinical observations of a pregnant therapist. _Social Work,_ 21:512–517.

25

Factors Affecting the Pre-Oedipal and Oedipal Paternal Relationship in Girls
The Collusion to Exclude Father
Eleanor Galenson

The widespread changes in the social structure of many countries of the western world that have taken place over the last 15 or 20 years have altered many of the conditions under which children are reared. Among the major social changes have been the tendency toward disruption of the nuclear family, the increased mobility of families, and the absence of more mothers from the home as the presence of women in the work force has increased. With the increased absence of the mother as primary caretaker, either by choice or because of economic necessity, a shift in the relationship of mothers to young children has gradually occurred. This shift in the mother's relationship has created an important change in many aspects of the marital relationship itself and in the role of the father in the resulting altered family structure.

Although these family changes have been the subject of many sociological studies, individual family dynamic constellations have received far less attention, in part because of the difficulty in identifying how specific factors in the environment influence normal development in children. While it is now well documented that different developmental pathways often lead to the same developmental destinations, there are limits beyond which such variations cannot extend without causing serious developmental damage; it is precisely those limits which need to be identified more precisely.

Normally there is a moderate increase in hostile aggression during the early months of the child's second year, resulting from the ambivalence of the separation-individuation process and the anal phase. Additional hostile aggression is connected with the early genital phase and the preoedipal castration complex that normally accompanies this early genital phase (Galenson and Roiphe, 1971).

The intensity of the hostile aggression toward the mother that arises from these three sources is normally considerably alleviated when the father is available as an alternative object for both libidinal and aggressive investment. Girls thrive on their father's acceptance of their genitality as they turn from the temporarily excessively hostile maternal relationship of the middle of the second year to the father, who under normal conditions responds positively both to the budding femininity of the girl and to her need to separate from her mother. Boys whose fathers are available to them during their first two years are able about the middle of the second year, to begin to disidentify with the mother as they move to increased separation-individuation from her and turn toward the father during the early genital phase in identification with his masculinity. Thus, the second year is for both sexes a critical period of development in object relations, psychosexual development, and various aspects of ego functioning. If the father is emotionally unavailable at this time or is absent, the girl remains fixed in a regressive identification with her mother; the boy struggles both in regard to separation-individuation and in relation to the establishment of a sense of his male identity.

During the baby's first two years, the mother tends to regress from the advanced genital level in the marital relationship. This regression stems from the combined impact of many factors: her prior experience in regard to her preoedipal relationship with her mother, the nature of her preoedipal relationship with her father, subsequent sexual experiences, and so forth. Most husbands are able to make some accommodation to such a postpartum regression in their wives. However, if the husband's pregenital needs are also strong, he cannot help his wife as she deals with her own regression. Under these circumstances, the marital relationship deteriorates and often disintegrates entirely during the months following the birth of a new child. The mother may become depressed, requiring a great deal of support from her immediate family and from outside sources. Such support is vital because it is during these early months of the infant's life that basic patterns of child-mother interaction are established. A great deal of attention has been paid in thechild development literature to the early mother-child reciprocal relationship. However, the critical role of the father at this time in relation to both mother and child has not been sufficiently explored.

Direct infant observational research and direct therapeutic intervention with psychologically deviant young infants offer a rich source of clarification of some of the features of normal development in general and of the normal paternal preoedipal role in particular (Cath, 1982; Gunsberg, 1982; Ross, 1982; Yogman, 1982). For example, direct infant observation and clinical treatment of infants have demonstrated the role of the father in the separation-individuation process (Abelin, 1971) and in the modulation of aggression (Herzog, 1982).

Historical data gathered in the course of psychoanalytic or psychotherapeutic treatment and literary biographies have offered considerable retrospective insight into the effects of the absence of fathers during the early years of infancy on the later development of the individual. These sources indicate that if there is only little contact with the father, or if his "absence" consists of his emotional distance from the child, the course of the infant's early development is profoundly affected, as is the character of the subsequent oedipal phase. All retrospective material is, however, subject to distortion and offers only limited understanding of normal developmental sequences.

The clinical case to be presented follows in this tradition: the effect of a father's "psychological absence"on the development of his young daughter is described, as are those factors which contributed to his "absence" and his subsequent rapprochement with the emergence of the child's oedipal phase development. The child and mother were treated conjointly in psychoanalytically oriented psychotherapy; one therapist treated the child, Janet, from her 21st month to her fifth year of life, while her mother was concurrently in intensive psychotherapy with another member of the therapeutic team in a treatment design that allows for the emergence and correlation of psychological content, which is then addressed in both treatment situations. This type of coordination of the treatment of mother and child provides a comparison of the themes covered with the child and mother and a better understanding of these themes.

Although the father was present in this family, he was "emotionally unavailable" during the first four years of the child's life for reasons that became clear only after two years of the mother's treatment. The effects of this emotional detachment on the child's early development will be described and discussed. Of particular interest were certain events that occurred when the child was four years old and that changed the child-father relationship to a remarkable degree, causing a marked shift in critical areas of the child's development after the emotional rapprochement with the father had taken place. The advent in the child of oedipal phase organization and its conflicts reactivated some of the mother's unconscious attitudes that had hitherto played a major role in the emotional disengagement of father and daughter prior to this critical juncture.

Prior to the child's oedipal development, the preoedipal conflicts of both parents, reactivated, as in most parents, by the specific very early developmental characteristics of their child, had caused serious developmental delays in the child. In fact, the distortion of her development was so great by the end of her second year that direct and immediate psychotherapeutic intervention with the child as well as with the parents was indicated. While the father's lack of participation in the conjoint treatment impeded the child's progress in many respects, his abstinence was useful in clarifying how the disturbed paternal relationship was interfering in the totality of the child's development and specifically in the application of our therapeutic design. It should be emphasized here that what had initially appeared to be the father's own abstinence and antagonism toward the treatment was due to his own psychological resistance only in part. His wife's unconscious need to exclude him from participation in treatment and from a more intimate relationship with his young child proved to be an even greater deterrent to his participation.

TREATMENT MODEL

The conjoint treatment method to which we refer in this chapter evolved out of many years of experience in treating psychopathological conditions of very young children in a treatment design in which parents were largely excluded from active participation in the treatment process. The results of those attempts, while partially satisfactory, were necessarily limited because the external environment – the parents – continued to provide the infant with those very experiences of daily living which had exerted pathological influence in the first place, despite direct therapeutic work with the child. Although treatment of the child had provided a more optimal type of relationship, that is, with the therapist, this often proved insufficient to the task of returning the child to a normal developmental course since the parental difficulties simply continued to impede resolution of the child parent disturbances.

Our therapeutic model of conjoint infant and parent treatment aims at avoiding the continued repetition of environmental traumata by addressing the *particular* parental psychodynamic conflicts that appear to be delaying or derailing the infant's current development. The infant remains the primary focus of the therapeutic work in all its aspects, despite the fact that one or both parents become deeply involved in the therapeutic work itself. Of course, it is never possible to confine work with parents altogether to those areas which have been or are currently the cause of conflict with the child, but we have been more successful than might have been expected in sustaining and limiting this focus upon the child as patient. Our relatively more successful outcomes appear to be due to the fact that unresolved preoedipal conflicts are revived in all parents by the birth of a child and remain relatively free from their former repression for several years thereafter. Fraiberg (1982) has emphasized this greater availability of young parents during the relatively short period of the infancy of their children. She utilized a therapeutic model similar in many respects to our own.

Our therapeutic model consists of two therapeutic processes carried out simultaneously. One process consists of two or three play therapy sessions each week with the infant in the presence of and with the participation of one of the parents, the housekeeper (if there is one), or some member of the extended family, such as a grandparent with whom the infant has considerable familiarity. These play sessions are carried out by a therapist trained in the psychotherapy of very young infants. Work with the infant is correlated with the other part of treatment, namely, therapeutic sessions with the parents carried out by another therapist. These individual sessions may include both parents at times, or either parent individually, depending on the nature of their problems. The sessions with the parents may take place as frequently as three times weekly or as infrequently as once every two weeks, again as the situation indicates. Close collaboration between the two therapists involves constant exchange of material of the treatment sessions and efforts at integrating the themes that derive from and are developed in the treatment of the child and of the parents. Since the unconscious conflicts and fantasies of the parents are communicated to the child and the infant acts out these fantasies, the conjoint treatment design offers insight into the nature of such joint fantasies and the mode by which they are communicated between parents and child.

In the case that follows, an interesting intergenerational phenomenon emerged: the mother repeated with her own child a pattern that had characterized her early relationship with her own parents. While this is not unusual, it was particularly clearly demonstrated in this instance.

CASE ILLUSTRATION

Twenty-one-month-old Janet, the only child of a professionally successful mother and a father some twenty years her senior, had been cared for by a nurse from the time of her birth. She was brought to see me because she had never spoken a word, although her gestural repertoire and her receptive language appeared to be adequate for her age. Other symptoms included conflicts over eating and excessive use of her bottle both during the day and at night, as well as the use of several pacifiers at night and often during the day as well. Her eating disturbance was more intense whenever her mother attempted to feed her, and at the time of the consultation the nurse had taken over the entire feeding situation.

It was a planned pregnancy. The mother had decided that she was getting older and could not safely postpone having a child; the father had agreed to the pregnancy only reluctantly since he felt he was too old to assume the role of a father of such a young child and already had grown children by a prior marriage. The mother related that she had had little desire to hold or be with her newborn child and had returned to her work six weeks postpartum, leaving Janet almost entirely in the nurse's care from that time on. The father was only occasionally involved with handling the child and expressed little feeling of any kind for her at the time of the consultation. Some type of attachment had obviously developed, however. Janet cried when her mother surreptitiously left the house each morning to go to work without preparing the child for her departure. There was no history of stranger anxiety at any time.

During their first visit to our playroom, this frail, tiny, pretty girl, who was accompanied by her mother, was immediately drawn to the toys in the room, paying little attention to the strange adults. While her gestures were complex and she effectively indicated her needs and wants, she was utterly silent throughout the session. She understood and complied with some complicated spoken requests, indicating that a high level of receptive language had been attained despite the serious delay in her expressive language. Neither auditory nor neurological impairment had been found on examinations completed some months earlier. Our diagnostic impression was that the delay in language development was secondary to a serious disturbance in object relationships.

During our subsequent sessions with the mother, Martha, we learned that she was the first born of two siblings. She described herself as her own mother's "perfect" child during her first eight or ten years of life: obedient and unfailingly helpful. She and her mother had maintained an intimate and happy relationship during this time, despite the fact that a younger sibling had been born when Martha was four years old. Martha's father was a busy and successful man who was at home only on weekends. His relationship with Martha had been a distant one during her first eight or ten years of life. The intimate relationship between Martha and her mother had been only slightly marred by Martha's eating disturbance, which dated from her earliest days and continued during early childhood and adolescence. Martha recalled many distressing feeding encounters with her mother, memories that were now all too reminiscent of the current feeding disturbances with her own child, Janet. Martha's compliance at home contrasted sharply with her fierce disobedience in school from her earliest nursery years onward. Although the school problems were repeatedly brought to the attention of her parents, they seemed to have paid little attention to them, and Martha continued to be a serious behavior problem at school although she was an excellent student despite her behavioral problems. (This split between home and school is discussed later.)

During her early 20s there was a brief and unsuccessful marriage, after which she entered a profession closely related to her father's. Identification with her father had begun during late adolescence, accompanied by an increasingly close relationship with him. This provided Martha with a solid feeling about her own professional competence and provided an important positive impetus for her pleasure in work in later years. Martha had never been separated from her own mother until adolescence; when this separation did occur, Martha experienced severe panic and suicidal ideas, which led to a brief period of psychotherapy at that time. The panic abated and was soon followed by her unsuccessful first marriage, terminated several years later.

Our patient Janet's, father was seen on several occasions in individual sessions during the initial period of evaluation. A chronically depressed man, inclined to comply with his wife's demands on him and obviously dependent on her both financially and emotionally, he was concerned primarily about himself. Several periods of unsuccessful psychotherapy in connection with his earlier, unsuccessful marriage and a return of more intense depressive moods more recently led to our discussion of his need for further treatment. He failed, however, to carry out arrangements made for treatment with another colleague after two initial visits.

The material that follows is a condensation of several years of treatment of the mother carried out during twice-a-week psychotherapy sessions by one therapist and Janet's twice weekly treatment by the other therapist. Janet's sessions took place in the presence and with the collaboration of the mother or housekeeper at first, and the father at other sessions as the treatment progressed.

The mother's ambivalence toward Janet was intense from the start; whether to have a baby at all, her dislike of small babies, her irritability when she was at home with the baby and yet her desire to return home from work to see and be with the baby, her conscious thoughts about dropping or strangling the baby when she found herself unable to comfort her. The relationship between mother and child was in jeopardy almost from the beginning. The mother had suffered many previous bouts of depression from which she had received some relief through periods of psychoanalytic and psychotherapeutic courses of treatment. Despite her emotional disturbance, however, she had been able to pursue a successful career, was at ease socially, and was unaware of any other emotional interference in her life until the birth of this child.

The decision concerning the type of therapy best suited for this family was dictated by the severe delay in Janet's development. Already in jeopardy, the mother–child relationship was worsening as intense hostile aggression emerged in both members of the mother--child dyad. Our aim in intensive psychotherapy with the mother was to attenuate her highly ambivalent relationship with her child as well as her early covert hostile aggression toward her own mother, which had been revived in the relationship with her young child almost from the beginning. Although her marriage appeared to be more troubled at this time than it had been prior to the infant's birth, the reason for the deterioration was not clear. It appeared that marital dissatisfaction had increased with the revival of her earlier attachment to her own mother, but it was now expressed toward her husband. The husband also represented the father of her childhood, whom she maintained as the outsider, reversing the situation that had prevailed during her own childhood when her father had "deserted" her.

Course of Treatment Over the Next Ten Months

Several major themes in the treatment of the child could be correlated with the maternal treatment material. Within two weeks of beginning treatment, Janet spoke her first word, "No," as she played out many games involving regressive oral and anal themes of separation fears. Increasingly angry and rebellious at home, she now became openly aggressive toward her mother, her angry moods replacing her former temper tantrums. Her moods annoyed and frightened her mother, and this was a difficult time for the whole family. The mother became even angrier at Janet and at her husband, and her depression increased as she struggled to find even one area of pleasurable interchange between herself and Janet. As Janet became embroiled in issues of separation in her treatment, her mother was becoming more emphatic about wanting to break up her marriage. However, as soon as she took a step in that direction, her fears of separation, of which she hd never been aware, began to emerge and she became extremely anxious about the prospect of remaining alone with her child.

During the second month of treatment, anal derivative games occupied many of Janet's sessions, and there was an increase in her outwardly directed aggression and she became constipated and resisted having her soiled diapers removed. With this upsurge in anality, many new words appeared. The concurrence of anal phase unfolding and the development of language has long been recognized as a clinical constellation and probably signals the advance in the expression of directed aggression that results from increased self-object differentiation. However, this very advance threatens the child with heightened fear of object loss, and Janet showed considerable regression in her play as she initiated a "tiny baby" game in which she took both passive and active roles, discarding the baby and being discarded herself.

As Janet's directed hostile aggression increased, her mother's depression deepened, and memories of her first long and intensely painful separation from her own mother at ten years of age now returned. She recalled her suicidal wishes when she had not been allowed to return home, and the gradual shift away from her mother had begun at that time. Her relationship with her father slowly flowered thereafter into a solid and often secret alliance with him against her mother.

During the fourth month of conjoint treatment, two-year-old Janet now became unwilling to remain with her nurse when her mother left for work. This evidence of the development of a closer relationship between mother and child reminded the mother about her own "obsessions," which she now recalled from before and after the time of Janet's birth: her fears of having a deformed child and being afraid to handle the baby once she was born lest she drop and damage her.

During the fifth month of treatment, Martha decided to stop working for several months and to replace the old nurse during this time, a decision that signaled a shift in Martha's feelings and a consolidation in her relationship with her child. Although the father remained an uneasy outsider, despite our continued efforts to involve him in Janet's treatment sessions as well as in her life outside of treatment, Janet's behavior indicated that some beginning attachment to her father, as well as other advances, seemed to be emerging. For example, she developed signal anxiety for the first time, and she seemed to be wistful and sad during her father's occasional business trips away from home. Also, there was increasing modulation of her affect in general as well as a wider variety of moods.

During the summer vacation, Janet, now 26 months old, began to masturbate and explore her genitals for the first time, at least eight or ten months later than this normally occurs. Heightened genital sensitivity, which normally emerges sometime between 16 and 19 months of age in both sexes, begins to serve as a source of focused pleasure (Galenson and Roiphe, 1971; Roiphe and Galenson, 1982; Galenson, 1984). Repetitive self-stimulation by manual and indirect means is accompanied by evidence of erotic arousal, including facial expressions of excitement and pleasure, flushing, rapid respiration, and perspiration. Overt affectionate behavior, initially toward the mother, accompanies this new genital self-stimulation and disappears after the first few weeks, to be replaced by the familiar inward gaze and self-absorbed look during self-stimulation, indicating that a fantasy feeling-state probably accompanies the genital stimulation for the first time. Many of the children who constituted our research sample then began to use nursing bottles, transitional-object blankets, stuffed animals, and dolls for their direct masturbatory manipulation. Genital-derivative behavior emerges soon after the beginning of masturbation in the form of elaborate doll play in girls, as well as many other types of behavior that simulate the structure of the experience simultaneously occurring at the genital zone itself. Graphic representation also takes place as the girl attempts to draw, paint, and otherwise express a behavior most nearly resembling the concrete representation of urination itself. The absence or presence of a penis is explored in relation to dolls, humans, and animals. Accompanying this intense curiosity about the genital difference is a regression, with revival of fears of object loss and general bodily disintegration, as the girl attempts to deal with her awareness of her own genital anatomy. Mood changes include increased irritability and anger toward the mother, reflecting the girl's conviction that the mother is responsible for her genital anatomy. Loss of zest, as well as more intensely depressed reactions, was a regular part of this early, preoedipal castration reaction in a group of girls studied in our direct infancy research.

Along with these negative reactions to the genital difference, a new erotic and flirtatious interest in the father emerged in most of the girls studied, a shift in object relations that signals, in our opinion, an early preparation for the positive oedipal attachment for the oedipal period soon to emerge. It should be emphasized, however, that the preoedipal turn to the father has as yet a dyadic conformation in contrast to the triadic relationship of the oedipal phase reaction. As had been predicted (Roiphe and Galenson, 1982), a certain number of the girls showed very intense symptomatology as the discovery of the genital difference affected every aspect of their general behavior. These were the girls who had experienced some untoward trauma in relation to body image development, such as an injury, physical illness, accident, or a trauma in connection with the relationship with the mother, such as prolonged separation from her or a depression in the mother.

But these young girls also developed coping devices that appeared particularly in those toddlers who had not experienced disturbances during the first year of life. Their play was more elaborate in its fantasy content as well as its structural aspects, and they showed very early attempts at graphic representation. These advancements in ego functioning represent, we think, efforts to cope with the anxiety provoked by the recognition of the genital difference.

Returning now to Janet and her mother, a breakthrough in the mother's therapy took place in connection with the anticipated summer vacation. She recounted for the first time her intense emotional reaction to the death of a very important male friend some ten years previously. This relationship represented both her ambivalent attachment to her own mother, which had never been sufficiently resolved, and the deeply repressed longing for her father, which had finally come to fruition during her adolescence. Her daughter, Janet, had unconsciously been planned as a partial replacement for this man whose death she had never really mourned. Martha wept for the first time in years. Her sad feelings were extremely painful and unwelcome. They could easily be equated and interpreted in connection with her intense fears of separation from her mother, which had finally led to her adolescent suicidal ideas during the summer separation and her forbidden oedipal wishes, which were partially gratified in adolescence. There were now faint recollections of sadness and yearning during her fifth and sixth years when her father was away on business trips, a reaction very similiar to the one already described in Janet.

At the end of the summer, 29-month-old Janet was a pleasant, sociable child capable of advanced semi-symbolic play. Interested in books and beginning to deciper words, she used many short sentences and showed considerable progress in other areas of ego development. However, she now often clung to her mother and had developed a rather severe sleep disturbance, which was evidence of her advancing separation-individuation process. Her sense of herself as a feminine person was also much more definite now, as she admired and wanted to wear shoes with high heels and jewelry and cosmetics belonging to her mother, in feminine identification with her. The heels and jewelry probably also represented phallic replacements, since she was still avidly exploring her own genitals and those of dolls, animals, and adults. Her human figure drawings demonstrated that she had a clear knowledge of the sexual genital difference but was still coping with her sense of loss and disturbance over this difference.

The mother reacted to the child's growing sense of separateness and femininity with a "paradoxical discouragement about her lack of progress," probably sensing the child's dawning preparation for oedipal development. The mother had become more and more attached to the child and was reluctant to return to her work full-time because of the separation from the child that it entailed.

The marriage continued to be unstable, with both parents threatening to leave on numerous occasions. It became possible, however, to clarify that the mother unconsciously resisted her own wishes to separate from her husband because of the intense fear of living alone with her child, a revival of her early severe separation anxiety, although she could not yet recognize her avoidance of the oedipal involvement entailed in the marriage.

As for Janet's development, her early genital phase, along with its genital derivative behavior, continued to emerge to a surprisingly rich degree, and now for the first time her father began to bring her to her sessions. He obviously enjoyed his daughter's new exhibitionism and flirtatiousness toward him, and his participation in her life in other areas also increased as the pull of Janet's oedipal attachment became more intense. Thus, her own developmental push was a considerable factor in the child's attaining a relationship with her father that our therapeutic efforts with him had previously failed to elicit, and it was the mother's increasing tolerance of his investment in the child that allowed the oedipal phase development to proceed.

Janet's language became increasingly fluent and articulate; her peer relationships became happy and free; and her school performance demonstrated that she was an intellectually gifted child who was now free to use her intellectual capacity in a new way. We have continued our efforts to enrich and support Janet's paternal relationship, while the mother's therapy has begun to help her resolve her severe separation anxiety and the effect on her object choices in both her marriages. The depressions that the mother experienced in the course of this treatment, in contrast to her earlier treatment attempts, have now become linked in her mind with her unresolved ambivalent attachment to her mother and her despair at ever being able to resolve this attachment.

DISCUSSION

We have presented a case in which the birth of a baby precipitated a major upheaval in the mother, interfering with the lifelong defenses that had allowed her to maintain a split of rather serious proportions in her self-representation. One aspect of her personality was the small child, ever fearful of separation from her mother, constantly attempting, in the beginning, to please her mother and later on, various mother-related figures in her life. The mother's ambivalence toward her own mother showed itself in the continuing bitter fights between them, despite their close attachment, and in her similar relationships with numerous men, who represented the disappointing mother she constantly sought. Her other major personality characteristic was represented most clearly in her professional life. She identified more and more from adolescence on with her father, despite her earlier oedipal disappointment in him. She was competent and clear-headed in this male identification, "thinking like a man," as she described it, generally in good humor and able to deal with her everyday life despite her recurrent depressions.

However, this identification with her father constantly threatened her ambivalent relationship with her mother, posing the ultimate danger of a final separation from her mother. She had good reason to fear this separation, having already experienced its drastic effect during early adolescence in the form of her serious depressive episode while she was away from home.

During the fourth month of the child's psychiatric treatment, a qualitative change in her relationship with her mother emerged: she became unwilling to remain with her nurse when her mother left for work. There was a parallel development in the mother, who was able to identify and empathize with her child's new separation anxiety, which developed as her attachment to her mother became more reliable and intense. The maternal shift had been facilitated by the emergence into consciousness of the intensity of the mother's negative feelings toward her child, feelings that had been reflected in her fear of having a deformed child and her dread of handling the baby lest she drop and hurt her. These negative feelings belonged to the mother's ambivalent relationship with her own mother but had found expression in her provocativeness everywhere but at home. Janet's birth had revived the mother's primitive ambivalence toward her own mother in all its preoedipal intensity and from a period before the splitting off of the anger had taken place.

Martha's father had been barred from her emotional life during her very early years by her mother. He had been unavailable to Martha in disengaging herself from her overly close and highly ambivalent relationship to her mother. Martha repeated this exclusionary pattern: Janet and her father were to remain uninvolved emotionally. The father's role in aiding the young child's neutralization of aggression during the early years has been stressed by Cath (1982) and Herzog (1982) and is well illustrated in this situation: both mother and child suffered from the impact of their excessive and unmodulated aggression towards one another. Regression to her earlier primitive aggression, the mother's predominant and lifelong defense of splitting off and displacing her aggression, had been disrupted by Janet's birth. It may well be that Janet would have followed the same route as her mother if treatment had not been instituted.

Perhaps the most striking feature of the family relationship was the father's apparent psychological abstinence from his daughter, as he continued to be excluded from the mother–infant dyad. It was only when the mother's very helpful adolescent relationship with her own father became clarified as treatment proceeded that she was able to permit Janet's father to function as a father, although not yet as a husband to herself. A truly genital level of object relatedness had not yet been achieved by the mother, although her adolescent identification with her father did allow her to succeed professionally. It may be that such an intense and highly ambivalent mother–daughter early relationship precludes the girl's preoedipal attachment to the father and distorts and inhibits the subsequent oedipal constellation. Direct and intensive treatment of both members of the mother–child dyad has proven to be extremely effective in providing an entrée for the father's psychological participation in forming both a preoedipal and oedipal relationship with his daughter, despite his relative exclusion from the treatment situation itself.

REFERENCES

Abelin, E. (1971), The role of the father in the separation-individuation process. In: *Separation-Individuation* ed. J. B. McDevitt & C. F. Settlage. New York: International Universities Press.

Cath, S. H. (1982), Divorce and the child: "The father question hour."In: *Father and Child,* ed. S. H. Cath, A. Gurwitt & J. M. Ross. Boston: Little, Brown, pp. 357–383.

Fraiberg, S. (1982), Pathological defense in infancy. *Psychoanal. Quart.,* 51:612–635.

Galenson, E. (1984), Infancy research and clinical implications for women. Unpublished manuscript.

_____ & Roiphe, H., (1971), Impact of early sexual discovery on mood, defensive organization and symbolization. *The Psychoanalytic Study of the Child,* 26:195–216. New Haven: Yale University Press.

Gunsberg, L. (1982), Selected critical review of psychological investigations of the early father-infant relationship. In: *Father and Child,* ed. S. H. Cath, A. Gurwitt & J. M. Ross. Boston: Little, Brown, pp. 65–86.

Herzog, J. M. (1982), On father hunger: The father's role in the modulation of aggressive drive and fantasy. In: *Father and Child,* ed. S. H. Cath, A. Gurwitt & J. M. Ross. Boston: Little, Brown, pp. 163–174.

Roiphe, H., & Galenson, E. (1982), *The Infantile Origins of Sexual Identity.* New York: International Universities Press.

Ross, J. M. (1982), The roots of fatherhood: Excursions into a lost literature. In: *Father and Child,* ed. S. H. Cath, A. Gurwitt & J. M. Ross. Boston: Little, Brown, pp. 3–20.

Yogman, M. W. (1982), Observations on the father-infant relationship. In: *Father and Child,* ed. S. H. Cath, A. Gurwitt, & J. M. Ross. Boston: Little, Brown, pp. 101–122.

26

Issues in Fathering and How They Are Reflected in the Psychoanalytic Treatment of Men

Linda Gunsberg

In Kenya, a man is not considered a man until he has a son.
— Stanley Cath, personal communication

Many men (and women) come into treatment claiming they had (have) inadequate fathers. During the course of psychoanalysis, it is often discovered that their fathers and their fathering experiences were and are indeed adequate.

As a female analyst, I have been impressed with a certain transference phenomenon, which I will call, in keeping with Atkins's (1982) contribution, the transitive vitalizing function of the mother and the transitive revitalizing function of the female analyst. What is specifically meant here is the mother's role in the patient's life and the female analyst's role in the transference and psychoanalysis in allowing the patient to have a relationship with father, either in the dyadic context of father and son or within the family triad of mother-father-son. Also, the patient is permitted to have a relationship with father uniquely developed by father and son, with its positive, negative, and ambivalent components. One might ask if this role and function cannot be assumed by either a female or male analyst, that is, is it tied to the gender of the analyst? The answer, based on my work with men patients, is that the form of transitive vitalization and revitalization yearned for mirrors that of the nuclear family, with a mother who loves, respects, and admires her husband and who can permit her son to do so in his own way. In one patient's words, "One thing I love about you. Here you are, a woman, who wants me to be a man. I never experienced that before." As can be seen, if father cannot be considered by mother to be a significant cornerstone of her son's masculine identity, then her son will have serious difficulties in his emerging identity as a man and father.

Very often, when a man comes into treatment, there is little, if any, mention of the father. A crucial part of the transitive revitalizing function of the analyst is to bring the father's presence into the analytic space, even in the face of strong opposition from the patient. Or, if only negative aspects of the father are mentioned as the patient's history unravels, the analyst may introduce positive character traits and achievements of the father, as well as positively remembered father-son experiences, to loosen the fixedness of the paternal figure's denigrated image.

Several issues are salient when one deals with fathering within the context of psychoanalytic treatment. First, men who have become fathers often feel excessive competition with their wives for the *mothering* role, a wish often misconstrued by both patient and analyst as a desire to assume a central paternal role. A possible explanation for this competition with their wives for the maternal role is suggested by Pruett (1983). Many of the men in his study of primary caretaking fathers were suspicious of the kind of mothering their wives would provide for their children.

Second, boys and men yearn for an "isogender attachment" with their fathers (Blos, 1985). That is, all the wishes, impulses, and gratifications in the father-son relationship cannot be reduced to conflictual oedipal struggles or homosexual yearnings. Rather, sons and fathers alike strive for a warm, loving, and constructive relationship, one not saddled with oedipal tensions. The early model for this relationship is the preoedipal father-son attachment.

Third, how does a father acknowledge his growing son's body? That is, how does he endorse his son's masculine body? On the other side, how does an adult son acknowledge his father's aging? The last question is particularly of interest when father ages very well and the adult son envies his father in this accomplishment. In addition, there is the issue of the erotization of the father-son relationship.

Fourth, sons can be very disappointed that their fathers have not given them enough. For example, a father who is not successful in the work world fails the son who wishes he could ride on his father's coattails of glory. Or a man may express disappointment with his father for not being taught my him to be a superior sexual lover.

Fifth, there are issues of aggression in the father-son relationship. Many fathers abandon their children either psychologically or through divorce because they fear the extent of their own aggression and murderous wishes toward their children (Ross and Herzog, 1985). Fathers more often than mothers tend to put their children in dangerous situations. There are several possible explanations for fathers' apparent need to have their sons face danger. First, fathers are keenly sensitive to situations that present castration threats. In addition, the male psyche is often riddled with what I have termed "circumcision anxiety" (Gunsberg, 1987). Many life experiences are perceived and experienced within these two contexts, namely castration threats and circumcision anxiety. Putting their sons in dangerous situations represents both *mastery* over castration and circumcision threats and *repetitions* of castration and circumcision experiences. One father left knives and scissors within his young child's reach. Another, who took his son along with him while he took photographs, left the infant in his stroller in the middle of the street, in danger of being run over by a passing car.

Fathers of girls, on the other hand, are much more protective in dangerous situations. For example, a colleague of mine, father of a five-year-old girl, was told that a boy was harassing his daughter a few feet away from him in the playground. He went up to the boy and said, "I'm her father. You look at me. You look at what you're messing with." I was there with my children, and I said to him, "Well done." He replied, "I don't know where it came from. No one did shit for me," indicating no memory of his father's protecting him the way he had come to the aid of his daughter.

For their part, boys and even adult sons need to be able to aggress against their fathers and to feel their fathers' retaliation and aggression toward them. Loewald (1980) states that aggression toward the father figure is a necessary component for individuation and the waning of the Oedipus complex. But how does a son challenge the father's authority and move to a resolution where both men can respect and love each other? Too often, the aggression that accompanies separation and oedipal struggles turns into chronic father denigration. Many adult men, like Abraham Lincoln (Strozier and Cath, this volume), never move from this state.

Others, like some of my male patients, wish to give their fathers AIDS. I am not convinced that this wish is a homosexual one. Rather,

I think it is a murderous – and indeed, torturous – death wish as well as a wish for union. Another patient fantasized sticking his mother with a needle contaminated with AIDS during the C-section birth of his sister.

The final issue to be emphasized when one deals with fathering within the context of psychoanalytic treatment is the denigration of the father figure and the coupling of mother and son. The work of the French school, particularly that of McDougall (1980) and Chasseguet-Smirgel (1986) on the development of perversions in men is pertinent here.

McDougall sees as the major problem in perversions the dis-avowal of both the differences between the sexes and the need the two sexes have to complement each other sexually. She feels that, although the child makes a significant contribution to this disavowal, both parents also contribute greatly. She is one of the very few psychoana-lytic writers who points out the prominent role of *actual* parent pathology. Sometimes mother will denigrate the father in front of the boy child and simultaneously idealize her own father. A coupling exists between the mother and her own idealized father, who has the grand phallus (as she does by affiliation). The boy child is promised that he too will have this through the tie to the mother. The boy feels that his normal wish to love and identify with father is unacceptble to the mother, therefore, his wish remains his secret. In collusion with mother he denigrates the father while in his secret life he idealizes the father.

Thus, there is a reversal in the oedipal scenario. Here, the boy child does not have a picture of father as having something he wants but cannot have. Rather, the father is the observer of the oedipal scene between the boy child and his mother, seeing the boy child as having what he (the father) wants and cannot have. (McDougall refers to this position of the father as the "Other.") As a result, the father, by being kept outside, is not internalized or introjected but instead is kept externalized and denigrated.

Chasseguet-Smirgel (1987) states that the developmental progres-sion in people with perversions is thwarted in two basic ways. First, destruction takes the form of a hatred of reality. Father, as an example of reality, needs to be hated and destroyed since his presence introduces the reality that union with mother is not possible. Second, the boy hates the mother for having another baby, another reality that makes union with mother impossible. In view of this Chasseguet-Smirgel cautions us to consider the defensive purposes of father idealization.

That is, it may represent a need to keep father at a distance or disregard his actual presence.

CASE ILLUSTRATION

A man in his mid-30s sought psychoanalysis when his wife became pregnant. The treatment began in the third month of his wife's pregnancy with his son, now 1½ years old. This case material elucidates the issues addressed earlier in this chapter.

Circumcision Anxiety, Vicissitudes of Triangulation, Rivalry with
Son for His Wife, and the Relationship Between Sadism and
Respect in His Relationship with His Father

The first session presented took place in the patient's expectant fatherhood days, shortly after amniocentesis revealed that he would have a son.

> P: I'm lonely. My wife is falling asleep at 8:30 p.m. I do all the cooking and cleaning up afterwards. She does the laundry. I'm cleaning up the house – streamlining – to make everything ready for the baby.
> A: But you're all alone in this.
> P: She finally woke up at 10:30 p.m. I did something good. I had an impulse to be angry at her. I told her I felt lonely when she was asleep.
> P: It was nice. It made me feel a lot better. I was cutting the inner sole out of my sneaker – for a moment I thought I had done it wrong. Then I wished Mimi was up and not asleep. I needed mothering or reassurance that I wasn't screwed up.
> A: Were you using a razor blade?
> P: I was surprised at how fast the razor blade cut the padding – like butter or water.
> A: It must have made you anxious.
> P: Oy yoy yoy. If you cut too much, you can't put it back.
> A: Sounds like you're concerned about the circumcision of your son.
> P: You're pretty smart. You'll love this. Last summer I went to a bris. I passed out. I never did that before. I didn't fall over, but it was pretty close. My job was to transfer the baby to someone who gave the baby to the moile. When he pulled the baby's pants down, I got woozy, and I blacked out. People were

shouting, where's Arthur? I watched the circumcision, then after I couldn't take it anymore. I had to watch. Some people turned away – they were chicken, cowardly not to watch – giving into the fear. In fact there was nothing to it. The moile put his finger in wine, and the baby was sucking on the moile's finger. It didn't look like enough for the baby.

It reminds me of something that happened with my father. In eighth grade I broke my ankle. I was in a cast. My father decided to take me to his doctor – some special grownup doctor. He wanted to have this little thing on my penis looked at. A sebaceous cyst, probably left over from my circumcision. Something wortlike, oval cartilage that was just trapped under the top layer of what had been the foreskin. It was always there, it didn't hurt, it wasn't that noticeable. My father decided he should have it looked at. I was afraid they would cut me. I was embarrassed and humiliated – two men (doctor and my father) looking at my little peepee.

Big successful doctor looking at my thing. I felt my father had sold me out. I didn't want anything taken out that was painful. The doctor told my father that it was nothing, that I had a cast on my foot and there was no reason to put me through anything now – trauma. The doctor said if I wanted to do something later, I could. I just hated my father. He brings me here and has me cut up. He wanted to have my dick chopped off.

Many years later, I was living with my girlfriend, who became my wife. No girlfriend had noticed I had a problem. But my cyst became infected. It was red, raw, and swollen. Mimi said, "I know what to do. Soak it in boric acid and everything will be fine." The whole mass, which had been there all my life, broke down and all disappeared.

Mimi, in a benevolent way, cured me of it and took away this flawed thing on my penis. I felt very grateful to her, I guess. It was something my father couldn't do. He couldn't take care of me in any way I could hold on to.

The next session took place toward the end of the expectant fatherhood phase. It examined the nature of his relationship with a very special teacher, Mrs. Wonderful. This session included the first transference dream in the psychoanalysis.

P: I had a dream last night that you were in. I think I lost part of it because I haven't thought about it since I woke up.

Dream: There was some sort of living room I was in with a bunch of people, and you were there. Something was going to happen, like a party of all your patients. What an absurd situation. I was going. I did get the address and time from you. Then I think you left. I was looking forward to going to this party and meeting everyone else, I guess.

Associations: In fourth grade, I had a very charismatic teacher with the appropriate name, Mrs. Wonderful. My mother said that was the year I woke up. Until then I had been dreamy and looking out the window. My mother mentioned that Mrs. W. was concerned about me. The teachers said I was a loner and a dreamer, but I was doing well in my subjects. Mrs. W. was very vivacious, dynamic, fair, and very demanding. It was thrilling to be in her class. She got you inspired to do things you never thought you could do.

My mother looks back at it as a turning point. "She lit a fire under you." I imagine that was true. The thing that made me think of Mrs. W. again when I described the dream wat that at the end of the year she had a picnic at her house. She lived in the country. There was a ballfield, games, a cookout. It was fun and exciting but also difficult for me because I imagined she had–I had–a special relationship with her in the class. I was the genius of Mrs. W. She made everyone feel so well. There were lots of kids there from previous years. Lots of kids. Not to mention her own family. So I probably felt shaken up and rejected to see other people she cared about as much as me or more–her own kids and husband. There's nothing new here.

> A: There is something new. Now the feelings are also being expressed toward me.
> P: Maybe it is the same old bullshit, but I had a kind of positive feeling about going to this party and that it was nice to feel–when I would expect to feel anxious–happy to be a member of the children.

This first direct transference dream of the treatment occurred less than one month before the birth of the patient's son. The way I understood it was that he had been successful in *temporarily* putting aside his tremendous difficulties in sharing whoever was most important to him. Now the family was going to become a triad, and he was trying to prepare himself for welcoming his son, who was also his rival for his wife's attention and love.

The session continues with discussion about an outstanding professional move, which was prompted by a wish to do better for his family and was the result of significant progress in the beginning phase phase of treatment. In addition, he expresses his exuberance at being in analysis and having a female analyst. The session's ending shows how this positive but temporary consolidation toward a family of three begins to unravel, with wishes to abandon his wife in childbirth and a wish to keep the baby from being born.

P: Perhaps after all those times of dread and panic I now feel positive, excited, ready. I now feel very close to Mimi. Why, why is this so? I've come out into a little bit of sunshine here, when I need it the most. When it comes close to the due date, I told myself it has to be a positive time. My friend and his wife – he left her without money to go to the hospital if she had to go. It called into question his role as a husband or father-to-be. Was he only thinking of himself? That's awful. Her trust was gone, and he had to built it up, brick by brick. Maybe I got all my crazy stuff out of the way early and come show time, I would be ready. That image is interesting because in high school I got involved in drama productions. The coach said, "I'm giving you this role because you are a good actor and you have good intelligence, but you don't look like Billy Bigelow."

Hey, this is important. I don't want you to be embarrassed with me. I burnt myself out. Here, I got it all out of the way. I even was sick. I had this idea that I would be sick when the baby comes.

A: Sounds like a wish.

P: The baby was conceived when we both had the flu. My wife said, let's forget it this month. I said, let's go for it. It was the night of a Christmas party. Great, we would both be sick when he was born.

A: What comes to your mind about this?

P: Life disaster, doom, curse, inescapable. There's a curse attached to me. I wasn't meant to make it in life and have happy experiences. Pain.

A: If you were sick, what would happen with the childbirth?

P: If I'm sick, I would have no stamina to stay in there and do my job – coaching, helping, massaging my wife's belly, compresses – all the things that require physical stamina. When I'm sick, I can barely stand up. You need mental and physical stamina for this.

A: If your wife is sick too?

P: She couldn't get through the labor. Her nose would be stuffed up, sore. She couldn't do the breathing.

A: So the baby wouldn't be born.

P: It would be the last chance to call it off.

At this point in the analysis, the baby is six months old. What has emerged is a full-blown rivalry with his son (Ross, 1960). Simultaneously, aggressive fantasies toward his son, aggressive wishes toward his own father and desires for his father to be aggressive with him have been stimulated.

P: Mimi belongs to me, and I have discounted her. Lately I have been feeling very positive toward her. I love her, I feel positive about her being the mother of my child. I had this idea about wanting women who are not mine. Maybe I have this idea that Mimi belongs to Andrew and actually I want her more because she's somebody else's. She happens to be my son's. Maybe that explains why I have a hard time with Andrew – he's a threat – he'll take Mimi away like I took my mother away from my father. On one level, why should I be nice to him? He'll think he can have my wife. I'll leave him in the road. [Here, reference is to leaving his son in stroller in the middle of a busy street while taking pictures with his camera.]

A: You feel your son wants your things, so you don't treat him well, you discard him, leave him in danger in the stroller. You feel you wanted your father's things – your mother – and you wish that he would discard you.

P: Two things come to mind, leap out. My father never had his own standards, his own set of positions. He would be called upon by my mother when she felt she would go ape with the children, but he never took over the job with gusto. He was a pushover. We never felt he stood for anything, was anything. He was a puppet of my mother.

A: One time, one Saturday, I was in 6th, 7th, or 8th grade. Maybe my mother was not feeling well. He did rounds of errands – dry cleaner, bank. He was doing it, and I was in the passenger seat of the car. But I definitely did something. I was being provocative or subtly disrespectful, treating him like nothing, secretly hoping he would react. Finally, we got to the parking lot of the bank, and he reacts. He was angry, for about 30 seconds. I was scared for a minute there, it looked like the real thing. I was scared, terrified. Then I got all excited. Then the thing fell apart, as if "who cares about you." I was hoping he would wale the hell out of me. I wound up remembering it for the rest of my life. I lost more respect for him. I was disappointed.

A: A second thing, two years ago I called him on the phone one night. He had been dishonest, and I was pissed. I berated and abused him. I said he was a coward, a liar. I said, "Stand up already, I'm trying to get a reaction from you." He said, "I don't like it. It's not my style. If you treat me badly, why should I have anything to do with you?"

I was disappointed and disgusted. Let's get it over with already, the punishment, justice. I treated him like a jerk for over 30 years, and he wouldn't be a man about it – so fuckin' mealy-mouthed. I hated it.

In a way, part of me wants to kick Andrew's ass in for his own good. There is a definite urge. I want to hold him and fly him around. He thinks it's cool. But another impulse is to treat him like a human football – I want to maul, mangle, torture, torment him. I just think there's some connection between the profound curiosity I have with inanimate objects, like coming upon empty soda bottles in an alley and the ecstasy in flinging them against a brick wall and exploding into powder. That was the greatest thing, to poke out, maul inanimate objects, paint cans. It is a displacement of wanting to mangle, maul someone else, physically. The force of my mother's punishments was devastating.

I think I created an extremely neurotic cat.

A: What did you do?

P: The quintessential thing I did, I made a sandwich. I put a pillow on my lap, I would grab her. I slammed her down on the pillow – I flipped two sides of the pillow like in a pillow vise. Then only the tip of her nose was showing. I would massage the top of her nose, then release her after a few minutes. It was the most unmitigated, pure acting out of twisted, sadistic impulses. I loved her so much, such a beautiful cat. A pretty, svelte re-creation of my relationship with my mother. I had great love and passion and admiration for my cat, but I owned her. She had no privacy, I had no respect for her body. I would have done the same thing with a girl if I had a girlfriend.

A: You are upset that your father wasn't sadistic toward you. But isn't it also that you wished he could intervene and stop the sadistic relationship between you and your mother?

P: Yes, he never protected me from my mother. He should have been sadistic toward me. Then I would have thought more highly of him.

Elaboration of Envy, Aggression, and Murderous Wishes Toward His Wife, Son, and Father

As the treatment unfolds, the wish to have his son possess his mother the way the patient possessed his own mother is reenacted. The exclusive union with mother reflects the desire to get rid of anyone who interferes with this bond and envy of anyone who can achieve this bond. His desire is ultimately to possess the mother, whom he views as having all the desirable female and male qualities. By being part of her, he too has all of these qualities.

The developmental achievement of differentiation allows a relationship to form between two separate people. This separateness between people can also promote envy of what the other has and murderous wishes toward the other. Dedifferentiation protects the son from these feelings, since the other person is he and he is the otherperson. There are no differences and thus no envy. The psychological consequences of such a position are many, but among them is that the child cannot be an object that gratifies and promotes the father's healthy narcissism. He is not proud of his son. Pride is fleeting. Most of his time is spent fantasizing that his son is castrated, is dead, or has no form. This evolution has also emerged in the transference, whereby my interpretations are snatched away from me and become words he can either use or discard; and I remain formless and separated from my interpretations.

The raw and primitive nature of the patient's associations causes me to cringe at times. One might wonder why this man needs to *feel* so cruel toward his son. Ross (personal communication) suggests that such murderous wishes towards one's child are usually not bald and undisguised but are accompanied by anxiety, guilt, obsessive overconcern, and depressive phenomena. Perhaps these wishes represent a defensive organization against even more disturbing self-castrating wishes. Or they may represent the remarkable failure in defense characteristic of a person with a perverse organization. Of course, although the patient's psychic life is filled with cruelty, in reality he has never actually harmed anyone physically, except his cat. There have however, been a few instances where he has put his son in dangerous situations. I have, on several occasions, forcefully suggested that he either not be with his son or that he be more careful if he takes his son with him. He responded with great relief to this analytic parameter. He felt that I understood that he was in trouble and needed guidance.

The following excerpt is from a session when his son was nine months old.

> P: I hate to say this. Sometimes I give Andrew a bath. When he's standing there in the bathtub I look at his penis and balls, and I have this fantasy of snipping them off with a shears. I feel terrible about it.
>
> Mimi loves Andrew so much. Several times she said she was glad she had a boy, and she didn't want to have a girl. Too tough to have a girl, a pain, all that stuff. How happy he [slip for she] is.
>
> A: She is he?
>
> P: She can get to be a he through Andrew. When she was pregnant and had the amnio, she would laugh about the strange feeling for a girl to feel there is a boy inside her growing. I remember she said, after Andrew was born, how strange it was that she had

grown testicles and penis.

A: She didn't grow them, he grew them. Both you and Mimi gave him the genes, and *he* grew.

P: Ah! You're right. Maybe I needed to hear she grew them.

A: Why?

P: Because I don't have to be the man if she's got that covered already. I don't know, it's just one of those things that sends me off the deep end.

A: You want to be both sexes, and you envy her fantasy. You would like to be able to transform yourself from one sex to the other whenever you wish.

P: I'm afraid I couldn't be around a very attractive woman because then I couldn't be me. They would want a man.

A: Let's go back to your feelings and thoughts when you look at Andrew's penis and balls.

P: I will indoctrinate him into the same thing. He is threatening to me. He is very clearly a boy.

A: What if you made him a girl and snipped off his penis?

P: Maybe I would feel closer to him – feel he wasn't superior to me. Or you could take it another way – then I would know what it is like to have a son and a daughter. Sometimes I think about that, friends who have daughters. Daughters are more gaga for their fathers, and boys are more gaga for their mothers.

A: You wish to turn Andrew into a girl expresses your envy and anger toward Andrew and Mimi for their loving bond from which you feel excluded. Also your envy of both of them being both male and female. By turning your son into a girl you are giving her the child she would hate.

P: Right.

The next excerpt is from a session when the patient's son was 14 months old. This dream about the death of his son and his wife reactivated his misunderstanding of his mother's message to him. He felt she denigrated his father, yet she never left the father for my patient. Thus the two intended lovers are united through death (son and his wife, his mother and him).

Dream: Mimi and I are looking at a house in a strange jungle under the Queensboro Bridge. Inside was a closet, and in there was a tube like what newspapers are delivered in. In one pouch of this translucent bag was Andrew's body – he was dead – balanced by another body in another bag. I don't know whose bag, but very big. Then I looked outside the house. We decided this was not the house for us. The bag was hanging on the doorknob, the scene is fresh.

The following excerpt is from a session one week later.

P: I'm destroying myself again. I'm feeling more and more worthless and like a failure–including as a parent. I don't know how I'm going to be any good as a father because I feel like a total empty shell as a person. What will Andrew see in me? An empty person with a shell, no depth. What kind of model am I setting in terms of passionate commitment? If it's both of us around, he prefers Mimi. If it's just him and me, it's okay. If I wasn't feeling insane, I would have a better sense of whether I am insane or it's appropriate for a 14 month old.

A: Insane?

P: I feel I want to break up this bond between them. Look what it did to me. Last week I came home from work, and I kissed Mimi, and I wanted him to know she's my wife and not just his mother. I am wrecked. It's too late for me, but maybe he can grow up normal. I get very uncertain about what constitutes spoiling him.

A: He has a cold. Last night he woke up screaming. After an hour he was asleep. He finally settled down. Mimi read him a book, and at each page she gave him a kiss on his head. Is this okay, motherly, or is it some special romance, and will he be screwed up like me?

A: What feelings do you have when you see your wife kissing his head?

P: Two things. I feel kind of shut out, like a spare part, and, if I really think about it, I wish I could trade places. I wish I had a sweet loving mommy. I feel helpless and hopeless. There's no role for me. Very, very sweet kisses planted on his head, and his head is sweet too. Whole thing is beautiful. A certain kind of innocence. Sometimes I can't get over how beautiful he is. There's something sexual there. The other night I carried him in from the car. His head smelled of him, smoothness, freshness. I wish I could be like that. Something sexual. His face is so close to mine and like a blur. I couldn't quite focus.

A: Sexual?

P: I'm thinking how small his face is. What could be as beautiful and sensuous? He's too small, he's a baby. Not like being with a woman. I don't know how to put my finger on it.

   He's so yummy. I wanted to rub him all over me, as if he was a bar of soap.

*The Beginning of Admiration for, Respect for, and Positive
Identification with Father*

In the following session, two years into the psychoanalysis, admiration for the father emerges in a dream.

> P: I think it [the dream] is about my father, although he's not in it.
>   It is brief but interesting.

> *Dream:* I'm standing in some room with a guy who is a pro
> quarterback. I'm throwing, and he's watching how I throw.
> "Very interesting, you have an interesting way to throw. There's
> something in your elbow keeping you from throwing." I say, "It's
> very interesting that you noticed about my throwing. You're on
> to something, I broke my elbow." He (the pro) throws. It's fluid,
> one motion, pssh, it looks great. I say, "You really are a pro
> quarterback." I don't know if I said it when he noticed my elbow.
> He rolled up his sleeve on his right arm. His elbow had a scar
> similar to one on my father's arm. He had a pin put in and couldn't
> rotate his elbow fully. This same arm is the arm for beautiful
> passes.
>   I thought about my father's arm. Maybe I had the dream
> Thanksgiving night after reading my father's article or
> Wednesday night after talking about him in the session on
> Wednesday.
>   *Associations:* (Patient's elbow is held up as he talks.) My
> father injured his arm (fell on the ice). In the dream, I admire my
> father. My right arm got hurt, and I'm left-handed, but he's
> right-handed. All that summer, when I had the cast on my arm, I
> felt great–attention, sympathy.

> A: How did you hurt your arm?
> P: At my job–I felt heroic. I went for a catch and stumbled. The
>   orthopedist put a fiberglass cast on so I could swim with it. When
>   the doctor was molding the cast, he said, "Hold your hand as if
>   you're fondling your breast. You're old enough to know about
>   this now." I was 19 or 20 years old. It was the summer after my
>   junior year in college.
>   There was something about this guy [the doctor]. He was 49
>   years old, ladies' man, athletic, handsome, macho guy, maybe
>   single. It was a little scary to me.
> A: Why?
> P: Because I was not like him, I would have liked to have been. I
>   was with a supermasculine guy. He was assuming I was in the
>   fraternity, and I didn't feel that way. There was so much in his

> attitude toward women, so obvious in his being. I was about to
> go to a new job. I could be a ladies' man, and I could have
> my pick in women. He [the doctor] was the real thing. The
> differences between him and me are great.
>
> A: One similarity is that you both broke your elbow.
>
> P: Joe Montana and Phil Simms – both quarterbacks. The guy in
> the dream is like Montana. Montana and Simms have injuries
> which kept them out, and, when they came back, they played
> better *after* their injuries.

Associations later in the same session focus on stacks of rings on
penises. What this man is working on is the turning around of his
identification with his circumcised father from negative – whereby
they both are circumcised and castrated men – to positive, whereby
they both can make "beautiful passes," demonstrating athletic prowess
among men and success with the ladies. The father, who has been
presented until this point in the analysis as repulsive and even frightening (big hands, big fingers, big penis), is now emerging as an exciting
man worthy of admiration, respect, and identification. The revulsion
was in fact, a defense against the patient's excitement about the father.
The father's competence in athletics, sculpture, photography, and
writing can now be discussed without quick denigration of the father.
The father is aging well, and this too can be admired.

The patient's task, once the positive aspects of the father are
allowed to emerge, is to integrate the positive and negative, the
frightening and exciting in his image of his father. He must acknowledge his father's successful marriage to the patient's mother and face his
aggression and denigration of his father and the father's aggression
toward him. As all of these aspects are worked on, his own paternal
identity will become more positive and he will become more competent and confident in his fathering. Much work is necessary in these
areas, with accompanying consolidation and structuralization. Further
work remains for him to become an adult man and father within the
larger world outside the nuclear family.

A major difficulty in working on these issues is that until recently
the maternal imago encapsulated everything good from both the
mother and the father. This man is looking for a father to internalize,
but his search has been to look for the father in the mother rather than
in the father. Lansky (this volume) alerts us to the condensations that
can occur in parental imagos. Another major component in working
on a dyadic relationship and its internalizations is the freedom to
rework this relationship within the context of a responsive triad. That

is, the man must have mother's (and analyst's) permission to have his relationship with his father on his terms.

CONCLUDING REMARKS

Although the focus of this chapter is the reverberations of the son-father relationship in the psychoanalytic treatment of men, the family triad is always the context. Mother plays a significant role in vitalizing the father's relationship with the child. Likewise, the female analyst, in her role as woman and analyst, acts as a transitive revitalizer of the son-father relationship. The female analyst becomes the woman who can allow the son-father relationship to exist and who can endorse it with her love.

My work has emphasized that the gender of the analyst can be crucial in what the patient works on in treatment, how he works on it, and how the transference evolves. The patient reported here needed *real* contact with a woman analyst who could provide both a corrective experience with women (mother) and allow the transference with its maternal, paternal, and sibling components to unfold. Patients with triangulation (triadic) disturbances may need to have a reconcretization of the nuclear family in the treatment situation in order to master this developmental achievement. To a great extent, this patient's mother was the impediment to his developmental progress, and thus a female analyst is crucial to the treatment's success.

The clinical material shows us the disequilibrium experienced within a family during the pregnancy and after the birth of a child. Among these shifts, we see that some of the wife's endorsement of her husband and nurturance of his narcissism is lost, as her attention turns to her preparation for her new role as mother. Many men do not react to this very well. As we look at the preoedipal father, we see not only his active contributions within the family as a husband and father, but also his frailties and vulnerabilities. This understanding of the father may shake the strong need for us as analysts to view the father as an idealized oedipal figure. We see that the preoedipal father is not the uncontaminated object that Mahler, Pine, and Bergman (1975) and Abelin (1971) proposed, but rather that he has a complex range of affects toward his child, as does his child towards him.

Moreover, it is misleading to think that a father's nurturing capacities are directly linked solely to the actual nurturing received from his mother and maternal identifications. Paternal nurturance can originate in the father-child relationship too.

Finally, too much emphasis has been placed on the father as a figure for masculine identification, and sufficient emphasis has only begun to be placed on sorely needed object ties with father. Classical Freudian theory, by saving the father in an idealized form for the oedipal phase, has certainly reinforced this misconception.

REFERENCES

Abelin, E. (1971), The role of the father in the separation-individuation process. In: *Separation-Individuation,* ed. J. B. McDevitt & C. F. Settlage. New York: International Universities Press, pp. 229–252.

Atkins, R. (1982), Discovering daddy: The mother's role. In: *Father and Child,* ed. S. H. Cath, A. Gurwitt & J. M. Ross. Boston: Little, Brown, pp. 139–149.

Blos, P. (1985), *Son and Father.* New York: Free Press.

Chasseguet-Smirgel, J. (1986). Clinical workshop conducted at Institute for Psychoanalytic Training and Research, New York, NY, December.

Gunsberg, L. (1987), Issues in fathering and how they are reflected in the psychoanalytic treatment of men. Presented at meeting of American Psychoanalytic Association, New York, NY.

Loewald, H. (1980), The waning of the Oedipus complex. In: *Papers on Psychoanalysis.* New Haven, CT: Yale University Press, pp. 384–404.

Mahler, M. S., Pine, F., & Bergman, A. (1975), *The Psychological Birth of the Human Infant.* New York: Basic Books.

McDougall, J. (1980), *Plea for a Measure of Abnormality.* New York: International Universities Press.

Pruett, K. (1983), Infants of primary nurturing fathers. *The Psychoanalytic Study of the Child,* 38:257–277. New Haven: Yale University Press.

Ross, J. & Herzog, J. (1985), The sins of the father: Notes on fathers, aggression, and pathogenesis. In: *Parental Influences in Health and Disease,* ed. E. J. Anthony & G. H. Pollock. Boston: Little, Brown, pp. 477–510.

Ross, N. (1960), Rivalry with the product. *J. Amer. Psychoanal. Assn.,* 8:450–463.

27

Fathers of Psychotic Children

Clinical Observations and Approaches to Treatment

Michael Schwartzman

Mental health professionals in clinical practice who work with psychotic children are often confronted with the bizarre behaviors and seemingly insatiable needs of their young patients. As communication with these patients is very difficult, clinicians are hard pressed to understand and respond to these needs. Based on the pioneering work of Margaret Mahler and her colleagues at the Masters Children's Center and Anni Bergman and her colleagues Gilbert Voyat and Linda Gunsberg at the City University Child Center, treatment programs that address the need for a more precise understanding of the psychotic child's behaviors have been developed.

These programs, which have achieved considerable success, typically involve working with the mother-child dyad instead of with the child alone. As a staff member of the City University Child Center, I extended this approach to include clinical work with the father-child dyad as well. Fathers and mothers seem to develop a keen sense of what their child is attempting to communicate, and, when this is brought into the treatment room, the therapist can intervene by helping the parents to understand their children better and thereby enrich their interactions with them.

Intrigued by these findings, I began to work with more fathers of psychotic children and ultimately conducted a research project (Schwartzman, 1983) aimed at describing who these men are, what their experience of fatherhood is like, and what kind of impact they have on their children. Throughout, my interest has been to better understand these men in order to incorporate them into the treatment plans for their children. The findings of this project and some thoughts about how to work clinically with these fathers follow.

Our knowledge and understanding of the father's role in the life of his psychotic child is incomplete. The studies that have been conducted focus on his role as supporter of the mother-child relationship, as an object of identification for the child, or as an emotional supporter of the mother (Kanner, 1943; Eisenberg and Kanner, 1956; Eisenberg, 1957; Donelly, 1960; Lidz, 1965; Gunsberg, 1982). They have not focused on the direct effect he has on his child's development. These studies have been of father's attitudes and beliefs regarding child rearing or of his characteristic ways of behaving with his child. The studies have been based on secondary sources of information such as reports of father by mother rather than on first-hand evidence provided by father himself.

A review of these studies reveals their findings to be inconclusive for two major reasons. Basing studies on secondary, often subjective, sources raises the question of the accuracy of representation of the father's behavior. Second, in the light of what has been written by developmental psychologists studying early infancy and childhood, isolating father's attitudes from his actual behaviors for purposes of controlled study also is misleading. Clearly, numerous factors, some less analyzable than others, contribute to his role as father and the part he plays in the development of his psychotic child. These include his attitudes about child rearing, his feelings about being a father, his perception and understanding of his child's needs, his relationship with his wife, his general state of well-being, and his characteristic ways of engaging his child in activity. The combination of these factors, seen in the context of the father's personality style, contributes to the influence a father has on his child and his child's ensuing development.

With regard to what has been studied in the past, my investigation was a first effort at assessing the influences that affect a father's attempts at fathering his psychotic child. It had three aims. The first aim was to establish some descriptive characteristics distinguishing the different behavioral styles of fathers during interactions with their psychotic sons. This was accomplished by naturalistically observing father-son interactions and assessing them by analyzing the components of the interaction using the Interpersonal Behavior Constructs

Scale (IBC), developed by Kogan and Gordon (1975). The second aim of the study was to investigate the attitudes and feelings fathers had about their role as father and their attitudes and feelings toward their sons. This was done by conducting semistructured interviews with the fathers. The third aim of the study was to draw some comparisons between fathers of normal children and fathers of psychotic children. Findings based on a comparable sample of fathers and their normal sons conducted by Strong (1978), which also utilized the IBC, were used as a comparison.

The sample of fathers studied in this investigation was small; fortunately, the number of psychotic children, and consequently the number of their fathers, is relatively small. Unfortunately, of this small group, even fewer are willing to participate in this kind of research study. Therefore, while I was able to obtain considerable detail about the participating fathers, the small sample size requires that the results of this study be used as a starting point for future inquiry and not as conclusions that can be generalized to all fathers of psychotic children.

The two fathers in this study were matched. Both were in their 40s, middle class, and married for the first time. Both were fathers of first-born sons who were also only children. Neither father revealed any history of mental illness. Both fathers volunteered for the study. The following clinical descriptions reveal factors that crucially affect father's interaction with his psychotic son.

CLINICAL ILLUSTRATIONS

Mr. D.

Mr. D is a 40-year-old, middle-class businessman. His son, P, is 5 years old. P.'s diagnosis, in accordance with DSM III, is 299.9, Childhood Onset, Pervasive Developmental Disorder.

An analysis of interview data regarding attitudes and feelings about fathering revealed that Mr. D had adopted an objective view of his son. He stated that this attitude contrasted with that of his "emotional wife." Consequently, he perceived his son as a child whose psychological development was disrupted by an illness. Originally upset over his son's condition, he quickly began a search that despite his anger at the many professionals he encountered, led him to a therapeutic program that provided a satisfactory explanation of the reasons for this deviant development and a promising plan of remediation. In accepting this program, Mr. D apparently adopted the role of

P.'s worker, bent on helping him, via behavioral exercises, to develop more suitable and appropriate means of adapting to the demands of everyday life.

In discussing his feeelings about being a father to this child, Mr. D consistently spoke almost with an air of professional detachment. He talked of working with his son but avoided talk of feelings engendered by the difficulties of this work. With some feeling, he stated that his son's needs kept him and his wife from having another child. Later, when confronted with the question of the dreams he had for P., Mr. D. appeared somewhat upset. This was quickly overridden by the statement, "I don't dream. I'm concerned more with what is happening now than where he is going to go. I need to know where he is so I know where to work and how to work."

Mr. D. attends behavior modification classes at P.'s school and stated that he applies its principles in a consistent manner when he interacts with P. Though he works hard at his job, he sees P. in the morning before work, in the evening, and on the weekends. At these times he plays physical games with him in an attempt to capture his attention. Then he imposes physical and verbal structures within their interaction in an effort to modify his son's behavior. Mr. D. stated that he attempts to create an atmosphere of pleasure, but, within his role as P.'s protector and trainer, he also must act as a disciplinarian and structurer of P.'s experience because that is what his child needs to ensure his continued development.

Mr. D. feels that he has had a strong impact on P. and that he has been successful in his goal of teaching him how to care for himself and behave appropriately. As we talked about the future, he explained that he hopes they will continue their "satisfying, friendly relationship" but on a more adult level when P. is able to communicate in a more sophisticated manner.

Consonant with Mr. D.'s attitudes and feelings are the IBC scores obtained from an analysis of his interactive style with his son. Scores reveal that, while exuding positive affect, Mr. D. worked consistently to capture his child's attention with exciting stimulating activity. By deciding both the rules and materials for their games, Mr. D. controlled their interactions. To accomplish this, he physically altered his son's behaviors so they appropriately met the requirements called for in the games.

As a last resort, when P. turned away, Mr. D. would physically alter his son's behavior, put an end to one activity, and initiate another. Within the transition from one activity to another, Mr. D. often accomplished his goal of recapturing P.'s attention with a physical act of endearment that was highly exciting and stimulating. Then he introduced objects with which they could share an activity.

For his part, P. quickly and with obvious pleasure responded to his father's lead and interacted with him for periods of time. These periods would eventually end with P.'s loss of interest and lapse into independent behavior. These lapses would immediately trigger another instance of Mr. D.'s physically restructuring P.'s behavior and initiating a joint activity. At times this intrusion on father's part was upsetting for P., and he would engage in some idiosyncratic behavior. Mr. D. would then discipline him with verbal or physical scolding and physically reengage him.

This interactive cycle continued as Mr. D., used repetitive behaviors to insure his son's focused attention and structured the situation. Although Mr. D. was asked to teach P. something new, when it became clear that P. could not accomplish the task, Mr. D. made it easier for him by changing the goal of the lesson. When it became clear that P. was getting upset and becoming involved in independent play rather than shared teaching or play activity, Mr. D. abandoned the task.

In the light of Mr. D.'s attitude regarding maintaining his son's attention in order to modify and teach behaviors, it is interesting that this also meant that P.'s attention had to be focused on an object-oriented or physical game they shared together. Little room was left for independent play in the presence of father, as this occasioned another instance of Mr. D.'s restructuring activity.

Mr. J.

Mr. J. is a 47-year-old, middle-class professional. His son, K. is 5 years old. K's diagnosis, in accordance with DSM III, is 299.9, Childhood Onset, Pervasive Developmental Disorder.

An analysis of the qualitative results regarding Mr. J.'s attitudes and feelings about fathering reveals that he loves children and would like to have more if it were not for the severity of K.'s problems. Mr. J. appears to feel very upset over K.'s condition despite his stated denials of his son's deviant behaviors. Describing his efforts at being a cool investigator, in contrast to his wife's perennial state of upset, Mr. J. has tried to find solutions to his sons's problems. Unlike Mr. D., he has not been able to find a suitable answer to his questions about his son's condition, nor has he been able to locate a program that he feels will satisfy his son's needs. He continues to feel confused about his son and the role he attempts to assume with regard to his development. At times, Mr. J. like his wife, will lapse into a state of emotional upset that borders on panic. He reports feeling guilty and worried about what will happen to his son.

Mr. J. says that, because of his confusion about K.'s condition, he has developed very inadequate means for fathering him. He assumes that his fathering efforts should change K.'s behavior so that K. is independent and safe and he uses reward and punishment to modify K.'s behaviors toward this end. While teaching his son is a primary aim, Mr. J. fears that his lack of understanding may lead him to hurt his son, and so often gives up. He sees himself as K.'s protector and satisfier of his needs but has no faith that K. understands the efforts he has made in this direction. He feels it important to protect K. by physically controlling him and structuring the situation, but he has not arrived at suitable ways of doing so. Repeated failures at engaging K. have led him to question whether K. even regards him as his father.

Mr. J. stated that he spends whatever time he can with K. before work, after work, and on weekends. As he described what they do together, he consistently said "I try to," and his statements revealed great confusion and uncertainty about what to do. Their main activities involve physical play and reading. He is very put off by K.'s behavioral and attentional inconsistencies and finds their interactions frustrating and fleeting. Often he has found himself having to control K. physically and is worried about the time when K. will be too big to control. When asked what needs to be improved between them, Mr. J. laughingly answered, "Everything." To cope with this onerous task, Mr. J. has lowered his expectations for K. but remains worried that K. will never be self-sufficient.

Being K.'s father means that Mr. J. often comes home to assume primary responsibility for his child's needs so that his wife can get some private time. He feels that a great deal of strain has developed between himself and his wife. At times they have contemplated institutionalizing K. This frustration over his efforts at being a father to K. is such that he hopes that K.'s problems can be handled medically with an operation.

Consonant with Mr. J.'s statements about his attitudes and feelings about fathering are the behaviors he exhibited during his observed interactions with K. In an unemotional way and showing great persistence, Mr. J. used physical and verbal means in an apparent effort to get K. to focus his attention and perform certain activities. Using a variety of objects, Mr. J. would reach in front of K.'s line of vision to attract his attention to an object. Often K. attended only briefly, and Mr. J. would quickly reengage K.'s attention with an exciting physical or verbal maneuver. Thus, they appeared to engage in repeated acts of shared activity. K. would submit to his father and comply by being still. After a short time he would try to move away and operate independently. Mr. J. would call to him and then use physical means to bring him back, if K. did not do so on his own. K.'s efforts at terminating his interaction with father appeared, at times, to be attempts to break away from his father's control. Eventually Mr. J. would read to K. K. would answer questions about the reading and learned some new answers. This activity seemed to be one that both had learned before and were repeating during the observation period. During the teaching portion of the interaction, using exaggerated sounds and movements repetitively, Mr. J. taught K. to place pegs in holes. As K. did this, Mr. J. would respond positively. K. would look and then continue, smiling with apparent pleasure. When K. appeared ready to give up the activity, Mr. J. would physically hold him back and reengage his attention. This continued until K. slipped away to engage in some idiosyncratic behavior.

DISCUSSION OF FINDINGS

An analysis of the qualitative findings reveals both similarities and differences between these two fathers with regard to their attitudes and feelings about fathering a psychotic child. The fathers' stated attitudes and feelings, are not simply the results of their experiencing children who has the same diagnosed illness; they also are dependent on the individual personality characteristics each father brings to the child-rearing situation. Each father has his own character style through which his fathering experience is filtered and by which his reported experience is colored.

Both men state their love for children but, aware of the severity of their child's problems, have chosen not to have other children at the present time. Each father notes his initial upset over observing his son's deviant development. Each one describes his own attitude of cool investigation in contrast to his wife's emotionality, although he, too, can become emotional. Each father describes a wish to teach the child how to take care of himself, and each sees himself as his child's protector. Both fathers appear to have adopted, with differing degrees of comfort, a behaviorist approach to training their children to behave adequately and appropriately in everyday situations. Each father sees his role as a structurer and discipliner of his son's experience. Both fathers note the importance of caring for their sons, but, unlike their wives, they also devote a great deal of their time to work outside the home. Each father is aware of wanting to see great changes in his child and notes various feelings that go along with his experience of waiting for these changes to occur.

The most important differences between the fathers appears to be a difference in the acceptance and understanding they have reached in their perceptions of their sons. Mr. D. appears much more satisfied and at peace in his relationship than does Mr. J. Mr. J., on the other hand, remains very confused about what is wrong and very upset with his relationship with his son. Mr. D. talks with confidence and certainty about his role as P.'s father and the impact he is having as a father; Mr. J. appears to be very unsure of the effect he is having on K. and talks of the frustration he feels fathering him.

The comparison of quantitative results obtained by analyzing the father-psychotic son interactions also reveals some similarities and differences in their interactional style. Though the sample size is too small to make general statements about the style and content of father-psychotic son interaction, patterns can be described.

The results of this study indicate that these psychotic children and their fathers engage in a form of transactive interaction, an interaction during which there is a give-and-take reciprocity between father and son. This finding appears to dispute what is commonly noted in the diagnostic literature, namely that this type of child does not engage in interpersonal interactions. The present findings indicate that these children are capable of interaction with their fathers. These results point to the usefulness of interactional measures in assessing the psychotic child's behavioral capacities.

Each father's efforts seem aimed initially at focusing his son's attention and then modifying his son's behaviors to insure a level of appropriate activity. For his part, the psychotic child used little language, had a short attention span, but appeared cooperative and responsive to his father for periods of time. Though their interaction was observed under varying conditions – playing, teaching, and unstructured – both fathers' interaction styles were consistent throughout and appeared to combine teaching and playing with their sons in repetitive, physical ways.

Compared with the fathers of normal children, fathers of psychotic children appear to be significantly more physical and to use verbal methods to take the lead in interactive situations, structuring what is to occur within them. The interactions between the normal pairs involve significantly more instances of independent activity wherein the child acts and the father watches. In the pairs studied here, there were significantly more instances of shared activity.

This difference in fathering raises the question of what accounts for the tendency of fathers of psychotic children to be so controlling. Eisenberg (1957) argues that the father of an autistic child is potentially pathological and provides little that is helpful for his child. Qualitative findings in the present study indicate that both fathers seemed to stress teaching their children appropriate behaviors. The fathers tended to interact by structuring their children's activities and intrusively altering their children's attention and behaviors to conform to their own wishes. They wanted the children's behavior to seem appropriate.

Given Bender's (1957) characterization of the autistic child as grossly impaired, one is led to speculate on the child's effect on the father and the compensatory alterations the father makes in his child-rearing attitudes and behaviors. Perhaps the father's need to control the child and structure his activity, as revealed in this study, is better understood in the light of Kogan and Gordon's (1975) finding that mothers of disturbed children face situations that parents of normal children do not. This often creates emotional reactions in parents that affect their interaction in subtle ways. Fathers' controlling behavior can be similarly understood as a consequence of the conditions inherent in this situation.

Like the sensorimotor child Piaget (1954) describes, the psychotic child's deviant development leaves him able to understand actions and objects primarily on a physical, action level. Unlike the normal child of five, who can more easily understand primitive conceptualizations, the psychotic child requires more active involvement with his partner if his interest is to be sustained. Perhaps, like the father of a normal two year old, the father of the psychotic child responds to this need and provides repetitive cues to his child because he finds that he can capture the child's attention and influence him in this way. Rather than being experienced as cold, harsh, and restrictive by the psychotic child, the father is understood by him. The father's repetitive actions seem to attract the psychotic child specifically because they provide a structure that the child understands and needs.

This conclusion is in accordance with Abelin's (1971) finding that the father of the two year old provides stimulating physical activity that the child finds appealing. The father is able to attract the child away from mother and facilitate his burgeoning abilities to explore the world. Father's physical activities act as a bridge, away from mother, to the rest of the external environment. For his part, the child learns from father by imitating father's behaviors and using them as he explores. More and more, he looks to father as a guide and identifies with him.

For the psychotic child, who is tied to mother for fear of being annihilated by stimuli he cannot face alone (Mahler, 1968), father may provide physical cues the child understands and can respond to. These cues help the child move out into the world and act more independently. Just as mother nurtures the infant's emotional needs, father nurtures the child's need to explore by providing physical ways of doing so (Parke, 1979). Father's physical cues, via repetition, situational structuring efforts, control, and direction, nurture the psychotic child's developing capacity for tolerating his fears and learning new things. In line with Mahler's (1952) formulation that the psychotic child is symbiotically tied to mother, it is not unexpected to observe a higher frequency of "shared activity" with father among these children than among normal children. Because the psychotic child has not achieved a sufficient sense of separateness from mother, this developmental inadequacy also appears with father. Perhaps submitting to father is the way that the child can tolerate being away from mother and still feel safe. One can speculate that experiences with someone other than mother, such as father, contribute to the psychotic child's cognitive development. Similar enough in style to mother, insuring continuity and emotional security, the father nurtures the child's development by providing new experiences for mastery.

Though further research is needed to confirm this finding, father's controlling style may be positive and useful to the child rather than negative, as suggested by Eisenberg (1957). Unlike language and mild physical prompts, father's clear physical cues, offered in a controlling manner, get through to the psychotic child. The child takes these cues and is emotionally secure by them. Additionally the cognitively stimulate him in ways that he is capable of taking in. This physically controlling style, as contrasted with mother's verbal style, may be what makes father the unique caregiver that he is.

While no conclusive answers can be offered to other questions about the father's role and his effect on his psychotic son, the present study suggests some ideas worthy of consideration. In line with Pittfield and Oppenheimer's (1964) conclusion that father's effect on his child is tied to the child's effect on his father, it is useful to look at the ways in which Mr. D. and Mr. J.'s perceptions of their roles and impact have been affected by their child-rearing experiences. Mr. D. sees his child as having become sick and that his illness has resulted in the loss of a year of development. Having found an explanation for his son's condition and a treatment program that he finds satisfactory, he appears no longer to feel upset about his son's illness. On the other hand, Mr. J. continues to be very confused about his son's problems and prognosis. He has not overcome his confusion and continues to be upset about it. Asked to talk about his role, he cannot help but lapse into talk of his distress.

Having overcome his upset, Mr. D. sees himself as a protector and teacher of his child. He thinks of himself as his child's worker, who will encourage his development by carrying out certain strategies. He feels himself to be an effective father. On the other hand, Mr. J. continues to be emotionally put off by his child's problems and is unable to establish a consistent role for himself or a way to feel good about his role. He feels unsure of his effect as a father and stands by passively unless his son is in danger.

APPROACHES TO TREATMENT

Given the foregoing clinical observations of fathers and their psychotic sons, it is clearly useful to involve the fathers in the treatment plans devised for the children. The father has much to offer the child and needs to be helped by the mental health professional in carrying out the plan. Generally this involves a three step process:

1. coming to terms with his feelings about losing a "normal child" and having an "impaired one," with all the meanings this may have for him in terms of his life experience;
2. understanding the specifics of his child's impairments, their causes, and the possible treatment approaches available;
3. understanding the emotional and physical expressions of his particular child and how to respond to them.

There are four approaches to working with the father in this three-step process. They are working with father individually, working with father and mother together, working with father in a group context, and working with father and child together.

Individual Work with Father

This approach relies on the assumption that father has many conscious and unconscious feelings about his child and his illness. He is confused about what is wrong with his child and what needs to be done as well as what can be done to help him with his problems.

From my research and therapy with fathers of psychotic children, I have found that the father needs to vent the myriad of feelings he has about his child. Interest in any therapy where acceptance of harsh realities is involved are feelings of loss and the need to mourn. Guilt, anger, and sadness must be tolerated. Fears need to be explored. A father cannot be expected to adjust to the needs and demands of his child if he has not come to terms with his own. A father must be brought first to some point of acceptance of what is wrong and then to a sense of hope for what can be done.

Once this process is underway, father will be better able to deal with what needs to be done to further his child's development. At this point it is useful to take a psychoeducational approach. The father is encouraged both to express his ideas about his child's needs and to state his questions and confusions about the child's needs and behaviors. The therapist should be very direct in offering his experience and knowledge in clarifying feelings and questions and then in answering them. This is best accomplished in an atmosphere of acceptance for the father is certain to experience a host of humiliating and shameful feelings about coming to depend on the help of the professional. The therapist must be sensitive to these feelings as he helps the father to sort out major questions about what he might do as caregiver to his needy child.

Ultimately, professional and father must address questions pertaining to his role as father. Father has two types of concerns. The first has to do with planning for the child's future. Planning and organizing for the future involves not only considerations of treatment approach but also issues about keeping the child at home. Father needs concrete help with these decisions. Second, father has questions about how best to care for the child on a day-to-day basis. He needs to learn about the specific needs of his child–his strengths, weaknesses, and limitations. He needs educative support for his efforts.

Work with Father and Mother

Underlying this approach is the assumption that father and mother have issues about their child that might stem from or impinge upon their marriage as well as questions about how to cooperatively give care to their child. The first issue involves problems that relate to the marital tensions that arise as a result of bearing a child with such a severe disorder as psychosis. Such issues as who is responsible and the onus of guilt require parents to communicate with each other despite the burden of their feelings, which will, at times, come between them. Parents need help with these feelings.

Parenting concerns, taken up with the couple, ultimately must touch on the fears and confusions that cause tension and distress between them. Again, it is useful for the professional to take a clarifying and educative approach. Just what are the questions parents have about their own and their partner's parenting? Their questions should be answered with understanding and supportive suggestions. Parents who can be brought together as mutual helpers, understanding each other's feelings, can also be be brought together to answer each other's questions about themselves and their child. It is useful to point out how much they each know about their child just from their own experiences with him.

Group Work with Fathers

This approach is grounded on the assumption that fathers can gain insight and understanding about themselves and their children by listening and talking with fathers with similar types of children. Groups can be sources of self-acceptance, educative information, and emotional support.

For example, one group of fathers, each of whom had a psychotic child, met for weekly one-hour sessions with two group leaders. One leader was a classroom teacher of the children, the other was a therapist. The group focused on the fathers' feelings about having disabled children and the "intrusion" this created in their lives. Fathers seemed relieved to find other fathers who were experiencing similar feelings, such as guilt over what they felt they had done to create their children's problems and anger over having to care for the children. Issues ranged from one father's wish to have another child, but being afraid that it too would be ill, to another father's wish that the government would give him money so that he could spend his days teaching his daughter rather than the government's paying a residential facility to care for her. The leaders responded to the fathers' concerns with empathy as well as educative support. At various times, each father struggled with such feelings of shame, guilt, and harassment that it was difficult for him to attend the group (Lansky and Simenstad, this volume). It was surprising how these fathers attempted to bear these feelings in silence. Once they opened up and each member expressed his feelings, the fathers became much more accepting of themselves and one another.

Work with Father and Child Together

This approach assumes that the psychotic child's behavior can be bizarre and extremely difficult for the father to understand. Therefore, the therapist, who has come to understand the child, can show the father how he might interact with his child.

For example, a psychotic girl was being treated on a three-times-a-week basis. Her father, who was being seen by the same therapist, was very confused and put off by his daughter's behavior. He did not know how to break into her idiosyncratic behaviors and interact with her. Father and daughter were brought to a playground familiar to the child. After the therapist had played with the girl in front of the father for a while, the father took the place of the therapist and, with the therapist offering instructions and discussion, played with his daughter. It quickly became evident that she wanted very much to be with her father. She grew very excited as he let her show him what she wanted to do rather than telling her what to do or ignoring her. Under the therapist's directive guidance, the father was able to enlarge his repertoire of ways of playing with his daughter, and the therapist could retreat into the background.

This directive approach was used at home as well. The therapist "walked through" such activities as mealtime, playtime, and bedtime with father and daughter. Learning how to do this with the active support of the therapist enabled the father to take on more of a direct role with the child. As he felt more secure in his ability to understand the child's signals, he became more flexible in his own behavioral and verbal response to them.

Within each of these four approaches the professional needs to be armed with several areas of expertise. A thorough understanding of normal and abnormal child development in the emotional, cognitive, and social spheres is essential. The professional should certainly have up-to-date information about childhood psychoses, their etiology, differential diagnosis considerations, treatment approaches, and prognostic issues. The father's trust in the clinician will hinge on the professional's ability to understand the father's plight, as well as to articulate a knowledgeable, informative understanding of the disorder. The clinician must be able at once to work with the father's feelings about the condition and to educate him about what can be done about it. Helping father involves facilitating his acceptance of his child and himself and helping him to cope with the lifelong struggle to create the most useful treatment approaches for his child. Of course, it is necessary to determine if the father evidences any psychopathology. Obviously, if the father is experiencing his own psychological problems, treatment recommendations and referral information need to be offered to him. Child psychosis, to father, is a real and emotionally threatening experience. The father needs the real emotional and educative support a professional has to offer.

IMPLICATIONS FOR FUTURE RESEARCH

In view of the paucity of pertinent literature, the present study was undertaken in an effort to evaluate such general issues as the father's interactional style and his feelings and attitudes toward his psychotic child. Some of the literature on child rearing has stressed that the development of the child is affected by triadic interactions. Accordingly, future research that focuses on the triad, and not the dyad, would be useful. Such a study would describe and assess the effects husband and wife have on each other's interaction with their child and how their child's illness contributes to their interaction, as well as describing and assessing the three-way interaction.

Also useful would be longitudinal studies of the father's interaction with his child. Father's style probably changes as his understanding of his child's particular development evolves over the developmental process. Such a study would assess these changes over time. It would assess how the degree of "organicity" in the child affects the father's relationship with his child. How is the father affected by the etiological factors in his particular child's case? To better understand this, fathers with children found to have organicity at the root of their psychosis and fathers with children found to have trauma at the root of their psychosis should be studied and compared.

The finding that a father's interaction with his psychotic child is positively influenced by an objective understanding of his child's behavior would be usefully employed in a follow-up study. Such a study would involve videotaping an interaction and reviewing it with a father. Not only would this effort support and encourage the father's continued involvement, it would offer him a means for gaining a more objective way of understanding his child and improving their interactions. Results of such a study would facilitate the design of badly needed treatment methods and programs.

REFERENCES

Abelin, E. (1971), The role of the father in the separation-individuation process. In *Separation-Individuation,* ed. J. B. McDevitt & C. F. Settlage. New York: International Universities Press, pp. 229–253.

Bender, L. (1957). Schizophrenia in childhood: its recognition, description and treatment. *Amer. J. Orthopsychiat.,* 27:499–506.

Donelly, E. (1960), The quantitative analysis of parent behavior toward psychotic children and their siblings. *Genetic Psychol. Monogr.,* 62:1–60.

Eisenberg, L. (1957), Father and autistic children. *Amer. J. Orthopsychiat.,* 27:2–37.

_____ & Kanner, L. (1956), Early infantile autism. *Amer. J. Orthopsychiat.,* 26:556–566.

Gunsberg, L. (1982), Selected critical review of psychological investigations of the early father-infant relationship. In: *Father and Child,* ed. S. Cath, A. Gurwitt & J. Ross. Boston: Little, Brown, pp. 65–87.

Kanner, L. (1943), Autistic disturbances of affective contact. *Nervous Child,* 2:217–250.

Kogan, K. & Gordon, B. (1975), Interpersonal behavior constructs: A means for analyzing video-taped dyadic interaction. Laboratory Manual, Parenting Clinic, University of Washington, Seattle.

Lidz, T. (1965), *The Family and Human Adaptation.* New York: International Universities Press.

Mahler, M. (1952), On child psychosis and schizophrenia: autistic and symbiotic infantile psychoses. *The Psychoanalytic Study of the Child,* 7:286–305. New York: International Universities Press.

_____ (1968), *On Human Symbiosis and the Vicissitudes of Individuation.* New York: International Universities Press.

Parke, R. (1979), Perspectives on father-infant interaction. In: *Handbook of Infant Development,* ed. J. Osofsky. New York: Wiley, pp. 3–16.

Piaget, J. (1954), *The Construction of Reality.* New York: Ballantine.

Pittfield, M. & Oppenheimer, A. (1964), Child rearing attitudes of mothers of psychotic children. *J. Child Psychol. and Psychiat. & Allied Disciplines,* 5:51–57.

Schwartzman, M. (1983), Father and atypical son: A study of social interaction. Unpublished doctoral dissertation, Yeshiva University.

Strong, G. (1978), Father-child interaction: A comparison with mother-child interaction. Unpublished Master's Thesis, University of Washington, Seattle.

28

Conflict and Resistance in the Treatment of Psychiatrically Hospitalized Fathers

Melvin R. Lansky

Ellen A. Simenstad

THE PROBLEM

Recognition of the treatment needs of severely disturbed fathers has scarcely begun. There is in fact a striking paucity of attention to the plight of the psychiatrically hospitalized father. Reasons for this neglect may include difficulties conceptualizing what activities constitute fathering as compared to the more experience-near dyadic caretaking behaviors usually designated as mothering. Clinically, one finds surprising difficulties focusing on treatment issues dealing with the paternal role of the hospitalized father. We will attempt to understand the failure of these patients and the staff treating them to form a working collaboration that addresses central issues in paternity.

Attention to these problems is painful. In previous writings (Lansky, 1984; Lansky, 1987; Lansky and Simenstad, 1986) we have noted patients' difficulties facing their problems as fathers. This chapter considers the result of a project of several years' duration, studying fathers admitted to a psychiatric hospital ward. That project attempted to survey the plight of the psychiatrically hospitalized father preparatory to specific hospital-based treatment strategies. We were able to locate and describe some of the massive deficits found in these men and the difficulties they had in acknowledging that the paternal role was an area for treatment focus. We have described in detail narcissistic injury and resultant shame endured by these men, and their defensive efforts, often symptomatic impulsive action, that compensate for and hide their sense of defectiveness (Lansky, in press).

We hope to pave the way for efforts aimed at treating these men as fathers. Our investigations pointed to overwhelming and generalized residual psychopathology in virtually all these men even at times of presumed remission. We saw few areas in which simple intervention would be of help and little symptomatic remission that took place as a result of sustained therapeutic focus on the problem or therapeutic zeal. We are prepared, then, to see clinical predicaments that are peppered with enormous difficulties and despair and futility arising from dysfunction in the paternal role, but we hope to introduce a sensitivity to the fact that treatment staff are not merely observers of the damage in these chronically impaired men; they are also vulnerable to a reactive futility that may reflect a collusion[1] with the patient, buttressing rather than minimizing the patient's own resistance to treatment. Such collusions, if they are discovered, would be dynamically overdetermined and deviation amplifying systems that risk premature dismissal of the clinical situation as hopeless. These collusions, then, pose serious hazards to the entire treatment enterprise and demand the fullest psychoanalytical understanding, preparatory to speculating about possibilities for such patient-staff collusive resistances. We will touch briefly on the background for our investigations and present an overview of our findings.

SETTING AND METHODOLOGY

Our interest in the problem of fathers hospitalized on our family-oriented inpatient unit came from many sources. The Family Treatment Program itself provided an especially favorable environment for

---

[1]By *collusion*, we refer to the unconscious dovetailing of defensive processes of persons in families or in other close collaborative relationships. This dovetailing serves, without a conscious agreement to do so, to regulate either expression or avoidance of certain situations of central dynamic significance to all parties concerned. These latent expressive and protective operations are concealed within the manifest, consciously agreed-upon activities of the collaboration. Collusion is a ubiquitous phenomenon in close relationships and should be considered pathological only if the latent issues are split off and disowned by all parties and exert a force that sabotages (rather than complementing) the manifest basis of the collaboration.

scrutiny of the problem. It is a hospital-based, 20-bed unit at the Brentwood V.A. Medical Center in Los Angeles, a hospital with close university ties and generously staffed with seasoned, psychoanalytically sophisticated therapists and UCLA psychiatric residents. Efforts are made to involve the family in every case. In the 12 years of the program's existence, we have come to appreciate the role in the family system of collusion that provides resistance to therapy in the hospital and to change in life outside the hospital. As we have come to recognize collusive-defensive patterns and to appreciate impulsive symptoms in the family context as the patient's attempt to control distance to intimates – that is, to prevent them from getting too close or too far away – we have come to appreciate the role of narcissistic vulnerability and other characterologic limitations posed by propensities of the personality to disorganize – and of resultant shame and defenses against it (Lansky, in press).

Our psychoanalytic orientation and our commitment to family involvement provided a synergistic impetus to the study of fathers. Understanding of the key role of father in facilitating the separation process in individual development has been noted (Abelin, 1971, 1975, 1980), and the multiple roles of father in development, not just as oedipal overlord but in a more complex way, has acquired enough recent momentum (Ross, 1979; Cath, Gurwitt, and Ross, 1982) to be considered a substantial body of knowledge available to enter the mainstream of psychoanalytic development thinking. Family therapy has progressed far beyond the presumption that the mother-child dyad is itself pathogenic and has focused on the entire family system in the genesis and momentum of psychopathology (Bowen, 1966). Our increasing sophistication in viewing psychopathology in crisis and remaining mindful of family systems has drawn our attention to absence as well as presence as significant phenomena: emotional absences of the chronically preoccupied father are often seen to amplify or precipitate more visible psychopathology – blaming or impulsive action – on the part of others in the family system (Lansky, 1985). Furthermore, we came to see the absence of family in hospitalized patients as a sign with a great deal of prognostic and therapeutic significance (Lansky, Bley, Simenstad, West, McVey and McVey, 1983) in patients who proved to be demanding, rageful, and intimidating with the ward staff in the hospital.

Consolidation of these areas of emphasis enabled us to remain curious about the familial, and especially paternal, role in psychiatrically hospitalized men who made every effort to minimize or even deny their contact with family during their hospitalizations. We uncovered a distinct reluctance to acknowledge problems in the paternal role. The more we tried to understand this role, the more the overdetermined nature of this reluctance to focus became clear. Patients tended either to externalize their problems or to overfocus on specific symptoms or turbulent circumstances. Staff felt reluctant to press these men to face their problems with their children or felt themselves overcome with the patients' depression when such an effort was made. A similar absence was noted in the clinical literature; a computerized literature search revealed no literature on the psychiatrically hospitalized father.

This absence of focus in patients, therapy teams, and the literature aroused our suspicions that we were dealing with yet another species of defensively overdetermined absence. Such a possibility alerted us to question resistances to straightforward collaboration in therapeutic tasks that might be contained within the patient-staff matrix in ways that might recapitulate similarly futile stalemates in the patient's current family situation or in the one in which he grew up.

Our appreciation of these resistances to treatment collaboration aimed at difficulties in the paternal role led to systematic efforts to explore the problem. Three different avenues were employed. *Clinical scrutiny* of psychiatrically hospitalized fathers included circumstances of admission, ward behavior, hospital course, and followup. The clinical treatment setting was the matrix in which other activities occurred. These included taped and transcribed *intergenerational interviews* with each father admitted to the service for an entire year (N=75, only 4 fathers refused). These three-generational interviews covered patients' recollections of their fathers as father; of their mothers as supporter of father's paternal role or in undercutting it; of their wives' support or lack of it for the patients' own paternal function; and finally of their own view of themselves as father to their children. Questions were deliberately open ended and general. Finally, *groups for hospitalized fathers* (continuing into the posthospital period) were begun. The groups were established primarily to explore the problems of these men and only secondarily for the purpose of treatment.

OVERVIEW OF FINDINGS

The results of these endeavors to study the psychiatrically hospitalized father, together with detailed case material, are found in other writings and will only be summarized here.

Clinical observation (Lansky, 1984) highlighted the patients' tendencies to represent their problems as illness (manic depressive, schizophrenic, alcoholic), as resulting solely from turmoil in circumstances (usually familial), or as isolated symptoms (drinking, voices). Even with staff emphasis on fathering, patients continued to resist focus on obvious and even overwhelming crises in the paternal role. Observations in a series of groups for fathers highlighted some of these difficulties (Lansky and Simenstad, 1986). Most of our recently admitted fathers welcomed the offer of such a group, but few attended and even fewer stayed. The groups tried to be supportive of members and to utilize common predicaments of the fathers as a basis for supportive group identifications. Groups homogeneous for predicament have been highly successful in our program for other difficulties, yet both therapists and patients alike experienced these groups as overwhelming and depressing. The patients that profited from these groups were those few fathers who had years before been cast out of their families but who had contact with their children thrust upon them recently by circumstances; that is, they had no choice but to deal with their children. In these few, a history of extreme narcissistic vulnerability with an inability to relate and constant preoccupation emerged as memories of their experiences of father when their children were young. More visible pathology (drunkenness, abusiveness, marital strife, desertion, violence) covered up these basic narcissistic defects, which were often compounded by frightening identifications with similar vulnerabilities and methods of handling them in the father's own father (Lansky, in press).

Intergenerational interviews showed ubiquitous and overwhelming damage in the fathers' capacities to fulfill the paternal role. These defects were experienced by the patients in ways that were characteristic of their particular diagnoses. For example, borderline patients consistently blamed their own fathers for abusing them and leaving them poorly prepared for the paternal role. They carried a conscious sense of being damaged and cheated, often accompanied by rage and a sense of entitlement, and an unconscious sense of being doomed to identify with their own fathers. They evidenced split views of women. Their mothers at first were idealized and seen as victims of their fathers, but later as much more like their wives—divisive and tending to pair off with children in coalitions, excluding and even provoking their husbands. Borderline fathers all felt that they were inadequate fathers themselves; even those who blamed their wives for divisiveness painfully acknowledged their inadequacies. Those borderline patients who identified themselves as uncontrollable alcoholics always viewed their lack of control with a conscious and pervasive sense of shame. These men, to avoid more shame and to protect their families from themselves, often voluntarily absented themselves from their children.

Schizophrenics (Lansky and Simenstad, draft a) seldom blamed either parents or spouses for their difficulties but tended to have an all-too-painful awareness of the devastating limitations imposed by their condition. Manic- depressive fathers usually combined the characteristics of borderlines and schizophrenics. Their histories showed severe familial trauma. None of our manic-depressive patients reported a satisfactory relationship with his own father. Almost all made conscious efforts to be a better father than his own father had been. Several of these men gave themselves good marks in achieving these goals, despite their pathology, and expressed gratitude toward their wives (Lansky and Simenstad, draft b). Our small sample of manic depressive fathers had a greater proportion of men for whom treatment had a positive response for their role as fathers than did any other diagnostic group. Manic-depressive fathers' talk was full of manicky affect and denial of emotional reality. Written transcripts of what they said, in contradistinction to the impression left by their personal discourse, revealed an overwhelming sensitivity to psychic reality and great pain at their developmental deficits and current limitations. These transcripts seemed strikingly incongruent with their affect while they spoke to the interviewers.

Our investigative activity illuminated global underlying psychopathology in these men and the complex mechanisms that hospitalized fathers of any diagnosis used to compensate for narcissistic vulnerability and lack of authority and status in the family. These mechanisms frequently consisted of impulsive actions such as violence, threats of violence, communication of suicidal intent, self-harm, binge drinking, and generally intimidating lifestyles that served for a time to control intimates in the family. These men were not bound to their intimates by the providing, protecting, and leadership function from which a father's authority is usually felt to be derived.

The matter of therapy remained problematic. Simple scrutiny and awareness of the problem and investigatory zeal were not enough. Most of our sample came and left with massive deficiencies and real as well as fantasied failures in the paternal role. This lack of initial therapeutic success was not due to denial that problems existed; there was usually a mutually agreed upon sense of enormity of the therapeutic tasks ahead of us. Yet many of the staff in our programs shared the patients' sense of depression and futility. Our staff is highly sophisticated and thoroughly seasoned in dealing with the same population from which our sample of fathers was drawn. Their response might have been due quite simply to the realization by both patients and staff that the limitations imposed by the patients' global incapacities were indeed overwhelming, chronic, and utterly devastating. That is to say, the pervasive sense of futility might, purely and simply, have arisen from genuine perception of bedrock pathology.

Alternatively, however, there is the possibility that such futility arose from a view of reality that appeared more grim than seemed to be the case to our staff during our efforts in studying these men. The issue is a crucial one, for if the futility felt by all concerned is seen to arise simply from appreciation of the clinical facts, then the situation can be presumed to be nearly hopeless. On the other hand, if the *futility itself* were a result of dynamically overdetermined collusion between patient and staff, the situation might be more hopeful. We feel, then, that an exploration of potential treatment obstacles, amplified by covert collusion in the patient-staff relationship – a situation homologous to transference resistance and transference-countertransference stalemates in the strictly analytic situation – should be considered. Accordingly, we view our findings with some sensitivity to the fact that unrecognized and unresolved conflict and resistance involving patients and staff may have contributed to the pessimism resulting from our study and undermined specific treatment efforts aimed at the problems uncovered.

CONFLICT AND RESISTANCE

We turn to a consideration of sources of conflict and resistance in patients and staff on a hospital ward. We do so neither to explain retrospectively our treatment difficulties, nor to imply that the outcome might have been better with improved awareness and handling of transference and countertransference. These fathers were severely impaired, and our staff were seasoned in the recognition and management of countertransference phenomena. Our intent here is to provide a perspective on the range of obstacles to treatment that we have seen over the years and to foster a sensitivity to the dynamics of such obstacles as they occur in a hospital setting.

Resistances and conflicts come from many sources. Some obstacles are not resistances in the true dynamic sense but arise from the disorder and realistic reactions to it. Such disorders as manic-depressive illness, schizophrenia, alcoholism, or crisis manifestations of borderline pathology are overwhelming when they are in exacerbation. Patients and staff alike may be overwhelmed either by the florid, acute disorder or by restitutive or controlling maneuvers of reactions against shame that pose symptomatic crises. Sophisticated staff may get beyond these more manifest features of the clinical situation to a view of the chronic deficits faced by the psychiatrically impaired father. Many of our staff, accustomed to working with this population, saw treatment difficulties as arising from florid illness, defense compensatory mechanisms, and bedrock residual pathology. Realistically based as any of these difficulties are, they may feed into deeper transferential issues and dovetail with countertransference problems.[2] Whatever the patient's basic disorder is, there is some endopsychic perception of a basic defectiveness that resonates with the hospitalized father's overall personality organization and becomes accentuated in the caretaking situation in the hospital. All of these hospitalized men responded to a basic neediness by seeking out caretakers for help and for soothing. This regressively reactivated neediness, related as it is to the inability to function and the designation as defective, produces a great deal of shame and envy and intensifies defenses against these feelings. Any tendency on the part of patients toward dyadic fixation – that is, the formation of close dyads perpetrating the omnipotent illusion of self-sufficiency – become amplified in the hospital. Such patient-staff dyads often antagonize other staff factions, thus resulting in staff splitting. Accordingly, pressure on staff members to form protective dyads increases the risk of staff splitting if patients are gratified by staff members, or of rageful acting out by the patient if they are not. Many of these patients tended to split off their need for caretaking and to disavow their dependent relationship to the hospital. Such splitting was, in part, a defense against the shame and envy that would accompany the patient's awareness of his dependent state and in part a manifestation of envy in his hostile-dependent relationship to the hospital staff.

The patients who did not provoke staff splits were often the most impaired. Those patients who saw their global limitations and their neediness clearly and who made no apparent attempt to take their hurt out on the staff did so at a fearful price. The fathers who were most collaborative were those who carried with them very little sense of self-worth of pride and were almost constantly suicidal.

In virtually all the fathers in our studies, the feelings of authority, worth, and status that come from having a truly generative, giving

---

[2]We use the word countertransfernece, unless otherwise specified, as a reaction of the treating persons to the patient's transferences, without presuming unresolved neurosis on the part of the staff.

relationship with spouse and child were absent entirely. These men were powerless, helpless, and defeated. Many overt symptoms could be understood as attempts to deal with these feelings of powerlessness and helplessness. Intimidation, violence, and suicidal bouts gave these men a certain control by intimidation. Several fathers in our sample were admitted in crisis involving suicide threats, wrist-slashing, or threats of violence. Such crises had served to control wives or children by inducing in them of a sense of panic or a feeling of responsibility for the chaos in the patient, who at the same time seemed alarmingly indifferent to the consequences of such acts. Self-soothing from drugs or alcohol frequently added to the intimidating scenario and provided transient chemical relief from their tensions and lowered their awareness of their humiliated plight. Such maneuvers tended either to repel spouses immediately or to draw spouses into pathologic involvement with the disorder. Consequently, the very sort of pathologic distance regulation that compensates for the basic weakness, disorganization, and helplessness these men felt made it unlikely that they could have continued relationships with caring and supportive spouses who had no emotional stake in the continuance of these pathological patterns.

We began to appreciate these same forces as countertransference pressures. Staff may, and usually do, react to pathologic distance regulation (Lansky, 1985; Lansky, in press) on the part of patients who control supportive persons by indirectly communicated violence, self-harm, or loss of control. As we acquired experience, we realized that the same phenomena were occurring in the current family, or ex-family, and on the ward (with the patient as perpetrator) and, often, in the family of origin (with the patient as victim). Nonetheless, the impact of pathologic distance regulation, or pathologic projective identification[3] is such as to create the constant danger of keeping the staff anxious, off balance, and feeling that matters of crisis are more their worry than the patient's. Risk is high that the staff will become overinvolved, split, exhausted and that they ultimately will reject the patient.

A problem clearly noticed in our staff was their infection by the

---

[3]We use the term pathologic distance regulation rather than projective identification because the usage of projective identification (Klein, 1946) leaves confusion about whether projective identification is pruely an intrapsychic fantasy (that unmanageable parts of the self reside in another), or whether significant behaviors occur in projective identification. Pathologic distance regulation focuses on observable control of the distance between ogjects, with the assumption that unconscious fantasy is operative in determining both the optimal distance and the fantasied means of control – taking in or putting out (Lansky, unpublished).

patient's affects of futility of depression, hopelessness, and shame. The similarities between these staff responses and those of patients who, in the intergenerational interviews, portrayed parents as unable to tolerate their darker and more negative feelings made us suspect that staff may to some extent have been drawn into a dramatization that replayed the patient's archaic conflicts with parents (and later spouses) who could not tolerate him and ultimately left him emotionally abandoned. What portion of the futility was realistically based, and what portion induced by the caretaking staff's participation in these archaic collusions, cannot be ascertained *a priori.*

Some conflicts can be presumed to have been posed by the structure of the ward and the gender of the persons involved. The ward is directed by a male physician. The patients are predominantly male, and the staff of psychotherapists, predominantly female and professional. Such an organization presents what the patients may see as a highly sexualized organization to the treatment scene. A dominant male is seen to be in charge of competent, caretaking females administering to a very damaged male population. Even outside the limits of professional propriety, very few of the men would consider themselves appropriate suitors for the staff women, yet all had intimate psychotherapeutic relationships with these staff women. The effect of this sort of intimacy on both sexes remains, of course, speculative but cannot be presumed to be negligible. For many of the men, control by strong women who made them feel ashamed and dominated was a significant theme both in family of origin and family of procreation; such themes dominated the intergenerational interviews of many of the men. An intimate relationship with women who served solely as caretakers could only be expected to reactivate conflict in these areas. Unresolved neurotic conflicts in the staff–fears of sexuality, excessive voyeurism, sadism, or outright castrativeness–of course, only intensify these issues (Ferholt and Gurwitt, 1982).

Related to, but not identical with these issues are both staff's and patients' fantasies about the paternal role. Unresolved oedipal awe (usually sustained by fear of father or a remote relationship with their own fathers) may leave as a residue an idealized view of what a father should be: always masterful, powerful, sexual, providing, protecting, guiding, and fearless. The shame, guilt, and anxiety of patients with these residual fantasies superimposed as goals on the treatment situation may dovetail with staff fantasies to make the psychiatrically hospitalized father's plight seem unduly hopeless and efforts to treat him unduly futile.

Any of these potential difficulties may exist as low-key, commonplace fantasies or may reflect neurotic conflicts of severe magnitude (that is, countertransference in the classical sense). Any may combine with the patient's difficulties with the resultant collusive agreement that the psychiatrically hospitalized fathers' affects, deficits and problem cannot be usefully acknowledged and addressed and in some cases are minimized. Such collusions then intensify very real problems to the point that these seem unmanageable or hopeless.

TREATMENT IMPLICATIONS

We cannot estimate the extent to which psychoanalytically enlighted approaches to conflict and resistance in the therapy of these men can alter the treatment situation. Such uncertainty is part of any approach that is truly psychoanalytic. That is to say, a major part of the problem with unconscious resistance is that significant dynamically determined resistances ususlly preclude either analyst's or patient's accurately assessing the magnitude of "reality" problems and developing appropriate strategies to cope with them. Many covert sources of resistance are apparent behind the overwhelming affect and failure of focus in these cases. These abound in the clinical field and undermine the collaborative therapeutic alliance around issues in paternity. These sources of resistance must be understood if straightforward treatment strategies are to succeed. Realization of this by the hospital staff is vital if that staff, or part of it, is to take leadership in clarifying the self-sabotage that is always the cost of collusive resistance.

The task of therapy, then, can best proceed if conflict and resistance are considered dynamically and are seen either as forces that flare up and obstruct the treatment or as forces that clarify and abate in the context of treatment by a staff that is willing to acknowledge and accept both chaos and shortcomings in themselves, and in the fathers who are in treatment, and still remain confident and caring. All too often, this is the kind of caretaking that the psychiatrically hospitalized father has never received himself and that he can not provide for his offspring. The hospital staff's ability to scrutinize and tolerate awareness of conflict and dynamically determine resistance to collaboration not only paves the way for straightforward strategy and problem solving, it also provides the potential for a *process of caretaking*. Such a process has the potential to interrupt cycles in collusion and self-defeat and provides the basis for modifying and corrective internalizations that may be the foundations for hopeful and useful treatment approaches.

REFERENCES

Abelin, E. (1971), The role of the father in the separation-individuation process. In: *Separation Individuation,* ed. J. B. McDevitt & C. Settlage. New York: International Universities Press, pp. 229–253.

—— (1975), Some further observations and comments on the earliest role of the father. *Internat. J. Psycho-Anal.,* 56:293–302.

—— (1980), Triangulation: The role of the father and the origins of core gender identity during the rapprochement subphase. In: *Rapprochement,* ed. R. Lax, S. Bach & J. A. Burland. New York: Aronson.

Bowen, M. (1966), The use of family theory in clinical practice. *Comp. Psychiat.,* 7:345–374.

Cath, S. H., Gurwitt, A. & Ross, J. M., ed. (1982), *Father and Child.* Boston: Little, Brown.

Ferholt, J. B. & Gurwitt, A. R. (1982), Involving fathers in treatment. In: *Father and Child,* ed. S. H. Cath. A. Gurwitt & J. M. Ross. Boston: Little, Brown, pp 557–568.

Klein, M. (1946), Notes on some schizoid mechanisms. *Internat. J. Psycho-Anal.,* 27:99–110.

Lansky, M. R. (1981), The psychiatrically hospitalized father. *Internat. J. Family Psychiat.,* 5:151–168.

—— (1984), The psychiatrically hospitalized father. *Internat. S. Family Psychiat.,* 5:151–168.

—— (1985), Preoccupation and pathologic distance regulation. *Internat. J. Psychoanal. Psychother.,* 11:409–425.

—— (1987), The borderline father: Reconstructions of young adulthood. *Psychoanal. Inq.,* 7:77–98.

—— (in press), The "explanation" of impulsive action. *Brit. J. Psychother.*

—— Bley, C. R., Simenstad, E. A., West, K. L. & McVey, G. G. (1983), The absent family of the hospitalized borderline patient. *Internat. J. Family Psychiat.,* 4:155–172.

—— Simenstad, E. A. (1986), Narcissistic vulnerability in a group for psychiatrically hospitalized fathers. *Group.* 10:149–159.

—— —— (draft a), The schizophrenic father.

—— —— (draft b), The manic-depressive father.

Ross, J. M. (1979), Fathering: A review of some psychoanalytic considerations. *Internat. J. Psycho-Anal.,* 60:317–328.

Epilogue

The editors are pleased to share their delight in the contributions of the authors in this book. A decade ago our initial goal was to study the epigenesis of paternal identity or how male children grow up and become fathers. In our "Issues in Paternity" seminars at the American Psychoanalytic Association meetings, we began to isolate important life-span variables around which interactive and transgenerational data could be gathered and collated by interdisciplinary observers. From the feedback we have gathered it seems we, among many others, have stimulated clinicians and researchers to reflect, more deeply than was their wont, about fathers in normative relations to mothers, children, and grandparents as well as on their importance in neurosogenesis and pathologies. Previously neglected areas of transference and counter-transference have been illuminated by clarifying the origins and dominance of paternal and maternal imagos.

We became convinced that by more definitely including the father in our formulations about the dynamics in the family, we could unearth more accurate intervention strategies and enhance therapeutic effectiveness. To do this required that we tease out the epigenesis of fatherhood, its roots in preoedipal, oedipal, and postoedipal phases in order to understand and rebalance the vital compensatory-nurturant roles men and women play for each other all their lives long. Fathers and grandparents fell under the same scrutiny, for they all had been a large part of the truly significant, seemingly unavailable, and therefore least analyzed past. We found colleagues grateful and enriched in their work when we called their attention to the strangely not obvious, lifelong neglect of the male members of the extended family.

Considering the historical habit of exonerating the male and blaming the female, we can be grateful to Ross for his expanded emphasis on the inordinate ambivalence of the men involved in that "quintissential oedpial parable of little Hans." As he does in his paper on the Laius complex of (1982), he reminds us here of the father's seemingly preordained contribution to this inevitable family struggle through generations.

Reflecting upon another, more abusive form of father-son relatedness in a novel by Pat Conroy (1986), the protagonist in a midlife reconciliation of primitive mental representations, meditates, "My life did not really begin until I summoned the power to forgive my father for making my childhood a long march of terror. But his eyes were the eyes of my father, and something in those eyes always loved me even when his hands could not" (p. 222). Later he told his father, "Dad, I learned everything I know about being a man from you. And I want to thank you for that. But I want to be a man like your father. I want to be weak and gentle and kind to every creature on this earth. And, Dad, I would rather be dead than to be the kind of man you taught me to be" (p. 577).

As we screened many new chapters, echoes of loving paternal voices (Tessman, this volume), reflecting very early introjects of both male and female progenitors, emerged. Exciting new paths for future exploration of the cross-gender constructive and unique contributions a father makes to the family system opened before us. Especially as we reflected on the variations of family attachments and cohabitations throughout the world today, the richness of the unexplored theoretical and clinical landscape led us to appreciate more fully the vital contributions of fathering and the varieties of fathers. Not only are there reluctant fathers, there are involuntary, teenage, first, multiple, early, late, adoptive fathers; those whose wives are artificially inseminated; those interrupted by the separations of military service, resurrected, single, step grand, and a host of others. Some fathers change for the better over time, and some flee when a dreaded child is born (Simons, 1984; Gurwitt, this volume). Most men are quite different as grandfathers. Even when fathers are deficient or abusive, they may be idealized or reconstructed as neutral in their child's mind ("silhouetted" in Michaels's, this volume, way of thinking).

Wherever we looked, the characteristics of a particular child, or its ordinal position contributed to the father's unfolding or nascent paternal imago, and the impact of the child's natural endowment had been underestimated positively or negatively. Or, at least, these characteristics resonated with something very much denied or repressed in the parent, explaining why previously reluctant fathers are often enthralled by certain of their young.[1] From the initial contact with the infant at birth to midlife, when adult sons may struggle to raise their own brood while caring for an aged, depleting parent, tremendous variability in self-image and a surprising degree of altruistic caretaking seems related to this simultaneous paternal and filial enthralldom. Lamb's survey of today's young fathers suggests that men seem available, accessible, and capable of this deep attachment – except that it is still mother to whom most children go with pain and problems. Cath's clinical experience at the other end of the life span teaches us that it is almost invariably daughters or daughers-in-law who, Cordelia-like, care for their elderly frail men either at home or in institutional settings. Nursing homes seem most uncomfortable for men, who can hardly wait to escape their oppressive atmospheres.

In the past, researchers (see, for example, Yogman, 1982) have affirmed the value of the different modes of child handling and rearing employed by each of the sexes. This finding is reiterated in Schopper's delineation of male and female forms of toilet training. Still other authors (for example,) Pruitt on primary caretakers, document overlapping, interchangeable, non-gender-specific functions in today's less traditional families.

Thus, both *Father and Child* (Cath, Gurwitt, and Ross, 1982) and *Fathers and Their Families* present much that increases our understanding of society's unconscious, final, common path of loading inordinate responsibilities upon madonna-like females. This is a cross-cultural phenomenon linked with inordinate idealization or ignoring of males.

In what we hope is a more balanced perspective of the family, we have presented a selection of the unique real and intrapsychic, nurturant and destructive contributions that men can make under both intact and separating family circumstances. With a few notable exceptions, most of the clinical papers reaffirm the hopeful potential for psycho-

---

[1]Enthrall can also mean to imprison.

analytically based psychotherapies and interventions in promoting growth and adapting to the stresses of family attachments. Finally, grandparenthood may offer a third, less ambivalent chance to be a nurturant part of the growing world. This opportunity is well timed, for in the last third of life, dealing with one of the greatest threats of all, namely annhiliation of self and the self-other world, new alliances are welcome indeed.

Medicine, psychology, and the media seem to be catching up with literature. For after being almost forgotten, a new appreciation of involving fathers is appearing in both professional and lay publications. In the media especially, new joys in co-parenting, co-nurturing and co-custody arrangements are claimed almost daily. "A new American father" seems to have emerged. But some of our contributors (Lamb and Oppenheimer and Gerson, for example) have dissected this phenomenon finely and shed a more reasoned, scientific light on the rewards and difficulties of being a contemporary father.

Most men have very different feelings toward each of their sons; fathers at 20 or 30 may be very different than in subsequent decades. Some men have very different feelings toward their young in a second marriage, at the safe distance of a generation removed, possibly because certain issues were played out the first time around. Similarly, in the ghetto or *shtetl* of pre-War Europe, the burden of preparing a son for the arduous task of survival "in this world" *(b'olom ha-zeh)* and for the world to come *(b'olom ha-ba)* often precluded tender friendship between father and son and continued to distance them when the boy reached adulthood. If fortunate, middle-aged Jewish men might find some isogender warmth with their sons-in-law. It follows that various sons may have various images of their fathers. Today most male patients start analysis wondering why it was so hard for their fathers to have affection for them. This sensed deficit often colors transferences in the initial phases of analysis with a male or female analyst. Again, the imago of the analyst may be very different in different phases of analysis.

We have tried to relate some of these vitalizing, self-mutating" life-span findings to modern changes in our society as together they meld with our own reflections in interludes and epilogue. It is true that some families may be better off with less of, if not completely without, their particular fathers. With therapeutic work, however, a more salutary outcome is possible (see Cath, Gunsberg, Solnit, Tessman, and others). Children raised in father-devalued, father-absented, or borderline homes may reject their fathers in part or in whole but still reach for a compatible relationship with a surrogate male. Some gifted people create their own versions of male progenitors by adopting fantasied, great fathers (see Strozier and Cath, this volume).

In general as well as in the psyche, we hold that father may donate much to the nurturant balance within a family. And, finally, as Conroy (1986) observed, the last word has yet to be said on the origins, forms, transitions, and the remarkable endurance of father love that grows out of the beauty, pain, and fear of kinship.

REFERENCES

Cath, S. H., Gurwitt, A. & Ross, J. M. (1982), *Father and Child*. Boston, MA: Little, Brown.

Conroy, P. (1986), *The Prince of Tides*. New York: Bantam Books.

Ross, J. M. (1982), Oedipus Revisited: Laius and the Laius Complex. *The Psychoanalytic Study of the Child*, 37:169–200. New Haven: Yale University Press.

Simons, R. (1984), Creativity, Mourning and the Dread of Paternity. *Internat. Rev. Psycho-Anal.* 11:181–198.

Yogman, M. (1982), Observations on the Father-Infant Relationship In: *Father and Child*, ed. S. H. Cath, A. Gurwitt & J. M. Ross. Boston, MA: Little, Brown, pp. 101–122.

Author Index

A

Abelin, E. L., 37, 44, 52, 57, 59, 69, 74, 79, 82, 94, 128, 142, 182, 186, 225, 227, 238, 239, 243, 244, 418, 421, 493, 505, 522, 533, 539, 543, 552

Adam, K., 58, 59

Adams, P., 410, 421

Adamson, L., 51, 60

Afterman, J., 128, 144, 150, 165

Alpert, J., 128, 142

Als, H., 51, 60, 113, 241, 244

Anthony, E. J., 66, 74, 121, 125

Arbeit, S. A., 148, 162

Arlow, J., 281, 282

Arons, E., 474, 490

Aschenbrenner, B. G., 147, 163

Asher, S. J., 432, 457

Ashway, J. A., 474, 489

Atkins, R. N., 4, 6, 10, 29, 37, 44, 103, 117, 179, 184, 186, 372, 382, 433, 438–40, 455, 456, 457, 507, 523

Azrin, N. H., 84, 94

B

Bach, G. R., 409–13, 415, 417, 421

Bahm, R., 409, 418, 421

Bak, R., 279, 282

Balint, M., 50, 59

Ballentine, C., 330, 335

Barnett, R. C., 17, 17, 24

Baruch, G. K., 16, 17, 24

Basler, R., 305, 306

Beavin, A. D., 53, 61

Beck, J., 84, 94

Becker, J. W., 84, 94

Becker, W. C., 84, 94

Behrends, R. S., 333, 335

Beller, E. K., 82, 94

Bellman, M., 86, 87, 94

Belsky, J., 13, 24, 145, 147, 148, 162

Bender, L., 533, 540

Benedek, T., 121, 125, 128, 139, 140, 142, 146, 149, 162, 185, 186, 395, 399, 403, 405, 488, 490

Bennett, L., 371, 382

Bergman, A., 52, *60*, 71, *74*, 77, 78, *96*,
   225, *239*, 240, *244*, 275, *283*, 522, 523
Berkes, N., 349–50, *362*
Berman, W., 160, *164*
Bernstein, N. R., 438, *457*
Berry, M., 373, *383*
Bettelheim B., 271, *282*
Beveridge, A. J., 293, *299*
Bibring, G. L., 146, 159, *162*
Biller, H. B., 180, *186*, 193, *195*, 409,
   410, 415, 418, *421*, *422*
Blanchard, R. W., 409, *422*
Blassingame, J., 373, *383*
Blatt, S. J., 333, *335*
Bley, C. R., 543, *552*
Block, J., 71–72, *74*
Bloom, B. L., 432, *457*
Blos, D., 371, *383*
Blos, P., Jr., 115, *117*, 248, 257, 259,
   262, 281, *282*, 309, *326*, 333, *336*,
   356, *362*, 401, *405*, 508, *523*
Blum, H., 88, *95*, 335
Boehm, F., 150, *162*
Boles, A. J., 147, 148, *163*
Bookstein, F. L., 19, *25*
Boscolo, L., 53, *61*
Bowen, M., 543, *552*
Bowlby, J., 48, 54, *59*
Brazelton, T. B., 51, *60*, 81, *95*, 241,
   244
Broberg, A., 19, *25*
Brooks, J. G., 85, *95*
Brough, D. I., 160, *163*
Browning, D. H., 474, *490*
Burlingham, D., 58, *60*, 409, *422*

C

Cahen, C., 348, *362*
Caliver, A., 371, *383*
Campos, J. J., 70, *74*
Cansever, G., 356, *362*
Caplan, G., 146, *162*
Carlson, B. F., 21, *24*
Cath, C., 114, *117*, 128, *142*, 186, *188*
Cath, S. H., 3, 8, 9, *10*, 77, 79, *95*, 100,
   102, 104, 108, 111, 112, 114, 115,
   117, 121, *125*, 179, *186*, 286, 288, *299*,
   303–4, 305, *306*, 339, 410, *422*, 425,

   430, 475, *490*, 493, 504, *505*, 507,
   509, 543, *552*, 555, 556, *557*
Cavenar, J. O., Jr., 151, *163*
Cecchin, G., 53, *61*
Çevik, A., 343–44, 352, *362*
Charnov, E. L., 11, 12, 15, 21, *25*
Chasseguet-Smirgel, J., 510–11, *523*
Chesler, P., 439, *457*
Chodorov, N., 141, *142*, 211, *222*
Choquet, M., 83, *95*
Clausen, J. A., 410, *422*
Clower, V. L., 411, *422*
Cobbs, P., 373, *383*
Cohen, D. J., 1609, *164*
Cohen, L. J., 70, *74*
Cohen, R., 184, *186*
Colarusso, C., 184, *186*
Cole, D. S., 474, 488, *490*
Colman, A., 184, *186*
Colman, L., 184, *186*
Comer, J. P., 344–45, 369, 378, *383*
Conlon, M. F., 179, *188*
Conroy, P., 554, *557*
Copans, S., 401, *405*
Corney, R. T., 354, *363*
Cowan, C. P., 145, 147, 148, 157, 161,
   163
Cowan, P. A., 145, 147, 148, 157, 161,
   163
Cowell, H., 309, *326*, 331, *336*
Cowell, S., 309, *326*, 331, *336*
Cox, M., 431, 433, 438–40, *457*
Cox, R., 431, 433, 438–40, *457*
Coyish, W. S., 147, 148, *163*
Crockenberg, S. B., 147, *165*
Culp, R. E., 121, 123–24, 184
Cummings, e. e., 205, *222*
Curtis, J. A., 151, *163*
Curtis-Boles, H., 147, 148, *163*

D

Davidson, F., 83, *95*
Demos, J., 343, *346*, 367, *383*
Derdeyn, A. P., 427, *430*, 438, *457*
Deutch, H., 205, *222*
Deutsch, L., 328, 333, *336*
Deutscher, M., 128, *142*, 184, *186*
Dinnerstein, D., 139, *142*
Dodson, F., 84–85, *95*

Doering, S. G., 147, *163*
Donelly, E., 526, *540*
Donini, G. P., 418, *422*
Douglas, J. W. B., 83, *A95*
Dwyer, T. F., 146, *162*

E

Easterbrooks, M. A., 21, 22, *24*
Edelman, M., 373, *383*
Eichler, C. S., 128, *143*
Eisenberg, L., 526, 533, 534, *540*
Eksi, A., 357, *362*
Eldred, M. M., 85, *95*
Elliott, S. A., 160, *163*
Ellis, W., 381, *383*
Elster, A. B., 14, *24*
Emms, E. M., 160, *164*
Entwisle, D. R., 147, *163*
Erikson, E. H., 104, *117*, 127, 140, 141, *142*, 160, *163*, 216, *222*, *244*
Erikson, J., 104, *117*
Escalona, S., 241, *244*
Esman, A., 88, *95*

F

Fairbairn, W. R. D., 50, 54, *60*
Feder, S., 309–11, 320, 321, 323, *326*, 329, 330, 332, 334, 335, *336*
Fein, R. A., 147, *163*
Feldman, J., 474, *490*
Feldman, S. S., 147, *163*
Fenster, S., 474, 475, *490*
Ferholt, J. B., 468, *471*, 550, *552*
Fichler, L., 184, *187*
Flapan, D., 83, *95*
Fletcher, J., 160, *164*
Forrest, T., 192, 193, *195*
Foxx, R. M., 84, *94*
Fraiberg, S. H., 82, 84, *95*, 333, *336*, 495, *505*
Frank, J. B., 160, *164*
Franklin, J., 370, *383*
Franzier, E., 370, 372, *383*
Freeman, T., 128 *142*, 150, *163*
Freud, A., 281, *282*, 409, 417, *422*, 427, 429, *430*, 460, *463*

Freud, S., 38–40, *44*, 50, *60*, 105, *117*, 178*n*, *186*, 268–72, 274–76, 278, 280, 281, *282*, 320, *326*, 333, *336*
Friedman, H. J., 440, *457*
Friendly, A., 350, *362*
Frodi, A. M., 14, 15, *25*
Frodi, M., 14, 15, 19, *24*, *25*
Furman, E., 411, *422*
Furstenberg, F., 343, *346*, 435, 439, *457*

G

Galenson, E., 83–84, *96*, 179, *187*, 492, 500, 501, *505*
Gamble, T. J., 72, *74*
Garrett, E., 147, 148, *163*
Gerson, M. J., 121–23, 127–29, *142,143*
Gesell, A., 82, *95*
Gibbs, J., Jr., 368, *383*
Gillespie, W. H., 279, *282*
Gilligan, C., 205, *222*
Gillman, R. D., 327, *336*
Gilstrap, B., 13, *24*
Ginath, Y., 151, *163*
Glenn, J., 268, *283*
Glover, E., 310, *326*
Glueck, C. J., 387, *388*
Gökçe, B., 360, *362*
Goldberg, W. A., 21, 22, *24*
Golding, E., 5*n*, *10*
Goldsmith, R., 18, *26*
Goldstein, J., 427, 429, *430*, 460, *463*
Goldstein, S., 427, 429, *430*
Gordon, B., 527, 533, *540*
Gordon, K. K., 147, *163*
Gordon, R. E., 147, *163*
Gould, R., 417, *422*
Graf, H., 268, *283*
Graf. M., 268, *283*
Greenacre, P., 91, *95*, 225, *239*, 260, *262*, 279, *283*, 317, *326*
Greenberg, M., 135, *143*, 168*n*, 179, 184, 185, *187*
Greenson, R. R., *44*, 80–81, 90, *95*, 180, *187*
Greenspan, S., 128, 139, *143*
Greer, W., 373, *383*
Greif, J., 438, *457*
Grigsby, N., 294, *299*

Grossman, F. K., 5n, *10,* 128, *143,* 184, *187*
Grossman, K. E., 19, *24*
Gudrun, B., 66–67, *74*
Gunsberg, L., 128, 141, *143,* 194, *195,* 493, *505,* 509, *523,* 526, *540*
Guntrip, H., 50, *60*
Gurwitt, A., 3, 8, *10,* 77, 79, *95,* 121, *125,* 127, 128, *143,* 149, 150, *163,* 179, 181–84, *186, 187,* 468, *471,* 475, *490,* 543, 550, *552,* 554, 555, *557*

H

Hacker, A., 432, 440, *457*
Hagan, M. S., 433, *458*
Hanks, D. F., 292–95, *299*
Hanson, S. H., 460, 462, *463*
Harnett, F., 474, *490*
Harper, P. A., 83, *96*
Harris, A., 371, 372, *383*
Hartmann, H., 40, *45,* 241, *244*
Heming, G., 147, 148, *163*
Herndon, W. H., 287, 289, 296–96, *299*
Hershberg, T., 343, *346*
Hertz, E., 305, *306*
Herzog, J. M., *10,* 128, 140, *143,* 149, *163,* 168, 179, 181, 182, *187, 188,* 260, *262,* 487, 488, *490,* 493, 504, *505,* 509, *523*
Hetherington, E. M., 410, 411, 418, *422,* 431–33, 438–40, *457, 458*
Hipgrave, T., 14, *24*
Holland, J. G., 294, *299*
Holland, N., 281, *299*
Holland, N., 281, *283*
Horovitz, J., 410, *421*
Hottinger, A., 361, *362*
Hudson, W. W., 157, *164*
Hult, G., 19, *25*
Huntington, D., 146, *162*
Huston, T., 157, *164*
Hwang, C. P., 14, 15, 19, *24, 25*
Hymel, S., 52, 55, *61*

I

Inhelder, B., 413, *423*
Irwin, E. M., 247, *263*
Itzkowitz, N., 349, 353, 361, *362, 363*

J

Jackson, D. D., 53, *61*
Jacobs, J. W., 438, 439, *458*
Jacobson, E., 40, *45,* 150, *164,* 205, *222,* 335, *336*
Jarvis, W., 183, *187,* 488, *490*
Johnson, A. M., 53, *60*
Johnston, J. D., 289–90, 293, 294, *299*
Jones, W., 102, *117*
Juster, F. T., 23, *24*

K

Kagan, J., 83, *96*
Kağitçbaşi, C., 355, 357, *362*
Kahn, C., 168, *187*
Kaif, L., 160, *164*
Kakar, S., 344, *346*
Kanner, L., 526, *540*
Kelly, J. B., 409, 410, *423,* 425, 430, 431, 440, *458,* 459, 462, *463*
Kernberg, O., 50, *60*
Kestenberg, J., 139, *143*
Kirkpatrick, J., 230–31, 309–11, 313, 317, *326,* 328, 334
Kitson, G. C., 431, 433, *458*
Kivnick, H., 100, 104, 111, 113, *117, 118*
Klein, M., 49, *60,* 549n, *552*
Klein, T., 85, *95*
Kogan, K., 527, 533, *540*
Kohlberg, L., 70, *75*
Kohut, H., 55, *60,* 140, 142, *143,* 203, *223,* 285, *299*
Kornhaber, A., 100, *118*
Koupernik, C., 66, *74*
Kramer, R., 84, *96*
Kristal, J., 410, *422*

L

Lacoursiere, R., 128, *143,* 150, 151, *164*
Laing, R. D., 53, 54, *60*
Lamb, M. E. 11–16, 19–21, 23, *24, 25,* 29, *45,* 49, *60,* 79, 84, *95,* 113, *118,* 128, *143,* 179, 184, 333, *336*
Lamon, W. H., 292, *299*

Lang, M. E., 145, 148, *162*
Lansky, M. R., 433, *458,* 541–46, 549, *552*
Laplanche, J., 27, *45*
Lasch, C., 403, *405*
Lawton, M. P., 111, *118*
Lax, R., 474, *490*
Leach, P., 84, *96*
Leifer, M., 147, *164*
Lelrner, D., 353, *362*
Levenson, R., 193, *196*
Levine, J. A., 11, 12, 14, 15, 20, 21, *25,* 83, *96*
Levine, M. I., 84, *96*
Levinson, D., 216, *223*
Lewis, B., 351, *362*
Lewis, G., 350,*362*
Lidz, R. W., 279, *283*
Lidz, T., 279, *283,* 367, *383,* 526, *540*
Liebeuberg, B., 488, *490*
Lincoln, A., 285, 286–98, *299*
Lincoln, S., 289, *300*
Loewald, H., 128, *143,* 227, *239,* 509, *523*
Loewenstein, R., 40, *45*
Lowe, T. L., 160, *164*

M

McDougall, J., 191, *196,* 510, *523*
Machtlinger, V., 418, *422*
Mack, A., 85, *96*
McLaughlin, M. M., 343, *346*
McNeil, T. K., 160, *164*
McVey, G. G., 543, *552*
Mahler, M. S., 52, 58, *60,* 77–79, *96,* 128, *143,* 225, *239,* 240, *244,* 275, *283,* 522, *523,* 534, *540*
Malmquist-Larsson, A., 160, *164*
Mangelsdorf, T. K., 88, *96*
Manson, S., 344, *346*
Marcus, H., 139, *143*
Masterson, J. F., 58, *60*
Maugham, W. S., 168, *187*
Mead, M., 104, 105, *118*
Meers, D., 372, *383*
Michaels, C. S., *422,* 555
Miller, J. B., 205, *223*
Minton, C., 83, *96*

Modell, J., 343, *346*
Morris, N., 134, *143, 187*
Mounts, N. S., 13, *26*
Muir, R. C., 54, 55, *60,* 179, 184, *187*
Muller, H. J., 349, *362*

N

Nadelson, C. C., 6, *10,* 179, 185, *188,* 204, *223,* 474, *490*
Naftolin, F., 160, *164*
Nash, J., 79, *96*
Nash, S. C., 147, *163*
Nelson, J., 182, *187*
Nemiroff, R., 184, *186*
Neubauer, P. B., 3, *10,* 63, 64, 72, *75,* 82, 83, *94, 95,* 344, 409, 420, *422*
Nicolay, H., 304, 305, *306*
Notman, M. T., 6, *10,* 179, 185, *188,* 205, *233,* 474, *490*

O

Offer, D., 285, *300,* 400, *405*
Offer, J., 400, *405*
Ogden, T., 54, *61*
Oppel, W. C. 83, *96*
Oppenheimer, A., 534, *540*
Osofsky, H. J., 8, 121, 123–24, 128, *143,* 145, 147, 152, *164*
Osofsky, J. D., 145, 147, 152, *164*
Özbek, A., 348, 352, 353, *362, 363*
Öztürk, O. M., 349, 355, 356, 359, *363*

P

Palkovitz, R., 17, *25*
Parens, H., 149, *164*
Parke, R. D. 13, *25,* 52, 55, *61,* 128, *143,* 145, 149, *164,* 534, *540*
Paykel, E. S., 160, *164*
Pederson, F. A., 70, *75*
Perlis, V., 308, 316, *326*
Phillips, S., 474, 475, *490*
Piaget, J., 413, *423,* 533, *540*
Pierce, C. M., 88, *96*
Pine, F., 52, *60,* 77, 78, *96,* 225, *239,* 240, *244,* 275, *283,* 522, *523*
Pittfield, M., 543, *540*
Pleck, J. H., 11, 12, 15, 17–21, 23, *25*

Polatnick, M., 13, 17, 18, *25*
Pollack, W. S., 5*n*, *10*
Pontalis, J. B., 27, *45*
Power, T. G., 52, 55, *61*
Prata, G., 53, *61*
Provence, S., 367, *383*
Pruett, K. D., 15, 21, *25,* 168, 179, 181,
   188, 345–46, 387, *388,* 389, 391, *405,*
   429, *430,* 508, *523*

Q

Quinn, R. P., 15, 17, *26*

R

Radin, N., 16–18, 20, 21, *26,* 409, 410,
   423
Radloff, L., 157, *164*
Rapoport, E. G., 474, 475, *490*
Rapoport, R. N., 343, *346*
Rassaby, E. S., 160, *164*
Rees, K., 193, *196*
Richardson, M. S., 128, *142*
Rider, R. V., 83, *96*
Ritvo, S., 248, *263*
Rizzuto, A.-M., 303, *306*
Roazen, P., 303, *306*
Robertson, J., 100, *118*
Robey, J. S., 438, *457*
Robson, K. S., 70, *75*
Roiphe, H., 83–84, *96,* 179, *187,* 492,
   500, 501, *505*
Roopnarine, J. L., 13, *26*
Ross, J. M., 3, 6, 8, *10,* 77, 79, 80, *95,*
   96, 105, *118,* 121, *125,* 139, 140, *144,*
   179, 183, *186, 188,* 191, 225, *239,*
   267, 268, *283,* 302–3, *306,* 333, *336,*
   475, *490,* 493, *505,* 509, *523,* 543, *552,*
   554, 555, *557*
Ross, N., 514, *523*
Ross Laboratories, 81, *96*
Rothenberg, M. B., 81, 84, *97*
Rovine, M., 13, *24,* 145, 148, *162*
Rubens, R. L., 50, *61*
Rubenstein, S., 381, *383*
Rugg, A. J., 160, *163*
Russell, G., 14, 16, 18, 20–22, *26*
Rutter, M., 58, *61,* 71, *75*

S

Sagi, A., 16, 21, *26*
Saks, B. R., 160, *164*
Salk, L., 84, *96*
Samaraweera, S., 1238, *142,* 186, *188*
Sander, L., 113, *118*
Sandler, A., 54, *61*
Sandler, J. J., 54, *61*
Santrock, J. W., 409, 410–11, *423*
Sarlin, C. N., 88, *96*
Schafer, R., 54, *61*
Schwartzman, M., 470, *526, 540*
Seides, S. W., 268, 281, *283*
Seligman, J. H., 84, *96*
Selvini-Palazzoli, M., 53, *61*
Shaw, E. Z., 349, *363*
Shaw, S. J., 348, 349, *363*
Shengold, L., 286, *300*
Shereshefsky, P. M., 147, 148, *165*
Shopper. M., 3, 8, 77, 86, *96, 97,* 179
Shuker, E., 74
Siegler, A. L., 410, 420, *423*
Silverman, M., *74,* 270, *283*
Simenstad, E. A., 541, 543, 545, 546,
   552
Simons, R., 181–83, *188,* 554, *557*
Slap, J.,, 271, *283*
Slater, P. E., 140, *144*
Slipp, S., 43, *45,* 463, *464*
Solnit, A. J., 72, 73, *75,* 367, *383,* 427,
   429, *430,* 460, *463*
Sossin, K., 139, *143*
Soule, B., 401, *405*
Spanier, G. B., 435, *457*
Sperling, M., 83, *97*
Spero, S., 371, 372, *383*
Spitz, R. A., 225, *239,* 241, *244*
Spock, B., 81, 84, *97*
Staines, G. L., 15, 17, *26*
Standley, K., 401, *405*
Stechler, G., 205, *223*
Steele, B. F., 179, *188*
Stein, A., 348, *363*
Steinberg, J., 14, *25*
Steinman, S., 432, *458*
Stevenson, R., 139, *143*
Stierlin, H., 53, *61*
Stoller, R. J., 79, 80, *97,* 225, *249,* 240,
   242, 279, *283*

Stratton, A., 352, *363*
Strelitz, Z., 343, *346*
Strong, G., 527, *540*
Strozier, C. B., 285, *300,* 303-4, 305, *306*
Sullivan, H., 140, *144*
Sümer, E. A., 349, 351, 353, *363*
Sümer, F., 351, *363*
Suppiger, J. E., 292, 294, *300*
Sussman, M. B., 431, 433, *458*
Sutherland, J. D., 50, *61*
Suzuki, P. T., 348, *363*
Szurek, S. A., 53, *60*

T

Tabin, J. K., 252-53, *263*
Taleporos, E., 411, 413, *423*
TenHouten, W. D., 410, *423*
Tessman, L. H., 167, 182, *188,* 192, *196,* 198, 203, *223,* 2423, *244,* 254, 261, *263,* 417, 418, *423*
Thomes, M., 409, *423*
Thompson, B., 409, *423*
Timur, S., 353, *363*
Tinsley, B., 13, *25,* 52, 55, *61,* 145, 149, *164*
Towne, R. D., 128, *144,* 150, *165*
Trethowan, W. H., 151, *165,* 179, *188*
Trombetta, D., 436-38, *458*
Tronick, E., 51, *60*
Turner, J. G., 288, *300*
Turner, L. L., 288, *300*
Tyson, P., 29, *45,* 79, *97,* 179, 180, *188*
Tyson, R. L., 70-71, *751*

U

Underwood, E. D., 474, *490*
Underwood, M. M., 474, *490*
Uysal, A. E., 351, *363*
Valentine, A. F., 146, *162*
Valliant, G., 401, 402, *405*
van Leeuwen, K., 150, *165*
Volkan, V. D., 343-44, 348, 349, 353-56, 359, 361, *363*
Volling, B. L., 145, *162*
Volkner, H. J., 19, *24*
Von Bertalanffy, L., 53, *61*

W

Wainwright, W. H., 150, *165*
Walker, W. E., 350, 351, *363*
Wallerstein, J. S., 67, *75,* 425, *430,* 431, 435, 436, 438, 440, *458,* 459, 462, *463*
Wallerstein, S. S., 409, 410, *423*
Watson, J. P., 160, *163*
Watzlawick, P., 53, *61*
Weddington, W. W., Jr., 151, *163*
Weik, J. W., 294, 296, *299*
Weisberger, E., 85, *97*
Weisman, P., 418, *423*
Weiss, E., 193, *195*
Weiss, S. D., 419, *422*
Weissman, S., 184, *186*
Weitzman, L. J., 429, *458*
Welch. L. S., 324, 326
Wente, A. S., 147, *165*
Wessel, M., *9n, 10*
West, K. L., 543, *552*
White, S. W., 432, *457*
Whitman, R. M., 88, *96*
Whitney, H. C., 292, *300*
Williamson, N., 192, *196*
Winnicott, D. W., 49-51, 57, *61,* 69, 74, *75,* 77, *97,* 225, *226n, 240,* 241, *244,* 260, *263*
Wise, S., 51, *60*
Wohlford, P., 410-11, *423*
Wolf, E., 55, *60*
Wolfenstein, M., 409, *423*
Woodson, C., 370, *383*
Woodward, K., 100, *1218*
Wordsworth, W. M., 387, *388*

Y

Yankelovich, D., 19, *26*
Yarrow, L. J., 147, 148, *165*
Yasa, I., 359, *364*
Yogman, M. W., 4, *10,* 13, *26,* 29, *45,* 48, 52, *61,* 113, *118,* 333, *336,* 493, *505,* 555, *557*
Yusufoğlu, N., 356, *364*

Z

Zigler, E., 72, *74*
Zilbach, J., 205, *223*

Subject Index

A

Absent fathers, 409–23, 462
  case illustrating effects of, 234–37
  data collection on, 414
  defining terms relating to study of,
    411–12
  development of boys vs. girls with,
    70–72
  early absence, 409
  fantasy of, 220–21
    or preschoolers, 410–23, 462
  findings on, 414–16
    discussion of, 416–21
  method of study, 412–13
  See also Single parents, fathers as
Absent parent, effects of, 63–64, 66–68
Abuse, meanings in different cultures
    and different times, 293
Accessibility, paternal, 12–13, 14
Acrimony, divorce and parental,
    438–39, 454–55
Acute phase of divorce, 436
Adaptation

divorce and factors affecting, 437–39
  in marriage, following birth of child,
    124–24
  during transition to parenthood, psy-
    chological, 148–51, 161
Adequacy, sense of, among Black fa-
    thers, 376
Adjustment to process of becoming par-
    ent, 146–47
Admiration for father, 519–21
Adolescence
  of nurturing fathers, 400–401
  oedipal involvement in, 261–62
  parents as grandparental gatekeepers
    to children in, 103–6
Adolescent daughter with disturbed and
    denigrated mother, father's contri-
    bution to, 245–47
  family triad and, 246–47
  father's involvement, 248–51
  presenting complaints, 247–48
  relationships with young men,
    251–52
  sexual development, 252–55

transference and course of analyses, 255–60
Adult development, father-daughter relationship and transformations during, 205–10
Affective tones in father-daughter relationship, 198–99, 211, 212, 216–17, 221, 222
Affectomotor stimulus patterns of parents, 52
Affluence, problems of, 374
Age of child
  anticipation of fatherhood and imagined, 130–31
  post-divorce adjustment and, 437–38
Aggression, 516–19
  in father-son relationship, 509
  hostile, in mother-child dyad, 492, 498, 499
  among slaves, 369–70
Aggressive overstimulation, 327–28, 332, 333–34
Aggressive strivings, effect of father's action on, 70–72
Aging. *See* Grandfatherhood
AIDS, 509–10
Alcoholism, 545–46
Alienation between Lincoln and his father, 291–92
Alliance
  between grandparents and grandchildren, 104–5
  parenting, 194
  of pregnancy, 184
Alternative caretakers to daughters of disturbed mothers, 260
Ambisexuality, 272
American father, expectations of, 366–68
Anal phase, concurrence of development of language and, 499
"Analysis of a Phobia in a Five-Year-Old Boy" (Freud), 267, 281
Analytic neutrality, 256
Androgenous transference, 194–95
Androgeny, 255, 256
Angst, 271
Anticipation of fatherhood, 122–23, 127–44
  anchored in traditional role, 139

discussion of data, 138–42
disjunction in development of paternal identity, 139–42
interview data on, 130–38
  age of child imagined, 130–31
  confidence and, 136–37
  idealized child images, 135–36
  images and fantasies of fatherhood, 131–36
  issues of great concern, 133–34
  views of own parents, 138
  views of pregnancy, 137
methods of study, 128–30
Antisocial behavior in boys, 71–72. *See also* Aggression
Anxiety
  castration, 227
  circumcision, 509, 511–16
Artistic imagination, 320
"As-if" child, 333–34, 339
Atatürk, 360–61
Attachment theory, 48–49
Attachment to father, 333
  isogender, 508
Attitudes
  divorce and sociocultural, 434
  of fathers as single parents, 65
  maternal, to nonresident father, 414–15, 416, 418–19
  sex-stereotyped, 21
  of fathers of psychotic children, 531–32
Auditory environment of Charles Ives, 314–189
Authority
  respect for, in rural Turkish family, 355
  sense of, in psychiatrically hospitalized fathers, 548–49
Autonomy, father-daughter relationship and, 216–17
Average expectable environment, concept of, 241

B

"Bad seed" phenomenon, 110
Bedwetting. *See* Enuresis
Behavioral styles of mothers and fathers, 13–15

Bias, matricentric, 3–4
Biological factors, flight from father-hood and, 179–180, 181
Birth
  concerns after, 154–55
  premature, reaction to, 149–51
Birth of sibling
  Ives perception of, 317
  Little Hans' response to, 268–69, 270, 272–80
Black church, influence of, 371, 380
Black fathers in U.S., 344–45, 365–83
  broad spectrum of, 366
  childrearing implications and interventions, 378–80
  clinical implications and intervention, 380–82
  historical social conditions and, 368–73
  social policy implications, 376–77
  synopses of, 373–76
  traditional and emerging fatherhood expectations and, 366–68
Black subculture, 374, 375
Black therapists, 381
Bladder control. See Toilet training
Body image
  of adolescent women with disturbed mothers, 258–59
  evolution of, 86
Book of Dede Korkut, The, 350–51
Borderline personality disorder
  genesis of, 58
  hospitalized fathers with, 545–46
Bowel control. See Toilet training
Boys
  antisocial behavior in, 71–72
  need to disidentify with mother, 80–81, 90
  reaction to stress in, 72
  sexual identity, development of, 267–68
  See also Father-son relationship
Breast-feeding, 355–56
Brentwood, V. A. Medical Center, 543

C

Calcium Light Night (Ives), 307, 311, 313–14, 321–24, 325

Capacity to father, 404
Caregiving objects, availability of other, 72–73
Caretaking
  competencies of mothers and fathers at, 13–14
  process of, 551
Caretaking nurturing, 168n
Castration, circumcision of Turkish boys as, 356
Castration anxiety, 227
Castration fears, 387–88
  Little Hans's case and, 268–69
Castration threats, 509
Center for Epidemiological Studies Depression Scale (CES-D), 157
Chapman, Harriet Hanks, 286
Child abuse, 381
Child-care programs in schools, 379–80
Child development
  paternal influence on, 5, 20–23, 225–44
    case illustrations, 227–38
    nurturing father as primary caretaker and, 390–91
    summary of, 226–27
  view of toilet training, 81–82
Child rearing
  among blacks, historical and social conditions, and, 368–73
  feeling left out during, 155
Children
  cloacal theories of, 86–87, 274
  of divorce, 459–63
    intensity of post-divorce activities with, 442–43
    postdivorce reactions and adjustments, 437–38
    use of, 455
  See also Psychotic children, fathers of
Church, Black, 371, 380
Circumcision, 154, 352, 356, 521
Circumcision anxiety, 509, 511–16
Cities
  of Ottoman Turkey, 352
  Turkish fathers and families in 360–62
Civil Rights Movement, 373
Clinical scrutiny of psychiatrically hospitalized father, 544–45

Cloacal theories of children, 86–87, 274
Cognitive competence, paternal influences on, 21
Collusion in patient-staff relationship, 542, 547, 551
Collusion to exclude father, 491–505, 510
  case illustration of, 496–503
  discussion of, 403–4
  treatment model for, 493, 494–96
Community-based institutions, black families and, 380
Compensatory hypothesis of paternal involvement, 16
Concord Sonata (Ives), 331
Confidence, anticipation of parenthood and, 136–37
Conflict in treatment of psychiatrically hospitalized fathers, 547–51
Conjoint treatment method, 493, 494–96
Continuity of care, 72
Controlling style of fathers of psychotic children, 532–534
Control mechanisms used by psychiatrically hospitalized fathers, 546
Cooperation between divorced spouses, 438–39, 461
Coping device, fantasy as, 417
Core fantasy of Lincoln, 296–99
Countertransference, 488
  manifestations of late-life relationships, 115–16
  with psychiatrically hospitalized fathers, 549
Coupling of mother and son, 510
Cowell, Henry, 313
Creativity, roots of. *See* Ives, Charles Edward
Crisis, pregnancy as period of, 146–47
Cross-cultural perspective on grandparenthood, 105
Cross cultural variations, *See* Black fathers in U.S.; Hispanic fathers; Nurturing fathers; Turkish fathers and their families
Crying by daughters of disturbed mothers, 258
Culture, father figure in public world and, 285–300

Custody issues, 460
  joint, 455
  See also Divorce; Noncustodial father

D

Daughter-preferring societies, 192
Daughters. *See* Father-daughter relationship
Death
  of father, daughter's reaction to, 219–20
  grandfatherhood and association with, 105, 110
Decision making role, transition to fatherhood and, 158, 159, 161
Defenses
  identification-with-aggressor, 369
  self-holding, 69
  transpersonal, 53, 54
Defiance, sex differences in, 82
Delinquency, parental processes in aetiology of, 53
Delivery of newborn, concerns during, 153–54
Denial, fantasy as, 417
Denigrated and disturbed mother, 245–63
Denigration of father figure, 510
Depression
  divorce and, 454
  transition to fatherhood and, 157–58, 161
Deprivation, parental, 182
  cases of paternal deprivation during preoedipal years, 227–38
Developing Toilet Habits (Ross Laboratories), 81
Diapering, father's avoidance of, 79–80
Differentiation
  developmental achievement of, 516–17
  single parents as disadvantage to, 70
Directive approach to therapy of father and psychotic child, 538
Discipline, anticipation of fatherhood and issue of, 133–34
Disclosure of paternity by therapist, 473–90

Discrimination, black families and racial, 370–75
Disidentification process from mother,
   80–81, 90
Disrupted families. *See* Absent fathers;
   Divorce
Distance regulation, pathologic, 549
Distortion of memory, 320
Divorce
   case illustrations, 433–35, 443–53
   children of, 459–63
      intensity of postdivorce activities
         with, 442–43
      postdivorce reactions and adjust-
         ments, 437–38
      use of, 455
   consequences to fathers in, 439–42
   cooperation between spouses in,
      438–39, 461
   depression and, 454
   effects of, 66–68
   factors affecting adaptation after,
      437–39
   grandfatherhood and, 108–9
   intrapsychic factors affecting outome,
      431–58
   noncustodial father, 425–30
   parental acrimony and, 438–39,
      454–55
   phases of, 435–37
   rates and causes, 431, 432–35
   social policy and, 456
   See also Single parents, fathers as
Divorce-custody issues, 460
Doll play, 253, 413
Dream, transference, 512–13

E

Early infantile identification, 335
Eating disorders, 249, 250, 257,
   496–503
Ego functioning, second year as critical
   period in, 492
Ego ideal
   of adolescent daughter with disturbed
      mother, 251, 256–57
   Ives's formation of, 309
   projections, 140–41

sex differences in, 205–6
transformations during women's adult
   development, 205–7
of young man, children embodying,
   140–41
Ego identification, 335
Elective mutism, case of, 175–78
Emotional engagement between father
   and daughter, 198
Emotions during acute postdivorce period, 440
Employment of mother, paternal involvement and, 12–13
Endeavor excitement, 198–99
   father's role in, 192–93
   mother's role in, 194
Engagement, extent of paternal, 12–13
Enlow, Abraham, 293
Enuresis
   female mode of toilet training and,
      88–89
   in first-born male, 92
   sex ration in, 83
Envious feelings, 151, 152
Environment
   auditory, of Charles Ives, 314–19
   average expectable, 241
Envy, 516–19
Erotic excitement, 198–99
   father's role in, 192–93
   mother's role in, 194
Erotization of father-son relationship,
   508
Essays Before A Sonata (Ives), 310
Ethnic background, father fantasies of
   preschoolers with nonresident fathers and, 415. *See also* Black fathers in U.S.; Hispanic fathers
Exclusion of father, collusion, in
   194–505, 510
   case illustration of, 496–503
   discussion of, 503–4
   treatment model for 493, 494–96
Expectations
   of fatherhood, traditional and emerg-
      ing, 366–68
   of grandfathers for grandchildren,
      101–2
Experience with infants and children of
   nurturing fathers, 403–5

Extended family in rural Turkey, 353, 354–55

F

Familial dysfunction, paternal imago and screens of, 37–38
Family
context of, 21
internalization of, 42
modes of relatedness in, 53, 54–58
structure and process, 51–52
Turkish patterns, 343–44
Family systems theory, 59
Family Treatment Program (Brentwood V.A. Medical Center), 542–43
Fantasies
about absent parent, 220–21
anticipation of fatherhood and, 131–33
conscious, maternal and paternal object representations in, 29
Lincoln's, of his heredity, 296–99
about paternal role, 550
plumber, of Little Hans, 274, 279
of preschoolers with absent father, 410–23, 462
findings on, 414–16
maternal attitude to absent father and, 414–15, 416, 418–19
purposes of, 417, 418
sexual
of adolescent daughters with disturbed mothers, 253, 254–55
affectionate father and, 419
"silhouette" father, 411–12, 415, 420
Father-daughter relationship, 191–223
affective tone in, 198–99, 211, 212, 216–17, 221, 222
autonomy and, 216–17
disturbed and denigrated mother and, 245–63
in formative years, 203–5
intentionality and, 202–4
overstimulation in, example of, 333–34
protectiveness, 509
research project on, 202–3
transformations during adult formation and, 205–10

transformations in, 210–22
Father figure
in public world of politics and culture, 285–300
Turklish mental representation of, 360–62
Fatherhood, anticipation of. *See* Anticipation of fatherhood
Fatherhood and father-child relationships, 11–26
advantages to child of relationship, 47–48
changing roles of fathers, 11
determinants of father involvement, 15–20
paternal influences on child development, 5, 20–23, 225–44
quantifying the new, 12–15
Fatherhood of child therapist, 468–69, 473–90
case illustrations of, 476–87
discussion of, 487–89
Father imago. *see* Paternal imago
Fatherliness
Benedek's definition of, 403–4
development of, 149
Father-son relationship, 554
acknowledgment of growing son's body, 508
aggression in, 509
disappointment of son in father, 508–9
erotization of, 508
Little Hans, riddle of, 267–83
reverberations in psychoanalytic treatment of men, 507–21
sadism and respect in, 511–16
See also Psychotic children, fathers of
Fear
of castration, 387–88
of loss of wife, 182
"Female mode" of toilet training, 80, 85–89
Feminine development, 191–95
endeavor and erotic excitement and, 192–92, 194
father and masculine identifications, 193–94
lack of mother's support and, 193
preference for daughter and, 192

See also Father-daughter relationship
Feminine identification, 502
  conflicted feminine-maternal, 183
  father's role in solidifying, 248
First born, concerns after birth of, 154
Flight from fatherhood, 124, 167–88
  biological factors and social forces in,
    179–81
  case illustration of, 169–78
  current life influences on, 184–85
  marital relationship and, 184–85
  psychological impediments to father-
    hood and, 181–84
Formative years, impact of father on
  daughter's, 203–5
Founders of U.S., Lincoln's attachment to, 296–99
Futility ina treatment of psychiatrically
  hospitalized fathers, sense of,
    546–47, 550

G

Gasterbeiter (guest workers), 348
Gatekeeper(s)
  mother as, 184–85
  parents as grandparental, 103–6
Gender
  anticipation of parenthood and,
    130–38
  effect of absent father and, 462–63
  father fantasies, nonresident father
    and, 415–16
  in grandparental destiny, 111–15
  of therapist, importance of, 522
Gender identity
  development of core, 226–27
  toilet training and, 80–81, 87–88
General systems theory, 53, 54–58
Genitals
  daughter's interest in, 230–31, 232,
    237, 242–43
  Little Hans's interest in, 269–70, 271
  negative reactions to differences,
    500–501
Genital sensitivity, emergence in child
  of, 500
Girls
  reaction to stress in, 72

"unitary" concept of excretion in,
    86–87
See also Father'daughter relationship
Good-enough parent, notion of, 238,
    241
Grandfatherhood, 99–118
  clinical vignettes of, 106–11
  conclusions on, 116–17
  expectations for grandchildren, 101–2
  as forced or dreaded experience,
    110–11
  parents as grandparental gatekeepers,
    103–6
  as positive maturational force, 106–10
  social role, 111–15
  stages of, 9, 102
  transference and countertransference
    implications, 115–16
  transgenerational rescreenings in late
    life, 99–101
Grandmothers, 112, 113
Grandparenthood, 556
Grandparents' acceptance of nurturing
  father as primary caregiver, 396–97
Group work
  with fathers of psychotic children, 537
  for hospitalized fathers, 544, 545

H

Hate for object, 51
Helpless feelings of psychiatrically hos-
  pitalized fathers, 548–49
Hispanic fathers, 385–88
Historical social conditions of Black
  fathers, 368–73
"Holding," maternal, absence of, 69–70
Homosexuality, 356–57, 435, 451
Hospitalized fathers, psychiatrically,
    470, 541–52
  conflict and resistance in, 547–51
  implications for, 551
  overview of findings, 544–47
  problem of, 541–42
  setting and methodology, 542–44
Hostile aggression in mother-child dyad,
    492, 498, 499
Housatonic at Stockbridge, The (Ives), 315
"How-to" books on toilet training,
    84–85

How to Father (Dodson), 85
How to Parent (Dodson), 85
Hypospadias, 90–91

I

Idealization
   of Lincoln, 304
   political, 285–300
Idealization, paternal, 470–71
   idealized perception of nonresident
      father, 418, 419
Idealized child images, 135–36
Identification
   of blacks under slavery, 370
   ego vs. early infantile, 335
   with father, 330–31, 503, 504,
      519–21
      by adolescent women, 261–62
   of father with child, 386–87
   feminine, 502
      conflicted feminine-maternal, 183
      father's role in solidyifying, 248
   masculine, 193–94
   maternal, of nurturing fathers, 402–3
   paternal, of nurturing fathers, a401–2
   projective, 54, 55, 549
   with infant, 390
Identification-with-aggressor defense
   mechanism, 369
Identity
   gender. *See* Gender identity
   masculine, 400
   paternal, disjunction in development
      of, 139–42
   procreative, 267, 270–71, 274, 276
   sexual, development of boy's, 267–68
Identity crisis of adolescent daughters
   with disturbed mothers, 258
Imagination, artistic, 320
Imitative process, father's role in,
   226–27
Immunocompetency,
   gender-determined, 112
Impulsive behavior, disclosure of therapist's upcoming paternity and pro-
   neess to, 488
Incest taboo, 356
Index of Self-Esteem (ISE) from Clinical
   Measurement Package, 157

India, family patterns in, 344
Individual work with father of
   psychotic children, 535–36
Industrial era, black families in, 371–72
Infant Care (U.S. Children's Bureau), 84
Infant swaddling, 355
Institutional practices, paternal involve-
   ment and, 5, 18–19
Insufficiency, paternal, 267
Intentionality, 202–4
   characteristics associated with high vs.
      low, 204
   defined, 202
   father-daughter relationship in forma-
      tive years and, 203–4
Interaction, child-parent
   of mothers vs. fathers, 13–15
   paternal involvement in terms of, 14
   styles of fathers of psychotic children,
      532–34
Interactional nurturing, 168n
Intercourse, fear of, 153
Intergenerational interviews with psychiatrically hospitalized fathers,
   544, 545–46
Internalization, 54
   of family, 42
   father's role in, 226–27
   paternal imago as indicator of, 44
Internal object relationship, 49
Interracial therapy, 381–82
Interventions for Black fathers and their
   families, 378–82
Introjects, devalued or damaged, 38, 42
Involvement, paternal with adolescent
   daughters with disturbed mothers,
   248–51
   determinants of, 15–20
   effects of increased, 20–22
   encouragement of, 185
   extent of, 12–13
   factors in, 5, 18–19
   mother-father relationship and, 4–5
   qualitative vs. quantitative, 22–23
   after remarriage, 440
   stability of increased, 20
   in terms of interaction, 14
Isogender attachment with fathers, 508
Isolation of nurturing fathers acting as
   primary caregiver 397–98

Ives, Charles Edward, 307–36
  auditory environment and early/loss,
    314–19
  childhood of, 329
  early memories of, 307–25
  major phases of adult life, 328–29
  means of presentation, 319–24
  melancholy element in, 320–21
  memories in music; 310–14
    music as matrix for reminiscence,
    324–25
  mourning, identification, and memo-
    rialization of father, 330–31, 335
  Oedipus complex of, 334
  overstimulation by father, 327–36
  relationship with mother, 315–16,
    334
  retirement from work and withdrawal
    from music, 331–32
Ives, George Edward, 307, 308–10,
  314–25, 329, 334
Ives, George Wilcox, 319
Ives, Mollie, 315–16

J

Johnston, John D., 286
Joint custody, 455
Jones, Jim, 285

K

Kemal, Mustafa (Atatürk), 349

L

Labor, concerns during wife's, 153–54
Laius Complex, 302
Lamon, Ward Hill, 288
Language, anal phase and development
  of, 499
Libidinal overstimulation, 327, 332,
  333–34
Lincoln, Abraham, 285, 286–99, 303–6
Lincoln, Mary, 288, 289, 304
Lincoln, Nancy Hanks, 296–97
Lincoln, Robert, 304

Lincoln, Sarah, 288, 292
Lincoln, Thomas, 286–99, 303–4
Little Hans, riddle of, 267–83
  clinical narrative, 269–80
  conclusions about, 280–82
Logan, Stephen T., 287
Loss of parent, 58, 64
Loss of wife, fear of, 182
Loving, father-daughter relationships
  and patterns of, 221

M

McCullough, Fanny, 305
Mainstream social skills, programs to
  provide Blacks with, 378–80
Male-Female Antagonism Scale, (MFAS),
  411, 413
"Male mode" of toilet training, 80,
  89–93
Manhood
  development of useful expressions of,
    380
  through paternity, 373, 374–75
Manic-depressive fathers, 546
Manzigert, Battle of (1071), 348–49
Marital satisfaction, transition to parenthood and, 147–48, 158–59, 161
Marriage
  flight from fatherhood and, 184–85
  following birth of child, adaptative
    challenges in, 123–24
  of nurturing fathers acting as primary
    caregiver, 395–96
  among Ottoman Turks, 352
  of parents of psychotic child, tensions
    in, 536–37
  in small Turkish towns, 359
Masculine identification, 193–94
Masculine identity, 400
Masculinity, phallic, 94
Masturbation, 86, 252–53, 270, 500
Maternal attitude to nonresident father,
  father fantasies and 414–15, 416,
    418–19
Maternal Attitude Toward Nonresident
  Father Sacle (MANRF), 411,
    412–13
Maternal deprivation, 182

Maternal "holding," absence of, 69–70
Maternal identification of nurturing fa-
    thers, 402–3
Maternal imago, 42, 521
    of adolescent women with disturbed
        mothers, 259–60
Maternal object representations, 29, 41
Matricentric bias of developmental
    thinking, 3–4
Matrix, music as, for Ives's reminiscense,
    324–25
Maturation
    enhancement of, by facilitation of se-
        paration/individuation process, 226
    grandfatherhood as positive force in,
        106–10
    during wife's pregnancy, 149
Mellowing of aging men, 113–14
Memorialization of father, 330–31, 335
Memories
    distortion of, 320
    early, of Charles Ives, 307–25
    in music, 310–14, 319–24
    music as matrix for reminiscence,
        325–25
    of own parents, anticipation of father-
        hood and, 133
    paternal imago, 6, 27–45, 469
        clinical illustrations. 30–36
        concept, 27–30
        implications for theory and practice,
            38–44
        mother's contribution to, 29–30
        overvalued, assimilated into
            self-representation, 309
        screening function, 38–44
        screens of familial dysfunction,
            37–38
        self-representation and, 42, 43–44
        split, 38
Memos (Kirkpatrick), 310
Mental illness, fatherhood and, 150–51
Mentors, 215–16, 257
Mirroring, 51, 55
Miscarriage, 153
Modeling hypothesis of paternal
    involvement, 16
Moon and Sixpence, The (Maugham), 168
Mortality, intimations of, grandparents
    and, 105, 110

Mother(s)
    attaitude toward men, 411
        nonresident father, 410, 411
    attitude toward paternal involvement,
        17–18
    authority of, noncustodial father's sup-
        port of, 428–29
    behavioral styles of, 13–15
    boy's need to disidentify with, 80–81,
        90
    daughter's rediscovery of values of,
        207, 1209–10
    as disturbed and denigrated figure,
        245–63
    oḟ disturbed children, 533, 534
    employed vs. unemployed, paternal
        involvement and, 12–13
    endeavor and erotic excitement and,
        194
    gatekeeping function, 184–85
    hostile aggression toward, 492, 498,
        499
    male mode of toilet training used by,
        91
    pregnancy experience, 146–47
    in rural Turkish family, 354–55
    transitive vitalization, 37
    See also Pregnancy
Mother and child, coordination of treat-
    ment of, 493
Mother and son, coupling of, 510
Mother-child relationship,
    overenmeshed, 57, 58
Mother-father relationship
    father involvement and, 4–5
    toilet training of boy and, 89
Mothering role, competition with wives
    for, 508
Motivation, paternal involvement and,
    15–16
Mourning of father, 330–31
Mozart, Wolfgang Amadeus, 337–38
Murderous wishes, 516–19
Music
    differences in tolerance for, 339–40
    of Ives, memory in, 310–14, 319–24
    as matrix for reminiscence,
        324–25
    quotation in, 330–31
Mutism, case of elective, 175–78

N

Narcissism, phallic, toilet training and, 89
Negative oedipal position, 269, 281
Neutrality, analytic, 256
Newborn, wife as facialitator of husband's connection to, 141. *See also* Birth
Noncustodial father, 425–30
Nonresident father. *See* Absent fathers
Normative process during transition to fatherhood, 160–61a
Nurturing, interactional and caretaking, 168*n*
Nurturing fathers, 345–46, 367, 368, 389–405
  adolescence of, 400–401
  case illustrations of, 394–99
  experience with infants and children and, 403–5
  families in study, 390
  initial findings on, 390–91
  maternal identification and, 402–3
  paternal identification and, 401–2
  sketch of men studied, 391–94
  social class and, 401
Nurturing role, predisposition for, 393

O

Obedience to maternal control, sex differences in, 83
Object
  caregiving, availability of other, 72–73
  father as, 51, 58
  hate for, 51
  meanings of, 49
Object constancy, father fantasies of preschoolers with nonresident fathers and, 419
Object hunger, loss of parent and, 68
Object relations
  case example of disturbance in child's, 496–503
  complexity of early, 70
  internal, 49
  second year as critical period in, 492
Object relations theory, 6–7, 49–51
  synthesis with family group relations and general systems approach, 54–55
  case illustration of, 55–58
Object representations, 40–41
  in conscious fantasy, 29
  maternal, 29, 41
  paternal, 29, 38, a41–42
Observational data on mothering vs. fathering, 29
Oedipal complex, 183, 281
  aggression in father-son relationship and, 509
  Ives's psyche and, 334
  negative oedipal position, 269, 281
  Papi phenomenon and, 387–88
  separation from parent and, 64
  Turkish family life and, 356, 357–58
Oedipal development, 58
  in adolescence, 261–62
  early preparation for positive oedipal attachment, 501
  Little Hans, case of, 267–83
  of one-parent child, 7–8
  primalry oedipal phase, 253
  reversal in, 510
Oghuz Turks, 348
  family life, 350–51
Old Song Deranged, An (Ives), 334
114 Songs (Ives), 310
One-parent child
  oedipal development of, 7–8
  studies of, 66–69
  See also Single parents, fathers as
Organicity, 539
Orgasm, 254, 255
Ottoman Turks, 349–50
  family life, 351–52
Overstimulation, 339
  aggressive, 327–28, 332, 333–34
  as contribution to psychopathology, 332–34
  by Ives's father, 327–36
  libidinal, 327, 332, 333–34
  sensory, 328, 332–34

P

Papi phenomenon, 385–88
Parental deprivation, 182
Parental style, 13–15, 343

Parenthood, anticipation of. *See* Antici-
    pation of fatherhood
Parenting alliance, 184
Parenting role behavior, 51–52
Parents
    anticipation of fatherhood and view of
        own, 138
    couple's adjustment to process of be-
        coming, 146–47
    good enough, notion of, 238, 241
    as grandparental gatekeepers, 103–6
Paternal deprivation, 182
    during preoedipal years of develop-
        ment, cases of, 227–38
    See also Absent fathers
Paternal idealization, 470–71
Paternal identification of nurturing fa-
    thers, 401–2
Paternal imago, 6, 27–45, 469
    clinical illustrations, 30–36
    concept, 27–30
    implications for theory and practice,
        38–44
    of Lincoln, 303–4
    mother's contribution to, 29–30
    overvalued, assimilated into
        self-representation, 309
    screening function, 38–44
    screens of familial dysfunction, 37–38
    self-representation and, 42, 43–44
    split, 38
Paternal insufficiency during second
    year of life, 267
Paternal involvement, *See* Involvement,
    paternal
Paternal object representations, 29, 38,
    41–42
Paternity
    manhood through, 373, 374–75
    transference and, 468–69, 473–90
        case illustrations of, 476–87
        discussion of, 487–89
        method of study of, 476–76
Paternity leave, 19
Pathologic distance regulation, 549
Pediatric view of toilet training, 81–82
Peer relationships, postdivorce, 436
Penis
    daughjter's interest in, 230–31, 232,
        237, 242–43

Little Hans' interest in, 269–70, 271
    See also Genitals
Perceptions of role of fathers of psy-
    chotic children, 435–35
Pervasive Development Disorder, father
    of child with, 527–31
Perversions, development of, 510–11
Phallic masculinity, developing, 94
Phallic narcissism, toilet training and, 89
Physical activity of father with
    psychotic child, 532–34
Play
    behavioral styles of mothers and fa-
        thers in, 13
    doll, 253, 413
    with grandfather, 113–14
    sessions in conjoint treatment model,
        495
Political idealization, 285–300
Pond, The (Ives), 307, 311–13, 319–20,
    324
Postdivorce phase of divorce, 436–37
Powerless feelings of psychiatrically
    hospitalized fathers, 548–49
Preferred child, 192
Pregnancy
    alliance of, 184
    anticipation of fatherhood and view
        of, 137
    biological impact of, 179–80
    concerns during, 152–53
    disequilibrium experienced within
        family during, 511–21, 522
    maturation during wife's, 149
    mother's experience, 146–47
    potential father's view of, 141
    psychological adaptation during,
        149–51, 161
Pregnancy envy, 182
Premature birth, reaction to, 149–51
Preoedipal relationships, 183, 501
Preschoolers, father fantasies of father-
    absent, 410–23, 462
Primary caretaker
    father as, 8, 345–46, 389–405
        case illustrations of, 394–99
        experience with infants and children
            and, 403–5
        families in study, 390
        initial findings on, 390–91

maternal identification and, 402–3
paternal identification and, 401–2
sketch of men studied, 301–94
stylistic differences between mothers
    and fathers as, 4
Primary oedipal phase, 253
Process of caretaking, 551
Procreative identity, 267, 270–71, 274,
    276
Projections, ego ideal, 140–41
Projective identification, 54, 55, 549
    with infant, 390
Protector, experience of father as, 140
Providers, fathers as, 367
Psychiatrically hospitalized fathers, 470,
    541–52
conflict and resistance in, 547–51
implications for, 551
overview of findings, 544–47
problem of, 541–42
setting and methodology, 542–44
Psychoanalytic treatment of men, issues
    in fathering and reflection in,
    507–23
case illustrations, 511–21
issues outlined, 507–11
Psychoeducational approach to treat-
    ment of fathers of psychotic chil-
    dren, 536
Psychological adaptation
to pregnancy, 149–51, 161
during transition to parenthood,
    148–51
Psychological impediments to father-
    hood, 181–84
Psychosexual development
modulation and regulation of, 227
second year as critical period in, 492
Psychosis, fatherhood and, 150
Psychosomatic symptoms during wives'
    pregnancies, 151
Psychotherapy, paternal transference
    phenomena in, 473–89
Psychotic children, fathers of, 470,
    525–40
approaches to treatment of, 535–39
group work with fathers, 537–39
individual work with father, 535–36
work with mother and father,
    536–37

attitudes and feelings of, 531–32
clinical illustrations, 527–31
discussion of findings on, 531–35
effect on child, 534–35
implications for future research, 539
interactional styles of, 532–34
role of, 536
perceptions of, 534–35
samples studied, 527
Psychotic regression, disclosure of thera-
    pist's upcoming paternity and
    proneness to, 488

Q

Quotation in music, use of, 330–31

R

Racial discrimination, black families
    and, 370–75
Rapprochement crises, 71
toilet training and, 78–79
Reality, development sense of, 227
Rearing of children. See Child rearing
Regression
to increased mother-child unity, toilet
    training and, 88
of mother during baby's first two
    years, 492–93
Relatedness, family modes of, 53, 54–58
Relational systems theory, 47–59
development of model, 52–53
father as significant contributor in,
    58–59
Winnicott's contributions and move-
    ment toward, 51
Reluctance to become father, case illus-
    tration, 169–72
Remarriage
father's involvement with his children
    and, 440
grandfather and, 108–9
Remote father, case illustration, 172–75
Rescreenings in late life, transgeneratio-
    nal, 99–101
Resistance
to treatment collaboration, 544

in treatment of psychiatrically hospitalized fathers, 547–51
Respect for father, 519–21
Responsibility, extent of paternal, 12–13, 14
Rights For Fathers, 439
Risala of Ibn Fadlan, 350
Risk factors in transition to fatherhood, 145–65
  birth of baby, concerns with, 154–55
  current study on, 156–62
  labor and delivery, concerns with, 153–54
  marital satisfaction and, 147–48, 158–59, 161
  pregnancy, concerns with, 152–53
  psychological adaptation and, 148–51
Risk-vulnerability intervention model, 66
Rivalry
  between Lincoln and his father, 292
Rivalry with son for wife, 511–16
Role behavior, parenting, 51–52
Role of father
  changing, 11
  with psychotic children, 534–35, 536
  See also Psychiatrically hospitalized fathers
Role reversal, use of address "Papi" and, 386
Roles, transition to parenthood and move toward traditional, 148
Rural family life in Turkey, 352, 353–58

S

Sadism
  coparental acrimony among divorcing parents, 454–55
  and respect in father-son relationship, 511–16
Satellite state, rural Turkish family as, 354, 355
Satisfaction, transition to parenthood and marital, 147–48, 158–59, 161
Schizophrenic fathers, 546
Schools, child-care programs in, 379–80
Screen memories, 38–44

"Screen Memories" (Freud), 39–40
Screens of familial dysfunction, paternal imago and, 37–38
Second individuation process, 248
Second Piano Sonata (Ives), 310
Second Symphony (Ives), 330
Self-confidence, paternal involvement and, 16–17
Self-esteem, transition to fatherhood and, 157–58, 161
Self-holding, defensive maneuver of, 69
Self-image, high intentionality and father's, 204
Self/object differentiation, female mode of toilet training and, 88
Self-representation
  overvalued father imago assimilated into, 309
  paternal imago and, 42, 43–44
Self-stimulation, genital, 500
Seljuk Turks, 348, 351
Sensitivity, developing, 16
Sensory overstimulation, 328, 332–34
Separation/individuation, 502
  of boys vs. girls, 70–71
  challenge/opportunity of becoming grandfather as fourth crisis of, 115
  effect of absence of parent on, 66
  enhancement of maturation by facilitation of, 226
  father's role in, 37, 57–58, 543
  fear of, 503–4
  grandparent-grandchild alliance and, 104–5
  inadequate or conflicted, 182–83
  in rural Turkish family, 355
  second individuation process, 248
  toilet training and, 78–79, 90
Sex
  after birth of baby, feelings about, 155
  concerns about, during pregnancy, 153
  curiosity about, emergence of, 84
  injury from divorce and pressure for, 442
Sex differences
  in defiance, 82, 83
  in ego ideal, 205–6
  toilet training and, 82–84
  See also Gender
Sex-role differentiation in rural Turkey, 356

Sex-stereotyped attitudes, paternal influences on, 21
Sexual development of adolescent daughters with disturbed mothers, 252–55
Sexual fantasies, 419
Sexual identity, development of boy's, 267–68
Sexuality
  Lincoln's doubts of his father's, 295–97
  paternity of therapist and introduction of, 475
Shame, overvalued parental imago assimilated into self-representation and, 309
Shantytowns, Turkish fathers and families in, 359–60
"Silhouette" father fantasies, 411–12, 415, 420
Sinan, 352
Single parents, fathers as, 63–75
  attitudes of, 65
  availability of other caregiving objects and, 72–73
  child's inner developmental need and, 65–66
  disadvantage to differentiating process, 70
  effects of absent parent, 63–64, 66–68
Skills, paternal involvement and, 16–17
Slavery, Black family and, 369–70, 371
Small town, Turkish fathers and families in, 358–59
Social class, nurturing fathers and, 401
Social forces, flight from fatherhood and, 180–81
Social policy
  divorce and, 456
  implications for Black families and, 376–77
Social role of grandparent, 111–15
"Social Skills Curriculum for Inner City Children, A," 378–80
Sociocultural attitudes, divorce and, 434
Somatic symptoms during wives' pregnancies, 151
Songs My Mother Taught Me (Ives), 334
Sons, conflictual feelings about, 154. *See also* Father-son relationship
Split representations, 38, 42

Stability of increased paternal involvement, 20
Status, sense of, in psychiatrically hospitalized fathers, 548–49
Stepmothers of daughters with disturbed biological mothers, 251
Stillbirth, 153
Stress
  reaction to, in boys vs. girls, 72
  during wife's pregnancy, 152–53
Structural theory, advent of, 40
Structure formation, Fairbairn on, 50
Style, parental, 13–15, 343
Subculture, Black, 374, 375
Suicide, 549
Support
  paternal involvement and, 17–18
Support-resoacurce, noncustodial father as, 427–29, 460
Swaddling of infants, 355

T

Taboo, incest, 356
Therapist
  Black, 381
  fatherhood of child therapist, 468–69, 473–90
    case illustrations of, 476–87
    discussion of, 487–89
  female, 550
    transitive revitalizing function of, 507–8
  openness to father's influence, 468
Things Our Fathers Loved, The (Ives), 323
Thoreau, Henry David, 325
Thought control, 328
"Three Essays, The" (Freud), 268
Timing in grandparental destiny, 111–15
Toddlerhood, use of address "Papi" in, 386
Toilet training, 8, 77–97
  child development view of, 81–82
  conclusions and recommendations on, 92–94
  father's role in, 79–80
  female psychology and "female mode" of, 80, 85–89
  gender identity and, 80–81, 87–88

"how-to" books on, 84–85
"male mode" of, 80, 89–93
review of psychoanalytic literature on, 78–84
in rural Turkish family, 356
sex differences and, 82–84
Towns, Turkish fathers and families in, 358–59
Transference
of adolescent daughters with disturbed mothers, 255–60
androgenous, 194–95
manifestations of late-life relationships, 115–16
paternity and, 468–69, 473–90
case illustrations of, 476–87
discussion of, 487–89
method of study of, 475–76
transitive revitalizing function of female analyst, 507–8
Transference dream, example of, 512–13
Transgenerational rescreenings in late life, 99–101
Transitional phase of divorce, 436
Transitional society. *See* Turkish fathers and their families
Transition to fatherhood, 121–24
normative process during, 160–61
risk factors in, 145–65
birth of baby, concerns with, 154–55
current study on, 156–62
labor and delivery, concerns with, 153–54
marital satisfaction and, 147–48, 158–59, 161
pregnancy, concerns with, 152–53
psychological adaptation and, 148–51
See also Anticipation of fatherhood; Flight from fatherhood
Transitive revitalization, female analyst and, 507–8
Transitive vitalization, 37
Transpersonal defenses, 53, 54
Transpersonal mode as adaptive or defensive, 53, 54–55
Trauma, overstimulation as, 327–36
Treatment collaboration, resistances to, 544

Treatment of mother and child, coordination of, 493
Triangulation, 192, 227, a420, 468, 511–16
Turkish fathers and their families, 343–44, 347–64
historical background of, 350–52
panoramic view of Turkish history, 347–50
of today, 352–62
in big cities, 360–62
in rural, 353–58
in shantytowns, 359–60
in small towns, 358–59
Turkomans, 348
Twichell, Harmony, 310, 334
Two-parent families
among Blacks, decline of, 376
involvement by fathers in, 12–13

U

Unanswered Question (Ives), 324
"Unitary" concept of excretion in girls, 86–87
Ural-Altaic Turks, 348
"Urinating and Weeping" (Greenacre), 91

V

Value of family, attitude toward protective, 434
Vigeland, Gustav, 181
Visitation by noncustodial father, 427–29
Vitalization, transitive, 37

W

Wife
as facilitator of husband's connection to newborn, 141
fear of loss of, 182
feelings about, after birth of baby, 155
See also Marriage; Mother(s); Pregnancy
Wish fulfillment, fantasies for, 417, 418
Womb envy, 182

Women, anticipation of parenthood,
133. *See also* Mother(s); Wife
Workplace, paternal involvement and,
19
Worth, sense of, in psychiatrically hospitalized fathers, 548–49

Y

Yale Child Study Center School Development Program, 378
Yale Development Schedules, 391